XSLT
Programmer's Reference

Michael Kay

Wrox Press Ltd. ®

About the Author

Michael Kay has spent most of his career as a software designer and systems architect with ICL, the IT services supplier. As an ICL Fellow, he divides his time between external activities and mainstream projects for clients, mainly in the area of electronic commerce and publishing. His background is in database technology: he has worked on the design of network, relational, and object-oriented database software products as well as a text search engine. In the XML world he is known as the developer of the open source Saxon product, the first fully-conformant implementation of the XSLT standard.

Michael lives in Reading, Berkshire with his wife and daughter. His hobbies, as you might guess from the examples in this book, include genealogy and choral singing.

Acknowledgements

Firstly, I'd like to acknowledge the work of the W3C XSL Working Group, who created the XSLT language. Without their efforts there would have been no language and no book. They've recently asked me to join the group as an Invited Expert, and I'm looking forward to working with them in future, but I'd like to say that this book was written entirely from an outsider's perspective.

More specifically, I'm grateful to James Clark, the editor of the XSLT and XPath specifications, who responded courteously and promptly to a great many enquiries, ranging from the extremely foolish to the highly challenging.

I've learnt a great deal of what I know about XSLT from the people on the XSL-List: not only from the experts like David Carlisle who answer so many of the questions, but also from the many beginners who ask them.

I'd like to thank Alex Homer and David Sussman, for helping to compile the MSXML appendix.

I owe a debt to ICL, my employers, who took my request to spend time on this project with great equanimity.

My editors at Wrox Press, and the technical reviewers, made an invaluable contribution by pointing out the many, many places where more explanations and examples were needed.

And finally, I couldn't have done this without the support of Penny and Pippa, who have suffered my non-participation in family life for the last five months with remarkable patience.

Goun

XSLT Programmer's Reference

wrox

Published by Wrox Press Ltd
Arden House, 1102 Warwick Road, Acock's Green, Birmingham B27 6BH, UK
Printed in USA
ISBN 1-861003-12-9

Trademark Acknowledgements

Wrox has endeavored to provide trademark information about all the companies and products mentioned in this book by the appropriate use of capitals. However, Wrox cannot guarantee the accuracy of this information.

Credits

Author
Michael Kay

Additional Material
Alex Homer
David Sussman

Technical Architect
Tony Davis

Technical Editors
Catherine Alexander
Claire Fletcher

Development Editor
Peter Morgan

Managing Editor
Paul Cooper

Project Manager
Chandima Nethisinghe

Proof Reader
Andy Nimmo

Technical Reviewers
David Carlisle
Robert Chang
Michael Corning
Jason Diamond
Craig McQueen
Paul Tchistopolskii
David Thompson
Linda van den Brink
Dan Wahlin

Design / Layout
Tom Bartlett
Mark Burdett
William Fallon
Jonathan Jones
Laurent Lafon

Cover Design
Chris Morris

Index
Michael Brinkman
Martin Brooks

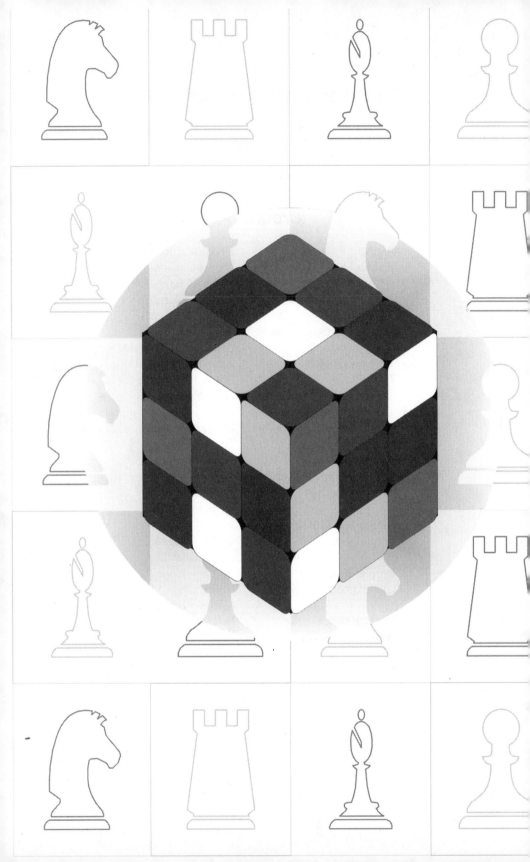

Table of Contents

Table of Contents

Table of Contents

Table of Contents

Table of Contents

Table of Contents

Table of Contents

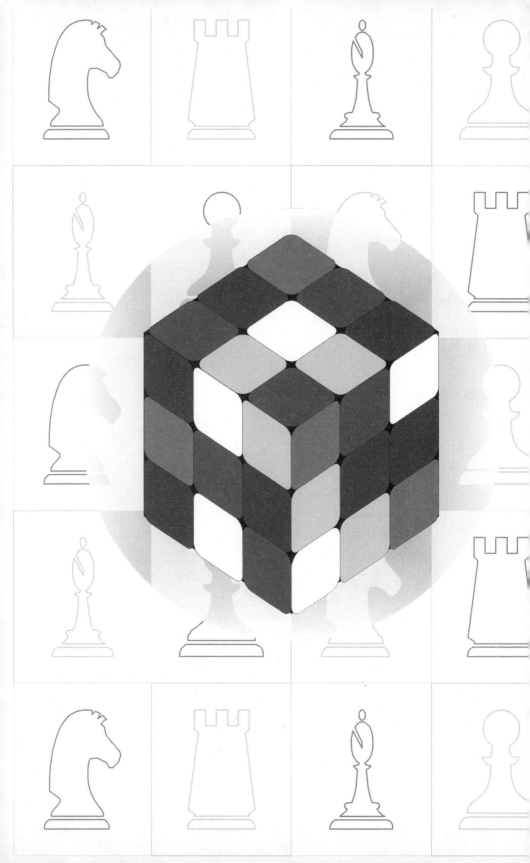

Introduction

It wouldn't be too extravagant to claim that XML is the biggest thing to hit the web since the whole thing started less than ten years ago. It's also one of the biggest things to hit the world of information management. Yet on its own, XML doesn't actually **do** anything, all it provides is a way of structuring information and sending it from one piece of software to another. Until now, if you wanted to write applications that took advantage of XML, you had to write some rather low-level code using interfaces (such as DOM and SAX) that required a very detailed knowledge of the way the data is organized.

It reminds me of the way people used to access databases before SQL came along (you've seen the gray hairs on the cover photo) – and when I first saw the XSL Transformation language, XSLT, I realized that this was going to be the SQL of the web, the high-level data manipulation language that would turn XML from being merely a storage and transmission format for data into an active information source that could be queried and manipulated in a flexible, declarative way.

Early in 1998, I was looking at ways of incorporating XML into ICL's content management toolkit for web-based publishing, and I started developing a Java library called Saxon to provide higher-level interfaces for manipulating XML. I was very critical of the first XSL proposals, but as the standardization process gathered pace I started to see a useful and powerful language emerging, and decided to change direction with the Saxon software to turn it into an XSLT processor. When the XSLT version 1.0 Recommendation finally came out on 16th November 1999, I was able to announce a fully-conformant open source implementation just 17 days later.

But although I could see the power and potential of the XSLT language, I could also see that it contained some new and difficult concepts which early users were struggling with. That also reminded me of the early days with SQL – it's hard to remember it now, but when SQL first emerged people had great difficulty understanding its radical new concepts such as inner and outer joins and three-valued logic.

So that's why I wrote the book. XSLT is an exciting and powerful language, but not an easy one to get to grips with. Until now, there have been very few resources available to help, apart from the official W3C specification itself, which is about as readable to most programmers as a piece of tax legislation. So I hope this book will fill the gap, and help to unleash the tremendous potential of this new language.

Who is this Book for?

I've written this book for practising software developers who have used a variety of languages in the past and now want to learn how to use XSLT to create new applications. I'm assuming you will have a basic understanding of XML, though I do recognize that if you ever knew what an external general parsed entity is, you've probably forgotten. I'm also assuming a basic understanding of the architecture of the web and of HTML.

I'm not assuming you are familiar with any particular programming language, though I have written on the basis that you have programming experience. If all the programming you've done is to write HTML pages with a little bit of Javascript, you might find some of the material tough going.

What does the Book Cover?

The book is primarily about XSLT as a language, and not about any particular product. In Chapter 10 I've given a survey of currently available products that implement the XSLT language, and in Appendix A I've included some extended coverage of Microsoft's latest MSXML3 product, which currently implements most of the standard. But I've kept the product information confined to a small part of the book, because I expect that over the next year or two there will be many new product developments and new players in the market, while the language itself will remain stable, just as XML itself has done.

The book **doesn't** cover the early dialect of XSL that Microsoft delivered when Internet Explorer 5 came out in 1998. XSLT has moved on a long way since that early draft, and I decided it would be just too confusing to describe two very different versions of a language in one book. In any case, Microsoft have stated (and demonstrated) their commitment to moving their technology forward to comply with the XSLT standard as published by W3C, so the IE5 1998 dialect clearly has no long-term future, even though it has shipped millions of copies.

How is the Book Structured?

The material in this book falls naturally into three parts.

The first part comprises Chapters 1 to 3. The purpose of these chapters is to explain the concepts of the XSLT language. Chapter 1 is about the role and purpose of the language, about its history and the factors that motivated its design – I could have called it *Why XSLT?* Chapter 2 explains what the concept of **transformation** means, and describes the processing model in which an XSLT stylesheet describes the relationship of an output tree to an input tree. Then Chapter 3 describes the internal structure of a stylesheet, the way in which stylesheet modules relate to each other, and the main things that you expect to find within a stylesheet.

The second part, Chapters 4 to 7, contains reference information. These chapters aim to give a complete description of every language feature, explaining its detailed syntax rules and its effect, giving usage advice and showing how it works using code examples. I've ordered the material in these chapters for ease of reference rather than for sequential reading: XSLT elements in Chapter 4, XPath expressions in Chapter 5, the syntax of Patterns in Chapter 6, and the standard function library in Chapter 7. Most of these chapters are arranged alphabetically so you can quickly find the information on a particular language feature.

The third part of the book, Chapters 8 through 10, is designed to help you exploit the XSLT language in developing real industrial applications. Chapter 8 explores a number of design patterns; Chapter 9 contains three in-depth worked examples; and Chapter 10 is a survey of current XSLT products: I'm not trying here to give you all the information you need to use each product, but rather to summarize the characteristics of each product so that you can decide which ones to investigate further.

Finally, Appendix A gives a much more detailed treatment of the recently-released Microsoft MSXML3 technology preview. This is of particular interest, not just because it's from Microsoft, but also because it's the first XSLT processor that is integrated with a web browser; something that adds a whole range of possibilities to the different ways of exploiting the power of the language. Appendix B gives a useful glossary of terms.

Other XSLT Resources

If you can't find what you need in this book, there are several good places to find an answer on the web. Rather than give a long list of XSLT-related sites, I'll just list one or two sites that maintain good collections of links.

❑ http://www.w3.org/Style/XSL/
    This is the official site of the World Wide Web Consortium. It contains all the published specifications and working drafts, plus a good number of news items, articles and white papers.

❑ http://www.xslinfo.com/
    This is a well-organized site run by James Tauber, consisting almost entirely of classified lists of XSL software, articles, tutorials, and other resources.

❑ http://www.oasis-open.org/cover/xsl.html
    Robin Cover's link pages provide remarkably comprehensive coverage of everything that's happening or has ever happened in the world of SGML and XML. The link given is to his XSL section.

❑ http://www.xml.com/
    A good site for opinion articles and news round-up covering the XML world generally.

❑ http://msdn.microsoft.com/xml/
    This URL gives a good jumping-off point to Microsoft's view of the XML and XSL world. Many useful articles and white papers, not always confined to their own products.

What do I Need to Use this Book?

Reading about a new language won't make you an expert in it; you also need to try it out and learn from your own experience. There are many examples in this book which I'd encourage you to run, but more importantly I hope they'll stimulate you to try out ideas of your own.

You can download all the worked examples from the main support page for this book, at http://www.wrox.com.

In Chapter 10 I've listed some of the XSLT products available, and the good news is that there's plenty of choice. Most of them are free, though you should always read the license conditions. The bad news is that the development tools are rather basic: don't expect sophisticated visual editing and debugging environments, the technology hasn't yet reached that level of maturity.

To get started, if you're using a Windows platform, I would suggest:

- ❑ **Instant Saxon**, available from:
  http://users.iclway.co.uk/mhkay/saxon/instant.html

- ❑ **Programmer's File Editor (PFE)**, available from various archive sites including:
  http://www.simtel.net/pub/simtelnet/win95/editor/pfe101i.zip

The recommendation for Instant Saxon is entirely biased; I wrote it. Its merits are that it's a complete implementation of the standard, it's free, and it's easy to install and run. The examples in this book are all tested with Saxon. They should also work with Xalan and with Oracle XSL, both excellent products that claim 100% conformance to the standard, but I haven't done extensive testing with them.

Like most of the other processors, Saxon requires you to create and edit your XML and stylesheet files in a text editor, and to run them from the operating system command line. If you've grown up entirely with Windows, that probably seems rather primitive. I recommend PFE because it contains an intuitive text editor that allows you to have lots of files open at once, and because it gives you access to the operating system command line in a Windows-friendly way. If you already have a different favorite, use that instead: I won't be mentioning PFE again.

For non-Windows platforms, several of the products described in Chapter 10 are written in Java and should run on almost anything. You'll have to install a Java Virtual Machine for your particular computer, and you'll have to become familiar with the mechanics of installing and running Java applications in that environment.

I wouldn't recommend using Microsoft's MSXML3 as a learning tool just yet, until the product matures a little. Its coverage of the XSLT standard is incomplete, its documentation is sketchy, and its diagnostics when you get things wrong can be very unhelpful. Use it once you've gained a little bit of experience, to explore the unique things you can do when running a stylesheet within the web browser. No doubt this situation is temporary, and I fully expect that in six months or a year Microsoft will have one of the best XSLT processors on the market. It will be interesting to see whether they live up to their promises on standards conformance.

Conventions

To help you get the most from the text and keep track of what's happening, a number of conventions have been used throughout the book.

Worked examples – those which you can download and try out for yourself – are generally in a box like this:

A specimen example

Source

This section gives the XML source data, the input to the transformation.

```
<source data="xml"/>
```

Stylesheet

This section describes the XSLT stylesheet used to achieve the transformation.

```
<xsl:stylesheet...
```

Output

This section shows the output when you apply this styesheet to this source data, either as an XML or HTML listing, or as a screenshot.

```
<html>...</html>
```

Any freestanding sections of code are generally shown in a shaded box, like this:

```
<data>
Some XML data or XSLT code
</data>
```

As for styles in the text:

❑   Important terms, when first introduced, are highlighted as follows: **important words**.

❑   Filenames, and code within the text appear like so: dummy.xml.

❑   Text on user interfaces, and URLs, are shown as: **File/Save As...**

❑   French quotation marks (chevrons or guillemots) are used in order to separate the code snippet clearly from the surrounding text, like this: «a=3;». These have been used in preference to the usual English single or double quotes partly because they stand out better, and partly to avoid any ambiguity with quotes that are part of the code sample: it means we can write examples such as «select="'Madrid'"», where the quotation marks («"» and «'») are part of the code sample, and the chevrons aren't.

❑   XML element names, function names and attribute names are written as: **<xsl:value-of>**, **concat()**, **href**.

In addition:

> **These boxes hold important, not-to-be forgotten information, which is directly relevant to the surrounding text.**

While the background style is used for asides to the current discussion.

Syntax rules (which appear mainly in Chapters 5 and 6) stick largely to the conventions used in the W3C standards, except that, again, chevrons have been used to surround literal text. The main notations used in these syntax rules are:

Expression	Meaning
clause | paragraph	A clause or a paragraph. The meaning of clause and paragraph will be defined in separate rules: these are **non-terminal symbols**. The vertical bar «|» is used to separate alternatives.
«!» | «?»	An exclamation mark or a question mark. Words or symbols enclosed by chevrons must be used as written: they are **terminal symbols**.
adjective noun «.»	An adjective followed by a noun followed by a full-stop (period).
adjective? noun	Either a noun on its own, or an adjective followed by a noun. The «?» indicates that the preceding symbol is optional.
adjective* noun	Zero or more adjectives followed by a noun.
adjective+ noun	One or more adjectives followed by a noun.
sentence («?» | «!»)	A sentence followed by either a question mark or an exclamation mark. The parentheses indicate grouping.

Customer Support

We have made all the source code for this book available at our web site, at the following address:

http://www.wrox.com

We've made every effort to make sure that there are no errors in the text or code. However, to err is human. If you find an error in the book, or have problems getting an example to work, first check whether it's a problem we already know about, by looking at the errata pages on the Wrox web site. If not, please let us know, so that we can help you with the problem and tell other readers about it. You'll find instructions for notifying errors and raising queries on the web site.

Wrox now has a commitment to supporting you not just while you read the book, but once you start developing your own applications. We provide you with a forum where you can put your questions to the authors, reviewers and fellow industry professionals. Check out the XML-related lists at:

http://p2p.wrox.com

Tell Us What You Think

The author and the Wrox team have worked hard to make this book a pleasure to read as well as being useful and educational, so we'd like to know what you think. Wrox are always keen to hear what you liked best and what improvements you think are possible. We appreciate feedback on our efforts and take both criticism and praise on board in our future editorial efforts. When necessary, we'll forward comments and queries to the author. If you've anything to say, let us know on:

feedback@wrox.com

Or via the feedback links on:

http://www.wrox.com

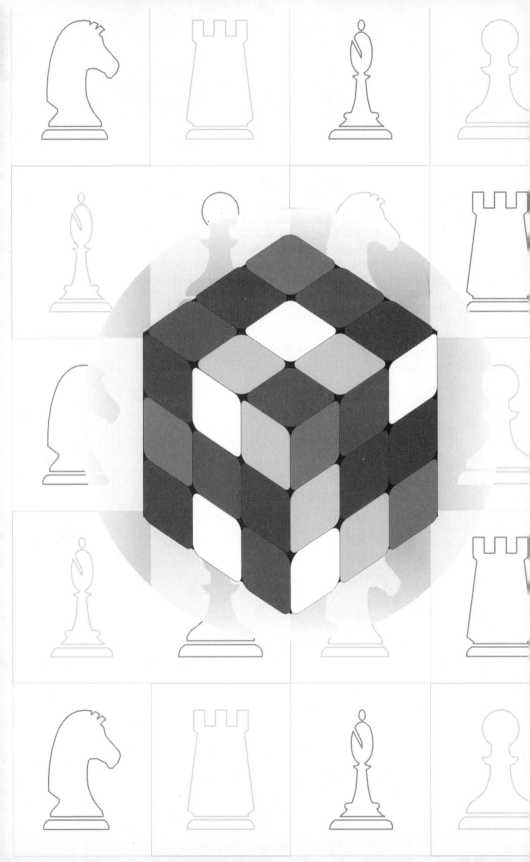

1

XSLT in Context

This chapter is designed to put XSLT in context. It's about the purpose of XSLT and the task it was designed to perform. It's about what kind of language it is, and how it came to be that way; and it's about how XSLT fits in with all the other technologies that you are likely to use in a typical web-based application. I won't be saying much in this chapter about what an XSLT stylesheet actually looks like or how it works: that will come later, in Chapters 2 and 3.

I shall begin by describing the task that XSLT is designed to perform – **transformation** – and why there is the need to transform XML documents. I'll then present a trivial example of a transformation in order to explain what this means in practice.

The chapter then moves on to discuss the relationship of XSLT to other standards in the growing XML family, to put its function into context and explain how it complements the other standards.

I'll describe what kind of language XSLT is, and delve a little into the history of how it came to be like that. If you're impatient you may want to skip the history and get on with using the language, but sooner or later you will ask "why on earth did they design it like that?" and at that stage I hope you will go back and read about the process by which XSLT came into being.

Finally, I'll have a few things to say about the different ways of using XSLT within the overall architecture of an application, in which there will inevitably be many other technologies and components each playing their own part.

What is XSLT?

XSLT, which stands for **eXtensible Stylesheet Language: Transformations**, is a language which, according to the very first sentence in the specification (found at http://www.w3.org/TR/xslt), is primarily designed for transforming one XML document into another. However, XSLT is more than capable of transforming XML to HTML and many other text-based formats, so a more general definition might be as follows:

> XSLT is a language for transforming the structure of an XML
> document.

Why should you want to do that? In order to answer this question properly, we first need to remind ourselves why XML has proved such a success and generated so much excitement.

Why Transform XML?

XML is a simple, standard way to interchange structured textual data between computer programs. Part of its success comes because it is also readable and writable by humans, using nothing more complicated than a text editor, but this doesn't alter the fact that it is primarily intended for communication between software systems. As such, XML satisfies two compelling requirements:

- ❑ **Separating data from presentation**. The need to separate information (such as a weather forecast) from details of the way it is to be presented on a particular device. This need is becoming ever more urgent as the range of internet-capable devices grows. Organizations that have invested in creating valuable information sources need to be able to deliver them not only to the traditional PC-based web browser (which itself now comes in many flavors), but also to TV sets and WAP phones, not to mention the continuing need to produce print-on-paper.

- ❑ **Transmitting data between applications**. The need to transmit information (such as orders and invoices) from one organization to another without investing in bespoke software integration projects. As electronic commerce gathers pace, the amount of data exchanged between enterprises increases daily and this need becomes ever more urgent.

Of course, these two ways of using XML are not mutually exclusive. An invoice can be presented on the screen as well as being input to a financial application package, and weather forecasts can be summarized, indexed, and aggregated by the recipient instead of being displayed directly. Another of the key benefits of XML is that it unifies the worlds of documents and data, providing a single way of representing structure regardless of whether the information is intended for human or machine consumption. The main point is that, whether the XML data is ultimately used by people or by a software application, it will very rarely be used directly in the form it arrives: it first has to be transformed into something else.

In order to communicate with a human reader, this something else might be a document that can be displayed or printed: for example an HTML file, a PDF file, or even audible sound. Converting XML to HTML for display is probably the most common application of XSLT today, and it is the one I will use in most of the examples in this book. Once you have the data in HTML format, it can be displayed on any browser.

In order to transfer data between different applications we need to be able to transform data from the data model used by one application to the model used in another. To load the data into an application, the required format might be a comma-separated-values file, a SQL script, an HTTP message, or a sequence of calls on a particular programming interface. Alternatively, it might be another XML file using a different vocabulary from the original. As XML-based electronic commerce becomes widespread, so the role of XSLT in data conversion between applications also becomes ever more important. Just because everyone is using XML does not mean the need for data conversion will disappear. There will always be multiple standards in use. For example, the newspaper industry is likely to use different formats for exchanging news articles from the format used in the TV industry. Equally, there will always be a need to do things like extracting an address from a purchase order and adding it to an invoice. So linking up enterprises to do e-Commerce will increasingly become a case of defining how to extract and combine data from one set of XML documents to generate another set of XML documents: and XSLT is the ideal tool for the job.

At the end of this chapter we will come back to specific examples of when XLST should be used to transform XML. For now, I just wanted to establish just a general feel for the importance and usefulness of transforming XML. Before we move on to discuss XSLT in more detail and have a first look at how it works, let's take a look at an example that clearly demonstrates the variety of formats to which we can transform XML, using XSLT.

An Example: Transforming Music

There is an excellent registry of XML vocabularies and schemas at http://www.xml.org/xmlorg_registry/index.shtml.

If you look there, you will find at least three different XML schemas for describing music; and if you follow the links, you will find several more. These were all invented with different purposes in mind: a markup language used by a publisher for printing sheet music has different requirements from one designed to let you listen to the music from a browser. MusicML, for example, is oriented to displaying music notation graphically; ChordML is designed for encoding the harmonic accompaniment to vocal lyrics, while the much more comprehensive Music Markup Language (MML) from the University of Pretoria is designed for serious musicological analysis, embracing Eastern and African as well as Western musical idioms.

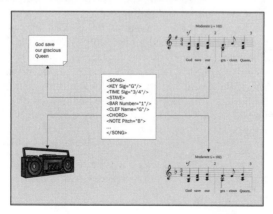

So you could use XSLT to process marked-up music in many different ways:

❑ You could use XSLT to convert music from one of these representations to another, for example from MusicML to MML.

❑ You could use XSLT to convert music from any of these representations into visual music notation, by generating the XML-based vector graphics format SVG.

❑ You could use XSLT to play the music on a synthesizer, by generating a MIDI (Musical Instrument Digital Interface) file.

❑ You could use XSLT to perform a musical transformation, such as transposing the music into a different key.

❑ You could use XSLT to extract the lyrics, into HTML or into a text-only XML document.

As you can see, XSLT is not just for converting XML documents to HTML!

How does XSLT transform XML?

By now you are probably wondering exactly how XSLT goes about processing an XML document in order to convert it into the required output. There are usually two aspects to this process:

❑ The first stage is a structural transformation, in which the data is converted from the structure of the incoming XML document to a structure that reflects the desired output.

❑ The second stage is formatting, in which the new structure is output in the required format such as HTML or PDF.

The second stage covers the ground we discussed in the previous section: the data structure that results from the first stage can be output as HTML, a text file or as XML. HTML output allows the information to be viewed directly in a browser by a human user or be input into any modern word processor. Plain text output allows data to be formatted in the way an existing application can accept, for example comma-separated values or one of the many text-based data interchange formats that were developed before XML arrived on the scene. Finally, XML output allows the data to be supplied to one of the new breed of applications that accepts XML directly. Typically this will use a different vocabulary of XML tags from the original document: for example an XSLT transformation might take the monthly sales figures as its XML input and produce a histogram as its XML output, using the XML-based SVG standard for vector graphics. Or you could use an XSLT transformation to generate VOXML output, for aural rendition of your data.

A white paper describing Motorola's VOXML Voice Markup Language can be found at http://www.voxml.com/downloads/VoxMNwp.pdf

Let's now delve into the first stage, transformation - the stage with which XSLT is primarily concerned and which makes it possible to provide output in all of these formats. This stage might involve selecting data, aggregating and grouping it, sorting it, or performing arithmetic conversions such as changing centimeters to inches.

So how does this come about? Before the advent of XSLT, you could only process incoming XML documents by writing a custom application. The application wouldn't actually need to parse the raw XML, but it would need to invoke an XML parser, via a defined Application Programing Interface (API), to get information from the document and do something with it. There are two principal APIs for achieving this: the Simple API for XML (SAX) and the Document Object Model (DOM).

The SAX API is an event-based interface in which the parser notifies the application of each piece of information in the document as it is read. If you use the DOM API, then the parser interrogates the document and builds a tree-like object structure in memory. You would then write a custom application (in a procedural language such as C++, Visual Basic, or Java, for example), which could interrogate this tree structure. It would do so by defining a specific **sequence of steps** to be followed in order to produce the required output. Thus, whatever parser you use, this process has the same principal drawback: every time you want to handle a new kind of XML document, you have to write a new custom program, describing a different sequence of steps, to process the XML.

> Both the DOM and the SAX APIs are fully described in the Wrox Press book *Professional XML, ISBN 1-861003-11-0.*

So how is using XSLT to perform transformations on XML better than writing "custom applications"? Well, the design of XSLT is based on a recognition that these programs are all very similar, and it should therefore be possible to describe what they do using a high-level **declarative** language rather than writing each program from scratch in C++, Visual Basic, or Java. The required transformation can be expressed as a set of rules. These rules are based on defining what output should be generated when particular patterns occur in the input. The language is declarative, in the sense that you describe the transformation you require, rather than providing a sequence of procedural instructions to achieve it. XSLT describes the required transformation and then relies on the XSL processor to decide the most efficient way to go about it.

XSLT still relies on a parser – be it a DOM parser or a SAX-compliant one – to convert the XML document in to a "tree structure". It is the structure of this tree representation of the document that XSLT manipulates, not the document itself. If you are familiar with the DOM, then you will be happy with the idea of treating every item in an XML document (elements, attributes, processing instructions etc.) as a node. With XSLT we have a high-level language that can navigate around a node tree, select specific nodes and perform complex manipulations on these nodes.

> The XSLT tree model is similar in concept to the DOM but it is not the same. The full XSLT processing model is discussed in Chapter 2.

The description of XSLT given thus far (a declarative language that can navigate to and select specific data and then manipulate that data) may strike you as being similar to that of the standard database query language: SQL. Let's take a closer look at this comparison.

XSLT and SQL: an Analogy

I like to think of an analogy with relational databases. In a relational database, the data consists of a set of tables. By themselves, the tables are not much use, the data might as well be stored in flat files in comma-separated values format. The power of a relational database doesn't come from its data structure; it comes from the language that processes the data, SQL. In the same way, XML on its own just defines a data structure. It's a bit richer than the tables of the relational model, but by itself it doesn't actually do anything very useful. It's when we get a high-level language expressly designed to manipulate the data structure that we start to find we've got something interesting on our hands: and for XML data that language is XSLT.

Superficially, SQL and XSLT are very different languages. But if you look below the surface, they actually have a lot in common. For starters: in order to process specific data, be it in a relational database or an XML document, the processing language must incorporate a declarative query syntax for selecting the data that needs to be processed. In SQL, that's the SELECT statement. In XSLT, the equivalent is the **XPath expression**.

The XPath expression language forms an essential part of XSLT, though it is actually defined in a separate W3C Recommendation (http://www.w3.org/TR/xpath) because it can also be used independently of XSLT (the relationship between XPath and XSLT is discussed further on page 23).

The XPath query syntax is designed to retrieve nodes from an XML document, based on a path through the XML document or the context in which the node appears. It allows access to specific nodes, while preserving the hierarchy and structure of the document. XSLT is then used to manipulate the results of these "queries" (rearranging selected nodes, constructing new nodes etc).

There are further similarities between XSLT and SQL:

❑ Both languages augment the basic query facilities with useful additions for performing basic arithmetic, string manipulation, and comparison operations.

❑ Both languages supplement the declarative query syntax with semi-procedural facilities for describing the sequence of processing to be carried out, and they also provide hooks to escape into conventional programming languages where the algorithms start to get too complex.

❑   Both languages have an important property called **closure**, which means that the output has the same data structure as the input. For SQL, this structure is tables, for XSLT it is trees – the tree representation of XML documents. The closure property is extremely valuable because it means operations performed using the language can be combined end-to-end to define bigger more complex operations: you just take the output of one operation and make it the input of the next operation. In SQL you can do this by defining views or subqueries; in XSLT you can do it by passing your data through a series of stylesheets.

In the real world, of course, XSLT and SQL have to coexist. There are many possible relationships, but typically data will be stored in relational databases and transmitted between systems in XML. The two languages don't fit together as comfortably as one would like, because the data models are so different. But XSLT transformations can play an important role in bridging the divide. A number of database vendors are working on products that integrate XML and SQL, though there are no standards in this area as yet.

> **SQL Server 2000 will support XPath queries on its data. Prior to the release of SQL Server 2000, Microsoft has released the XML SQL Technology Preview, which allows access to data in a SQL Server 6.5 or 7.0 databases in XML form.**
>
> **The XML SQL Technology Preview is available from http://msdn.microsoft.com/workshop/xml/articles/xmlsql/sqlxmlset up.exe.**

Before we move on to look at a simple working example of an XSLT transformation, we need to briefly discuss a few of the XSLT processors that are available to effect these transformations.

XSLT Processors

The principle role of an XSLT processor is to apply an XSLT stylesheet to an XML source document and produce a result document. It is important to note that each of these is an application of XML and so the underlying structure of each is a tree. So, in fact, the XSLT processor handles three trees.

There are several XSLT processors to choose from. Here I'll mention three: Saxon, xt, and Microsoft MSXML3. All of these can be downloaded free of charge (but do read the licensing conditions).

These three processors and several others are described in Chapter 10.

Saxon is an open source XSLT processor developed by the author of this book. It is a Java application, and can be run directly from the command prompt: no web server or browser is required. The Saxon program will transform the XML document to, say, a HTML document, which can then be placed on a web server. In this example, both the browser and web server only deal with the transformed document.

If you are running Windows (95/98/NT/2000) the simplest way to use it is to download Instant Saxon, which is packaged as a Windows executable. You will need to have Java installed, but that will be there already if you have any recent version of Internet Explorer. On non-Windows platforms you will need to install the full Saxon product and follow the instructions that come with it. You can download Instant Saxon for free from http://users.iclway.co.uk/mhkay/saxon/instant.html. Saxon will run with any XML parser that implements the SAX interface (in its original Java form).

xt is another open source XSLT processor developed by James Clark, the editor of the XSLT specification. Like Saxon, this is a Java application that can be run from the command prompt; it too has a simple packaged version for the Windows platform and a full version for other environments. This time the download is from http://www.jclark.com/xml/xt.html. Like Saxon, xt can operate with any SAX-compliant parser.

Alternatively, you can run XSLT stylesheets actually within Internet Explorer. You'll need to install Internet Explorer 5 and the latest version of the **Microsoft MSXML processor**, which you can find at http://www.microsoft.com/xml. The information here is correct for the 15 March 2000 technology preview, referred to as **MSXML3**, but Microsoft has promised a rapid sequence of new releases, so check the latest position. MSXML3 comes with a new version of the MSXML parser.

Download and install both the SDK and the run-time package. Installing the SDK creates a program called `xmlinst.exe`, typically in the windows\system directory. Run this program to establish MSXML3 as the default XML processor to be used by Internet Explorer (if you don't do this, IE5 will try to use the old 1998 MSXML processor, which implements an obsolete dialect of XSL that is quite different from the language described in this book: see Chapter 10 for details). The big advantage of Microsoft's technology is that the XSLT processing can take place on the browser.

I've avoided talking about specific products in most of the book, because the information is likely to change quite rapidly. It's best to get the latest status from the web. Some good places to start are:

- ❑ http://www.w3.org/Style/XSL
- ❑ http://www.xslinfo.com/
- ❑ http://www.xml.com/
- ❑ http://www.oasis-open.org/cover

An Example Stylesheet

Now we're ready to take a look at an example of using XSLT to transform a very simple XML document.

Example: A "Hello, world!" XSLT Stylesheet

Kernighan and Ritchie in their classic *The C Programming Language* originated the idea of presenting a trivial but complete program right at the beginning of the book, and ever since then the "Hello world" program has been an honored tradition. Of course, a complete description of how this example works is not possible until all the concepts have been defined: so if you feel I'm not explaining it fully, don't worry – the explanations will come later.

Input

What kind of transformation would we like to do? Let's try transforming the following XML document:

```
<?xml version="1.0" encoding="iso-8859-1"?>
<greeting>Hello, world!</greeting>
```

A simple node-tree-representation of this document would look as follows:

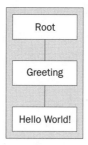

There is one root node per document. The root node in the XSLT model performs the same function as the document node in the DOM model. The XML declaration is not visible to the parser and, therefore, is not included in the tree.

Output

Our required output is the following HTML, which will simply change the browser title to "Today's Greeting" and display whatever greeting is in the source XML file:

```
<html>
<head>
   <title>Today's greeting</title>
</head>
<body>
   <p>Hello, world!</p>
</body>
</html>
```

XSLT StyleSheet

Without any more ado, here's the XSLT stylesheet to effect the transformation:

```
<?xml version="1.0" encoding="iso-8859-1"?>
<xsl:stylesheet
   version="1.0"
   xmlns:xsl="http://www.w3.org/1999/XSL/Transform">

<xsl:template match="/">
   <html>
   <head>
      <title>Today's greeting</title>
   </head>
   <body>
      <p><xsl:value-of select="greeting"/></p>
   </body>
   </html>
</xsl:template>

</xsl:stylesheet>
```

Running the Stylesheet

You can run this stylesheet using any of the three processors described in the previous section.

Saxon

With Saxon, the steps are:

❏   Download the processor

❏   Install the executable saxon.exe in a suitable directory, and make this the current directory

❏ Using Notepad, type the two files above into `hello.xml` and `hello.xsl` respectively, within this directory (or get them from the Wrox web site at `http://www.wrox.com`)

❏ Bring up an MSDOS-style console window (Start | Programs | MSDOS Prompt)

❏ Type the following at the command prompt:
`saxon hello.xml hello.xsl`

❏ Admire the HTML displayed on the standard output

If you want to view the output using your browser, simply save the command line output as an HTML file, in the following manner:

```
Saxon hello.xml hello.xsl > hello.html
```

xt

The procedure is very similar if you use xt. This time the command to use the Windows executable is `xt` rather than `saxon`. It should give the same result.

MSXML3

Finally, you can run the stylesheet actually within Internet Explorer. You need to modify the XML source file to include a reference to the stylesheet, so it now reads:

```
<?xml version="1.0" encoding="iso-8859-1"?>
<?xml-stylesheet type="text/xsl" href="hello.xsl"?>
<greeting>Hello, world!</greeting>
```

Now you should simply be able to double-click on the **hello.xml** file, which will bring up IE5 and load `hello.xml` into the browser. IE5 reads the XML file, discovers what stylesheet is needed, loads the stylesheet, executes it to perform the transformation, and displays the resulting HTML. If you don't see the text "Hello, world!" on the screen, but just the XML file, this is because you're using the original XSL interpreter that Microsoft issued with IE5, not the MSXML3 version. If you see the stylesheet displayed, this also indicates that you haven't completed the installation process correctly: remember to run the `xmlinst.exe` program.

How it Works

If you've succeeded in running this example, or even if you just want to get on with reading the book, you'll want to know how it works. Let's dissect it:

```
<?xml version="1.0" encoding="iso-8859-1"?>
```

19

This is just the standard XML heading. The interesting point is that an XSLT stylesheet is itself an XML document. I'll have more to say about this later in the chapter. I've used iso-8859-1 character encoding (which is the official name for the character set that Microsoft calls "ANSI") because in Western Europe and North America it's the character set that most text editors support. If you've got a text editor that supports UTF-8 or some other character encoding, feel free to use that instead.

```
<xsl:stylesheet
    xmlns:xsl="http://www.w3.org/1999/XSL/Transform"
    version="1.0">
```

This is the standard XSLT heading. In XML terms it's an element start tag, and it identifies the document as a stylesheet. The xmlns:xsl attribute is an XML Namespace declaration, which indicates that the prefix xsl is going to be used for elements defined in the W3C XSLT specification: XSLT makes extensive use of XML namespaces, and all the element names defined in the standard are prefixed with this namespace, to avoid any clash with names used in your source document. The version attribute indicates that the stylesheet is only using features from version 1.0 of the XSLT standard, which at the moment is the only version there is.

Let's move on:

```
<xsl:template match="/">
```

An <xsl:template> element defines a template rule to be triggered when a particular part of the source document is being processed. The attribute match="/" indicates that this particular rule is triggered right at the start of processing the source document. Here «/» is an XPath expression which identifies the **root node** of the document: an XML document has a hierarchic structure, and in the same way as UNIX uses the special filename «/» to indicate the root of a hierarchic filestore, XPath uses «/» to represent the root of the XML content hierarchy. The DOM model calls this the Document object, but in XPath it is called the root.

```
<html>
<head>
    <title>Today's greeting</title>
</head>
<body>
    <p><xsl:value-of select="greeting"/></p>
</body>
</html>
```

Once this rule is triggered, the body of the template says what output to generate. Most of the template body here is a sequence of HTML elements and text to be copied into the output file. There's one exception: an <xsl:value-of> element, which we recognize as an XSL instruction because it uses the namespace prefix xsl. This particular instruction copies the value of a node in the source document to the output document. . The SELECT attribute of the element specifies the node for which the value should be evaluated. The XPath expression «greeting>> means: "find the set of all <greeting> elements that are children of the node that this template rule is currently processing". In this case, this means the <greeting> element that's the outermost element of the source document. The <xsl:value-of> instruction then extracts the text node of this element, and copies it to the output at the relevant place, in other words within the generated <p> element.

All that remains is to finish what we started:

```
</xsl:template>

</xsl:stylesheet>
```

In fact, for a simple stylesheet like the one shown above, you can cut out some of the red tape. Since there is only one template rule, the <xsl:template> element can actually be omitted. The following is a complete, valid stylesheet equivalent to the preceding one:

```
<html xsl:version="1.0"
      xmlns:xsl="http://www.w3.org/1999/XSL/Transform">
<head>
   <title>Today's greeting</title>
</head>
<body>
   <p><xsl:value-of select="greeting"/></p>
</body>
</html>
```

This simplified syntax is designed to make XSLT look familiar to people who have learnt to use proprietary template languages which allow you to write a skeleton HTML page with special tags (analogous to <xsl:value-of>) to insert variable data at the appropriate place. But as we'll see, XSLT is much more powerful than that.

Why would you want to place today's greeting in a separate XML file and display it using a stylesheet? One reason is that you might want to show the greeting in different ways depending on the context; for example, it might be shown differently on a different device. In this case you could write a different stylesheet to transform the same source document in a different way. This raises the question of how a stylesheet gets selected at run-time. There is no single answer to this question. As we saw above, Saxon and xt have interfaces that allow you to nominate both the stylesheet and the source document to use. The same thing can also be achieved with the Microsoft XSLT product, though it requires some scripting on the HTML page: the `<?xml-stylesheet?>` processing instruction which I used in the example above only works if you want to use the same stylesheet every time.

It's time now to take a closer look at the relationship between XSLT and XPath and other XML-related technologies.

The Place of XSLT in the XML Family

XSLT is published by the World Wide Web Consortium (W3C) and fits into the XML family of standards, most of which are also developed by W3C. In this section I will try to explain the sometimes-confusing relationship of XSLT to other related standards and specifications.

XSLT and XSL

XSLT started life as part of a bigger language called **XSL (eXtensible Stylesheet Language)**. As the name implies, XSL was (and is) intended to define the formatting and presentation of XML documents for display on screen, on paper, or in the spoken word. As the development of XSL proceeded, it became clear that this was usually a two-stage process: first a structural transformation, in which elements are selected, grouped and reordered, and then a formatting process in which the resulting elements are rendered as ink on paper, or pixels on the screen. It was recognized that these two stages were quite independent, so XSL was split into two parts, XSLT for defining transformations, and "the rest" – which is still officially called XSL, though some people prefer to call it **XSL-FO (XSL Formatting Objects)** – the formatting stage.

XSL Formatting is nothing more than another XML vocabulary, in which the objects described are areas of the printed page and their properties. Since this is just another XML vocabulary, XSLT needs no special capabilities to generate this as its output. XSL Formatting is outside the scope of this book. It's a big subject (the draft specification currently available is far longer than XSLT), the standard is not yet stable, and the only products that implement it are at a very early stage of development. What's more, you're far less likely to need it than to need XSLT. XSL Formatting provides wonderful facilities to achieve high-quality typographical output of your documents. However, for most people translating them into HTML for presentation by a standard browser is quite good enough, and that can be achieved using XSLT alone, or if necessary, by using XSLT in conjunction with Cascading Style Sheets (CSS or CSS2), which I shall return to shortly.

The XSL Formatting specifications, which at the time of writing are still evolving, can be found at http://www.w3.org/TR/xsl.

XSLT and XPath

Halfway through the development of XSLT, it was recognized that there was a significant overlap between the expression syntax in XSLT for selecting parts of a document, and the XPointer language being developed for linking from one document to another. To avoid having two separate but overlapping expression languages, the two committees decided to join forces and define a single language, **XPath**, which would serve both purposes. XPath version 1.0 was published on the same day as XSLT, 16 November 1999.

XPath acts as a sublanguage within an XSLT stylesheet. An XPath expression may be used for numerical calculations or string manipulations, or for testing Boolean conditions, but its most characteristic use (and the one that gives it its name) is to identify parts of the input document to be processed. For example, the following instruction outputs the average price of all the books in the input document:

```
<xsl:value-of select="sum(//book/@price) div count(//book)"/>
```

Here the `<xsl:value-of>` element is an instruction defined in the XSLT standard, which causes a value to be written to the output document. The **select** attribute contains an XPath expression, which calculates the value to be written: specifically, the total of the **price** attributes on all the `<book>` elements, divided by the number of `<book>` elements.

The separation of XPath from XSLT works reasonably well, but there are places where the split seems awkward, and there are many cases where it's difficult to know which document to read to find the answer to a particular question. For example, an XPath expression can contain a reference to a variable, but creating the variable and giving it an initial value is the job of XSLT. Another example: XPath expressions can call functions, and there is a range of standard functions defined. Those whose effect is completely freestanding, such as **string-length()**, are defined in the XPath specification, whereas additional functions whose behavior relies on XSLT definitions, such as **key()**, are defined in the XSLT specification.

Because the split is awkward, I've written this book as if XSLT+XPath were a single language. For example, all the standard functions are described together in Chapter 7. In the reference sections, I've tried to indicate where each function or other construct is defined in the original standards, but the working assumption is that you are using both languages together and you don't need to know where one stops and the other one takes over. The only downside of this approach is that if you want to use XPath on its own, for example to define document hyperlinks, then the book isn't really structured to help you.

XSLT and Internet Explorer 5

Very soon after the first draft proposals for XSL were published, back in 1998, Microsoft shipped a partial implementation as a technology preview for use with IE4. This was subsequently replaced with a rather different implementation when IE5 came out. This second implementation, known as MSXSL, remained in the field essentially unchanged until very recently, and is what many people mean when they refer to XSL. Unfortunately, though, Microsoft jumped the gun, and the XSLT standard changed and grew, so that when the XSLT Recommendation version 1.0 was finally published on 16 November 1999, it bore very little resemblance to the initial Microsoft product.

> **A Recommendation is the most definitive of documents produced by the W3C. It's not technically a standard, because standards can only be published by government-approved standards organizations. But I will often refer to it loosely as "the standard" in this book.**

Many of the differences, such as changes of keywords, are very superficial but some run much deeper: for example, changes in the way the equals operator is defined.

So the Microsoft IE5 dialect of XSL is also outside the scope of this book. Please don't assume that anything in this book is relevant to the original Microsoft XSL: even where the syntax appears similar to XSLT, the meaning of the construct may be completely different.

You can find information about the original IE5 dialect of XSL in the Wrox book XML IE5 Programmer's Reference, ISBN 1-861001-57-6.

Microsoft has fully backed the development of the new XSLT standard, and on 26 January 2000 they released their first attempt at implementing it. It's a partial implementation, packaged as part of a set of XML tools called MSXML, but enough to run quite a few of the examples in this book – and the parts they have implemented conform quite closely to the XSLT specifications. A further update to this product (MSXML3) was released on 15 March 2000, bringing the language even closer to the standard. They've announced that they intend to move quickly towards a full implementation, so by the time you read this, the Microsoft product may comply fully with the W3C standard: check their web site for the latest details.

Microsoft has also released a converter to upgrade stylesheets from the old XSL dialect to the new. However, this isn't the end of the story, because, of course, there are millions of copies of IE5 installed that only support the old version. If you want to develop a web site that delivers XML to the browser and relies on the browser interpreting its XSLT stylesheet, you've currently got your work cut out to make sure all your users can handle it.

If you are using Microsoft technology on the server, there is an ISAPI extension called XSLISAPI that allows you to do the transformation in the browser where it's supported, and on the server otherwise. Until the browser situation stabilises, however, **server-side** transformation of XML to HTML, driven from ASP pages or from Java servlets, is really the only practical option for a serious project.

There's more information about products from Microsoft and other vendors in Chapter 10 – but do be aware that it will become out of date very rapidly.

XSLT and XML

XSLT is essentially a tool for transforming XML documents. At the start of this chapter we discussed the reasons why this is important, but now we need to look a little more precisely at the relationship between the two. There are two particular aspects of XML that XSLT interacts with very closely: one is XML Namespaces; the other is the XML Information Set. These are discussed in the following sections.

XML Namespaces

XSLT is designed on the basis that **XML namespaces** are an essential part of the XML standard. So when the XSLT standard refers to an XML document, it really means an XML document that also conforms to the XML Namespaces specification, which can be found at http://www.w3.org/TR/REC-xml-names.

> *For a full explanation of XML Namespaces, see Chapter 7 of the Wrox Press book* Professional XML, ISBN 1-861003-11-0.

Namespaces play an important role in XSLT. Their purpose is to allow you to mix tags from two different vocabularies in the same XML document. For example, in one vocabulary `<table>` might mean a two-dimensional array of data values, while in another vocabulary `<table>` refers to a piece of furniture. Here's a quick reminder of how they work:

❑ Namespaces are identified by a Unique Resource Identifier (URI). This can take a number of forms. One form is the familiar URL, for example `http://www.wrox.com/namespace`. Another form, not fully standardized but being used in some XML vocabularies (see for example `http://www.biztalk.org`) is a URN, for example `urn:java:com.icl.saxon`. The detailed form of the URI doesn't matter, but it is a good idea to choose one that will be unique. One good way of achieving this is to use the URL of your own web site. But don't let this confuse you into thinking that there must be something on the web site for the URL to point to. The namespace URI is simply a string that you have chosen to be different from other people's namespace URIs: it doesn't need to point to anything.

❑ Since namespace URIs are often rather long and use special characters such as «/», they are not used in full as part of the element and attribute names. Instead, each namespace used in a document can be given a short nickname, and this nickname is used as a prefix of the element and attribute names. It doesn't matter what prefix you choose, because the real name of the element or attribute is determined only by its namespace URI and its local name (the part of the name after the prefix). For example, all my examples use the prefix **xsl** to refer to the namespace URI http://www.w3.org/1999/XSL/Transform, but you could equally well use the prefix **xslt**, so long as you use it consistently.

❑ For element names, you can also declare a default namespace URI, which is to be associated with unprefixed element names. The default namespace URI, however, does not apply to unprefixed attribute names.

A namespace prefix is declared using a special pseudo-attribute within any element tag, with the form:

```
xmlns:prefix = "namespace-URI"
```

This declares a namespace prefix, which can be used for the name of that element, for its attributes, and for any element or attribute name contained in that element. The default namespace, which is used for elements having no prefix (but not for attributes), is similarly declared using a pseudo-attribute:

```
xmlns = "namespace-URI"
```

XSLT can't be used to process an XML document unless it conforms to the XML Namespaces recommendation. In practice this isn't a big problem, because most people are treating XML Namespaces as if it were an inherent part of the XML standard, rather than a bolt-on optional extra. It does have certain implications, though. In particular, serious use of Namespaces is virtually incompatible with serious use of Document Type Definitions, because DTDs don't recognize the special significance of prefixes in element names; so a consequence of backing Namespaces is that XSLT provides very little support for DTDs, choosing instead to wait until the replacement facility, XML Schemas, eventually emerges.

The XML Information Set

XSLT is designed to work on the information carried by an XML document, not on the raw document itself. This means that, as an XSLT programmer, you are given a tree view of the source document in which some aspects are visible and others are not. For example, you can see the attribute names and values, but you can't see whether the attribute was written in single or double quotes, you can't see what order the attributes were in, and you can't tell whether or not they were written on the same line.

One messy detail is that there have been many attempts to define exactly what constitutes the **essential** information content of a well-formed XML document, as distinct from its accidental punctuation. All attempts so far have come up with slightly different answers. The most recent, and the most definitive, attempt to provide a common vocabulary for the content of XML documents is the **XML Information Set** definition, which may be found at http://www.w3.org/TR/xml-infoset.

Unfortunately this came too late to make all the standards consistent. For example, some treat comments as significant, others not; some treat the choice of namespace prefixes as significant, others take them as irrelevant. I shall describe in Chapter 2 exactly how XSLT (or more accurately, XPath) defines the Tree Model of XML, and how it differs in finer points of detail from some of the other definitions such as the Document Object Model or DOM.

XSL and CSS

Why are there two stylesheet languages, XSL (i.e. XSLT plus XSL Formatting Objects) as well as Cascading Style Sheets (CSS and CSS2)?

It's only fair to say that in an ideal world there would be a single language in this role, and that the reason there are two is that no-one has been able to invent something that achieved the simplicity and economy of CSS for doing simple things, combined with the power of XSL for doing more complex things.

CSS (by which I include CSS2, which greatly extends the degree to which you can control the final appearance of the page) is mainly used for rendering HTML, but it can also be used for rendering XML directly, by defining the display characteristics of each XML element. However, it has serious limitations. It cannot reorder the elements in the source document, it cannot add text or images, it cannot decide which elements should be displayed and which omitted, it cannot calculate totals or averages or sequence numbers. In other words, it can only be used when the structure of the source document is already very close to the final display form.

Having said this, CSS is simple to write, and it is very economical in machine resources. It doesn't reorder the document, so it doesn't need to build a tree representation of the document in memory, and it can start displaying the document as soon as the first text is received over the network. Perhaps most important of all, CSS is very simple for HTML authors to write, without any programming skills. In comparison, XSLT is far more powerful, but it also consumes a lot more memory and processor power, as well as training budget.

It's often appropriate to use both tools together. Use XSLT to create a representation of the document that is close to its final form, in that it contains the right text in the right order, and then use CSS to add the finishing touches, by selecting font sizes, colors, and so on. Typically you would do the XSLT processing on the server, and the CSS processing on the client (in the browser), so another advantage of this approach is that you reduce the amount of data sent down the line, which should improve response time for your users as well as postponing the next expensive bandwidth increase.

The History of XSL

Like most of the XML family of standards, XSLT was developed by the World Wide Web Consortium (W3C), a coalition of companies orchestrated by Tim Berners-Lee, the inventor of the web. There is an interesting page on the history of XSL, and styling proposals generally, at http://www.w3.org/Style/History/.

Pre-history

HTML was originally conceived by Berners-Lee as a set of tags to mark the logical structure of a document: headings, paragraphs, links, quotes, code sections, and the like. Soon people wanted more control over how the document looked: they wanted to achieve the same control over the appearance of the delivered publication as they had with printing and paper. So HTML acquired more and more tags and attributes to control presentation: fonts, margins, tables, colors, and all the rest that followed. As it evolved, the documents being published became more and more browser-dependent, and it was seen that the original goals of simplicity and universality were starting to slip away.

The remedy was widely seen as separation of content from presentation. This was not a new concept; it had been well developed through the 1980s in the development of **Standard Generalized Markup Language (SGML)**, whose architecture in turn was influenced by the elaborate (and never implemented) work done in the ISO Open Document Architecture (ODA) standards.

Just as XML was derived as a greatly simplified subset of SGML, so XSLT has its origins in an SGML-based standard called **DSSSL (Document Style Semantics and Specification Language)**. DSSSL (I pronounce it *Dissel*) was developed primarily to fill the need for a standard device-independent language to define the output rendition of SGML documents, particularly for high-quality typographical presentation. SGML was around for a long time before DSSSL appeared in the early 1990s, but until then the output side had been handled using proprietary and often extremely expensive tools, geared towards driving equally expensive phototypesetters, so that the technology was only really taken up by the big publishing houses.

C. M. Sperberg-McQueen and Robert F. Goldstein presented an influential paper at the WWW '94 conference in Chicago under the title *A Manifesto for Adding SGML Intelligence to the World-Wide Web*. You can find it at: http://www.ncsa.uiuc.edu/SDG/ IT94/Proceedings/Autools/sperberg-mcqueen/sperberg.html.

The authors presented a set of requirements for a stylesheet language, which is as good a statement as any of the aims that the XSL designers were trying to meet. As with other proposals from around that time, the concept of a separate transformation language had not yet appeared, and a great deal of the paper is devoted to the rendition capabilities of the language. There are many formative ideas, however, including the concept of fallback processing to cope with situations where particular features are not available in the current environment.

It is worth quoting some extracts from the paper here:

> *Ideally, the style sheet language should be declarative, not procedural, and should allow style sheets to exploit the structure of SGML documents to the fullest. Styles must be able to vary with the structural location of the element: paragraphs within notes may be formatted differently from paragraphs in the main text. Styles must be able to vary with the attribute values of the element in question: a quotation of type "display" may need to be formatted differently from a quotation of type "inline". They may even need to vary with the attribute values of other elements: items in numbered lists will look different from items in bulleted lists.*

At the same time, the language has to be reasonably easy to interpret in a procedural way: implementing the style sheet language should not become the major challenge in implementing a Web client.

The semantics should be additive: It should be possible for users to create new style sheets by adding new specifications to some existing (possibly standard) style sheet. This should not require copying the entire base style sheet; instead, the user should be able to store locally just the user's own changes to the standard style sheet, and they should be added in at browse time. This is particularly important to support local modifications of standard DTDs.

Syntactically, the style sheet language must be very simple, preferably trivial to parse. One obvious possibility: formulate the style sheet language as an SGML DTD, so that each style sheet will be an SGML document. Since the browser already knows how to parse SGML, no extra effort will be needed.

We recommend strongly that a subset of DSSSL be used to formulate style sheets for use on the World Wide Web; with the completion of the standards work on DSSSL, there is no reason for any community to invent their own style-sheet language from scratch. The full DSSSL standard may well be too demanding to implement in its entirety, but even if that proves true, it provides only an argument for defining a subset of DSSSL that must be supported, not an argument for rolling our own. Unlike home-brew specifications, a subset of a standard comes with an automatically predefined growth path. We expect to work on the formulation of a usable, implementable subset of DSSSL for use in WWW style sheets, and invite all interested parties to join in the effort.

In late 1995, a W3C-sponsored workshop on stylesheet languages was held in Paris. In view of the subsequent role of James Clark as editor of the XSLT Recommendation, it is interesting to read the notes of his contribution on the goals of DSSSL, which can be found at http://www.w3.org/Style/951106_Workshop/report1.html#clark.

What follows is a few selected paragraphs from these notes:

DSSSL contains both a transformation language and a formatting language. Originally the transformation was needed to make certain kinds of styles possible (such as tables of contents). The query language now takes care of that, but the transformation language survives because it is useful in its own right.

Both simple and complex designs should be possible, and the styles should be suitable for batch formatting as well as interactive applications. Existing systems should be able to support DSSSL with only minimal changes (a DSSSL parser is obviously needed).

The language is strictly declarative, which is achieved by adopting a functional subset of Scheme. Interactive style sheet editors must be possible.

A DSSSL style sheet very precisely describes a function from SGML to a flow object tree. It allows partial style sheets to be combined ('cascaded' as in CSS): some rule may override some other rule, based on implicit and explicit priorities, but there is no blending between conflicting styles.

James Clark closed his talk with the remark:

Creating a good, extensible style language is hard!

One suspects that the effort of editing the XSLT Recommendation didn't cause him to change his mind.

The First XSL Proposal

Following these early discussions, the W3C set up a formal activity to create a stylesheet language proposal. The remit for this group specified that it should be based on DSSSL.

As an output of this activity came the first formal proposal for XSL, dated 21 August 1997. It can be found at http://www.w3.org/TR/NOTE-XSL.html.

There are eleven authors listed. They include five from Microsoft, three from Inso Corporation, plus Paul Grosso of ArborText, James Clark (who works for himself), and Henry Thompson of the University of Edinburgh.

The section describing the purpose of the language is worth reading:

XSL is a stylesheet language designed for the Web community. It provides functionality beyond CSS (e.g. element reordering). We expect that CSS will be used to display simply-structured XML documents and XSL will be used where more powerful formatting capabilities are required or for formatting highly structured information such as XML structured data or XML documents that contain structured data.

Web authors create content at three different levels of sophistication:

❑   *markup: relies solely on a declarative syntax*

❑   *script: additionally uses code "snippets" for more complex behaviors*

❑   *program: uses a full programming language*

XSL is intended to be accessible to the "markup" level user by providing a declarative solution to most data description and rendering requirements. Less common tasks are accommodated through a graceful escape to a familiar scripting environment. This approach is familiar to the Web publishing community as it is modeled after the HTML/JavaScript environment.

The powerful capabilities provided by XSL allow:

- ❏ *formatting of source elements based on ancestry/descendency, position, and uniqueness*
- ❏ *the creation of formatting constructs including generated text and graphics*
- ❏ *the definition of reusable formatting macros*
- ❏ *writing-direction independent stylesheets*
- ❏ *extensible set of formatting objects*

The authors then explained carefully why they had felt it necessary to diverge from DSSSL, and described why a separate language from CSS (Cascading Style Sheets) was thought necessary.

They then stated some design principles:

- ❏ *XSL should be straightforwardly usable over the Internet.*
- ❏ *XSL should be expressed in XML syntax.*
- ❏ *XSL should provide a declarative language to do all common formatting tasks.*
- ❏ *XSL should provide an "escape" into a scripting language to accommodate more sophisticated formatting tasks and to allow for extensibility and completeness.*
- ❏ *XSL will be a subset of DSSSL with the proposed amendment. (As XSL was no longer a subset of DSSSL, they cannily proposed amending DSSSL so it would become a superset of XSL).*
- ❏ *A mechanical mapping of a CSS stylesheet into an XSL stylesheet should be possible.*
- ❏ *XSL should be informed by user experience with the FOSI stylesheet language.*
- ❏ *The number of optional features in XSL should be kept to a minimum.*
- ❏ *XSL stylesheets should be human-legible and reasonably clear.*
- ❏ *The XSL design should be prepared quickly.*
- ❏ *XSL stylesheets shall be easy to create.*
- ❏ *Terseness in XSL markup is of minimal importance.*

As a requirements statement, this doesn't rank among the best. It doesn't read like the kind of list you get when you talk to users and find out what they need. It's much more the kind of list designers write when they know what they want to produce, including a few political concessions to the people who might raise objections. But if you want to understand why XSLT became the language it did, this list is certainly evidence of the thinking.

The language described in this first proposal contains many of the key concepts of XSLT as it finally emerged, but the syntax is virtually unrecognizable. It was already clear that the language should be based on templates that handled nodes in the source document matching a defined pattern, and that the language should be free of side-effects, to allow "progressive rendering and handling of large documents". I'll explore the significance of this requirement in more detail on page 34, and discuss its implications on the way stylesheets are designed in Chapter 8. The basic idea is that if a stylesheet is expressed as a collection of completely independent operations, each of which has no external effect other than generating part of the output from its input (for example, it cannot update global variables), then it becomes possible to generate any part of the output independently if that particular part of the input changes. Whether the XSLT language actually achieves this objective is still an open question.

Microsoft shipped their first technology preview four months after this proposal appeared, in January 1998.

To enable W3C to make an assessment of the proposal, Norman Walsh produced a requirements summary, which was published in May 1998. It is available at http://www.w3.org/TR/WD-XSLReq.

The bulk of his paper is given over to a long list of the typographical features that the language should support, following the tradition both before and since that the formatting side of the language gets a lot more column inches than the transformation side. But as XSLT fans that need not worry us: the success of standards has always been inversely proportional to their length.

What Walsh has to say on the transformation aspects of the language is particularly terse, and although he clearly had reasons for thinking these features were necessary, it's a shame that he doesn't tell us why he put these in and left others, such as sorting, grouping, and totaling, out:

> *Ancestors, children, siblings, attributes, content, disjunctions, negation, enumerations, computed select based upon arbitrary query expressions.*

> *Arithmetic Expressions; arithmetic, simple boolean comparisons, boolean logic, substrings, string concatenation.*

> *Data Types: Scalar types, units of measure, Flow Objects, XML Objects*

> *Side effects: No global side effects.*

> *Standard Procedures: The expression language should have a set of procedures that are built in to the XSL language. These are still to be identified.*

> *User Defined Functions: For reuse. Parameterized, but not recursive.*

Following this activity, the first Working Draft of XSL (not to be confused with the Proposal) was published on 18 August 1998, and the language started to take shape, gradually converging on the final form it took in the 16 November 1999 Recommendation through a series of Working Drafts, each of which made radical changes, but kept the original design principles intact.

So let's look now at the essential characteristics of XSLT as a language.

XSLT as a Language

What are the most significant characteristics of XSLT as a language, which distinguish it from other languages? In this section I shall pick three of the most striking features: the fact that it is written in XML syntax, the fact that it is a language free of side-effects, and the fact that processing is described as a set of independent pattern-matching rules.

Use of XML Syntax

As we've seen, the use of SGML syntax for stylesheets was proposed as long ago as 1994, and it seems that this idea gradually became the accepted wisdom. It's difficult to trace exactly what the overriding arguments were, and when you find yourself writing something like:

```
<xsl:variable name="y">
    <xsl:call-template name="f">
        <xsl:with-param name="x"/>
    </xsl:call-template>
</xsl:variable>
```

to express what in other languages would be written as « y = f(x); », then you may find yourself wondering how such a decision came to be made.

In fact, it could have been worse: in the very early drafts, the syntax for writing what are now XPath expressions was also expressed in XML, so instead of writing `select="book/author/first-name"` you had to write something along the lines of:

```
<select>
    <path>
        <element type="book">
        <element type="author">
        <element type="first-name">
    </path>
</select>
```

The most obvious arguments for expressing XSLT stylesheets in XML are perhaps:

❑   There is already an XML parser in the browser, so it keeps the footprint small if this can be re-used.

❑ Everyone had got fed up with the syntactic inconsistencies between HTML/XML and CSS, and didn't want the same thing to happen again.

❑ The syntax of DSSSL was widely seen as a barrier to its adoption; better to have a syntax that was already familiar in the target community.

❑ Many existing popular templating languages are expressed as an outline of the output document with embedded instructions, so this is a familiar concept.

❑ All the lexical apparatus is reusable, for example Unicode support, character and entity references, whitespace handling, namespaces.

❑ It's occasionally useful to have a stylesheet as the input or output of a transformation (witness the Microsoft XSL converter as an example), so it's a benefit if a stylesheet can read and write other stylesheets.

❑ Providing visual development tools easily solves the inconvenience of having to type lots of angle brackets.

Like it or not, the XML-based syntax is now an intrinsic feature of the language that has both benefits and drawbacks. It does require a lot of typing: but in the end, the number of keystrokes has very little bearing on the ease or difficulty of solving particular transformation problems.

No Side-effects

The idea that XSL should be a declarative language free of side-effects appears repeatedly in the early statements about the goals and design principles of the language, but no-one ever seems to explain *why*: what would be the user benefit?

A function or procedure in a programming language is said to have side-effects if it makes changes to its environment, for example if it can update a global variable that another function or procedure can read, it can write messages to a log file, or prompt the user. If functions have side-effects, it becomes important to call them the right number of times and in the correct order. Functions that have no side-effects (sometimes called pure functions) can be called any number of times and in any order. It doesn't matter how many times you evaluate the area of a triangle, you will always get the same answer; but if the function to calculate the area has a side-effect such as changing the size of the triangle, or if you don't know whether it has side-effects or not, then it becomes important to call it once only.

I expand on this concept in the section on Computational Stylesheets in Chapter 8, page 545.

It is possible to find hints at the reason why this was considered desirable in the statements that the language should be equally suitable for batch or interactive use, and that it should be capable of **progressive rendering**. There is a concern that when you download a large XML document, you won't be able to see anything on your screen until the last byte has been received from the server. Equally, if a small change were made to the XML document, it would be nice to be able to determine the change needed to the screen display, without recalculating the whole thing from scratch. If a language has side effects then the order of execution of the statements in the language has to be defined, or the final result becomes unpredictable. Without side-effects, the statements can be executed in any order, which means it is possible, in principle, to process the parts of a stylesheet selectively and independently.

Whether XSLT has actually achieved these goals is somewhat debatable. Certainly, determining which parts of the output document are affected by a small change to one part of the input document is not easy, given the flexibility of the expressions and patterns that are now permitted in the language. Equally, all existing XSLT processors require the whole document to be loaded into memory. However, it would be a mistake to expect too much too soon. When E. F. Codd published the relational calculus in 1970, he made the claim that a declarative language was desirable because it was possible to optimize it, which was not possible with the navigational data access languages in use at the time. In fact it took another fifteen years before relational optimization techniques (and, to be fair, the price of hardware) reached the point where large relational databases were commercially viable. But in the end he was proved right, and the hope is that the same principle will also eventually deliver similar benefits in the area of transformation and styling languages.

What being side-effect free means in practice is that you cannot update the value of a variable. This restriction is something you may find very frustrating at first, and a big price to pay for these rather remote benefits. But as you get the feel of the language and learn to think about using it the way it was designed to be used, rather than the way you are familiar with from other languages, you will find you stop thinking about this as a restriction. In fact, one of the benefits is that it eliminates a whole class of bugs from your code! I shall come back to this subject in Chapter 8, where I outline some of the common design patterns for XSLT stylesheets, and in particular, describe how to use recursive code to handle situations where in the past you would probably have used updateable variables to keep track of the current state.

Rule-based

The dominant feature of a typical XSLT stylesheet is that it consists of a sequence of template rules, each of which describes how a particular element type or other construct should be processed. The rules are not arranged in any particular order; they don't have to match the order of the input or the order of the output, and in fact there are very few clues as to what ordering or nesting of elements the stylesheet author expects to encounter in the source document. It is this that makes XSLT a declarative language: you say what output should be produced when particular patterns occur in the input, as distinct from a procedural program where you have to say what tasks to perform in what order.

This rule-based structure is very like CSS, but with the major difference that both the patterns (the description of which nodes a rule applies to) and the actions (the description of what happens when the rule is matched) are much richer in functionality.

Example: Displaying a Poem

Let's see how we can use the rule-based approach to format a poem. Again, we haven't introduced all the concepts yet, so I won't try to explain every detail of how this works, but it's useful to see what the template rules actually look like in practice.

Input

Let's take this XML source as our poem. The source file can be found on the web site for this book at http://www.wrox.com, under the name poem.xml, and the stylesheet is there as poem.xsl.

```
<poem>
    <author>Rupert Brooke</author>
    <date>1912</date>
    <title>Song</title>
    <stanza>
        <line>And suddenly the wind comes soft,</line>
        <line>And Spring is here again;</line>
        <line>And the hawthorn quickens with buds of green</line>
        <line>And my heart with buds of pain.</line>
    </stanza>
    <stanza>
        <line>My heart all Winter lay so numb,</line>
        <line>The earth so dead and frore,</line>
        <line>That I never thought the Spring would come again</line>
        <line>Or my heart wake any more.</line>
    </stanza>
    <stanza>
        <line>But Winter's broken and earth has woken,</line>
        <line>And the small birds cry again;</line>
        <line>And the hawthorn hedge puts forth its buds,</line>
        <line>And my heart puts forth its pain.</line>
    </stanza>
</poem>
```

Output

We'll write a stylesheet such that this document appears in the browser as shown below:

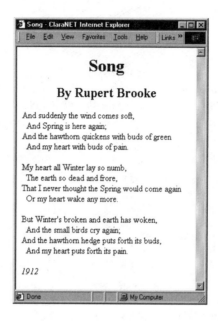

Stylesheet

It starts with the standard header:

```
<xsl:stylesheet
    xmlns:xsl="http://www.w3.org/1999/XSL/Transform"
    version="1.0">
```

Now we'll write one template rule for each element type in the source document. The rule for the <poem> element creates the skeleton of the HTML . output, defining the ordering of the elements in the output (which doesn't have to be the same as the input order). The <xsl:value-of> instruction inserts the value of the selected element at this point in the output. The <xsl:apply-templates>instructions cause the selected child elements to be processed, each using its own template rule.

```
<xsl:template match="poem">
    <html>
    <head>
    <title><xsl:value-of select="title"/></title>
    </head>
```

```
<body>
<xsl:apply-templates select="title"/>
    <xsl:apply-templates select="author"/>
    <xsl:apply-templates select="stanza"/>
    <xsl:apply-templates select="date"/>
  </body>
  </html>
</xsl:template>
```

The template rules for the `<title>`, `<author>`, and `<date>` elements are very simple: they take the content of the element (denoted by «`select="."`»), and surround it within appropriate HTML tags to define its display style:

```
<xsl:template match="title">
    <div align="center"><h1><xsl:value-of select="."/></h1></div>
</xsl:template>

<xsl:template match="author">
    <div align="center"><h2>By <xsl:value-of select="."/></h2></div>
</xsl:template>

<xsl:template match="date">
    <p><i><xsl:value-of select="."/></i></p>
</xsl:template>
```

The template rule for the `<stanza>` element puts each stanza into an HTML paragraph, and then invokes processing of the lines within the stanza, as defined by the template rule for lines:

```
<xsl:template match="stanza">
    <p><xsl:apply-templates select="line"/></p>
</xsl:template>
```

The rule for `<line>` elements is a little more complex: if the position of the line within the stanza is an even number, it precedes the line with two non-breaking-space characters (` `). The `<xsl:if>` instruction tests a boolean condition, which in this case calls the **position()** function to determine the relative position of the current line. It then outputs the contents of the line, followed by an empty HTML `<br>` element to end the line.

```
<xsl:template match="line">
    <xsl:if test="position() mod 2 = 0">  </xsl:if>
    <xsl:value-of select="."/><br/>
</xsl:template>
```

And to finish off, we close the `<xsl:stylesheet>` element:

```
</xsl:stylesheet>
```

Although template rules are a characteristic feature of the XSLT language, we'll see that this is not the only way of writing a stylesheet. In Chapter 8, I will describe four different design patterns for XSLT stylesheets, only one of which makes extensive use of template rules. In fact, the *Hello World* stylesheet I presented earlier in this chapter doesn't make any real use of template rules: it fits into the design pattern I call *fill-in-the-blanks*, because the stylesheet essentially contains the fixed part of the output with embedded instructions saying where to get the data to put in the variable parts.

Where to use XSLT

In this final section of this chapter I shall try and identify what tasks XSLT is good at, and by implication, tasks for which a different tool would be more suitable. I shall also look at alternative ways of using XSLT within the overall architecture of your application.

Broadly speaking, as I discussed at the beginning of the chapter, there are two main scenarios for using XSLT transformations: data conversion, and publishing; and we'll consider each of them separately.

Data Conversion Applications

Data conversion is not something that will go away just because XML has been invented. Even though an increasing number of data transfers between organizations or between applications within an organization are likely to be encoded in XML, there will still be different data models, different ways of representing the same thing, and different subsets of information that are of interest to different people (recall the example at the beginning of the chapter, where we were converting music between different XML representations and different presentation formats). So however enthusiastic we are about XML, the reality is that there are going to be a lot of comma-separated-values files, EDI messages, and any number of other formats in use for a long time to come.

When you have the task of converting one XML data set into another XML data set, then XSLT is an obvious choice.

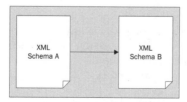

It can be used for extracting the data selectively, reordering it, turning attributes into elements or vice versa, or any number of similar tasks. It can also be used simply for validating the data. As a language, XSLT is best at manipulating the structure of the information as distinct from its content: it's a good language for turning rows into columns, but for string handling (for example removing any text that appears between square brackets) it's rather laborious compared with a language like Perl. However, you can always tackle these problems by invoking procedures written in other languages, such as Java or Javascript, from within the stylesheet.

XSLT is also useful for converting XML data into any text-based format, such as comma-separated values, or various EDI message formats. Text output is really just like XML output without the tags, so this creates no particular problems for the language.

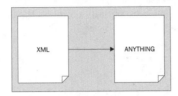

Perhaps more surprising is that XSLT can often be useful to convert from non-XML formats into XML or something else:

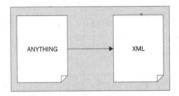

In this case you'll need to write some kind of parser that understands the input format; but you would have had to do that anyway. The benefit is that once you've written the parser, the rest of the data conversion can be expressed in a high-level language. This separation also increases the chances that you'll be able to reuse your parser next time you need to handle that particular input format. I'll show you an example in Chapter 9, page 610, where the input is a rather old-fashioned and distinctly non-XML format widely used for exchanging data between genealogy software packages. It turns out that it isn't even necessary to write the data out as XML before using the XSLT stylesheet to process it: all you need to do is to make your parser look like an XML parser, by making it implement one of the standard parser interfaces: SAX or DOM. Most XSLT processors will accept input from a program that implements the SAX or DOM interfaces, even if the data never saw the light of day as XML.

One caveat about data conversion applications: today's XSLT processors all rely on holding all the data in memory while the transformation is taking place. The tree structure in memory can be as much as ten times the original data size, so in practice, the limit on data size for an XSLT conversion is a few megabytes. Even at this size, a complex conversion can be quite time-consuming: it depends very much on the processing that you actually want to do.

One way around this is to split the data into chunks and convert each chunk separately – assuming, of course, that there is some kind of correspondence between chunks of input and chunks of output. But when this starts to get complicated, there comes a point where XSLT is no longer the best tool for the job. You might be better off, for example, loading the data into a relational or object database, and using the database query language to extract it again in a different sequence.

If you need to process large amounts of data serially, for example extracting selected records from a log of retail transactions, then an application written using the SAX interface might take a little longer to write than the equivalent XSLT stylesheet, but it is likely to run many times faster. Very often the combination of a SAX filter application to do simple data extraction, followed by an XSLT stylesheet to do more complex manipulation, can be the best solution in such cases.

Publishing

The difference between data conversion and publishing is that in the former case, the data is destined for input to another piece of software, while in the latter case it is destined to be read (you hope) by human beings. Publishing in this context doesn't just mean lavish text and multimedia, it also means data: everything from the traditional activity of producing and distributing reports so that managers know what's going on in the business, to producing online phone bills and bank statements for customers, and rail timetables for the general public. XML is ideal for such data publishing applications, as well as the more traditional text publishing, which was the original home territory of SGML.

XML was designed to enable information to be held independently of the way it is presented, which sometimes leads people into the fallacy of thinking that using XML for presentation details is somehow bad. Far from it: if you were designing a new format for downloading fonts to a printer today, you would probably make it XML-based. Presentation details have just as much right to be encoded in XML as any other kind of information. So we can see the role of XSLT in the publishing process as being converting data-without-presentation to data-with-presentation, where both are, at least in principle, XML formats.

The two important vehicles for publishing information today are print-on-paper, and the web. The print-on-paper scene is the more difficult one, because of the high expectations of users for visual quality. XSL Formatting Objects attempts to define an XML-based model of a print file for high quality display on paper or on screen. Because of the sheer number of parameters needed to achieve this, the standard is taking a while to complete, and will probably take even longer to implement. But the web is a less demanding environment, where all we need to do is convert the data to HTML and leave the browser to do the best it can on the display available. HTML, of course, is not XML, but it is close enough so that a simple mapping is possible. Converting XML to HTML is the most common application for XSLT today. It's actually a two-stage process: first convert to an XML-based model that is structurally equivalent to the target HTML, and then serialize this in HTML notation rather than strict XML.

The emergence of XHTML 1.0 of course tidies up this process even further, because it is a pure XML format, but how quick the take-up of XHTML will be remains to be seen.

When to do the Conversion?

The process of publishing information to a user is illustrated in the diagram below:

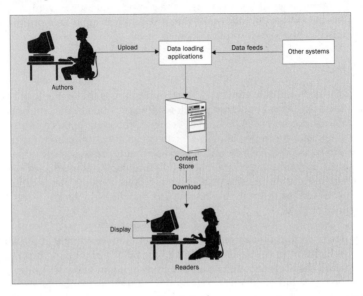

There are several points in such a system where XSLT transformations might be appropriate:

❑ Information entered by authors using their preferred tools, or customized form-filling interfaces, can be converted to XML and stored in that form in the content store.

❑ XML information arriving from other systems might be transformed into a different flavor of XML for storage in the content store. For example, it might be broken up into page-size chunks.

❑ XML can be translated into HTML on the server, when the users request a page. This can be controlled using technology such as Java servlets or Java Server Pages. On a Microsoft server you can use the XSL ISAPI extension available from http://msdn.microsoft.com/xml, or if you want more application control, you can invoke the transformation from script on ASP pages.

❑ XML can be sent down to the client system, and translated into HTML within the browser. This can give a highly interactive presentation of the information, but it relies on all the users having a browser that can do the job.

❑ XML data can also be converted into its final display form at publishing time, and stored as HTML within the content store. This minimizes the work that needs to be done at display time, and is ideal when the same displayed page is presented to very many users.

There isn't one right answer, and often a combination of techniques may be appropriate. Conversion in the browser is an attractive option once XSLT becomes widely available within browsers, but that is still some way off. Even when this is done, there may still be a need for some server-side processing to deliver the XML in manageable chunks, and to protect secure information. Conversion at delivery time on the server is a popular choice, because it allows personalization, but it can be a heavy overhead for sites with high traffic. Some busy sites have found that it is more effective to generate a different set of HTML pages for each section of the target audience in advance, and at page request time, to do nothing more than selecting the right pre-constructed HTML page.

Summary

This introductory chapter described the whys and wherefores of XSLT: it tried to answer questions such as:

❑   What kind of language is it?

❑   Where does it fit into the XML family?

❑   Where does it come from and why was it designed the way it is?

❑   Where should it be used?

You now know that XSLT is a declarative high-level language designed for transforming the structure of XML documents; that it has two major applications: data conversion and presentation; and that it can be used at a number of different points in the overall application architecture, including at data capture time, at delivery time on the server, and at display time on the browser. You also have some idea why XSLT has developed in the way it has.

Now it's time to start taking an in-depth look inside the language to see how it does this job. In the next chapter, we'll look at the way transformation is carried out by treating the input and output as tree structures, and using patterns to match particular nodes in the input tree and define what nodes should be added to the result tree when the pattern is matched.

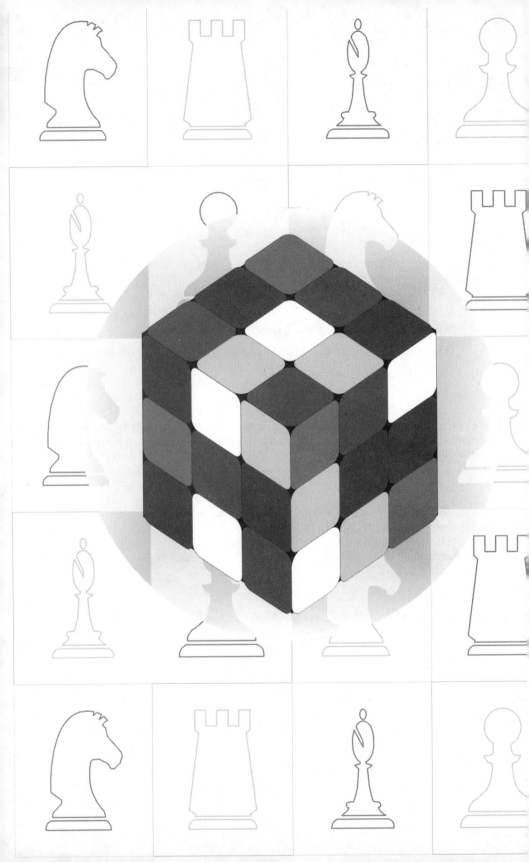

2

The XSLT Processing Model

In this chapter, we'll take a bird's eye view of what an XSLT processor does. We'll start by looking at a system overview: what are the inputs and outputs of the processor.

Then we'll look in some detail at the data model, in particular the structure of the tree representation of XML documents. An important message here is that XSLT transformations do not operate on XML documents as text, they operate on the abstract tree-like information structure represented by the text.

Having established the data model, I'll describe the processing sequence that occurs when a source document and a stylesheet are brought together. XSLT is not a conventional procedural language: it consists of a collection of template rules defining output that is produced when particular patterns are matched in the input. As seen in Chapter 1, this rule-based processing structure is one of the distinguishing features of the XSLT language.

Finally, we'll look at the way in which variables and expressions can be used in an XSLT stylesheet, and also look at the various data types available.

XSLT: A System Overview

This section looks at the structure of the process performed by XSLT.

A Simplified Overview

The core task of an XSLT processor is to apply a stylesheet to a source document and produce a result document. This is shown in the simplified diagram below:

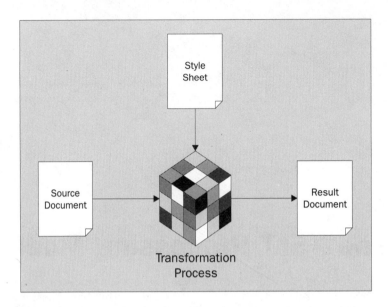

As a first approximation we can think of the source document, the stylesheet, and the result document as each being an XML document. XSLT performs a **transformation** process because the **output** (the result document) is the same kind of object as the **input** (the source document). This has immediate benefits: for example, it is possible to do a complex transformation as a series of simple transformations, and it is possible to do transformations in either direction using the same technology.

> *The choice of Rubik's cube to illustrate the transformation process is not entirely whimsical. The mathematics of Rubik's cube relies on group theory, which is where the notion of closure comes from: every operation transforms one instance of a type into another instance of the same type. We're transforming XML documents rather than cubes, but the principle is the same.*

The name **stylesheet** has stuck for the document that defines the transformation, even though purists prefer to call it a **transformation sheet**. The name reflects the reality that a very common kind of transformation performed using XSLT is to define a display style for the information in the source document, so that the result document contains information from the source document augmented with information controlling the way it is displayed on some output device.

Trees, not Documents

In practice though, we don't always want the input or output to be XML in its textual form. If we want to produce HTML output (a very common requirement) we want to produce it directly, rather than having an XML document as an intermediate form. Similarly, we might want to take input from a database or (say) an LDAP directory, or an EDI message, or a data file using comma-separated values syntax. We don't want to spend a lot of time converting these into XML documents if we can avoid it, nor do we want another raft of converters to install.

So instead, XSLT defines its operations in terms of a representation of an XML document called the **tree**. The tree is an abstract data type. There is no defined API and no defined data representation, only a conceptual model that defines the objects in the tree, their properties and their relationships. The tree is similar in concept to the W3C DOM, except that the DOM does have a defined API. Some implementors do indeed use the DOM as their internal tree structure. Others use a data structure that corresponds more closely to the XPath tree model, while some are experimenting with internal data structures that are only distantly related to this model: it's a conceptual model we are describing, not something that necessarily exists in an implementation.

Taking the inputs and output of the XSLT processors as trees produces a new diagram, as shown below:

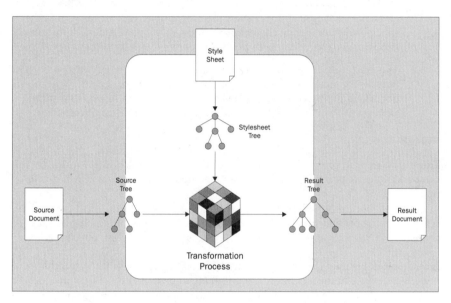

The formal conformance rules say that an XSLT processor must be able to read a stylesheet and use it to transform a source tree into a result tree. This is the part of the system shown in the oval box. There's no official requirement to handle the parts of the process shown outside the box, namely the creation of a source tree from a source XML document, or the creation of a result XML document from the result tree. In practice, though, most real products are likely to handle this part as well.

Later in this chapter we will examine the data model for the trees in more detail, and see how it relates to the structure of the XML documents.

Different Output Formats

Although the final process of converting the result tree to an output document is outside the conformance rules of the XSLT standard, this doesn't mean that XSLT has nothing to say on the subject. In fact, there is a substantial section of the specification devoted to the subject, and although everything it says is non-binding, most implementations have followed it very closely. The main control over this process is the `<xsl:output>` element, which is described in detail in Chapter 4, page 250.

The <xsl:output> element defines three output formats or methods, namely xml, html, and text. In each case the result tree is written to a single output file.

❑   With the xml output method, the output file is an XML document. We'll see later that it need not be a complete XML document; it can also be an XML fragment. The <xsl:output> element allows the stylesheet writer some control over the way in which the XML is written, for example the character encoding used, and the use of CDATA sections.

❑   With the html output method, the output file is an HTML document, typically HTML 4.0, though products may support other versions if they wish. With HTML output, the XSLT processor will recognize many of the conventions of HTML and structure the output accordingly. For example it will recognize elements such as <hr> that have a start tag and no end tag, as well as the special rules for escape characters within a <script> element. It may also (if it chooses) generate references to built-in entities such as «é».

❑   The text output method is designed to allow output in **any other text-based format**. For example, the output might be a comma-separated-values file, a document in Microsoft's Rich Text Format (RTF) or in Adobe's Portable Document Format (PDF), or it might be an electronic data interchange message, or a script in SQL or JavaScript. It's entirely up to you.

There is no explicit provision for XHTML output, but since XHTML is pure XML, it can be written using the XML method in the same way as any other XML document type.

If the <xsl:output> element is omitted, the processor makes an intelligent guess, choosing HTML if the output starts with an <html> tag, and XML otherwise.

Implementations may include output methods other than these three, but this is outside the scope of the standard. One mechanism provided by several products is to feed the result tree to a user-supplied document handler. This will generally be written to conform to the DocumentHandler interface defined as part of the SAX API specification available at http://www.megginson.com/, or in the Wrox publication *Professional XML*, ISBN 1-861003-11-0. Some products are starting to support the new version of this standard, SAX2, which can also be found at this link.

So, while the bulk of the XSLT Recommendation describes the transformation process from a source tree to a result tree, there is one section (specifically, section 16, *Output*) that describes another process, the output process. This is sometimes referred to as **serialization**, because it turns a tree structure into a serial file. XSLT processors can implement this at their discretion, and it fits into our diagram as shown below:

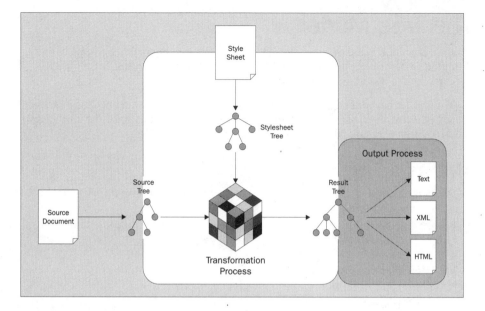

Multiple Inputs and Outputs

In real life the processing model is further complicated because there can be multiple inputs and outputs.

Specifically:

- [ ] There can be multiple input documents. The stylesheet can use the `document()` function (described in Chapter 7, page 440) to load secondary input documents, based on URI references held in the source document or the stylesheet. Each input document is processed as a tree in its own right, in exactly the same way as the principal input document.

- [ ] The stylesheet too can consist of multiple documents. There are two directives that can be used in the stylesheet, `<xsl:include>` and `<xsl:import>`, to load additional stylesheet modules and use them as extensions of the first. Splitting a stylesheet in this way allows modularity: in a complex environment different aspects of processing can be described in component stylesheets that can be incorporated into several different parent stylesheets. There is a detailed discussion of how to split a stylesheet into modules in Chapter 3.

- [ ] Several XSLT implementations also allow a single run of the XSLT processor to produce multiple output documents. This allows a single source document to be split into several output files: for example, the input might contain the text of an entire book, while the output contains one HTML file for each chapter, all connected using suitable hyperlinks. However, this capability is not present in the current version of the XSLT standard, and it is provided in different ways in different products. For details, see Chapter 10.

49

The Tree Model

Let's now look at the tree model used in XSLT in a little more detail. Actually this model is described partly in the XPath standard, and partly in XSLT itself: we'll combine the two to make things simpler.

The XSLT tree model is similar in many ways to the XML Document Object Model (DOM). However, there are a number of differences of terminology and some subtle differences of detail. I'll point some of these out as we go along.

XML as a Tree

At a simple level, the equivalence of the textual representation of an XML document with a tree representation is very straightforward.

Example: An XML Tree

Consider a document like this:

```
<definition>
    <word>export</word>
    <part-of-speech>vt</part-of-speech>
    <meaning>Send out (goods) to another country.</meaning>
    <etymology>
        <language>Latin</language>
        <parts>
            <part>
                <prefix>ex</prefix>
                <meaning>out</meaning>
            </part>
            <part>
                <word>portare</word>
                <meaning>to carry</meaning>
            </part>
        </parts>
    </etymology>
</definition>
```

We can consider each piece of text as a leaf node, and each element as a containing node, and build an equivalent tree structure, which looks like the diagram below. I've shown the tree after the stripping of all whitespace nodes: for discussion of this process, see Chapter 3, page 129. In this diagram each node is shown with potentially three pieces of information: in the top cell, the type of node, in the middle cell, the **name** of the node, and in the bottom one, its **string-value**. For the root node and for elements, I have shown the string-value simply as an asterisk: in fact, the string-value of these nodes is defined to be the concatenation of the string-values of all the element and text nodes at the next level of the tree.

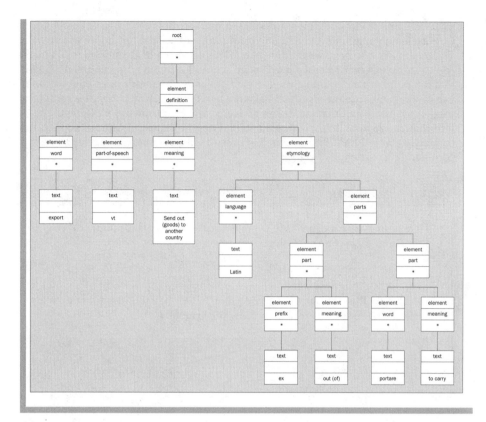

It is easy to see how other aspects of the XML document, for example attributes and processing instructions, can be similarly represented in this tree view by means of additional kinds of node.

At the top of every tree there is a **root** node. This performs the same function as the Document node in the DOM model: it doesn't correspond to any particular part of the source document, but you can regard it as representing the document as a whole. The children of the root node are the top level elements, comments, processing instructions and so on.

The XSLT tree model can represent every well-formed XML document, but it can also represent structures that are not well-formed according to the XML definition. Specifically, in well-formed XML, there must be a single outermost element containing all the other elements and text nodes; this element (the XML specification calls it the document element, though XSLT does not use this term) can be preceded and followed by comments and processing instructions, but cannot be preceded by other elements or text nodes.

The XSLT tree model does not enforce this constraint: the root can have any children that an element might have, including multiple elements and text nodes in any order. The root might also have no children at all. This corresponds to the XML rules for the content of an **external general parsed entity**, which is a freestanding fragment of XML that can be incorporated into a well-formed document by means of an entity reference. I shall sometimes use the term **well-balanced** to refer to such an entity: this term is not used in the XSLT specification, rather I have borrowed it from the XML fragment interchange proposal (http://www.w3.org/TR/WD-xml-fragment). The essential feature of a well-balanced XML fragment is that every element start tag is balanced by a corresponding element end tag.

Example: Well-balanced XML Fragment

Here is an example of an XML fragment that is well-balanced but not well-formed, as there is no enclosing element:

```
The <noun>cat</noun> <verb>sat</verb> on the <noun>mat</noun>.
```

And here is the corresponding XPath tree. In this case it is important to retain whitespace, so spaces are shown using the symbol ♦:

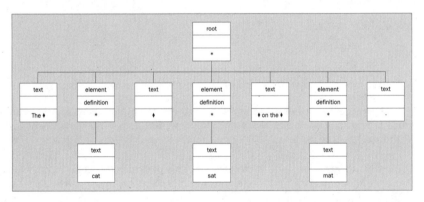

The string-value of the root node in this example is simply «The cat sat on the mat.».

Nodes in the Tree Model

An XPath tree is made up of nodes. There are seven types of node. The different types of node correspond fairly directly to the components of the source XML document:

Node Type	Description
Root node	The root node is a singular node; there is one for each document. The root node in the XSLT model performs the same function as the document node in the DOM model. Do not confuse the root with the document element, which in a well-formed document is the outermost element that contains all others.
Element node	An element is the part of a document bounded by start and end tags, or represented by a single empty-element tag such as `<TAG/>`.
Text node	A text node is a sequence of consecutive characters in a `PCDATA` part of an element. Text nodes are always made as big as possible: there will never be two adjacent text nodes in the tree, because they will have been merged together. In DOM terminology, the text nodes are **normalized**.
Attribute node	An attribute node includes the name and value of an attribute written within an element start tag (or empty element tag). An attribute that was not present in the tag, but which has a default value defined in the DTD, is also represented as an attribute node on each separate element instance. A namespace declaration (an attribute whose name is `xmlns` or whose name begins with `xmlns:`) is, however, **not** represented by an attribute node in the tree.
Comment node	A comment node represents a comment written in the XML source document between the delimiters «`<!--`» and «`-->`».
Processing instruction node	A processing instruction node represents a processing instruction written in the XML source document between the delimiters «`<?`» and «`?>`». The *PITarget* from the XML source is taken as the node's name and the rest of the content as its value. Note that the XML declaration `<?xml version="1.0"?>` is not a processing instruction, even though it looks like one, and it is not represented by a node in the tree.
Namespace node	A namespace node represents a namespace declaration, except that it is copied to each element that it applies to. So each element node has one namespace node for every namespace declaration that is in scope for the element. The namespace nodes belonging to one element are distinct from those belonging to another element, even when they are derived from the same namespace declaration in the source document.

2

Processing Model

There are several possible ways of classifying these nodes. We could distinguish those that can have children (elements and the root), those that have a parent (everything except the root), those that have a name (elements, attributes, namespaces, and processing instructions) or those that have their own textual content (attributes, text, comments, processing instructions, and namespace nodes). Since each of these criteria gives a different possible class hierarchy, the XSLT tree model instead leaves the hierarchy completely flat, and defines all these characteristics for all nodes, using null or empty values for nodes where the characteristic isn't applicable. So if we show the class hierarchy in UML notation , we get the simple diagram below.

UML (Unified Modelling Language) is a set of diagrammatic conventions for object-oriented analysis and design. For an example, see http://www.rational.com.

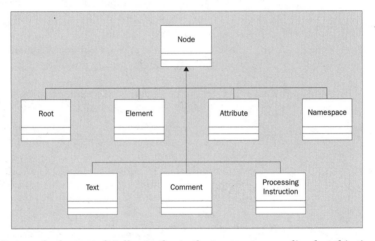

This diagram looks superficially similar to the tree we saw earlier, but this time I'm not showing a specific tree, I'm showing a class hierarchy: the boxes represent classes or types, and the arrow represents an "is-a-kind-of" relationship: for example a comment is-a-kind-of node. The earlier diagram was just one example of a particular tree, whereas now we are considering the structure of all possible trees.

I've already hinted at some of the properties and relationships of these nodes. Let's list the properties and relationships in more detail, and then add them to the diagram.

Property/Relationship	Description
name	A node has a name.
	For the root node, comments, and text nodes this is the empty string. (Note that this differs from the DOM, where names such as «#comment» are used)
	For elements and attributes it is the name that appears in the source XML, expanded using the applicable namespace declarations.

Property/Relationship	Description
name	For a processing instruction it is the *PITarget* from the source XML: this is not subject to namespace rules. The name of a namespace node is, by convention, the namespace prefix. A name itself has three parts: the prefix, which is the part of the name before the «:» as written in the source XML; the namespace URI, which is the URI associated with the prefix by means of a namespace declaration; and the local part, which is the part of the name after any «:» in the source document. For example, the name of the `<xsl:stylesheet>` element has: prefix: `"xsl"` URI: `"http://www.w3.org/1999/XSL/Transform"` local part: `"stylesheet"` Two names are considered equivalent if they have the same URI and local part, even if the prefix is different.
string-value	A node has a string-value, which is a sequence of Unicode characters. For a text node this is the text as it appears in the source XML document, except that the XML parser will have replaced every end-of-line sequence by a single new line ($\#xA$) character. For a comment, it is the text of the comment, minus the delimiters. For a processing instruction, it is the data part of the source processing instruction, not including the white space that separates it from the *PITarget*. For an attribute, it is the attribute value. For a root or element node, it is defined as the concatenation of the string-values of all the element and text children of this node. Or to look at it another way: the concatenation of all the PCDATA contained in the element (or for the root node, the document) after stripping out all Markup. (This again differs from the DOM, where the `nodeValue` property in these cases is null.) For a namespace node the string-value is, by convention, the URI of the namespace being declared.

Property/ Relationship	Description
base-URI	A node has a base URI. This should not be confused with its namespace URI. The base URI of a node depends on the URI of the source XML document it was loaded from, or more accurately, the URI of the external entity it was loaded from, since different parts of the same document might come from different XML entities. The base URI is used when evaluating a relative URI that occurs as part of the value of this node, for example an `href` attribute: this is always interpreted relative to the base URI of the node it came from.
	In fact, the base URI is only maintained explicitly for element nodes and processing instruction nodes. For attributes, text nodes, comments, and namespace nodes the base URI is the same as the URI of its parent node. For the root node, it is the URI of the document entity. This is a little ad-hoc, since a text node need not come from the same external entity as its parent element, but it reflects the decision that text nodes should be joined up irrespective of entity boundaries.
child	A node has a list (an ordered set) of child nodes. This one-to-many relationship is defined for all nodes, but the list will be empty for all nodes except the root node and element nodes. So you can ask for the children of an attribute, and you will get an empty node-set returned.
	The children of an element are the elements, text nodes, processing instructions, and comments contained textually between its start and end tags, provided that they are not also children of some lower-level element
	The children of the root node are all the elements, text nodes, comments, and processing instructions that aren't contained in another element. For a well-formed document the children of the root node will be the document element plus any comments or processing instructions that come before or after the document element.
	The attributes of an element are not regarded as child nodes of the element; neither are its namespace nodes.
parent	Every node, except the root, has a parent. The parent relationship is **not** the exact inverse of the child relationship: specifically, attribute nodes and namespace nodes have an element node as their parent, **but they are not considered to be children of that element**. In other cases, however, the relationship is symmetric: elements, text nodes, processing instructions, and comments are always children of their parent node, which will always be either an element or the root.

Property/ Relationship	Description
has-attribute	This relationship only exists in a real sense between element nodes and attribute nodes, and this is how it is shown on the diagram below. It is a one-to-many relationship: one element has zero or more attributes. In fact, the relationship `has-attribute` is defined for all nodes, but if you ask for the attributes of any node other than an element, the result will be an empty node-set.
has-namespace	This relationship only really exists between element nodes and namespace nodes, and this is how it is shown on the diagram. It is a one-to-many relationship: one element has zero or more namespaces. Like the `has-attribute` relationship, the relationship `has-namespace` is defined for all nodes, so if you ask for the namespaces of any node other than an element, the result will be an empty node-set. Note that each namespace node is owned uniquely by one element. If a namespace declaration in the source document has a scope that includes many elements, then a corresponding namespace node will be generated for each one. These nodes will all have the same name and string-value, but they will be distinct nodes for the purposes of counting and using the union operator.

It's now possible to draw a more complete picture of the UML class diagram as follows. In this version:

❑ I have brought out `Container` as a separate class, to distinguish those nodes that have children (the root, and elements) from those that do not. This is for illustration only: the concept of a container node is not explicit in the formal model.

❑ I have identified the `has-parent` relationship between any node and its parent.

❑ I have identified the separate relationships between an element and its attributes, and between an element and its namespace nodes.

❑ I have identified the additional class `UnparsedEntity`. This is not itself a node on the tree. It corresponds to an unparsed entity declaration within the document's DTD, and the information is accessible only using the `unparsed-entity-uri()` function.

❑ I have identified two additional properties on the Element node: `BaseURI`, which is the URI of the entity that the element start and end tags were found in, and ID, which is the ID attribute value for this element if it has one.

57

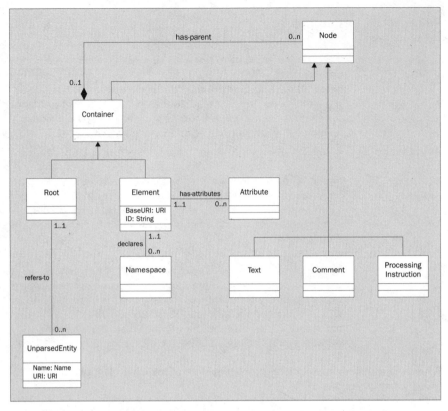

It's worth mentioning that the XSLT tree model never uses null values in the sense that SQL or Java use null values. If a node has no string-value, then the value returned is the empty string, a string of length zero. If a node has no children, then the value returned is the empty node-set, a set containing no members. There's no distinction made between an empty string and an absent string, or between an empty set and an absent set. In the specification, the words null and empty are used interchangeably.

Let's look briefly at some of the features of this model.

Names and Namespaces

XSLT and XPath are designed very much with the use of XML Namespaces in mind, and although many source documents may make little or no use of namespaces, an understanding of the XML Namespaces recommendation (found in http://www.w3.org/TR/REC-xml-names) is essential.

Expanding on the description in Chapter 1(page 25), here's a summary of how namespaces work:

❏ A namespace declaration defines a namespace prefix and a namespace URI. The namespace prefix only needs to be unique within a local scope, but the namespace URI is supposed to be unique globally. Globally here really does mean globally: not just unique in the document, but unique across all documents around the planet. To achieve that, the advice is to use a URI based on a domain name that you control, for example «http://www.my-domain.com/namespace/billing». However, as far as XSLT is concerned, it does not have to conform to any particular syntax. For example, «abc», «42», and «?!*» are all acceptable as namespace URIs. It is just a character string, and two namespace URIs are considered equal if they contain the same sequence of Unicode characters.

❏ The namespace URI does not have to identify any particular resource, and although it is recommended to use a URL based on a domain name that you own, there is no implication that there is anything of interest to be found at that address. The two strings «c:\this.dtd» and «C:\THIS.DTD» are both acceptable as namespace URIs, whether or not there is actually a file of this name; and they represent different namespaces even though when read as filenames they might identify the same file.

❏ A namespace declaration for a non-null prefix is written as follows. This associates the namespace prefix my-prefix with the namespace URI http://my.com/namespace:

```
<a xmlns:my-prefix="http://my.com/namespace">
```

❏ A namespace declaration may also be present for the null prefix. This is known as the default namespace. The following declaration makes http://your.com/namespace the default namespace URI:

```
<a xmlns="http://your.com/namespace">
```

❏ The scope of a namespace declaration is the element on which it appears and all its children and descendants, excluding any subtree where the same prefix is associated with a different URI. This scope defines where the prefix is available for use. Within this scope, any name with the given prefix is automatically associated with the given namespace URI.

❏ A name has three properties: the prefix, the local part, and the namespace-URI. If the prefix is not null, the name is written in the source document in the form prefix:local-part, for example in the name xsl:template, the prefix is xsl and the local-part is template. The namespace-URI of the name is found from the innermost element that carries a namespace declaration of the relevant prefix. (In theory this allows you to use the same prefix with different meanings in different parts of the document, but such overloading is easily avoided since you have a completely free choice of prefixes.)

❏ The XML Namespaces recommendation defines two kinds of name that may be qualified by means of a prefix: element names, and attribute names. The XSLT recommendation extends this to many other kinds of name which appear in the values of XML attributes, for example variable names, template names, names of keys, and so on. All these names can be qualified by a namespace prefix.

❏ If a name has no prefix, then its namespace URI is considered to be the default namespace URI in the case of an element name, or a null URI in the case of an attribute name or any other kind of name (such as XSLT variable names and template names). However, within an XPath expression, the default namespace URI is never used for unprefixed names, even if the name is an element name.

❏ Two names are considered equal if they have the same local part and the same namespace-URI. The combination of the local-part and the namespace-URI is called the **expanded name**. The expanded name is never actually written down, and there is no defined syntax for it: it is a conceptual value made up of these two components.

❏ The prefix of a name is arbitrary in that it does not affect comparison of names; however it is available to applications so it can be used as the default choice of prefix in the result tree, or in diagnostic output messages.

In the XPath tree model, there are two ways namespace declarations are made visible:

❏ For any node such as an element or attribute, the three components of the name (the prefix, the local-part, and the namespace URI) are each available, via the functions `name()`, `local-name()`, and `namespace-uri()`. The application doesn't need to know, and cannot find out, where the relevant namespace was declared.

❏ For any element, it is possible to determine all the namespace declarations that were in force for that element, by retrieving the associated namespace nodes. These are all made available as if the namespace declarations were repeated on that specific element. Again the application cannot determine where the namespace declaration actually occurred in the source document.

Although the namespace declarations are originally written in the source document in the form of XML attributes, they are not retained as attribute nodes on the tree, and cannot be processed by looking for all the attribute nodes.

IDs

An `ID` is a string value that identifies an element node uniquely within a document. If an element has an `ID`, it becomes easy and (one hopes) efficient to access that element if the `ID` value is known. The `ID` always appears as the value of an attribute declared in the DTD as being of type `ID`. Each element has zero or one `ID` values and each `ID` value (if it is present at all) identifies one element.

For example, in an XML dataset containing details of employees, each `<employee>` element might have a unique `ssn` attribute giving the employee's social security number. For example:

```
<personnel>
<employee ssn="123-45-6789">
  <name>John Doe</name>
  ...
```

```
  </employee>
  <employee ssn="123-45-6890">
    <name>Jane Stag</name>
    ...
  </employee>
</personnel>
```

As the ssn attribute is unique, it can be declared in the DTD as an ID attribute using the following declaration:

```
<!ATTLIST employee ssn ID #REQUIRED>
```

Attributes of type ID are often given the name ID as a reminder of their role; unfortunately this sometimes leads people to believe that the attribute name ID is somehow special. It isn't; an ID attribute is any attribute defined in the DTD as having type ID, regardless of the attribute name.

An ID value is constrained to take the form of an XML **Name**. This means, for example, that it must start with a letter, and that it may not contain characters such as «/» or space.

In XML, attributes can also be defined as being of type IDREF or IDREFS if they contain ID values used to point to other elements in the document (an IDREF attribute contains one ID value, and IDREFS attribute contains a whitespace-separated list of ID values). However, XPath does not make any use of this information. XPath provides a function, id() (see page 466), which can be used to locate an element given its ID value. This function is designed so that an IDREF or IDREFS attribute can be used as input to the function, but equally, so can any other string that happens to contain an ID. Therefore, IDREF and IDREFS attributes do not appear explicitly in the tree model.

There is a slight complication with the use of ID values, in that XPath is not constrained to process only valid XML documents. If an XML document is well-formed (or merely well-balanced) but not valid, then values which are supposed to be IDs may be duplicated, and they might not obey the syntactic rules for an XML Name. The XPath specification says that if an ID value appears more than once, all occurrences except the first are ignored. It doesn't say what happens if the ID value contains invalid characters such as spaces: it's quite likely in this case that the id() function will fail to find the element but will otherwise appear to work correctly. If you use ID values, it's probably a good idea to use a validating XML parser to prevent this situation occurring.

XSLT also provides a more flexible approach to finding elements (or other nodes) by content, namely keys. With keys you can do anything that IDs achieve, other than enforcing uniqueness. Keys are declared in the stylesheet using the <xsl:key> element (see Chapter 4, page 222), and they can be used to find a node by means of the key() function (see Chapter 7, page 469).

Characters

In the **XML Information Set** definition (http://www.w3.org/TR/xml-infoset) each individual character is distinguished as an object (or **information item**). This is a useful model conceptually, because it allows one to talk about the properties of a character and the position of a character relative to other characters, but it would be very expensive to represent each character as a separate object in a real tree implementation.

The XPath model has chosen not to represent characters as nodes. It would be nice if it did, because the XPath syntax could then be extended naturally to do character manipulation within strings, but instead the designers chose to provide a separate set of string-manipulation functions. These functions are described in Chapter 7.

The string-value of any node is a sequence of zero or more characters. Each character is a Char as defined in the XML standard. Loosely, this is a Unicode character. More precisely, it is one of the following:

❏ One of the four whitespace characters tab #x9, linefeed #xA, carriage return #xD, or space #x20.

❏ An ordinary 16-bit Unicode character in the range #x21 to #xD7FF or #xE000 to #xFFFD.

❏ An extended Unicode character in the range #x10000 to #x10FFFF. Internally such a character is usually represented as a **surrogate pair**, using two 16-bit codes in the range #xD800 to #xDFFF, but as far as XPath is concerned, it is one character rather than two. This affects functions that count characters in a string or that make use of the position of a character in a string, specifically the functions string-length(), substring(), and translate(). Here XPath differs from Java, which counts a surrogate pair as two characters. (Unicode surrogate pairs are not at present widely used, but they are starting to be defined and are likely to be encountered more frequently in the future).

Note that line endings are normalized to a single newline #xA character, regardless how they appear in the original XML source file.

It is not possible in a stylesheet to determine how a character was written in the source file. For example, the following strings are all identical as far as the XPath data model is concerned:

❏ >

❏ >

❏ >

❏ >

❏ >

❏ <![CDATA[>]]>

The XML parser handles these different character representations. In most implementations, the XSLT processor will use a standard XML parser underneath, and the XSLT processor couldn't treat these representations differently even if it wanted to, because they all look the same once the XML parser has dealt with them.

The only exception to this rule is in the area of whitespace handling. The way in which whitespace in the source XML document is handled, and the interaction of the XML parser and the XSLT processor in this respect, are surprisingly complex topics, and I shall discuss them in some detail in Chapter 3.

What Does the Tree Leave Out?

The debate in defining a tree model is about what to leave out. What information from the source XML document is significant, and what is an insignificant detail? For example, is it significant whether the CDATA notation was used for text? Are entity boundaries significant? What about comments?

Many newcomers to XSLT ask questions like "How can I get the processor to use single quotes around attribute values rather than double quotes?" or "How can I get it to output « » instead of « »?" – and the answer is that you can't, because these distinctions are considered to be things that the recipient of the document shouldn't care about, and they were therefore left out of the XPath tree model.

Generally the features of an XML document fall into one of three categories: definitely significant, definitely insignificant, and debatable. For example, the order of elements is definitely significant; the order of attributes within a start element tag is definitely insignificant; but the significance of comments is debatable.

The XML standard itself doesn't define these distinctions particularly clearly. It defines certain things that must be reported to the application, and these are certainly significant. There are other things that are obviously significant (such as the order of elements) about which it says nothing. Equally, there are some things that it clearly states are insignificant, such as the choice of CR-LF or LF for line endings, but many others about which it stays silent, such as choice of «"» versus «'» to delimit attribute values.

One result of this is that different standards in the XML family have each made their own decisions on these matters, and XSLT and XPath are no exception.

The debate arises partly because there are two kinds of application. Applications that only want to extract the information content of the document are usually interested only in the core information content. Applications such as XML editing tools tend also to be interested in details of how the XML was written, because when the user makes no change to a section of the document, they want the corresponding output document to be as close to the original as possible.

To resolve these questions and get some commonality across the different standards, the W3C set up an activity to define a common model of the information in an XML document: the so-called XML Information Set. Their current conclusions are published at http://www.w3.org/TR/xml-infoset.

The XML information set they define includes core information items and peripheral information items, as illustrated in the diagram below. Core information items must be reported to the application, peripheral information items may optionally be reported.

For the core information items, the Information Set defines both core properties and peripheral properties: the core properties must be reported, and the peripheral properties may optionally be reported.

The diagram below illustrates which information items are in the core, which are peripheral, and which are excluded from the information set entirely. The diagram does not attempt to show which properties of core items are core, and which are peripheral.

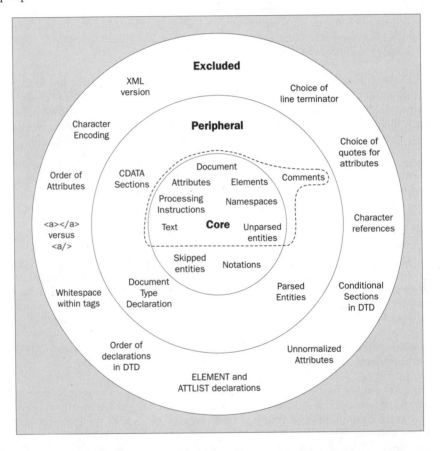

The dotted line on the diagram surrounds those information items that are present in the XSLT/XPath tree model, and which therefore are accessible to an XSLT stylesheet. As you can see, this model follows the Information Set recommendation fairly closely, but not absolutely precisely.

There are two information items which the Information Set regards as core, but which are not available to the writer of an XSLT stylesheet, namely notations and references to skipped entity references.

❑   Since notations are rarely used their omission is unlikely to cause any practical problems. However, the XML standard does say that notations should be notified to the application, so the XSLT model is taking liberties here. In the small print at the back they promise (though not in quite so many words) to put this right in the next version.

❑   Skipped entity references are entity references that a non-validating parser has chosen not to expand: see section 4.4.3 of the XML Recommendation for details. If the parser chooses not to expand an entity, it is supposed to tell the application that it has skipped it. In practice most parsers do expand all entity references, and there seems to be an implicit assumption in XSLT that they will do so, in which case skipped entity references can't exist.

There are some other minor mismatches between the XSLT/XPath tree model and the core Information Set:

❑   The XSLT model includes comments, which are not core information items in the Information Set. This can lead to problems when the XSLT processor is built on top of other software, such as a SAX-compatible XML parser, which treats comments as irrelevant and doesn't pass them on.

❑   The XSLT model makes available the namespace prefixes in the source tree, but it does not give the stylesheet author complete control over the namespace prefixes in the output, on the principle that two XML documents that differ only in their choice of namespace prefixes are equivalent. In the current draft of the Information Set, however, namespace prefixes are a core item.

❑   The XSLT model defines for every node in the tree a Base URI, which (at least in the case of elements and processing instructions) is the URI of the external entity that the node came from. This property isn't accessible directly; in fact it is used only when the document() function (described in Chapter 7, page 440) is executed, to provide a URI to use as a baseline for turning relative URIs into absolute URIs. In the Information Set, this property is considered peripheral. As with comments, there is therefore a potential problem that the XSLT processor may have difficulty getting hold of the information.

❑   Unparsed entities are a core part of the Information Set, but XSLT provides very limited access to them, and provides no way of generating them in the result document. An unparsed entity is an entity defined in the DTD using a declaration of the form:

```
<!ENTITY weather-map SYSTEM "weather.jpeg" NDATA JPEG>
```

It's the NDATA (meaning "not XML data") that makes it an unparsed entity; and because it is an unparsed entity, it can't be referenced using a normal entity reference of the form «&weather-map;». Instead it must be referenced by name in an attribute of type ENTITY or ENTITIES, for example «map="weather-map"».

The XSLT tree model only allows you to do one thing with unparsed entities: if you know the name of the entity (weather-map), then using the unparsed-entity-uri() function you can find out its system identifier (weather.jpeg). This is a lot less than the Information Set implies. The unparsed-entity-uri() function is described in Chapter 7, page 529.

What can be Controlled at the Output Stage?

The transformation processor, which generates the result tree, generally gives the user control only over the core information items and properties (plus comments). The output processor or serializer gives a little bit of extra control over how the result tree is converted into a serial XML document. Specifically, it allows control over:

- ❏ Use of CDATA sections
- ❏ XML version
- ❏ Character encoding
- ❏ Standalone property
- ❏ DOCTYPE declaration

Some of these things are considered peripheral in the Information Set, and some are excluded from it entirely. The features that can be controlled during the output stage do not include all the peripheral properties (for example, it is not possible to generate entity references), and they certainly do not include all the excluded features. For example, there is no way of controlling the order in which attributes are written, or the choice of <a/> versus <a></a> to represent empty elements, the disposition of whitespace within a start tag, or the presence of a newline character at the end of the document.

In short, the set of things that you can control in the output generation stage of processing bears some resemblance to the classification of features in the Information Set, but not as much resemblance as one might expect. Perhaps if the Information Set had been defined earlier, there would be greater consistency between the different W3C specifications.

To underline all this, let's list some of the things you can't see in the input tree, and some of the things you can't control in an XML output file.

Invisible Distinctions

In the table below, the constructs in the two columns are considered equivalent, and in each case you can't tell as a stylesheet writer which one was used in the source document. If one of them doesn't seem to have the required effect, don't bother trying the other: it won't make any difference:

Construct	Equivalent
`<item/>`	`<item></item>`
`&gt;`	`&#62;`
`<e>&quot;</e>`	`<e>"</e>`
`<![CDATA[ a < b ]]>`	`a &lt; b`

`<a xmlns="one.uri">`
`<b/>`
`</a>`
	`<a xmlns="one.uri">`
	`<b xmlns="one.uri"/>`
	`</a>`

`<rectangle x="2" y="4"/>`	`<rectangle y='4'`
	`           x='2'`
	`/>`

In all these cases, except `CDATA`, it's equally true that you have no control over the format of the output: the alternatives are equivalent, so you aren't supposed to care which is used.

Why make a distinction for `CDATA` on output? Perhaps because where a passage of text contains a large number of special characters, for example in a book where you want to show examples of XML, the use of character references can become very unreadable. It is after all one of the strengths of XML, and one of the reasons for its success, that XML documents are easy to read and edit by hand. Also, perhaps, because there is actually some controversy about the meaning of `CDATA`: there are disputes, for example, about whether «`<![CDATA[    ]]>`» is allowed in circumstances where XML only permits white space.

DTD Information

The XPath designers decided not to include all the DTD information in the tree. Perhaps they were anticipating the introduction of XML Schemas, which are widely expected to replace DTDs in the future, and which represent schema information in XML form, which would allow the same tree model to be used.

The XSLT processor (but not the application) needs to know which attributes are of type `ID`, so that the relevant elements can be retrieved when the `id()` function is used. It is part of the tree model that a particular element has a particular `ID` value, but apart from this, there is no information about attribute types explicitly present in the tree model.

The Transformation Process

I've described how the essential process performed by XSLT is to transform a source tree to a result tree under the control of a stylesheet, and we've looked at the structure of these trees. Now it's time to look at how the transformation process actually works, which means taking a look inside the stylesheet.

Template Rules

As we saw in Chapter 1, most stylesheets will contain a number of template rules. Each template rule is expressed in the stylesheet as an `<xsl:template>` element with a `match` attribute. The value of the `match` attribute is a pattern. The pattern determines which nodes in the source tree the template rule matches.

For example, the pattern «/» matches the root node; the pattern «title» matches a <title> element, and the pattern «chapter/title» matches a <title> element whose parent is a <chapter> element.

When you invoke an XSLT processor to apply a particular stylesheet to a particular source document, the first thing it does is to read and parse these documents and create internal tree representations of them in memory. Once this preparation is complete, the transformation process can start.

The first step in the transformation process is to find a template rule that matches the root node of the source tree. If there are several possible candidates, there is a conflict resolution policy to choose the best fit (see page 75 for details). If there is no template rule that matches the root node, a built-in template is used. The XSLT processor then instantiates the contents of this template rule.

The content of the <xsl:template> element in the stylesheet is a sequence of elements and text nodes. Comments and processing instructions in the stylesheet are ignored, as are whitespace text nodes, unless they belong to an <xsl:text> element or to one with an appropriate xml:space attribute. I refer to this sequence as a **template body** The XSLT specification itself refers to it simply as a template, but this terminology is often confusing, so I have avoided it.

Elements in the template body are classified as either instructions or data, depending on their namespace. Text nodes are always classified as data. When the template is instantiated, the instructions in the template body are executed, and the data nodes are copied to the result tree. Elements that are classified as data are officially termed **literal result elements**.

Contents of a Template Body

Consider the following template rule:

```
<xsl:template match="/">
   <xsl:message>Started!</xsl:message>
   <xsl:comment>Generated from XSLT</xsl:comment>
   <html>
      . . .
   </html>
   The end
</xsl:template>
```

The body of this template rule consists of two instructions(<xsl:message> and <xsl:comment>), a literal result element (the <html> element) and some text («The end»). When this template is instantiated, the instructions are executed according to the rules for each individual instruction, and literal result elements and text nodes are copied (as element nodes and text nodes respectively) to the result tree.

It's simplest to think of this as a sequential process, where instantiating a template body causes instantiation of each of its components in the order they appear. Actually, because XSLT is largely side-effect-free, they could be executed in a different order, or in parallel. The important thing is that after instantiating this template body, the result tree will contain, below its root node, a comment node (produced by the <xsl:comment> instruction), an <html> element node (produced by the <html> literal result element), and the text node «The end».

Actually <xsl:message> is an exception to the rule that XSLT is side-effect-free. If there are several <xsl:message> instructions in a template body, then the sequence in which the messages appear is not guaranteed.

If I hadn't included the «...» within the <html> element, this would be the end of the matter. But when a literal result element such as <html> is instantiated, its content is treated as a template body in its own right, and this is instantiated in the same way. It can again contain a mixture of instructions, literal result elements, and text.

Nested Template Bodies

Now suppose the template rule actually looks like this:

```
<xsl:template match="/">
    <xsl:message>Started!</xsl:message>
    <xsl:comment>Generated from XSLT</xsl:comment>
    <html>
        <head>
            <title>My first generated HTML page</title>
        </head>
        <body>
            <xsl:apply-templates/>
        </body>
    </html>
    The end
</xsl:template>
```

Here the <html> element contains two child elements, <head> and <body>. These are both literal result elements, so they are instantiated by copying them from the stylesheet to the result tree. The <head> element contains a <title> literal result element, which contains some text, so the whole structure is copied to the result tree.

When the <body> element is instantiated, however, it contains an XSL instruction, namely <xsl:apply-templates/>. This particular instruction has critical importance: when written as here, without any attributes, it means "select all the children of the current node in the source tree, and for each one, find the matching template rule in the stylesheet, and instantiate it".

What actually happens at this point depends both on what is found in the source document, and on what other template rules are present in the stylesheet. Typically, because we are currently processing the root node of the source document tree, it will have just one child node, namely the document element (the outermost element of the source XML document). Suppose this is a <doc> element. Then the XSLT processor will search the stylesheet looking for a template rule that matches the <doc> element.

The simplest situation is where it finds just one rule that matches this element, for example one declared as:

```
<xsl:template match="doc">
```

If it finds more than one matching template rule, it again has to use its conflict resolution policy to choose the best fit. The other possibility is that there is no matching template rule: in this case it invokes the built-in template rule for element nodes, which simply executes `<xsl:apply-templates/>`: that is, it selects the children of this element, and tries to find template rules that match these children. There's also a built-in template rule for text nodes, which copies the text node to the output. If the element has no children, `<xsl:apply-templates/>` does nothing.

Simple Recursive-Descent Processing

The simplest way to process a source tree is thus to write a template rule for each kind of node that can be encountered, and for that template rule to produce any output required, as well as calling `<xsl:apply-templates>` to process the children of that node.

Example: Simple Recursive-Descent Processing

Here's an example stylesheet that does just that. You can find the files on the web site for this book at http://www.wrox.com. Note, however, that this stylesheet uses the `<xsl:number/>` instruction to generate a sequence number. At the time of writing Microsoft's MSXML3 processor does not support this instruction.

Input

The source document, books.xml, is a simple book catalog:

```xml
<?xml version="1.0"?>
<books>
   <book category="reference">
      <author>Nigel Rees</author>
      <title>Sayings of the Century</title>
      <price>8.95</price>
   </book>
   <book category="fiction">
      <author>Evelyn Waugh</author>
      <title>Sword of Honour</title>
      <price>12.99</price>
   </book>
   <book category="fiction">
      <author>Herman Melville</author>
      <title>Moby Dick</title>
      <price>8.99</price>
   </book>
   <book category="fiction">
      <author>J. R. R. Tolkien</author>
      <title>The Lord of the Rings</title>
      <price>22.99</price>
   </book>
</books>
```

Stylesheet

Say you want display this data in the form of a sequentially numbered booklist. The following stylesheet, `books.xsl`, will do the trick:

```
<xsl:stylesheet
          xmlns:xsl="http://www.w3.org/1999/XSL/Transform"
          version="1.0"
>
<xsl:template match="books">
    <html><body>
    <h1>A list of books</h1>
    <table width="640">
    <xsl:apply-templates/>
    </table>
    </body></html>
</xsl:template>

<xsl:template match="book">
<tr>
    <td><xsl:number/></td>
    <xsl:apply-templates/>
    </tr>
</xsl:template>

<xsl:template match="author | title | price">
    <td><xsl:value-of select="."/></td>
</xsl:template>

</xsl:stylesheet>
```

What's happening here? There's no template for the root node, so the built-in template gets invoked. This processes all the children of the root node.

There's only one child of the root node, the `<books>` element. So the template for the `<books>` element is instantiated. This outputs some standard HTML elements to the result tree, and eventually calls `<xsl:apply-templates/>` to cause its own children to be processed. These children are all `<book>` elements, so they are all processed by the template rule whose match pattern is «match="book"». This template rule outputs an HTML `<tr>` element, and within it a `<td>` element, which it fills by executing the `<xsl:number/>` instruction whose effect is to get the sequence number of the current node (the book element) within its parent element. It then calls `<xsl:apply-templates/>` once again to process the children of the `<book>` element in the source tree.

The children of the `<book>` element are all `<author>`, `<title>`, or `<price>` elements, so as it happens they all match the template rule whose match pattern is «match="author | title | price"» (you can read «|» as "or"). This template rule outputs an HTML `<td>` element which it fills by executing an instruction: `<xsl:value-of select="."/>`. This instruction evaluates an XPath expression, and writes its result (a string) as text to the result tree. The expression is «.» which returns the string-value of the current node, that is the textual content of the current `<author>`, `<price>`, or `<title>` element.

This template makes no further call on `<xsl:apply-templates>`, so its own children are not processed, and control returns all the way up.

Output

```
<html>
   <body>
      <h1>A list of books</h1>
      <table width="640">
         <tr>
            <td>1</td>
<td>Nigel Rees</td>
            <td>Sayings of the Century</td>
            <td>8.95</td>
         </tr>
         <tr>
            <td>2</td>
            <td>Evelyn Waugh</td>
            <td>Sword of Honour</td>
            <td>12.99</td>
         </tr>
etc
      </table>
   </body>
</html>
```

I call this style of processing recursive-descent because each element is processed by essentially the same logic: output some data values or markup relevant to the element, and call `<xsl:apply-templates/>` to process the child elements. Some people also refer to it as **push** processing: it is as if the processor is pushing the nodes out of the door, saying "is anyone interested in dealing with this one?"

Controlling Which Nodes to Process

Simple recursive-descent processing works very well when the data in the output is to have the same structure and sequence as the data in the input, and all we want to do is add a few tags or perform other simple editing of values as we go along.

In the above example, it wouldn't work so well if the properties of each book were less predictable, for example if some of the books had no price, or if the title and author could appear in either order. In this case the HTML table that we generated wouldn't be nicely arranged in columns any more, because generating a new cell for each property we encounter is not necessarily the right thing to do.

In such circumstances, we've got two choices:

❑   We can be more precise about which nodes to process, rather than just saying *process all children of the current node.*

❑   We can be more precise about how to process them, rather than just saying *choose the best-fit template rule.*

Let's try the first option.

Example: Controlling the Sequence of Processing

We can gain greater control over **which** nodes are to be processed by changing the `<book>` template in `books.xsl`, as follows:

```
<xsl:template match="book">
  <tr>
  <td><xsl:number/></td>
  <xsl:apply-templates select="author"/>
  <xsl:apply-templates select="title"/>
  <xsl:apply-templates select="price"/>
  </tr>
</xsl:template>
```

Instead of selecting all child elements and finding the appropriate template rule for each one, this now explicitly selects first the `<author>` child element, then the `<title>` child element, and then the `<price>` child element.

This will still work, and it's more robust than our previous attempt, but it will still produce a ragged table if there are any `<book>` elements without an `<author>` (say), or with more than one.

As we want a regular structure in the output and because we know a lot about the structure of the source document, we'd probably be better off in this situation defining all the processing in the `<book>` template rather than relying on templates to match each of its child elements.

Example: Selecting Nodes Explicitly

We can gain greater control over **how** nodes are to be processed by writing the `<book>` template in the following manner:

```
<xsl:template match="book">
  <tr>
  <td><xsl:number/></td>
  <td><xsl:value-of select="author"/></td>
  <td><xsl:value-of select="title"/></td>
  <td><xsl:value-of select="price"/></td>
  </tr>
</xsl:template>
```

Some people call this **pull** processing, because instead of the template pushing nodes out of the door to be picked up by another template, it is pulling the nodes in and handling them itself.

2

Processing Model

The pattern-matching, or push, style of processing is the most characteristic feature of XSLT, and it works very well in applications where it makes sense to describe the handling of each type of node in the source document independently. However, there are many other techniques available, all of which are equally valuable. From within a template rule that is processing one particular node, the main alternatives if you want access to information in other nodes are:

❑ Call `<xsl:apply-templates>` to process those nodes using their appropriate template rules.

❑ Call `<xsl:apply-templates>` in a particular **mode** (see below) to process those nodes using the template rules for the relevant mode.

❑ Call `<xsl:value-of>` to extract the required information from the nodes directly.

❑ Call `<xsl:for-each>` to perform explicit processing of each of the nodes in turn.

❑ Call `<xsl:call-template>` to invoke a specific template by name, rather than relying on pattern matching to decide which template to invoke.

Further discussion of the different approaches to writing a stylesheet is included in Chapter 8, *Design Patterns*.

Modes

Sometimes you want to process the same node in the source tree more than once, in different ways. The classic example is to produce a table of contents. When generating the table of contents, you want to handle all the section headings in one way, and when producing the body of the document, you want to handle them in a different way.

One way around this problem is to use push processing on one of these passes through the data, and pull processing on all the other occasions. However, this could be very constraining. Instead, you can define different modes of processing, one for each pass through the data. You can name the mode of processing when you call `<xsl:apply-templates>`, and the only template rules that will be considered are those that specify the same mode. For example, if you specify:

```
<xsl:apply-templates select="heading-1" mode="table-of-contents"/>
```

Then the selected template rule might be one defined as:

```
<xsl:template match="heading-1" mode="table-of-contents">
  . . .
</xsl:template>
```

Further details of how to use modes are in Chapter 4, page 150 and an example of how to use them to generate a table of contents is in Chapter 9, page 573.

Built-in Template Rules

What happens when `<xsl:apply-templates>` is invoked to process a node, and there is no template rule in the stylesheet that matches that node?

The answer is that a **built-in template rule** is invoked.

There is a built-in template rule for each type of node. The built-in rules work as follows:

Node type	Built-in template rule
root	Call `<xsl:apply-templates>` to process the children of the root node, in the same mode as the calling mode
element	Call `<xsl:apply-templates>` to process the children of this node, in the same mode as the calling mode
attribute	Copy the attribute value to the result tree, as text – not as an attribute node
text	Copy the text to the result tree
comment	Do nothing
processing-instruction	Do nothing
namespace	Do nothing

The built-in template rules will only be invoked if there is no rule that matches the node anywhere in the stylesheet.

There is no way to override the built-in template for namespace nodes, because there is no pattern that will match a namespace node. If you call `<xsl:apply-templates>` to process namespace nodes, nothing happens. If you want to process all the namespace nodes for an element, use:

```
<xsl:for-each select="namespace::*">
```

Conflict Resolution Policy

Conversely, what happens when there is more than one template rule whose pattern matches a particular node? As I mentioned earlier, the conflict resolution policy comes into play.

This works as follows:

❑ First the **import precedence** of each rule is considered. As we will see in Chapter 3, one stylesheet may import another using the `<xsl:import>` element, and this part of the policy basically says that when stylesheet A imports stylesheet B, the rules in A take precedence over the rules in B.

❑ Then the **priority** of each rule is examined. The priority is a numeric value: the higher the number, the higher the priority. You can either specify the priority explicitly in the `priority` attribute of the `<xsl:template>` element, or you can leave the system to allocate a default priority. In this case, the system allocates a priority that is designed to reflect whether the pattern is very general or very specific, for example the pattern «subsection/title» (which matches any `<title>` element whose parent is a `<subsection>` element) gets higher priority than the pattern «*», which matches any element. System-allocated priorities are always in the range –0.5 to +0.5: user-allocated priorities will normally be 1 or more, but there are no restrictions. For more details, see the description of the `<xsl:template>` element in Chapter 4, page 288.

❑ Finally, if there is more than one rule with the same import precedence and priority, the XSLT processor has a choice: it can either report an error, or it can choose whichever rule appears last in the stylesheet. Different processors will behave differently in this situation, which gives you a slight portability problem to watch out for: it is best to ensure this ambiguity never happens.

Variables, Expressions, and Data Types

The system of data types lies at the core of any language, and the way expressions are used to compute values and assign these to variables is closely tied up with the type system. So, we will now examine further these aspects of the language.

Variables

XSLT allows global variables to be defined, which are available throughout the whole stylesheet, as well as local variables, which are available only within a particular template body. The name and value of a variable are defined in an `<xsl:variable>` element. For example:

```
<xsl:variable name="width" select="50"/>
```

This defines a variable whose name is `width` and whose value is the number 50. The variable can subsequently be referenced in an XPath expression as `$width`. If the `<xsl:variable>` element appears at the top level of the stylesheet (as a child of the `<xsl:stylesheet>` element) then it is a global variable; if it appears within the body of an `<xsl:template>` element then it is a local variable.

Similarly, XSLT also allows global and local parameters to be defined, using an `<xsl:param>` element. Global parameters are set from outside the stylesheet (for example, from the command line or from an API – the actual mechanism is implementor-defined). Local parameters to a template are set using an `<xsl:with-param>` element when the template is called.

Variables and parameters are not statically typed: they take whatever type of value is assigned to them. The five data types defined in XSLT and XPath are:

❑ **String** (any sequence of Unicode characters permitted in XML)

❑ **Number** (a double-precision floating point number as defined in IEEE 754)

❑ **Boolean** (the value true or false)

❑ **Node-set** (a set of nodes in the source tree)

❑ **Tree** (a data structure conforming to the tree model described earlier in this chapter). In the XSLT specification, this is referred to as a **Result Tree Fragment**, but apart from being longwinded this is rather misleading: it is a full tree, not a fragment, and it is not actually part of the result tree, though it can be copied to the result tree when required.

These data types are described in more detail later in the chapter, starting on page 80. In addition, most XSLT processors also allow an extra data type for use with external functions, namely an arbitrary object (for example, a Java object). By allowing XSLT variables to identify an external object, external functions are able to pass arbitrary values to each other.

The use of variables is superficially very similar to their use in conventional programming and scripting languages. They even have similar scoping rules. However, there is one key difference: once a value has been given to a variable, it cannot be changed. This difference has a profound impact on the way programs are written, so it is discussed in detail in the section *Programming Without Assignment Statements* in Chapter 8, page 546.

Expressions

The syntax of expressions is defined in the XPath Recommendation, and is described in detail in Chapter 5.

XPath expressions are used in a number of contexts in an XSLT stylesheet. They are used as attribute values for many XSLT elements, for example:

```
<xsl:value-of select="($x + $y) * 2"/>
```

In this example `$x` and `$y` are references to variables, and the operators «+» and «*» have their usual meanings of addition and multiplication.

Many XPath expressions, like this one, follow a syntax that is similar to other programming languages. The one that stands out, however, and the one that gave XPath its name, is the **Path Expression**.

A Path Expression defines a navigation path through the document tree. Starting at a defined origin, usually either the current node or the root, it follows a sequence of steps in defined directions. At each stage the path can branch, so for example you can find all the attributes of all the children of the origin node. The result is always a set of nodes. It might be empty or contain only one node, but it is still treated as a set.

The directions of navigation through the tree are called **axes**. The various axes are defined in detail in Chapter 5. They include:

❑ the child axis, which finds all the children of a node.

❑ the attribute axis, which finds all the attributes of a node.

❑ the ancestor axis, which finds all the ancestors of a node.

❑ the following-siblings axis, which finds the nodes that come after this one and share the same parent.

❑ the preceding-siblings axis, which finds the nodes that come before this one and share the same parent.

As well as specifying the direction of navigation through the tree, each step in a path expression can also qualify which nodes are to be selected. This can be done in several different ways:

❑ by defining the name of the nodes (completely or partially).

❑ by defining the type of nodes (e.g. elements or processing instructions).

❑ by defining a predicate that the nodes must satisfy – an arbitrary boolean expression.

❑ by defining the relative position of the node along the axis: for example it is possible to select only the immediately preceding sibling.

The syntax of a path expression uses «/» as an operator to separate the successive steps. A «/» at the start of a path expression indicates that the origin is the root node; otherwise it is generally the current node. Within each step, the axis is written first, separated from the other conditions by the separator «::». However, the child axis is the default, so it may be omitted; and the attribute axis may be abbreviated to «@».

For example:

```
child::item/attribute::category
```

is a path expression of two steps, the first selects all the child <item> elements of the current node, and the second step selects their category attributes. This can be abbreviated to:

```
item/@category
```

Predicates that the nodes must satisfy are written in square brackets, for example:

```
item[@code='T']/@category
```

This selects the `category` attributes of those child `<item>` elements that have a `code` attribute whose value is 'T'.

There are many ways of abbreviating path expressions to make them easier to write, but the basic structure remains the same. The full detail appears in Chapter 5.

Context

The way in which expressions are evaluated is to some extent context-dependent. For example, the value of the expression `$x` depends on the current value of the variable `x`, and the value of the expression «.» depends on which node is currently being processed in the source document.

There are two aspects to the context: the static context, which depends only on where the expression appears in the stylesheet, and the dynamic context, which depends on the state of processing at the time the expression is evaluated.

The static context consists of:

- ❏ The set of namespace declarations in force at the point where the expression is written. This determines the validity and meaning of any namespace prefixes used in the expression.

- ❏ The set of variable declarations (that is, `<xsl:variable>` and `<xsl:param>` elements) in scope at the point where the expression is written. This determines the validity of any variable references used in the expression.

The dynamic context consists of:

- ❏ The current values of all the variables that are in scope for the expression. These may be different each time the expression is evaluated.

- ❏ The current location in the source tree. The current location comprises:

  - ❏ The **current node**: this is the node in the source tree that is currently being processed: a node becomes the current node when it is processed using the `<xsl:apply-templates>` or `<xsl:for-each>` instructions. The current node can be referenced using the `current()` function.

  - ❏ The **context node**: this is normally the same as the current node, except in a predicate used to qualify a step within a path expression, when it is the node currently being tested by the predicate. The context node can be referenced using the expression «.», or the longer form «self::node()». For example, «a[.='Madrid']» selects all the `<a>` elements whose string-value is 'Madrid'.

79

❏ The **context position**: this is an integer (1) that indicates the position of the context node in the current node list. The context position can be referenced using the position() function. When <xsl:apply-templates> or <xsl:for-each> are used to process a list of nodes, that list becomes the current node list, and the context position therefore takes the values 1..n as each of the nodes in the list is processed. When a predicate is used within a path expression, the context position is the position of the node being tested within the set of nodes being tested. So, for example, «child::a[position() != 1]» selects all the child elements named <a>, except the first.

❏ The **context size**: this is an integer (1) that indicates the number of nodes in the current node list. The context size can be referenced using the last() function. So, for example, «child::a[position() != last()]» selects all the child elements named <a>, except the last.

The XSLT and XPath specifications use different terminology to describe the context. XSLT uses the concepts of current node and current node list, while XPath uses the concepts of context node, context position, and context size. When the <xsl:apply-templates> or <xsl:for-each> instructions are executed, the current node list is set to the list of nodes being processed, and the current node is set of each of these nodes in turn. When an XPath expression is evaluated, the context node is set to the current node; the context position is set to the position of the current node within the current node list; and the context size is set to the size of the current node list.

Some system functions that can be used in expressions have other dependencies on the context, for example the document() function depends on the Base URI of the stylesheet element in which it appears; but the list above covers all the context information that is directly accessible to user-written expressions.

Data Types

XSLT is a dynamically typed language, in that types are associated with values rather than with variables. In this respect it is similar to VBScript or JavaScript.

There are five data types available and conversion between is generally carried out implicitly when the context requires it. However, the functions boolean(), number(), and string() are also available to carry out explicit conversions. The table below summarizes the conversions between the five data types:

To From	boolean	number	string	node-set	tree
boolean	**not applicable**	false 0 true 1	false 'false' true 'true'	not allowed	not allowed
number	0 false other true	**not applicable**	convert to decimal format	not allowed	not allowed
string	null false other true	parse as a decimal number	**not applicable**	not allowed	not allowed

To From	boolean	number	string	node-set	tree
node-set	empty false other true	convert via string	string-value of first node in document order	**not applicable**	not allowed
tree	convert via string	convert via string	concatenate all text nodes in the fragment	not allowed (see note below)	**not applicable**

More detailed information is given in the descriptions of the functions `boolean()`, `number()`, and `string()` in Chapter 7.

It should be noted that several products provide an extension function to convert a tree to a node-set: the resulting node-set contains a single node, the root of the tree, from which the other nodes can be found using path expressions. However, this useful function is not available in the current XSLT standard. See Chapter 10 for details of extension functions in particular vendors' products.

Boolean Values

The Boolean data type in XPath contains the two values: true and false.

There are no constants to represent true and false, instead the values can be written using the function calls `true()` and `false()`.

Boolean values may be obtained by comparing values of other data types using operators such as «=» and «!=», and they may be combined using the two operators «and» and «or» and the function `not()`.

XPath differs from SQL in that it does not use three-valued logic. A Boolean value is always either true or false; it can never be undefined or null. The nearest equivalent to an SQL null value in XPath is an empty node-set, and when you compare an empty node-set to a string or number the result is always false, regardless of which comparison operator you use. For example, if the current element has no `name` attribute, then the expressions «@name='Boston'» and, «@name!='Boston'» both return false. However, the expression «not(@name='Boston')» returns true.

For more information on the sometimes-strange behavior of the equality and inequality operators when applied to node-sets, see the sections EqualityExpr and RelationalExpr in Chapter 5.

Number Values

A number in XPath is always a double-precision (64-bit) floating-point number, and its behavior is defined to follow the IEEE 754 standard. This standard (*IEEE Standard for Binary Floating-Point Arithmetic. ANSI/IEEE Std. 754-1985*) has been widely implemented by many microprocessors for some years, but it is only through its adoption in the Java language that it has become familiar to high-level language programmers. If you understand how floating point behaves in Java, the contents of this section will be quite familiar; if not, they may be rather strange.

Unlike most other programming languages, XPath does not use scientific notation for floating-point numbers, either on input or on output. If you want to enter the number one trillion, you must write 1000000000000, not 1.0E12. The only exception is that scientific notation is available when you output a number using the format-number() function, which is described in Chapter 7, page 455.

IEEE 754 defines the following range of values for a double-precision number:

Value	Description
Finite nonzero values	These are values of the form $s \times m \times 2^x$, where s (the sign) is +1 or –1, m (the mantissa) is a positive integer less than 2^{53}, and x (the exponent) is an integer between –1075 and 970, inclusive.
Positive zero	This is the result of subtracting a number from itself. It can also result from dividing any positive number by infinity, or from dividing a very small number by a very large number of the same sign.
Negative zero	This is the result of dividing any negative number by infinity. It can also result from dividing a positive number by minus infinity, or from dividing a very small negative number by a very large positive number, or vice versa.
Positive infinity	This is the result of dividing any positive number by zero. It can also result from multiplying two very large numbers with the same sign. Note that division by zero is not an error: it has a well-defined result.
Negative infinity	This is the result of dividing any negative number by zero. It can also result from multiplying two very large numbers with different sign.
NaN	Not a Number. This is the result of attempting to convert a non-numeric string value to a number. It can also be used to mean "unknown" or "not applicable", like the SQL null value.

These values cannot all be written directly as XPath constants. However they can be expressed as the result of expressions, for example:

Value	XPath expression
Negative zero	–0 (see note)
Positive Infinity	1 div 0
Negative Infinity	–1 div 0
NaN	number("NaN")

Note: Unlike the Java language specification, the XPath standard is not explicit that unary minus means negation, in fact it can be read as saying that unary minus means subtraction from zero, in which case –0 would represent positive zero. James Clark says that the intended meaning is as shown here, but some processors may implement it differently.

Except for NaN, number values are **ordered**. Arranged from smallest to largest, they are:

- ❏ negative infinity
- ❏ negative finite nonzero values
- ❏ negative zero
- ❏ positive zero
- ❏ positive finite nonzero values
- ❏ positive infinity.

This ordering determines the result of less-than and greater-than comparisons, and also the result of sorting using `<xsl:apply-templates>` or `<xsl:for-each>` with a sort key specified using `<xsl:sort data-type="number">`.

NaN is **unordered**, so the operators «<», «<=», «>», and «>=» return false if either or both operands are NaN. This means that when `<xsl:sort>` is used to sort a sequence of numeric values that includes one or more NaN values, the position of any NaN values in the final sequence is undefined.

Positive zero and negative zero compare equal. This means that the operators «=», «<=», and «>=» return true, while «!=», «<», and «>» return false. However, other operations can distinguish positive and negative zero; for example, «1.0 div $x» has the value positive infinity if $x is positive zero, and negative infinity if $x is negative zero.

The equals operator «=» returns false if either or both operands are NaN, and the not-equals operator «!=» returns true if either or both operands are NaN. Watch out for the apparent contradictions this leads to: for example «$x=$x» can be false, and «$x<$y» doesn't necessarily give the same answer as «$y>$x».

The simplest way to test whether a value $x is NaN is:

```
<xsl:if test="$x!=$x">
```

If this seems too obscure for your taste, then provided you know that $x is numeric you can write:

```
<xsl:if test="string($x)='NaN'">
```

If you are familiar with null values in SQL, some of this logic might seem familiar, but there are some subtle differences. For example, in SQL the condition «null=null» has the value null, so that «not(null=null)» is also null; while in XPath «NaN=NaN» is false, so that «not(NaN=NaN)» is true.

XPath provides a number of operators and functions that act on numeric values:

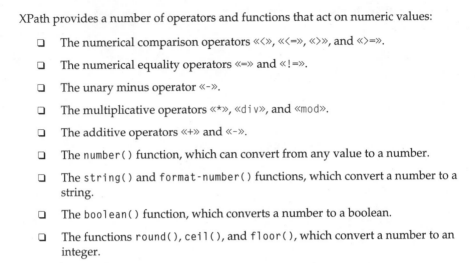

- ❑ The numerical comparison operators «<», «<=», «>», and «>=».

- ❑ The numerical equality operators «=» and «!=».

- ❑ The unary minus operator «-».

- ❑ The multiplicative operators «*», «div», and «mod».

- ❑ The additive operators «+» and «-».

- ❑ The number() function, which can convert from any value to a number.

- ❑ The string() and format-number() functions, which convert a number to a string.

- ❑ The boolean() function, which converts a number to a boolean.

- ❑ The functions round(), ceil(), and floor(), which convert a number to an integer.

- ❑ The function sum(), which totals the numeric values of a set of nodes.

Operators on numbers behave exactly as specified by IEEE 754. XPath is not as strict as Java in defining exactly what rounding algorithms should be used for inexact results, and in what sequence operations should be performed. Many implementations, however, will follow the Java rules.

XPath numeric operators and functions never produce an error. An operation that overflows produces positive or negative infinity, an operation that underflows produces positive or negative zero, and an operation that has no other sensible result produces NaN. All numeric operations and functions with NaN as an operand produce NaN as a result. For example, if you apply the sum() function to a node-set, then if the string value of any of the nodes cannot be converted to a number, the result of the sum() function will be NaN.

String Values

A string value in XPath is any sequence of zero or more characters, where the alphabet of possible characters is the same as in XML: essentially the characters defined in Unicode.

String values can be written in XPath expressions in the form of a literal, using either single quotes or double quotes, for example 'John' or "Mary". In theory the string can contain the opposite quote character as part of the value, for example "John's". In practice, however, XPath expressions are written within XML attributes, so the opposite quote character will generally already be in use for the attribute delimiters. For more details, see the section *Literal* in Chapter 5, page 362.

There is no special null value, as there is in SQL. Where no other value is appropriate, a zero-length string is used. In fact the terms null string and empty string are used interchangeably to refer to a zero-length string.

The only ASCII control characters permitted (codes below #x20) are the whitespace characters #x9, #xA, and #xD (tab, carriage return, and newline).

Strings may be compared using the «=» and «!=» operators. They are compared character by character (there is no space-padding as in SQL). The implementation is allowed to normalize the strings before comparing them, to handle different Unicode representations of the same accented character, but it is not required to do so. There is no operator or function provided to compare two strings ignoring case: the best you can achieve (if you know the strings are restricted to a limited alphabet such as ASCII) is to convert from lowercase to uppercase, or vice versa, using the translate() function. Otherwise, use an external user-defined function.

When counting characters in a string, for example in the string-length() function, it is the number of XML characters that is relevant, not the number of 16-bit Unicode codes. This means that Unicode surrogate pairs are counted as a single character. Unicode surrogate pairs, which are used to extend Unicode beyond 65,535 characters, are very rarely encountered in practice, though their use may increase in the future.

Node-set Values

A node-set is a set of nodes in the source document tree. If there are multiple source document trees, a node-set may contain nodes from more than one tree. The nodes in a node-set may be any type of node, and different types of node can be mixed in the same node-set. It is a pure mathematical set: each node can appear at most once, and there is no intrinsic order.

There is no data type to represent a single node; instead a node-set with a single member is used. For example, when you use the expression «@name» to find the value of the name attribute of the current element, the result is a node-set containing a single attribute node if the element has a name attribute, or an empty set if it does not.

When a node-set value is converted to a boolean, an empty node-set is treated as false and a node-set containing one or more nodes as true. So you can use the test:

```
<xsl:if test="@name">
```

to find out whether the current element has a name attribute.

The nodes in a node-set may have children, but the children are not regarded as members of the node-set. For example, the expression «/» returns a node-set containing a single node, the root. The other nodes subordinate to the root can be reached from this node, but they are not themselves members of the node-set, and the value of count(/) is therefore always 1.

A node-set is not intrinsically ordered, though in many contexts the nodes are processed in **document order**. Where two nodes come from the same document, their relative position in document order is based on their position in the document tree: for example an element precedes its children in document order, and sibling nodes are listed in the same order as they appear in the original source document. Where two nodes come from different documents, their relative order is undefined. The ordering of attribute and namespace nodes is defined only partially: an element node is followed by its namespace nodes, then its attributes, and then its children, but the ordering of the namespace nodes among themselves, and of the attribute nodes among themselves, is undefined.

Tree Values

A value of type tree – or result tree fragment, to give it its full XSLT name – always contains a root node, and the root node may have children. A tree does not necessarily correspond to a well-formed XML document, for example the root node can own text nodes directly, and it can have more than one element node among its children. However, it must conform to the same rules as an XML external parsed entity, for example all the attributes belonging to an element node must have distinct names.

Example: Tree Values

A tree is constructed by instantiating the body of an `<xsl:variable>` declaration, for example:

```
<xsl:variable name="rtf">
  AAA
  <xsl:element name="x">
  <xsl:attribute name="att">att-value</xsl:attribute>
    BBB
  </xsl:element>
  <xsl:element name="y"/>
  CCC
</xsl:variable>
```

This creates the tree illustrated in the diagram below. Each box shows a node; the three layers are respectively the node type, the node name, and the string-value of the node. Once again, an asterisk indicates that the string-value is the concatenation of the string-values of the child nodes.

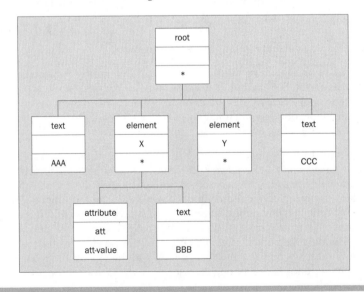

In standard XSLT there are only two things you can do with a tree once it has been constructed: you can copy it to the current destination tree (which may be the final result tree or another tree variable) using the `<xsl:copy-of>` instruction, or you can convert its value to a string. Converting it to a string gives the concatenation of all the text nodes in the tree: in the above example this is «AAABBBCCC».

Several products provide an extension function allowing a tree to be converted to a node-set. This returns a node-set containing a single node, the root node of the tree. The other nodes can then be found by following paths from the root node. Details are given in Chapter 10; however, this useful facility is not part of the current XSLT standard.

Summary

In this chapter we explored the important concepts needed to understand what an XSLT processor does.

- ❑ We examined the overall system architecture, in which a stylesheet controls the transformation of a source tree into a result tree.

- ❑ We saw in some detail the tree model used in XSLT, and the way it relates to the XML standards: also some of the ways it differs from the DOM model.

- ❑ We learned how template rules are used to define the action to be taken by the XSLT processor when it encounters particular kinds of node in the tree.

- ❑ And we looked at the way in which expressions, data types, and variables are used in the XSLT language to calculate values.

In the next chapter we will look at the structure of an XSLT stylesheet in more detail.

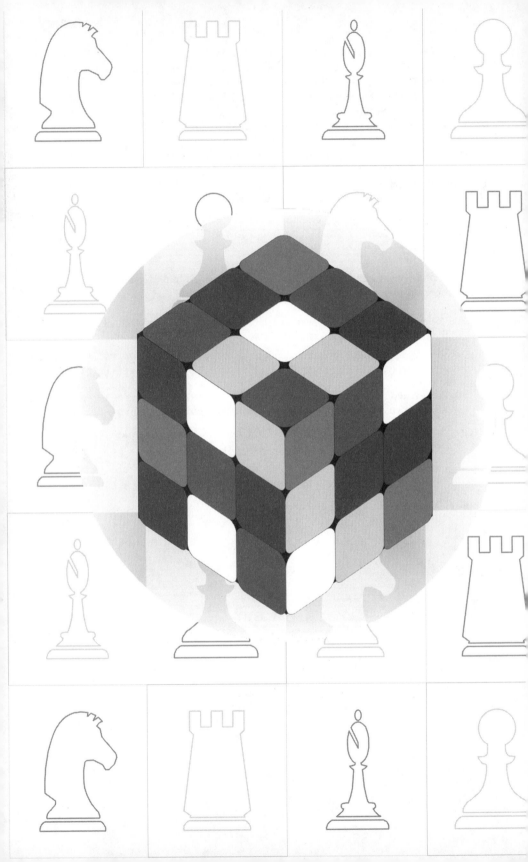

Stylesheet Structure

This chapter describes the overall structure of a stylesheet. The aim of the chapter is to explain some of the concepts used in writing stylesheets, before we get into the main reference section of the book in Chapters 4 through 7. Some of these concepts are tricky: they are areas that often cause confusion, which is why I have tried to explain them in some detail. However, it's not necessary to master everything in this chapter before you can write your first stylesheet – so use it as a reference, coming back to topics as and when you need to understand them more deeply.

The topics covered in this chapter are:

❑ **Stylesheet modules**: we will discuss how a stylesheet program can be made up of one or more stylesheet modules, linked together with `<xsl:import>` and `<xsl:include>` elements.

❑ The `<xsl:stylesheet>` (or `<xsl:transform>` element), which is the outermost element of most stylesheet modules.

❑ The `<?xml-stylesheet?>` processing instruction which can be used to link a source document to its associated stylesheet, and which also allows stylesheets to be embedded directly in the source document whose style they define.

❑ A brief description of the **top-level elements** found in the stylesheet, that is, the immediate children of the `<xsl:stylesheet>` or `<xsl:transform>` element: the full specifications are in Chapter 4.

❑ Simplified stylesheets, in which the `<xsl:stylesheet>` and `<xsl:template match="/">` elements are omitted, to make an XSLT stylesheet look more like the simple template languages that some users may be familiar with.

❑ The idea of a **template body**, a sequence of text nodes and literal result elements to be copied to the result tree, and instructions and extension elements to be executed.

❑ **Attribute value templates**, which are used to define variable attributes not only of literal result elements, but of certain XSL elements as well.

❑ Facilities allowing the specification to be extended, both by vendors and by W3C itself, without adversely affecting the portability of stylesheets.

❑ Handling of **whitespace** in the source document, in the stylesheet itself, and in the result tree.

The Modular Structure of a Stylesheet

In the previous chapter we described the XSLT processing model, in which a stylesheet defines the rules by which a source tree is transformed into a result tree.

Stylesheets, like programs in other languages, can become quite long and complex, and so there is a need to allow them to be divided into separate modules. This allows modules to be reused, and combined in different ways for different purposes: for example, we might want to use two different stylesheets to display press releases on screen and on paper, but there might be components that both of these stylesheets share in common. These shared components can go in a separate module that is used in both cases.

We can regard the complete collection of modules as a **stylesheet program**, and refer to its components as **stylesheet modules**.

> *The XSLT standard does not use this terminology. In fact it uses the term stylesheet sometimes for the stylesheet program and sometimes for the stylesheet module as defined here.*

One of the stylesheet modules is the **principal stylesheet module**. This is in effect the main program, the module which is identified to the stylesheet processor by the use of an `<?xml-stylesheet?>` processing instruction in the source document, or whatever command line parameters or API the vendor chooses to provide. The principal stylesheet module may fetch other stylesheet modules using `<xsl:include>` and `<xsl:import>` elements: these may in turn fetch others, and so on.

Example: Using <xsl:include>

Source

The input document, `sample.xml`, looks like this:

```
<?xml version="1.0" encoding="iso-8859-1"?>
<document>
    <author>Michael Kay</author>
    <title>XSLT Programmer's Reference</title>
    <copyright/>
    <date/>
    <abstract>A comprehensive guide to the XSLT and XPath recommendations
    published by the World Wide Web Consortium on 16 November
      1999</abstract>
</document>
```

Stylesheets

The stylesheet uses `<xsl:include>`. The effect of this stylesheet is to copy the source document unchanged to the result, except that any `<date>` elements are set to the current date, and any `<copyright>` elements are set to a string identifying the copyright owner.

The three modules of this stylesheet program are as follows: `principal.xsl`, `date.xsl`, and `copyright.xsl`. The `date.xsl` module uses an extension function, it is written to work with xt and Saxon, but will need to be modified to work with other XSLT processors.

You only need to name the principal stylesheet module as your stylesheet, the other modules will be fetched automatically. The way this stylesheet is written, all the modules must be in the same directory.

principal.xsl

The first module, `principal.xsl`, contains the main logic of the stylesheet:

```
<?xml version="1.0" encoding="iso-8859-1"?>
<xsl:stylesheet
      xmlns:xsl="http://www.w3.org/1999/XSL/Transform"
      version="1.0"
>
<xsl:include href="date.xsl"/>
<xsl:include href="copyright.xsl"/>

<xsl:output method="xml" encoding="iso-8859-1" indent="yes"/>
<xsl:strip-space elements="*"/>

<xsl:template match="date">
    <date><xsl:value-of select="$date"/></date>
</xsl:template>

<xsl:template match="copyright">
    <copyright><xsl:call-template name="copyright"/></copyright>
</xsl:template>

<xsl:template match="*">
    <xsl:copy>
        <xsl:copy-of select="@*"/>
        <xsl:apply-templates/>
    </xsl:copy>
</xsl:template>

</xsl:stylesheet>
```

It starts with two <xsl:include> elements to bring in the other modules. The <xsl:output> element indicates that the output should be in XML format, using the ISO 8859/1 character set (which makes it easy to view with a text editor), and with indentation to show the XML structure. The <xsl:strip-space> element indicates that whitespace nodes in the source document are to be ignored: I'll have a lot more to say about whitespace handling later in this chapter. Then there are three template rules, one for <date> elements, one for <copyright> elements, and one for everything else.

The template rule for <date> elements outputs the value of the variable named $date. This variable isn't defined in this stylesheet module, but it is present in the module date.xsl, so it can be accessed from here.

The template rule for <copyright> elements similarly calls the template named copyright. Again, there is no template of this name in this module, but there is one in the module copyright.xsl, so it can be called from here.

Finally, the template rule that matches all other elements («match="*"») has the effect of copying the element unchanged from the source document to the output. The <xsl:copy> (page 180) and <xsl:copy-of> (page 183) instructions are explained in Chapter 4.

date.xsl

The next module date.xsl declares a global variable containing today's date. This calls the Java «java.util.Date» class to get the date, referencing it as an external function. External functions are introduced later in this chapter.

```
<xsl:stylesheet
     xmlns:xsl="http://www.w3.org/1999/XSL/Transform"
     version="1.0"
>
<xsl:variable name="date"
     select="Date:to-string(Date:new())"
     xmlns:Date="http://www.jclark.com/xt/java/java.util.Date"/>

</xsl:stylesheet>
```

copyright.xsl

Finally, the module copyright.xsl contains a named template that outputs a copyright statement. This template is called by the <xsl:call-template> instruction in the principal stylesheet. The template uses a variable $owner to construct the copyright statement: we'll see later how this is useful.

The rather strange way of writing the <xsl:template> start tag is to avoid outputting a newline before the copyright text. Later in the chapter I'll describe other ways of achieving this.

```
<?xml version="1.0" encoding="iso-8859-1"?>
<xsl:stylesheet
        xmlns:xsl="http://www.w3.org/1999/XSL/Transform"
        version="1.0"
>
<xsl:variable name="owner">Wrox Press</xsl:variable>

<xsl:template name="copyright"
>Copyright © <xsl:value-of select="$owner"/> 2000</xsl:template>

</xsl:stylesheet>
```

The reason for separating this stylesheet program into three modules is that the date.xsl and copyright.xsl modules are reusable in other stylesheets. Functionally, the stylesheet would have exactly the same effect if the variable $date and the templated named copyright were defined directly in the principal stylesheet.

Output

```
<?xml version="1.0" encoding="iso-8859-1" ?>
<document>
    <author>Michael Kay</author>
    <title>XSLT Programmer's Reference</title>
    <copyright>Copyright © Wrox Press 2000</copyright>
    <date>Sat Mar 18 10:27:44 GMT+00:00 2000</date>
    <abstract>A comprehensive guide to the XSLT and XPath recommendations
    published by the World Wide Web Consortium on 16 November
1999</abstract>
    </document>
```

There is no syntactic difference between a principal module and any other module; in fact any module can be used as a principal module.

This means that <xsl:include> and <xsl:import> can be used in any module, not only the principal module. So the stylesheet program is actually a tree of stylesheet modules, with the principal module at its root.

A stylesheet module is generally one XML document (the exception, an **embedded stylesheet,** will be described later on page 99). The document element (the outermost element of the XML document) is then either an <xsl:stylesheet> element or an <xsl:transform> element: the two names are synonymous. The elements immediately subordinate to the <xsl:stylesheet> or <xsl:transform> element are called **top-level** elements (it might have been clearer to call them second-level elements, but top-level is the term the standard uses). The XSLT-defined top-level elements are listed on page 102.

The <xsl:include> and <xsl:import> elements are always top-level elements. They take an href attribute whose value is a URI: most commonly, it will be a relative URL, defining the location of the included or imported stylesheet module relative to the parent module. For example, <xsl:include href="mod1.xsl"/> causes the module named mod1.xsl, located in the same directory as the parent module, to be fetched.

The difference between <xsl:include> and <xsl:import> is that conflicting definitions are resolved differently:

❑ <xsl:include> effectively does a textual inclusion of the referenced stylesheet module, minus its containing <xsl:stylesheet> element, at the point where the <xsl:include> element is written. The included module is treated exactly as if its top-level elements, with their contents, appeared in the parent module in place of the <xsl:include> element itself.

❑ <xsl:import> also incorporates the top-level elements from the referenced stylesheet module, but in this case the definitions in the imported module have lower **import precedence** than the definitions in the parent module. If there are conflicting definitions, the one with higher import precedence will generally win. The detailed rules actually depend on the type of definition, and are given in the specification of <xsl:import> on page 207, in Chapter 4. Importing a module is thus rather like defining a subclass: the parent module can use some definitions unchanged from the imported module, and override others with definitions of its own.

The most obvious kind of definition is the definition of a template rule, using an <xsl:template> element with a match attribute. As we saw in the previous chapter, if there are several template rules that match a particular node in the source tree, the first step in deciding which to use is to look at their import precedence, and discard all those with import precedence less than the highest. So a template rule defined in a particular stylesheet module will automatically take precedence over another matching rule in a module that it imports.

Where one module A imports two others, B and C, as shown in the diagram on the right, then A takes precedence over both B and C, and C also takes precedence over B, assuming that the <xsl:import> element that loads B precedes the <xsl:import> element that loads C.

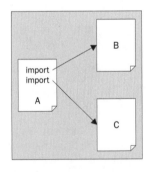

When a stylesheet incorporates another using <xsl:include>, the definitions in the included stylesheet have the same import precedence as those in the parent stylesheet.

Where two definitions have the same import precedence (because they were in the same stylesheet module, or because one was in a module incorporated in the other using <xsl:include>), the rules for resolving conflicts depend on the kind of definition. In some cases, for example definitions of named templates or variables, duplicate definitions with the same name are always reported as an error. In some other cases, for example definitions of template rules, the implementer has the choice of reporting an error or choosing the definition that occurs later in the stylesheet. Some implementers may pass this choice on to the user. The detailed rules are given in Chapter 4 for each kind of top-level element, and they are summarized in the section for <xsl:import>, page 207.

Example: Using <xsl:import>

This extends the previous `<xsl:include>` example, showing how to use
`<xsl:import>` to incorporate the definitions in another stylesheet module while
overriding some of them.

Source

The input document for this example is `sample.xml`.

Stylesheet

Recall that the `copyright.xsl` module used a variable, `$owner`, to hold the name of
the copyright owner. Suppose that we want to use the `copyright` template, but
with a different copyright owner. We can achieve this by writing a revised
principal stylesheet as follows (this is called `principal2.xsl` in the downloadable
sample files).

This stylesheet uses `<xsl:import>` instead of `<xsl:include>` to incorporate the
`copyright.xsl` module, and it then contains a new declaration of the `$owner`
variable, which will override the declaration in the imported module. Note that the
`<xsl:import>` element must come first.

```xml
<?xml version="1.0" encoding="iso-8859-1"?>
<xsl:stylesheet
        xmlns:xsl="http://www.w3.org/1999/XSL/Transform"
        version="1.0"
>
<xsl:import href="copyright.xsl"/>
<xsl:variable name="owner">Wrox Press Ltd</xsl:variable>
<xsl:include href="date.xsl"/>

<xsl:output method="xml" encoding="iso-8859-1" indent="yes"/>
<xsl:strip-space elements="*"/>

<xsl:template match="date">
   <date><xsl:value-of select="$date"/></date>
</xsl:template>

<xsl:template match="copyright">
   <copyright><xsl:call-template name="copyright"/></copyright>
</xsl:template>

<xsl:template match="*">
   <xsl:copy>
      <xsl:copy-of select="@*"/>
      <xsl:apply-templates/>
   </xsl:copy>
</xsl:template>

</xsl:stylesheet>
```

Output

```
<?xml version="1.0" encoding="iso-8859-1" ?>
<document>
    <author>Michael Kay</author>
    <title>XSLT Programmer's Reference</title>
    <copyright>Copyright © Wrox Press Ltd 2000</copyright>
    <date>Sat Mar 18 11:11:37 GMT+00:00 2000</date>
    <abstract>A comprehensive guide to the XSLT and XPath recommendations
        published by the World Wide Web Consortium on 16 November
1999</abstract>
    </document>
```

This example wouldn't work if you used <xsl:include> rather than
<xsl:import>. It would complain that the variable $owner was declared twice.
This is because with <xsl:include>, the two declarations have the same import
precedence, so neither can override the other.

It is an error for a stylesheet module to import or include itself, directly or indirectly.
This would define an infinite loop.

It isn't an error, however, for a stylesheet module to be included or imported at more
than one place in the stylesheet program. The following isn't an error:

```
<xsl:stylesheet xmlns:xsl="http://www.w3.org/1999/XSL/Transform" version="1.0">
    <xsl:import href="date.xsl"/>
    <xsl:import href="date.xsl"/>
</xsl:stylesheet>
```

This may seem rather pointless, but in a highly modular structure it can sometimes
happen by accident and be harmless: for example, several of your stylesheet modules
might independently reference a commonly used module such as date.xsl. The effect
is simply to load two copies of all the definitions in date.xsl, exactly as if two
identical files with different names had been imported.

If the same module is fetched twice using <xsl:include>, the included definitions will
have the same import precedence, which is likely to cause an error: for example, if the
included module defines a global variable or a named template, duplicate definitions
will be reported. In other cases, for example where the file uses the <xsl:attribute-
set> element to define named attribute sets, the duplicate definitions are harmless (the
<xsl:attribute-set> element is described on page 162, in Chapter 4). However, if
there is a risk of loading the same module twice, it makes sense to use <xsl:import>
rather than <xsl:include>.

The <xsl:stylesheet> Element

The <xsl:stylesheet> element (or <xsl:transform>, which is a synonym) is the
outermost element of every stylesheet module.

The name \<xsl:stylesheet\> is a conventional name. The first part, xsl, is a prefix that identifies the namespace to which the element name belongs. Any prefix can be used so long as it is mapped, using a namespace declaration, to the URI http://www.w3.org/1999/XSL/Transform. There is also a mandatory version attribute. So the start tag of the \<xsl:stylesheet\> element will usually look like this:

```
<xsl:stylesheet
   xmlns:xsl="http://www.w3.org/1999/XSL/Transform"
   version="1.0"
>
```

> *If you come across a stylesheet that uses the namespace URI*
> *http://www.w3.org/TR/WD-xsl, then the stylesheet is written in a*
> *Microsoft dialect of XSL based on an early working draft of the standard. This*
> *version was released with Internet Explorer 5. There are many differences*
> *between the IE5 dialect of XSL and the final XSLT specification described in*
> *this book. For details of IE5 XSL, see the Wrox Press book* XML IE5
> Programmer's Reference, *ISBN 1-861001-57-6. Microsoft has since released*
> *an updated version of their XSL processor, which supports most of the XSLT*
> *specification: see Chapter 10, page 661, for details.*

The other attributes that may appear on this element are described under \<xsl:stylesheet\> in Chapter 4, page 278. Specifically, they are:

❑ id, to identify the stylesheet if it appears as an embedded stylesheet within another document. Embedded stylesheets are described in the next section.

❑ extension-element-prefixes, a list of namespace prefixes that denote elements used for vendor-defined or user-defined extensions to the XSLT language.

❑ exclude-result-prefixes, a list of namespaces used in the stylesheet that should not be copied to the result tree unless they are actually needed. I'll explain how this works in the section *Literal Result Elements* on page 109.

These attributes affect only the stylesheet module in which this \<xsl:stylesheet\> element appears; they do not affect what happens in included or imported stylesheet modules.

The \<xsl:stylesheet\> element will often contain further namespace declarations. Indeed, if the extension-element-prefixes or exclude-result-prefixes attributes are used, then any namespace prefixes they mention must be declared by means of a namespace declaration on the \<xsl:stylesheet\> element. For example, if you want to declare «saxon» as an extension element prefix, the start tag of the \<xsl:stylesheet\> element would look like this:

```
<xsl:stylesheet
   xmlns:xsl="http://www.w3.org/1999/XSL/Transform"
   xmlns:saxon="http://icl.com/saxon"
   version="1.0"
   extension-element-prefixes="saxon"
>
```

3

Stylesheet Structure

97

Namespace declarations on the `<xsl:stylesheet>` element, and indeed anywhere else in the stylesheet, apply only to the stylesheet module in which they appear. They are not inherited by included or imported modules.

The `<?xml-stylesheet?>` Processing Instruction

This processing instruction is not part of the XSLT or XPath standard, rather it has a short W3C Recommendation all to itself, which you can find at http://www.w3.org/TR/xml-stylesheet. XSLT mentions it, but only in an example, so there is no implication that an XSLT processor is required to support it.

The `<?xml-stylesheet?>` processing instruction is used within a source XML document to identify the stylesheet that should be used to process it. There can be several `<?xml-stylesheet?>` processing instructions present, defining different stylesheets to be used under different circumstances.

The processing instruction has an `href` attribute whose value is the URI of the stylesheet (that is, the principal stylesheet module), and a `type` attribute that indicates the language in which the stylesheet is written. This doesn't have to be an XSLT stylesheet, it could be CSS. The W3C Recommendation says that for XSL the media type should be either `text/xml` or `application/xml`; however, with Microsoft's implementation in Internet Explorer 5 it must be `text/xsl`.

Technically, XML processing instructions do not contain attributes, they contain a name (here `xml-stylesheet`) followed by character data. However, many people like to structure the character data as a sequence of `name="value"` pairs, like the attributes in an element start tag, and the xml-stylesheet recommendation follows this practice. It refers to the `name="value"` pairs as pseudo-attributes.

The full list of pseudo-attributes in the `<?xml-stylesheet?>` processing instruction is as follows:

Attribute name	Value	Meaning
href *mandatory*	URI	The URI of the stylesheet. This may be a full URL of the XML document containing the stylesheet, or it may contain a fragment identifier (e.g. #styleB) used to locate the stylesheet within a larger file: see *Embedded Stylesheets* below
type *mandatory*	Mime type	Identifies the language in which the stylesheet is written: typically text/xml or text/xsl (see discussion above).

Attribute name	Value	Meaning
title *optional*	String	If there are several `<?xml-stylesheet?>` processing instructions, each should be given a title to distinguish them. The user can then be allowed to choose which stylesheet is wanted. For example, there may be special stylesheets that use large print or aural rendition.
media *optional*	String	Description of the output medium, for example "print", "projection", or "aural". The list of possible values is defined in the HTML 4.0 specification. This value can be used to select from the available stylesheets.
charset *optional*	Character encoding name, e.g. iso-8859-1	This attribute is not useful with XSLT stylesheets, since as XML documents they define their character encoding themselves.
alternate *optional*	"yes" or "no"	If "no" is specified, this is the preferred stylesheet. If "yes" is specified, it is an alternative stylesheet.

An `<?xml-stylesheet?>` processing instruction must appear, if it appears at all, as part of the document prolog, that is, before the start tag of the document element. The href attribute identifies the location of the stylesheet by an absolute or relative URL. For example:

```
<?xml-stylesheet type="text/xsl" href="../style.xsl"?>
```

It isn't mandatory to use the `<?xml-stylesheet?>` processing instruction, and most products will offer some other way of saying which stylesheet you want to apply to a particular document. It's mainly useful when you want to apply a stylesheet to an XML document within the browser: specifying this processing instruction means that the browser can apply a default stylesheet to the document without any extra scripting being needed.

Clearly, one of the reasons for separating the stylesheet from the source XML document is so that the same information can be transformed or presented in different ways depending on the user, their equipment, or the particular mode of access. The various attributes of the `<?xml-stylesheet?>` processing instruction are designed to define the rules controlling the selection of an appropriate stylesheet. The mechanism is geared towards stylesheets that are used to display information to users: it has less relevance to the more general use of XSLT for performing data transformations.

Embedded Stylesheets

There is one exception to the rule that the stylesheet module must be an XML document. The principal stylesheet module can be **embedded** within another XML document, typically the document whose style it is defining.

The ability to embed stylesheets within the source document is best regarded as a carryover from CSS. It can be useful if you have a freestanding document that you want to distribute as a self-contained unit, but in most situations it is better to use an external stylesheet that can be used for many different source documents. Some people like to embed stylesheets to reduce download time, but this can be counter-productive, because it means the browser cannot spot that the stylesheet is already present in its cache.

> **Not all XSLT processors support embedded stylesheets. Check the documentation for your particular product before using them.**

The outermost element of the stylesheet is still an `<xsl:stylesheet>` or `<xsl:transform>` element, but it will no longer be the outermost element of the XML document (that is, the document element). The `<xsl:stylesheet>` element will generally have an `id` attribute to identify it, and will be referenced within its containing document using the `<?xml-stylesheet?>` processing instruction, for example:

Example: Embedded Stylesheets

This example shows a stylesheet embedded within an XML source document containir a list of books.

Source

The data file, `embedded.xsl`, containing both source document and stylesheet, is as follows:

```xml
<?xml version="1.0"?>
<?xml-stylesheet type="text/xml" href="#style1"?>
<books>
    <book category="reference">
        <author>Nigel Rees</author>
        <title>Sayings of the Century</title>
        <price>8.95</price>
    </book>
    <book category="fiction">
        <author>Evelyn Waugh</author>
        <title>Sword of Honour</title>
        <price>12.99</price>
    </book>
    <book category="fiction">
        <author>Herman Melville</author>
        <title>Moby Dick</title>
        <price>8.99</price>
    </book>
    <book category="fiction">
        <author>J. R. R. Tolkien</author>
        <title>The Lord of the Rings</title>
        <price>22.99</price>
    </book>
```

```
<xsl:stylesheet id="style1" version="1.0"
    xmlns:xsl="http://www.w3.org/1999/XSL/Transform">

<xsl:template match="xsl:stylesheet"/>

<xsl:template match="books">
    <html><body>
        <h1>A list of books</h1>
        <table>
            <xsl:apply-templates/>
        </table>
    </body></html>
</xsl:template>

<xsl:template match="book">
    <tr><xsl:apply-templates/></tr>
</xsl:template>

<xsl:template match="author | title | price">
    <td><xsl:value-of select="."/></td>
</xsl:template>

</xsl:stylesheet>
</books>
```

You can run this stylesheet using Saxon with a command of the form:

```
saxon -a embedded.xsl
```

The -a option tells Saxon to look for an <?xml-stylesheet?> processing instruction in the supplied source document, and to process the source document using that stylesheet. (Saxon will always use the first <?xml-stylesheet?> processing instruction it finds, ignoring attributes such as media and alternate).

Output

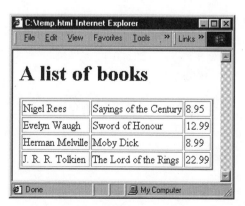

Note the empty template rule that matches the `<xsl:stylesheet>` element. This is needed because without it, the stylesheet will try to process itself along with the rest of the document. The empty template rule ensures that when the `<xsl:stylesheet>` element is matched, no output is generated, and its child elements are not processed. You may need to take care to avoid matching other elements in the stylesheet as well. For example, if the stylesheet looks for book titles using an expression such as «//title», this could accidentally match a `<title>` literal result element within the embedded stylesheet.

An embedded stylesheet module will generally be used as the principal stylesheet module. The standard doesn't explicitly say whether or not an embedded stylesheet can be included or imported into another. In practice, the details of what is supported are likely to vary from one product to another: few of the current products have much to say about embedded stylesheets in their documentation.

Top-Level Elements

The term **top-level element** means an element that is an immediate child of the `<xsl:stylesheet>` or `<xsl:transform>` element. The term second-level element might have been more accurate, but **top-level element** is the one used in the standard.

It is not permitted to have text nodes as immediate children of the `<xsl:stylesheet>` or `<xsl:transform>` element, unless they consist entirely of whitespace characters. Processing instructions and comments may appear, and the XSLT processor will ignore them.

Top-level elements can appear in any order in the stylesheet, except that if there are any `<xsl:import>` elements, they must come first. In most cases the order in which the elements appear is of no significance; however, if there are conflicting definitions, the XSLT processor sometimes has the option of either reporting an error or taking whichever definition comes last. If you want your stylesheet to be portable, you cannot rely on this behavior, and should ensure that conflicting definitions don't arise.

The elements that may appear at the top level fall into three categories:

- ❏ XSL-defined top-level elements
- ❏ Implementer-defined top-level elements
- ❏ User-defined top-level elements

Let us now examine further these three categories.

XSL-Defined Top-Level Elements

An XSL-defined top-level element must be one of the elements listed below:

```
<xsl:attribute-set>        <xsl:key>                    <xsl:preserve-space>
<xsl:decimal-format>       <xsl:namespace-alias>        <xsl:strip-space>
<xsl:import>               <xsl:output>                 <xsl:template>
<xsl:include>              <xsl:param>                  <xsl:variable>
```

The meaning of these elements is explained in Chapter 4. No other XSL element (that is, no other element with the namespace URI http://www.w3.org/1999/XSL/Transform) may be used at the top level.

Implementer-Defined Top-Level Elements

An implementer-defined top-level element must belong to a namespace with a non-null URI, different from the XSL namespace. This will generally be a namespace defined by the vendor: for example with the Saxon product, the relevant namespace URI is http://icl.com/saxon. The meaning of elements in this category is entirely at the discretion of the vendor, though the specification states a rule that such elements must not be used to change the meaning of any standard XSLT constructs. Note that these top-level elements are not technically extension elements, and their namespace does not have to be declared in the extension-element-prefixes attribute for them to be effective.

Several vendors supply top-level elements that allow you to define scripts or external functions that can be invoked from XPath expressions in the stylesheet. Others might use such elements to define debugging or tracing options. Some of these extensions are described in Chapter 10.

User-Defined Top-Level Elements

A **user-defined top-level element** must also belong to a namespace with a non-null URI, different from the XSL namespace, and preferably different from the namespace URI used by any vendor. These elements are ignored by the XSLT processor. They are useful, however, as a source of lookup data, error messages, and the like. It is possible to reference these elements from within the stylesheet by treating the stylesheet as an additional source document, and loading it using the document() function - which is described in Chapter 7, page 440. If the first argument to this function is an empty string, it is interpreted as a reference to the stylesheet module in which the document() function appears.

So for example, if the stylesheet contains a user-defined top-level element as follows:

```
<user:data xmlns:user="http://acme.com/">
   <message nr="1">Source document is empty</message>
   <message nr="2">Invalid date</message>
   <message nr="3">Sales value is not numeric</message>
</user:data>
```

then the same stylesheet can contain a named template to display a numbered message as follows:

```
<xsl:template name="display-message">
   <xsl:param name="message-nr"/>
   <xsl:message xmlns:user="http://acme.com/">
      <xsl:value-of
        select="document('')/*/user:data/message[@nr=$message-nr]"/>
   </xsl:message>
</xsl:template>
```

3

Stylesheet Structure

103

The `<xsl:value-of>` element evaluates the XPath expression in its `select` attribute as a string, and writes the value to the result tree. In this case the XPath expression is a path expression starting with «`document('')`», which selects the root node of the stylesheet module, followed by «`*`», which selects its first child (the `<xsl:stylesheet>` element), followed by «`user:data`», which selects the `<user:data>` element, followed by «`message[@nr=$message-nr]`», which selects the `<message>` element whose `nr` attribute is equal to the value of the `$message-nr` parameter in the stylesheet.

This named template might be invoked from elsewhere in the stylesheet using a sequence such as:

```
<xsl:if test="string(number(@sales))='NaN'">
    <xsl:call-template name="display-message">
        <xsl:with-param name="message-nr" select="3"/>
    </xsl:call-template>
</xsl:if>
```

The `<xsl:if>` element tests whether the `sales` attribute of the current source element is numeric: if not, the result of converting it to a number and then to a string will be the value `NaN`, meaning Not-A-Number. In this case, the code will call the template we defined earlier to display the message "Sales value is not numeric". (The destination of messages output using `<xsl:message>` is not defined in the standard. It might produce an alert box, or simply a message in the web server log file.)

The advantage of this technique is that it gathers all the messages together in one place, for ease of maintenance. The technique can also be readily extended to use different sets of messages depending on the user's preferred language.

Simplified Stylesheets

A simplified stylesheet uses an abbreviated syntax in which the `<xsl:stylesheet>` element and all the top-level elements are omitted.

The XSLT specification calls this facility **Literal Result Element As Stylesheet.**[104] Its purpose is to allow people with HTML authoring skills but no programming experience to write simple stylesheets with a minimum of training. A simplified stylesheet has a skeleton that looks like the target document (which is usually HTML, though it doesn't have to be), and uses XSLT instructions to fill in the variable parts.

A stylesheet module is interpreted as a simplified stylesheet if the outermost element is not `<xsl:stylesheet>` or `<xsl:transform>`. The outermost element can have any name, provided it is not in the XSL namespace. It must still contain a declaration of the XSL namespace, and it must have an `xsl:version` attribute. For this version the value should be 1.0. When the `xsl:version` attribute is not equal to 1.0, forwards compatible processing mode is enabled. This is discussed later on page 127.

Example: A Simplified Stylesheet

This example shows a stylesheet that takes the form of an HTML skeleton page, with XSLT instructions embedded within it to pull data from the source document. The stylesheet is in the download file obtainable from http://www.wrox.com. It has the filename `simplified.xsl`, and can be used together with the data file `books.xml`.

The complete stylesheet is as follows:

```
<html xmlns:xsl="http://www.w3.org/1999/XSL/Transform"
      xsl:version="1.0">
<head><title>A list of books</title></head>
<body>
<h1>A list of books</h1>
    <table border="2">
    <xsl:for-each select="//book">
        <xsl:sort select="author"/>
        <tr>
            <td><xsl:value-of select="author"/></td>
            <td><xsl:value-of select="title"/></td>
            <td><xsl:value-of select="@category"/></td>
            <td><xsl:value-of select="price"/></td>
        </tr>
    </xsl:for-each>
    </table>
</body>
</html>
```

When you run this against the file `books.xml` (which is listed on page 70 in Chapter 2), the output is a sorted table showing the books, as follows:

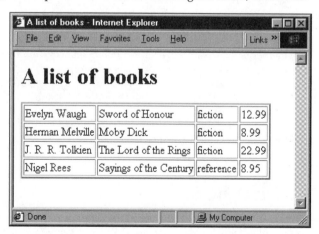

A simplified stylesheet is equivalent to a stylesheet in which the outermost element (typically the `<html>` element) is wrapped first in an `<xsl:template>` element with «`match="/"`», and then in an `<xsl:stylesheet>` element. The `xsl:version` attribute of the outermost element becomes the `version` attribute of the `<xsl:stylesheet>`. So the expanded form of the above example would be:

```
<xsl:stylesheet xmlns:xsl="http://www.w3.org/1999/XSL/Transform" version="1.0">
<xsl:template match="/">
<html>
<head><title>A list of books</title></head>
<body>
<h1>A list of books</h1>
   <table border="2">
   <xsl:for-each select="//book">
      <xsl:sort select="author"/>
      <tr>
        <td><xsl:value-of select="author"/></td>
        <td><xsl:value-of select="title"/></td>
        <td><xsl:value-of select="@category"/></td>
        <td><xsl:value-of select="price"/></td>
      </tr>
   </xsl:for-each>
   </table>
</body>
</html>
</xsl:template>
</xsl:stylesheet>
```

The significance of «`match="/"`» is that this identifies the template rule as the first one to be processed when the stylesheet is activated. As we saw in Chapter 2, processing always starts at the root node of the source document tree, and whichever template rule matches the root node is the first one to be invoked. The match pattern «`/`» matches the root node. In a simplified stylesheet, this will generally be the only template to be invoked.

There are many things a simplified stylesheet cannot do, because it cannot have any top-level XSL elements. For example, a simplified stylesheet can't include or import another stylesheet, it can't have global variables or parameters, and it can't define keys. But when you need these extra capabilities, you can always "unsimplify" the stylesheet by adding the surrounding `<xsl:stylesheet>` and `<xsl:template>` elements.

It is possible in theory for a stylesheet to include or import a simplified stylesheet, which would be expanded exactly as described above – but it would be a rather unusual thing to do.

Template Bodies

The content of an `<xsl:template>` element, after any parameter definitions contained in `<xsl: param>` elements, is a **template body**. The XSLT specification calls this simply a **template**, but since this term is often used casually to mean an `<xsl:template>` element, I have avoided this usage.

Many other XSL elements are also defined to have a template body as their content. This simply refers to the rules for what contents may appear within the element, it does not mean that there must actually be an `<xsl:template>` element present. For example, the contents of an `<xsl:variable>` or `<xsl:if>` element follow exactly the same rules as the content of an `<xsl:template>` (ignoring `<xsl: param>` elements), and these too are template bodies. It follows that one template body may be contained within another. For example, consider the following template rule:

```
<xsl:template match="para">
    <xsl:if test="position()=1">
       <hr/>- o - O - o -<hr/>
    </xsl:if>
    <xsl:apply-templates/>
    <xsl:if test="position()=last()">
       <hr/>- o - O - o -<hr/>
    </xsl:if>
</xsl:template>
```

Viewed as a tree, using the notation introduced in Chapter 2, this has the structure shown in the diagram below. There are three template bodies, indicated by the dotted lines. Within the template bodies on this tree, there are three kinds of nodes: text nodes, XSL instructions (such as `<xsl:if>`), and literal result elements (such as `<hr>`) which are elements to be written to the result tree.

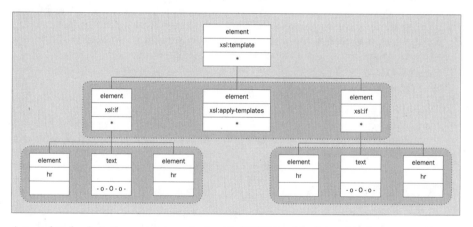

A template body is the nearest equivalent in XSLT to a block in a block-structured programming language such as C or Java; and like blocks in C or Java, it defines the scope of any local variables declared within the block.

A template body is a sequence of sibling nodes in the stylesheet. Comment and processing instruction nodes are allowed, but the XSLT processor ignores them. The nodes of interest are text nodes and element nodes.

Text nodes appearing within a template body are copied to the result tree when the template body is instantiated. However, text nodes in a template body that consist entirely of whitespace will be ignored, unless the `xml:space` attribute is used on an enclosing element to define them as significant.

Text nodes containing whitespace only are also significant if they appear as the content of an `<xsl:text>` element, but in that case they are not part of a template body.

Element nodes within a template body are one of three kinds: XSL instructions, extension elements, and literal result elements. I'll describe these in the next three sections.

XSL Instructions

An XSL instruction is one of the following elements:

```
<xsl:apply-imports>      <xsl:copy>          <xsl:message>
<xsl:apply-templates>    <xsl:copy-of>       <xsl:number>
<xsl:attribute>          <xsl:element>       <xsl:processing-
<xsl:call-template>      <xsl:fallback>      instruction>
<xsl:choose>             <xsl:for-each>      <xsl:text>
<xsl:comment>            <xsl:if>            <xsl:value-of>
                                             <xsl:variable>
```

No other element in the XSL namespace may appear directly in a template body. Other XSL elements, for example `<xsl:with-param>`, `<xsl:sort>`, and `<xsl:otherwise>`, are not regarded as instructions, because they cannot appear directly in a template body – they may only appear in very specific contexts. The `<xsl:param>` element is a bit anomalous: it can appear as a child or an `<xsl:template>` element, but it is constrained to appear before other elements, and is therefore not considered to be part of the template body. So it is not classified as an instruction.

I shall explain the meaning of all these XSL instructions in Chapter 4.

If an unknown element in the XSL namespace is encountered in a template body, the action taken depends on whether **forwards-compatible mode** is enabled. This is discussed later on page 127.

Extension Elements

An **extension element** is an instruction defined by the vendor or the user, as distinct from one defined in the XSLT standard. In both cases, they are recognized as extension elements because they belong to a namespace that is listed in the `extension-element-prefixes` attribute of the containing `<xsl:stylesheet>` element, or in the `xsl:extension-element-prefixes` attribute of the element itself, or of a containing literal result element or extension element.

In practice, extension elements are more likely to be defined by vendors than by users. Several vendors have provided extension elements to direct the stylesheet output to multiple output files. Another example: the Saxon product provides the `<saxon:group>` extension element to perform grouping (like the SQL GROUP BY construct), a capability which is awkward and inefficient to achieve using standard XSLT facilities.

3

Stylesheet Structure

Not all products allow users to implement their own extension elements, and with those that do, it may well involve some rather complex system-level programming. In practice, it is usually simpler to escape to user-written code by using extension functions, which are much easier to write.

The following example shows an `<acme:instruction>` element which would be treated as a literal result element were it not for the `xsl:extension-element-prefixes` attribute, which turns it into an extension element:

```
<acme:instruction
   xmlns:acme="http://acme.co.jp/xslt"
   xsl:extension-element-prefixes="acme"/>
```

The way in which new extension elements are implemented is not defined in the XSLT specification, and is likely to vary for each vendor. In fact, XSLT processors are not required to provide a mechanism for defining new extension elements. The only requirement is that they should recognize an extension element when they see one, and distinguish it from a literal result element.

What happens if a stylesheet that uses an extension element defined in the Xalan product (say) is processed using a different product (say Microsoft's)? If the processor encounters an extension element that it cannot instantiate (typically because it was invented by a different vendor), the action it must take is clearly defined in the XSLT standard: if the stylesheet author has defined an `<xsl:fallback>` action, it must execute that, otherwise it must report an error. The one thing it must not do is to treat the extension element as a literal result element and copy it to the result tree.

The `<xsl:fallback>` instruction allows you to define how an XSLT processor should deal with extension elements it does not recognize. It is described in more detail on page 126, and full specifications are on page 197, in Chapter 4.

Any element found in a template body that is not an XSL instruction or an extension element is interpreted as a **literal result element** (for example, the `<hr/>` elements in the previous template bodies example above). When the template body is instantiated, the literal result element will be copied to the result tree.

So in effect there are two kinds of nodes in a template body: instructions and data. Instructions are obeyed according to the rules of the particular instruction, and data nodes (text nodes and literal result elements) are copied to the result tree.

Literal result elements play an important role in the structure of a stylesheet, so the next section examines them in more detail.

Literal Result Elements

A literal result element is an element within a template body in the stylesheet that cannot be interpreted as an instruction, and which is therefore treated as data to be copied to the current output destination.

We'll describe literal result elements using the same structure as we'll be using to describe XSL elements in Chapter 4.

Format

Position

A literal result element always appears directly within a template body.

Attributes

Name	Value	Meaning
xsl:exclude-result-prefixes *optional*	Whitespace-separated list of namespace prefixes (see note below)	Each prefix in the list must identify a namespace that is in scope at this point in the stylesheet module. The namespace identified is not to be copied to the result tree.
xsl:extension-element-prefixes *optional*	Whitespace-separated list of namespace prefixes (see note below)	Each prefix in the list must identify a namespace that is in scope at this point in the stylesheet module. Elements that are descendants of this literal result element, and whose names are in one of these identified namespaces, are treated as extension elements rather than literal result elements.
xsl:version *optional*	Number	If the value is «1.0», then any XSL element that is a descendant of the literal result element must be an XSL element defined in version 1.0 of the Recommendation. If the value is any other value, forwards-compatible mode is enabled: see below.
xsl:use-attribute-sets *optional*	Whitespace-separated list of QNames identifying named <xsl:attribute-set> elements (see note below)	The attributes defined in the named attribute sets are instantiated and copied as attributes of this literal result element in the output destination.

Name	Value	Meaning
other attributes (optional)	Attribute value template	Any XPath expressions occurring between curly braces in the value are evaluated, and the resulting string forms the value of an attribute copied to the current output destination. Attribute Value Templates are described on page 118.

Note

Several of the attributes take the form of whitespace-separated lists. This is simply a list of names (or prefixes) in which the various names are separated by any of the XML-defined whitespace characters: tab, carriage return, newline, or space. For example, you could write:

```
<TD xsl:use-attribute-sets="blue italic centered"/>
```

Here the names `blue`, `italic`, and `centered` must match the names of `<xsl:attribute-set>` elements elsewhere in the stylesheet.

Content

The content of a literal result element is a template body. It may thus contain XSL instructions, extension elements, literal result elements, and/or text nodes.

Usage

The literal result element is copied to the result tree, and its content is instantiated.

Consider a template body containing a single literal result element:

```
<TD>Product code</TD>>
```

In this case a `<TD>` element will be written to the result tree with a child text node whose content is «Product code». When the result tree is output to an XML or HTML file, it will regenerate the text as it appeared in the stylesheet – or something equivalent. There is no guarantee that it will be character-for-character identical, for example, the processor may add or remove whitespace within the tags, or it may represent characters using character or entity references.

If the literal result element has content, then the content must be another template body, and this template body is itself instantiated; any nodes generated in the result tree in the course of this process will become children of the element created from the literal result element.

For example, if the template body is:

```
<TD><xsl:value-of select="."/></TD>
```

then when the `<TD>` element is instantiated, its content will also be instantiated. The content in this case is a template body consisting of a single XSL instruction, and the effect is that this instruction is instantiated to create a text node which will be a child of the `<TD>` element in the result tree. The instruction `<xsl:value-of select=".">` outputs the string-value of the current node in the source tree. So if this value is «`$83.99`», the result would be:

```
<TD>$83.99</TD>
```

It is tempting to think of this as a sequence of three steps:

❑   The `<TD>` start tag causes a `<TD>` start tag to be written to the output.

❑   The `<xsl:value-of>` element is evaluated and the result («`$83.99`») is written to the output.

❑   The `</TD>` end tag causes a `</TD>` end tag to be written to the output.

However, this is not a true picture of what is going on, and it is best not to think about it this way, because otherwise you will start wondering, for example, how to delay writing the end tag until some condition is encountered in the input.

> **The transformation process writes nodes to the result tree, it does not write tags to a sequential file. The `<TD>` node in the stylesheet causes a `<TD>` node to be written to the result tree. You cannot write half a node to the tree – the start and end tags are not written as separate operations. The `<TD>` and `</TD>` tags are generated only when the result tree is serialized as XML or HTML.**

The following diagram might help to illustrate this:

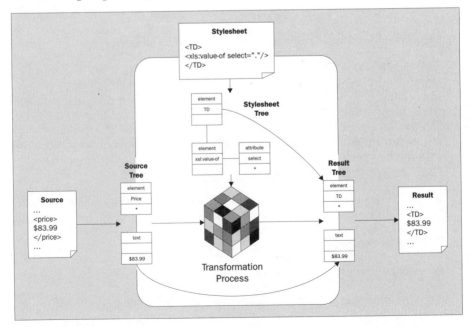

112

If you do find yourself thinking about where you want tags to appear in the output, it is a good idea to draw a sketch showing the required shape of the result tree, and then think about how to write the stylesheet to produce the required nodes on the tree.

Attributes of a Literal Result Element

If the literal result element has attributes, other than the special xsl-prefixed ones in the list above, then these attributes too will be copied to the current output destination. So if the template body contains:

```
<TD><IMG src="picture1.gif"/></TD>
```

then the output will contain a copy of this whole structure. The outer <TD> element is copied to the result tree as before, and this time its content consists of another literal result element, the <IMG> element, which is copied to the result tree as a child of the <TD> element, along with its src attribute. This time both the stylesheet tree and the result tree take the form shown here:

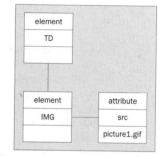

If the value of an attribute of a literal result element contains curly braces («{» and «}»), then it is treated as an **attribute value template** (discussed further in the next section). The text between the curly braces is treated as an XPath expression, and is evaluated as a string; the attribute written to the result tree contains this string in place of the expression. For example, suppose we apply the following template to the books.xml file used earlier:

```
<xsl:template match="/">
<xsl:""for-each select="//book">
<div id="div{position()}">
  <xsl:value-of select="title"/>
</div>
</xsl:for-each>
</xsl:template>
```

Because the position() function takes the values 1, 2, 3 and 4, as we move through the set of books, the output will take the form:

```
<div id="div1">Sayings of the Century</div>
<div id="div2">Sword of Honour</div>
<div id="div3">Moby Dick</div>
<div id="div4">The Lord of the Rings</div>
```

It is also possible to generate attributes for a literal result element by two other mechanisms:

❑ The attribute can be generated by an `<xsl:attribute>` instruction. This instruction does not need to be textually within the content of the literal result element in the stylesheet, but it must be instantiated before any child nodes (elements or children) have been generated.

The reason for this rule is to allow the XSLT processor to avoid building the result tree in memory. Many processors will write XML syntax direct to an output file as the nodes are generated, and the rule that attributes must be generated before child elements or text nodes ensures that this is possible. The rule is phrased as if execution of the stylesheet has to be sequential, but of course any implementation strategy that produces the same effect is acceptable.

❑ A collection of attributes can be generated by use of a named attribute set. The literal result element must contain an `xsl:use-attribute-sets` attribute that names the attribute sets to be incorporated: these names must correspond to `<xsl:attribute-set>` elements at the top level of the stylesheet. The named attribute sets each contain a sequence of `<xsl:attribute>` instructions, and these cause attributes to be added to the generated element as if they were present directly in the content of the literal result element. Named attribute sets are useful to maintain a collection of related attributes such as font name, color, and size, which together define a style that will be used repeatedly in the output document; they are a direct parallel to the styles found in simpler languages such as CSS.

Attributes are added to the generated element node in a defined order: first attributes incorporated using `xsl:use-attribute-sets`, then attributes present on the literal result element itself, and finally attributes added using `<xsl:attribute>` instructions. The significance of this sequence is that if two or more attributes with the same name are added, it is the last one that counts. It doesn't mean that they will necessarily appear in this order when the result tree is serialized.

Namespaces for a Literal Result Element

The namespace nodes of a literal result element are also copied to the current output destination. This is often the source of some confusion. The literal result element in the stylesheet will have a namespace node for every namespace declaration that is in scope: that is, every `xmlns` attribute or `xmlns:*` attribute on the literal result element itself, or on any of its ancestor elements in the stylesheet. The only exception is that the attribute «`xmlns=""`» does not act as a namespace declaration, rather it cancels any earlier declaration for the default namespace.

In the result tree, the element created from the literal result element is guaranteed to have a namespace node for every namespace node present on the literal result element in the stylesheet, except the following:

❑ a namespace node for the XSLT namespace URI `http://www.w3.org/1999/XSL/Transform` will not be copied.

❑ a namespace node for a namespace declared as an extension element namespace will not be copied. A namespace is declared as an extension element namespace by including its prefix in the value of the `extension-element-prefixes` attribute of the `<xsl:stylesheet>` element, or in the value of the `xsl:extension-element-prefixes` attribute of this literal result element or of any ancestor literal result element or extension element.

❑ a namespace node for an excluded namespace will not be copied. A namespace is declared as an excluded namespace by including its prefix in the value of the `exclude-result-prefixes` attribute of the `<xsl:stylesheet>` element, or in the value of the `xsl:exclude-result-prefixes` attribute of this literal result element or of any ancestor literal result element.

For example, consider the following stylesheet:

```
<xsl:stylesheet
   xmlns:xsl="http://www.w3.org/1999/XSL/Transform"
   version="1.0"
   xmlns:date="http://www.jclark.com/xt/java.util.Date"
>

<xsl:template match="/"
      xmlns = "urn:acme-com:gregorian">
   <date><xsl:value-of select="$today"/></date>
</xsl:template>

<xsl:param name="today" select="date:new()"/>

</xsl:stylesheet>
```

There are three namespaces in scope for the `<date>` element, namely the XSL namespace, the namespace «`http://www.jclark.com/xt/java.util.Date`», and the default namespace «`urn:acme-com:gregorian`». The XSL namespace is not copied to the result tree, but the other two are. So the `<date>` element added to the result tree is guaranteed to have these two namespaces «`http://www.jclark.com/xt/java.util.Date`», and «`urn:acme-com:gregorian`» in scope.

> *The stylesheet above uses an extension function «`date:new()`». As explained later in the chapter (page 122), the way in which extension functions work varies from one XSLT processor to another. The above example is written so that it should work with both Saxon and xt. To run it with a different XSLT processor, you will need to make minor changes: see chapter 10 for details.*

If the `$today` parameter is supplied as the value «`2000-13-18`», the output would be as follows (regardless of the source document):

```
<date xmlns="urn:acme-com:gregorian"
      xmlns:date="http://www.jclark.com/xt/java.util.Date ">2000-13-18</date>
```

3

Stylesheet Structure

The first namespace declaration is necessary, because it defines the namespace for the element name <date>. However, you probably don't really want the xmlns:date declaration here. It's not doing any harm, but it's not doing any good either. It's there because the XSLT processor can't tell that it's unwanted. If you want this declaration to be omitted, use the xsl:exclude-result-prefixes attribute as follows:

```
<xsl:stylesheet
    xmlns:xsl="http://www.w3.org/1999/XSL/Transform"
    version="1.0"
    xmlns:date="http://www.jclark.com/xt/java.util.Date"
>


<xsl:template match="/"
        xmlns = "urn:acme-com:gregorian">
    <date xsl:exclude-result-prefixes="date">
        <xsl:value-of select="$today"/>
    </date>
</xsl:template>


<xsl:param name="today" select="date:new()"/>


</xsl:stylesheet>
```

The fact that an element in the result tree has a namespace node does not necessarily mean that when the result tree is written out as an XML document, the corresponding element will have a namespace declaration for that namespace. The XSLT processor is likely to omit the namespace declaration if it is redundant, in other words, if it duplicates a namespace declaration on a containing element. It can't be omitted, however, simply on the basis that it is not used. This is because namespace declarations might affect the meaning of the data in the output document in a way that the XSLT processor is unaware of. Applications are perfectly entitled to use namespace declarations to scope identifiers and names appearing in attribute values or text.

An element in the result tree generated from a literal result element may also have additional namespace nodes beyond those described above. For example, it may well inherit namespace nodes that were generated on a containing element. In addition, because the XSLT processor is required to generate output that conforms to the XML namespaces recommendation, the generated element will also have namespace nodes corresponding to any namespace prefixes used in the element name or in any attribute name, even if these have been declared as excluded namespaces. The specification isn't explicit on this point: an XSLT processor could instead decide to report an error in this situation.

Namespace Prefixes

The namespaces generated in the result tree when a literal result element is instantiated will normally have the same prefix and the same URI as the corresponding namespace in the stylesheet.

There are unusual circumstances when the XSLT processor may need to change the prefix for a namespace. For example, it is possible to create two attributes that use the same namespace prefix to refer to different namespace URIs, as in the following example:

```
<output>
   <xsl:attribute name="out:file"
      xmlns:out="http://domain-a.com/">a</xsl:attribute>
   <xsl:attribute name="out:dir"
      xmlns:out="http://domain-b.com/">b</xsl:attribute>
</output>
```

The generated output in this case will look something like this:

```
<output
   out:file="a"
   ns1:dir="b"
   xmlns:out="http://domain-a.com/"
   xmlns:ns1="http://domain-b.com/"/>
```

The XSLT processor has no choice but to invent a prefix for one of the namespaces, because the supplied prefix is already in use with a different meaning. But because namespace prefixes are essentially arbitrary (it's only the URI that has any real significance) the meaning of the output file is not affected.

> *This rather contradicts what I said a moment ago, that namespace declarations are copied into the result tree even if they appear to be unused, because you might be using them in data values where the XSLT processor can't be aware of them. If you use namespace prefixes in your data, it would be very damaging if the XSLT processor changed them arbitrarily. Fortunately it is only in very obscure cases that the system needs to allocate a different prefix, and the implication in the spec, while not spelt out in so many words, is that in all other cases the processor is expected to leave them unchanged.*

Namespace Aliasing

In some circumstances, instead of changing the namespace prefix when a literal result element is copied to the result tree, it is necessary to change the namespace URI. The most obvious situation where this arises is when the output document is itself a stylesheet. This isn't as esoteric a requirement as it may appear: generating a stylesheet can sometimes be a useful technique. For example, if your company changes its house-style to use different fonts and colors, you could write an XSLT transformation to convert all your existing stylesheets to the new standard.

When you generate a stylesheet, you will want to generate XSL elements such as <xsl:template> in the result tree; but you can't include such elements as literal result elements in the stylesheet, because they would be mistaken for instructions. So the answer is to include them in the stylesheet with a different namespace, and to declare in an <xsl:namespace-alias> element that the URI should be changed when the literal result element is copied to the result tree.

For more details, see <xsl:namespace-alias> in Chapter 4, on page 233.

Attribute Value Templates

As we've seen, an attribute value template is a special form of parameterized attribute value. There are two ways they can be used:

❑ On a literal result element, an attribute value template provides a way of generating an attribute whose value is computed at run-time rather than always taking the same value: for example `<TD WIDTH="{$width}">`. You could achieve the same effect with the `<xsl:attribute>` instruction, but attribute value templates are easier to write and easier to understand.

❑ On some XSL elements, certain attributes can be computed at run-time. For example, when sorting, instead of writing «order="ascending"» or «order="descending"», you could write «order="{$order}"» so that the order varies depending on a run-time parameter. Note that there are very few attributes where this facility is available: they are listed later in this section.

The term **template** here has nothing to do with XSLT template rules, template bodies, or `<xsl:template>` elements: attribute value templates are simply a notation for embedding variable components into an otherwise fixed attribute value.

An attribute value template is a string in which XPath expressions may be embedded within curly braces («{» and «}»). The XPath expression is evaluated, the result is converted to a string using the conversion rules described on page 80 in Chapter 2, and this string is then substituted into the attribute value in place of the expression.

For example, suppose you have a set of images representing an alphabet such as the following, and you want to use these to represent the first character of a paragraph of text.

You could write a template rule to achieve this as follows (ignoring practical details such as how to deal with paragraphs that don't start with a capital letter). It uses the `substring()` function, which is described in Chapter 7, on page 512.

```
<xsl:template match="para">
  <p><img src="fancy{substring(.,1,1)}.gif">
  <xsl:value-of select="substring(.,2)" /></p>
</xsl:template>
```

A paragraph that starts with the letter A (like this one) will cause the `src` attribute of the `<img>` element to be evaluated as «img src="fancyA.gif"», so it will be displayed in the browser like this:

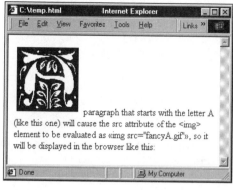

If you want to include the characters «{» or «}» in an attribute value with their ordinary meaning (this is sometimes useful when generating dynamic HTML), they should be doubled as «{{» or «}}». However, you should only do this in an attribute that is being interpreted as an attribute value template. In other attributes, curly braces have no special meaning.

Curly brackets can never be nested. You can only use them to include an XPath expression in the text of a stylesheet attribute; they cannot be used within an XPath expression itself. You can always achieve the required effect some other way; for example, instead of:

```
<a href="#{id( 'A{@nr}' )}">  /* WRONG */
```

write:

```
<a href="#{id( concat('A', @nr) )}">
```

The `concat()` function, described on page 430, in Chapter 7, performs concatenation of strings.

Attribute value templates cannot be used anywhere you like in the stylesheet. They can only be used for those attributes that are specifically identified as attribute value templates in the XSLT Recommendation. The following table gives a complete list of all the places you can use Attribute Value Templates:

Element	Attributes interpreted as Attribute Value Templates
Literal result elements	All attributes except those in the XSL namespace
Extension elements	As defined by the specification of each extension element
`<xsl:attribute>`	`name`, `namespace`
`<xsl:element>`	`name`, `namespace`
`<xsl:number>`	`format`, `lang`, `letter-value`, `grouping-separator`, `grouping-size`
`<xsl:processing-instruction>`	`name`
`<xsl:sort>`	`lang`, `data-type`, `order`, `case-order`

In all other contexts, don't even think of trying to use them: the curly braces will either be ignored, or will cause an error to be reported. It can be very tempting: if you want to use <xsl:call-template>, for example, and the name of the template you want to call is in a variable, you might badly want to write:

```
<!-WRONG-->
<xsl:param name="tname"/>
<xsl:call-template name="{$tname}"/>
<!-WRONG-->
```

However, you can't, because the name attribute of <xsl:call-template> (nor any other attribute of <xsl:call-template> for that matter) is not in the above list of places where attribute value templates can be used.

Why are attribute value templates rationed so severely? A few of the restrictions do appear to be purely arbitrary, but most are there deliberately to make life easier for the XSLT processor:

❑ Attribute value templates are never allowed for attributes of top-level elements. This ensures that the values are known before the source document is read, and are constant for each run of the stylesheet.

❑ Attribute value templates are never allowed for attributes whose value is an XPath expression or a pattern. This ensures that expressions and patterns can be compiled when the stylesheet is read, and do not need to be re-parsed each time they are evaluated.

❑ Attribute value templates are generally not allowed for attributes whose value is the name of another object in the stylesheet, for example a named template or a named attribute set. This ensures that references from one stylesheet object to another can be resolved once and for all when the stylesheet is first read. They are allowed, however, for names of objects being written to the result tree.

❑ Attribute value templates are not allowed for attributes interpreted by the XML parser, specifically xml:space, xml:lang, and namespace declarations (xmlns and xmlns:prefix). This is because the XML parser reads the value before the XSLT processor gets a chance to expand it.

The remaining restrictions must be seen as arbitrary. For example it is hard to see any good reason why the terminate attribute of <xsl:message> can't be an attribute value template, but the fact is that the spec doesn't allow it.

When an XPath expression within an attribute value template is evaluated, the context is the same as for any other expression in the stylesheet. The idea of an expression having a context was introduced in Chapter 2, on page 79: it determines the meaning of constructs such as «.», which refers to the context node, and «position()», which refers to the context position. Variables and namespace prefixes may only be used within the expression if they are in scope at that point in the stylesheet. The context node, context position, and context size are determined from the current node and current node list being processed in the most recent call of <xsl:apply-templates> or <xsl:for-each>; if there is no such call (which can happen while a global variable is being evaluated, for example), the current node and current node list contain just the root node.

Extensibility

Bitten by years of experience with proprietary vendor extensions to HTML, the W3C committee responsible for XSLT took great care to allow vendor extensions in a tightly controlled way.

The extensibility mechanisms in XSLT are governed by several unstated design principles:

❏ Namespaces are used to ensure that vendor extensions cannot clash with facilities in the standard (including facilities introduced in future versions), or with extensions defined by a different vendor.

❏ It is possible for an XSLT processor to recognize where extensions have been used, including extensions defined by a different vendor, and to fail cleanly if it cannot implement those extensions.

❏ It is possible for the writer of a stylesheet to test whether particular extensions are available, and to define fallback behavior if they are not. For example, the stylesheet might be able to achieve the same effect in a different way, or it might make do without some special effect in the output.

The principal extension mechanisms, which I will describe below, are extension functions and extension elements. However, it is also possible for vendors to define other kinds of extensions, or to provide mechanisms for users or third parties to do so. These include the following:

❏ XSLT-defined elements can have additional vendor-defined attributes, provided they use a non-null namespace URI, and that they do not change the behavior of standard elements and attributes. For example, a vendor could add an attribute such as `acme:debug` to the `<xsl:template>` element, whose effect is to pause execution when the template is instantiated. But adding an attribute `acme:repeat="2"` whose effect is to execute the template twice would be against the conformance rules. (Whether vendors will pay any attention to the conformance rules, of course, is another matter.)

❏ Vendors can define additional top-level elements; again provided that they use a non-null namespace URI, and that they do not change the behavior of standard elements and attributes. An example of such an element is Microsoft's `<msxsl:script>` element, for defining external functions in VBScript or JScript. Any processor that doesn't recognize the namespace URI will ignore such top-level elements.

❏ Certain XSLT-defined attributes have an open-ended set of values, where vendors have discretion on the range of values to be supported. Examples are the `lang` attribute of `<xsl:number>` and `<xsl:sort>`, which provides language-dependent numbering and sorting, the `method` attribute of `<xsl:output>`, which defines how the result tree is output to a file, and the `format` attribute of `<xsl:number>`, which allows the vendor to provide additional numbering sequences beyond those defined in the standard. The list of system properties supplied in the first argument of the `system-property()` function is similarly open-ended.

Extension Functions

Extension functions provide a mechanism for extending the capabilities of XSLT by escaping into another language such as Java or JavaScript. The most usual reasons for doing this are:

❑ To improve performance (for example, when doing complex string manipulations)

❑ To exploit system capabilities and services

❑ To reuse code that already exists in another language

❑ For convenience: complex algorithms and computations can be very verbose when written in XSLT

The term **extension function** is used both for functions supplied by the vendor beyond the core functions defined in the XSLT and XPath standards (those described in Chapter 7), and for functions written by users and third parties.

The XSLT Recommendation does not define how extension functions are written, or how they are bound to the stylesheet, and it does not define which languages should be supported. In fact, it does not require that an XSLT processor should provide a mechanism for writing extension functions at all, only that it should behave in a particular way when it encounters extension functions that it cannot invoke: for example it says how Microsoft's XSLT processor should behave when it encounters an Oracle extension function.

This means that it is quite difficult to write extension functions that work with more than one vendor's XSLT processor, even though there are some conventions that several vendors have adopted, as described in Chapter 10. Generally speaking, if you want your stylesheet to work with more than one XSLT processor, you will have to include some conditional logic when calling extension functions.

A function name in the XPath expression syntax (see Chapter 5) is a QName, that is, a name with an optional namespace prefix. If there is no prefix, the name must be one of the core functions defined in the standard: for example the core function not() can be invoked as:

```
<xsl:if test="not( @name = 'Mozart' )">
```

If there is a prefix, the function is assumed to be an extension function. The namespace URI associated with the prefix is used to identify the function library in which the implementation of the function can be found, but the way in which this happens is entirely vendor-defined. For example, the following example invokes an extension function xt:intersection(), but says nothing about where this function can be loaded from. In this case the namespace URI is one that the xt product will recognize as referring to its own built-in extension functions.

```
<xsl:variable name="x" select="xt:intersection($y, $z)"
xmlns:xt="http://www.jclark.com/xt"/>
```

Several XSLT processors provide a mechanism (described on page 632 in Chapter 10 as *Common Java Binding*) in which the namespace URI ends with the fully qualified name of a Java class. When a function is called, this Java class is loaded and inspected (using Java's introspection mechanisms) to find a method whose name and parameters match the name and arguments used in the XSLT call, and the relevant method is then called. This mechanism means all the information needed to identify and call the function is contained within the namespace URI itself.

Again using xt as an example, this allows you to output the current date and time by using the standard Java class «java.util.Date». The default constructor for this class creates a Date object whose value is the current date, and the «toString()» method on this object creates a default string representation of the date. So you can write in your stylesheet:

```
<xsl:template name="show-date"
    xmlns:Date="http://www.jclark.com/xt/java/java.util.Date">
    <xsl:variable name="today" select="Date:new()"/>
    <xsl:value-of select="Date:toString($today)"/>
</xsl:template>
```

In the expression «Date:new()», Date is a namespace prefix referring to a namespace URI that ends with «java.util.Date», so the processor knows that it is being asked to create an instance of this Java class. As a result, the variable «$today» will hold a value which is a Java object of type «java.util.Date». This is not one of the recognized XSLT data types, but vendors are allowed to extend the standard set of data types with their own. This variable is then passed to the «toString()» method on the same class (because it too has the namespace prefix «Date»). By convention, the object that is the target of the method is written as its first argument; so writing «toString($date)» in an XPath expression is the equivalent of writing «date.toString()» in Java. The effect is that the named template writes the current date to the result tree.

The details of how Java methods are invoked varies a little from one processor to another, as does the mapping of XSLT data types (such as node-set) to Java types. Further details are given for some popular products in Chapter 10. This is all likely to change in future: a standard interface for writing extension functions is one of the facilities promised for a future version of the XSLT standard.

Other XSLT processors, notably Microsoft's, have provided the ability to write Javascript functions in vendor-defined top-level elements, and to invoke these as extension functions. Indeed, such a mechanism was defined in early drafts of the XSLT standard, though it was removed before the final Recommendation was published, presumably because of difficulties in defining a rigorous specification.

Here is an example of a simple extension function implemented using this mechanism with Microsoft's XSLT processor, and an expression that calls it:

```
<msxsl:script
    xmlns:msxsl="urn:schemas-microsoft-com:xslt"
    language="VBScript"
    implements-prefix="ms"
```

3

Stylesheet Structure

```
>
Function ToMillimetres(inches)
    ToMillimetres = inches * 25.4
End Function
</msxsl:script>
```

```
<xsl:template match="/" >
    <xsl:variable name="test" select="12"/>
    <size><xsl:value-of select="ms:ToMillimetres($test)"/></size>
</xsl:template>
```

You can test whether a particular extension function is available by using the function-available() function. For example:

```
<xsl:choose xmlns:acme="http://acme.co.jp/xslt">
    <xsl:when test="function-available('acme:moonshine')">
        <xsl:value-of select="acme:moonshine($x)"/>
    </xsl:when>
    <xsl:otherwise>
        <xsl:text>*** Sorry, moonshine is off today ***</xsl:text>
    </xsl:otherwise>
</xsl:choose>
```

The specification says that an XSLT processor that doesn't recognize the extension function acme:moonshine() shouldn't fail simply because the stylesheet references it: it should only fail if it is actually called. In this situation no failure should occur, because function-available() is used first to check the availability of the function, and will return false if the function is not present.

Extension functions, because they are written in general-purpose programming languages, can have side-effects. For example, they can write to databases, they can ask the user for input, or they can maintain counters. The documentation of one product, Xalan, goes to some lengths to explain how to implement a counter using extension functions, effectively circumventing the restriction that XSLT variables cannot be modified in-situ. However, extension functions with side effects should be used with great care, because the XSLT specification doesn't say what order things are supposed to happen in. For example, it doesn't say whether a variable is evaluated when its declaration is first encountered, or when its value is first used. One product in particular, xt, adopts a lazy evaluation strategy in which variables are never evaluated until they are used. If extension functions with side-effects are used to evaluate such variables, the results can be very surprising, because the order in which the extension functions are called becomes quite unpredictable. For example, if one function writes to a log file and another closes this file, you could find that the log file is closed before it is written to.

Extension Elements

An extension element is an element occurring within a template body, that belongs to a namespace designated as an extension namespace. A namespace is designated as an extension namespace by including its namespace prefix in the extension-element-prefixes attribute of the <xsl:stylesheet> element, or in the xsl:extension-element-prefixes attribute of the element itself, or of a containing extension element or literal result element.

For example, Saxon provides an extension element <saxon:while> to perform looping while a condition remains true. There is no standard XSLT construct for this because without side-effects, a condition once true can never become false. But when used in conjunction with extension functions, <saxon:while> can be a useful addition.

The following named template takes a string as a parameter and splits it up into words, outputting each word as a separate element. It uses the standard Java class java.util.StringTokenizer to provide extension functions:

```
<xsl:template name="tokenize" xmlns:Tokenizer="/java.util.StringTokenizer">
   <xsl:param name="sentence"/>
   <xsl:variable name="tok" select="Tokenizer:new($sentence)"/>
   <saxon:while test="Tokenizer:hasMoreTokens($tok)"
         xsl:extension-element-prefixes="saxon"
         xsl:exclude-result-prefixes="Tokenizer"
         xmlns:saxon="http://icl.com/saxon">
      <word>
        <xsl:value-of select="Tokenizer:nextToken($tok)"/>
      </word>
   </saxon:while>
</xsl:template>
```

Note that for this to work, «saxon» must be declared as an extension element prefix, otherwise <saxon:while> would be interpreted as a literal result element and would be copied to the output. The xsl:exclude-result-prefixes attribute is not strictly necessary, but it prevents the output being cluttered with unnecessary namespace declarations.

If this template is called with the parameter value "The cat sat on the mat", as follows:

```
<xsl:template match="/">
  <xsl:call-template name="tokenize">
    <xsl:with-param name="sentence">The cat sat on the mat</xsl:with-param>
  </xsl:call-template>
</xsl:template>
```

it will produce the output:

```
<word>The</word><word>cat</word><word>sat</word><word>on</word>
<word>the</word><word>mat</word>
```

3

Stylesheet Structure

If you have extra namespaces declared on the `<xsl:stylesheet>` element, they will be copied into the `<word>` elements. To get rid of them, add the unwanted namespace prefix to the `xsl:exclude-result-prefixes` attribute.

As with extension functions, the term **extension element** covers both non-standard elements provided by the vendor, and non-standard elements implemented by a user or third party. There is no requirement that an XSLT implementation must allow users to define new extension elements, only that it should behave in a particular way when it encounters extension elements that it cannot process.

Where a product does allow users to implement extension elements (two products that do so are Saxon and Xalan), the mechanisms and APIs involved are likely to be rather more complex than those for extension functions, and the task is not one to be undertaken lightly. However, extension elements can offer capabilities that would be very hard to provide with extension functions alone: several vendors, for example, offer an extension element that switches output to a new file. These extensions are described in Chapter 10.

If there is an extension element in a stylesheet, then all XSLT processors will recognize it as such, but in general some will be able to handle it and others won't (because it is defined by a different vendor). As with extension functions, the rule is that a processor mustn't fail merely because an extension element is present, it should fail only if an attempt is made to instantiate it.

There are two mechanisms to allow stylesheet authors to test whether a particular extension element is available: the `element-available()` function, and the `<xsl:fallback>` instruction.

The `element-available()` function works in a very similar way to `function-available()`. For example:

```
<xsl:choose xmlns:acme="http://acme.co.jp/xslt">
    <xsl:when test="element-available('acme:moonshine')">
        <acme:moonshine select="$x" xsl:extension-element-prefixes="acme"/>
    </xsl:when>
    <xsl:otherwise>
        <xsl:text>*** Sorry, moonshine is off today ***</xsl:text>
    </xsl:otherwise>
</xsl:choose>
```

Note that at the time `element-available()` is called, the prefix for the extension element (here «acme») must have been declared in a namespace declaration, but it does not need to have been designated as an extension element.

The `<xsl:fallback>` instruction (which is fully described on page 197, in Chapter 4) provides an alternative way of specifying what should happen when an extension element is not available. The following example is equivalent to the previous one:

```
<acme:moonshine select="$x"
   xmlns:acme="http://acme.co.jp/xslt" xsl:extension-element-prefixes="acme">
   <xsl:fallback>
      <xsl:text>*** Sorry, moonshine is off today ***</xsl:text>
   </xsl:fallback>
</acme:moonshine>
```

When an extension element is instantiated, and the XSLT processor does not know what to do with it, it should instantiate any child <xsl:fallback> element. If there are several <xsl:fallback> children, it should instantiate each of them. Only if there is no <xsl:fallback> element should it report an error. Conversely, if the XSLT processor can instantiate the element, it should ignore any child <xsl:fallback> element.

The specification doesn't actually say that an extension element must allow an <xsl:fallback> child to be present. There are plenty of XSLT instructions that do not allow <xsl:fallback> as a child, for example <xsl:copy-of> and <xsl:value-of>. However, an extension element that didn't allow <xsl:fallback> would certainly be against the spirit of the standard.

Vendor-defined or user-defined elements at the top level of the stylesheet are not technically extension elements, because they don't appear within a template body; therefore the namespace they appear in does not need to be designated as an extension namespace.

Forwards Compatibility

Whereas extensibility, as discussed in the previous section, is about how to write stylesheets that are resilient to vendor and user extensions to the XSLT language, forwards compatibility is about how to achieve resilience to differences between versions of the XSLT standard. The two questions are, of course, closely related.

So far there has only been one version of the XSLT Recommendation, version 1.0 (the six earlier working drafts don't count). So compatibility between versions is not yet an issue. However, the language designers have had the foresight to anticipate that it will become an issue, and that it is necessary even in version 1.0 to incorporate provisions that allow for future change.

Firstly, the stylesheet is required to carry a version number: typically «version=1.0» as an attribute of the <xsl:stylesheet> element. This declares that the stylesheet will only be using facilities defined in XSLT version 1.0. If the XSLT processor finds that the stylesheet uses elements, attributes, or functions with names in the XSLT namespace, but which are not defined in the version 1.0 Recommendation, then it must reject them and report an error.

If an XSLT processor that was written to support XSLT version 1.0 reads a stylesheet and finds that the version attribute of the <xsl:stylesheet> has a value other than «1.0» (for example if it finds <xsl:stylesheet version="3.2">), then it must assume that the stylesheet is using XSLT facilities defined in a version of the standard that has been published since the software was released. The processor, of course, won't know what to do with these facilities, but it must assume that the stylesheet author is using them deliberately. It treats them in much the same way as vendor extensions that it doesn't understand:

- ❏ It must report an error for XSLT elements it doesn't understand only if they are instantiated, and if there is no child `<xsl:fallback>` instruction.

- ❏ It must ignore attributes it doesn't recognize, and unrecognized values for recognized attributes.

- ❏ It must report an error for functions it doesn't recognize, or that have the wrong number or arguments, only if the function is actually called. You can avoid this error condition by using `function-available()` to test whether the function exists before calling it.

- ❏ It must report syntax errors in XPath expressions that use syntax which isn't allowed in version 1.0 only if the expression is actually evaluated.

This behavior only occurs when forwards-compatible mode is enabled, which happens only if the `<xsl:stylesheet>` element specifies a version other than «1.0». Forwards-compatible mode can also be specified for a portion of a stylesheet by specifying the `xsl:version` attribute on any literal result element, again with a value other than «1.0». If forwards-compatible mode is not enabled, that is, if the version is specified as «1.0», then any use of an XSLT element, attribute, or function that isn't in the XSLT version 1.0 standard, or of XPath syntax that isn't in the XPath 1.0 standard, is an error and must be reported, whether it is actually executed or not.

> *It's a matter for speculation how this rule will evolve in future versions of the standard. If the stylesheet specifies «version="1.2"», for example, will the processor be expected to reject the use of a facility first introduced in version 1.3? We can only wait and see.*

Forwards compatible processing is an issue for implementers today, because version 1.0 products need to behave sensibly when confronted with version 2.0 stylesheets. It will only become an issue for stylesheet authors once there are several versions of the standard around, at which point you may want to write a stylesheet that exploits facilities in version 2.0 while still behaving sensibly when run with an XSLT processor that only supports version 1.0. To achieve this, you will be able to use the same mechanisms as you use for handling vendor extensions: the `function-available()` and `element-available()` functions, and the `<xsl:fallback>` element.

There is also one other mechanism you can use: you can use the `system-property()` function (described on page 524, in Chapter 7) to discover which version of XSLT the processor implements, or which processor is being used. For example, you could write code such as:

```
<xsl:if test="system-property('xsl:version')=2.0 or
    starts-with(system-property('xsl:vendor', 'xalan'))">
  <xsl:new-facility/>
</xsl:if>
```

Relying on the version number this returns is a rather crude mechanism: there are plenty of processors already in the field that return «1.0» as the value of «system-property('xsl:version')» but which do not implement the XSLT standard in full, and no doubt this will remain true. But testing which vendor's processor is in use is handy for portability, especially when vendors have not kept strictly to the conformance rules.

Whitespace

Whitespace handling can be a considerable source of confusion. When the output is HTML, you can get away without worrying too much about it, because, except in some very specific contexts, HTML generally treats any sequence of spaces and newlines in the same way as a single space. But with other output formats, getting spaces and newlines where you want them, and avoiding them where you don't, can be crucial.

There are two issues:

❑ Controlling which whitespace in the source document is significant, and therefore visible to the stylesheet.

❑ Controlling which whitespace in the stylesheet is significant, because significant whitespace in the stylesheet is likely to get copied to the output.

Whitespace is defined as any sequence of the following four characters:

Character	Unicode Symbol
tab	#x9
newline	#xA
Carriage return	#xD
space	x20

The definition in XSLT is exactly the same as in XML itself. Other characters such as non-breaking-space (#xA0), which is familiar to HTML authors as the entity reference « », may use just as little black ink as these four, but they are not included in the definition.

There are some additional complications about the definition. Writing a character reference « » is in many ways exactly the same as hitting the space bar on the keyboard, but in some circumstances it behaves differently. The character reference « » will be treated as whitespace by the XSLT processor, but not by the XML parser, so you need to understand which rules are applied at which stage of processing.

The XML standard makes some attempt to distinguish between significant and insignificant whitespace: whitespace in elements with element-only content is considered insignificant, whereas whitespace in elements that allow #PCDATA content is significant. However, the distinction depends on whether a validating parser is used or not, and in any case, the standard requires both kinds of whitespace to be notified to the application. The writers of the XSLT specification decided that the handling of whitespace should not depend on anything in the DTD, and should not depend on whether a validating or non-validating parser was used. Instead the handling of whitespace is controlled entirely from the source document (using the xml:space attribute) or from the stylesheet (using the <xsl:strip-space> and <xsl:preserve-space> directives), which are fully described in Chapter 4.

The first stages in whitespace handling are the job of the XML parser, and are done long before the XSLT processor gets to see the data:

❑ End-of-line appearing in the textual content of an element is always normalized to a single newline «#xA» character. This eliminates the differences between line endings on Unix, Windows, and Macintosh systems.

❑ The XML parser will normalize attribute values. A tab or newline will always be replaced by a single space, unless it is written as a character reference such as «	» or «&#A;»; for some types of attribute (anything except type CDATA), the XML parser will also remove leading and trailing whitespace, and normalize other sequences of whitespace to a single space character.

This attribute normalization can be significant when the attribute in question is an XPath expression in the stylesheet. For example, suppose you want to test whether a string value contains a newline character. You can write this as:

```
<xsl:if test="contains(address, '&#xA')">
```

It's important to use the character reference «
» here, rather than a real newline, because a newline character would be converted to a space by the XML parser, and the expression would then actually test whether the supplied string contains a space.

What this means in practice is that if you want to be specific about whitespace characters, write them as character references; if you just want to use them as separators and padding, use the whitespace characters directly.

Once the XML parser has done its work, the XSLT processor then applies some processing of its own. By this time entity and character references have been expanded, so there is no difference between a space written as a space and one written as « ».

❑ Adjacent text nodes are merged into a single text node.

❑ Then, if a text node consists entirely of whitespace, it is removed from the tree if the containing element is listed in an <xsl:strip-space> definition in the stylesheet. The detailed rules are more complex than this, and also take into account the presence of the xml:space attribute in the source document: see the <xsl:text> element on page 299, in Chapter 4, for details.

This process never removes whitespace characters that are adjacent to non-whitespace characters. For example, consider:

```
<article>
    <title>Abelard and Heloise</title>
    <subtitle>Some notes towards a family tree</subtitle>
    <author>Brenda M Cook</author>
    <abstract>
```

```
        The story of Abelard and Heloise is best recalled
nowadays from the stage drama of 1970 and it is perhaps inevitable that Diana Rigg
stripping off for Keith Mitchell should be the most enduring image of this historic
couple in some people's minds.
        </abstract>
    </article>
```

There are five whitespace-only text nodes in this fragment, one before each of the child elements <title>, <subtitle>, <author>, and , and another between the end of the and the end of the <article>. The whitespace in these nodes is passed by the XML parser to the XSLT processor, and it is up to the stylesheet whether to take any notice of it or not. Typically in this situation this whitespace is of no interest and it can be stripped from the tree by specifying <xsl:strip-space elements="article"/>.

The whitespace within the cannot be removed by the same process. The newline characters at the start and end of the abstract, and at the end of each line, are part of the text passed by the parser to the application, and it is not possible in the stylesheet to declare them as being irrelevant. They will always be present in the tree model of the source document. What you can do is to call the normalize-space() function when processing these nodes on the source tree: this will remove leading and trailing whitespace, and replace all other sequences of one or more whitespace characters by a single space. The normalize-space() function is described on page 492 in Chapter 7.

To emphasize this, XSLT makes a very firm distinction between text nodes that comprise whitespace only, and those that hold something other than whitespace. A whitespace text node can only exist where there is nothing between two pieces of markup other than whitespace characters.

To take another example, consider the following document:

```
<person>
    <name>Michael Kay</name>
    <employer>ICL</employer>
    <place-of-work>
        Lovelace Road
        Bracknell, UK
        RG12 8SN
    </place-of-work>
</person>
```

Where are the whitespace nodes? Let's look at it again, this time making the whitespace characters visible:

```
<person>↵
→<name>Michael Kay</name>↵
→<employer>ICL</employer>↵
→<place-of-work>↵
```

```
→♦♦♦Lovelace Road↵
→♦♦♦Bracknell, UK↵
→♦♦♦<zip>RG12 8SN</zip>♦↵
→</place-of-work>↵
</person>
```

The newline and tab between `<person>` and `<name>` are not adjacent to any non-whitespace characters, so they constitute a whitespace node. So do the characters between `</name>` and `<employer>`, and between `</employer>` and `<place-of-work>`. However, most of the whitespace characters within the `<place-of-work>` element are in the same text node as non-whitespace characters, so they do not constitute a whitespace node. To make it even clearer, let's show the characters in whitespace nodes in white on a black background:

```
<person>↵
→<name>Michael Kay</name>↵
→<employer>ICL</employer>↵
→<place-of-work>↵
→♦♦♦Lovelace Road↵
→♦♦♦Bracknell, UK↵
→♦♦♦<zip>RG12 8SN</zip>♦↵
→</place-of-work>↵
</person>
```

Why is all this relevant? As we've seen, the `<xsl:strip-space>` element allows you to control what happens to whitespace nodes (those shown in white on black above), but it doesn't let you do anything special with whitespace characters that appear in ordinary text nodes (those shown in black on white).

All the whitespace nodes in this example are immediate children of the `<person>` element, so they could be stripped by writing:

```
<xsl:strip-space elements="person"/>
```

Whitespace nodes are retained on the source tree unless you ask for them to be stripped.

Whitespace Nodes in the Stylesheet

For the stylesheet itself, whitespace nodes are all stripped, with one exception, namely whitespace within an `<xsl:text>` element. So if you explicitly want to copy a whitespace text node from the stylesheet to the result tree, write it within an `<xsl:text>` element, like this:

```
<xsl:value-of select="address-line[1]"/>
<xsl:text>&#xA;</xsl:text>
<xsl:value-of select="address-line[2]"/>
```

The only reason for using «
» here rather than an actual newline is that it's more clearly visible to the reader; it's also less likely to be accidentally turned into a newline followed by tabs or spaces. Writing the whitespace as a character reference doesn't stop it being treated as whitespace by XSLT, because the character references will have been expanded by the XML parser before the XSLT processor gets to see them.

The Effect of Stripping Whitespace Nodes

There are two main effects of stripping whitespace nodes, say on the <person> element in the example above:

❑ When you use <xsl:apply-templates/> to process all the children of the <person> element, the whitespace nodes aren't there, so they don't get selected. If they had been left on the source tree, then by default they would be copied to the result tree.

❑ When you use <xsl:number> or the position() or count() functions to count nodes, the whitespace nodes aren't there, so they aren't counted. If you had left the whitespace nodes on the tree, then the <name>, <employer> and <place-of-work> elements would be nodes 2, 4, and 6 instead of 1, 2, and 3.

There are cases where it's important to keep the whitespace nodes. Consider the following:

```
<para>
Edited by <name>James Clark</name>♦<email>jjc@jclark.com</email>
</para>
```

The diamond represents a space character that needs to be preserved, but because it is not adjacent to any other text, it would be eligible for stripping.

If you want to strip all the whitespace nodes from the source tree, you can write:

```
<xsl:strip-space elements="*"/>
```

If you want to strip all the whitespace nodes except those within certain named elements, you can write:

```
<xsl:strip-space elements="*"/>
<xsl:preserve-space elements="para h1 h2 h3 h4"/>
```

If any elements in the document (either the source document or the stylesheet) use the XML-defined attribute «xml:space="preserve"», this takes precedence over these rules: whitespace nodes in that element, and in all its descendants, will be kept on the tree unless the attribute is cancelled on a descendant element by specifying «xml:space="default"». This allows you to control on a per-instance basis whether whitespace is kept, whereas <xsl:strip-space> controls it at the element-type level.

Solving Whitespace Problems

There are two typical problems with whitespace in the output: too much of it, or too little.

If you are generating HTML, a bit of extra whitespace usually doesn't matter, though there are some places where it can slightly distort the layout of your page. With some text formats, however (a classic example is comma-separated values) you need to be very careful to output whitespace in exactly the right places.

Too Much Whitespace

If you are getting too much whitespace, there are three possible places it can be coming from:

❑ The source document

❑ The stylesheet

❑ Output indentation

First ensure that you set «indent="no"» on the <xsl:output> element, to eliminate the last of these possibilities.

If the output whitespace is adjacent to text, then it probably comes from the same place as that text.

❑ If this text comes from the stylesheet, use <xsl:text> to control more precisely what is output. For example, the following code outputs a comma between the items in a list, but it also outputs a newline after the comma, because the newline is part of the same text node as the comma:

```
<xsl:for-each select="item">
    <xsl:value-of select="."/>,
</xsl:for-each>
```

If you want the comma but not the newline, change this so that the newline is in a text node of its own, and is therefore stripped:

```
<xsl:for-each select="item">
    <xsl:value-of select="."/>,<xsl:text/>
</xsl:for-each>
```

❑ If the text comes from the source document, use normalize-space() to trim leading and trailing spaces from the text before outputting it.

If the offending whitespace is between tags in the output, then it probably comes from whitespace nodes in the source tree that have not been stripped, and the remedy is to add an <xsl:strip-space> element to the stylesheet.

Too Little Whitespace

If you want whitespace in the output and aren't getting it, use `<xsl:text>` to generate it at the appropriate point. For example, the following code will output the lines of a poem in HTML, with each line of the poem being shown on a new line:

```
<xsl:for-each select="line">
    <xsl:value-of select="."><br/>
</xsl:for-each>
```

This will display perfectly correctly in the browser, but if you want to view the HTML in a text editor, it will be difficult because everything goes on a single line. It would be useful to start a newline after each `<br>` element – you can do this as follows:

```
<xsl:for-each select="line">
    <xsl:value-of select="."><br/><xsl:text>&#xa;</xsl:text>
</xsl:for-each>
```

Another trick I have used to achieve this is to exploit the fact that the non-breaking-space character (#xa0), although invisible, is not classified as whitespace. So you can achieve the required effect by writing:

```
<xsl:for-each select="line">
    <xsl:value-of select="."><br/> 
</xsl:for-each>
```

This works because the newline after the « » is now part of a non-whitespace node.

Summary

The purpose of this chapter was to study the overall structure of a stylesheet, before going into the detailed specification of each element in the next chapter.

❑   First I explained how a stylesheet program can be made up of one or more stylesheet modules, linked together with `<xsl:import>` and `<xsl:include>` elements. I described how the concept of import precedence allows one stylesheet to override definitions in those it imports.

❑   I introduced the `<xsl:stylesheet>` (or `<xsl:transform>` element), which is the outermost element of most stylesheet modules.

❑   I described the `<?xml-stylesheet?>` processing instruction which can be used to link from a source document to its associated stylesheets, and explained how this can be used to allow a stylesheet to be embedded directly in the source document whose style it defines.

❑   I then covered the top-level elements found in the stylesheet, that is, the immediate children of the `<xsl:stylesheet>` or `<xsl:transform>` element, including the ability to have user-defined or vendor-defined elements here.

❑   Very simple stylesheets can be written as a single template, so you saw how the `<xsl:stylesheet>` and `<xsl:template match="/">` elements can be omitted, to make an XSLT stylesheet look more like the simple template languages that some users may be familiar with.

❑   A structure that occurs throughout a stylesheet is the idea of a template body, a sequence of text nodes and literal result elements to be copied to the result tree, and instructions and extension elements to be executed. This led naturally to a discussion of literal result elements, and of attribute value templates which are used to define variable attributes not only of literal result elements, but of certain XSL elements as well.

❑   I then explained how the W3C standards committee has tried to ensure that the specification can be extended, both by vendors and by W3C itself, without adversely affecting the portability of stylesheets. You saw how to make a stylesheet work even if it uses proprietary extension functions and extension elements that may not be available in all implementations.

❑   Finally I discussed, in some detail, how XSLT stylesheets handle whitespace in the source document, in the stylesheet itself, and in the result tree.

You have now reached the end of the preamble. The next four chapters contain detailed specifications of the XSL elements you can use in a stylesheet, the XPath expressions you can use in the attributes of some of these elements, the node-matching patterns you can use to establish template rules, and the standard functions that are available for use within XPath expressions.

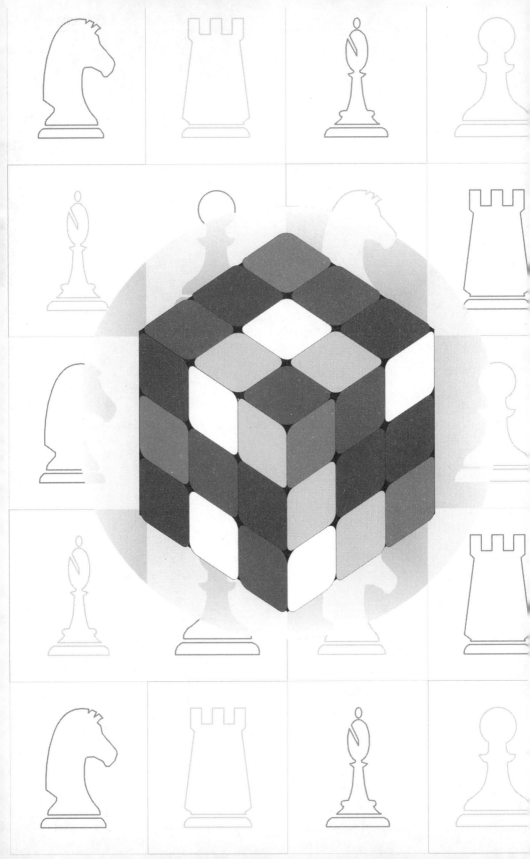

XSLT Elements

This chapter provides an alphabetical list of reference entries, one for each of the XSLT elements. Each entry gives:

❑ a short description of the purpose of the element

❑ an indication of where in the XSLT specification the element is described

❑ a proforma summary of the format, defining where the element may appear in the stylesheet, what its permitted attributes are, and what its content (child elements) may be

❑ a definition of the formal rules defining how this element behaves

❑ a section giving usage advice on how to exploit this XSLT element

❑ finally, coding examples of the element, showing the context in which it might be used

The *Format* section for each element includes a syntax skeleton designed to provide a quick reminder of the names and types of the attributes and any constraints on the context. The format of this is designed to be intuitive: it only gives a summary of the rules, because you will find these in full in the sections *Position*, *Attributes*, and *Content* which follow.

There are a number of specialized terms used in this chapter, and it is worth becoming familiar with them before you get in too deeply. There are fuller explanations in Chapters 2 and 3, and the following descriptions are really intended just as a quick memory-jogger.

For a more comprehensive glossary of terms, refer to Appendix B.

Term	Description
attribute value template	An attribute whose value may contain expressions nested with curly braces, for example «url="../{$href}"». The term *template* here has nothing to do with any other kind of template in XSLT. Embedded expressions may only be used in an attribute value (or are only recognized as such) if the attribute is one that is explicitly designated as an attribute value template. Attribute value templates are described in more detail in Chapter 3, page 118
document order	An ordering of the nodes in the source tree which corresponds to the order in which the corresponding items appeared in the source XML document: an element precedes its children, and the children are ordered as they appeared in the source.
Expression	Many XSLT elements have attributes whose value is an Expression. This always means an XPath expression: a full definition of XPath Expressions is given in Chapter 5. An expression returns a value, which may be a string, a number, a Boolean, a node-set, or a result tree fragment. These data types are described fully in Chapter 2, page 80
instantiate	Instructions and template bodies can be instantiated. This may seem a rather grandiose way of saying that the instruction is obeyed or executed, but there is some logic to it: we can regard a template body in the stylesheet as being a proforma for lots of pieces of the output document, each of which is formed by creating a new instance of the proforma.
instruction	Any element used in a template body that is not a literal result element: specifically, an XSLT instruction or an extension element. The <xsl:if> element is an instruction, but <xsl:strip-space> isn't, because <xsl:if> appears in a template body and <xsl:strip-space> doesn't. Extension elements are described in Chapter 3, page 108.
literal result element	An element in the stylesheet, used in a *template body*, which is copied to the output document: for example (if you are generating HTML) <p> or <td>. Literal result elements are described in Chapter 3, page 109.
Pattern	Some XSLT elements have attributes whose value must be a Pattern: the syntax of Patterns is defined in Chapter 6. A Pattern is a test that can be applied to nodes to see if they match. For example, the Pattern «title» matches all <title> elements, and the Pattern «text()» matches all text nodes.
QName	An XML name, optionally qualified by a namespace prefix. Examples of QNames with no prefix are «color» and «date-due». Examples of prefixed names are «xsl:choose» and «html:table». Where the name has a prefix, this must always match a namespace declaration that is in scope at the place in the stylesheet where the QName is used. For more information on namespaces, see Chapter 2, page 58.

stylesheet	In general, references to the **stylesheet** mean the principal stylesheet module plus all the stylesheet modules incorporated into it using `<xsl:include>` and `<xsl:import>` elements. When I want to refer to one of these components individually, I call it a **stylesheet module**.
template body	A sequence of instructions and literal result elements contained within (that is, that are children of) another XSLT element. The containing element need not be an `<xsl:template>` element; many other XSLT elements, such as `<xsl:if>` and `<xsl:variable>`, also have a template body as their content. The XSLT specification calls this simply a **template**, but I have avoided this because it is easily confused with a **template rule** (an `<xsl:template>` element with a `match` attribute) and a **named template** (an `<xsl:template>` element with a `name` attribute).
template rule	An `<xsl:template>` element that has a `match` attribute.
XSLT element	Any of the standard elements in the XSLT namespace listed in this chapter, for example `<xsl:template>` or `<xsl:if>`

I decided to list the different XSLT elements in alphabetical order for ease of reference, because I know how difficult it is to find them in the XSLT Recommendation, where they are organised on functional lines. This is fine when you know what you are looking for, but if you are using this book as your introduction to XSLT, it does create the problem that related things won't be found together. And if you try to read sequentially, you'll start with `<xsl:apply-imports>`, which on a training course is something I would probably cover rather quickly on the Friday afternoon.

So here's an attempt at some kind of ordering and grouping, to suggest which entries you might look at first if you're new to the subject:

Grouping	Elements

Elements used to define template rules and control the way they are invoked	`<xsl:template>`
	`<xsl:apply-templates>`
	`<xsl:call-template>`

Elements defining the structure of the stylesheet	`<xsl:stylesheet>`
	`<xsl:include>`
	`<xsl:import>`

Elements used to generate output	`<xsl:value-of>`
	`<xsl:element>`
	`<xsl:attribute>`
	`<xsl:comment>`
	`<xsl:processing-instruction>`
	`<xsl:text>`

Elements used to define variables and parameters	`<xsl:variable>`
	`<xsl:param>`
	`<xsl:with-param>`

Elements used to copy information from the source document to the result	`<xsl:copy>` `<xsl:copy-of>`

Grouping	Elements

Elements used for conditional processing and iteration	`<xsl:if>`
	`<xsl:choose>`
	`<xsl:when>`
	`<xsl:otherwise>`
	`<xsl:for-each>`

Elements to control sorting and numbering	`<xsl:sort>` `<xsl:number>`
Elements used to control the final output format	`<xsl:output>`

This covers all the most commonly-used elements; the rest can only really be classified as 'miscellaneous'.

xsl:apply-imports

The `<xsl:apply-imports>` instruction is used in conjunction with imported stylesheets. A template rule in one stylesheet module can override a template rule in an imported stylesheet module. Sometimes, you want to supplement the functionality of the rule in the imported module, not to replace it entirely. `<xsl:apply-imports>` is provided so that the overriding template rule can invoke the overridden template rule in the imported module.

There is a clear analogy here with object-oriented programming. Writing a stylesheet module that imports another is like writing a subclass, whose methods override the methods of the superclass. `<xsl:apply-imports>` behaves analogously to the super() function in object-oriented programming languages, allowing the functionality of the superclass to be incorporated in the functionality of the subclass.

Defined in

XSLT section 5.6

Format

```
<xsl:apply-imports />
```

Position

`<xsl:apply-imports>` is an instruction, and is always used within a template body.

Attributes

None.

Content

None, the element is always empty.

Effect

`<xsl:apply-imports>` relies on the concept of a *current template rule*. A template rule becomes the current template rule when it is invoked using `<xsl:apply-templates>`. Using `<xsl:call-template>` does not change the current template rule. However, using `<xsl:for-each>` makes the current template rule null, until such time as the `<xsl:for-each>` terminates, at which time the previous value is reinstated. The current template rule is also null while global variables are being evaluated.

`<xsl:apply-imports>` searches for a template rule that matches the current node, using the same search rules as `<xsl:apply-templates>`, but considering only those template rules that (a) have the same mode as the current template rule and (b) are defined in a stylesheet that was imported into the stylesheet containing the current template rule. For details of import precedence, see `<xsl:import>` on page 207.

The specification doesn't say exactly what **imported into** *means. A reasonable interpretation is a stylesheet that is a descendant of this one in the import tree. A stylesheet S becomes a child of another stylesheet T in the import tree by being referenced in an* `<xsl:import>` *statement within T, or within a stylesheet that is included in T directly or indirectly by means of* `<xsl:include>` *statements. If stylesheet S is imported into stylesheet T, then templates defined in S will always have lower import precedence than templates defined in T.*

It is not possible to specify parameters on `<xsl:apply-imports>`. If the called template rule declares any parameters, they will all take their default values.

Usage and Examples

The intended usage pattern behind `<xsl:apply-imports>` is illustrated by the following example.

One stylesheet, `a.xsl`, contains general-purpose rules for rendering elements. For example, it might contain a general-purpose template rule for displaying dates, as follows:

```
<xsl:template match="date">
  <xsl:value-of select="day"/>
  <xsl:text>/</xsl:text>
  <xsl:value-of select="month"/>
  <xsl:text>/</xsl:text>
  <xsl:value-of select="year"/>
</xsl:template>
```

A second stylesheet, `b.xsl`, contains special-purpose rules for rendering elements. For example, stylesheet `b.xsl` might want to display dates that occur in a particular context in the same way, but in bold face. It could write:

```
<xsl:template match="timeline/date">
   <b>
   <xsl:value-of select="day"/>
   <xsl:text>/</xsl:text>
   <xsl:value-of select="month"/>
   <xsl:text>/</xsl:text>
   <xsl:value-of select="year"/>
   </b>
</xsl:template>
```

However, this involves duplicating most of the template body, which is a bad idea from a maintenance point of view. So, in b.xsl we could import a.xsl, and write instead:

```
<xsl:import href="a.xsl"/>
<xsl:template match="timeline/date">
   <b>
   <xsl:apply-imports/>
   </b>
</xsl:template>
```

Note that the facility only allows a template rule to invoke one of lower **import precedence**, not one of lower **priority**. The import precedence depends on how the stylesheet module was loaded, as explained under <xsl:import> on page 207. The priority can be specified individually for each template rule, as explained under <xsl:template> on page 288. The code above will work only if the «timeline/date» template rule is in a stylesheet that directly or indirectly imports the «date» template rule. It will not work, for example, if they are in the same stylesheet but defined with different priority.

In most situations the same effect can be achieved equally well by giving the general-purpose template rule a name, and invoking it from the special-purpose template rule by using <xsl:call-template> (see page 167). This technique also works when overriding a template rule of lower priority (and equal import precedence). The one time this alternative technique is not possible is when the general-purpose template rule was written by someone else and cannot be changed. For example this situation might arise if users of web pages were allowed to create XSLT stylesheets that modified the behavior of an author-supplied stylesheet.

There is a more complete example of the use of <xsl:apply-imports> in the section for <xsl:import>.

See also

<xsl:import> on page 207

xsl:apply-templates

The `<xsl:apply-templates>` instruction defines a set of nodes to be processed, and causes the system to process them by selecting an appropriate template rule for each one.

Defined in

XSLT section 5.4

Format

```
<xsl:apply-templates select=Expression mode=QName >
    ( <xsl:with-param> | <xsl:sort> ) *
</xsl:apply-templates>
```

Position

`<xsl:apply-templates>` is an instruction, and is always used within a template body.

Attributes

Name	Value	Meaning
select **optional**	Expression	The node-set to be processed. If omitted, all children of the current node are processed.
mode	QName	The processing mode. Template rules used to process the selected nodes must have a matching mode.

The constructs Expression and QName are defined at the beginning of this chapter and more formally in Chapter 5.

Content

Zero or more `<xsl:sort>` elements
Zero or more `<xsl:with-param>` elements

Effect

The `<xsl:apply-templates>` element selects a set of nodes in the input tree, and processes each of them individually by finding a matching template rule for that node. The set of nodes is determined by the `select` attribute; the order in which they are processed is determined by the `<xsl:sort>` elements (if present), and the parameters passed to the template rules are determined by the `<xsl:with-param>` elements (if present). The behavior is explained in detail in the following sections.

The select Attribute

If the select attribute is present, the Expression defines the nodes that will be processed. This must be an XPath Expression that returns a node-set. (The concept of a node-set is explained along with other XSLT data types in Chapter 2, page 85). For example `<xsl:apply-templates select="*"/>` selects the set of all element nodes that are children of the current node. Writing `<xsl:apply-templates select="@width+3"/>` would be an error, because the value of the expression is a number, not a node-set.

The expression may select nodes relative to the current node (the node currently being processed), as in the example above. Alternatively it may make an absolute selection from the root node (for example `<xsl:apply-templates select="//item"/>`), or it may simply select the nodes by reference to a variable initialized earlier (for example `<xsl:apply-templates select="$sales-figures"/>`. For further details of XPath expressions, see Chapter 5.

If the select attribute is omitted, the nodes processed will be the children of the current node: that is, the elements, text nodes, comments, and processing instructions that occur directly within the current node. Text nodes that consist only of whitespace will be processed along with the others, unless they have been stripped from the tree: for details, see `<xsl:strip-space>` on page 277. In the XPath tree model, described in Chapter 2, attribute nodes and namespace nodes are **not** regarded as children of the containing element, so they are not processed: if you want to process attribute nodes, you must include an explicit select attribute, for example `<xsl:apply-templates select="@*"/>`. However, it is more usual to get the attribute values directly using the `<xsl:value-of>` instruction, described on page 305.

Omitting the select attribute has exactly the same effect as specifying a node-set expression of «child::node()». This selects all the nodes (elements, text nodes, comments, and processing instructions) that are children of the current node. If the current node is anything other than a root node or an element node, then it has no children, so `<xsl:apply-templates/>` does nothing, because there are no nodes to process.

For each node in the selected node-set, in turn, one template rule is selected and its template body is instantiated. In general this may be a different template rule for each selected node. Within this template body, this node becomes the new current node, so it can be referred to using the XPath expression «.».

The called template can also determine the relative position of this node within the list of nodes selected for processing: specifically, it can use the position() function to give the position of that node in the list of nodes being processed (the first node processed has position()=1, and so on), and the last() function to give the number of nodes in the list being processed. These two functions are described (with examples) in Chapter 7, pages 500 and 478 respectively. They enable the called template to output sequence numbers for the nodes as they are processed, or to take different action for the first and the last nodes, or perhaps to use different background colors for odd-numbered and even-numbered nodes.

Sorting

If there are no child <xsl:sort> instructions, the selected nodes are processed in *document order*. In the normal case where the nodes all come from the same input document this means they will be processed in the order they are encountered in the original source document: for example, an element node is processed before its children. Attribute nodes belonging to the same element, however, may be processed in any order, because the order of attributes in XML is not considered significant. If there are nodes from several different documents in the node-set, which can happen when you use the document() function described in Chapter 7 (page 440), the relative order of nodes from different documents is not defined, though it is consistent if the same node-set is processed more than once.

If there are one or more <xsl:sort> instructions as children of the <xsl:apply-templates> instruction, the nodes are sorted before processing. Each <xsl:sort> instruction defines one sort key. For details of how sorting is controlled, see <xsl:sort> on page 272. If there are several sort keys defined, they apply in major-to-minor order. For example if the first <xsl:sort> defines sorting by Country and the second by State, then the nodes will be processed in order of State within Country. If two nodes have equal sort keys, they will be processed in document order.

Note that the ordering of the axis used to select the nodes is irrelevant. (The ordering of different axes is described in Chapter 5). For example, «select="preceding-sibling::*"» will process the preceding siblings of the current node in document order (starting with the first sibling) even though the preceding-sibling axis is in reverse document order. The axis ordering affects only the meaning of any positional qualifiers used within the select expression. For example, «preceding-sibling::*[1]» will select the first preceding sibling element in axis order – that is, the element immediately before the current node, if there is one.

Choosing a Template Rule

For each node to be processed, a template rule is selected. The choice of a template rule is made independently for each selected node; they may all be processed by the same template rule, or a different template rule may be chosen for each one.

The template rule selected for processing a node will always be either an <xsl:template> with a match attribute, or a built-in template rule provided by the XSLT processor.

An <xsl:template> element will be used to process a node only if it has a matching *mode*: that is, the mode attribute of the <xsl:apply-templates> element must match the mode attribute of the <xsl:template> element. This means they must both be absent, or they must both be present. If they are both present, they must be matching names: if the mode name contains a namespace prefix, it is the namespace URI that must match, not necessarily the prefix itself.

Note that if the mode attribute is omitted, it makes no difference what mode was originally used to select the template rule containing the <xsl:apply-templates> instruction. The mode is not sticky: it reverts to the default mode as soon as <xsl:apply-templates> is used with no mode attribute.

An `<xsl:template>` element will be used to process a node only if the node matches the pattern defined in the `match` attribute of the `<xsl:template>` element.

If there is more than one `<xsl:template>` element that matches a selected node, one of them is selected based on its **import precedence** and **priority**, as detailed under `<xsl:template>` on page 288.

If there is no `<xsl:template>` element that matches a selected node, a built-in template rule is used. The action of the built-in template rule depends on the type of node, as follows:

Node Type	Action of Built-In Template Rule
root	Call apply-templates to process each child of the root node, using the mode specified on the call to `<xsl:apply-templates>`. This is as if the contents of the template were: `<xsl:apply-templates mode="mode"/>`
element	Call apply-templates to process each child node of the element, using the mode specified on the call to `<xsl:apply-templates>`. This is as if the contents of the template were: `<xsl:apply-templates mode="mode"/>`
text	Copy the text value of the node to the output. This is as if the content of the template were: `<xsl:value-of select="."/>`
attribute	Copy the value of the attribute to the output, as text. This is as if the content of the template were: `<xsl:value-of select="."/>`
processing instruction	No action
comment	No action
namespace	No action

For the root node and for element nodes, the built-in template rule processes the children of the selected node in document order, matching each one against the available template rules as if the template body contained an explicit `<xsl:apply-templates>` element with no `select` attribute. Unlike the situation with explicit template rules, the mode *is* sticky: it is carried through automatically to the template rules that are called. So if you execute `<xsl:apply-templates mode="m"/>` for an element that has no matching template rule, the built-in template rule will execute `<xsl:apply-templates mode="m"/>` for each of its children. This process can of course recurse to process the grandchildren, and so on.

Parameters

If there are any `<xsl:with-param>` elements present as children of the `<xsl:apply-templates>` element, they define parameters which are made available to the called template rules. The same parameters are made available to each template rule that is instantiated, even though different template rules may be invoked to process different nodes in the list.

Each `<xsl:with-param>` element is evaluated in the same way as an `<xsl:variable>` element. Specifically:

❏ if it has a `select` attribute, this is evaluated as an XPath expression

❏ if there is no `select` attribute and the `<xsl:with-param>` element is empty, the value is an empty string

❏ otherwise, the value of the parameter is a result tree fragment obtained by instantiating the template body making up the content of the `<xsl:with-param>` element. Result tree fragments are described in Chapter 2, and again more formally under `<xsl:variable>` on page 308.

It is not defined whether the parameter is evaluated once only, or whether it is evaluated repeatedly, once for each node in the node-set. If the value isn't needed (for example, because the node-set is empty, or because none of the nodes match a template that uses this parameter) then it isn't defined whether the parameter is evaluated at all. Usually this doesn't matter, because evaluating the parameter repeatedly will have exactly the same effect each time. But it's something to watch out for if the parameter is obtained by calling an external function that has a side-effect, such as reading the next record from a database.

If the name of a child `<xsl:with-param>` element matches the name of an `<xsl:param>` element in the selected template rule, then the value of the `<xsl:with-param>` element is assigned to the relevant `<xsl:param>` variable name.

If there is a child `<xsl:with-param>` element that does not match the name of any `<xsl:param>` element in the selected template rule, then it is ignored. This is not treated as an error.

If there is an `<xsl:param>` element in the selected template rule with no matching `<xsl:with-param>` element in the `<xsl:apply-templates>` element, then the parameter is given a default value: see `<xsl:param>` on page 262 for details. Again, this is not an error.

Result Value

A called template rule does not return a result in the conventional way that functions in many programming languages (and indeed in XPath) return a result. The only thing a template rule can do to leave a record of its existence is to write nodes to the current output destination.

When execution of the stylesheet starts, the current output destination is the final result tree produced by executing the stylesheet, so any output produced by a template goes to the final output document.

Within the body of an `<xsl:variable>`, `<xsl:param>`, or `<xsl:with-param>` element, the current destination is changed to be a new result tree fragment, which when complete becomes the value of that variable or parameter.

Some other XSLT instructions also change the output destination. Examples are `<xsl:attribute>`, `<xsl:comment>`, and `<xsl:processing-instruction>`. In these cases the new output destination is the text value of the node being created, and it is an error if nodes other than text nodes are written to the destination. Another example is `<xsl:message>`, where the new output destination is the text of the message to be written. In this case it is permitted to write nodes other than text nodes, but it's up to the implementation to decide what to do with them.

Calling `<xsl:apply-templates>` does not change the current output destination. So if `<xsl:apply-templates>` is called within the body of an `<xsl:variable>` element, the output from the called template rules, and from any template rules which they in turn call, is added to the result tree fragment that becomes the value of this variable.

Usage

The following sections give some hints and tips about using `<xsl:apply-templates>`. First I'll discuss when to use `<xsl:apply-templates>` and when to use `<xsl:for-each>`. Then I'll explain how to use modes.

<xsl:apply-templates> Versus <xsl:for-each>

`<xsl:apply-templates>` is most useful when processing an element that may contain children of a variety of different types in an unpredictable sequence. This is a *rule-based* design pattern: the body of each individual template rule declares which nodes it is interested in, rather than the template rule for the parent node defining in detail how each of its children should be processed. The rule-based approach works particularly well when the document design is likely to evolve over time. As new child elements are added, template rules to process them can also be added, without changing the logic for the parent elements in which they might appear.

This style of processing is sometimes called **push** processing. It will be familiar if you have used text processing languages such as awk or perl, but it may be unfamiliar if you are more used to procedural programming in C++ or Visual Basic.

Where the structure is more regular and predictable, it may be simpler to navigate around the document using `<xsl:for-each>`, or by accessing the required data directly using `<xsl:value-of>`. This is sometimes called **pull** processing. The `<xsl:value-of>` instruction allows you to fetch data from the XML document using an arbitrarily complex XPath expression. In this sense it is similar to a SELECT statement in SQL.

A unique strength of XSLT is the ability to mix these two styles of programming. I'll discuss both approaches, and their relative merits, in more detail in Chapter 8.

Modes

Modes are useful where the same data is to be processed more than once. A classic example is when building a table of contents. The main body of the output can be produced by processing the nodes in default mode, while the table of contents is produced by processing the same nodes with «mode="TOC"».

The following example does something very similar to this: it displays a scene from a play, adding at the start of the page a list of the characters who appear in this scene:

Example: Using Modes

Source

The source file, scene.xml, contains a scene from a play (specifically, Act I Scene 1 of Shakespeare's *Othello* – marked up in XML by Jon Bosak).

It starts like this:

```
<?xml version="1.0"?>
<SCENE><TITLE>SCENE I.   Venice. A street.</TITLE>
<STAGEDIR>Enter RODERIGO and IAGO</STAGEDIR>

<SPEECH>
<SPEAKER>RODERIGO</SPEAKER>
<LINE>Tush! never tell me; I take it much unkindly</LINE>
<LINE>That thou, Iago, who hast had my purse</LINE>
<LINE>As if the strings were thine, shouldst know of this.</LINE>
</SPEECH>

<SPEECH>
<SPEAKER>IAGO</SPEAKER>
<LINE>'Sblood, but you will not hear me:</LINE>
<LINE>If ever I did dream of such a matter, Abhor me.</LINE>
</SPEECH>
etc.
</SCENE>
```

Stylesheet

The stylesheet scene.xsl is designed to display this scene in HTML. This is how it starts:

```
<xsl:transform
 xmlns:xsl="http://www.w3.org/1999/XSL/Transform"
 version="1.0"
>
<xsl:template match="SCENE">
<html><body>
    <xsl:apply-templates select="TITLE"/>
    <xsl:variable name="speakers"
        select="//SPEAKER[not(.=preceding::SPEAKER)]"/>
    <h2>Cast: <xsl:apply-templates
        select="$speakers" mode="cast-list"/></h2>
    <xsl:apply-templates select="*[not(self::TITLE)]"/>
</body></html>
</xsl:template>
```

The template rule shown above matches the <SCENE> element. It first displays the <TITLE> element (if there is one) using the appropriate template rule. Then it sets up a variable called «speakers» to be a node-set containing all the distinct <SPEAKER> elements that appear in the document. The rather complex select attribute uses the expression «//SPEAKER» to select all <SPEAKER> elements that are descendants of the root (in other words, all of them), and then qualifies this with a predicate in square brackets that eliminates those speakers that are the same as a previous speaker. The result is a list of the speakers in which each one appears once only.

The template rule then calls <xsl:apply-templates> to process this set of speakers in mode «cast-list» (a nice side-effect is that they will be listed in order of appearance). Finally it calls <xsl:apply-templates> again, this time in the default mode, to process all elements («*») that are not <TITLE> elements (because the title has already been processed).

The stylesheet carries on as follows:

```
<xsl:template match="SPEAKER" mode="cast-list">
    <xsl:value-of select="."/>
    <xsl:if test="not(position()=last())">, </xsl:if>
</xsl:template>
```

This template rule defines how the <SPEAKER> element should be processed when it is being processed in «cast-list» mode. The template body has the effect of outputting the speaker's name, followed by a comma if it is not the last speaker in the list.

Finally the remaining template rules define how each element should be output, when processed in default mode:

```
<xsl:template match="TITLE">
<h1><xsl:apply-templates/></h1>
</xsl:template>

<xsl:template match="STAGEDIR">
<i><xsl:apply-templates/></i>
</xsl:template>

<xsl:template match="SPEECH">
<p><xsl:apply-templates/></p>
</xsl:template>

<xsl:template match="SPEAKER">
<b><xsl:apply-templates/></b><br/>
</xsl:template>
```

```
<xsl:template match="LINE">
<xsl:apply-templates/><br/>
</xsl:template>

</xsl:transform>
```

Output

The precise layout of the HTML will depend on which XSLT processor you are using, but apart from layout details, it should start like this:

```
<html>
    <body>
        <h1>SCENE I.  Venice. A street.</h1>
        <h2>Cast: RODERIGO, IAGO, BRABANTIO</h2>
        <i>Enter RODERIGO and IAGO</i>
        <p>
            <b>RODERIGO</b><br>
            Tush! never tell me; I take it much unkindly<br>
            That thou, Iago, who hast had my purse<br>
            As if the strings were thine, shouldst know of this.<br>
        </p>
        <p>
            <b>IAGO</b><br>
            'Sblood, but you will not hear me:<br>
            If ever I did dream of such a matter, Abhor me.<br>
        </p>
    </body>
</html>
```

It is sometimes useful to use named modes, even where they are not strictly necessary, to document more clearly the relationship between calling templates and called templates, and to constrain the selection of template rules rather more visibly than can be achieved by relying on template rule priorities. This might even improve performance by reducing the number of rules to be considered, though the effect is likely to be marginal.

For example, suppose that a <poem> consists of a number of <stanza> elements, and that the first <stanza> is to be output using a different style from the rest. The orthodox way to achieve this would be as follows:

```
<xsl:template match="poem">
. . .
    <xsl:apply-templates select="stanza"/>
. . .
</xsl:template>

<xsl:template match="stanza[1]">
. . .
</xsl:template>
```

```
<xsl:template match="stanza">
. . .
</xsl:template>
```

This relies on the default priority rules to ensure that the correct template rule is applied to each stanza – as explained under `<xsl:template>` on page 288, the default priority for the pattern «stanza[1]» is higher than the default priority for «stanza»

Another way of doing it, perhaps less orthodox but equally effective, is as follows:

```
<xsl:template match="poem">
. . .
    <xsl:apply-templates select="stanza[1]" mode="first"/>
    <xsl:apply-templates select="stanza[position() &gt; 1]" mode="rest"/>
. . .
</xsl:template>

<xsl:template match="stanza" mode="first">
. . .
</xsl:template>

<xsl:template match="stanza" mode="rest">
. . .
</xsl:template>
```

Another solution, giving even finer control, would be to use `<xsl:for-each>` and `<xsl:call-template>` to control precisely which template rules are applied to which nodes, avoiding the pattern-matching mechanisms of `<xsl:apply-templates>` altogether.

Which you choose is largely a matter of personal style, and it is very hard to argue that one is better than the other in all cases. However, if you find that the match patterns used in defining a template rule are becoming extremely complex and context-dependent, then you probably have both a performance and a maintenance problem on your hands, and controlling the selection of template rules in the calling code, by using modes or by calling templates by name, may well be the answer.

Examples

`<xsl:apply-templates/>`	Processes all the children of the current node
`<xsl:apply-templates select="para"/>`	Process all the `<para>` elements that are children of the current node
`<xsl:apply-templates select="//*" mode="toc"/>`	Processes every element in the document in mode «toc»

```<xsl:apply-templates select="para"> <xsl:with-param name="indent" select="$n+4"/> </xsl:apply-templates>```	Process all the `<para>` elements that are children of the current node, setting the value of the `indent` parameter in each called template to the value of the variable `$n` plus 4.
```<xsl:apply-templates select="//book "> <xsl:sort select="@isbn"/> </xsl:apply-templates>```	Process all the `<book>` elements in the document, sorting them in ascending order of their `isbn` attribute.

See also

`<xsl:for-each>` on page 201
`<xsl:template>` on page 288
`<xsl:with-param>` on page 318

xsl:attribute

The `<xsl:attribute>` element outputs an attribute name and value to the current output destination. It is successful only if an element node has been added to this output tree and if no nodes other than attributes have been added since the element was added.

Defined in

XSLT section 7.1.3

Format

```
<xsl:attribute name={QName} namespace={uri}>
    template-body
</xsl:attribute>
```

Position

`<xsl:attribute>` may be used either as an instruction within a *template-body*, or within an `<xsl:attribute-set>` element.

Attributes

Name	Value	Meaning
name mandatory	Attribute value template returning a `QName`	The name of the attribute to be generated
namespace optional	Attribute value template returning a URI	The namespace URI of the generated attribute

4

Elements

Content

A template-body

Effect

An <xsl:attribute> instruction may appear within a template body, or within an
<xsl:attribute-set> element.

Both the name and the namespace attributes may be given as attribute value templates:
that is, they may contain expressions nested within curly braces, for example
<xsl:attribute name="{$chosenName}"/>. Attribute value templates are explained
in detail in Chapter 3, page 118.

The <xsl:attribute> instruction must be instantiated in the course of instantiating an
instruction to add an element node to the result tree. This might be an <xsl:element>
or <xsl:copy> instruction, or a literal result element. Moreover, the attribute must be
instantiated before any child nodes (text nodes, elements, comments, or processing
instructions) are added to the element node. Very often the <xsl:attribute>
instruction will be contained directly in the instruction that writes the element, for
example:

```
<table>
    <xsl:attribute border="2"/>
</table>
```

but this is not essential, for example you could also do:

```
<table>
    <xsl:call-template name="set-border"/>
</table>
```

and then create the attribute from within the «set-border» template.

The rule that the attributes of an element must be written to the result tree before any
children are added is there for the convenience of implementers. It means that the
XSLT processor doesn't actually need to build the result tree in memory, instead each
node can be written out to an XML file as soon as it is generated. If it weren't for this
rule, the software wouldn't be able to write the first start tag until right at the end,
because there would always be a chance of an attribute being added to it.

If, at the time <xsl:attribute> is instantiated, there is already an attribute on the
current element node with the same name as this one (that is, another attribute whose
name has the same local part and namespace URI), then the new attribute overwrites
the earlier one. This is not an error: in fact, when named attribute sets are used to add
attributes to an output element, it is an important mechanism. Named attribute sets are
described under <xsl:attribute-set> on page 162.

Attribute Name

The name of the new attribute is obtained by expanding the name attribute. The result of expanding the attribute value template must be a QName: that is, a valid XML name with optional namespace prefix. In the most common case, this will be a simple name with no colon, and the output attribute name is then the same as this QName.

The local part of the name of the output attribute will always be the same as the local part of the QName supplied as the value of the name attribute. The prefix may be different, as discussed below.

Attribute Namespace

I introduced XML namespaces in Chapter 2 (page 58). The namespace attribute of the <xsl:attribute> instruction lets you define the namespace URI of the attribute being generated.

The XSLT specification explicitly states that you cannot use <xsl:attribute> to generate namespace declarations by giving an attribute name of «xmlns» or «xmlns:*». Namespace declarations will be added to the output tree automatically whenever you generate elements or attributes that require them.

If the <xsl:attribute> element has a namespace attribute, then its value (after expanding the attribute value template) should be a URI identifying a namespace. However, the system does not check that it conforms to any particular URI syntax, so in effect any string can be used.

The prefix of the name of the output attribute will normally be the same as the prefix of the supplied QName, but this is not guaranteed, and there are some circumstances where the system may need to allocate a different prefix. One such situation is when two attributes are added to the same element using the same prefix but with different namespace URIs; another is when the prefix takes the reserved value «xmlns». If this happens, the system can allocate any namespace prefix it likes. The prefix has to be consistent, of course, between the attribute name and the corresponding namespace declaration.

If there is no namespace attribute:

❑ If the supplied QName includes a prefix, the prefix must be a namespace prefix that is in scope at this point in the stylesheet. The namespace URI in the output will be that of the namespace associated with this prefix in the stylesheet.

❑ Otherwise, the supplied QName is used directly as the output attribute name. The default namespace (as declared using «xmlns="uri"») is **not** used.

If there is a namespace attribute, the name of the output attribute will have the namespace URI obtained by evaluating the namespace attribute. The namespace URI associated with any prefix in the QName obtained from the name attribute will then be ignored (though it must still be valid). The XSLT processor may need to generate a prefix for the output attribute name if none was supplied. For example, if you write:

4

Elements

```
<table>
<xsl:attribute name="width" namespace="http://acme.org/">
  <xsl:text>200</xsl:text>
</xsl:attribute>
</table>
```

then the output might be:

```
<table ns0001:width="100" xmlns:ns0001="http://acme.org"/>
```

Attribute Value

The value of the new attribute is the string value obtained by instantiating the template body. It is an error if instantiating the template body generates any nodes other than text nodes.

Usage

There are many different ways to generate an attribute in the result tree: this section compares the different approaches.

Where an output element is generated using a literal result element, the simplest way to specify attributes is normally to include them as attributes on the literal result element itself. You can do this even when the value is derived from information in the source document, because the value can be generated using an attribute value template, for example:

```
<body bgcolor="#{@red}{@green}{@blue}">
```

This concatenates three attributes of the current node in the source tree to create a single attribute in the result tree. Attribute value templates are described in Chapter 3, page 118.

Using <xsl:attribute> gives you more control than writing the attribute directly in this way. It is useful where one of the following conditions applies:

❑ The parent element is output using <xsl:element> or <xsl:copy> (rather than a literal result element)

❑ There is conditional logic to decide whether to output the attribute or not

❑ The name of the attribute is computed at run-time

❑ There is complex logic to calculate the value of the attribute

❑ The attribute is one of a set that can conveniently be grouped together using an <xsl:attribute-set>

❑ The output attribute belongs to a namespace that is not present in the source document or the stylesheet.

A third way to output attributes is to copy them from the source tree to the result tree by using <xsl:copy> or <xsl:copy-of>. This works only if the attribute you want to generate has the same name and same value as an attribute in the source.

`<xsl:copy>` can be used when the current node in the source document is an attribute node. It's not necessary that the owning element was output using `<xsl:copy>`, for example the following code ensures that the `width`, `height`, and `depth` attributes of the source `<parcel>` element are copied to the output `<package>` element, but its `value` and `owner` attributes are discarded:

```
<xsl:template match="parcel">
<package>
    <xsl:apply-templates select="@*"/>
</package>
</xsl:template>

<xsl:template match="parcel/@width | parcel/@height | parcel/@depth">
    <xsl:copy/>
</xsl:template>

<xsl:template match=" parcel/@value | parcel/@owner"/>
```

This example uses `<xsl:apply-templates>` to process all the attributes of the `<parcel>` element. Some of these match one template rule, which copies the attribute to the output element, while others match an empty template rule that does nothing.

The same effect could be achieved more easily with `<xsl:copy-of>`, as follows:

```
<xsl:template match="parcel">
<package>
    <xsl:copy-of select="@width | @ height | @depth"/>
</package>
</xsl:template>
```

The `select` expression here selects a node-set that contains all the `width`, `height`, and `depth` attributes of the current node, and the `<xsl:copy-of>` instruction copies this node-set. The «|» operator, described in Chapter 5, creates the union of two node-sets.

If you want to copy all attributes of the current node to the result tree, the simplest way to achieve it is `<xsl:copy-of select="@*"/>`.

Examples

The following example outputs an HTML `<OPTION>` element, with a `SELECTED` attribute included only if the Boolean variable `$selected` is true. (The XML output would be `<OPTION SELECTED="SELECTED">`, but the HTML output method will convert this to `<OPTION SELECTED>`.)

Example: Generating an Attribute Conditionally

Source

The source file is `countries.xml`

```
<?xml version="1.0"?>
<countries>
<country name="France"/>
<country name="Germany"/>
<country name="Israel"/>
<country name="Japan"/>
<country name="Poland"/>
<country name="United States" selected="yes"/>
<country name="Venezuela"/>
</countries>
```

Stylesheet

The stylesheet file is `options.xsl`

This is a complete stylesheet using the simplified stylesheet syntax described in Chapter 3, page 104. It outputs an HTML selection box in which the selected attribute is set for the option marked as «`selected="yes"`» in the XML source document.

```
<html xsl:version="1.0"
      xmlns:xsl="http://www.w3.org/1999/XSL/Transform">
<body>
<h1>Please select a country:</h1>
<select id="country">
<xsl:for-each select="//country">
    <option value="{@name}">
    <xsl:if test="@selected='yes'">
        <xsl:attribute name="selected">selected</xsl:attribute>
    </xsl:if>
    <xsl:value-of select="@name"/>
    </option>
</xsl:for-each>
</select>
<hr/>
</body>
</html>
```

The output (shown with the selection box opened) is as follows:

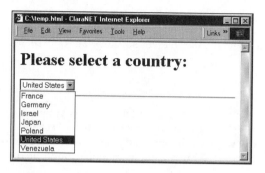

The following example outputs a `<promotion>` element with either a `code` or `reason-code` attribute depending on the variable `$schema-version`. This kind of logic can be useful in an application that has to handle different versions of the output document schema.

Example: Deciding the Attribute Name at Run-Time

Source

This example works with any source file.

Stylesheet

The stylesheet can be found in file `conditional.xsl`

The stylesheet declares a global parameter «schema-version» which controls the name of the attribute used in the output file.

```
<xsl:stylesheet xsl:version="1.0"
     xmlns:xsl="http://www.w3.org/1999/XSL/Transform">

<xsl:param name="schema-version" select="4.0"/>

<xsl:template match="/">
<promotion>
   <xsl:variable name="attname">
      <xsl:choose>
      <xsl:when test="$schema-version &lt; 3.0">code</xsl:when>
      <xsl:otherwise>reason-code</xsl:otherwise>
      </xsl:choose>
   </xsl:variable>
   <xsl:attribute name="{$attname}">17</xsl:attribute>
</promotion>

</xsl:template>
</xsl:stylesheet>
```

161

Output

With the default value of the parameter «schema-version», the output is:

```
<promotion reason-code="17"/>
```

When run with the parameter «schema-version» set to 2.0, the output is:

```
<promotion code="17"/>
```

In the above example it would be equally valid, of course, to use `<xsl:attribute>` with a fixed attribute name in both arms of the `<xsl:choose>` element; the advantage of doing the way we have shown would start to become apparent if the template body of the `<xsl:attribute>` instruction were more complicated than the simple constant «17».

This leads naturally to the next example, where `<xsl:attribute>` is used because the value requires a calculation. In this example, the value of the output attribute is a whitespace-separated list of the id attributes of the child `<item>` elements of the current node:

```
<basket>
<xsl:attribute name="value">
    <xsl:for-each select="item">
        <xsl:value-of select="@id"/>
        <xsl:if test="not(position()=last())">
            <xsl:text> </xsl:text>
        </xsl:if>
    </xsl:for-each>
    </xsl:attribute>
</basket>
```

See also

`<xsl:element>` on page 192
`<xsl:copy>` on page 180

xsl:attribute-set

The `<xsl:attribute-set>` element is a top-level XSLT element used to define a named set of attribute names and values. The resulting attribute set can be applied as a whole to any output element, providing a way of defining commonly-used sets of attributes in a single place.

Named attribute sets provide a capability similar to named styles in CSS.

Defined in

XSLT section 7.1.4

Format

```
<xsl:attribute-set    name=QName
   use-attribute-sets=list-of-QNames >
      <xsl:attribute> *
</xsl:attribute-set>
```

Position

`<xsl:attribute-set>` is a top-level element, so it must always occur as an child of the `<xsl:stylesheet>` element.

Attributes

Name	Value	Meaning
name mandatory	QName	The name of the attribute set
use-attribute-sets optional	Whitespace-separated list of QName	The names of other attribute sets to be incorporated into this attribute set

Content

Zero or more `<xsl:attribute>` elements.

Effect

The `name` attribute is mandatory, and defines the name of the attribute set. It must be a `QName`: a name with or without a namespace prefix. If the name uses a prefix, it must refer to a namespace declaration that is in scope at this point in the stylesheet, and as usual it is the namespace URI rather than the prefix that is used when matching names.

The `use-attribute-sets` attribute is optional. It is used to build up one attribute set from a number of others. If present, its value must be a whitespace-separated list of tokens each of which is a valid `QName` that refers to another named attribute set in the stylesheet. For example:

```
<xsl:attribute-set name="table-cell"
   use-attribute-sets="small-font gray-background centered"/>
<xsl:attribute-set name="small-font">
   <xsl:attribute name="font-name">Verdana</xsl:attribute>
   <xsl:attribute name="font-size">6pt</xsl:attribute>
</xsl:attribute-set>
<xsl:attribute-set name="grey-background">
   <xsl:attribute name="bgcolor">#xBBBBBB</xsl:attribute>
</xsl:attribute-set>
<xsl:attribute-set name="centered">
   <xsl:attribute name="align">center</xsl:attribute>
</xsl:attribute-set>
```

4

Elements

163

The references must not be circular: if A refers to B, then B must not refer directly or indirectly to A. The order is significant: specifying a list of named attribute sets is equivalent to copying the `<xsl:attribute>` elements that they contain, in order, to the **beginning** of the list of `<xsl:attribute>` elements contained in this `<xsl:attribute-set>` element.

It is not an error for two attributes in the same attribute set to have the same name: all but the last will be ignored. This means that an attribute defined directly within the `<xsl:attribute-set>` element takes precedence over one that was obtained from another attribute set referenced in the `use-attribute-sets` attribute.

If several attribute sets in the same stylesheet have the same name, they are merged. If this merging finds two attributes with the same name, then the one in the attribute set with higher import precedence will take precedence. Import precedence is discussed under `<xsl:import>` on page 207. If they both have the same precedence, the XSLT processor has the option of using the one that came later in the stylesheet, or reporting an error.

The XSLT specification doesn't say explicitly how the `use-attribute-sets` attribute is handled during this merging process, in particular, it doesn't say whether the referenced attribute sets are incorporated before or after the merging. This is therefore an area where implementations might differ from each other.

Usage

The most common use of attribute sets is to define packages of attributes that constitute a display style, for example a collection of attributes for a font or for a table.

A named attribute set is used by referring to it in the `use-attribute-sets` attribute of the `<xsl:element>` or `<xsl:copy>` elements, or in the `xsl:use-attribute-sets` attribute of a literal result element, or, of course, in the `use-attribute-sets` attribute of another `<xsl:attribute-set>`. The first three cases all write an element node to the current output destination, and have the effect of adding the attributes in the named attribute set to that element node. Any attributes added implicitly from a named attribute set can be overridden by attribute nodes added explicitly by the invoking code.

An attribute set is not simply a textual macro. The attributes contained in the attribute set each have a template body to define the value, and although this will often be a simple text node, it may also, for example, declare variables or invoke other XSLT instructions such as `<xsl:call-template>` and `<xsl:apply-templates>`.

The rules for the scope of variables, described under `<xsl:variable>` on page 308, are the same as anywhere else, and are defined by the position of the definitions in the source stylesheet document. This means that the only way to parameterize the values of attributes in a named attribute set is by reference to global variables and parameters: there is no other way of passing parameters to an attribute set. However, the value of the generated attributes may depend on the context in the source document. The context is not changed when the attribute-set is used, so the current node («.») and current node list are exactly the same as in the calling template.

This is shown in the following example:

Example: Using an Attribute Set for Numbering

Let's suppose we want to copy an XML file containing a poem, but with the `<line>` elements in the poem output in the form `<line number="3" of="18">` within the stanza.

Source

The source file `poem.xml` has the following structure (I'm only showing the first stanza):

```
<?xml version="1.0"?>
<poem>
<author>Rupert Brooke</author>
<date>1912</date>
<title>Song</title>
<stanza>
<line>And suddenly the wind comes soft.</line>
<line>And Spring is here again;</line>
<line>And the hawthorn quickens with buds of green</line>
<line>And my heart with buds of pain.</line>
</stanza>
</poem>
```

Stylesheet

The stylesheet `number-lines.xsl` copies everything unchanged except the `<line>` elements, which are copied with a named attribute set:

```
<xsl:transform
 xmlns:xsl="http://www.w3.org/1999/XSL/Transform"
 version="1.0"
>
<xsl:strip-space elements="*"/>
<xsl:output method="xml" indent="yes"/>

<xsl:template match="*">
   <xsl:copy>
   <xsl:apply-templates/>
   </xsl:copy>
</xsl:template>

<xsl:template match="line">
   <xsl:copy use-attribute-sets="sequence">
   <xsl:apply-templates/>
   </xsl:copy>
</xsl:template>
```

4

Elements

```
    <xsl:attribute-set name="sequence">
       <xsl:attribute name="number"><xsl:value-of
                    select="position()"/></xsl:attribute>
       <xsl:attribute name="of"><xsl:value-of
                    select="last()"/></xsl:attribute>
    </xsl:attribute-set>
    </xsl:transform>
```

Output

The output (again showing only the first stanza) looks like this:

```
<poem>
    <author>Rupert Brooke</author>
    <date>1912</date>
    <title>Song</title>
    <stanza>
       <line number="1" of="4">And suddenly the wind comes soft,</line>
       <line number="2" of="4">And Spring is here again;</line>
       <line number="3" of="4">And the hawthorn quickens with
                    buds of green</line>
       <line number="4" of="4">And my heart with buds of pain.</line>
    </stanza>
</poem>
```

Examples

The following example defines an attribute set designed for generated HTML `<table>` elements:

```
<xsl:attribute-set name="full-width-table">
    <xsl:attribute name="border">1</xsl:attribute>
    <xsl:attribute name="cellpadding">3</xsl:attribute>
    <xsl:attribute name="cellspacing">0</xsl:attribute>
    <xsl:attribute name="width">100%</xsl:attribute>
</xsl:attribute-set>
```

This attribute set can be used when generating an output element, as follows:

```
<table xsl:use-attribute-set="full-width-table">
<tr></tr>
</table>
```

This produces the following output:

```
<table border="1" cellpadding="3" cellspacing="0" width="100%">
<tr></tr>
</table>
```

Alternatively it is possible to use the attribute set while overriding some of its definitions and adding others, for example:

```
<table border="2" rules="cols" xsl:use-attribute-set="full-width-table">
<tr></tr>
</table>
```

The output now becomes:

```
<table border="2" rules="cols" cellpadding="3"
                        cellspacing="0" width="100%">
<tr></tr>
</table>
```

If this combination of attributes is also used repeatedly, it could be defined as an attribute in its own right, as:

```
<xsl:attribute-set name="ruled-table" use-attribute-set="full-width-table">
   <xsl:attribute name="border">2</xsl:attribute>
   <xsl:attribute name="rules">cols</xsl:attribute>
</xsl:attribute-set>
```

Then this new attribute set could also be invoked by name from a literal result element, an <xsl:element> instruction, or an <xsl:copy> instruction.

See also

<xsl:element> on page 192
<xsl:copy> on page 180
Literal Result Elements in Chapter 3, page 109

xsl:call-template

The <xsl:call-template> instruction is used to invoke a named template. Its effect is analogous to a procedure call or subroutine call in other programming languages.

Defined in

XSLT section 6

Format

```
<xsl:call-template   name=QName>
   <xsl:with-param> *
</xsl:call-template>
```

Position

<xsl:call-template> is an instruction; it is always used within a template body.

4

Elements

Attributes

Name	Value	Meaning
name mandatory	QName	The name of the template to be called

Content

Zero or more `<xsl:with-param>` elements.

Effect

The sections below describe the rules for the template name, the rules for supplying parameters to the called template, and the way the context is affected.

The Template Name

The mandatory `name` attribute must be a `QName`, and it must match the `name` attribute of an `<xsl:template>` element in the stylesheet. If the name has a namespace prefix, the names are compared using the corresponding namespace URI in the usual way. If there is no prefix, the namespace URI is null (the default namespace is not used). It is an error if there is no `<xsl:template>` element with a matching name.

If there is more than one `<xsl:template>` in the stylesheet with a matching name, they must have different **import precedence**, and the one with highest import precedence is used. For information about import precedence, see `<xsl:import>` on page 207.

The name of the template to be called must be written explicitly in the `name` attribute. There is no way of writing this name as a variable or expression to be evaluated at run-time. If you want to make a run-time decision which of several named templates to call, the only way to achieve this is to write an `<xsl:choose>` instruction.

Parameters

If the name of a child `<xsl:with-param>` matches the name of an `<xsl:param>` element in the called `<xsl:template>`, then the `<xsl:with-param>` element is evaluated (in the same way as an `<xsl:variable>` element) and the value is assigned to the relevant `<xsl:param>` variable name within that named template.

If there is a child `<xsl:with-param>` that does not match the name of any `<xsl:param>` element in the selected `<xsl:template>`, then it is ignored. This is not treated as an error.

If there is an `<xsl:param>` element in the selected `<xsl:template>` with no matching `<xsl:with-param>` element in the `<xsl:call-template>` element, then the `<xsl:param>` variable is given a default value: see `<xsl:param>` on page 262 for details. Again, this is not an error.

Context

The selected <xsl:template> is executed with no change to the context: it uses the same current node and current node list, and the same output destination, as the calling template. There is also no change to the *current template rule* (a concept that is used only by <xsl:apply-imports>, described on page 142).

Usage and Examples

The <xsl:call-template> element is similar to a subroutine call in conventional programming languages, and the parameters behave in the same way as conventional call-by-value parameters. It is useful wherever there is common logic to be called from different places in the stylesheet.

Returning a Result

There is no direct way of returning a result from <xsl:call-template>. However, if <xsl:call-template> is called from within an <xsl:variable> element, that variable becomes the current output destination, so any data written by the called template (for example, using <xsl:value-of>) will be accessible as part of the value of this variable. The variable will always be a result tree fragment, but in practice it will usually be used as a string.

For example, the following template outputs the supplied string enclosed in parentheses:

```
<xsl:template name="parenthesize">
   <xsl:param name="string"/>
   <xsl:value-of select="concat('(',$string,')')"/>
</xsl:template>
```

This may be called as follows:

```
<xsl:variable name="credit-in-paren">
   <xsl:call-template name="parenthesize"/>
      <xsl:with-param name="string" select="@credit"/>
   </xsl:call-template>
</xsl:variable>
```

If the value of the credit attribute is «120.00», the resulting value of the variable «$credit-in-paren» will be «(120.00)»

Changing the Current Node

If you want to use <xsl:call-template> to process a node that is not the current node, the easiest way to achieve this is to nest the <xsl:call-template> inside an <xsl:for-each> element. An alternative, however, is to give the target template a distinctive mode name, and call it using <xsl:apply-templates> with the specified mode.

For example, suppose you have written a template that outputs the depth of the current node (the number of ancestors it has). The template has been given a unique name and an identical mode name.

```
<xsl:template name="depth-of-node" mode="depth-of-node" match="node()">
    <xsl:value-of select="count(ancestor::node())"/>
</xsl:template>
```

Now suppose you want to obtain the depth of a node other than the current node – let's say the depth of the next node in document order, which might be above, below, or on the same level as the current node. You can call this template in either of two ways.

Using <xsl:call-template>:

```
<xsl:variable name="next-depth">
    <xsl:for-each select="following::node()[1]">
        <xsl:call-template name="depth-of-node"/>
    </xsl:for-each>
</xsl:variable>
```

or using <xsl:apply-templates> with a special mode:

```
<xsl:variable name="next-depth">
    <xsl:apply-templates select="following::node()[1]" mode="depth-of-node"/>
</xsl:variable>
```

In both cases the variable $next-depth will, on return, hold a value which is the depth in the tree of the node following the current node. Technically the value will be a result tree fragment, but because a result tree fragment can be freely converted to a string or a number where the context requires it, it can be used without formality in contexts such as arithmetic expressions. For example, you could write a test such as <xsl:if test="$next-depth > 4">.

Recursion: Processing a List of Values

Named templates are sometimes used to process a list of values. As XSLT has no updateable variables like a conventional programming language, it also has no conventional *for* or *while* loop, because these constructs can only terminate if there is a control variable whose value is changing. Instead, to process a list of items in XSLT you need to use recursion.

The typical logic used is illustrated by the following pseudo-code:

```
function process-list(list L) {
    if (not-empty(L)) {
        process(first(L));
        process-list(remainder(L));
    }
}
```

That is, the function does nothing if the list is empty; otherwise it processes the first item in the list, and then calls itself to process the list containing all items except the first. The net effect is that each item in the list will be processed and the function will then exit.

There are two main kinds of list that this logic is applied to: node-sets, and strings containing separator characters. I will show one example of each kind; there are further, more complex examples in Chapters 8 and 9.

Example: Using Recursion to Process a Node-Set

Here's an example for processing a node-set. XPath provides built-in functions for counting nodes and for totaling their values, but it doesn't provide a max() or min() function, so to do this we have to walk through the set of nodes comparing the value with the previous highest or lowest. Of course we can't use a variable to record the highest or lowest so far, so we need to turn to recursion for the solution. (There's another solution, which involves sorting the node-set, but that is best avoided on performance grounds.)

Conceptually it's trivial: the maximum value of a set of numbers is either the first number or the maximum of the set of the numbers after the first, whichever is larger. We use XPath predicates for manipulating the node-sets: in particular, «[1]» to find the first node in the set, and «[position()!=1]» to find the remainder.

Let's use this approach to find the longest speech in a scene of a play.

Source

The source file scene.xml is the scene of a play. It starts like this:

```
<?xml version="1.0"?>
<SCENE><TITLE>SCENE I.   Venice. A street.</TITLE>
<STAGEDIR>Enter RODERIGO and IAGO</STAGEDIR>

<SPEECH>
<SPEAKER>RODERIGO</SPEAKER>
<LINE>Tush! never tell me; I take it much unkindly</LINE>
<LINE>That thou, Iago, who hast had my purse</LINE>
<LINE>As if the strings were thine, shouldst know of this.</LINE>
</SPEECH>

<SPEECH>
<SPEAKER>IAGO</SPEAKER>
<LINE>'Sblood, but you will not hear me:</LINE>
<LINE>If ever I did dream of such a matter, Abhor me.</LINE>
</SPEECH>
etc.
</SCENE>
```

Stylesheet

The stylesheet longest-speech.xsl is shown below. It starts by defining a named template «max». This template takes a node-set called «list» as its parameter.

The first thing it does is to test whether this node-set is empty (<xsl:when test="$list">). If it is, is gets the number of <LINE> element children of the first node in the list into a variable «$first». Then the template calls itself recursively, passing all nodes except the first as the parameter, to determine the maximum value for the rest of the list. It then returns either the first value, or the maxumum for the rest of the list, whichever is greater. Finally, if the supplied list was empty, it returns zero.

The template rule for the root node of the source document simply calls the «max» template, passing the list of all <SPEECH> elements as a parameter.

```
<xsl:transform
 xmlns:xsl="http://www.w3.org/1999/XSL/Transform"
 version="1.0"
>
<xsl:template name="max">
<xsl:param name="list"/>
<xsl:choose>
<xsl:when test="$list">
    <xsl:variable name="first" select="count($list[1]/LINE)"/>
    <xsl:variable name="max-of-rest">
        <xsl:call-template name="max">
            <xsl:with-param name="list" select="$list[position()!=1]"/>
        </xsl:call-template>
    </xsl:variable>
    <xsl:choose>
    <xsl:when test="$first &gt; $max-of-rest">
        <xsl:value-of select="$first"/>
    </xsl:when>
    <xsl:otherwise>
        <xsl:value-of select="$max-of-rest"/>
    </xsl:otherwise>
    </xsl:choose>
</xsl:when>
<xsl:otherwise>0</xsl:otherwise>
</xsl:choose>
</xsl:template>

<xsl:template match="/">
Longest speech is <xsl:text/>
    <xsl:call-template name="max">
        <xsl:with-param name="list" select="//SPEECH"/>
    </xsl:call-template>
<xsl:text/> lines.
</xsl:template>
</xsl:transform>
```

Output

The output is simply a message giving the length of the longest speech in this scene:

```
<?xml version="1.0" encoding="utf-8" ?>
Longest speech is 26 lines.
```

Similar logic is often used to process a list presented in the form of a string containing a list of tokens. The easiest form to process is a whitespace-separated list, because the normalize-space() function is available to ensure that each item in the list is separated by exactly one space character.

Example: Using Recursion to Process a Separated String

In this example we will print out all lines in scene.xml where the line contains the name of a person appearing in that scene. An example of such a line is:

```
<LINE>That thou, Iago, who hast had my purse</LINE>
```

To do this we will first need to normalize the line to convert punctuation into spaces and to convert lower-case into uppercase. Then we will need to process the line word by word. The only way to do this is by recursion: test whether the first word in the line is the name of a speaker, then apply the same logic to the rest of the line after the first word.

Source

The source file scene.xml is the same as in the previous example.

Stylesheet

The stylesheet naming-lines.xsl starts by declaring a global variable whose value is the set of <SPEAKER> elements anywhere in the document:

```
<xsl:transform
 xmlns:xsl="http://www.w3.org/1999/XSL/Transform"
 version="1.0"
>

<xsl:variable name="speakers" select="//SPEAKER"/>
```

Now comes the recursive named template. It takes a parameter called «line». The first thing it does is to massage this line, first by converting lower case to upper case and punctuation to spaces using the translate() function, and then by replacing multiple spaces by a single space, and adding a another single space at the end, using the normalize-space() and concat() functions. (These functions are all described in Chapter 7).

Then the template extracts the first word in the line by using substring-before(). If this word is present in the global node-set «$speakers» it returns the value «true». Otherwise it applies the same test to the rest of the line (obtained using substring-after()) by calling itself recursively.

If the end of the line is reached, the template returns the value «false».

```
<xsl:template name="contains-name">
    <xsl:param name="line"/>
    <xsl:variable name="line1"
        select="translate($line,
          'abcdefghijklmnopqrstuvwxyz.,:?!;',
                        'ABCDEFGHIJKLMNOPQRSTUVWXYZ        ')"/>
    <xsl:variable name="line2"
        select="concat(normalize-space($line1), ' ')"/>
    <xsl:variable name="first" select="substring-before($line2,' ')"/>
    <xsl:choose>
    <xsl:when test="$first">
      <xsl:choose>
      <xsl:when test="$speakers[.=$first]">true</xsl:when>
      <xsl:otherwise>
          <xsl:variable name="rest" select="substring-after($line2,' ')"/>
          <xsl:call-template name="contains-name">
              <xsl:with-param name="line" select="$rest"/>
          </xsl:call-template>
      </xsl:otherwise>
      </xsl:choose>
    </xsl:when>
    <xsl:otherwise>false</xsl:otherwise>
    </xsl:choose>
</xsl:template>
```

Then comes the "main program", the template rule that matches the root node. This simply calls the named template for each <LINE> element in the document, copying the element to the output if the named template returns the value «true»:

```
<xsl:template match="/">

<xsl:for-each select="//LINE">
    <xsl:variable name="contains-name">
        <xsl:call-template name="contains-name">
            <xsl:with-param name="line" select="."/>
        </xsl:call-template>
    </xsl:variable>
    <xsl:if test="$contains-name='true'">
        <xsl:copy-of select="."/>;
    </xsl:if>
</xsl:for-each>
</xsl:template>
</xsl:transform>
```

174

The output lists all the `<LINE>` elements containing the name of a `<SPEAKER>` in the scene:

```
<?xml version="1.0" encoding="utf-8" ?>
    <LINE>That thou, Iago, who hast had my purse</LINE>;
    <LINE>It is as sure as you are Roderigo.</LINE>;
    <LINE>Were I the Moor, I would not be Iago:</LINE>;
    <LINE>What, ho, Brabantio! Signior Brabantio, ho!</LINE>;
    <LINE>Awake! what, ho, Brabantio! thieves! thieves! thieves!</LINE>;
    <LINE>My name is Roderigo.</LINE>;
    <LINE>Most grave Brabantio,</LINE>;
    <LINE>This thou shalt answer; I know thee, Roderigo.</LINE>;
    <LINE>Is nought but bitterness. Now, Roderigo,</LINE>;
    <LINE>May be abused? Have you not read, Roderigo,</LINE>;
    <LINE>On, good Roderigo: I'll deserve your pains.</LINE>;
```

When processing strings in this way, the only thing you need to be specially careful about is ensuring that there is a single space between each pair of words and another one at the end (because otherwise the `substring-before()` call would fail when there is one word left in the list). This is achieved using the `normalize-space()` and `concat()` functions. The way these are used here is rather inefficient, because the line only needs to be normalized once, not on each recursive call, but I have left that inefficiency in to keep the example code simpler.

One other case where recursion is needed is the simple matter of doing something a fixed number of times. For example, suppose you need to create four empty cells in a table. The following code achieves this, by producing one cell, and then calling itself to produce the rest, stopping only when the number requested reaches zero.

```
<xsl:template name="produce-empty-cells">
    <xsl:param name="count"/>
    <xsl:if test="$count != 0">
        <td> </td>
        <xsl:call-template name="produce-empty-cells">
            <xsl:with-param name="count" select="$count - 1"/>
        </xsl:call-template>
    </xsl:if>
</xsl:template>
```

To produce four empty cells, call this with the «count» parameter set to four, thus:

```
<xsl:call-template name="produce-empty-cells">
    <xsl:with-param name="count" select="4"/>
</xsl:call-template>
```

See also

`<xsl:apply-templates>` on page 145
`<xsl:param>` on page 262
`<xsl:with-param>` on page 318

xsl:choose

The `<xsl:choose>` instruction defines a choice between a number of alternatives.

If there are two alternatives it performs the equivalent of `if-then-else` in other languages; if there are more than two, it performs the equivalent of a `switch` or `select` statement.

Defined in

XSLT section 9.2

Format

```
<xsl:choose>
   <xsl:when> +
   <xsl:otherwise> ?
</xsl:choose>
```

Position

`<xsl:choose>` is an instruction: it is always used within a template body.

Attributes

None.

Content

One or more `<xsl:when>` elements.
Optionally, an `<xsl:otherwise>` element, which must come last if it is present at all.

Effect

The `<xsl:choose>` element is instantiated as follows:

❑ The first `<xsl:when>` element whose `test` *expression* is true is selected. Subsequent `<xsl:when>` elements are ignored whether or not their `test` *expression* is true.

❑ If none of the `<xsl:when>` elements has a `test` *expression* that is true, the `<xsl:otherwise>` element is selected. If there is no `<xsl:otherwise>` element, no element is selected, and the `<xsl:choose>` element therefore has no effect.

❑ The selected child element (if any) is executed by instantiating its template body in the current context. So the effect is as if the relevant template body appeared in place of the `<xsl:choose>` instruction.

It is not defined whether the `test` *expression* in a `<xsl:when>` element after the selected one is evaluated or not, so if it calls extension functions that have side-effects, or if it contains errors, the result is undefined.

Usage

The <xsl:choose> instruction is useful where there is a choice of two or more alternative courses of action. It thus performs the functions of both the if-then-else and switch or Select Case constructs found in other programming languages.

Using <xsl:choose> with a single <xsl:when> instruction and no <xsl:otherwise> is permitted, and means exactly the same as <xsl:if>. Some people suggest writing every <xsl:if> instruction this way, to save rewriting it later when you discover that you want an else branch after all.

When <xsl:choose> is used within the body of an <xsl:variable> (or <xsl:param> or <xsl:with-param>) element, the effect is a conditional assignment: the relevant variable is assigned a different value depending on the conditions. Note however that the value of the variable in such cases will always be a result tree fragment.

Examples

The following example outputs the name of a State in the USA based on a two-letter abbreviation for the State. If the abbreviation is not that of a recognized State, it outputs the abbreviation itself.

```
<xsl:choose>
    <xsl:when test="state='AZ'">Arizona</xsl:when>
    <xsl:when test="state='CA'">California</xsl:when>
    <xsl:when test="state='DC'">Washington DC</xsl:when>
    ......
    <xsl:otherwise><xsl:value-of select="state"/></xsl:otherwise>
</xsl:choose>
```

The following example declares a variable called width and initializes its value to the width attribute of the current node, if there is one, or to 100 otherwise.

```
<xsl:variable name="width">
    <xsl:choose>
        <xsl:when test="@width">
            <xsl:value-of select="@width"/>
        </xsl:when>
        <xsl:otherwise>100</xsl:otherwise>
    </xsl:choose>
</xsl:variable>
```

Note: you might be tempted to write this as follows:

```
<!--WRONG-->
<xsl:choose>
    <xsl:when test="@width">
        <xsl:variable name="width">
            <xsl:value-of select="@width"/>
        </xsl:variable>
    </xsl:when>
    <xsl:otherwise>
```

```
          <xsl:variable name="width" select="100"/>
      </xsl:otherwise>
   </xsl:choose>
   <!--WRONG-->
```

This is legal XSLT, but it does not achieve the required effect. This is because both the variables called «width» have a scope which is bounded by the containing element, so they are inaccessible outside the <xsl:choose> instruction.

See also

<xsl:when> on page 317
<xsl:otherwise> on page 249
<xsl:if> on page 204

xsl:comment

The <xsl:comment> instruction is used to write a comment to the current output destination.

Defined in

XSLT section 7.4

Format

```
<xsl:comment>
   template-body
</xsl:comment>
```

Position

<xsl:comment> is an instruction: it is always used within a template body.

Attributes

None.

Content

A template-body.

Effect

The template-body contained in the <xsl:comment> instruction may only generate text nodes, it is an error if it generates other nodes such as elements, attributes, or nested comments.

The comment should not include the sequence «--», and it should not end in «-», because these sequences are not allowed in XML comments. The XSLT processor may recover from these errors by adding extra spaces to the comment or it may report an error. If you want your stylesheet to be portable, you must therefore avoid generating these sequences.

178

In XML or HTML output, the comment will appear as:

```
<!-- comment text -->
```

Usage

In theory, a comment has no meaning to the software that processes the output document, it is intended only for human readers. Comments are therefore useful to record when and how the document was generated, or perhaps to explain the meaning of the tags.

Comments can be particularly useful for debugging the stylesheet: if each `<xsl:template>` in the stylesheet starts with an `<xsl:comment>` instruction, you will find it much easier to trace back from the output to your stylesheet.

Comments in HTML output are used for some special markup conventions, for example surrounding Dynamic HTML scripts. The purpose of the comment here is to ensure that browsers that don't understand the script will skip over it rather than displaying it as text. An example is shown below.

Examples

The following example uses an extension function, if it is available, to output a comment containing the date at which the stylesheet was generated. Extension functions are described in Chapter 3, page 122.

```
<xsl:if test="function-available(Date:toString)"
                            xmlns:Date="/java.util.Date">
   <xsl:comment>Generated at:
      <xsl:value-of select="Date:toString()"/>
   </xsl:comment>
</xsl:if>
```

Typical output might be:

```
<!--Generated at Tue Dec 07 23:38:08 GMT 1999-->
```

The following example outputs a piece of client-side JavaScript to an HTML output file:

```
<script language="JavaScript">
   <xsl:comment>
      function bk(n) {
         parent.frames['content'].location="chap" + n + ".1.html";
      }
   //</xsl:comment>
</script>
```

The output will look like this:

```
<script language="JavaScript">
  <!--
    function bk(n) {
        parent.frames['content'].location="chap" + n + ".1.html";
    }
  //-->
</script>
```

The comment cannot be written as a comment in the stylesheet, of course, because then the XSLT processor would ignore it entirely. Comments in the stylesheet are not copied to the output destination.

See also

`function-available( )` in Chapter 7, page 459 .

xsl:copy

The `<xsl:copy>` instruction copies the current node in the source document to the current output destination. This is a shallow copy: it does not copy the children, descendants, or attributes of the current node, only the current node and (if it is an element) its namespaces.

Defined in

XSLT section 7.5

Format

```
<xsl:copy use-attribute-sets=list-of-QNames >
   template-body
</xsl:copy>
```

Position

`<xsl:copy>` is an instruction. It is always used within a template body.

Attributes

Name	Value	Meaning
use-attribute-sets *optional*	Whitespace-separated list of QNames	The names of attribute sets to be applied to the generated node, if it is an element

Content

An optional template-body: used only if the current node is a root node or an element.

Effect

The action depends on the node type of the current node, as follows:

Type of current node in source document	Action
root	Nothing is written to the output destination (it is never necessary to write a root node to the output destination, because it is created implicitly). The use-attribute-sets attribute is ignored. The only effect of calling <xsl:copy> is that the template body is instantiated.
element	An element node is added to the current output destination, as if by a call on <xsl:element>. This will have the same name as the current element node in the source document. The namespace nodes associated with the current element node are also copied. The use-attribute-sets attribute is expanded: it must be a whitespace-separated list of QNames that identify named attribute-sets in the stylesheet. The attributes within these named attribute sets are evaluated in the order they appear, and added to the output destination. The template body is then instantiated.
text	A new text node is written to the output destination, with the same value as the current text node in the source document. The use-attribute-sets attribute and the template body are ignored.
attribute	An attribute node is added to the current output destination, as if by a call on <xsl:attribute>. This will have the same name and value as the current attribute node in the source document. If the output destination does not currently have an open element node to hold this attribute, an error is reported. If the open element node already holds an attribute with the same name, the new attribute overwrites the old. The use-attribute-sets attribute and the template-body are ignored. The XSLT specification does not explicitly say that any necessary namespace nodes are copied, though this is implicit in the requirement to generate output that conforms to the XML Namespaces specification.

4

Elements

Type of current node in source document	Action
processing instruction	A processing instruction node is added to the current output destination, with the same name and value (target and data in XML terminology) as the current processing instruction node in the source document. The use-attribute-sets attribute and the template body are ignored.
comment	A comment node is added to the current output destination, with the same content as the current comment node in the source document. The use-attribute-sets attribute and the template-body are ignored.
namespace	The XSLT specification does not define the effect of copying a namespace node. It should never be necessary, and it is best not attempted.

Usage

The main use of <xsl:copy> is when doing an XML-to-XML transformation in which parts of the document are to remain unchanged. It is also useful when the source XML document contains XHTML fragments within it, for example if the simple HTML formatting elements such as <i> and <b> are used within textual data in the source, and are to be copied unchanged to an HTML output document.

Although <xsl:copy> does a shallow copy, it is easy to construct a deep copy by applying it recursively. The typical manner of use is to write a template rule that effectively calls itself:

```
<xsl:template match="@*|node()" mode="copy">
   <xsl:copy>
      <xsl:apply-templates select="@*" mode="copy"/>
      <xsl:apply-templates mode="copy"/>
   </xsl:copy>
</xsl:template>
```

This template rule matches any node except a namespace or root node. This is because «@*» matches any attribute node, and «node()», which is short for «child::node()», matches any node that is the child of something. Once this template rule is applied to a node, it copies that node, and if it is an element node, it applies the same template rule first to its attributes and then to its child nodes – I am assuming there is no other template rule with mode="copy" that has a higher priority.

An easier way of doing a deep copy is to use <xsl:copy-of>. However, the recursive use of <xsl:copy> allows control over exactly which nodes are to be included in the output.

Examples

The following template rule is useful if the source document contains HTML-like tables that are to be copied directly to the output, without change to the structure.

```
<xsl:template match=" table | tbody | tr | th | td ">
   <xsl:copy>
      <xsl:for-each select="@*">
         <xsl:copy/>
      </xsl:for-each>
      <xsl:apply-templates/>
   </xsl:copy>
</xsl:template>
```

The effect is that any of these elements are copied to the output destination, along with their attributes, but their child elements are processed using whatever template rule is appropriate, which might be this one in the case of a child element that is part of the table model, or it might be a different template for some other element. This template rule could be simplified by copying the attributes using <xsl:copy-of>, thus:

```
<xsl:template match=" table | tbody | tr | th | td ">
   <xsl:copy>
      <xsl:copy-of select="@*"/>
      <xsl:apply-templates/>
   </xsl:copy>
</xsl:template>
```

The following template rule matches any elements in the source document that are in the SVG namespace, and copies them unchanged to the output, along with their attributes. The SVG namespace node itself will also be included automatically in the output tree. (SVG stands for Scalable Vector Graphics, it is an XML-based standard currently under development designed to fill the long-standing need for including vector graphics in web pages. The SVG namespace may change when the final standard is published).

```
<xsl:template match="svg:*"
              xmlns:svg="http://www.w3.org/Graphics/SVG/SVG-19991203.dtd >
   <xsl:copy>
      <xsl:copy-of select="@*">

      <xsl:apply-templates/>
   </xsl:copy>
</xsl:template>
```

See also

<xsl:copy-of>.

xsl:copy-of

The main purpose of the <xsl:copy-of> instruction is to copy a result tree fragment or a node-set to the current output destination. This is a deep copy – when a node is copied, its descendants are also copied.

Defined in

XSLT section 11.3

Format

```
<xsl:copy-of select=Expression /> Position
```

Position

`<xsl:copy-of>` is an instruction. It is always used within a template-body.

Attributes

Name	Value	Meaning
select mandatory	Expression	The result tree fragment, node-set, or other value to be copied to the output destination

Content

None; the element is always empty.

Effect

If the result of evaluating the select expression is a result tree fragment (this will only happen if the expression is a VariableReference), the result tree fragment is copied to the current output destination. The root node of the result tree fragment is not copied (because a tree can only have one root) but all the nodes that are children of this root are copied, in the order they appear, together with their namespaces, their attributes, and their children, recursively.

If the result of evaluating the select expression is a node-set, each of the nodes in the node-set is copied, in document order, to the current output destination. This is a deep copy: copying a node copies its namespaces, its attributes, and its children, recursively.

If the result is any other type, `<xsl:copy-of>` has the same effect as `<xsl:value-of>`. The value is converted to a string using the rules of the string() function, and the string is written to the current output destination as a text node.

Usage and Examples

There are two principal uses for `<xsl:copy-of>`: it can be used when the same data is needed in more than one place in the output document, and it can be used for copying a subtree unchanged from the input document to the output.

Repeated Output Fragments

The use of `<xsl:copy-of>` in conjunction with result tree fragments arises primarily when you want to write the same collection of nodes to the output in more than one place. This might arise, for example, with page headers and footers. The construct allows you to assemble the required output fragment as the value of a variable, and then copy it to the final output destination as often as required.

Example: Using <xsl:copy-of> for Repeated Output

Source

The source file `soccer.xml` holds details of a number of soccer matches played during the World Cup finals in 1998.

```xml
<?xml version="1.0"?>
<results group="A">
<match>
<date>10-Jun-98</date>
<team score="2">Brazil</team>
<team score="1">Scotland</team>
</match>
<match>
<date>10-Jun-98</date>
<team score="2">Morocco</team>
<team score="2">Norway</team>
</match>
<match>
<date>16-Jun-98</date>
<team score="1">Scotland</team>
<team score="1">Norway</team>
</match>
<match>
<date>16-Jun-98</date>
<team score="3">Brazil</team>
<team score="0">Morocco</team>
</match>
<match>
<date>23-Jun-98</date>
<team score="1">Brazil</team>
<team score="2">Norway</team>
</match>
<match>
<date>23-Jun-98</date>
<team score="0">Scotland</team>
<team score="3">Morocco</team>
</match>
</results>
```

Stylesheet

The stylesheet is in file `soccer.xsl`.

It constructs an HTML table heading as a global tree-valued variable, and then uses `<xsl:copy-of>` every time it wants to output this heading. In this particular case the heading is fixed, but it could contain data from the source document, so long as the heading is the same each time it is output. If it contained calculated values, there would be a possible performance benefit it coding it this way rather than regenerating the heading each time.

```
<xsl:stylesheet version="1.0"
     xmlns:xsl="http://www.w3.org/1999/XSL/Transform">

<xsl:variable name="table-heading">
    <tr>
        <td><b>Date</b></td>
        <td><b>Home Team</b></td>
        <td><b>Away Team</b></td>
        <td><b>Result</b></td>
    </tr>
</xsl:variable>

<xsl:template match="/">
<html><body>
    <h1>Matches in Group <xsl:value-of select="/*/@group"/></h1>
    <xsl:for-each select="//match">
    <h2><xsl:value-of select="concat(team[1], ' versus ', team[2])"/></h2>
    <table bgcolor="#cccccc" border="1" cellpadding="5">
        <xsl:copy-of select="$table-heading"/>
        <tr>
        <td><xsl:value-of select="date"/> </td>
        <td><xsl:value-of select="team[1]"/> </td>
        <td><xsl:value-of select="team[2]"/> </td>
        <td><xsl:value-of
           select="concat(team[1]/@score, '-', team[2]/@score)"/> </td>
        </tr>
    </table>
    </xsl:for-each>
</body></html>
</xsl:template>

</xsl:stylesheet>
```

Output

(Apologies to soccer fans who know full well that all these matches were played in France, on neither team's home territory. It's only an example!)

There are only really two things you can do with a result tree fragment: you can copy it to another tree using <xsl:copy-of>, and you can convert it to a string. Several XSLT implementations also provide a function to convert a result tree fragment to a node-set, which greatly expands the usefulness of result tree fragments because they can then be used as working data structures. Unfortunately this feature is not yet in the standard, but because it has been prototyped in several products it is a strong candidate for inclusion in a future version.

Deep Copy

The other use for <xsl:copy-of>, which is easily overlooked because of the way the XSLT specification describes its use, is that it provides a simple way of copying an entire sub-tree of the input document directly to the output. As <xsl:copy-of> does a deep copy, this is simpler than using <xsl:copy>, though it can only be used when the whole subtree is to be copied without change. For example, an XML document defining a product description might have an element called <overview> whose content is pure XHTML. You could copy this to the output HTML document with a template rule such as:

```
<xsl:template match="overview">
   <div>
      <xsl:copy-of select="node()">

   </div>
</xsl:template>
```

Unlike the examples using <xsl:copy>, there is no recursive application of template rules here: each child node of the <overview> element is copied to the output destination in a single operation, along with all its children.

See also

<xsl:copy> on page 180
<xsl:variable> on page 308

xsl:decimal-format

The <xsl:decimal-format> element is used to define the characters and symbols used when converting numbers into strings using the format-number() function.

Note that <xsl:decimal-format> only affects the format-number() function. It has no effect on the way <xsl:number> formats numbers for display, nor on the default number-to-string conversion used by the string() function, nor on the format used when <xsl:value-of> is used to output a number as a string.

Defined in

XSLT section 12.3

Format

```
<xsl:decimal-format
    name=QName
    decimal-separator=character
    grouping-separator=character
    infinity=string
    minus-sign=character
    NaN=string
    percent=character
    per-mille=character
    zero-digit=character
    digit=character
    pattern-separator=character  />
```

Position

`<xsl:decimal-format>` is a top-level element. It may appear any number of times in a stylesheet, but only as an immediate child of the `<xsl:stylesheet>` element.

Attributes

Name	Value	Meaning
name optional	QName	The name of this decimal format. If omitted, the attributes apply to the default decimal format.
decimal-separator optional	character	Character to be used to separate the integer and the fraction part of a number. Default is «.»
grouping-separator optional	character	Character used to separate groups of digits. Default is «,»
infinity optional	string	String used to represent the numeric value infinity. Default value is «Infinity»
minus-sign optional	character	Character used as the default minus sign. Default is «-».
NaN optional	string	String used to represent the numeric value NaN (not a number). Default value is «NaN»
percent optional	character	Character used to represent a percentage sign. Default value is «%»
per-mille optional	character	Character used to represent a per-mille (i.e. per-thousand) sign. Default value is «‰»
zero-digit optional	character	Character used in a format pattern to indicate a place where a leading zero digit is required. Default value is «0»
digit optional	character	Character used in a format pattern to indicate a place where a digit is required. Default value is «#»

Name	Value	Meaning
pattern-separator optional	character	Character used in a format pattern to separate the subpattern for positive numbers from the subpattern for negative numbers. Default value is «;»

Content

None; the element is always empty.

Effect

If a name attribute is supplied, the `<xsl:decimal-format>` element defines a named decimal format; otherwise it defines attributes of the default decimal format. A named decimal format is used by the `format-number()` function when it is called with three arguments (the third argument is the name of a decimal format); the default decimal format is used when the `format-number()` function is called without a third argument.

It is an error to have more than one `<xsl:decimal-format>` element for the default decimal format, or more than one for a decimal format with a given name, unless all non-default attribute values are identical. This is true even if the different `<xsl:decimal-format>` elements have different import precedence.

The `<xsl:decimal-format>` element does not directly define the display format of a number. Rather it defines the characters and strings used to represent different logical symbols. Some of these logical symbols occur in the *format pattern* used as an argument to the `format-number()` function, some of them occur in the final output number itself, and some are used in both. The actual display format of a number depends both on the format pattern and on the choice of decimal format symbols.

For example, if there is a `<xsl:decimal-format>` element as follows:

```
<xsl:decimal-format name="european"
                    decimal-separator=","
                    grouping-separator="." >
```

then the function call:

```
format-number(1234.5, '#.##0,00', 'european')
```

will produce the output:

```
1.234,50
```

The use of the «.» and «,» characters in both the format pattern and the output display is determined by the named `<xsl:decimal-format>` element, but the number of digits displayed, and the use of leading and trailing zeroes is determined solely by the format pattern.

The structure of a format pattern is defined in the description of the `format-number()` function in Chapter 7, page 455. The syntax of the format pattern uses a number of special symbols: the actual characters used for these symbols are defined in the relevant `<xsl:decimal-format>` element. These symbols are:

4

Elements

```
decimal-separator
grouping-separator
percent
per-mille
zero-digit
digit
pattern-separator
```

The `<xsl:decimal-format>` element also defines characters and strings which are used, when required, in the actual output value. Some of these are the same as characters used in the format pattern, others are different. These characters and strings are:

```
decimal-separator
grouping-separator
infinity
minus-sign
NaN
percent
per-mille
zero-digit
```

For example, if the `<xsl:decimal-format>` element defines the infinity string as «***», then the output of «format-number(1 div 0, $format)» will be «***», regardless of the format pattern.

Usage

The `<xsl:decimal-format>` element is used in conjunction with the `format-number()` function to output numeric information. It is designed primarily to provide localization of the format for display to human readers, but it can also be useful when you need to produce an output data file using, for example, a fixed number of leading zeroes. It is typically used for numbers in the source data or computed from the source data, whereas the `<xsl:number>` element, which has its own formatting capabilities, is generally used for sequence numbers.

Each `<xsl:decimal-format>` element defines a style of localized numbering, catering for the variations that occur in different countries and languages, and for other local preferences such as the convention in the accountancy profession whereby parentheses are used to indicate negative numbers.

Examples

The following tables illustrate some of the effects achievable using the `<xsl:decimal-format>` element in conjunction with different format patterns.

Example 1

This decimal format is used in many Western European countries: it uses a comma as a decimal point and a period (full stop) as a thousands separator, the reverse of the custom in Britain and North America.

The left hand column shows the number as it would be written in XSLT. The middle column shows the format pattern supplied as the second argument to the format-number() function. The right-hand column shows the string value returned by the format-number() function.

The patterns used in this example use the following symbols:

❏ «.» which I have defined as my thousands separator

❏ «,» which I have defined as my decimal point

❏ «#» which is a position where a digit can occur, but where the digit is omitted if it is an insignificant zero

❏ «0» which is a position where a digit will always occur, even if it is an insignificant zero

❏ «%» which indicates that the number should be expressed as a percentage

❏ «;» which separates the pattern used for positive numbers from the pattern used for negative numbers

```
<xsl:decimal-format decimal-separator="," grouping-separator="."/>
```

Number	Format Pattern	Result
1234.5	#.##0,00	1.234,50
123.456	#.##0,00	123,46
100000	#.##0,00	1.000.000,00
-59	#.##0,00	-59,00
1 div 0	#.##0,00	Infinity
1234	###0,0###	1234,0
1234.5	###0,0###	1234,5
.00035	###0,0###	0,0004
0.25	#00%	25%
0.736	#00%	74%
1	#00%	100%
-42	#00%	-4200%
-3.12	#,00;(#,00)	(3,12)
-3.12	#,00;#,00CR	3,12CR

Example 2

This example shows how digits other than the Western digits 0–9 can be used. Since such digits will be unfamiliar to most readers, I'll illustrate the effect using letters instead. This works perfectly well, though it isn't very useful:

```
<xsl:decimal-format zero-digit="a" minus-sign="~"/>
```

191

Number	Format Pattern	Result
10	aa	ba
12.34	##.##	bc.de
−9999999	#,###,###	~j,jjj,jjj

Example 3

This example shows how the exceptional numeric values NaN and Infinity can be shown, for example in a statistical table.

```
<xsl:decimal-format NaN="Not Applicable" infinity="Out of Range"/>
```

Number	Format Pattern	Result
'a'	any	Not Applicable
1 div 0	any	Out of Range
−1 div 0	any	−Out of Range

See also

format-number() function in Chapter 7, page 455
<xsl:number> on page 237.

xsl:element

The <xsl:element> instruction is used to output an element node to the current output destination.

It provides an alternative to using a literal result element, and is useful especially when the element name or namespace are to be calculated at run-time.

Defined in

XSLT section 7.1.2

Format

```
<xsl:element name={QName} namespace={uri}
    use-attribute-sets=list-of-QNames  >
        template-body
</xsl:element>
```

Position

<xsl:element> is used as an instruction within a template-body.

Attributes

Name	Value	Meaning
name mandatory	Attribute value template returning a QName	The name of the element to be generated
namespace optional	Attribute value template returning a URI	The namespace URI of the generated element
use-attribute-sets optional	Whitespace-separated list of QNames	List of named attribute sets containing attributes to be added to this output element

Content

A template-body.

Effect

The name of the generated element node is determined using the name and namespace attributes.

Attributes may be added to the element node either by using the use-attribute-sets attribute, or by writing attribute nodes to the output destination using <xsl:attribute> or <xsl:copy> or <xsl:copy-of>: this must be done before anything else is written to the output destination. Any attributes written using <xsl:attribute> or <xsl:copy> or <xsl:copy-of> will overwrite attributes of the same name written using the use-attribute-sets attribute.

The child nodes of the element are produced by instantiating the contained *template-body*.

The XSLT specification is written in terms of writing nodes to a result tree. Sometimes it is convenient to think in terms of the start tag of the <xsl:element> element producing a start tag in the output XML file and the end tag of the <xsl:element> element producing the corresponding end tag, with the intervening *template-body* producing the contents of the output element. However, it is dangerous to extend this analogy too far, because writing the start tag and end tag are not separate operations that can be individually controlled, they are simply two things that happen together as a consequence of the <xsl:element> instruction being instantiated. This is explained in more detail in the section on *Literal Result Elements* in Chapter 3, page 109.

Both the name and the namespace attributes may be given as attribute value templates: that is, they may contain expressions nested within curly braces.

4

Elements

Element Name

The name of the new element is obtained by expanding the name attribute. The result of expanding the attribute value template must be a QName: that is, a valid XML name with an optional namespace prefix. For example, «table» or «fo:block». If there is a prefix, it must correspond to a namespace declaration that is in scope at this point in the stylesheet, unless there is also a namespace attribute, in which case it is taken as referring to that namespace.

If the name is not a valid QName, the XSLT processor is required either to report the error, or to leave this element node out of the generated tree, while still including its children. Different processors may thus handle this error differently.

The local part of the name of the output element will always be the same as the local part of the QName supplied as the value of the name attribute.

Element Namespace

As explained in Chapter 2, the result tree will always conform to the XML Namespaces specification. You can choose, of course, to generate all the output elements in the default namespace, but as namespaces become more widely used you may need to define the namespace URI of the generated element name.

If the <xsl:element> instruction has a namespace attribute, then its value (after expanding the attribute value template) should be a URI identifying a namespace. This namespace does **not** need to be in scope at this point in the stylesheet, in fact it usually won't be. The system does not check that the value conforms to any particular URI syntax, so in effect any string can be used.

If the value is empty, the element will have a null namespace URI. Otherwise, the XSLT processor will output any necessary namespace declarations to ensure that the element name is associated with this namespace URI in the result tree.

The prefix of the name of the output element will normally be the same as the prefix of the supplied QName, but the XSLT processor is allowed to allocate a different prefix if it chooses, so long as it is associated with the correct URI. This might happen, for example, if there are several different prefixes associated with the same namespace URI.

If there is no namespace attribute:

❑ If the supplied QName includes a prefix, the prefix must be a namespace prefix that is in scope at this point in the stylesheet: in other words, there must be an xmlns:prefix attribute either on the <xsl:element> instruction itself or on some containing element The namespace URI in the output will be that of the namespace associated with this prefix in the stylesheet.

❑ Otherwise, the default namespace is used. This is the namespace declared, in some containing element in the stylesheet, with an «xmlns="uri"» declaration. Note that this is one of the few places in XSLT where the default namespace is used to expand a QName having no prefix: in nearly all other cases, a null namespace URI is used. The reason is to ensure that the behavior is consistent with that for an element name used in the start tag of a literal result element.

The generated element node will automatically contain all the namespace declarations it needs to define the prefixes used on its own name and on the names of all its attributes.

Generating Attributes

If the use-attribute-sets attribute is present it must be a whitespace-separated list of QNames that identify named <xsl:attribute-set> elements in the stylesheet. The attributes within these named attribute sets are instantiated in the order they appear, and are added to the new element node. If two attributes with the same name are added during this process, the last one added overwrites any earlier ones.

Subsequently, further attribute nodes may be added to the element using <xsl:attribute>. The <xsl:attribute> instruction will often be a child of the <xsl:element> instruction, but it does not need to be; it could be invoked, for example, by using <xsl:call-template>. Once a node other than an attribute node is added to the element (typically a text node or a child element node), no further attributes can be added.

> *The reason for this rule is to allow the implementation the flexibility to generate the output as an XML file, without having to build the result tree in memory first. If attributes could be added at any time, the whole result tree would need to be kept in memory.*

Again, if any attribute is added with the same name as an attribute already present on the element node, the new value takes precedence.

Element Content

The contents of the new element, that is, its child and descendant nodes, are the nodes produced by instantiating the template-body contained in the <xsl:element> instruction.

Usage

In most cases, output elements can be generated either using literal result elements in the stylesheet, or by copying a node from the source document using <xsl:copy>.

The only situations where <xsl:element> is absolutely needed are therefore where the element type in the output file is not fixed, and is not the same as the element type in the source document.

Using <xsl:element> rather than a literal result element can also be useful where different namespaces are in use. It allows the namespace URI of the generated element to be specified explicitly, rather than being referenced via a prefix. This means the namespace does not have to be present in the stylesheet itself, thus giving greater control over exactly which elements the namespace declarations are attached to.

Example: Converting Attributes to Child Elements

Source

The source document `book.xml` contains a single `<book>` element with several attributes:

```xml
<?xml version="1.0"?>
<book title="Object-oriented Languages"
    author="Michel Beaudouin-Lafon"
    translator="Jack Howlett"
    publisher="Chapman &amp; Hall"
    isbn="0 412 55800 9"
    date="1994"/>
```

Stylesheet

The stylesheet `atts-to-elements.xsl` handles the book element by processing each of the attributes in turn (the expression «@*» selects all the attribute nodes): for each one, it outputs an element whose name is the same as the attribute name and whose content is the same as the attribute value.

The stylesheet is as follows:

```xml
<xsl:transform
  xmlns:xsl="http://www.w3.org/1999/XSL/Transform"
  version="1.0"
>
<xsl:output indent="yes"/>
<xsl:template match="book">
  <book>
      <xsl:for-each select="@*">
        <xsl:element name="{name()}">
        <xsl:value-of select="."/>
        </xsl:element>
      </xsl:for-each>
  </book>
</xsl:template>
</xsl:transform>
```

This selects all the attribute of the `<book>` element (using the expression «@*»), and for each one, it generates an element whose name is the same as the name of that attribute, and whose content is the value of that attribute.

Output

The XML output (from Saxon) as shown below. Actually, this stylesheet isn't guaranteed to produce exactly this output. This is because the order of attributes is undefined. This means that the `<xsl:for-each>` loop might process the attributes in any order, so the order of child elements in the output is also unpredictable.

```
<book>
    <author>Michel Beaudouin-Lafon</author>
    <date>1994</date>
    <isbn>0 412 55800 9</isbn>
    <publisher>Chapman &amp; Hall</publisher>
    <title>Object-oriented Languages</title>
    <translator>Jack Howlett</translator>
</book>
```

See also

<xsl:attribute> on page 155
<xsl:copy> on page 180
Literal Result Elements in Chapter 3, page 109

xsl:fallback

The <xsl:fallback> instruction is used to define processing that should occur if no implementation of its parent instruction is available.

Defined in

XSLT section 15

Format

```
<xsl:fallback>
    template-body
</xsl:fallback>
```

Position

<xsl:fallback> is an instruction. It is always used within a template-body.

Attributes

None.

Content

A template-body.

Effect

There are two circumstances where <xsl:fallback> can be useful:

❑ In a stylesheet that uses XSLT features defined in a version later than 1.0, to indicate what should happen if the stylesheet is used with an XSLT processor that implements an earlier version of the standard (for example, version 1.0). This facility will not be useful until a later version of XSLT is defined, but it has been specified now to ensure that XSLT version 1.0 implementations support this mechanism.

❑ In a stylesheet that uses extension elements provided by a vendor, by the user, or by a third party, to indicate what should happen if the stylesheet is used with an XSLT processor that does not support these extensions.

If the `<xsl:fallback>` instruction is encountered in a template body that the processor can instantiate normally, it is ignored, along with its contents.

An XSLT processor recognizes an element as an instruction if it occurs in a template body **and** it is:

❑ either in the XSLT namespace,

❑ or in a namespace designated as an extension namespace by its inclusion in:

  ❑ the `extension-element-prefixes` attribute of the `<xsl:stylesheet>` element

  ❑ or the `xsl:extension-element-prefixes` attribute of the element itself, or of a containing literal result element or extension element.

If an element recognized as an instruction is known to the XSLT processor, it is instantiated. Exactly what "known to the XSLT processor" means is implementation-dependent. Typically it means that either the instruction is a vendor-specific extension implemented by that vendor, or it is a user-defined extension that has been installed or configured according to the instructions given by the vendor.

If an element is recognized as an instruction but is **not** known to the XSLT processor, the action taken is as follows:

❑ For an element in the XSLT namespace, if the effective version is «1.0», an error is reported. If the effective version is anything other than «1.0», fallback processing is invoked.

❑ For an extension element, fallback processing is invoked.

The effective version is the value of the `xsl:version` attribute on the nearest enclosing literal result element that has such an attribute, or the `version` attribute on the `<xsl:stylesheet>` element otherwise. It isn't made clear whether the comparison is a string comparison or a numeric one, so it's safest to write the version number strictly as «1.0», and not for example «1» or «1.00». The idea is that a stylesheet, or a portion of a stylesheet, that uses facilities defined in some future XSLT version, 2.1 (say), should be given an effective version of «2.1».

Fallback processing means that if the unknown instruction has an <xsl:fallback> child element, the <xsl:fallback> instruction is instantiated; otherwise, an error is reported.

<xsl:fallback> is concerned only with fallback behavior for instructions within templates. Top level elements that the implementation doesn't recognize are simply ignored. An unrecognized element in another context (for example, an unrecognized child of an <xsl:choose> or <xsl:call-template> instruction) is an error.

Note that both the version (or xsl:version) attribute and the extension-element-prefixes (or xsl:extension-element-prefixes) attribute apply only within the stylesheet module in which they occur: they do not apply to stylesheet modules incorporated using <xsl:include> or <xsl:import>.

Usage

When a future version of XSLT appears, the <xsl:fallback> mechanism will allow a stylesheet to be written that behaves sensibly in different environments. This is motivated very much by the experience of web developers with HTML, and especially by the difficulty of writing web pages that work correctly on different browsers. Once XSLT support becomes widespread within browsers, you will need to think about how to ensure that your stylesheet runs correctly in any browser.

Similarly, it is very likely that each vendor of an XSLT processor (or each browser vendor) will add some bells and whistles of their own – indeed, this is already happening. For server-side stylesheet processing you might be prepared to use such proprietary extensions and thus lock yourself into the products of one vendor; but more likely, you want to keep your stylesheets portable. The <xsl:fallback> mechanism allows you to do this, by defining within any proprietary extension element what the XSLT processor should do if it doesn't understand it. This might be, for example:

❑   do nothing, if the behavior is inessential, such as keeping statistics

❑   invoke an alternative implementation that achieves the same effect

❑   output fallback text to the user explaining that a particular facility cannot be offered and suggesting how they should upgrade.

An alternative way of defining fallback behavior when facilities are not available is to use the element-available() function, and to avoid executing the relevant parts of a stylesheet. This function is described in Chapter 7, page 449. The two mechanisms are overlapping: use whichever you find most convenient.

Examples

Example 1: XSLT Forwards Compatibility

The following example shows a stylesheet written to exploit a hypothetical new XSLT feature in version 6.1 of the standard that inserts a document identified by URI straight into the result tree (this is one of the features that appears in the list of possible enhancements published as an appendix to the standard). The stylesheet is written so that if this feature is not available, the same effect is achieved using existing facilities.

199

```
<xsl:template match="boilerplate"/>
  <div id="boilerplate" xsl:version="6.1">
     <xsl:copy-to-output href="boilerplate.xhtml">
        <xsl:fallback>
           <xsl:copy-of select="document('boilerplate.xhtml')"/>
        </xsl:fallback>
     </xsl:copy-to-output>
  </div>
</xsl:template>
```

Example 2: Vendor Portability

Writing a stylesheet that uses vendor extensions but is still portable is not particularly easy, but the mechanisms are there to achieve it, especially in the case where several vendors provide similar extensions but in slightly different ways.

For example, several products (certainly xt, Saxon, and Xalan) provide a feature to generate multiple output files from a single stylesheet. This facility isn't in the XSLT standard, so unsurprisingly, each product has invented its own syntax. If you want to write a stylesheet that works with all three products you could do it like this:

```
<xsl:template match="preface">
<a href="preface.html"
     xmlns:saxon="http://icl.com/saxon"
     xmlns:xt="http://www.jclark.com/xt"
     xmlns:xalan="com.lotus.xsl.extensions.Redirect"
     xsl:extension-element-prefixes="saxon xt xalan">
  <saxon:output file="preface.html">
     <xsl:call-template name="write-preface"/>
     <xsl:fallback/>
  </saxon:output>
  <xt:document href="preface.html">
     <xsl:call-template name="write-preface"/>
     <xsl:fallback/>
  </xt:document>
  <xalan:write file="preface.html">
     <xsl:call-template name="write-preface"/>
     <xsl:fallback/>
  </xalan:write>
Preface</a>
</xsl:template>
```

Hopefully with the next version of the XSLT Recommendation this little nightmare will disappear: support for multiple output files is high on the shopping list of new facilities. However, by then the vendors, no doubt, will have thought of other good ideas to include as non-standard extensions.

See also

Extensibility in Chapter 3, page 121
Literal result elements in Chapter 3, page 109
element-available() function in Chapter 7, page 449

xsl:for-each

The `<xsl:for-each>` instruction selects a set of nodes using an XPath expression, and performs the same processing for each node in the set.

Defined in

XSLT section 8

Format

```
<xsl:for-each select=Expression>
    <xsl:sort> *
    template-body
</xsl:for-each>
```

Position

`<xsl:for-each>` is an instruction, it is always used within a template body.

Attributes

Name	Value	Meaning
select mandatory	Expression returning a node-set	The set of nodes to be processed

Content

Zero or more `<xsl:sort>` elements, followed by a template body.

Effect

The effect of the `<xsl:for-each>` instruction is to instantiate the template body that it contains once for each node in the selected node-set. The following sections describe how this is done.

The select Attribute

The `select` attribute is mandatory. The `Expression` defines the nodes that will be processed. This may be any XPath expression, as defined in Chapter 5, so long as it returns a node-set. The expression may select nodes relative to the current node (the node currently being processed) or it may make an absolute selection from the root node, or it may simply select the nodes by reference to a variable initialized earlier. By using the `document()` function (described in Chapter 7, page 440) it may also select the root node of another XML document.

The template body contained within the `<xsl:for-each>` element is instantiated once for each node selected. Within this template body, the current node is the node being processed (one of the selected nodes); the `position()` function gives the position of that node in order of processing (the first node processed has `position()`=1, and so on), and the `last()` function gives the number of nodes being processed.

Sorting

If there are no child <xsl:sort> elements, the selected nodes are processed in *document order*. In the normal case where the nodes all come from the same input document this means they will be processed in the order they are encountered in the original source document: for example, an element node is processed before its children. Attribute nodes belonging to the same element, however, may be processed in any order. If there are nodes from several different documents in the list, the relative order of nodes from different documents is not defined (and may therefore differ from one product to another).

If there are one or more <xsl:sort> elements as children of the <xsl:apply-templates> instruction, the nodes are sorted before processing. Each <xsl:sort> element defines one sort key. For details of how sorting is controlled, see <xsl:sort> on page 272. If there are several sort keys defined, they apply in major-to-minor order. For example if the first <xsl:sort> defines sorting by Country and the second by State, then the nodes will be processed in order of State within Country. If two selected nodes have equal sort keys, they will be processed in document order.

Note that the ordering of the axis used to select the nodes is irrelevant (The various axes, and the way they are ordered, are described in Chapter 5.) For example, «select="preceding-sibling::*"» will process the preceding siblings of the current node in document order (starting with the first sibling) even though the preceding-sibling axis is in reverse document order. The axis ordering affects only the meaning of any positional qualifiers used within the select expression. For example, «preceding-sibling::*[1]» will select the first preceding sibling element in axis order – that is, the element immediately before the current node, if there is one. If you want to process the nodes in reverse document order, specify:

```
<xsl:sort select="position()" order="descending">
```

Usage and Examples

The main purpose of <xsl:for-each> is to iterate over a set of nodes. It can also be used, however, simply to change the current node. These two styles of use are illustrated in the following sections.

Iterating Over a Set of Nodes

The principal use of <xsl:for-each> is to iterate over a set of nodes. As such it provides an alternative to <xsl:apply-templates>. Which you use is largely a matter of personal style: arguably <xsl:apply-templates> (*push* processing) ties the stylesheet less strongly to the detailed structure of the source document and makes it easier to write a stylesheet that can accommodate some flexibility in the structures that will be encountered, while <xsl:for-each> (*pull* processing) makes the logic clearer to the reader. It may even improve performance because it bypasses the need to identify template rules by pattern matching, though the effect is likely to be very small.

The following example processes all the attributes of the current element node, writing them out as elements to the result tree. This example is presented in greater detail under <xsl:element> on page 192.

```
<xsl:template match="book">
   <book>
      <xsl:for-each select="@*">
         <xsl:element name="{name()}">
            <xsl:value-of select="."/>
         </xsl:element>
      </xsl:for-each>
   </book>
</xsl:template>
```

The next example is a general one that can be applied to any XML document.

Example: Showing the Ancestors of a Node

The following example stylesheet can be applied to any XML document. For each element it processes all its ancestor elements, in reverse document order (that is, starting with the parent node and ending with the document element), and outputs their names to a comment that shows the position of the current node.

Source

This stylesheet can be applied to any source document.

Stylesheet

This stylesheet is in file nesting.xsl.

```
<xsl:transform
 xmlns:xsl="http://www.w3.org/1999/XSL/Transform"
 version="1.0"
>
<xsl:template match="*">
   <xsl:comment>
      <xsl:value-of select="name()"/>
      <xsl:for-each select="ancestor::*">
         <xsl:sort select="position()" order="descending"/>
         <xsl:text> within </xsl:text>
         <xsl:value-of select="name()"/>
      </xsl:for-each>
   </xsl:comment>
   <xsl:apply-templates/>
</xsl:template>

</xsl:transform>
```

Output

An example of the output this might produce is:

4

Elements

```
<!--BOOKS within BOOKLIST-->
  <!--ITEM within BOOKS within BOOKLIST-->
  <!--TITLE within ITEM within BOOKS within BOOKLIST-->Number, the
                                      Language of Science
  <!--AUTHOR within ITEM within BOOKS within BOOKLIST-->Danzig
  <!--PRICE within ITEM within BOOKS within BOOKLIST-->5.95
  <!--QUANTITY within ITEM within BOOKS within BOOKLIST-->3
```

Changing the Current Node

Another use of <xsl:for-each> is simply to change the current node. For example, if you want to use the key() function (described in Chapter 7, page 469) to locate nodes in some ancillary document, you must first establish some node in that document (typically the root) as the current node, because the key() function will only find nodes in the same document as the current node.

For example, you might write:

```
<xsl:variable name="county">
  <xsl:for-each select="document('county-code.xml')">
    <xsl:value-of select="key('county-code', $code)/@name"/>
  </xsl:for-each>
</xsl:variable>
```

The effect is to assign to the variable the value of the name attribute of the first element whose county-code key matches the value of the $code variable.

The <xsl:for-each> statement here selects a single node, because the document() function when used like this will return at most one node. We don't even use the node that it returns; the only effect is to make this the current node, which affects the result of the key() function.

See also

<xsl:apply-templates> on page 145.
<xsl:sort> on page 272.
document() function in Chapter 7, page 440.
key() function in Chapter 7, page 469.

xsl:if

The <xsl:if> instruction encloses a template body that will be instantiated only if a specified condition is true.

<xsl:if> is analogous to the *if* statement found in many programming languages. There is no else branch: if you need one, use the <xsl:choose> instruction described on page 176.

Defined in

XSLT section 9.1

Format

```
<xsl:if test=Expression >
   template-body
</xsl:if>
```

Position

`<xsl:if>` is an instruction. It is always used within a template body.

Attributes

Name	Value	Meaning
test mandatory	Expression	The Boolean condition to be tested

Content

A template-body.

Effect

The test expression is evaluated and the result is converted if necessary to a Boolean using the rules defined for the `boolean()` function. If the result is true, the contained template-body is instantiated; otherwise, no action is taken.

Any XPath value may be converted to a Boolean. In brief, the rules are:

❑   if the expression is a node-set, it is treated as true if the node-set contains at least one node.

❑   if the expression is a string or a result tree fragment, it is treated as true if the string is not empty.

❑   if the expression is a number, it is treated as true if the number is non-zero.

Usage

The `<xsl:if>` instruction is useful where an action is to be performed conditionally. It performs the functions of the if-then construct found in other programming languages. If there are two or more alternative actions (the equivalent of an if-then-else or switch or Select Case in other languages), use `<xsl:choose>` instead.

One common use of `<xsl:if>` is to test for error conditions. In this case it is often used with `<xsl:message>`.

Examples

The following example outputs an `<hr>` element after processing the last of a sequence of `<para>` elements:

```
<xsl:template match="para">
   <p><xsl:apply-templates/></p>
   <xsl:if test="position()=last()">
      <hr/>
   </xsl:if>
</xsl:template>
```

The following example reports an error if the `percent` attribute of the current element is not a number between 0 and 100. The expression returns true if:

❑   that the `percent` attribute does not exist, or

❑   the value cannot be interpreted as a number (so that «`number(@percent)`» is NaN), or

❑   the numeric value is less than zero, or

❑   the numeric value is greater than 100

```
<xsl:if test="not(@percent) or
                (string(number(@percent))='NaN') or
                (number(@percent) &lt; 0) or
                (number(@percent) &gt; 100)">
   <xsl:message>
      percent attribute must be a number between 0 and 100
   </xsl:message>
</xsl:if>
```

The following example formats a list of names, using `<xsl:if>` to produce punctuation that depends on the position of each name in the list.

Example: Formatting a List of Names

Source

The source file `authors.xml` contains a single `<book>` element with a list of authors.

```
<?xml version="1.0"?>
<book>
     <title>Design Patterns</title>
     <author>Erich Gamma</author>
     <author>Richard Helm</author>
     <author>Ralph Johnson</author>
     <author>John Vlissides</author>
</book>
```

Stylesheet

The stylesheet `authors.xsl` processes the list of authors, adding punctuation depending on the position of each author in the list.

```
<xsl:transform
 xmlns:xsl="http://www.w3.org/1999/XSL/Transform"
 version="1.0"
>

<xsl:template match="book">
  <xsl:value-of select="title"/>
  by <xsl:for-each select="author">
    <xsl:value-of select="."/>
    <xsl:if test="position()!=last()">, </xsl:if>
    <xsl:if test="position()=last()-1">and </xsl:if>
</xsl:for-each>
</xsl:template>

</xsl:transform>
```

Output

```
Design Patterns
by Erich Gamma, Richard Helm, Ralph Johnson, and John Vlissides
```

See also

`<xsl:choose>` on page 176

xsl:import

`<xsl:import>` is a top-level element used to import the contents of one stylesheet module into another. The definitions in the importing stylesheet module have a higher *import precedence* than those in the imported module, which usually means that they will be used in preference; but the detailed rules vary for each top-level element type.

Defined in

XSLT section 2.6.2

Format

```
<xsl:import href=uri />
```

Position

`<xsl:import>` is a top-level element, which means that it must appear as a child of the `<xsl:stylesheet>` element. Within an `<xsl:stylesheet>` element, the `<xsl:import>` child elements must come before any other children.

207

Attributes

Name	Value	Meaning
href mandatory	URI	The URI of the stylesheet to be imported

Content

None; the element is always empty.

Effect

The URI contained in the href attribute may be an absolute URI or a relative URI. If relative, it is interpreted relative to the the base URI of the XML document or external entity containing the <xsl:import> element. For example, if a file main.xsl contains the element <xsl:import href="date.xsl"/> then the system will look for date.xsl in the same directory as main.xsl.

The URI must identify an XML document that is a valid XSLT stylesheet. The top level elements of this stylesheet are logically inserted into the including stylesheet at the point where the <xsl:import> element appears. However:

❑ Imported top-level elements have a lower *import precedence* than the top-level elements defined directly in the importing stylesheet, or incorporated into it using <xsl:include>. This is explained in more detail below.

❑ Imported elements retain their base URI, so anything that involves referencing a relative URI is done relative to the original URI of the imported stylesheet. This includes, for example, expansion of further <xsl:import> elements, or use of URIs as arguments to the document() function.

❑ When a namespace prefix is used (typically within a QName, but it also applies to freestanding prefixes such as those in the xsl:exclude-result-prefixes attribute of a literal result element) is it is interpreted using only the namespace declarations in the original stylesheet module in which the QName occurred. An imported stylesheet module does not inherit namespace declarations from the module that imports it. This includes QNames constructed at execution time as the result of evaluating an expression, for example an expression used within an attribute value template for the name or namespace attribute of <xsl:element>.

❑ The values of the version, extension-element-prefixes, and exclude-result-prefixes attributes that apply to an element in the included stylesheet, as well as xml:lang and xml:space, are those that were defined in the <xsl:stylesheet> element of their own stylesheet module, not those on the <xsl:stylesheet> element of the importing module.

The imported stylesheet module may use the *literal-result-element-as-stylesheet* syntax described in Chapter 3. This allows an entire module to be defined as the content of an element such as <HTML>. It is then treated as if it were a stylesheet module containing a single template, whose match pattern is «/» and whose content is the literal result element.

The imported stylesheet module may contain `<xsl:include>` statements to include further stylesheet modules, or `<xsl:import>` statements to import them. A stylesheet module must not directly or indirectly import itself.

It is not an error to import the same stylesheet module more than once, either directly or indirectly, but it is not usually a useful thing to do. The effect is that the same definitions or templates will be present with several different import precedences. The situation is exactly the same as if two stylesheet modules with different names but identical contents had been imported.

Import Precedence

Each stylesheet module that is imported has an import precedence. The rules are:

- ❑ The precedence of a module that is imported is always lower than the precedence of the module importing it

- ❑ If one module imports several others, then the one it imports first has lower precedence than the next, and so on.

This means that in the structure shown here, the highest precedence module is A; after that C, then F, then B, then E and finally D.

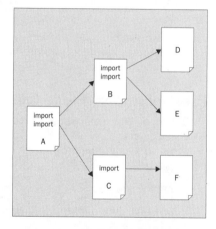

If one stylesheet module incorporates another using `<xsl:include>` rather than `<xsl:import>`, then it has the same import precedence as the module that includes it. This is shown in the next diagram.

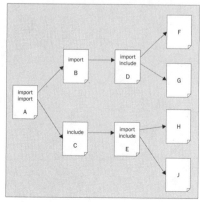

Here J is included in E, so it has the same import precedence as E, and similarly E has the same import precedence as C. If we attach numeric values to the import precedence to indicate the ordering (the absolute values don't matter, the only significance is that a higher number indicates higher precedence) we could do so as follows:

A	B	C	D	E	F	G	H	J
6	3	5	2	5	1	2	4	5

The import precedence of a stylesheet module applies to all the top-level elements in that module, so for example the `<xsl:template>` elements in module E have a higher import precedence than those in G.

As `<xsl:import>` statements must occur before any other top-level elements in a stylesheet module, the effect of these rules is that if each `<xsl:import>` statement were to be replaced by the content of the module it imports, the top-level elements in the resulting combined stylesheet would be in increasing order of import precedence. This makes life rather easier for implementers. However, it does not mean that `<xsl:import>` is a straightforward textual substitution process, because there is still a need to distinguish cases where two objects (for example template rules) have the same import precedence because they came originally from the same stylesheet or from stylesheets that were included rather than imported.

Effect of Import Precedence

The import precedence of a top-level element affects its standing relative to other top-level elements of the same type, and may be used to resolve conflicts. The effect is as shown in the table below for each kind of top-level element.

Element type	Rules
`<xsl:attribute-set>`	If there are two attribute sets with the same expanded name, they are merged. If there is an attribute that is present in both, then the one from the attribute set with higher import precedence wins. It is an error if there is no clear winner from this process (that is, if there are two or more values for the attribute that have the same precedence, and this is the highest precedence). The XSLT processor has the choice of reporting the error or choosing the one that was specified last. The attribute-sets named in the use-attribute-sets attributes of the two merged attribute sets are also merged, but the specification does not give precise details of how this should be done

Element type	Rules
`<xsl:decimal-format>`	The import precedence of an `<xsl:decimal-format>` element is of no significance. It is an error to include more than one `<xsl:decimal-format>` element with the same name (or, presumably, with no name) unless the definitions are equivalent. On this occasion the XSLT processor is required to report the error.
`<xsl:import>` and `<xsl:include>`	No conflicts arise; the import precedence of these elements is immaterial, except in determining the import precedence of the referenced stylesheet module.
`<xsl:key>`	All the key definitions are used, regardless of their import precedence. See `<xsl:key>` on page 222 for details.
`<xsl:namespace-alias>`	If several aliases for the same stylesheet prefix are defined, the one with the highest import precedence is used. It is an error if there is no clear winner. The XSLT processor has the choice of reporting the error or choosing the one that was specified last.
`<xsl:output>`	All the `<xsl:output>` elements in the stylesheet are effectively merged. In the case of the cdata-section-elements attribute, an element is output in CDATA format if it is declared as such on any of the `<xsl:output>` elements. For all the other attributes, if the value is explicitly present on more than one `<xsl:output>` element then the one with highest import precedence wins. It is an error if there is no clear winner. The XSLT processor has the choice of reporting the error or choosing the one that was specified last.
`<xsl:strip-space>` and `<xsl:preserve-space>`	If there is more than one `<xsl:strip-space>` or `<xsl:preserve-space>` element that matches a particular element name in the source document, then the one with highest import precedence is used. If this still leaves several that match, each one is assigned a priority, using the same rules as for the match pattern in `<xsl:template>`. Specifically, an explicit QName has higher priority than the form «prefix:*», which in turn has higher priority than «*». The one with highest priority is then used.

4

Elements

Element type	Rules
	It is an error if this leaves more than one match. The XSLT processor has the choice of reporting the error or choosing the one that was specified last. (The specification says that this rule is used to resolve conflicts. It could be argued that specifying the same element name in two different `<xsl:strip-space>` elements, or in two different `<xsl:preserve-space>` elements, is not a conflict: but don't rely on it.)
	If there are no matches for an element, whitespace nodes are preserved.
`<xsl:template>`	When selecting a template rule for use with `<xsl:apply-templates>`, firstly all the template rules with a matching mode are taken. Of these, all those with a match pattern that matches the selected node are considered. If this leaves more than one, only those with the highest import precedence are considered. If this still leaves more than one, the one with highest priority is chosen: the rules for deciding the priority are given under `<xsl:template>` on page 288. It is an error if this still doesn't identify a clear winner. The XSLT processor has the choice of reporting the error or choosing the template rule that was specified last.
	When selecting a template for use with `<xsl:call-template>`, all the named templates with a matching name are considered. If there are several, the one with highest import precedence is used. It is an error to have several named templates with the same name and the same import precedence: the XSLT processor is required to report this error, even if the templates are never referenced.
`<xsl:variable>` and `<xsl:param>`	In resolving a VariableReference in an expression or pattern, the XSLT processor first tries to find a matching local variable or parameter definition, that is, one defined in a template. If it can't find one that is in scope, it looks for a global variable or parameter – that is, a top-level `<xsl:variable>` or `<xsl:param>` element with the same expanded name as the VariableReference. This may occur anywhere in the stylesheet, either in the same module or in a different module, and there is no restriction on forward references. If there is more than one global variable or parameter that matches, the one with highest import precedence is used. (The specification doesn't actually say this explicitly, but the implication is clear enough.)

Element type	Rules
	It is an error to have more than one global variable or parameter in the stylesheet with the same expanded name and the same import precedence. This is true even if the variable is never referenced, or if it is masked by another variable of the same name with higher import precedence. The XSLT processor must report this error.

Usage

The rules for `<xsl:import>` are so pervasive that one would imagine the facility is central to the use of XSLT, rather in the way inheritance is central to writing in Java. In practice, however, many stylesheets never need to use `<xsl:import>`, and most of those that do are likely to use it in a very simple way. It is an advanced feature needed only in the more demanding of applications.

Like inheritance in object-oriented languages, `<xsl:import>` is designed to allow the creation of a library or reusable components, only in this case, the components are fragments of stylesheets. And the mechanism works in a very similar way to inheritance. For example, you might have a stylesheet that simply defines your corporate color scheme, as a set of global variables defining color names. Another stylesheet might be defined to produce the basic framesets for your site, referring to these color names to supply the background detail. Now if you want to use this general structure but to vary some detail, for example to modify one of the colors because it clashes with an image you are displaying on a particular page, you can define a stylesheet for this particular page that does nothing apart from redefining that one color. This is illustrated in the diagram below.

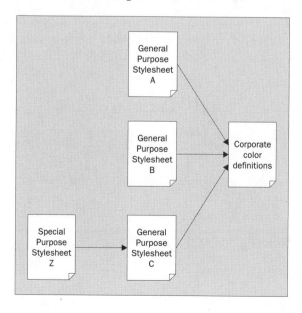

Suppose the stylesheet module for corporate color definitions looks like this:

```
<xsl:stylesheet xmlns:xsl="http://www.w3.org/1999/XSL/Transform"
    xmlns:color="http://acme.co.nz/colors"
        version="1.0">
<xsl:variable name="color:blue" select="'#0088ff'"/>
<xsl:variable name="color:pink" select="'#ff0088'"/>
<xsl:variable name="color:lilac" select="'#ff00ff'"/>
</xsl:stylesheet>
```

Now all the general-purpose stylesheets could <xsl:include> these definitions (no need to <xsl:import> them unless they are being modified). This makes it easier to maintain the corporate brand image, because things are defined in one place only.

However, there are cases where we want to depart from the general rule, and we can do so quite easily. If a particular document wants to use stylesheet C, but needs to vary the colors used, we can define stylesheet Z for it, as follows:

```
<xsl:stylesheet xmlns:xsl="http://www.w3.org/1999/XSL/Transform"
    xmlns:color="http://acme.co.nz/colors"
        version="1.0">
<xsl:import href="general-stylesheet-C.xsl"/>
<xsl:variable name="color:lilac" select="'#cc00cc'"/>
</xsl:stylesheet>
```

In fact, this might be the entire stylesheet (apart from the <xsl:stylesheet> element, of course). In common English, style Z is the same as style C but with a different shade of lilac. Note that all the references to variable «color:lilac» are interpreted as references to the definition in Z, even if the references occur in the same stylesheet module as a different definition of «color:lilac».

As a general principle, to incorporate standard content into a stylesheet without change, use <xsl:include>. If there are definitions you want to override, use <xsl:import>.

Examples

The first example is designed to show the effect of <xsl:import> on variables.

Example 1: Precedence of Variables

This example demonstrates the precedence of global variables when the principal stylesheet module and an imported module declared variables with the same name.

Source

This example can be run with any source XML file.

Stylesheet

The principal stylesheet module is `variables.xsl`.

```
<?xml version="1.0" encoding="iso-8859-1"?>
<xsl:stylesheet version="1.0"
    xmlns:xsl="http://www.w3.org/1999/XSL/Transform"
    xmlns:acme="http://acme.com/xslt"
    exclude-result-prefixes="acme">

<xsl:import href="boilerplate.xsl"/>
<xsl:output encoding="iso-8859-1" indent="yes"/>

<xsl:variable name="acme:company-name" select="'Acme Widgets Limited'"/>

<xsl:template match="/">
<c><xsl:value-of select="$acme:copyright"/></c>
</xsl:template>

</xsl:stylesheet>
```

The imported stylesheet module is `boilerplate.xsl`:

```
<?xml version="1.0" encoding="iso-8859-1"?>
<xsl:stylesheet version="1.0"
                 xmlns:xsl="http://www.w3.org/1999/XSL/Transform"
                 xmlns:co="http://acme.com/xslt">

<xsl:variable name="co:company-name" select="'Acme Widgets Incorporated'"/>

<xsl:variable name="co:copyright"
                 select="concat('Copyright © ', $co:company-name)"/>

</xsl:stylesheet>
```

Output

The output of this stylesheet will be:

```
<?xml version="1.0" encoding="iso-8859-1" ?>
<c>Copyright © Acme Widgets Limited</c>
```

This is because in the variable declaration of «$co:copyright», the reference to variable «$co:company-name» matches the declaration of this variable in the principal stylesheet, because that has higher import precedence than the declaration in `boilerplate.xsl`.

The fact that different namespace prefixes are used in the two stylesheets is, of course, irrelevant: the prefix «acme» in the principal stylesheet maps to the same namespace URI as the prefix «co» in `boilerplate.xsl`, so the names are considered equivalent.

215

This example explicitly specifies encoding="iso-8859-1" for both the stylesheet modules and the output. Most of my examples only use ASCII characters, and since the default character encoding UTF-8 is a superset of ASCII, that works fine. This time, though, I've used the symbol «©», which is not an ASCII character, so it's important to specify the character encoding that my text editor uses, which is iso-8859-1 (actually it's the Microsoft variant of it known as Windows ANSI, but that's close enough not to make a difference).

The second example shows the effect of `<xsl:import>` on template rules.

Example 2: Precedence of Template Rules

In this example I shall define a complete stylesheet standard-style.xsl to display poems in HTML, and then override one of its rules in an importing stylesheet. The files required are all in the subdirectory import in the download file for this chapter.

Source

This example works with the poem that we used in Chapter 1. In the download file it's available as poem.xml. It starts like this:

```
<?xml version="1.0"?>
<poem>
<author>Rupert Brooke</author>
<date>1912</date>
<title>Song</title>
<stanza>
<line>And suddenly the wind comes soft,</line>
<line>And Spring is here again;</line>
<line>And the hawthorn quickens with buds of green</line>
<line>And my heart with buds of pain.</line>
</stanza>
etc.
</poem>
```

Stylesheet A

Here is standard-style.xsl:

```
<xsl:stylesheet version="1.0"
                xmlns:xsl="http://www.w3.org/1999/XSL/Transform">

<xsl:template match="/">
   <html>
   <head>
   <title><xsl:value-of select="//title"/></title>
   </head>
   <body>
```

```
          <xsl:apply-templates/>
      </body>
      </html>
</xsl:template>

<xsl:template match="title">
    <h1><xsl:apply-templates/></h1>
</xsl:template>

<xsl:template match="author">
    <div align="right"><i>by </i>
        <xsl:apply-templates/>
    </div>
</xsl:template>

<xsl:template match="stanza">
    <p><xsl:apply-templates/></p>
</xsl:template>

<xsl:template match="line">
    <xsl:apply-templates/><br/>
</xsl:template>

<xsl:template match="date"/>
</xsl:stylesheet>
```

Output A

When you run this stylesheet, the output starts like this (the actual layout may vary, of course, depending on which XSLT processor you use).

```
<html>
    <head>
    <title>Song</title>
    </head>
    <body>
        <div align="right"><i>by </i>Rupert Brooke</div>
        <h1>Song</h1>
        <p>
            And suddenly the wind comes soft,<br>
            And Spring is here again;<br>
            And the hawthorn quickens with buds of green<br>
            And my heart with buds of pain.<br>
        </p>
```

Stylesheet B

Now we want to create a variant of this in which the lines of the poem are numbered. This will act as the principal style sheet when we want this form of output. Here it is in `numbered-style.xsl`:

4

Elements

```
<xsl:stylesheet version="1.0"
                    xmlns:xsl="http://www.w3.org/1999/XSL/Transform">

<xsl:import href="standard-style.xsl"/>

<xsl:template match="line">
    <xsl:number level="any" format="001"/>  
    <xsl:apply-imports/>
</xsl:template>

</xsl:stylesheet>
```

Note the use of the character reference « » to output a non-breaking space. In HTML this is normally done by writing « ». You can use this entity reference in the stylesheet if you like (it's simply a symbolic name for the Unicode character #xa0), but only if you declare it as an entity in the DTD. It's usually simpler just to use the numeric character reference.

Output B

This time the output starts like this. Again, the precise format depends on the processor (for example, some processors may output « »; or « » instead of « ») but it should look the same when displayed in the browser.

```
<html>
    <head>
    <title>Song</title>
    </head>
    <body>
        <div align="right"><i>by </i>Rupert Brooke</div>
        <h1>Song</h1>
        <p>
            001  
            And suddenly the wind comes soft,<br>
            002  
            And Spring is here again;<br>
            003  
            And the hawthorn quickens with buds of green<br>
            004  
            And my heart with buds of pain.<br>
        </p>
```

All the template rules defined in standard-style.xsl are used as normal, except where the current node matches the pattern «line». In this situation there are two possible templates that match the node, so the one with higher import precedence is chosen. This is the one in the importing stylesheet module, namely numbered-style.xsl. As a result, the lines of the poem are output with a preceding line number, calculated using the <xsl:number> instruction, which is described on page 237. The use of <xsl:apply-imports> means that once the line number has been output, the line is then displayed in the normal way, using the template rule from the standard-style.xsl stylesheet.

See also

<xsl:include>
<xsl:apply-imports> on page 142

xsl:include

<xsl:include> is a top-level element used to include the contents of one stylesheet module within another. The definitions in the included stylesheet modulehave the same *import precedence* as those in the including module, so the effect is exactly as if these definitions were textually included at the point in the including module where the <xsl:include> element appears.

Defined in

XSLT section 2.6.1

Format

<xsl:include href=uri />

Position

<xsl:include> is a top-level element, which means that it must appear as a child of the <xsl:stylesheet> element. There are no constraints on its ordering relative to other top-level elements in the stylesheet.

Attributes

Name	Value	Meaning
href mandatory	URI	The URI of the stylesheet to be included

Content

None; the element is always empty.

Effect

The URI contained in the href attribute may be an absolute URI or a relative URI. If relative, it is interpreted relative to the the base URI of the XML document or external entity containing the <xsl:include> element. For example, if a file main.xsl contains the element <xsl:include href="date.xsl"/> then the system will look for date.xsl in the same directory as main.xsl.

The URI must identify an XML document that is a valid XSLT stylesheet. The top level elements of this stylesheet are logically inserted into the including stylesheet module at the point where the <xsl:include> element appears. However:

❑ These elements retain their base URI, so anything that involves referencing a relative URI is done relative to the original URI of the included stylesheet. This rule applies, for example, when expanding further `<xsl:include>` and `<xsl:import>` elements, or when using relative URIs as arguments to the `document()` function.

❑ When a namespace prefix is used (typically within a `QName`, but it also applies to freestanding prefixes such as those in the `xsl:exclude-result-prefixes` attribute of a literal result element) is it is interpreted using only the namespace declarations in the original stylesheet module in which the `QName` occurred. An included stylesheet module does not inherit namespace declarations from the module that includes it. This even applies to `QNames` constructed at execution time as the result of evaluating an expression, for example an expression used within an attribute value template for the `name` or `namespace` attribute of `<xsl:element>`.

❑ The values of the `version`, `extension-element-prefixes`, and `exclude-result-prefixes` attributes that apply to an element in the included stylesheet module, as well as `xml:lang` and `xml:space`, are those that were defined on its own `<xsl:stylesheet>` element, not those on the `<xsl:stylesheet>` element of the including stylesheet module.

❑ An exception is made for `<xsl:import>` elements in the included stylesheet module. `<xsl:import>` elements must come before any other top-level elements, so instead of placing them in their natural sequence in the including module, they are promoted so they appear after any `<xsl:import>` elements, but before any other top-level elements, in the including stylesheet module. This is relevant to situations where there are duplicate definitions and the XSLT processor is allowed to choose the one that comes last.

The included stylesheet module may use the *literal-result-element-as-stylesheet* syntax, described in Chapter 3. This allows an entire stylesheet module to be defined as the content of an element such as `<HTML>`. It is then treated as if it were a module containing a single template, whose match pattern is «/» and whose content is the literal result element.

The included stylesheet module may contain `<xsl:include>` statements to include further stylesheets, or `<xsl:import>` statements to import them. A stylesheet must not directly or indirectly include itself.

It is not an error to include the same stylesheet module more than once, either directly or indirectly, but it is not a useful thing to do. It may well cause errors due to the presence of duplicate declarations, in fact if the stylesheet contains definitions of global variables or named templates, and is included more than once at the same import precedence, such errors are inevitable. In some other situations it is implementation-defined whether an XSLT processor will report duplicate declarations as an error, so the behavior may vary from one product to another.

Usage

<xsl:include> provides a simple textual inclusion facility analagous to the #include directive in C: it is purely a way of writing a stylesheet in a modular way so that commonly used definitions can be held in a library and used wherever they are needed.

If you are handling a wide range of different document types, the chances are they will have some elements in common, which are to be processed in the same way regardless where they occur. For example, these might include standard definitions of toolbars, backgrounds, and navigation buttons to go on your web pages, as well as standard styles applied to data elements such as product names, email contact addresses, or dates.

To incorporate such standard content into a stylesheet without change, use <xsl:include>. If there are definitions you want to override, use <xsl:import>.

It can make a difference where in your stylesheet the <xsl:include> statement is placed. There are some kinds of objects – notably template rules – where if there is no other way of deciding which one to use, the XSLT processor has the option of giving priority to the one that occurs last in the stylesheet. This isn't something you can easily take advantage of, because in all these cases the processor also has the option of reporting an error. As a general principle, it's probably best to place <xsl:include> statements near the beginning of the file, because then if there are any accidental overlaps in the definitions, the ones in your principal stylesheet will either override those included from elsewhere, or be reported as errors.

Examples

Example: Using <xsl:include> with Named Attribute Sets

Source

This example can be used with any source document.

Stylesheet

Consider a principal stylesheet picture.xsl that includes a stylesheet attributes.xsl, as follows:

Module picture.xsl:

```
<xsl:stylesheet version="1.0"
                xmlns:xsl="http://www.w3.org/1999/XSL/Transform">

<xsl:include href="attributes.xsl"/>

<xsl:template match="/">
   <picture xsl:use-attribute-sets="picture-attributes">
      <xsl:attribute name="color">red</xsl:attribute>
   </picture>
```

```
        </xsl:template>
    </xsl:stylesheet>
```

Module `attributes.xsl`:

```
<xsl:stylesheet version="1.0"
                    xmlns:xsl="http://www.w3.org/1999/XSL/Transform">

<xsl:attribute-set name="picture-attributes">
    <xsl:attribute name="color">blue</xsl:attribute>
    <xsl:attribute name="transparency">100</xsl:attribute>
</xsl:attribute-set>

</xsl:stylesheet>
```

The named attribute set in the included stylesheet is used exactly as if it were defined in the principal stylesheet, at the point where the `<xsl:include>` statement appears.

Output

The resulting output is:

```
<picture transparency="100" color="red"/>
```

This is because attributes generated using `<xsl:attribute>` override those generated by using a named attribute set; it has nothing to do with the fact that the attribute-set came from an included stylesheet.

See also

`<xsl:import>` on page 207.

xsl:key

The `<xsl:key>` element is a top-level element used to declare a named key, for use with the `key()` function in expressions and patterns.

Defined in

XSLT section 12.2

Format

```
<xsl:key  name=QName  match=Pattern  use=Expression />
```

Position

<xsl:key> is a top-level element, which means that it must be a child of the <xsl:stylesheet> element. It may appear any number of times in a stylesheet.

Attributes

Name	Value	Meaning
name mandatory	QName	The name of the key
match mandatory	Pattern	Defines the nodes to which this key is applicable
use mandatory	Expression	The expression used to determine the value of the key for each of these nodes

The constructs QName and Expression are defined in Chapter 5, and Pattern is defined in Chapter 6.

Neither the Pattern in the match attribute, nor the Expression in the use attribute, may contain a VariableReference. This is to prevent circular definitions. Key definitions are effectively processed before global variable definitions: this means you can use keys when defining the value of a global variable, but you cannot use global variables when defining a key.

Content

None, the element is always empty.

Effect

The name attribute specifies the name of the key. It must be a valid QName; if it contains a namespace prefix, the prefix must identify a namespace declaration that is in scope on the <xsl:key> element. The effective name of the key is the expanded name, consisting of the namespace URI and the local part of the name. Namespaces are described in Chapter 2, page 58.

The match attribute specifies the nodes to which the key applies. The value is a Pattern, as described in Chapter 6. If a node doesn't match the pattern, then it has no values for the named key. If a node does match the pattern, then the node has zero or more values for the named key, as determined by the use attribute.

The simplest case is where the key values are unique. For example, consider the following source document:

```
<vehicles>
<vehicle reg="P427AGH" owner="Joe Karloff"/>
<vehicle reg="T788PHT" owner="Prunella Higgs"/>
<vehicle reg="V932TXQ" owner="William D. Abikombo"/>
</vehicles>
```

In the stylesheet you can define a key for the registration number of these vehicles, as follows:

```
<xsl:key name="vehicle-registration" match="vehicle" use="@reg"/>
```

The use attribute specifies an expression used to determine the value or values of the key. This expression doesn't have to be an attribute, like «@reg» in the example above: it could, for example, be a child element. If this is a repeating child element, you can create an index entry for each instance. The formal rules are as follows: for each node that matches the pattern, the expression is evaluated with that node as the current node, and with the current node list containing that node only.

❑   If the result is a node-set, each node in the result contributes one value for the key. The value of the key is the string-value of that node.

❑   Otherwise, the result is converted to a string, and this string acts as the value of the key.

There is no rule that stops two nodes having the same key value, for example, declaring a key for vehicle registration numbers in the example above does not mean that each registration number must be different. So a node can have more than one key, and a key can refer to more than one node.

More formally, each named key can be considered as a set of node-value pairs. A node can be associated with multiple values and a value can be associated with multiple nodes. The value is always a string. A node-value pair (N, V) is added to the set if node N matches the pattern specified in the match attribute, and if the expression in the use attribute, when applied to node N, produces either a node-set containing a node whose string-value is V, or a value that is not a node-set and which, on conversion to a string, is equal to V. To complicate things a bit further, there can be more than one key definition in the stylesheet with the same name. The set of node-value pairs for the key is then the union of the sets produced by each key definition independently. The import precedence of the key definitions makes no difference.

A key can be used to select nodes in any document, not just the principal source document. The key() function always returns nodes that are in the same document as the context node at the time it is called. It is therefore best to think of there being one set of node-value pairs for each named key for each document.

The effect of calling key(K, V), where K is a key name and V is a string value, is to locate the set of node-value pairs for the key named K and the context document, and to return a node-set containing the node from each pair where the value is V.

If you like to think in SQL terms, imagine a table KEY-VALUES with four columns, KEY-NAME, DOCUMENT, NODE, and VALUE. Then calling key('K', 'V') is equivalent to the SQL statement:

```
SELECT DISTINCT NODE FROM KEY-VALUES WHERE
    KEY-NAME='K' AND
    VALUE='V' AND
    DOCUMENT=current-document;
```

Usage and Examples

Declaring a key has two effects: it simplifies the code you need to write to find the nodes with given values, and it is likely to make access faster.

The performance effect, of course, depends entirely on the implementation. It would be quite legitimate for an implementation to conduct a full search of the document each time the key() function was called. In practice, however, most implementations are likely to build an index, so there will be a one-time cost in building the index (for each document), but after that, access to nodes whose key value is known should be very fast.

The <xsl:key> element is usually used to index elements, but in principle it can be used to index any kind of node except namespace nodes.

Using a Simple Key

The detailed rules for keys seem complicated, but most practical applications of keys are very simple. Consider the following key definition:

```
<xsl:key name="product-code" match="product" use="@code"/>
```

This defines a key whose name is «product-code», and which can be used to find <product> elements given the value of their code attribute. If a product has no code attribute, it won't be possible to find it using this key.

To find the product with code value «ABC-456», we can write, for example

```
<xsl:apply-templates select="key('product-code', 'ABC-456')"/>
```

Note that we could just as well choose to index the attribute nodes:

```
<xsl:key name="product-code" match="product/@code" use="."/>
```

To find the relevant product we would then write:

```
<xsl:apply-templates select="key('product-code', 'ABC-456')/.."/>
```

I've used <xsl:apply-templates> here as an example: this will select all the <product> elements in the current document that have code «ABC-456» (we never said it had to be a unique identifier) and apply the matching template to each one in turn, processing them in document order, as usual. I could equally have used any other instruction that uses an XPath expression, for example I could have assigned the node-set to a variable, or used it in an <xsl:value-of> element.

The second argument to the key function is normally a string. It won't usually be a literal, as in my example, but is more likely to be a string obtained from somewhere else in the source document, or perhaps supplied as a parameter to the stylesheet. It may well have been passed as one of the parameters in the URL used to select this stylesheet in the first place: for example a web page might display a list of available products such as:

Select from the following list of products:
Baked Beans
Tomato Ketchup
Fish Fingers
Cornflakes

Behind each of these hyperlinks shown to the user might be a URL such as:

```
http://www.cheap-food.com/servlet/product?code=ABC-456
```

You then write a servlet (or an ASP page if you prefer) on your web server that extracts the query parameter code, and fires off your favorite XSLT processor specifying products.xml as the source document, show-product.xsl as the stylesheet, and «ABC-456» as the value to be supplied for the global stylesheet parameter called prod-code. Your stylesheet then would look like this:

```
<xsl:param name="prod-code"/>
<xsl:key name="product-code" match="product" use="@code"/>
<xsl:template match="/">
    <html>
    <body>
    <xsl:variable name="product"
                          select="key('product-code', $product-code)"/>
    <xsl:if test="not($product)">
       <p>There is no product with this code</p>
    </xsl:if>
    <xsl:apply-templates select="$product"/>
    </body>
    </html>
</xsl:template>
```

Multi-valued Keys

A key can be multi-valued, in that a single node can have several values each of which can be used to find the node independently. For example, a book may have several authors, and each author's name can be used as a key value. This could be defined as follows:

```
<xsl:key name="book-author" match="book" use="author/name"
```

The use expression, «author/name», is a node-set expression, so the string value of each of its nodes (that is, the name of each author of the book) is used as one of the values in the set of node-value pairs that makes up the key.

In this particular example, as well as one book having several authors, each author may have written several books, so when we use an XPath expression such as:

```
<xsl:for-each select="key('book-author', 'Agatha Christie')">
```

We will be selecting all the books in which Agatha Christie was one of the authors. There's no direct way of using the key to find books written by two known authors, we just have to use one of them as the key value and then filter out the books that don't meet the other criteria.

At least two products, Saxon and xt, support an extension function
`intersection()`, *allowing you to write*
«`intersection(key(A, value1), key(A, value2))`».
However, this isn't in the standard.

We can supply a node-set as the second argument to the key function. For example, we might write:

```
<xsl:variable name="ac" select="key('book-author', 'Agatha Christie')">
<xsl:for-each select="key('book-author', $ac/author/name)">
```

The result of the select expression in the `<xsl:for-each>` instruction is the set of all books in which one of the authors is either Agatha Christie or a co-author of Agatha Christie. This is because $ac is the set of all books of which Agatha Christie is an author, so «`$ac/author/name`» is the set of all authors of these books, and using this set of named authors as the value of the key produces the set of books in which **any** of them is an author. As we have already mentioned, there is no direct way of finding books in which they are **all** named as authors.

Example: Multi-valued Non-unique keys

This example shows how a node can have several values for one key, and a given key value can identify more than one node. It uses author name as a key to locate `<book>` elements.

Source

The source file is `booklist.xml`:

```
<booklist>
<book>
    <title>Design Patterns</title>
    <author>Erich Gamma</author>
    <author>Richard Helm</author>
    <author>Ralph Johnson</author>
    <author>John Vlissides</author>
</book>
<book>
    <title>Pattern Hatching</title>
    <author>John Vlissides</author>
</book>
<book>
    <title>Building Applications Frameworks</title>
    <author>Mohamed Fayad</author>
    <author>Douglas C. Schmidt</author>
    <author>Ralph Johnson</author>
</book>
<book>
    <title>Implementing Applications Frameworks</title>
    <author>Mohamed Fayad</author>
    <author>Douglas C. Schmidt</author>
    <author>Ralph Johnson</author>
```

```
    </book>
  </booklist>
```

Stylesheet

The stylesheet is `author-key.xsl`.

It declares the key and then simply copies the `<book>` elements that match the author name supplied as a parameter. As it can be difficult to supply parameters containing spaces, the stylesheet is written so that an underscore in the supplied parameter is translated to a space. So you can call this stylesheet with a call such as:

```
saxon booklist.xml author-key.xsl author=Ralph_Johnson
```

For convenience in trying out this stylesheet, a default value has been supplied for the parameter.

```
<xsl:transform
 xmlns:xsl="http://www.w3.org/1999/XSL/Transform"
 version="1.0"
>

<xsl:key name="author-name" match="book" use="author"/>

<xsl:param name="author" select="'John Vlissides'"/>

<xsl:template match="/">
<xsl:copy-of select="key('author-name', translate($author, '_', ' '))"/>
</xsl:template>

</xsl:transform>
```

Output

With the parameter set to its default value «John Vlissides», the output is as follows:

```
<?xml version="1.0" encoding="utf-8" ?>
<book>
    <title>Design Patterns</title>
    <author>Erich Gamma</author>
    <author>Richard Helm</author>
    <author>Ralph Johnson</author>
    <author>John Vlissides</author>
</book>
<book>
    <title>Pattern Hatching</title>
    <author>John Vlissides</author>
</book>
```

Multiple Named Keys

There is nothing to stop us defining several keys for the same nodes. For example:

```
<xsl:key name="book-isbn" match="book" use="isbn"/>
<xsl:key name="book-author" match="book" use="author/surname"/>
```

This allows you to find a book if either the author or the ISBN is known.

It's worth thinking twice before doing this, however. Assuming the XSLT processor implements the key by building an index, rather than by searching the whole document each time, you have to weigh the cost of building the index against the cost of finding the information by a search. If you only need to find a single book using its ISBN number, it might be simpler and faster to write:

```
<xsl:for-each select="//book[isbn='0-13-082676-6']"/>
```

and not use a key at all.

Multiple Definitions for the Same Key

It's also possible to have several key definitions with the same name. For example:

```
<xsl:key name="artist-key" match="book" use="author/name"/>
<xsl:key name="artist-key" match="CD" use="composer"/>
<xsl:key name="artist-key" match="CD" use="performer"/>
```

Now we can use the key() function in an expression such as:

```
<xsl:apply-templates select="key('artist-key', 'Ringo Starr')"/>
```

The set of nodes this returns will be either <book> elements or <CD> elements or a mixture of the two; the only thing we know for certain is that each one will either be a book with Ringo Starr as one of the authors, or a CD with Ringo Starr listed either as the composer or as a performer.

If the use expression were the same in each case, we could simplify this. For example to find books and CDs with a particular publisher, we could write:

```
<xsl:key name="publisher-key" match="book | CD" use="publisher"/>
```

This example uses the UnionPattern «book | CD» which matches all <book> elements and all <CD> elements. Like other patterns, the UnionPattern is described on page 409 in Chapter 6.

The different definitions do not all need to be in the same stylesheet module; all the key definitions in included and imported stylesheets are merged together regardless of their import precedence.

See also

key() function in Chapter 7, page 469.

xsl:message

The `<xsl:message>` instruction outputs a message, and optionally terminates execution of the stylesheet.

Defined in

XSLT section 13

Format

```
<xsl:message  terminate="yes" | "no" >
    template-body
</xsl:message>
```

Position

`<xsl:message>` is an instruction. It is always used as part of a *template body*.

Attributes

Name	Value	Meaning
terminate *optional*	«yes» | «no»	The value «yes» indicates that processing is terminated after the message is output. The default is «no».

Content

A *template body*. There is no requirement that this should only generate text nodes; it can produce any XML fragment. What happens to any markup, however, is not defined in the standard.

Effect

If the `terminate` attribute is omitted, the value «no» is assumed.

The value obtained by expanding the *template* is output where the user can be expected to see it. The XSLT specification does not actually say where it goes: this is implementation-dependent, and it might be determined by configuration options. The specification suggests an alert box on the screen and a log file as two possible destinations.

If the `terminate` attribute has the value «yes», execution of the stylesheet is abandoned immediately, and any output generated so far is discarded.

Usage

The `<xsl:message>` instruction is generally used to report error conditions detected by the stylesheet logic. An example might be where an element such as `<sales>` is expected to have a numeric value, but is found to have a non-numeric value.

❑ With «terminate="no"» (the default), the stylesheet can report the error and continue processing.

❑ With «terminate="yes"», the stylesheet can report the error and quit.

Before using `<xsl:message>` in a production environment, check what happens to the messages and whether they can be redirected. You need to be particularly clear about whether your messages are intended to be read by the source document author, the stylesheet author, or the end user: this will affect the way in which you write the text of the message.

The output produced by `<xsl:message>` can be unpredictable, because the sequence of execution of a stylesheet is not defined in the standard. For example, some products (notably xt) defer evaluation of a variable until the variable is first used, which means that the order in which different variables are evaluated is difficult to predict. If evaluation of a variable triggers execution of `<xsl:message>`, the order of the messages may be surprising. Certainly, it can vary from one XSLT processor to another.

A common use of `<xsl:message>` is to generate diagnostic output so you can work out why your stylesheet isn't behaving as expected. This works well with products like Saxon and Xalan that have a fairly predictable sequence of execution, but it can be rather bewildering with xt, which often does things in a different order from the one you would expect. Placing diagnostics as comments into the result tree (using `<xsl:comment>`) is probably a more flexible solution. Some products, of course, have vendor-defined debugging aids built-in.

Examples

The following example issues a message and quits if the value of the `<sales>` element is non-numeric:

```
<xsl:if test="string(number(sales))='NaN'">
  <xsl:message terminate="yes">
    <xsl:text>Sales value is not numeric</xsl:text>
  </xsl:message>
</xsl:if>
```

Unfortunately there is no mechanism defined in the XSLT standard that allows the location of the error in the source document to be included in the message.

The following example extends this by allowing several such errors to be reported in a single run, terminating the run only after all errors have been reported. It works by assigning a global variable to the set of nodes in error.

```
<xsl:variable name="bad-sales"
                select="//sales[string(number(current()))='NaN']"/>
<xsl:template match="/">
   <xsl:for-each select="$bad-sales">
      <xsl:message>Sales value <xsl:value-of select="."/>
         is not numeric
      </xsl:message>
   </xsl:for-each>
...
   <xsl:if test="$bad-sales">
      <xsl:message terminate="yes">
         <xsl:text>Processing abandoned</xsl:text>
      </xsl:message>
   </xsl:if>
</xsl:template>
```

Localized Messages

XSLT is designed very much with internationalization in mind, and no doubt the requirement to localize message text was discussed by the working group. They clearly decided that no special facilities were needed, and instead included a detailed example in the XSLT specification showing how the message text can be localized (output in the user's native language). The example is worth repeating because it shows a general technique.

Messages for a particular language are stored in a file whose name identifies the language, for example German messages might be in messages/de.xml. The message file might have the structure:

```
<messages>
   <message name="started">Angefangen</message>
   <message name="please-wait"/>Bitte warten!</message>
   <message name="finished"/>Fertig</message>
</messages>
```

A stylesheet that wishes to produce messages in the appropriate local language will need a parameter to identify that language (it might also be obtainable via the system-property() function described in Chapter 7, on page 524, but not in a portable way). It can then get access to the messages file for the appropriate language, and read the messages from there:

```
<xsl:param name="language" select="'en'"/>
<xsl:template name="output-message">
   <xsl:param name="name"/>
   <xsl:variable name="message-file"
                select="concat('messages/', $language, '.xml')"/>
   <xsl:variable name="message-text"
                select="document($message-file)/messages"/>
   <xsl:message>
      <xsl:value-of select="$message-text/message[@name=$name]"/>
   </xsl:message>
</xsl:template>
```

The same technique can of course be used for producing localized text to include in the output file from the stylesheet.

> **The example in the XSLT Recommendation starts**
>
> ```
> <xsl:param name="lang" select="en"/>
> ```
>
> **This is a classic mistake. This will default the** lang **parameter to the string-value of the child** <en> **element if there is one. It is clearly intended that the default should be the literal value «en», which requires the two pairs of quotes.**

xsl:namespace-alias

The <xsl:namespace-alias> element allows a namespace used in the stylesheet to be mapped to a different namespace used in the output.

Defined in

XSLT section 7.1.1

Format

```
<xsl:namespace-alias
      stylesheet-prefix=NCName
      result-prefix=NCName />
```

Position

<xsl:namespace-alias> is a top-level element, which means it must be a child of the <xsl:stylesheet> element. It may be repeated any number of times in a stylesheet.

Attributes

Name	Value	Meaning
stylesheet-prefix mandatory	NCName | «#default»	A namespace prefix used in the stylesheet
result-prefix mandatory	NCName | «#default»	The prefix of the corresponding namespace to be used in the output

Content

None. The <xsl:namespace-alias> element is always empty.

Effect

The `<xsl:namespace-alias>` element affects the treatment of namespaces on literal result elements.

If there are several `<xsl:namespace-alias>` elements that specify the same `stylesheet-prefix`, the one with highest import precedence is used; if there is more than one with this import precedence, the implementation can either report an error or choose the one that comes last in the stylesheet.

Normally, when an element node is output by processing a literal result element, the output element name will have the same local part, the same prefix, and the same namespace URI as the literal result element itself. It isn't required that it should have the same prefix, but it usually will. The same applies to the attributes of the literal result element, and less obviously, to its namespace nodes. (The XSLT specification states that when processing a literal result element, all the namespaces that are in scope for the element in the stylesheet, with certain defined exceptions, will also be present in the output, even if they aren't used. Redundant namespace nodes can be suppressed by using the `xsl:exclude-result-prefixes` attribute. For more details on this, see the section *Literal Result Elements*, on page 109, in Chapter 3.)

Suppose you want the output document to be an XSLT stylesheet. Then you need to create elements such as `<xsl:template>` that are in the XSLT namespace. However, you can't use `<xsl:template>` as a literal result element, because by definition, if an element uses the XSLT namespace, it is treated as an XSLT element.

The answer is to use a different namespace on the literal result element in the stylesheet, and include an `<xsl:namespace-alias>` declaration to cause this to be mapped to the XSLT namespace when the literal result element is output. So your literal result element might be `<out:template>`, and you could use an `<xsl:namespace-alias>` element to indicate that the stylesheet prefix «out» should be mapped to the result prefix «xsl».

The `<xsl:namespace-alias>` element declares that one namespace URI, the stylesheet URI, should be replaced by a different URI, the result URI, when literal result elements are output. The namespace URIs are not given directly, but are referred to by using prefixes that are bound to these namespace URIs as a result of namespace declarations that are currently in force. Either one of the namespace URIs may be the default namespace URI, which is referred to using the pseudo-prefix «#default».

So although the `<xsl:namespace-alias>` element describes the mapping in terms of prefixes, it is not the prefix that is changed, but the URI. The prefix may be changed as well, but that is implementation-defined: the specification makes no guarantee about what prefix will be used in the output document.

Note

The XSLT specification does not say whether namespace aliasing should take place at the time a literal result element is written to a result tree fragment, or at the time the result tree fragment is copied to the final output destination. Since there is no standard way of examining the nodes in a result tree fragment, the question may seem academic. However, several XSLT implementations provide extension functions that allow conversion of a result tree fragment to a node-set for further processing, and the interaction of this facility with namespace aliasing could cause some surprises.

Usage and Examples

The main justification for this facility is to enable stylesheets to be written that generate stylesheets as output. This is not as improbable a scenario as it sounds: there are many possible reasons for using this technique, including the following:

❑ There are many proprietary templating languages currently in use. Translating these templates into XSLT stylesheets creates an attractive migration route, and there is no reason why these translators should not be written in XSLT.

❑ There may be a continuing need for a templating language that is less complex and powerful than XSLT, for use by non-programmers. Again, these simple templates can easily be translated into XSLT stylesheets.

❑ There are some parts of an XSLT stylesheet that cannot easily be parameterized. For example, it is not possible to construct an XPath expression programmatically and then execute it (XSLT is not a reflexive language). The requirement to do this arises when visual tools are developed to define queries and reports interactively. One way of implementing such tools is to construct a customized stylesheet from a generic stylesheet, and again this is a transformation that can be assisted by using XSLT.

❑ You might have developed a large number of stylesheets that all have some common characteristic, for example they might all generate HTML that uses the `<CENTER>` tag. As the `<CENTER>` tag is deprecated, you now want to modify these stylesheets to use `<DIV ALIGN="CENTER">`. Why not write an XSLT transformation to convert them?

❑ When XML schema languages become more advanced, there is every prospect that it will be possible to generate default stylesheets from a schema. Since both the schema and the stylesheet are XML documents, this is an XML to XML transformation, so it should be possible to write it in XSLT.

In fact, having gone to all the trouble of defining XSLT stylesheets as well-formed XML documents, it would be very surprising if it then proved impossible to manipulate them using XSLT itself.

There may be other situations where <xsl:namespace-alias> is useful. The XSLT specification mentions one, the need to avoid using namespace URIs that have recognized security implications in the area of digital signatures. Another might arise if stylesheets and other documents are held in a configuration management system: there might be a need to ensure that namespaces recognized by the configuration management system, for example to describe the authorship and change history of a document, were not used directly in the stylesheet.

Example of <xsl:namespace-alias>

The following example generates an XSLT stylesheet consisting only of a single global variable declaration, whose name and default value are supplied as parameters. Although this is a trivial stylesheet, it could be useful when incorporated into another more useful stylesheet using <xsl:include> or <xsl:import>.

This example is available for download as alias.xsl.

Source

This stylesheet can be used with any source XML document. The source document is not used (though it must exist).

Stylesheet

```
<xsl:stylesheet version="1.0"
                xmlns:xsl="http://www.w3.org/1999/XSL/Transform"
                xmlns:out="output.xsl">


<xsl:param name="variable-name">v</xsl:param>
<xsl:param name="default-value"/>
<xsl:output indent="yes"/>


<xsl:namespace-alias
             stylesheet-prefix="out"
             result-prefix="xsl"/>


<xsl:template match="/">
   <out:stylesheet version="1.0">
   <out:variable name="{$variable-name}">
      <xsl:value-of select="$default-value"/>
   </out:variable>
   </out:stylesheet>
</xsl:template>


</xsl:stylesheet>
```

If you default the values of the parameters «variable-name» and «default-value», the output should be as follows:

```
<?xml version="1.0" encoding="utf-8" ?>
<xsl:stylesheet version="1.0"
        xmlns:xsl="http://www.w3.org/1999/XSL/Transform">
    <xsl:variable name="v"/>
</xsl:stylesheet>
```

See also

Literal result elements in Chapter 3, on page 109.

xsl:number

The <xsl:number> element performs two functions. It can be used to allocate a sequential number to the current node, and it can be used to format a number for output. These functions are often performed together, but they can also be done separately.

Note that the facilities for number formatting in the <xsl:number> element are quite separate from those offered by the format-number() function and the <xsl:decimal-format> element.

Defined in

XSLT section 7.7

Format

```
<xsl:number
    level="single" | "multiple" | "any"
    count=Pattern
    from=Pattern
    value=Expression
    format={format-string}
    lang={language-code}
    letter-value={ "alphabetic" | "traditional" }
    grouping-separator={character}
    grouping-size={number} />
```

Position

<xsl:number> is an instruction. It is always used within a template body.

Attributes

Name	Values	Meaning
level optional	«single» | «multiple» | «any»	Controls the way in which a sequence number is allocated based on the position of the node in the tree
count optional	Pattern	Determines which nodes are counted to determine a sequence number
from optional	Pattern	Determines a cut-off point, a point in the document from which sequence numbering starts afresh
value optional	Expression	A user-supplied number to be formatted (instead of using a node sequence number)
format optional	Attribute value template, returning a format string, as defined below	Determines the output format of the number
lang optional	Attribute value template, returning a language code, as defined in XML for the xml:lang attribute	Indicates a language whose conventions for number formatting should be used
letter-value optional	Attribute value template, returning «alphabetic» | «traditional»	Distinguishes between different numbering schemes used with the same language
grouping- separator optional	Attribute value template, returning a single character	A character to be used to separate groups of digits (for example, a comma as a thousands separator)
grouping-size optional	Attribute value template, returning a number	The number of digits in each group, indicating where the grouping-separator should be inserted

For the syntax of an Expression, see Chapter 5.
For the syntax of a Pattern, see Chapter 6.

Content

None, the element is always empty.

Effect

The <xsl:number> instruction performs four tasks:

- ❏ Determine a sequence number
- ❏ Analyze the format string into a sequence of format tokens
- ❏ Format each part of the sequence number using the appropriate format token
- ❏ Write the resulting string to the current output destination as a text node.

These steps are considered individually in the following sections.

Determining a Sequence Number

If the value attribute is specified, the sequence number is obtained by evaluating the expression in the value attribute, converting the result if necessary to a number using the rules for the number() function (page 498), and then rounding it to an integer using the rules for the round() function (page 504) . In this case, the level, count, and from attributes are ignored. The XSLT specification doesn't say what happens if the number is negative: <xsl:number> is primarily designed to handle positive integers.

If no value attribute is specified, <xsl:number> determines a sequence number based on the position of the current node in the source document.

The rules for determining a sequence number depend on the value of the level, count, and from attributes. If any of these attributes is omitted, the default is as follows:

Attribute	Default value
level	«single»
count	A pattern that matches nodes of the same node type as the current node; and if the current node has a name, that matches nodes with the same name. As always, names with namespace prefixes are matched using the relevant namespace URI rather than the prefix.
from	A pattern that matches no nodes, for example «*[false()]»

The sequence number is in general a list of positive integers. If the level attribute is «single» or «any» the sequence number will normally contain a single integer, if it is «multiple» then it may contain several (for example «3.6.1»). It is also possible for the list to be empty, and in the case of «any» it is possible for the sequence number to be zero.

The sequence number is determined as follows:

level	Rules
single	This is designed for numbering of peer nodes at the same level in the structure, for example the items in a list. If the current node matches the count pattern, the target node is the current node. Otherwise, the processor searches for an ancestor of the current node that matches the count pattern, and makes that the target node. It stops the search when an ancestor is found that matches the from pattern, if there is one. If a target node is found, the sequence number is determined by counting how many preceding siblings of the target node match the count pattern, and adding one for the target node itself. For example, if the target node has six preceding siblings that match the count pattern then the sequence number is 7. If no target node is found, the sequence number will be an empty list.
any	This is designed for numbering nodes that can appear at any level of the structure, for example the footnotes or equations in a chapter of a book. Starting at the current node, the processor walks backwards through the document in reverse document order, counting the number of nodes that match the count pattern, and stopping when a node is found that matches the from pattern, if there is one. The sequence number is the number of nodes counted. If the current node does not match the count pattern, the result can be zero. Attribute and namespace nodes are never counted.
multiple	This is designed to produce a composite sequence number that reflects the hierarchic position of a node, for example «2.17.1». The processor makes a list of all the ancestors of the current node, plus the current node itself, but stopping when an ancestor is reached that matches the from pattern, if there is one. The node that matches the from pattern is not included in the list. It puts this list into document order, that is, with the outermost ancestor first. For each node in this list that matches the count pattern, the processor counts how many preceding siblings it has that also match the count pattern, and adds one for the node itself. The resulting list of numbers makes up the composite sequence number.

These rules appear complex but in practice most common cases are quite straightforward: see the following examples.

Analysing the Format String

Once the sequence number has been determined, the next stage is to format it into a string.

Recall that the sequence number is in general a list of zero or more integers. When these are obtained by counting nodes they will generally be positive integers, though with «level="any"», the value zero can also arise. When a sequence number is supplied using the value attribute, there is nothing to stop the number being negative, or for that matter infinity or NaN (not a number). The XSLT specification doesn't define how negative integers or these other special values should be formatted, so the results are implementation-dependent. The <xsl:number> element is designed for handling the natural numbers that arise from counting nodes: if you want to handle other cases, it's better to use the format-number() function described in Chapter 7, on page 455.

The formatting is controlled primarily using the format string supplied in the format attribute. If this is omitted, the default value is «1».

The format string consists of a sequence of alternating formatting tokens and punctuation tokens. Any sequence of consecutive alphanumeric characters is taken as a formatting token, any other sequence is taken as a punctuation token. For example, if the format attribute is «1((a))», this is broken up into a formatting token «1», a punctuation token «((», a formatting token «a», and a punctuation token «))». The term *alphanumeric* is based on Unicode character categories, and is defined to include letters and digits from any language.

In the most common case the sequence number is a single number. In this situation, the output string consists of the initial punctuation token if there is one, followed by the result of formatting the number using the first format token, followed by the final punctuation token if there is one. So if the sequence number is «42» and the format attribute is «[1]», then the final output is «[42]».

Where the sequence number is a list of numbers, the rules are a little more complex but still have intuitive results, for example if the list of numbers is «3, 1, 6» and the format attribute is «1.1(a)» then the final output is «3.1(f)» (because «f» is the sixth letter in the alphabet). The detailed rules are as follows:

❏ The *n*th formatting token is used to format the *n*th number in the list where possible, using the rules in the following section

❏ If there are more numbers in the list than formatting tokens, then the excess numbers are formatted using the last formatting token. For example, if the list is «3,1,2,5» and the format attribute is «A.1», then the output will be «C.1.2.5»

❏ If there are no formatting tokens, then a formatting token of «1» is used

❏ If there are more formatting tokens than numbers in the list, the excess formatting tokens are ignored

❑ Each number is preceded in the output by the punctuation token that precedes the formatting token used to format that number, if there is one. If there is no preceding punctuation token, and the number is not the first in the list, it is preceded by «.»

❑ If the formatting string ends with a punctuation token, this is added to the end of the output string.

Note that if the list of numbers is empty, the result will consist of the initial and final punctuation tokens. For example if the format string is «[1]», an empty list will be formatted as «[]». The most likely reason for an empty list is that «level="multiple"» was specified, and no ancestor nodes matched the count pattern.

Formatting the Parts of the Sequence Number

This section describes how a single number is formatted using a single formatting token to construct a string that will form part of the final output string.

The XSLT specification defines this process only partially. There are some definitive rules, some guidance for the implementer, and many other cases that are left unspecified.

The definitive cases are listed in the table below:

Formatting token	Output sequence
1	1, 2, 3, 4…
01	01, 02, 03, … 10, 11, 12. More generally, if the format token is a «1» preceded by n zeros, the output numbers will be in decimal notation with a minimum of $n+1$ digits
other Unicode digits	The above two rules also apply to any other Unicode digits equivalent to zero and one, for example Thai or Tamil digits. The number is output using the same family of digits as are used in the formatting token
a	a, b, c, d, … x, y, z, aa, ab, ac …
A	A, B, C, D, … X, Y, Z, AA, AB, AC …
i	i, ii, iii, iv, … x, xi, xii, xii, xii, xiv, …
I	I, II, III, IV, … X, XI, XII, XIII, XIV, …

The attributes grouping-separator and grouping-size can be used to control the separation of groups of digits. For example, setting «grouping-separator=" "» (a single space) and «grouping-size="2"» would cause the number 12345 to be output as «1 23 45». The groups will always be formed by counting digits from the right-hand side.

For other formatting tokens, the XSLT specification is not prescriptive. It indicates that any formatting token may be used to indicate a sequence starting with that token, provided the implementation supports such a sequence; if the implementation does not support such a sequence, it may format the number using the format token «1». So, for example, if an implementation supports the numbering sequence «eins, zwei, drei, vier», then you can invoke this sequence using a format token of «eins»; if it supports the numbering sequence « , , , », then you can invoke this sequence with a format token of « ».

In case the format token does not identify a numbering sequence unambiguously, two attributes are provided to give greater control.

❑ The lang attribute is intended to indicate the target language: for example the sequence starting «a» might be different for English («lang="en"») and for Swedish («lang="se"»). The language code is intended to take the same form as the xml:lang attribute defined in the XML specification.

❑ The letter-value attribute is intended for languages such as Hebrew that have several possible sequences starting with the same token. The two permitted values are «alphabetic» and «traditional».

The detailed effect of these attributes is left entirely to the implementer, so you can't expect different products necessarily to behave in the same way.

All the attributes controlling formatting are attribute value templates, so they can be parameterized using expressions enclosed in curly braces. This is mainly useful if you want to select the values from a localization file based on the preferred language of the current user. To achieve this, you can use the same techniques as are described for localizing messages: see <xsl:message> on page 230.

Outputting the Number

The final action of <xsl:number> is to write the generated string to the current output destination, as a text node.

If you want to do something else with the number (perhaps to write it as an attribute or to copy it to every page heading), you can save it as the value of a variable, as follows:

```
<xsl:variable name="section-number"><xsl:number/></xsl:variable>
```

Writing the value to a variable also allows you to perform further manipulation. For example, if you want to use the traditional numbering sequence for footnotes (*, †, ‡, §, ¶) you cannot do this directly in <xsl:number> because these characters are punctuation symbols rather than alphanumerics. What you can do, however, is to use conventional decimal numbering and then convert, for example:

```
<xsl:template match="footnote"/>
<xsl:variable name="footnote-number">
    <xsl:number level="any" from="section"/>
</xsl:variable>
<xsl:value-of select="translate($footnote-number, '12345', '*†‡§¶')"/>
```

In practice it might be safer to use character references for these special characters to avoid them being mangled by a text editor that doesn't understand Unicode. The translate() function replaces characters in its second argument by the corresponding character in the third argument: it is described on page 526, in Chapter 7.

I have dodged a tricky question here, which is that if you want footnote numbers to start at one on each page, you can't allocate them until you have paginated the document. Some kinds of numbering are really the domain of XSL Formatting rather than XSL Transformations.

Usage and Examples

Although the rules for <xsl:number> are very general and sometimes complex, most common cases are quite straightforward.

The general rules allow for numbering any kind of node, but in practice the <xsl:number> instruction is almost invariably used for numbering elements. So in this section, I'll assume that the current node is an element.

level="single"

This option (the default) is used to number sibling elements.

The simplest way of using <xsl:number> is without any attributes: just

```
<xsl:number/>
```

If the current element is the eighth <item> element owned by its parent element, say, then this will write the text value «8» to the current output destination. Technically, the processor is counting all the elements that match the pattern in the count attribute, and the default for the count attribute in this case is a pattern that matches <item> elements.

For this simple kind of numbering, it is often better to use the position() function, particularly if there are many nodes to be numbered. This is because with a typical implementation, each node that is numbered using <xsl:number> will result in the preceding siblings being counted, which will take an increasingly long time as the number of siblings increases. With the position() function, it is much more likely that the system already knows the position and doesn't have to do any special walking around the tree and pattern matching. Of course this is only possible where «position()» and <xsl:number/> produce the same answer, which will happen when the current node list being processed consists of all the sibling elements of a particular element type.

The count attribute can be used in two ways.

Firstly, it is useful if there are several different kinds of sibling elements that we want to count. For example, we might have a an element containing a mixture of <item> and <special-item> children, as follows:

```
<shopping-list>
   <item>bananas</item>
   <item>apples</item>
   <special-item>flowers for Grandma</special-item>
   <item>grapes</item>
   <special-item>chocolate for Aunt Maud</special-item>
   <item>cherries</item>
</shopping-list>
```

If we want to number these in a single sequence, we can write:

```
<xsl:template match="item | special-item">
   <xsl:number count="item | special-item"/>
   <xsl:text> </xsl:text>
   <xsl:value-of select="."/><br/>
</xsl:template>
```

which, when we process the `<shopping-list>` element, will result in the output:

```
1 bananas<br/>
2 apples<br/>
3 flowers for Grandma<br/>
4 grapes<br/>
5 chocolate for Aunt Maud<br/>
6 cherries<br/>
```

In this case we could also use «count="*"» to achieve this effect. If we omitted the count attribute, the output would be:

```
1 bananas<br/>
2 apples<br/>
1 flowers for Grandma<br/>
3 grapes<br/>
2 chocolate for Aunt Maud<br/>
4 cherries<br/>
```

because each element is numbered taking into account only other elements with the same name.

Another use for the count attribute is to specify that it is not the current node that should be counted, but an ancestor node. For example, the template rule for a `<title>` element can use `<xsl:number>` to determine the number of the section that the title belongs to by writing

```
<xsl:template match="title">
   <xsl:number count="section"/>
. . .
</xsl:template>
```

This usage is less common: it would be just as easy in most cases to output the section number from the template that handles the `<section>` element itself.

The from attribute is rarely needed with «level="single"». In fact it is difficult to construct an example that isn't completely artificial.

4

Elements

If you want numbering to start at a value other than one, or perhaps to proceed in increments other than one, you can capture the result of <xsl:number> in a variable and manipulate it using XPath expressions. For example, the following template rule numbers the items in a list starting at an offset passed in as a parameter:

```
<xsl:template match="item">
    <xsl:param name="first-number" select="1"/>
    <xsl:variable name="number"><xsl:number/></xsl:variable>
    <xsl:value-of select="$first-number + $number - 1"/>
. . .
</xsl:template>
```

level="any"

This option is useful when numbering objects within a document that have a numbering sequence of their own, independent of their position within the hierarchic structure. Examples are figures and illustrations, tables, equations, footnotes, actions from a meeting.

The count attribute can usually be defaulted. For example to number quotations within a document, write a template rule such as

```
<xsl:template match="quotation">
<table><tr>
<td width="90%" valign="top">
    <i><xsl:value-of select="."/></i></td>
<td><xsl:number level="any"/></td>
</tr></table>
</xsl:template>
```

Again, the count attribute is useful when several different element types are included in the same numbering sequence, for example there might be a single sequence that includes both diagrams and photographs.

Note that each evaluation of <xsl:number> is quite independent of any previous evaluations. The result depends only on the relative position of the current element in the source document, and not on how many times the <xsl:number> element has been evaluated. So there is no guarantee that the numbers in the output document will be consecutive. In fact, if the output order is different from the input order then the numbers definitely won't be consecutive. If you want to number things based on their position in the output document, the only real way to achieve this is by using the position() function: if this isn't adequate, you may need to perform a second pass on the output document, using another stylesheet, to add the sequence numbers.

The from attribute is useful to indicate where numbering should restart:

```
<xsl:template match="footnote">
    <xsl:number level="any" from="chapter"/>
    <xsl:text> </xsl:text>
    <xsl:value-of select="."/>
</xsl:template>
```

The above code would number footnotes consecutively within a chapter, starting again at 1 for each chapter.

Example: Numbering the Lines of a Poem

The following example numbers the lines of a poem, showing the number to the right of every third line. We assume the input structure contains a <poem> element, a <stanza> element, and a <line> element: the lines are to be numbered within the poem as a whole, not within each stanza.

Source

This stylesheet can be used with the source file poem.xml used in Chapter 1.

Stylesheet

This stylesheet is poem.xsl. It uses <xsl:number> to get the number of every line, but displays it only every third line, using the «mod» operator to get the remainder when the line number is divided by three.

```
<xsl:stylesheet version="1.0"
      xmlns:xsl="http://www.w3.org/1999/XSL/Transform">

<xsl:template match="/">
<html><body>
<p><xsl:apply-templates select="/poem/stanza"/></p>
</body></html>
</xsl:template>

<xsl:template match="stanza">
<p><table><xsl:apply-templates/></table></p>
</xsl:template>

<xsl:template match="line">
<tr>
<td width="350"><xsl:value-of select="."/></td>
<td width="50">
   <xsl:variable name="line-nr">
      <xsl:number level="any" from="poem"/>
   </xsl:variable>
   <xsl:if test="$line-nr mod 3 = 0">
      <xsl:value-of select="$line-nr"/>
   </xsl:if>
</td>
</tr>
</xsl:template>
</xsl:stylesheet>
```

Output

level="multiple"

This option is typically used to produce the hierarchic sequence numbers often found in technical or legal documents, for example 1.12.3, or A2(iii).

Note that an alternative way to produce such numbers is to use several calls on
<xsl:number> with «level="single"» and different count attributes, for example:

```
<xsl:number count="chapter"/>.<xsl:number count="section"/>
   (<xsl:number count="clause"/>)
```

Another technique, which might be marginally faster, is to evaluate the chapter number once and pass it as a parameter to the template handling the section, and then pass both the chapter number and section number (or their concatenation) as parameters to the template handling each clause.

However, using «level="multiple"» is convenient, and in some cases (particularly with recursive structures, where <section> elements are contained within <section> elements) may be the only way of achieving the required effect.

The count attribute defines which ancestor elements should be included. Usually this is expressed as a union pattern, as in the example below:

```
<xsl:template match="clause">
   <xsl:number
       format="1.1.1. "
       level="multiple"
       count="chapter | section | clause"/>
   <xsl:apply-templates/>
</xsl:template>
```

The effect of the rules is that a composite sequence number will be formed containing one component number for each ancestor (or the element itself) that is a <chapter>, <section>, or <clause>. If the structure is regular, so that chapters, sections and clauses are neatly nested, then each clause will be output preceded by a number such as 1.13.5, where 1 is the chapter number, 13 is the number of the section within the chapter, and 5 is the number of the clause within the section.

If the structure isn't regular, for example if there are sections that don't belong to a chapter, or if there are clauses that have sections as siblings at the same level, or if there are sections nested within other sections, then the effects can be surprising, but a careful reading of the rules should explain what's going on.

A problem that sometimes occurs is that the numbering is context-sensitive. For example, within a regular chapter, clauses are numbered 1.2.3, but in an appendix, they are numbered A.2.3. It's possible to achieve this effect by exploiting the fact that the format pattern is an attribute value template; for example you could write:

```
<xsl:template match="clause">
   <xsl:variable name="format">
      <xsl:choose>
         <xsl:when test="ancestor::chapter">1.1.1. </xsl:when>
         <xsl:otherwise>A.1.1 </xsl:otherwise>
      </xsl:choose>
   </xsl:variable>
   <xsl:number
      format="{$format}"
      level="multiple"
      count="appendix | chapter | section | clause"/>
   <xsl:apply-templates/>
</xsl:template>
```

See also

position() function in Chapter 7, on page 500.
format-number() function, on page 455 in Chapter 7
<xsl:decimal-format> on page 187.

xsl:otherwise

The <xsl:otherwise> element is used within an <xsl:choose> instruction to indicate the action that should be taken when none of the <xsl:when> conditions is satisfied.

Defined in

XSLT section 9.2

Format

```
<xsl:otherwise>
   template-body
</xsl:otherwise>
```

Position

`<xsl:otherwise>` can only appear as a child of an `<xsl:choose>` element. If it is present at all, it must be the last child of the `<xsl:choose>` element, and it may not appear more than once.

Attributes

None.

Content

A *template body*.

Effect

The template body of the `<xsl:otherwise>` element is instantiated if (and only if) none of the `<xsl:when>` elements in the containing `<xsl:choose>` element evaluates to true.

Usage and Examples

See `<xsl:choose>` on page 176.

See also

`<xsl:choose>`
`<xsl:when>` on page 317.

xsl:output

The `<xsl:output>` element is a top-level element used to control the format of the stylesheet output. An XSLT stylesheet is processed conceptually in two stages: the first stage is to build a result tree, and the second is to write out the result tree to a serial output file. The `<xsl:output>` element controls this second stage.

This second stage of processing, to serialize the tree as an output document, is not a mandatory requirement for an XSLT processor; the standard allows the processor to make the tree available in some other way, for example via the DOM API. A processor that does not write the tree to an output file is allowed to ignore this element.

Defined in

XSLT section 16

Format

```
<xsl:output
    method="xml" | "html" | "text" | QName.
    version=NMtoken
    encoding=string
```

```
omit-xml-declaration="yes" | "no"
standalone="yes" | "no"
doctype-public=string
doctype-system=string
cdata-section-elements=list-of-QNames
indent="yes" | "no"
media-type=string />
```

Position

<xsl:output> is a top-level element, which means it must be a child of the
<xsl:stylesheet> element. It may appear any number of times in a stylesheet.

Attributes

Name	Value	Meaning
method optional	«xml» | «html» | «text» | QName	Defines the required output format
version optional	NMtoken	Defines the version of the output format
encoding optional	string	Defines the character encoding
omit-xml- declaration optional	«yes» | «no»	Indicates whether an XML declaration is to be included in the output
standalone optional	«yes» | «no»	Indicates that a standalone declaration is to be included in the output, and gives its value
doctype-public optional	string	Indicates the public identifier to be used in the DOCTYPE declaration in the output file
doctype-system optional	string	Indicates the system identifier to be used in the DOCTYPE declaration in the output file
cdata-section- elements optional	Whitespace separated list of QNames	Names those elements whose text content is to be output in the form of CDATA sections
indent optional	«yes» | «no»	Indicates whether the output should be indented to indicate its hierarchic structure
media-type optional	string	Indicates the media-type (often called MIME type) to be associated with the output file

4

Elements

Content

None, the element is always empty.

Effect

There may be more than one ‹xsl:output› element in the stylesheet. If there are several, the attributes they define are in effect combined into a single conceptual ‹xsl:output› element as follows:

❑ For the cdata-section-elements attribute, the lists of QNames supplied on the separate ‹xsl:output› elements are merged – if an element name is present in any of the lists, it will be treated as a CDATA section element.

❑ For all other attributes, an ‹xsl:output› element that specifies a value for the attribute take precedence over one that leaves it defaulted. If several ‹xsl:output› elements specify a value for the attribute, the one with highest import precedence is used. If this leaves more than one value, the XSLT processor may either report an error, or use the one that occurs last in the stylesheet. (The specification leaves it unclear whether "more than one value" includes the case where the value is specified several times but is the same each time).

The method attribute controls the format of the output, and this in turn affects the detailed meaning and the default values of the other attributes.

Three output formats are defined in the specification: «xml», «html», and «text». Alternatively, the output format may be given as a QName, which must include a non-null prefix that identifies a namespace that is currently in scope. This option is provided for vendor extensions, and the meaning is not defined in the standard. A vendor-defined format can attach its own interpretations to the meanings of the other attributes on the ‹xsl:output› element, and it can also define additional attributes on the ‹xsl:output› element, provided they are not in the default namespace.

If the method attribute is omitted, the output will be in XML format, unless the result tree is recognizably HTML. The result tree is recognized as HTML if:

❑ The root node has at least one element child, and

❑ The first element child of the root node is named ‹html›, in any combination of upper and lower case, and has a null namespace URI, and

❑ There are no text nodes before the ‹html› element, other than, optionally, a text node containing whitespace only.

Rules for XML output

When the output method is «xml», the output file will usually be a well-formed XML document, but the actual requirement is only that it should be a well-formed XML external general parsed entity: in other words, something that could be incorporated into an XML document by using an entity reference such as «&doc;». The following example shows a well-formed external general parsed entity that is not a well-formed document:

```
A <b>bold</b> and <emph>emphatic</emph> statement
```

The specification is a little bit ambiguous in this area. Although it appears to state that the output will always be a well-formed external general parsed entity, the context makes it clear that it can also include things such as a standalone document declaration and a document type declaration which according to XML syntax can only appear in a document entity, and not in an external general parsed entity.

An example of a well-formed document that is not a well-formed external general parsed entity is:

```
<?xml version="1.0" encoding="utf-8" standalone="yes"?>
<p>A <b>bold</b> and <emph>emphatic</emph> statement</p>
```

The rules for document entities and external general parsed entities overlap, as shown in the following diagram:

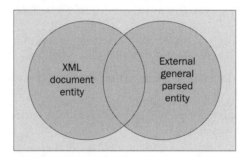

Essentially, an XSLT stylesheet can output anything that fits in the darker shaded area: anything that is a well-formed XML document entity, a well-formed external general parsed entity, or both.

Well, almost anything:

❑ it must also conform to the namespaces recommendation

❑ there is no explicit provision for generating an internal DTD subset, though it can be achieved with difficulty by generating text and disabling output escaping.

❑ similarly, there is no explicit provision for generating entity references, though this can also be achieved in the same way.

In the XML standard, the rules for an external general parsed entity are given as

```
extParsedEnt ⇒ TextDecl ? content
```

while the rule for the document entity is effectively:

```
document ⇒ XMLDecl ? Misc * doctypedecl ? Misc * element Misc *
```

where Misc permits whitespace, comments, and processing instructions.

253

So the principal differences between the two cases are:

- ❑ A `TextDecl` (text declaration) is not quite the same thing as an `XMLDecl` (XML declaration)

- ❑ A document may contain a `doctypedecl` (document type declaration), but an external general parsed entity may not. A document type declaration is the `<!DOCTYPE ... >` header identifying the DTD and possibly including an internal DTD subset.

- ❑ The body of a document is an `element`, while the body of an external parsed entity is `content`. Here `content` is effectively the contents of an element but without the start and end tags.

The `TextDecl` (text declaration) looks at first sight very like an XML declaration: for example `<?xml version="1.0" encoding="utf-8"?>` could be used either as an XML declaration or as a text declaration. There are differences, however:

- ❑ In an XML declaration, the `version` attribute is mandatory, but in a text declaration it is optional

- ❑ In an XML declaration, the `encoding` attribute is optional, but in a text declaration it is mandatory

- ❑ An XML declaration may include a `standalone` attribute, but a text declaration may not.

The `content` part is a sequence of components including child elements, character data, entity references, CDATA sections, processing instructions, and comments, each of which may appear any number of times and in any order.

So the following are all examples of well-formed external general parsed entities:

```
<quote>Hello!</quote>
```

```
<quote>Hello!</quote><quote>Goodbye!</quote>
```

```
Hello!
```

```
<?xml version="1.0" encoding="utf-8"?>Hello!
```

The following is a well-formed XML document, but it is *not* a well-formed external general parsed entity, both because of the `standalone` attribute, and because of the document type declaration. However, even though the XSLT specification states that the output is always a well-formed external general parsed entity, the context makes it clear that this is also legitimate output:

```
<?xml version="1.0" encoding="utf-8" standalone="no"?>
<!DOCTYPE quote SYSTEM "hello.dtd">
<quote>Hello!</quote>
```

The following is neither a well-formed XML document nor a well-formed external general parsed entity.

```
<?xml version="1.0" encoding="utf-8" standalone="no"?>
<!DOCTYPE quote SYSTEM "hello.dtd">
<quote>Hello!</quote>
<quote>Goodbye!</quote>
```

It cannot be an XML document because it has more than one top-level element, and it cannot be an external general parsed entity because it has a `<!DOCTYPE>` declaration. The XSLT standard isn't very explicit about what happens in this situation – it's certainly possible to request such output using XSLT – but the processor probably ought to treat it as an error.

The XSLT specification also places two other constraints on the form of the output, although these are rules for the implementer to follow rather than rules that directly affect the stylesheet author. These rules are:

❑ The output must conform to the rules of the XML Namespaces recommendation. If it is an XML document, the meaning of this is clear enough, but if it is merely an external entity, some further explanation is needed. The standard provides this by saying that when the entity is pulled into a document by adding an element tag around its content, the resulting document must conform with the XML Namespaces rules.

❑ The output file must faithfully reflect the result tree. This requirement is easy to state informally, but the specification includes a more formal statement of the requirement, which is surprisingly complex.

Although the output is required to be well-formed XML, there is no rule that says it has to be valid XML (recall that a valid XML document is, roughly speaking, an XML document that conforms to the rules in its own DTD). If you generate a document type declaration that refers to a specific DTD, don't expect the XSLT processor to check that the output document actually conforms to that DTD: that's entirely your responsibility as the stylesheet author.

With the «xml» output method, the other attributes of `<xsl:output>` are interpreted as follows:

Attribute	Interpretation
version	The version of XML used in the output document. Currently the only version of XML that exists is version 1.0, but this anticipates the possibility that there will be other versions in the future. The default value, and the only value you should consider using at present, is «1.0»

Attribute	Interpretation
encoding	This specifies the preferred character encoding for the output document. All XSLT processors are required to support the values «UTF-8» and «UTF-16» (which are also the only values that XML parsers are required to support). This encoding name will be used in the encoding attribute of the XML or Text declaration at the start of the output file, and all characters in the file will be encoded using these conventions. The standard encoding names are not case-sensitive. If the encoding is one that does not allow all XML characters to be represented directly, for example «iso-8859-1», then characters outside this subset will be represented where possible using XML character references (such as «₤»). It is an error if such characters appear in contexts where character references are not recognized (for example within a processing instruction or comment, or in an element or attribute name).
indent	If this attribute has the value «yes», the idea is that the XML output should be indented to show its hierarchic structure. The XSLT processor is not obliged to respect this request, and if it does so, the precise form of the output is not defined. There are some constraints on how indentation should be achieved: in effect, it can only be done by adding whitespace-only text nodes to the tree, and these cannot be added adjacent to an existing text node. Whitespace that is already in the result tree cannot be removed, so if the output already contains multi-line text nodes, the scope to produce aesthetically-pleasing output is limited. Note that even with these restrictions, adding whitespace nodes to the output may affect the way the recipient interprets it: this is particularly true with mixed content models where an element can have both elements and text nodes as its children.
cdata-section-elements	This is a list of element names, each expressed as a QName, separated by whitespace. Any prefix in a QName is treated as a reference to the corresponding namespace URI in the normal way, using the namespace declarations in effect on the actual <xsl:output> element where the cdata-section-elements attribute appears; because these are element names, the default namespace is assumed where the name has no prefix. When a text node is output, if the parent element of the text node is identified by a name in this list, then the text node is output as a CDATA section. For example, the text value «James» is output as «<![CDATA[James]]>», and the text value «AT&T» is output as «<![CDATA[AT&T]]>».

Attribute	Interpretation
	Otherwise, this value would probably be output as «AT&T». The XSLT processor is free to choose other equivalent representations if it wishes, for example a character reference, but the standard says that it should not use CDATA unless it is explicitly requested. (However, note the word *should*: this means the rule is advisory, not a conformance requirement.) The CDATA section will be split into parts if necessary, perhaps because the terminator sequence «]]>» appears in the data, or because there is a character that can only be output using a character reference because it is not supported directly in the chosen encoding.
omit-xml-declaration	If this attribute has the value «yes», the XSLT processor should not output an XML declaration (or, by implication, a text declaration: recall that XML declarations are used at the start of the document entity, text declarations at the start of an external general parsed entity). If the attribute is omitted, or has the value «no», then a declaration should be output. The declaration should include both the version and encoding attributes (to ensure that it is valid both as an XML declaration and as a text declaration). It should include a standalone attribute only if a standalone attribute is specified in the <xsl:output> element.
standalone	If this attribute is set to «yes», then the XML declaration will specify «standalone="yes"». If this attribute is set to «no», then the XML declaration will specify «standalone="no"». If the attribute is omitted, then the XML declaration will not include a standalone attribute. This will make it a valid text declaration, enabling its use in an external general parsed entity. This attribute should not be used unless the output is a well-formed XML document.
doctype-system	If this attribute is specified, the output file should include a document type declaration after the XML declaration and before the first element start tag. The name of the document type will be the same as the name of the first element. The value of this attribute will be used as the system identifier in the document type declaration. This attribute should not be used unless the output is a well-formed XML document.
doctype-public	This attribute is ignored unless the doctype-system attribute is also specified. It defines the value of the public identifier to go in the document type declaration. If no public identifier is specified, none is included in the document type declaration.

4

Elements

Attribute	Interpretation
media-type	This attribute defines the media type of the output file (often referred to as its MIME type). The default value is «text/xml». The specification doesn't say what use is made of this information: it doesn't affect the contents of the output file, but it may affect the way it is named, stored, or transmitted, depending on the environment. For example, the information might find its way into an HTTP protocol header.

Rules for HTML output

When the method attribute is set to «html», or when it is defaulted and the result tree is recognized as representing HTML, the output will be an HTML file. By default it will conform to HTML 4.0.

The XSLT specification doesn't mention the possibility of producing XHTML output, which is not really surprising as it was published before the XHTML specification. XHTML is pure XML, so if you want to generate XHTML, use the XML output method.

HTML is output in the same way as XML, except where specific differences are noted. These differences are:

❏ Certain elements are recognized as empty elements. They are recognized in any combination of upper and lower case. These elements are output with a start tag and no end tag. For HTML 4.0 these elements are:

```
<area>        <frame>       <isindex>
<base>        <hr>          <link>
<basefont>    <img>         <meta>
<br>          <input>       <param>
<col>
```

❏ The <script> and <style> elements (again in any combination of upper and lower case) do not require escaping of special characters. In the text content of these elements, a «<» character will be output as «<», not as «<».

❏ HTML attributes whose value is a URI (for example, the href attribute of the <a> element, or the src attribute of the <img> element) are recognized, and special characters within the URI are escaped as defined in the HTML specification. For example, non-ASCII characters in the URI should be represented by converting each byte of the UTF-8 representation of the character to «%HH» where HH represents the byte value in hexadecimal; spaces will be represented as «%20».

❏ Special characters may be output using character entity references such as «é» where these are defined in the relevant version of HTML. This is at the discretion of the XSLT processor, it doesn't have to use these entity names.

❑ Processing instructions are terminated with «>» rather than «?>». Processing instructions are not often used in HTML, but the HTML 4.0 standard recommends that any vendor extensions should be implemented this way, rather than by adding element tags to the language. So it is possible they will be seen more frequently in the future.

❑ Attributes that are conventionally written with a keyword only, and no value, will be recognized and output in this form. Common examples are `<TEXTAREA READONLY>` and `<OPTION SELECTED>`. This is shorthand, permitted in SGML but not in XML, for an attribute that has only one permitted value, which is the same as the attribute name. In XML, these tags must be written as `<TABLE BORDER="BORDER">` and `<OPTION SELECTED="SELECTED">`. The HTML output method will normally use the abbreviated form, as this is the only form that older HTML browsers will recognize.

❑ The special use of the ampersand character in dynamic HTML attributes is recognized. For example, the tag `<TD WIDTH="&{width};">` is correct HTML, though it would not be correct in XML, because of the ampersand character. To produce this output from a literal result element, the tag in the stylesheet would need to be written as `<TD WIDTH="&amp;{{width}};">`: note the double curly braces, to prevent them being interpreted with their special meaning in attribute value templates.

The attributes on the `<xsl:output>` element are interpreted as follows when HTML output is selected.

Attribute	Interpretation
version	The version of HTML used in the output document. It is up to the implementation which versions of HTML should be supported, though all implementations can be expected to support the default version, namely version 4.0
encoding	This specifies the preferred character encoding for the output document. This will be used to generate a `charset` attribute of a `<META>` element inserted immediately after the start tag of the `<HEAD>` element, if there is one. If the encoding is one that does not allow all XML characters to be represented directly, for example «iso-8859-1», then characters outside this subset will be represented where possible using either character entity references or numeric character references. It is an error if such characters appear in contexts where character references are not recognized (for example within a script element, within a comment, or in an element or attribute name).
indent	If this attribute has the value «yes», the idea is that the HTML output should be indented to show its hierarchic structure. The XSLT processor is not obliged to respect this request, and if it does so, the precise form of the output is not defined.

4

Elements

Attribute	Interpretation
	When producing indented output, the processor has much more freedom to add or remove whitespace than in the XML case, because of the way whitespace is handled in HTML: the processor can add or remove whitespace anywhere it likes so long as it doesn't change the way a browser would display the HTML.
cdata-section-elements	This attribute is not applicable to HTML output.
omit-xml-declaration	This attribute is not applicable to HTML output.
standalone	This attribute is not applicable to HTML output.
doctype-system	If this attribute is specified, the output file will include a document type declaration immediately before the first element start tag. The name of the document type will be «HTML» or «html». The value of the attribute will be used as the system identifier in the document type declaration.
doctype-public	If this attribute is specified, the output file will include a document type declaration immediately before the first element start tag. The name of the document type will be «HTML» or «html». The value of the attribute will be used as the public identifier in the document type declaration.
media-type	This attribute defines the media type of the output file (often referred to as its MIME type). The default value is «text/html». The specification doesn't say what use is made of this information: it doesn't affect the contents of the output file, but it may affect the way it is named, stored, or transmitted, depending on the environment. For example, the information might find its way into an HTTP protocol header.

Rules for Text Output

When «method="text"», the result tree is output as a plain text file. The values of the text nodes of the tree are copied to the output, and all other nodes are ignored. Within text nodes, all character values are output using the relevant encoding as determined by the encoding attribute: there are no special characters such as «&» to be escaped.

The way in which line endings are output (for example LF or CRLF) is not defined: the implementation might choose to use the default line-ending conventions of the platform on which it is running.

The attributes that are relevant to text output are listed below. All other attributes are ignored.

Attribute	Interpretation
encoding	This specifies the preferred character encoding for the output document. The default value is implementation-defined, and may depend on the platform on which it is running. If the encoding is one that does not allow all XML characters to be represented directly, for example «iso-8859-1», then any character outside this subset will be reported as an error.

Attribute	Interpretation
media-type	This attribute defines the media type of the output file (often referred to as its MIME type). The default value is «text/plain». The specification doesn't say what use is made of this information: it doesn't affect the contents of the output file, but it may affect the way it is named, stored, or transmitted, depending on the environment. For example, the information might find its way into an HTTP protocol header.

Usage

The defaulting mechanisms ensure that it is usually not necessary to include an <xsl:output> element in the stylesheet. By default, the XML output method is used unless the first thing output is an <HTML> element, in which case the HTML output method is assumed. (This means that if you want to generate XHTML, it might be a good idea to specify <xsl:output method="xml"/> explicitly).

The <xsl:output> element is concerned with how your result tree is turned into an output file. If the XSLT processor allows you to do something else with the result tree, for example passing it to the application as a DOM Document, then the <xsl:output> element is irrelevant.

The encoding attribute can be very useful to ensure that the output file can be easily viewed and edited. Unfortunately, though, the set of possible values varies from one XSLT implementation to another, and may also depend on the environment. For example, many XSLT processors are written in Java and use the Java facilities for encoding the output stream, but the set of encodings supported by each Java VM is different. However, support for iso-8859-1 encoding is fairly universal, so if you have trouble viewing the output file because it contains UTF-8 Unicode characters, setting the encoding to iso-9959-1 is often a good remedy.

Examples

The following example requests XML output using ISO 8859/1 encoding. The output will be indented for readability, and the contents of the <script> element, because it is expected to contain many special characters, will be output as a CDATA section. The output file will reference the DTD booklist.dtd: note that it is entirely the user's responsibility to ensure that the output of the stylesheet actually conforms to this DTD, and, indeed, that it is a well-formed XML document.

```
<xsl:output
    method="xml"
    indent="yes"
    encoding="iso-8859-1"
    cdata-section-elements="script"
    doctype-system="booklist.dtd" />
```

The following example might be used if the output of the stylesheet is a comma-separated-values file using US ASCII characters only.

```
<xsl:output
    method="text"
    encoding="us-ascii" />
```

xsl:param

The <xsl:param> element is used either at the top level, to describe a global parameter, or immediately within an <xsl:template> element, to describe a local parameter to a template. It specifies a name for the parameter and a default value, which is used if the caller supplies no value for the parameter.

Defined in

XSLT section 11

Format

```
<xsl:param name=QName select=Expression >
    template-body
</xsl:param>
```

Position

<xsl:param> may appear as a top-level element (a child of the <xsl:stylesheet> element), or as an immediate child element of <xsl:template>. In the latter case, <xsl:param> elements must come before any other child elements.

Attributes

Name	Value	Meaning
name mandatory	QName	The name of the parameter
select optional	Expression	The default value of the parameter if no explicit value is supplied by the caller

The constructs QName (on page 388) and Expression (on page 351) are defined in Chapter 5.

Content

An optional *template body*. If a select attribute is present, the element should be empty.

Effect

An <xsl:param> element at the top level of the stylesheet declares a global parameter; an <xsl:param> element appearing as a child of an <xsl:template> element declares a local parameter for that template.

The `<xsl:param>` element defines the name of the parameter, and a default value. The default value is used only if no other value is explicitly supplied by the caller.

An explicit value can be supplied for a local parameter by using the `<xsl:with-param>` element when the template is invoked using `<xsl:apply-templates>` or `<xsl:call-template>`.

The way in which explicit values are supplied for global parameters is implementer defined (for example, they may be defined on the command line or through environment variables, or they may be supplied via a vendor-defined API).

There is no way of supplying an explicit value for a local parameter when the template rule is invoked using `<xsl:apply-imports>`.

The Value of the Parameter

The default value of the parameter may be given either by the `Expression` in the `select` attribute, or by the contents of the contained *template-body*. If there is a `select` attribute, the `<xsl:param>` element should be empty. If there is no `select` attribute and the template body is empty, the default value of the parameter is an empty string.

If the value is given by an `Expression`, the data type of the value will be Boolean, number, string, or node-set, depending on the expression. If the value is given by a non-empty template body, the data type will always be a result tree fragment. This is all exactly the same as with the `<xsl:variable>` element, described on page 308.

The Name of the Parameter

The name of the parameter is defined by `QName`. Normally this will be a simple name (such as «num» or «list-of-names»), but it may be a name qualified with a prefix, for example «my:value». If it has a prefix, the prefix must correspond to a namespace that is in scope at that point in the stylesheet. The true name of the parameter, for the purpose of testing whether two names are the same, is determined not by the prefix but by the namespace URI corresponding to the prefix: so two variables «my:value» and «your:value» have the same name if the prefixes «my» and «your» refer to the same namespace URI. If the name has no prefix, it is treated like an attribute name: that is, it has a null namespace URI – it does not use the default namespace URI.

Parameter names are referenced in exactly the same way as variables, by prefixing the name with a dollar sign (for example «$num») and all the rules for uniqueness and scope of names are exactly as if the `<xsl:param>` element was replaced by an `<xsl:variable>` element. The only difference between parameters and variables is the way they acquire an initial value.

Usage

Global parameters are particularly useful to select which part of the source document to process. A common scenario is that the XSLT processor will be running within a web server. The user request will be accepted by a Java Server Page or by a Java servlet, or indeed by an ASP page, the request parameters will be accepted, and the stylesheet processing will be kicked off using an API defined by each vendor. Generally this API will provide some way of passing the parameters that came from the HTTP request into the stylesheet as the initial values of global `<xsl:param>` elements.

Local parameters are used more often with `<xsl:call-template>` than with `<xsl:apply-templates>`, though they are available to both. The actual value of the parameter is set by the caller using an `<xsl:with-param>` element. Parameters are often needed by the recursive algorithms used in XSLT to handle lists of items: there are examples of such algorithms under `<xsl:call-template>` on page 167.

Examples

Example: Using <xsl:param> with a Default Value

Source

This stylesheet works with any XML source file.

Stylesheet

The stylesheet is `call.xsl`.

It contains a named template that outputs the depth of a node (defined as the number of ancestors). The node may be supplied as a parameter; if it is not supplied, the parameter defaults to the current node.

The stylesheet includes a template rule for the root node that invokes this named template, defaulting the parameter, to display the name and depth of every element in the source document.

```
<xsl:transform
 xmlns:xsl="http://www.w3.org/1999/XSL/Transform"
 version="1.0"
>
<xsl:output method="text"/>

<xsl:template match="/">
<xsl:for-each select="//*">
    <xsl:value-of select="concat(name(), ' -- ')"/>
    <xsl:call-template name="depth"/>;
</xsl:for-each>
</xsl:template>

<xsl:template name="depth">
    <xsl:param name="node" select="."/>
    <xsl:value-of select="count($node/ancestor::node())"/>
</xsl:template>
</xsl:transform>
```

Output

If the stylesheet is run against the file poem.xml, the output is as follows:

```
poem -- 1;
author -- 2;
date -- 2;
title -- 2;
stanza -- 2;
line -- 3;
line -- 3;
line -- 3;
line -- 3;
stanza -- 2;
line -- 3;
line -- 3;
line -- 3;
line -- 3;
stanza -- 2;
line -- 3;
line -- 3;
line -- 3;
line -- 3;
```

See also

<xsl:apply-templates> on page 145.
<xsl:call-template> on page 167.
<xsl:variable> on page 308.
<xsl:with-param> on page 318.

xsl:preserve-space

The <xsl:preserve-space> element, along with <xsl:strip-space>, is used to control the way in which whitespace nodes in the source document are handled.

Defined in

XSLT section 3.4

Format

```
<xsl:preserve-space elements=list-of-NameTests />
```

Position

<xsl:preserve-space> is a top-level element, meaning that it must be a child of the <xsl:stylesheet> element. There are no constraints on its ordering relative to other top-level elements.

Attributes

Name	Value	Meaning
elements mandatory	Whitespace-separated list of NameTests	Defines the elements in the source document whose whitespace-only text nodes are to be preserved

The NameTest construct is defined on page 368, in Chapter 5. It may be an actual element name, the symbol «*» meaning all elements, or the construct «prefix:*» meaning all elements in a particular namespace.

Content

None, the element is always empty

Effect

This element, together with <xsl:strip-space> defines the way that whitespace-only text nodes in the source document are handled. Unless contradicted by an <xsl:strip-space> element, <xsl:preserve-space> indicates that whitespace-only text nodes occurring as children of a specified element are to be retained in the source tree.

Preserving whitespace-only text nodes is the default action, so this element only needs to be used where it is necessary to contradict an <xsl:strip-space> element. The interaction of the two is explained below.

The concept of whitespace-only text nodes is explained at some length, starting on page 129, in Chapter 3.

This element also affects the handling of whitespace-only text nodes in any document loaded using the document() function. It does not affect the handling of whitespace-only text nodes in the stylesheet when used in its role as a stylesheet, but it does affect the stylesheet in the same way as any other document if a copy of the stylesheet is loaded using the document() function.

A whitespace-only text node is a text node whose text consists **entirely** of a sequence of whitespace characters, these being space, tab, carriage return, and linefeed (#x20, #x9, #xD, and #xA). The <xsl:preserve-space> element has no effect on whitespace contained in text nodes that also contain non-whitespace characters: such whitespace is always preserved and is part of the value of the text node.

Before a node is classified as a whitespace-only text node, the tree is normalized by concatenating all adjacent text nodes. This includes the merging of text that originated in different XML entities.

A whitespace-only text node may either be stripped or preserved. If it is stripped, it is removed from the tree. This means it will never be matched, it will never be copied to the output, and it will never be counted when nodes are numbered. If it is preserved, it is retained on the tree in its original form, subject only to the end-of-line normalization performed by the XML parser.

If a whitespace-only text node has an ancestor with an xml:space attribute and the nearest ancestor with such an attribute has the value «xml:space= "preserve"», then the text node is preserved regardless of the ‹xsl:preserve-space› and ‹xsl:strip-space› elements in the stylesheet.

The elements attribute of ‹xsl:preserve-space› must contain a whitespace-separated list of NameTests. The form of a NameTest is defined in the XPath expression language: see Chapter 5, page 368. Each form of NameTest has an associated priority. The different forms of *NameTest* and their meanings are:

Syntax	Examples	Meaning	Priority
QName	title svg:width	Matches the full element name, including its namespace URI	0
NCName «:*»	svg:*	Matches all elements in the namespace whose URI corresponds to the given prefix	−0.25
«*»	*	Matches all elements	−0.5

The priority is used when conflicts arise. For example, if the stylesheet specifies:

```
<xsl:strip-space elements="*"/>
<xsl:preserve-space elements="para clause"/>
```

then whitespace-only text nodes appearing within a ‹para› or ‹clause› will be preserved. Even though these elements match both the ‹xsl:strip-space› and the ‹xsl:preserve-space›, the NameTest in the latter has higher priority (0 as compared to −0.5).

An ‹xsl:strip-space› or ‹xsl:preserve-space› element containing several NameTests is equivalent to writing a separate ‹xsl:strip-space› or ‹xsl:preserve-space› element for each NameTest individually.

A whitespace-only text node is preserved if there is no ‹xsl:strip-space› element in the stylesheet that matches its parent element.

A whitespace-only text node is removed from the tree if there is an ‹xsl:strip-space› element that matches the parent element, and no ‹xsl:preserve-space› element that matches.

If there is both an `<xsl:strip-space>` element that matches the parent element, and an `<xsl:preserve-space>` element that matches, then the decision depends on the import precedence and priority of the respective rules. Taking into consideration all the `<xsl:strip-space>` and `<xsl:preserve-space>` elements that match the parent element of the whitespace-only text node, take the one with highest import precedence (as defined in the rules for `<xsl:import>` on page 207). If there is more than one with this import precedence, take the one with highest priority, as defined in the table above. If there is still more than one, the XSLT processor may either report an error, or choose the one that occurs last in the stylesheet. If the chosen element is `<xsl:preserve-space>`, the whitespace-only text node is preserved on the tree, if it is `<xsl:strip-space>`, it is removed from the tree.

In deciding whether to strip or preserve a whitespace-only text node, only its immediate parent element is considered in the above rules. The rules for its other ancestors make no difference. The element itself, of course, is never removed from the tree: the stripping process will only ever remove text nodes.

If an individual element has the XML-defined attribute «xml:space="preserve"» or «xml:space="default"» this overrides anything defined in the stylesheet. These values, unlike `<xsl:preserve-space>` and `<xsl:strip-space>`, do affect descendant elements as well as the element on which the attribute appears. If an `<xsl:strip-space>` doesn't seem to be having any effect, one possible reason is that the element type in question is declared in the DTD to have an xml:space attribute with a default value of «preserve». There is no way of overriding this in the stylesheet.

Usage

For many categories of source document, especially those used to represent data structures, whitespace-only text nodes are never significant, so it is useful to specify:

```
<xsl:strip-space elements="*"/>
```

which will remove them all from the tree. There are two main advantages in stripping these unwanted nodes:

❑   when `<xsl:apply-templates>` is used with a default select attribute, all child nodes will be processed. If whitespace-only text nodes are not stripped, they too will be processed, probably leading to the whitespace being copied to the output destination.

❑   when the position() function is used to determine the position of an element relative to its siblings, the whitespace-only text nodes are included in the count. This often leads to the significant nodes being numbered 2, 4, 6, 8 ...

Generally speaking, it is a good idea to strip whitespace-only text nodes belonging to elements that have element content, that is, elements declared in the DTD as containing child elements but no #PCDATA.

It also usually does no harm to strip whitespace-only text nodes from elements declared as having #PCDATA content, that is, elements whose only children are text nodes. In most cases, an element containing whitespace text is equivalent to an empty element, so stylesheet logic can be simplified if elements containing whitespace only are normalized to be empty by removing the text node.

By contrast, stripping whitespace-only text nodes from elements with MIXED content, that is, elements declared in the DTD to contain both child elements and #PCDATA, is often a bad idea. For example, consider the element below:

```
<quote>He went to <edu>Balliol College</edu> <city>Oxford</city> to read
<subject>Greats</subject></quote>
```

The space between the <edu> element and the <city> element is a whitespace-only text node, and it should be preserved, because otherwise when the tags are removed by an application that's only interested in the text, the words «College» and «Oxford» will run together.

Examples

To strip whitespace nodes from all elements of the source tree:

```
<xsl:strip-space elements="*"/>
```

To strip whitespace nodes from selected elements:

```
<xsl:strip-space elements="book author title price"/>
```

To strip whitespace nodes from all elements except the <description> element:

```
<xsl:strip-space elements="*"/>
<xsl:preserve-space elements="description"/>
```

To strip whitespace nodes from all elements except those in the namespace with URI http://mednet.org/text:

```
<xsl:strip-space elements="*"/>
<xsl:preserve-space elements="mednet:*"
                    xmlns:mednet="http://mednet.org/text" />
```

See also

<xsl:strip-space> on page 277

xsl:processing-instruction

The <xsl:processing-instruction> instruction is used to write a processing instruction node to the current output destination.

4

Elements

Defined in

XSLT section 7.3

Format

```
<xsl:processing-instruction name=QName >
   template-body
</xsl:processing-instruction>
```

Position

`<xsl:processing-instruction>` is an instruction. It is always used as part of a template-body.

Attributes

Name	Value	Meaning
name mandatory	Attribute value template returning an NCName	The name (target) of the generated processing instruction.

Content

A template-body.

Effect

The name of the generated processing-instruction (in XML terms, the `PITarget`), is determined by the `name` attribute. This may be expressed as an attribute value template. The name must be valid as a `PITarget` as defined in the XML specification, and XSLT imposes the additional rule that it must be a valid `NCName`, as defined in the XML Namespaces recommendation. This means it must be an XML `Name` that doesn't contain a colon (to make it an `NCName`) and that isn't the name «xml» in any mixture of upper and lower case (to make it a `PITarget`).

The specification is quite explicit that `<xsl:processing-instruction>` cannot be used to generate an XML declaration at the start of the output file. The XML declaration looks like a processing instruction, but technically it isn't one; and the ban on using the name «xml» makes this quite explicit. The XML declaration in the output file is generated automatically by the XSLT processor, and can be controlled to a limited extent using the `<xsl:output>` element.

The data part of the processing instruction is generated from the contained *template-body*. The space that separates the `PITarget` from the data is output automatically. The output generated by the template body must contain text nodes only, and it must not contain the string «?>» which terminates a processing instruction. Implementations are allowed to trap the «?>» and replace it by «? >» (with an embedded space); unfortunately they are also allowed to report this as an error, so if you want your stylesheet to be portable, you need to make sure this condition can't happen.

The data part of a processing instruction cannot contain character references such as «₤», so it is an error to output any characters that can't be represented directly in the chosen character encoding of the output file. Some processing instructions may accept data that contains a character reference, but that's an application-level convention, not something defined in the XML standard, so the XSLT processor will never generate such a reference automatically.

Usage

Use this instruction when you want to output a processing instruction.

Processing instructions are not widely used in most XML applications, so you will probably not need to use this instruction very often. They are used even less in HTML, though HTML 4.0 does recommend that any vendor-specific extensions should be implemented this way. In HTML the terminator for a processing instruction is «>» rather than «?>», and this difference is handled automatically by the HTML output method: see <xsl:output> on page 250.

Note that you cannot generate a processing instruction in the output by writing a processing instruction in the stylesheet. Processing instructions in the stylesheet are ignored completely. You can, however, use <xsl:copy> or <xsl:copy-of> to copy processing instructions from the source tree to the result tree.

Examples

The following example outputs an <?xml-stylesheet?> processing instruction at the start of the output file.

```
<xsl:processing-instruction name="xml-stylesheet">
<xsl:text>href="housestyle.css" type="text/css"</xsl:text>
</xsl:processing-instruction>
```

The generated output is:

```
<?xml-stylesheet href="housestyle.css" type="text/css"?>
```

Writing an XSLT stylesheet that produces an XML document which itself refers to a CSS stylesheet isn't such a crazy thing to do as it might seem. It often makes sense to do the first stage of processing of an XML file on the server, and the second stage on the client (in other words, in the browser). The first stage will extract the data that the user wants to see – and, most importantly, remove any information they are not allowed to see. The second stage applies the detailed rules for output formatting. The second stage can often be done just as easily with CSS as with XSL, because anything CSS can't cope with, such as adding or reordering textual content, can be done in the first stage with XSLT.

4

Elements

One point to watch out for in generating an `<?xml-stylesheet?>` processing instruction, and which might well apply to other processing instructions, is the use of pseudo attributes and pseudo character and entity references. The text «`href="housestyle.css"`» in the above example is designed to look like an XML attribute, but it is not actually an XML attribute, it is purely part of the processing instruction data. It is parsed by the application, not by the XML parser. As it is not a true XML attribute, you cannot generate it as an attribute node using the `<xsl:attribute>` instruction; rather, it is generated as text.

The rules for the `<?xml-stylesheet?>` processing instruction are defined in a short W3C Recommendation called *Associating Style Sheets with XML documents*, available at http://www.w3.org/TR/xml-stylesheet. As well as defining the data part of this processing instruction in the form of pseudo-attributes, the rules also allow the use of numeric character references such as «`&#x20A4;`» and predefined entity references such as «`&gt;`» and «`&amp;`». Again, these are not true character references and entity references that the XML parser will recognize, and as a result they will not be generated by the XSLT processor either. If you want to include «`&#x20A4;`» as part of the data of the processing instruction, write, for example,

```
<xsl:processing-instruction name="xml-stylesheet">
<xsl:text>href="housestyle.css" type="text/css" </xsl:text>
<xsl:text>title="A title containing &amp;#x20A4;" </xsl:text>
</xsl:processing-instruction>
```

xsl:sort

The `<xsl:sort>` element is used to define a sort key, to specify the order in which nodes selected by `<xsl:apply-templates>` or `<xsl:for-each>` are processed.

Defined in

XSLT section 10

Format

```
<xsl:sort
    select=Expression
    order={"ascending" | "descending"}
    case-order={"upper-first" | "lower-first"}
    lang={language-code}
    data-type={"text" | "number" | QName }/>
```

Position

`<xsl:sort>` is always a child of `<xsl:apply-templates>` or `<xsl:for-each>`. Any number of sort keys may be specified, in major-to-minor order. When used in `<xsl:for-each>`, any `<xsl:sort>` elements must appear before the *template-body* of the `<xsl:for-each>` statement. When used in `<xsl:apply-templates>`, the `<xsl:sort>` elements can come before or after any `<xsl:with-param>` elements.

Attributes

Name	Value	Meaning
select optional	Expression	Defines the sort key. The default is the string value of the node (the expression «string(.)»).
order optional	Attribute value template returning: «ascending» | «descending»	Defines whether the nodes are processed in ascending or descending order of this key. The default is «ascending».
case-order optional	Attribute value template returning: «upper-first» | «lower-first»	Defines whether upper-case letters are to be collated before or after lower-case letters. The default is language-dependent.
lang optional	Attribute value template returning a language code	Defines the language whose collating conventions are to be used. The default depends on the processing environment.
data-type optional	Attribute value template returning: «text» | «number» | QName	Defines whether the values are to be collated alphabetically or numerically, or using a user-defined data type. The default is «text».

Content

None, the element is always empty.

Effect

The list of <xsl:sort> elements within an <xsl:apply-templates> or <xsl:for-each> element determines the order in which the selected nodes are processed. The nodes are sorted first by the first sort key; any group of nodes that have duplicate values for the first sort key are then sorted by the second sort key, and so on. If a group of nodes have duplicate values for all the sort keys, this group is sorted in document order. Similarly, when no sort keys are specified at all, the nodes are processed in document order.

The value of the sort key for each node in the node-set is established by evaluating the expression given in the select attribute. This is evaluated with that node as the current node, and with the current node list being the complete node-set, in document order.

The XSLT specification actually says "in unsorted order", but it's reasonable to interpret this here as meaning document order.

This means that if you want to process the nodes in reverse document order, you can specify a sort key as:

```
<xsl:sort select="position()"
                data-type="number"
                order="descending" />
```

The result of the expression is always converted to a string, and if the data-type is «number» this string will then be converted to a number.

The way in which sort keys are compared is determined by the other attributes of the <xsl:sort> element. Some of these rules are defined precisely in the XSLT specification, some are given merely as guidance for the implementer, and some are left entirely implementation-defined. The specification explicitly warns that different implementations may produce different results.

The data-type may be either «text» or «number». With «text» order, you would expect to see «10» appear before «5», while with «number» order, you would expect «5» to come before «10».

❑ Ordering of numbers is well defined in most cases. The specification says that they are sorted according to the numeric value: but it doesn't define what happens to NaN (not a number) values. The implementation can put them first or last, or (as some products currently do) leave them scattered around the list more or less at random. As the sort key is converted first to a string, and then back to a number, any keys whose numeric value is Infinity or minus Infinity will also be converted to NaN values by this process.

❑ Ordering of text strings is very loosely defined. The concept of alphabetic order is language-dependent, so the intention is that it should be controlled by the lang attribute. For example, in modern German «ä» is collated immediately after «a» (in older works, it is collated as if it were the pair of letters «ae»), while in Swedish, «ä» is a separate letter that appears at the end of the alphabet after «z». The XSLT specification refers implementers for guidance to a Unicode white paper on international sorting: Unicode Technical Report #10, *Unicode Collation Algorithm*. (See http://www.unicode.org/unicode/reports/tr10/index.html). However, it doesn't make any of the rules mandatory.

Knowing the language doesn't help you decide whether upper-case or lower-case letters should come first (every dictionary in the world has its own rules on this), so XSLT makes this a separate attribute, case-order. Generally case-order will be used only to decide the ordering of two words that compare equal if case is ignored. For example, in German, where an initial upper-case letter can change the meaning of a word, some dictionaries list the adjective *drall* (meaning plump or buxom) before the unrelated noun *Drall* (a swerve, twist, or bias), while others reverse the order. Specifying «case-order="lower-first"» would place *drall* immediately before *Drall*, while «case-order="upper-first"» would have *Drall* immediately followed by *drall*.

The specification isn't absolutely explicit about how `case-order` and `order` interact: does «`upper-first`» mean first in the collating sequence, or first in the output?. The intention is probably that «`case-order="upper-first"`» with «`order="descending"`» means that in the final output order, *Drall* comes **after** *drall*.

The `order` attribute specifies whether the order is ascending or descending. Descending order will generally produce the opposite result of ascending order – though even that isn't strictly guaranteed, for example the implementation could choose to put numbers whose value is NaN (not a number) at the start of the list in both cases.

The option to set «`data-type="QName"`» was a last-minute addition to the language before version 1.0 was frozen, and its behavior is not precisely defined. It's really a hook to allow vendor extensions, or perhaps to allow extensions in a subsequent addendum to the standard: there is a recognized requirement to enable sorting of data types such as dates and times that are likely to be defined in the forthcoming XML Schema recommendation.

The final sorted order of the nodes determines the sequence in which they are processed by the containing `<xsl:apply-templates>` or `<xsl:for-each>` statement, and also the value of the `position()` function when each node comes to be processed. The value of `position()` will reflect its position in the sorted list.

Usage

XSLT is designed to be capable of handling serious professional publishing applications, and clearly this requires some fairly powerful sorting capabilities. In practice, however, the most demanding applications almost invariably have domain-specific collating rules: the rules for sorting personal names in a telephone directory are unlikely to work well for geographical names in a gazetteer. For these applications, vendors are already providing hooks to allow user-defined collating algorithms.

Examples

I'll start with a couple of simple examples, and then show a full working example which you can download and try yourself.

Example 1: To process all the `<book>` children of the current node, sorting them by the value of the `isbn` attribute:

```
<xsl:apply-templates select="book">
   <xsl:sort select="@isbn"/>
</xsl:apply-templates>
```

Example 2: To output the contents of all the `<city>` elements in the document, in alphabetical order, including each distinct city once only:

```
<ul>
<xsl:for-each select="//city[not(.=preceding::city)]">
   <xsl:sort select="."/>
   <li><xsl:value-of select="."/></li>
</xsl:for-each>
</ul>
```

If «select=" . "» was omitted from the <xsl:sort> element, the effect would be the same, because this is the default; however, I prefer to include it for clarity.

Example: Sorting on the Result of a Calculation

This example outputs a list of products, sorted by the total sales of each product, in descending order.

Source

This is the file products.xml.

```
<products>
<product name="strawberry jam">
   <region name="south" sales="20.00"/>
   <region name="north" sales="50.00"/>
</product>
<product name="raspberry jam">
   <region name="south" sales="205.16"/>
   <region name="north" sales="10.50"/>
</product>
<product name="plum jam">
   <region name="east" sales="320.20"/>
   <region name="north" sales="39.50"/>
</product>
</products>
```

Stylesheet

products.xsl is a complete stylesheet written using the simplified stylesheet syntax, in which the entire stylesheet module is written as a single literal result element. Simplified stylesheets are described in Chapter 3, on page 104.

The <xsl:sort> element sorts the selected node-set (containing all the <product> elements) in descending order of the numerical total of the the sales attribute over all their <region> child elements. The total is calculated using the sum() function (discussed on page 520), and displayed using the format-number() function (shown on page 455).

```
<products xsl:version="1.0"
        xmlns:xsl="http://www.w3.org/1999/XSL/Transform">
<xsl:for-each select="products/product">
    <xsl:sort select="sum(region/@sales)"
                           data-type="number"
                           order="descending"/>
    <product name="{@name}"
            sales="{format-number(sum(region/@sales), '$####0.00')}"/>
</xsl:for-each>
</products>
```

Output

I have added line breaks for readability:

```
<products>
<product name="plum jam" sales="$359.70"/>
<product name="raspberry jam" sales="$215.66"/>
<product name="strawberry jam" sales="$70.00"/>
</products>
```

See also

<xsl:apply-templates> on page 145.
<xsl:for-each> on page 201.

xsl:strip-space

The <xsl:strip-space> element, along with <xsl:preserve-space>, is used to control the way in which whitespace nodes in the source document are handled. The <xsl:strip-space> element identifies elements in which whitespace-only text nodes are considered insignificant, so they can be removed from the source tree.

Defined in

XSLT section 3.4

Format

```
<xsl:strip-space  elements=list-of-NameTests />
```

Position

<xsl:strip-space> is a top-level element, which means it is always a child of the <xsl:stylesheet> element. There are no constraints on where it appears relative to other top-level elements.

Attributes

Name	Value	Meaning
elements mandatory	Whitespace-separated list of NameTests	Defines elements in the source document whose whitespace-only text nodes are to be removed

The construct NameTest is defined in Chapter 5, on page 368.

Content

None, the element is always empty.

Effect, Usage, and Examples

See `<xsl:preserve-space>` on page 265. The two elements `<xsl:strip-space>` and `<xsl:preserve-space>` are closely related, so we have presented the rules and usage guidance in one place.

See also

`<xsl:preserve-space>` on page 265.
`<xsl:text>` on page 299.

xsl:stylesheet

The `<xsl:stylesheet>` element is the outermost element of a stylesheet. The synonym `<xsl:transform>` can be used as an alternative.

Defined in

XSLT section 2.2

Format

```
<xsl:stylesheet
    id=identifier
    version="1.0"
    xmlns:xsl="http://www.w3.org/1999/XSL/Transform"
    extension-element-prefixes=list-of-prefixes
    exclude-result-prefixes=list-of-prefixes >
        top-level-element *
</xsl:stylesheet>
```

Position

`<xsl:stylesheet>` appears as the outermost element of every stylesheet module, except one that uses the *literal-result-element-as-stylesheet* syntax described on page 104, in Chapter 3. It is used both on a principal stylesheet and on one that is imported or included into another stylesheet.

As well as being the outermost element of the stylesheet module, the `<xsl:stylesheet>` element is usually the document element of an XML document – but not always: as described in Chapter 3, a stylesheet can also be embedded in another XML document.

Namespace Declarations

There will always be at least one namespace declaration on the `<xsl:stylesheet>` element, typically:

```
xmlns:xsl="http://www.w3.org/1999/XSL/Transform"
```

This is necessary to identify the document as an XSLT stylesheet. The URI part must be written exactly as shown. The prefix «xsl» is conventional, and is used in all XSLT documentation including this book and the standard itself, but you could choose a different prefix if you wanted, for example «XSLT». You would then have to name the element <XSLT:stylesheet> instead of <xsl:stylesheet>.

You can also make this the default namespace by using the following declaration:

```
xmlns="http://www.w3.org/1999/XSL/Transform"
```

In this case the element name will simply be <stylesheet>, and other XSLT elements will similarly be unprefixed, for example <template> rather than <xsl:template>. Although this works, it is not generally recommended, because the default namespace is then not available for literal result elements. The technique that works best is to reserve the default namespace for literal result elements that you want to go in the default namespace of the output document.

If you come across a stylesheet that uses the namespace declaration:

```
xmlns:xsl="http://www.w3.org/TR/WD-xsl"
```

then it is probably not an XSLT stylesheet at all, but one written in the early dialect of XSL that Microsoft shipped when Internet Explorer was shipped in 1998. See Chapter 10 for details of Microsoft XSL products.

Attributes

Name	Value	Meaning
id optional	XML Name	An identifier used to identify the <xsl:stylesheet> element when it is embedded in another XML document.
version mandatory	Number	Defines the version of XSLT required by this stylesheet. Until future versions of the XSLT specification are published, this should be set to «1.0».
extension- element-prefixes optional	Whitespace-separated list of NCNames	Defines the namespaces used in this stylesheet to identify extension elements.
exclude-result- prefixes optional	Whitespace-separated list of NCNames	Defines the namespaces used in this stylesheet that should not be copied to the output destination, unless they are actually used in the result document.

Content

The `<xsl:stylesheet>` element may contain XSLT elements referred to as **top-level elements**. These elements are:

```
<xsl:attribute-set>     <xsl:key>                  <xsl:preserve-
<xsl:decimal-format>    <xsl:namespace-alias>      space>
<xsl:import>            <xsl:output>               <xsl:strip-space>
<xsl:include>           <xsl:param>                <xsl:template>
                                                   <xsl:variable>
```

If there are any `<xsl:import>` elements, they must come before other top-level elements.

The `<xsl:stylesheet>` element may also contain other elements provided they use a non-null namespace URI which is different from the XSLT namespace URI. If the namespace URI is recognized by the XSLT processor, it may interpret such elements in any way the vendor chooses, provided that the correct functioning of the stylesheet is not affected. If it does not recognize these elements, it should ignore them.

Effect

The rules are described below for each of the attributes.

The id Attribute

This attribute is there to allow an `<xsl:stylesheet>` element to be referenced when it is contained within another XML document.

The precise usage is not defined in the standard, but the expectation is that this id attribute will allow an embedded stylesheet to be referenced in an `<?xml-stylesheet?>` processing instruction. An example is given in Chapter 3.

The version Attribute

The version attribute defines the version of the XSLT specification that the stylesheet is relying on. At present there is only one version of the XSLT standard, namely version 1.0, so this attribute should always take this value.

Implementations of XSLT, even if they only implement version 1.0 of the standard, are required to behave in a particular way if the version specified is anything other than 1.0.

❑ If the version attribute is «1.0», the implementation must report any elements in the XSLT namespace that it doesn't recognize as errors. For example, if it encounters the element `<xsl:apply_template>` it will flag this as an error (because the correct spelling is `<xsl:apply-templates>`).

❑ If the version attribute is any other value (including, oddly, a lower value than 1.0), the implementation must assume that the stylesheet is trying to use features defined in some version of XSLT that the software is unaware of. So if the version attribute is «1.1», and the element <xsl:apply_template> appears, the software has to assume that this is a new element defined in version 1.1 of the standard. The XSLT specification calls this *forwards compatible processing mode*. In this mode, the <xsl:apply_template> element will be rejected only if (a) an attempt is made to instantiate it, and (b) it has no <xsl:fallback> child element. If it does have an <xsl:fallback> child element, this will be instantiated in place of the unrecognized parent element. This is described in greater detail under <xsl:fallback> on page 197.

Forwards compatible mode also affects the handling of other apparent errors. For example if the version attribute is «1.0», then any unrecognized attributes or values of attributes on an XSLT element are reported as errors, but in forwards compatible mode, such attributes are ignored.

The version attribute applies to the entire stylesheet, except any parts contained within a literal result element that has an xsl:version attribute. Its scope is the stylesheet module, not the full stylesheet tree constructed by applying <xsl:include> and <xsl:import> elements.

The extension-element-prefixes Attribute

This attribute identifies a set of namespaces used for extension elements. Extension elements may be defined by an implementer, by a user, or by a third party. They can be used anywhere an instruction can be used, that is, within a template-body. If an element is found in a template body that is not in the XSLT namespace, then it must either be an extension element or a literal result element. If its namespace is the same as a namespace identified in the extension-element-prefixes attribute of the containing <xsl:stylesheet> element, then it will be treated as an extension element, otherwise it will be treated as a literal result element.

The value of the attribute is a whitespace-separated list of prefixes; each of these prefixes must identify a namespace declaration present on the <xsl:stylesheet> element. The default namespace (the namespace declared using the xmlns attribute) may be designated as an extension element namespace by including the pseudo-prefix «#default».

The list of namespaces used for extension elements may be augmented for a section of the stylesheet by using the xsl:extension-element-prefixes attribute of a literal result element or an extension element. This does not override the declarations at the stylesheet level, it supplements them.

The scope of the extension-element-prefixes attribute is the stylesheet module, not the full stylesheet tree constructed by applying <xsl:include> and <xsl:import> elements.

If a namespace is designated as an extension element namespace, then every XSLT processor will recognize that these elements are extension elements. However, some XSLT processors may be unable to instantiate them. For example, if the namespace `http://www.jclark.com/xt/extensions` is designated as an extension namespace, then both xt and Xalan will recognize that these elements are extensions, but the likelihood is that xt will know how to handle them and Xalan won't. If the processor knows how to instantiate the element, it does so; otherwise, it looks to see if the element contains an `<xsl:fallback>` instruction. If it does, the `<xsl:fallback>` instruction is instantiated, otherwise, an error is reported.

It is only necessary to designate a namespace as an extension element namespace to distinguish extension elements from literal result elements. At the top level of the stylesheet, there is no risk of confusion. Any implementation can define its own top-level elements, using its own namespace, and other implementations will simply ignore these elements, treating them as data. So the `extension-element-prefixes` attribute is not needed to identify top-level elements used as vendor or user extensions.

The exclude-result-prefixes Attribute

This attribute defines a set of namespaces which are **not** to be copied into the result tree.

The XSLT processor is required to produce a correct tree that conforms with the data model (as described on page 46, in Chapter 2) and with the XML Namespaces rules, so you will never find yourself with an output file using namespace prefixes that have not been declared. However, you can easily find yourself with a file containing unnecessary and unwanted namespace declarations, for example, declarations of namespaces that occur on nodes in your source document but which are not used in the output document, or namespaces that are used only in the stylesheet. These extra namespace declarations usually don't matter, because they don't affect the meaning of the output file, but they can clutter it up. They can also affect validation if you are trying to create a result document that conforms to a particular DTD. So this attribute is provided to help you get rid of them.

More specifically, the XSLT specification requires that when a literal result element in the stylesheet is instantiated, the element is copied into the result tree along with all its namespace nodes, except for the XSLT namespace and any namespace that defines extension elements. An element has a namespace node for every namespace that is in scope, including namespaces defined on ancestor elements as well as on the element itself, so the namespaces copied over include not only the namespaces defined on the literal result element, and those that are actually used on the literal result element, but even those that are merely *available* for use.

Very often, of course, one literal result element will be a child or descendant of another, and the namespace nodes on the child element will include copies of all the namespace nodes on the parent element. For example, consider the stylesheet below:

```
<xsl:stylesheet version="1.0"
                 xmlns:xsl="http://www.w3.org/1999/XSL/Transform"
/>

<xsl:template match="/">
   <acme:document xmlns:acme="http://acme.com/xslt">
      <acme:chapter>
         Once upon a time ...
      </acme:chapter>
   </acme:document>
</xsl:template>

</xsl:stylesheet>
```

This can be represented by the tree shown in the diagram below, using the same notation as previously seen in Chapters 2 and 3. Although there are only two namespace declarations, these are propagated to all the descendant elements, so for example the `<acme:chapter>` element has two namespace nodes even though there are no namespace declarations on the element.

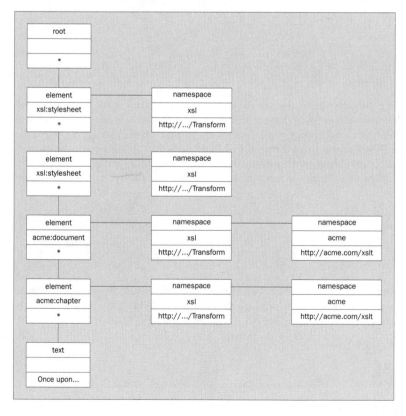

The specification says that each literal result element is copied with all its namespace nodes (but excluding the XSLT namespace), so the result tree will look like this:

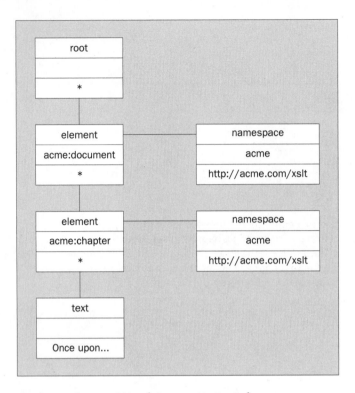

Both elements, `<acme:document>` and `<acme:chapter>`, have a namespace node for the «acme» namespace. However, this doesn't mean that the namespace declaration will be repeated unnecessarily in the output file: we're talking here about the abstract tree that is created, not the final serialized XML file. Avoiding duplicate namespace declarations is entirely the job of the XSLT processor, and most processors will produce the following output, shown indented for clarity:

```
<acme:document xmlns:acme="http://acme.com/xslt">
   <acme:chapter>
      Once upon a time ...
   </acme:chapter>
</acme:document>
```

The `exclude-result-prefixes` attribute isn't there to get rid of duplicate declarations, it's there to get rid of declarations that aren't wanted at all, which is a different matter entirely. For example suppose the stylesheet was like this:

```
<xsl:stylesheet version="1.0"
   xmlns:xsl="http://www.w3.org/1999/XSL/Transform"
xmlns:var="http://another.org/xslt"
/>

<xsl:variable name="var:x" select="17"/>
```

```
<xsl:template match="/">
   <acme:document xmlns:acme="http://acme.com/xslt">
      <acme:chapter>
         Once upon a time ...
      </acme:chapter>
   </acme:document>
</xsl:template>

</xsl:stylesheet>
```

Then although the template body has not changed, the `<acme:document>` and `<acme:chapter>` elements each now have an extra namespace node, and this will be copied to the output file even though it is unused, resulting in the output:

```
<acme:document xmlns:acme="http://acme.com/xslt"
               xmlns:var="http://another.org/xslt">
   <acme:chapter>
      Once upon a time ...
   </acme:chapter>
</acme:document>
```

Why can't the XSLT processor simply include all the namespaces that are actually used in element and attribute names, and omit the rest? The thinking is that many XML applications, like XSLT itself, will use the namespace mechanism to create unique values within their own data. For example, namespace prefixes might be used in attribute values as well as attribute names. The XSLT processor can't distinguish these from ordinary values, so it has to play safe.

So if there are namespaces you don't want in the output tree, you can specify them in the `exclude-result-prefixes` attribute of the `<xsl:stylesheet>` element. The attribute is a list of namespace prefixes, separated by whitespace, and with the option to include the default namespace under the pseudo-prefix «#default».

The prefix, as always, is simply a way of referring to the associated namespace URI: it is the namespace URI that is really being excluded, not the prefix itself. So if the same namespace URI is declared again with a different prefix, it is still an excluded namespace.

The `exclude-result-prefixes` attribute on the `<xsl:stylesheet>` element provides a way of controlling namespace exclusion for the entire stylesheet. Additional prefixes to be excluded may be specified in the `xsl:exclude-result-prefixes` attribute of the literal result element itself: these only affect that element and its descendants.

The `xsl:exclude-result-prefixes` and `exclude-result-prefixes` attributes apply only to namespace nodes copied from the stylesheet using literal result elements. They do not affect namespace nodes copied from the source document using `<xsl:copy>` or `<xsl:copy-of>`: there is no way of suppressing these.

Like the other attributes on the `<xsl:stylesheet>` element, the `exclude-result-prefixes` attribute applies only to elements within the physical stylesheet, not to those brought in using `<xsl:include>` or `<xsl:import>`.

4

Elements

The XSLT specification doesn't say what happens if you try to exclude a namespace that is actually needed because it is used in the result tree. The XSLT processor is obliged to generate output that conforms to the Namespaces recommendation, so it should either report an error, or ignore the request to exclude this namespace.

Usage and Examples

The `<xsl:stylesheet>` element is always the outermost element of the stylesheet (though the stylesheet may be embedded in another document). It will always include:

```
<xsl:stylesheet
        xmlns:xsl="http://www.w3.org/1999/XSL/Transform"
        version="1.0"
>
```

The various possible attributes are considered in the sections that follow.

The id Attribute

If the XSLT processor you are using supports embedding of stylesheets within the source document that they are to transform, then the typical layout will be like this:

```
<?xml version="1.0"?>
<?xml-stylesheet href="#style" type="text/xsl"?>
<data>
  ...
  ...
  <xsl:stylesheet id="style" version="1.0"
     xmlns:xsl="http://www.w3.org/1999/XSL/Transform"
  >
  <xsl:include href="module1.xsl"/>
  <xsl:include href="module2.xsl"/>
  <xsl:template match="xsl:*"/>
  </xsl:stylesheet>
</data>
```

Note that when this structure is used, the stylesheet will be presented with the entire source document, including a copy of itself. The stylesheet therefore needs to be written to handle its own elements in an appropriate way: hence the null template that matches all elements in the XSLT namespace.

The version Attribute

So long as XSLT 1.0 remains the latest version of the standard, always specify «version="1.0"» on the `<xsl:stylesheet>` element.

When a later version of the specification is released, use the new version number only if you actually change the stylesheet to use the new features. And if you still want your stylesheet to run with products that don't support the new features yet, it might be best to leave the `<xsl:stylesheet>` element saying «version="1.0"», and put the new version number only on a literal result element around the parts of the stylesheet that use the new features, in an `xsl:version` attribute.

The extension-element-prefixes Attribute

This attribute should be set to a list of all the prefixes you are using for extension elements in your stylesheet. The most common cases are either to omit it entirely, or to include a single prefix for the namespace used by the vendor for their own proprietary extensions. There will always be a namespace declaration for that namespace on the `<xsl:stylesheet>` element as well.

For example, if you are using Saxon:

```
<xsl:stylesheet
        version="1.0"
        xmlns:xsl="http://www.w3.org/1999/XSL/Transform"
        xmlns:saxon="http://icl.com/saxon"
        extension-element-prefixes="saxon"
        >
```

Don't include the vendor's prefix unless you are actually using their proprietary extensions in the stylesheet. You don't need to include this attribute to use proprietary top-level elements, only if you want to use proprietary features as instructions within a template body, where they would otherwise be assumed to be literal result elements.

If your usage of vendor extensions is highly localized within the stylesheet, it is better to identify them using the `xsl:extension-element-prefixes` attribute of the extension element itself, or of a literal result element that surrounds the template body where the extensions are actually used. This aids portability and makes it easier to see which parts of the stylesheet are standard and which parts use proprietary extensions.

If you want to use extensions supplied by several different vendors, you can list them all in this attribute. An XSLT processor from one vendor won't object to finding another vendor's namespace in the list, it will only object if it is actually asked to instantiate a proprietary instruction that it doesn't understand: and even then, if there is an `<xsl:fallback>` child element that defines the fallback behavior it will carry on calmly executing that in place of the unrecognized instruction.

Although extension elements supplied by XSLT product vendors are likely to be the most common case, it's also possible in principle to install third-party extensions or write your own (the APIs for doing so will be different for each vendor, however). So everything we've said about the vendor's extensions applies equally to your own extensions or those acquired from a third party.

For more information about the extensions provided by various vendors in their products, see Chapter 10.

The exclude-result-prefixes Attribute

The simplest way to decide which namespace prefixes to list here is by trial and error: run the stylesheet, and if the output document contains namespace declarations that clearly serve no useful purpose, add them to the `exclude-result-prefixes` attribute and run the stylesheet again.

Namespaces that are used only within the stylesheet will normally be excluded automatically: these include the XSLT namespace itself, and namespaces used for extension elements. It may not apply, however, to namespaces used for your own top-level elements in the stylesheet.

The most common cause of unwanted namespace declarations finding their way into the result document is where your stylesheet needs to refer to namespaces used in the source document, for example in a template `match` pattern, but where none of these elements is copied into the destination document.

For example:

```
<xsl:stylesheet
        version="1.0"
        xmlns:xsl="http://www.w3.org/1999/XSL/Transform"
        xmlns:po="http://accounting.org/xslt"
        exclude-result-prefixes="po"
>
<xsl:template match="po:purchase-order"/>
    <order-details>
    ...
    </order-details>
</xsl:template>
</xsl:stylesheet>
```

Here the «po» namespace would be copied into the result document if it weren't for the `exclude-result-prefixes` attribute, because it is in scope when the literal result element `<order-details>` is instantiated.

As with the other `<xsl:stylesheet>` attributes, you don't have to apply the exclusion to the whole stylesheet if you don't want to, you can also apply it to any part of the stylesheet by using the `xsl:exclude-result-prefixes` attribute on any literal result element. It's probably a good idea in practice to keep the declaration of a namespace and the directive that excludes it from the result document together in one place.

See also

`<xsl:transform>` on page 304.

xsl:template

The `<xsl:template>` element defines a template for producing output. It may be invoked either by matching nodes against a pattern, or explicitly by name.

Defined in

XSLT section 5.3

Format

```
<xsl:template
name=QName
match=Pattern
mode=QName
priority=Number >
      <xsl:param> *
      template-body
</xsl:template>
```

Position

<xsl:template> is a top-level element, which means that it always appears as a child
of the <xsl:stylesheet> element.

Attributes

Name	Value	Meaning
match optional	Pattern	A pattern that determines which nodes are eligible to be processed by this template. If this attribute is absent, there must be a name attribute.
name optional	QName	The name of the template. If this attribute is absent, there must be a match attribute.
priority optional	Number	A number (positive or negative, integer or real) that denotes the priority of this template, used when several templates match the same node.
mode optional	QName	The mode. When <xsl:apply-templates> is used to process a set of nodes, the only templates considered are those with a matching mode.

The constructs QName (page 388) and Number (page 375) are defined in Chapter 5. The
construct Pattern is defined in Chapter 6.

Content

Zero or more <xsl:param> elements, followed by a *template-body*.

Effect

There must be either a `match` attribute, or a `name` attribute, or both.

❑ If there is a `match` attribute, the `<xsl:template>` element defines a template rule that can be invoked using the `<xsl:apply-templates>` instruction.

❑ If there is a `name` attribute, the `<xsl:template>` element defines a named template that can be invoked using the `<xsl:call-template>` instruction.

❑ If both attributes are present, the template can be invoked in either of these ways.

The match Attribute

The match attribute is a `Pattern`, as defined in Chapter 6. The pattern is used to define which nodes this template rule applies to.

The pattern must not contain a `VariableReference`, that is, a reference to a variable such as «$var». This is to prevent circular definitions: the template body of a global variable is allowed to include an `<xsl:apply-templates>` instruction, so it must be possible to evaluate the pattern before the values of global variables are known.

To see what might happen if variables were allowed in the match attribute, consider the following:

```
<xsl:variable name="x">
    <xsl:apply-templates select="//item"/>
</xsl:variable>
<!-- WRONG -->
<xsl:template match="item[$x]">
    <xsl:value-of select="3"/>
</xsl:template>
<!-- WRONG -->
```

When `<xsl:apply-templates>` is used to process a selected set of nodes, each node is processed using the best-fit template rule for that node, as described under `<xsl:apply-templates>` on page 145.

A template is only considered as a candidate if the node matches the pattern supplied in the `match` attribute and if the value of the `mode` attribute is the same name as the `mode` attribute of the `<xsl:apply-templates>` instruction.

If more than one template rule meets these criteria, they are first considered in order of import precedence (as described under `<xsl:import>` on page 207), and only those templates with the highest import precedence are considered further.

If there is still more than one template rule (in other words, if two template rules that both match the node have the same import precedence) they are next considered in order of priority. The priority is given either by the value of the `priority` attribute, described below, or is a default priority that depends on the `match` pattern.

If this leaves one pattern with a numerically higher priority than all the others, that one is chosen. If there are several with the same priority, which is higher than all the others, the XSLT processor has the choice of reporting an error, or choosing from the remaining templates the one that appears last in the stylesheet.

The name Attribute

The name attribute is a QName: that is, a name optionally qualified with a namespace prefix. If there is a prefix, it must correspond to a namespace declaration that is in scope on this element (which means it must be defined either on this element itself, or on the <xsl:stylesheet> element). If there is no prefix, the namespace URI is null: the default namespace is not used.

This name is used when the template is invoked using <xsl:call-template>. The name attribute of the <xsl:call-template> element must match the name attribute of the <xsl:template> element. Two names match if they have the same local part and the same namespace URI: the prefix can be different.

If there is more than one named template in the stylesheet with the same name, the one with higher import precedence is used; for details, see <xsl:import> on page 207. It is an error to have two templates in the stylesheet with the same name and the same import precedence, even if the template is never called.

The priority Attribute

The priority attribute is a number, for example «17», «0.5», or «-3»: more specifically, a Number as defined on page 375 in the XPath expression syntax given in Chapter 5, with an optional leading minus sign.

The priority attribute is used to decide which template to invoke when <xsl:apply-templates> is called and there are several possible candidates. For each selected node, a template is chosen using the following procedure:

❑ First select all the templates that have a match attribute.

❑ From these, select all the templates that have the same mode as is used on the call of <xsl:apply-templates>. If the <xsl:apply-templates> element has no mode attribute, the selected templates must have no mode attribute.

❑ From these, select all those whose pattern matches the selected node.

❑ If there is more than one, select those that have the highest import precedence.

❑ If there is still more than one, select those that have the numerically highest priority.

If there are several matching templates left, and they all have the same import precedence and priority, the XSLT processor can either choose the one that occurs last in the stylesheet, or report an error.

If there are no templates that match the selected node, the built-in template for the relevant node type is used. Built-in templates are described under <xsl:apply-templates> on page 148.

The default priority depends on the pattern, and is decided according to the following rules. A numerically higher value indicates a higher priority.

Pattern syntax	Default priority
Pattern1 «|» Pattern2	Treat it as if there were two completely separate template rules specified, one for Pattern1 and one for Pattern2, and calculate the default priority of Pattern1 and Pattern2 independently.
QName «@» QName «child::» QName «attribute::» QName «processing-instruction» «(» Literal «)»	0.0
NCName «:*» «@» NCName «:*» «child::» NCName «:*» «attribute::» NCName «:*»	–0.25
NodeTest «@» NodeTest «child::» NodeTest «attribute::» NodeTest	–0.5
otherwise	0.5

These default priorities are carefully chosen. They reflect the selectivity of the pattern:

❑ The patterns «node()» and «text()» and «*» are not very selective at all, they match any node of the right node type, so they have a low priority of –0.5.

❑ Patterns of the form «abc:*» or «@xyz.*» are more selective, they will only match element or attribute nodes belonging to a particular namespace, so they have a higher priority than the previous category.

❑ Patterns such as «title» or «@isbn» are the ones most commonly encountered; their default priority of 0.0 reflects the fact that in terms of selectivity, they are typical.

❑ Patterns that are more specific than this, for example «book[@isbn]» or «chapter/title» or «para[1]» have a higher priority, so they will be chosen in preference to templates whose patterns are respectively «book», «title», or «para». Note however that this category can also include patterns that turn out not to be very selective at all, for example «//node()».

All these values are chosen to leave you free to allocate your own priorities as natural numbers, for example «1», «2», «3», and such templates will always be chosen ahead of those with a system-allocated default priority.

You may find that stylesheets are easier to understand and less error-prone if you avoid relying on default priorities, and use explicit priorities whenever you have more than one template that can match the same node.

The mode Attribute

If present, the mode attribute must be a QName, that is, a name with an optional namespace prefix. When <xsl:apply-templates> is used with a specific mode, only templates with that same mode will be considered, and when <xsl:apply-templates> is used with no mode attribute, only templates with no mode attribute will be considered.

The modes are compared using the usual rules for QNames: both names are expanded using the namespace declarations in effect on their respective stylesheet elements (not including any default namespace declaration), and they match if the local name and namespace URI both match.

The mode specified on the <xsl:template> template is **not** propagated to any <xsl:apply-templates> elements within its body. Although it is common practice to process an entire subtree in a single mode, and therefore for a template to continue using the mode it was called in, this is not the default behavior except in the case of built-in templates.

If you have a mode attribute on a template but no match attribute, this is not an error, but it is redundant because the mode will never be used.

If you have a mode attribute on a template and there is no <xsl:apply-templates> element with the same mode anywhere in the stylesheet, this again is not an error, though it means the template will never be selected by any <xsl:apply-templates> call. This can be a handy way of commenting out a template.

Instantiating a Template

Once an <xsl:template> element is selected for processing the following occurs:

❑ If called using <xsl:apply-templates>, the current node and current node list are set up as required.

❑ A new stack frame is allocated, to hold a new instance of each local variable defined within the template.

❑ All parameters listed in <xsl:param> elements contained within the <xsl:template> element are evaluated. These <xsl:param> elements must come before any instructions in the template body. For each parameter, if a value was supplied by the caller (using an <xsl:with-param> element with matching name), that value is assigned to the parameter, otherwise the <xsl:param> element is evaluated directly: see <xsl:param> on page 262 for details.

❑ The template body is instantiated. This means that the child nodes of the <xsl:template> element are instantiated in turn. XSLT instructions and extension elements are processed using their individual rules; literal result elements and text nodes are written to the current output destination.

When processing of the template body is complete, the stack frame containing its local variables is deleted, control returns to the calling template, and the current node and current node list revert to their previous values.

> *The implementation, of course, is free to do things in a different order if it has the same effect. Some products use lazy evaluation, where the parameters are only evaluated when they are first used. This will only show up if you use extension functions that have side-effects, or if you use `<xsl:message>` to trace the sequence of execution.*

Usage and Examples

We'll look first at using template rules, then give some advice on the use of modes, and finally discuss named templates.

Using Template Rules

A *template rule* is an `<xsl:template>` element with a `match` attribute, that can therefore be invoked using the `<xsl:apply-templates>` instruction.

This rule-based approach to processing is the characteristic way of writing XSLT stylesheets, though it is by no means the only way. Its biggest advantage is that the output for each element type can be defined independently of the context that the element appears in, which makes it very easy to reuse element types in different contexts, or to add new element types to an existing document definition without rewriting the stylesheet templates for all the possible containing elements. A classic example of this approach to processing arises when converting semantic markup in a document to rendition markup, as the following example demonstrates.

Example: Template Rules

Source

The source file is `soloist.xml`.

In a text featuring the work of a singer, the name of a composer might be tagged `<composer>`, the title of a musical work might be tagged `<work>`, and the name of a publication might be tagged `<publication>`. So a fragment of marked up text might read:

```
<cv>
<para>
<publication>Early Music Review</publication> said of his debut Wigmore
concert with <group>Ensemble Sonnerie</group> in 1998: <quote>One of the
finest concerts I have ever heard ... a singer to watch out for</quote>.
Other highlights include a televised production of
<composer>Bach</composer>'s <work>St. Matthew Passion</work> conducted by
<artist>Jonathan Miller</artist>, in which he played <role>Judas</role>.
</para>
</cv>
```

Stylesheet

The stylesheet file is `soloist.xsl`.

In presenting this text to a human reader, the main task is to select typographical conventions to be used for each piece of semantic markup. The designer might choose, for example, to display the titles of works in italics, titles of publications in a sans serif font, and composers' names in the ordinary paragraph font. This could be achieved by the following stylesheet definitions (assuming the output is HTML):

```
<xsl:stylesheet version="1.0"
<xsl:stylesheet version="1.0"
      xmlns:xsl="http://www.w3.org/1999/XSL/Transform">

<xsl:template match="/">
<html><body>
<xsl:apply-templates/>
</body></html>
</xsl:template>

<xsl:template match="para">
    <p><xsl:apply-templates/></p>
</xsl:template>

<xsl:template match="publication">
    <font face="arial"><xsl:apply-templates/></font>
</xsl:template>

<xsl:template match="quote">
    <xsl:text/>"<xsl:apply-templates/>"<xsl:text/>
</xsl:template>

<xsl:template match="work">
    <I><xsl:apply-templates/></i>
</xsl:template>

<xsl:template match="role">
    <u><xsl:apply-templates/></u>
</xsl:template>

</xsl:stylesheet>
```

Note that some of the markup is ignored, for example `<artist>`. The default template for elements simply discards the tags and outputs the text, which is exactly what we want here.

Output

If the generated HTML is copied into a word processor, it will look like this.

> Early Music Review said of his debut Wigmore concert with Ensemble Sonnerie in 1998: "One of the finest concerts I have ever heard ... a singer to watch out for". Other highlights include a televised production of Bach's *St. Matthew Passion* conducted by Jonathan Miller, in which he played <u>Judas</u>.................

(Incidentally, this way of getting printed output from an XSLT stylesheet is often overlooked. It won't give nearly as much control as the advanced features of the XSL Formatting proposals, but while you're waiting for that standard to be finished and for products to appear, using HTML as an intermediate format is not a bad compromise.)

The great advantage of this approach is that the rules are written making no assumptions about the way the markup tags are nested in the source document. It is very easy to add new rules for new tags, and to reuse rules if an existing tag is used in a new context.

With document structures where the nesting of elements is more rigid, for example in some data interchange files, this very flexible rule-based (or 'push') style of processing may have fewer benefits, and a 'pull' programming style using conventional flow-of-control constructs such as `<xsl:for-each>`, `<xsl:if>`, and `<xsl:call-template>` may be preferable. For more discussion of the different design approaches, see Chapter 8.

Using Modes

The classic reason for using modes is to enable the same content to be processed more than once in different ways: for example, the first pass through the document might generate the table of contents, the second pass the actual text, and the third pass an index.

Example: Using modes

The source document is a biography of a singer, in the same format as the previous example. This time, however, we want to produce at the end of the biography a list of works mentioned in the text.

Source

The source file is `soloist.xml`. See previous example.

Stylesheet

The stylesheet file is `soloist+index.xml`.

This stylesheet extends the previous one using `<xsl:import>`. After outputting the text as before, it now creates a table listing the singer's performances, completing what information is known about the composer, the work, the date of the performance, and the venue.

The « » characters (better known to HTML authors as a non-breaking space, « »), are used to ensure that there is something in each table cell: this gives a cleaner appearance in the browser. It would be quite possible to use the entity reference « » in the stylesheet so long as it was properly declared as an XML entity in a `<!DOCTYPE>` declaration at the start of the file.

```
<xsl:stylesheet version="1.0"
    xmlns:xsl="http://www.w3.org/1999/XSL/Transform">

<xsl:import href="soloist.xsl"/>

<xsl:template match="/">
<html><body>
    <xsl:apply-templates/>
    <table bgcolor="#cccccc" border="1" cellpadding="5">
    <tr>
        <td><b>Date</b></td>
        <td><b>Venue</b></td>
        <td><b>Composer</b></td>
        <td><b>Work</b></td>
        <td><b>Role</b></td>
    </tr>
    <xsl:apply-templates mode="index"/>
    </table>
</body></html>
</xsl:template>

<xsl:template match="performance" mode="index">
    <tr>
    <td><xsl:value-of select="date"/> </td>
    <td><xsl:value-of select="venue"/> </td>
    <td><xsl:value-of select="composer"/> </td>
    <td><xsl:value-of select="work"/> </td>
    <td><xsl:value-of select="role"/> </td>
    </tr>
</xsl:template>

</xsl:stylesheet>
```

Output

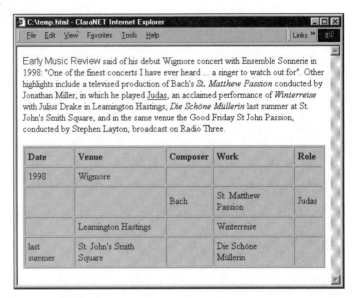

This time we are generating a hyperlink for each person and place mentioned (an `<a>` element with an `href` attribute). We are again using `generate-id()`, to ensure that each entry in the index links to the relevant place in the text. The actual index entry is the value of the `name` attribute.

Then we can generate the index, using logic such as:

```
<xsl:apply-templates select="//person | //place" mode="index">
    <xsl:sort select="@name"/>
</xsl:apply-templates>
```

This will generate an index containing all the tagged persons and places in the document, each with a hyperlink to the place they appear in the text.

(It will not combine multiple references to the same person or place into a single entry, and it will not include details such as a page number. That requires more advanced techniques, and probably a processing sequence involving multiple stylesheets and intermediate documents.)

Using Named Templates

Named templates provide the equivalent of a subroutine mechanism in XSLT. If a template has a name attribute, it can be invoked using the `<xsl:call-template>` instruction.

For examples of the use of named templates, see `<xsl:call-template>` on page 167.

See also

`<xsl:apply-templates>` on page 145
`<xsl:apply-imports>` on page 142
`<xsl:call-template>` on page 167
`generate-id()` function in Chapter 7, on page 463.

xsl:text

The `<xsl:text>` instruction is used within a template body to output literal text to the current output destination.

Defined in

XSLT section 7.2

Format

```
<xsl:text disable-output-escaping="yes" | "no">
   text ?
</xsl:text>
```

Position

`<xsl:text>` is an instruction. It is always used as part of a *template body*.

Attributes

Name	Value	Meaning
disable-output-escaping optional	«yes» | «no»	The value «yes» indicates that special characters in the output (such as «<») should be output as is, rather than using an XML escape form such as «<». Default is «no».

Content

A text node. The element may also be empty. It may not contain other elements such as `<xsl:value-of>`.

Effect

Text appearing within a template in the stylesheet is copied to the current output destination whether it is enclosed by `<xsl:text>` or not. The only direct effect of enclosing text in an `<xsl:text>` element is that the handling of whitespace is different. A whitespace node appearing in the stylesheet (that is, a text node which consists only of whitespace) is copied to the output tree only if

❑ it appears within an `<xsl:text>` element, or

❑ an enclosing element has the attribute «xml:space="preserve"», and this is not overridden by an inner enclosing element specifying «xml:space="default"».

The disable-output-escaping attribute controls whether special characters such as «<>» should be escaped (that is, converted to a character reference or entity reference such as «<») if they appear in the text. The default value is «yes». The value «no» may be ignored in some circumstances, for example if the current output destination is a result tree fragment.

Usage

There are two main reasons for using `<xsl:text>`: to control the output of whitespace, and to disable escaping of special characters. These are discussed in the next two sections.

Whitespace Control

The most obvious case where `<xsl:text>` is useful is to force output of whitespace. An example is given in the XSLT specification. If you write:

```
<xsl:value-of select="first-name"/> <xsl:value-of select="last-name"/>
```

the space between the first name and last name will be lost, because it is part of a node that contains whitespace only (a single space character). To force a space to appear between the first name and last name, write:

```
<xsl:value-of select="first-name"/>
<xsl:text> </xsl:text>
<xsl:value-of select="last-name"/>
```

The arrangement on three lines here is purely for readability, but it does not affect the output, because the newline characters are now in whitespace-only nodes that will not be output.

If you find this long-winded, another way of achieving the same effect is to write:

```
<xsl:value-of select="concat(first-name, ' ', last-name)"/>
```

The concat() function forms a string by concatenating its arguments: it is described on page 430 in Chapter 7.

The other side of the problem is to prevent the output of unwanted whitespace. Fortunately in HTML output extra whitespace doesn't matter, because the browser will ignore it. For XML or text output, however, avoiding unwanted white space can be important.

If you are suffering from excess whitespace in your output, the first thing to establish is whether it comes from the source document or from the stylesheet. If the whitespace is adjacent to text copied from the source document, then it probably comes from there; if it is adjacent to text that appears in the stylesheet, then that is the most likely source.

The <xsl:text> element can be used to suppress unwanted whitespace that originates in the stylesheet. For example, consider the following template:

```
<xsl:template match="stage-direction">
    [ <xsl:value-of select="."/> ]
</xsl:template>
```

The intention here is to output a stage direction enclosed in square brackets. But the text nodes containing the opening and closing square brackets also contain a newline character and several spaces, which will be written to the output destination along with the brackets themselves. To prevent this behavior, the simplest way is to use empty <xsl:text> elements before and after, thus:

```
<xsl:template match="stage-direction">
    <xsl:text/>[ <xsl:value-of select="."/> ]<xsl:text/>
</xsl:template>
```

The effect of this is that the extra newlines and spaces now belong to whitespace-only nodes, which are stripped from the stylesheet and ignored.

Note that it is incorrect to use an <xsl:text> element around the <xsl:value-of> element, as <xsl:text> elements must contain text data only. So the following is wrong:

```
<!-- WRONG -->
    <xsl:text>[ <xsl:value-of select="."/> ]</xsl:text>
<!-- WRONG -->
```

Controlling Output Escaping

Normally, when you try to output a special character such as «<» or «&» in a text node, the special character will be escaped in the output file using the normal XML escaping mechanisms. The XSLT processor is free to choose whichever mechanism it wants, for example it can write «<» as «<» or «<» or «<![CDATA[<]]>», because these are all equivalent according to the XML standard. The one thing it will not write is «<». So, it doesn't matter how you write the «<» in your input: the XSLT processor sees a «<» and escapes it in the output.

There are several valid reasons why you might not want this behavior. For example:

❑ The output is not XML or HTML at all; it is (say) a data file in comma-separated-values format.

❑ The output is HTML and you want to exploit one of the many HTML quirks where special characters are needed without escaping, for example a «<» sign in a piece of client-side JavaScript on your HTML page.

❑ The output is XML and you want to achieve some special effect that the XSLT processor won't let you do, for example to output an entity reference such as «&current-date;» or a document type declaration containing an entity declaration.

❑ The output is some format that uses angle-bracket syntax but is not pure XML or HTML: for example, ASP pages or Java Server Pages, which both use «<%» and «%>» as delimiters. (If you are generating Java Server Pages, note that these have an alternative syntax that is pure XML.)

If the output is not XML or HTML at all, then rather than using disable-output-escaping it is better to set «method="text"» on the <xsl:output> element.

Now here's an example of a bad reason for disabling output escaping. You want to get markup tags into the output document that you can't see how to achieve with the regular facilities of <xsl:element> or literal result elements. For example, you might want to do something like:

```
<!-- WRONG -->
<xsl:template match="bullet"/>
    <xsl:if test='not(preceding::*[self::list-item])'>
        <ul>
    </xsl:if>
    <li><xsl:value-of select="."/></li>
    <xsl:if test='not(following::*[self::list-item])'>
        </ul>
    </xsl:if>
</xsl:template>
<!-- WRONG -->
```

The intended effect here is to output a <ul> tag if the preceding element is not a list-item, and to output a </ul> tag when the following element is not a list-item. Of course it doesn't work, because the <ul> and </ul> tags are not properly nested: this template will be thrown out by the XML parser before the XSLT processor even gets to look at it.

So your next thought might be to write the tags as text, as follows:

```
<xsl:template match="bullet"/>
    <xsl:if test='not(preceding::*[self::list-item])'>
        <xsl:text disable-output-escaping="yes">&lt;ul&gt;</xsl:text>
    </xsl:if>
    <li><xsl:value-of select="."/></li>
    <xsl:if test='not(following::*[self::list-item])'>
        <xsl:text disable-output-escaping="yes">/&lt;ul&gt;</xsl:text>
    </xsl:if>
</xsl:template>
```

You now have something which is legal XML and indeed legal XSLT, but it's not guaranteed to work in all circumstances. In particular, it may fail if there is something downstream that cares about the structure of the output XML. So it's a trick that may or may not work.

With a bit of thought you can usually find a way to achieve the output you want without resorting to such devices.

The first thing is to think in terms of outputting a result tree containing nodes, not a text file containing tags. Don't try to generate the ⟨ul⟩ start tag and the ⟨/ul⟩ end tag as two separate actions; try to generate a ⟨ul⟩ element node as a single action, and then generate its children.

The aim is to produce a ⟨ul⟩ element for every ⟨bullet⟩ in the source that is not preceded by another bullet, so we can start by writing:

```
<xsl:template match="bullet[not(preceding-sibling::*[1][self::bullet])]>
    <ul>
        . . .
    </ul>
</xsl:template>
```

This template rule matches every ⟨bullet⟩ element that either has no preceding sibling, or whose immediately preceding sibling is not a ⟨bullet⟩ element.

For each such bullet, we want to process the list of following siblings until the next non-bullet is reached. To do this we need a recursive template:

```
<xsl:template match="bullet[not(preceding-sibling::bullet)]>
    <ul>
        <xsl:call-template name="bullet-list">
    </ul>
</xsl:template>

<xsl:template name="bullet-list">
    <li>
        <xsl:value-of select="."/>
    </li>
    <xsl:variable name="next" select="following-sibling::*[1]"/>
    <xsl:for-each select="$next[self::bullet]">
        <xsl:call-template name="bullet-list"/>
    </xsl:for-each>
</xsl:template>
```

Rather than processing the following bullets in a loop, we process them by recursion: the bullet-list template outputs the current ⟨bullet⟩ element, and if the next element is also a ⟨bullet⟩, it calls itself to process that one. Note that the ⟨xsl:for-each⟩ element here is not looping, it is processing a node-set which will contain one element if the next element is a ⟨bullet⟩, and zero elements otherwise.

303

Examples

1) Output first-name and last-name, separated by a space:

```
<xsl:value-of select="first-name"/>
<xsl:text> </xsl:text>
<xsl:value-of select-"last-name"/>
```

Another way to achieve the same effect is to use the concat() function:

```
<xsl:value-of select="concat(first-name, ' ', last-name)"/>
```

2) Output a comma-separated list of values:

```
<xsl:output method="text"/>
<xsl:template match="book">
    <xsl:value-of select="title"/>,<xsl:text/>
    <xsl:value-of select="author"/>,<xsl:text/>
    <xsl:value-of select="price"/>,<xsl:text/>
    <xsl:value-of select="isbn"/><xsl:text>
</xsl:text>
</xsl:template>
```

The purpose of the empty `<xsl:text/>` elements is to split the comma and the following newline character into separate text nodes; this ensures that the newline character becomes part of a whitespace-only node, and is therefore not copied to the output. The final `<xsl:text>` element ensures that a newline is written at the end of each record.

3) Output an « » entity reference:

```
<xsl:text disable-output-escaping="yes"> </xsl:text>
```

Note that outputting a #xa0 (or #160) character will generally have exactly the same effect, to do this you can simply write:

```
<xsl:text> </xsl:text>
```

See also

`<xsl:value-of>` on page 305.

xsl:transform

This is a synonym of `<xsl:stylesheet>`, described on page 278. The two element names may be used interchangeably.

Why is it useful to have two names for the same thing? Probably because it's the easiest way for a standards committee to keep all its members happy. More seriously, the existence of these two names is indicative of the fact that some people see XSLT as being primarily a language for transforming trees, while others see its main role as defining presentation styles. Take your pick.

Format

```
<xsl:transform
    id=identifier
    version="1.0"
    xmlns:xsl="http://www.w3.org/1999/XSL/Transform"
    extension-element-prefixes=list-of-prefixes
    exclude-result-prefixes=list-of-prefixes >
        top-level-element *
</xsl:transform>
```

Defined in

XSLT section 2.2

See also

`<xsl:stylesheet>` on page 278.

xsl:value-of

The `<xsl:value-of>` instruction writes the string value of an expression to the result tree.

Defined in

XSLT section 7.6.1

Format

```
<xsl:value-of select=Expression
disable-output-escaping="yes" | "no"/>
```

Position

`<xsl:value-of>` is an instruction. It is always used as part of a *template-body*.

Attributes

Name	Value	Meaning
select mandatory	Expression	The value to be output.
disable-output- escaping optional	«yes» | «no»	The value «yes» indicates that special characters in the output (such as «<») should be output as is, rather than using an XML escape form such as «<». Default is «no».

Content

None, the element is always empty.

Effect

The expression is evaluated as a string; if necessary it is first converted to a string, as follows:

❑   If the value is a Boolean, the output will be one of the strings «true» or «false».

❑   If the value is a number, it is converted to a string representation of the number in decimal notation, for example «93.7». (If you want to control the formatting of the number, use the <xsl:number> element or the format-number() function instead).

❑   If the value is a node-set, all nodes other than the first (in document order) are ignored. If the node-set is empty, nothing is output. Otherwise, the string value of the first node is output. The string value of a node depends on the type of node: for a text node, it is the textual content; for an attribute node, it is the attribute value; for a comment, it is the text of the comment; for a processing instruction, it is the data part of the processing instruction (excluding the *target*). For an element node, it is the concatenation of the values of all the descendant nodes: in other words, the text contained in the element, without any markup or attributes. Similarly for the root, the string-value is all the text in the document, with markup removed.

Note the very different behavior between a node-set that contains many elements and a node-set that contains a single element which itself has many children. The expression «//para» returns a node-set containing all the <para> elements in the document. The string value of this is the string-value of the first <para> element, so <xsl:value-of select="//para"> will only display one paragraph. By contrast, the expression «/» represents a node-set containing one node only, namely the root. The string-value of this is all the text in the document, so <xsl:value-of select="/"/> will output all this text.

❑   If the value is a result tree fragment, it is converted to a string as if it were a node-set containing a single node, the single node acting as a root for the result-tree-fragment. In effect this means that the result is the concatenation of all the text nodes within the result tree fragment. If you want to copy the nodes in the result tree fragment to the output destination, rather than just their string value, use <xsl:copy-of> described on page 183.

The disable-output-escaping attribute has the same effect as with <xsl:text>. Special characters such as «<» in the string value of the select expression will be escaped just as if they occurred in literal text, and the disable-output-escaping attribute can be used to suppress this in the same way. For details, see <xsl:text> on page 299.

Usage

The `<xsl:value-of>` element is the most common way of writing text to the result tree (or to the current output destination, if that is different).

The other ways of writing text nodes to the result are to include text literally in the stylesheet (perhaps within an `<xsl:text>` instruction) or to use `<xsl:copy>` or `<xsl:copy-of>`. Surprisingly, you could make do without using `<xsl:value-of>` at all, because `<xsl:value-of select="X"/>` can always be rewritten as `<xsl:copy-of select="string(X)"/>`.

Another alternative is to use `<xsl:apply-templates>` on a text node and rely on the built-in template for text nodes, which is equivalent to `<xsl:value-of select="."/>`

The `<xsl:value-of>` instruction is often an effective alternative to navigating the source tree recursively using `<xsl:apply-templates>`. For example:

```
<xsl:template match="book">
   <book>
      <publisher><xsl:value-of select="../@name"/></publisher>
      <title><xsl:value-of select="@title"/></title>
      <author><xsl:value-of select="@author"/></author>
      <isbn><xsl:value-of select="@isbn"/></isbn>
   </book>
</xsl:template>
```

As `<xsl:value-of>` writes to the current output destination, not necessarily the final result tree, it is used to return a result from a called template. For example we can write a named template that replaces characters in a filename as follows:

```
<xsl:template name="change-filename">
   <xsl:param name="filename"/>
   <xsl:value-of select="translate($filename, '\', '/')"/>
</xsl:template>
```

This template can then be called as follows, to get the result into the variable `$new-filename`:

```
<xsl:variable name="new-filename">
   <xsl:call-template name="change-filename">
      <xsl:with-param name="$old-filename"/>
   </xsl:call-template>
</xsl:variable>
```

Technically the variable `$new-filename` is a result tree fragment, but for all practical purposes it can be treated as a string.

Examples

`<xsl:value-of select="."/>`	Output the string-value of the current node
`<xsl:value-of select="title"/>`	Output the string-value of the first child `<title>` element of the current node
`<xsl:value-of select="sum(@*)"/>`	Output the sum of the values of the attributes of the current node, converted to a string. If there is any non-numeric attribute, the result will be "NaN".
`<xsl:value-of select="$x"/>`	Output the value of variable $x, after converting it to a string

See also

`<xsl:copy-of>` on page 183
`<xsl:text>` on page 299

xsl:variable

The `<xsl:variable>` element is used to declare a local or global variable in a stylesheet, and to give it a value.

Defined in

XSLT section 11

Format

```
<xsl:variable name=QName select=Expression >
    template-body
</xsl:variable>
```

Position

The `<xsl:variable>` element may appear either as a top-level element (that is, as a child of the `<xsl:stylesheet>` element), or as an instruction within a *template-body*.

Attributes

Name	Value	Meaning
name mandatory	QName	The name of the variable
select optional	Expression	An expression that is evaluated to give the value of the variable. If omitted, the value is determined from the contents of the `<xsl:variable>` element

The constructs QName (page 388) and Expression (page 351) are defined in Chapter 5.

Content

An optional *template body*. If a select attribute is present, the <xsl:variable> element should be empty.

Effect

An <xsl:variable> element may appear either at the top level of the stylesheet (in which case it declares a global variable) or as an instruction within a *template-body* (in which case it declares a local variable).

The Value of the Variable

The value of the variable may be given either by the Expression in the select attribute, or by the contents of the contained *template-body*. If there is a select attribute, the <xsl:variable> element should be empty. If there is no select attribute and the template body is empty, the value of the variable is an empty string.

If the value is given by an Expression, the data type of the value will be Boolean, number, string, or node-set, depending on the expression. If the value is given by a non-empty template body, the data type will always be a result tree fragment.

Note that if an expression is used to assign a literal string value to a variable, the String literal must be enclosed in quotes, and these quotes are additional to the quotes used around the XML attribute. So to assign the value «London» to the variable named «city», you can write either of the following:

```
<xsl:variable name="city" select="'London'"/>
<xsl:variable name="city" select='"London"'/>
```

We can also write:

```
<xsl:variable name="city">London</xsl:variable>
```

Technically the value is then a result tree fragment rather than a string, but it can be used exactly as if it were a string, so there is no difference in practice.

A common mistake is to write:

```
<xsl:variable name="city" select="London"/> <!-- WRONG -->
```

This sets the value of «$city» to a node-set containing all the element children of the current node that have element name <London>. This will probably be an empty set, so if you use the variable as a string, its value will be the empty string. You won't get any error message if you make this mistake, because it's a perfectly valid thing to write, it will just cause your stylesheet to produce the wrong output.

You won't be alone if you make this mistake, there's an example of it in the XSLT specification itself (in section 13, if you want to find it).

309

The Name of the Variable

The name of the variable is defined by a QName. Normally this will be a simple name such as «city» or «total-sales», but it may be a name qualified with a prefix, for example «my:value». If it has a prefix, the prefix must correspond to a namespace that is in scope at that point in the stylesheet. The true name of the variable, for the purpose of testing whether two names are the same, is determined not by the prefix but by the namespace URI corresponding to the prefix: so two variables «my:value» and «your:value» have the same name if the prefixes «my» and «your» refer to the same namespace URI. If the name has no prefix, it has a null namespace URI – it does not use the default namespace URI.

The scope of a global variable is the entire stylesheet, including any stylesheets that are included or imported. A global variable may even be referenced before it is declared. The only constraint is that circular definitions are not allowed: if variable x is defined in terms of y, then y may not be defined directly or indirectly in terms of x.

The scope of a local variable is block-structured: it may be referenced in any following sibling element or in a descendant of a following sibling. This is illustrated in the diagram below.

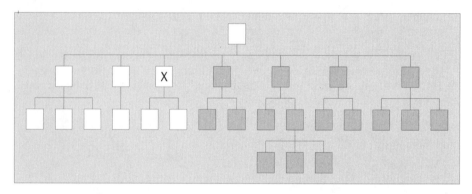

The diagram shows for a variable X, the elements that may contain a reference to X: the shaded elements may refer to X, the unshaded elements may not. Specifically, a local variable may be referenced in any following sibling element, or in a descendant of a following sibling. It cannot be referenced within its own descendants, and it goes out of scope when the end tag for its parent element is encountered. Unlike global variables, a forwards reference to a local variable is not allowed.

Two global variables may have the same name only if they have different *import precedence*: that is, if one of them was in an imported stylesheet (for further details, see <xsl:import> on page 207). In this case, the definition with higher import precedence wins (the spec doesn't actually say this, but it's clearly what's intended). Note that the higher-precedence definition applies everywhere, even within the imported stylesheet that contains the lower-precedence definition. This means it is not a good idea to rely on precedence to resolve accidental name clashes: better to use namespaces.

Two local variables may have the same name only if neither variable is defined within the scope of the other. However, a local variable may have the same name as a global variable, in which case the global variable is inaccessible within the scope of the local variable.

These rules on uniqueness and scope of names apply equally to parameters declared using `<xsl:param>`; the `<xsl:param>` instruction is effectively just another way of declaring a variable.

Usage

Variables are useful, as in any programming language, to avoid calculating the same result more than once.

Global variables are useful for defining constants, such as a color value, that will be used in many places throughout the stylesheet.

Unlike variables in many programming languages, XSLT variables cannot be updated. Once they are given an initial value, they retain that value until they go out of scope. This feature has a profound effect on the programming style used when a stylesheet needs to do calculations. The subject of *programming without variables* is discussed in detail in Chapter 8.

Examples

Most XSLT variables fall into one of three categories:

❑ Variables used to avoid repeating a common expression in more than one place. This might be simply to make the code more readable, or to ensure that you only have to make a change in one place if the value changes, or perhaps because it gives a performance benefit.

❑ Variables used to capture context-sensitive information, allowing the variable to be used after the context has changed

❑ Variables holding a tree value (a result tree fragment in the language of the spec).

In each case the variable might be local or global. I'll show some examples of each kind.

Convenience Variables

Consider this example, which calculates the number of goals scored by, and against, a soccer team.

```
<xsl:variable name="for"
              select="sum($matches/team[.=$this]/@score)"/>
<xsl:variable name="against"
              select="sum($matches[team=$this]/team/@score) - $for"/>
. . .
<td><xsl:value-of select="$for"/></td>
<td><xsl:value-of select="$against"/></td>
```

This uses two rather complex expressions to construct the variables «for» and «against», which calculate the number of goals scored by, and against, the team identified by the variable «$team». If you want to understand the logic in more detail, it is given as a fully worked example under the description of the sum() function in Chapter 7, on page 520.

It would be quite possible in this case to avoid using the variable «against». The expression that calculates its value could equally be written at the point where the variable is used, in the second <xsl:value-of> instruction. The same is true of the «for» variable, though this time the expression would need to be written twice, in both places where the variable is used, and this might give a performance penalty. However, the fact is, these variables are really being used only for clarity; it would be quite possible to write the stylesheet without them.

This is true because nothing can change between the variables being defined and being used. The source document can't change, and the values of the variables $team and $matches can't change. The context (for example the current position in the source document) can change, but in this example (a) it doesn't, and (b) the expressions don't depend on the context anyway.

I call these *convenience variables* because you could get by without them if you had to (though there might be a performance hit). They can be used either as global variables or as local variables. Creating global convenience variables that refer to node-sets in the source document is often a useful programming technique, for example:

```
<xsl:variable name="group-A-matches" select="//match[@group='A']"/>
```

These act rather like views in an SQL database.

Variables to capture context-sensitive Values

These variables are most often useful in conjunction with <xsl:for-each>, which changes the current node. Consider the following example:

Example: Using a Variable for Context-sensitive Values

Source

The source file is opera.xml. It contains a list of operas and details of their composers.

```
<?xml version="1.0"?>
<programme>
   <opera>
      <title>The Magic Flute</title>
      <composer>Mozart</composer>
      <date>1791</date>
   </opera>
   <opera>
      <title>Don Giovanni</title>
      <composer>Mozart</composer>
      <date>1787</date>
```

```
    </opera>
    <opera>
        <title>Ernani</title>
        <composer>Verdi</composer>
        <date>1843</date>
    </opera>
    <opera>
        <title>Rigoletto</title>
        <composer>Verdi</composer>
        <date>1850</date>
    </opera>
    <opera>
        <title>Tosca</title>
        <composer>Puccini</composer>
        <date>1897</date>
    </opera>
    <composer name="Mozart">
        <fullname>Wolfgang Amadeus Mozart</fullname>
        <born>1756</born>
        <died>1791</died>
    </composer>
    <composer name="Verdi">
        <fullname>Guiseppe Verdi</fullname>
        <born>1813</born>
        <died>1901</died>
    </composer>
    <composer name="Puccini">
        <fullname>Giacomo Puccini</fullname>
        <born>1858</born>
        <died>1924</died>
    </composer>
</programme>
```

Stylesheet

The stylesheet is file opera.xsl. This is a complete stylesheet: it uses the
simplified stylesheet syntax described on page 104, in Chapter 3.

The stylesheet contains two nested <xsl:for-each> loops. In the outer loop, it
sets a variable «c» to the context node (the current composer). In the expression
controlling the inner loop, this variable is used. It would not be correct to use «.»
in place of «$c», because the <composer> element is no longer the context node.
In this example it would be possible to use the current() function here (this
function is described on page 437, in Chapter 7), but there are other cases where a
variable is necessary.

```
<html
    xmlns:xsl="http://www.w3.org/1999/XSL/Transform"
    xsl:version="1.0">

<body><center>
    <h1>Programme</h1>
    <xsl:for-each select="/programme/composer">
        <h2><xsl:value-of
                select="concat(fullname, ' (', born, '-', died, ')')"/></h2>
        <xsl:variable name="c" select="."/>
        <xsl:for-each select="/programme/opera[composer=$c/@name]">
            <p><xsl:value-of select="title"/></p>
        </xsl:for-each>
    </xsl:for-each>
</center></body>
</html>
```

Output

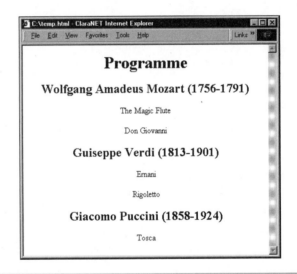

One case where context variables are very useful is when handling multiple source documents.

In any stylesheet that handles multiple source documents, it is useful to include a global variable that refers to the root node of the principal source document, thus:

```
<xsl:variable name="root" select="/"/>
```

This means it is always possible to refer to the source document by using this variable. Without this, when the context node is in a secondary document, there is no way of accessing data from the principal document.

For example, the expression «//item» refers to all <item> elements in the same document as the context node. If you actually want all <item> elements in the principal source document, then (provided you have included the global variable declaration above) you can use the expression «$root//item».

If there is a document referenced from the stylesheet, for example to hold lookup data such as messages or tax rates, it is also useful to define this in a global variable, for example:

```
<xsl:variable name="tax-rates" select="document('tax-rates.xml')"/>
```

Tree-valued Variables

The value of a variable is a tree (or result tree fragment) if it is defined using the content of the <xsl:variable> element rather than the select attribute. In many cases the tree will only contain a single text node, in which case it behaves exactly like a string variable.

A local variable can often be useful for expanding the default value of an attribute. For example:

```
<xsl:variable name="width">
   <xsl:choose>
      <xsl:when test="@width">
         <xsl:value-of select="@width"/>
      </xsl:when>
      <xsl:otherwise>0</xsl:otherwise>
   </xsl:choose>
</xsl:variable>
```

Subsequently the variable $width can be used in calculations in place of the attribute @width, without worrying about the case where the attribute was omitted. The fact that the variable is technically a tree rather than a string does not affect the way it can be used.

> *Beginners often try to write this as:*
>
> ```
> <xsl:choose>
>    <xsl:when test="@width">
>       <xsl:variable name="width" select="@width"/>
>    </xsl:when>
>    <xsl:otherwise>
>       <xsl:variable name="width" select="0"/>
>    </xsl:otherwise>
> </xsl:choose>
> ```
>
> *This won't work, because when you get to the end tag of the <xsl:choose> element, both variable declarations will have gone out of scope!*

Tree-valued variables are also needed whenever you want to use <xsl:call-template> to calculate a value which you then want to manipulate further, as shown in the next example.

315

Example: Getting the Result of <xsl:call-template> in a Variable

Source

The source file is the list of operas and composers used in the previous example, `operas.xml`.

Stylesheet

The stylesheet is the file `composers.xsl`.

This stylesheet uses a general-purpose named template («`make-list`») to output a list of names in the form «`A, B, C, and D`». It passes this template a node-set containing the names of all the composers in the source document. On return from the «`make-list`» template, it extracts the result of this template into a variable (which will be a tree containing a single text node), and passes this variable into the `translate()` function (described in Chapter 7) to convert the commas to semicolons. The `translate()` function converts its first argument to a string, which in this case extracts the value of the text node from the tree.

```
<xsl:stylesheet
    xmlns:xsl="http://www.w3.org/1999/XSL/Transform"
    xsl:version="1.0">

<xsl:template match="/">
    <xsl:variable name="list">
        <xsl:call-template name="make-list">
            <xsl:with-param name="names"
                            select="/programme/composer/fullname"/>
        </xsl:call-template>
    </xsl:variable>
    This week's composers are:
    <xsl:value-of select="translate($list, ',', ';')"/>
</xsl:template>

<xsl:template name="make-list">
    <xsl:param name="names"/>
    <xsl:for-each select="$names">
        <xsl:value-of select="."/>
        <xsl:if test="position()!=last()">, </xsl:if>
        <xsl:if test="position()=last()-1">and </xsl:if>
    </xsl:for-each>
</xsl:template>

</xsl:stylesheet>
```

Output

```
This week's composers are:
Wolfgang Amadeus Mozart; Guiseppe Verdi; and Giacomo Puccini
```

See also

<xsl:param> on page 262

xsl:when

The <xsl:when> element always appears as a child of <xsl:choose>. It defines a condition to be tested and the action to be performed if the condition is true.

Defined in

XSLT section 9.2

Format

```
<xsl:when test=Expression>
   template-body
</xsl:when>
```

Position

<xsl:when> is always a child element of <xsl:choose>. There must be at least one <xsl:when> element within an <xsl:choose> element.

Attributes

Name	Value	Meaning
test mandatory	Expression	The Boolean condition to be tested

Content

A *template body*.

Effect

The <xsl:choose> element is instantiated as follows:

❏ The first <xsl:when> element whose test Expression is true is selected; subsequent <xsl:when> elements are ignored whether or not their *Expression* is true.

❏ If none of the <xsl:when> elements has a test Expression that is true, the <xsl:otherwise> element is selected. If there is no <xsl:otherwise> instruction, no element is selected.

❏ The selected child element (if any) is executed by instantiating its template body in the current context: that is, the effect is as if the relevant template body appeared in place of the <xsl:choose> instruction.

It is not defined whether the test Expression in a <xsl:when> element after the selected one is evaluated or not, so if it calls functions that have side-effects, or if it contains errors, the result is undefined.

Any XPath value may be converted to a Boolean. In brief, the rules are:

- ❏ if the expression is a node-set, it is treated as true if the node-set is not empty
- ❏ if the expression is a string or a result tree fragment, it is treated as true if the string value is not empty
- ❏ if the expression is a number, it is treated as true if the number is non-zero

Usage and Examples

See <xsl:choose> on page 176

See also

```
<xsl:choose>
<xsl:otherwise> on page 249
<xsl:if> on page 204
```

xsl:with-param

The <xsl:with-param> element is used to set the values of parameters when calling a template, either when using <xsl:call-template>, or when using <xsl:apply-templates>.

Defined in

XSLT section 11.6

Format

```
<xsl:with-param name=QName select=Expression >
    template-body
</xsl:with-param>
```

Position

<xsl:with-param> is always a child of either <xsl:apply-templates> or <xsl:call-template>

Attributes

Name	Value	Meaning
name mandatory	QName	The name of the parameter
select optional	Expression	The value of the parameter to be supplied to the called template

The constructs QName (page 388) and Expression (page 351) are defined in Chapter 5.

Content

An optional *template-body*. If a select attribute is present, the <xsl:with-param> element should be empty.

Effect

An <xsl:with-param> element can appear only as the immediate child of an <xsl:call-template> or <xsl:apply-templates> instruction.

The <xsl:with-param> element assigns a value to a parameter. The value of the parameter can be used within the called template.

The value of the parameter is established in exactly the same way as for the <xsl:variable> element. That is, the value is taken from the select expression if present, or by instantiating the template body if not.

If the called template has an <xsl:param> element whose name matches that of the <xsl:with-param> element, then the value assigned to the <xsl:with-param> element is available within the template. If the called template has no such parameter, the value is ignored: this is not an error. In the case of <xsl:apply-templates>, the parameter value is available in each of the templates that is called (one per selected node). The parameter is effectively evaluated once only – it will have the same value for each of these templates.

The name of the parameter is defined by a QName. Normally this will be a simple name such as «city» or «total-sales», but it may be a name qualified with a prefix, for example «my:value». If it has a prefix, the prefix must correspond to a namespace that is in scope at that point in the stylesheet. The true name of the parameter, for the purpose of matching it with an <xsl:param> element in the called template, is determined not by the prefix but by the namespace URI corresponding to the prefix: so the name «my:value» will match a parameter declared as «your:value» if the prefixes «my» and «your» refer to the same namespace URI. If the name has no prefix, it has a null namespace URI – it does not use the default namespace URI.

The <xsl:with-param> element does not actually declare a variable, so there is no problem if the name is the same as that of a variable that is currently in scope. In fact it is quite normal to pass a parameter in the form:

```
<xsl:with-param name="current-user" select="$current-user"/>
```

This is used to ensure that the variable «$current-user» in the called template has the same value as the variable «$current-user» in the calling template.

It is not possible to use <xsl:with-param> in conjunction with <xsl:apply-imports>.

Usage and Examples

Parameters to templates take on considerable significance in XSLT because variables cannot be updated. This means that many tasks which in conventional programming languages are done by updating variables in a loop are done instead in XSLT using recursive calls and parameters. The consequences of this are explained in Chapter 8, and there are some detailed examples of the technique in Chapter 9.

Examples of recursive calls are also included in this chapter under `<xsl:call-template>` on page 167.

See also:

`<xsl:apply-templates>` on page 145
`<xsl:call-template>` on page 167
`<xsl:param>` on page 262

Summary

Phew! This has been a long chapter, but I'm sure you'll agree that every page was worth it! We have examined all of the XSLT elements in detail and have provided working examples to bolster your understanding of how they are used. We will now move on to look at *Expressions* in the same way.

4

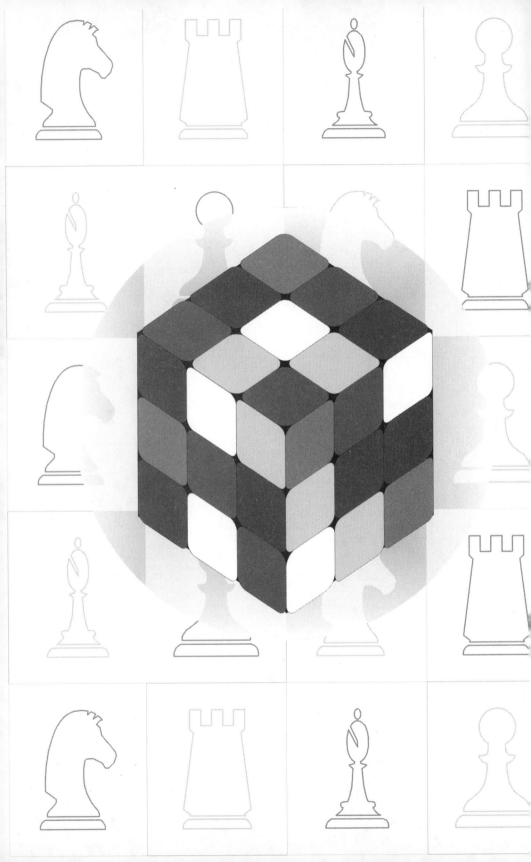

Expressions

This chapter defines the syntax and meaning of XPath expressions. XPath expressions are used in many places within an XSLT stylesheet to select data from the source document and to manipulate it to generate data to go in the result document. XPath is defined by W3C as a free-standing language, so it can also be used in other contexts, for example in defining links from one XML document to another (see the W3C XLink and XPointer specifications); however, all our examples will concentrate on the way it is used in XSLT.

As with other programming languages, the syntax is defined in a set of **production rules**. Each rule defines the structure of a particular construct as a set of choices, sequences, or repetitions. There is one section in this chapter for each production rule.

I have taken the formal production rules directly from the XPath specification document, http://www.w3.org/TR/xpath. I have reordered the rules into alphabetical order for ease of reference, and I have made minor changes to the typography for ease of reading. I have also pulled in those rules from the XML and XML Namespaces standards that the XPath syntax references. I've also included a reference to allow you to find the relevant rule in the original specification if you need to. However, I have tried to include all the information you need from the XPath specification, so this should only be necessary if you need to see the precise wording of the standard.

Most of the information you need to write XPath expressions is in this chapter. The key concepts were explained in Chapter 2, in particular the tree model (page 50) and the idea of the context of an expression (page 79) – both concepts are essential to a full understanding of this chapter. The system of data types was also explained in Chapter 2 (page 80). XPath expressions can include function calls: the standard functions defined within the XPath and XSLT Recommendations are described in Chapter 7 of this book.

Notation

As in the rest of the book, I have used French quotation marks «thus» (also known as chevrons or guillemots) to surround pieces of XPath text that you write: I chose this convention partly because these marks stand out more clearly, but more importantly to distinguish these quotation marks unambiguously from quotation marks that are actually part of the expression. So if we write, for example, that literals can be enclosed either in «"» or «'» marks, then it's clear that you don't actually write the chevrons. XPath syntax doesn't use chevrons with any special meaning (though like any other Unicode character, you can use them in literals), so you can be sure that any chevron you see is not to be included in the expression.

The production rules in XPath implicitly define the precedence of the different operators: for example the rule for OrExpr defines it as a sequence of AndExpr operands separated by «or» operators. This is a convenient way of defining that the «and» operator binds more tightly than «or».

One consequence of this style of definition is that the simplest OrExpr consists of a single AndExpr with no «or» operator present at all. This gives us a problem, because when we want to talk about an expression that uses an «or» operator, we can't call it an OrExpr. So we'll refer to an OrExpr with no «or» operator as a **trivial** OrExpr, and to a real one (with one or more «or» operators) as a **non-trivial** OrExpr. In the section of text that describes the effect of an OrExpr, we'll always concentrate on the non-trivial case. The same situation arises for many other constructs.

Although the production rules in XPath define the operator precedence, they do not impose any type checking. This would be hard to achieve, because variables are untyped, and because in most contexts a value of one type can be implicitly converted to a value of the required type, so for example «3 or 'bread'» is a perfectly legal expression (and evaluates to true). There are contexts that require a value that is a node-set, and values of other types cannot be converted to node-sets; however, the designers of the language chose not to build this in to any of the production rules. This means that the expression «3|'bread'» (where «|» is the set union operator) is also syntactically valid according to the production rules, though it is clearly an error because it violates the rule that the operands of «|» must be node-sets. Think of an analogy with English – there are sentences that are perfectly grammatically correct, but still nonsense: "An easy apple only trumpets yesterday."

Where to Start

Some people prefer to present the syntax of a language bottom-up, starting with the simplest constructs such as numbers and names, while others prefer to start at the top, with a construct like Program or Expression. As no single order of presentation suits everyone, and because you're likely to have to follow cross-references from one section to another anyway, we've chosen to list the production rules in alphabetical order. If you're the sort of person who likes the serendipity of browsing at random through an encyclopedia, you might enjoy reading the sections sequentially; or you could just as sensibly start at the end and work backwards. For a top-down approach, start with Expr on page 351: this is the top-level production rule for an XPath expression. For a bottom-up approach, look at the syntax tree shown on the following page and select the terms that are furthest from the root. Or if you want to start in the middle, take a look at Step, which is one of the key concepts that gives XPath its power.

Many languages distinguish the lexical rules, which define the format of basic tokens such as names, numbers, and operators, from the syntactic rules, which define how these tokens are combined to form expressions and other higher-level constructs. The XPath specification includes both syntactic and lexical production rules, but they are not quite as clearly separated as in some languages. As some constructs appear in both, I've kept them bundled together, showing the lexical rules in the same alphabetical sequence as the syntax rules, but distinguishing them in the text. The main distinction between the two kinds of rule is that whitespace can be freely used between lexical tokens but not within a lexical token. The top-level lexical rule is ExprToken.

A Syntax Tree

To help you find your way around the syntax, I have compiled the charts below, which show all the syntax rules (but not the purely lexical rules) arranged in a hierarchy. The children of each syntactic construct are the other constructs it references in its syntax rule.

The first chart contains all the expressions down to PathExpr: This part of the hierarchy is very straightforward: apart from MultiplyOperator, each construct defines a type of expression constructed using operands and operators, and the hierarchy reflects the precedence of the operators. For example, the chart shows that an AndExpr can contain an EqualityExpr, which implies that an operator used in an EqualityExpr (such as «=») has higher precedence and therefore binds more tightly than the «and» operator used in an AndExpr.

```
Expr
    OrExpr
        AndExpr
            EqualityExpr
                RelationalExpr
                    AdditiveExpr
                        MultiplicativeExpr
                            MultiplyOperator
                        UnaryExpr
                            UnionExpr
                                PathExpr
```

The next chart expands PathExpr. Where a name is followed by an asterisk, its expansion is to be found elsewhere in the hierarchy.

```
PathExpr
    LocationPath
        RelativeLocationPath *
        AbsoluteLocationPath
        RelativeLocationPath *
        AbbreviatedAbsoluteLocationPath
            RelativeLocationPath *
    FilterExpr
        PrimaryExpr
```

```
                VariableReference
                Expr *
                Literal
                Number
                    Digits
                FunctionCall
                    FunctionName
                        QName
                    Argument
                        Expr *
        Predicate
            PredicateExpr
                Expr *
    RelativeLocationPath
        Step
            AxisSpecifier
                AxisName
                AbbreviatedAxisSpecifier
            NodeTest
                NameTest
                    NCName
                    QName
                NodeType
                Literal *
            Predicate *
            AbbreviatedStep
        AbbreviatedRelativeLocationPath
        RelativeLocationPath *
```

Notice how once you hit PathExpr, the syntax gets much more complicated. Perhaps this isn't surprising in a language called XPath, because the main purpose of the language is to define paths through an XML document, and this is specifically what a PathExpr does. The reason the syntax gets messy below this level is that it's full of shortcuts, which make it much easier to write commonly-used path expressions, but which are difficult to define formally. For more details see the section PathExpr on page 379.

The following sections describe the syntactic constructs in alphabetical order.

AbbreviatedAbsoluteLocationPath

An AbbreviatedAbsoluteLocationPath is an expression used to select all nodes in the document that satisfy some condition.

Expression	Syntax
AbbreviatedAbsoluteLocationPath	«//» RelativeLocationPath

Defined in

XPath section 2.5, rule 10.

Used in

AbsoluteLocationPath

Usage

The initial «//» indicates that the selection path starts at the document root; the relative location path indicates how it then proceeds.

This form of expression can be expensive to evaluate, because the XSLT processor will generally have to search the whole document to find the selected nodes. If you can specify a more restricted search it is generally a good idea to do so – for example, if you know that all the <book> elements are children of the document element, then specifying «/*/book» will generally be more efficient than writing «//book». Of course, actual performance characteristics of different products may vary.

Examples

Expression	Description
//figure	Selects all <figure> elements in the document.
//book[@category='fiction']	Selects all <book> elements in the document that have a category attribute with the value «fiction».
//*/*	Selects all element nodes that have an element as a parent, in other words all elements except those that are immediate children of the root node. Here «*» is a NameTest that matches any element.
//book/title	Selects all <title> elements that have a <book> element as their parent.

Technically «//X» is an abbreviation for «/descendant-or-self::node()/X». So «//figure[1]» means «/descendant-or-self::node()/figure[1]»; that is, any <figure> element in the document that is the first <figure> child of its parent element. If you want to select the first figure element in the document, write «/descendant::figure[1]», or «(//figure)[1]».

AbbreviatedAxisSpecifier

An AbbreviatedAxisSpecifier indicates that the axis for selecting nodes in a path expression is either the child axis, or the attribute axis.

Expression	Syntax
AbbreviatedAxisSpecifier	«@» ?

Note the question mark: this means the «@» is optional. In other words, an AbbreviatedAxisSpecifier may be a completely empty string.

Defined in

XPath section 2.5, rule 13.

5

Expressions

Used in

AxisSpecifier

Usage

An abbreviated axis specifier may be either «@», to indicate the attribute axis, or nothing, to indicate the child axis. The abbreviated axis specifier «@» is an abbreviation for «attribute::», while the empty abbreviated axis specifier «» is an abbreviation for «child::». Looking at the syntax for AxisSpecifier on page 342, we see that an AxisSpecifier itself can be empty, which means (looking now at Step on page 394) that a Step can consist of a NodeTest on its own, or followed by one or more Predicates.

What this means in practice is that in a path expression «A/@B», B is referring to an attribute of A, while in the path expression «A/B», B is referring to a child element of A.

Examples in Context

Expression	Description
@category	This is a RelativeLocationPath consisting of a single Step, which itself consists of an AbbreviatedAxisSpecifier «@» followed by a NodeTest that is a NameTest, or more specifically a QName. The effect of the expression is to select any attribute node of the context node that is named «category». The full form of the expression would be «./attribute::category».
title	This is a RelativeLocationPath consisting of a single Step, which itself consists of an empty AbbreviatedAxisSpecifier followed by a NodeTest that is a NameTest, or more specifically a QName. The effect of the expression is to select any child element of the context node that is named «title». The full form of the expression would be «./child::title».

AbbreviatedRelativeLocationPath

An AbbreviatedRelativeLocationPath is a relative location path that uses the «//» operator, which is a shorthand way of requesting all the descendants of a node rather than just the immediate children.

Expression	Syntax
AbbreviatedRelativeLocationPath	RelativeLocationPath «//» Step

Defined in

XPath section 2.5, rule 11.

Used in

RelativeLocationPath

Usage

An abbreviated relative location path is a shorthand notation for selecting the descendants of a given node.

As with «//» used at the beginning of a path, this construct may be expensive, because the XSLT processor has to search all the descendants of the given node. If you can restrict the search it is a good idea to do so, for example if you know that the required nodes are all grandchildren of the starting node it is better to write «$A/*/B» rather than «$A//B». Of course, the actual performance may vary between different products.

Technically an expression such as «$chapters//diagram» is an abbreviation for «$chapters/descendant-or-self::node()/diagram»: which means: for each element in the node-set «$chapters», find all the descendant nodes of that element, and for each of these descendant nodes, find any children that are <diagram> elements. At first sight this seems to be the same as «$chapters/descendant::diagram», but there is a subtle difference when positional predicates are used, as seen in the example below:

Example: Comparing the // Operator with /descendant::

Consider the two expressions «$chapters//diagram[1]» and «$chapters/descendant::diagram[1]»:

❑ «$chapters//diagram[1]» means «$chapters/descendant-or-self::node()/diagram[1]», that is, every <diagram> element that is the first <diagram> child of its parent element and that is a descendant of a node in $chapters.

❑ «$chapters/descendant::diagram[1]» means the first <diagram> element (taking them in document order) that is a descendant of a node in $chapters. Another way of writing this is «($chapters//diagram)[1]».

To see the difference, consider the following source document:

```
<chapter>
<section>
    <diagram nr="12"/>
    <diagram nr="13"/>
</section>
<diagram nr="14"/>
<section>
    <diagram nr="15"/>
```

```
      <diagram nr="16"/>
   </section>
</chapter>
```

With this document, if the node-set $chapters contains only the outer
<chapter> element, «$chapters//diagram[1]» will select diagrams 12, 14, and
15, while both «$chapters/descendant::diagram[1]» and
«($chapters//diagram)[1]» will select diagram 12 only.

Examples

Expression	Description
chapter//footnote	Selects all <footnote> elements that are descendants of a <chapter> element that itself is a child of the context node. The context node is explained in the entry for Expr on page 351.
.//footnote	Selects all <footnote> elements that are descendants of the context node.
document('lookup.xml')//entry	Selects all <entry> elements within the document identified by the relative URL lookup.xml. The document() function is described in Chapter 7, page 440.
$winners//*/@name	Selects the name attribute of all elements that are descendants of a node that belongs to the node-set identified by the variable $winners.
.//..	This strange but perfectly legal expression combines «//» which finds the descendants of a node, and «..» which finds its parent. The effect is to find all nodes that are the parent of a descendant of the context node, plus the parent of the context node itself.

AbbreviatedStep

An AbbreviatedStep is a shorthand way to select the context node or the parent of the
context node.

Expression	Syntax
AbbreviatedStep	«.» | «..»

Defined in

XPath section 2.5, rule 12.

Used in

Step

Usage

The production rule AbbreviatedStep defines the two common symbols «.» which refers to the context node, and «..» which refers to the parent of the context node. (For a discussion of the meaning of context node, see Expr on page 351.) These symbols are abbreviations for «self::node()» and «parent::node()» respectively.

Although «.» is technically a Step, and can thus be used on the right-hand side of the path operator «/», it rarely makes sense to do so, since it is in effect a null step, a step that goes nowhere. The two places where «.» is commonly used are:

❑ with the operator «//» in a relative path expression such as «.//A», which (loosely speaking) selects all the descendant <A> elements of the context node. The «.» is necessary here because if the expression started with «//» it would select all descendants of the root node.

❑ On its own, to mean a node-set containing the context node only. This usually arises in expressions such as «.=3» or «string-length(.)» where we want to test the value of the context node, or in the XSLT instruction <xsl:value-of select="."/>, which outputs the string-value of the context node to the result tree.

Some people also like to use the «.» operator for clarity at the start of a relative path expression such as «./TITLE», but in fact this is precisely equivalent to «TITLE» on its own.

The «..» notation to refer to the parent is also found most commonly at the start of a relative path expression, for example «../@name» selects the name attribute of the parent of the context node. It is possible to use «..» anywhere in a path expression, though the need rarely arises. For example, «//@width/..» selects all elements in the document that have a width attribute. The same result could be achieved, perhaps more naturally, by writing «//*[@width]».

Note that every node except the root node has a parent (so «/..» is always an empty node-set; and «not(..)» is a simple way of testing whether the context node is the root). As explained in Chapter 2, the element containing an attribute is considered to be the parent of the attribute, even though the attribute is not a child of the element. So you can select all elements containing an attribute named ID with an expression such as «//@ID/..» (though «//*[@ID]» achieves the same thing and might be more efficient). Unlike biological relationships, in XSL the "parent" and "child" relationships are not the inverse of each other. The same applies to namespace nodes.

5

Expressions

Examples in Context

XSLT Instruction	Description
`<xsl:value-of select="."/>`	Outputs the string-value of the context node.
`<xsl:value-of select="../@name"/>`	Outputs the value of the name attribute of the parent of the context node.

AbsoluteLocationPath

An `AbsoluteLocationPath` represents a location path starting at the root node.

Expression	Syntax
`AbsoluteLocationPath`	«/» RelativeLocationPath ? | AbbreviatedAbsoluteLocationPath

Defined in

XPath section 2, rule 2.

Used in

`LocationPath`

Usage

The simplest `AbsoluteLocationPath` is «/», which selects the root node. More specifically, when there are multiple input documents, it selects the root node of the document that contains the context node. (So the term absolute is something of a misnomer).

This syntax is familiar to anyone who has used UNIX filenames, though it is not actually very logical. The symbol «/» is used both as an expression to refer to the root node, and as an operator to separate the parts of a path. I find it helpful to think of an `AbsoluteLocationPath` «/X» as an abbreviation for an imaginary expression «®/X», and «/» as an abbreviation for «®», where «®» represents the document root node.

The `AbbreviatedAbsoluteLocationPath`, which takes the form «//X», is discussed in its own section on page 326.

If you are writing a stylesheet that loads several source documents using the `document()` function, there is no direct way of selecting the root of the principal source document when the context node is in a different one. To solve this problem it is useful to include in your stylesheet a global variable declaration of the form `<xsl:variable name="root" select="/"/>`. You can then refer to the root of the principal document at any time as «$root».

Examples

Expression	Description
/	Selects the root node of the document containing the context node.
/price-list	Selects the document element, provided its name is **<price-list>**.
/*	Selects the document element, whatever its type.
/child::node()	Selects all nodes that are immediate children of the document root, that is the document element plus any comments or processing instructions that come before or after the document element. (However, note that the `<?xml version="1.0"?>` at the start of a document is **not** a processing instruction: in fact it is not a node at all, and is not accessible using XPath).
/*/xsl:*	Selects all element nodes with names in the namespace associated with the «xsl:» namespace prefix that are immediate children of the document element. (If applied to an XSLT stylesheet, this would select all the top-level XSL elements).
//figure	This `AbbreviatedAbsoluteLocationPath` selects all the `<figure>` elements in the document.

AdditiveExpr

A non-trivial `AdditiveExpr` is used to add or subtract numeric values.

Expression	Syntax
AdditiveExpr	MultiplicativeExpr | AdditiveExpr «+» MultiplicativeExpr | AdditiveExpr «-» MultiplicativeExpr

Defined in

XPath section 3.5, rule 25.

Used in

RelationalExpr

Usage

A non-trivial `AdditiveExpr` consists of two or more `MultiplicativeExpr` operands separated by the plus «+» or minus «-» operators. A trivial `AdditiveExpr` consists of a single `MultiplicativeExpr` with no plus or minus operator.

5

Expressions

When using the minus operator, take care that it does not get confused with a hyphen within a name. If it immediately follows a name, use a space to separate it. Note that «price-discount» (without spaces) is a single hyphenated name, whereas «price - discount» (with spaces) performs a subtraction.

Numbers in XSLT are always double-length floating point, so the calculation is carried out using floating point arithmetic, according to the rules of IEEE 754. See the description of the number data type in Chapter 2, page 81.

If an operand of the AdditiveExpr is not already a number, it is converted to a number as if the number() function was used. If the value cannot be converted to an ordinary number, it is converted to the special value NaN (Not-a-Number), and in this case the result of the addition or subtraction will also be NaN.

Examples in Context

Expression	Description
$X + 1	The result of adding 1 to the value of the variable $X.
last()-1	One less than the position of the last node in the context list.
@price - @discount	The value of the price attribute of the context node, converted to a number, minus the value of the discount attribute of the context node, converted to a number.
count($list) mod 5 + 1	The number of nodes in the node-set $list modulo 5, plus one. The result will be a number in the range 1 to 5. (For more on modulo, see page 367.)
42	The number 42 is a trivial AdditiveExpr, so it can be used anywhere that an AdditiveExpr is allowed.

AndExpr

A non-trivial AndExpr is used to test whether two or more Boolean conditions are all true.

Expression	Syntax
AndExpr	EqualityExpr	 AndExpr «and» EqualityExpr

Defined in

XPath section 3.4, rule 22.

Used in

OrExpr

Usage

A non-trivial `AndExpr` consists of one or more `EqualityExpr` operands separated by the «and» operator. A trivial `AndExpr` consists of a single `EqualityExpr` with no «and» operator.

An `AndExpr` is evaluated by evaluating each `EqualityExpr` in turn, from left to right, and converting it to a Boolean value, until one is found that is false. As soon as one is found that is false, evaluation stops and the expression returns false. If each `EqualityExpr` is true, the final result is true.

> *The XPath specification is quite explicit about the order of evaluation; however, since XPath expressions are free of side effects, it normally makes no difference. The only case where it might affect the outcome is if an operand invokes user-defined extension functions that have side-effects. However, since the order of evaluation of a stylesheet is generally undefined anyway, writing extension functions with side-effects is not good practice.*

The rules for converting the value to a Boolean are the same as for the `boolean()` function, described in Chapter 7, page 426. For example, a string is false if it is zero-length, and a node-set is false if it is empty.

Examples

Expression	Description
`$x &gt; 3 and $x &lt; 8`	True if the value of variable $x is greater than 3 and less than 8.
`@name and @address`	True if the context node has both a `name` and an `address` attribute. (Both the operands are node-sets, which are converted to the Boolean true if they contain a node, and to false if they are empty).
`string(@name) and string(@address)`	True if the context node has both a `name` and an `address` attribute and if neither is a zero length string. (Both the operands are strings, which are converted to the Boolean true if their length is zero. If an attribute is absent, the node-set will be empty, and its string value will therefore be the empty string.)
`true()`	A trivial `AndExpr` consisting of a single function call.

Argument

An `Argument` is used to represent the value supplied as input to a `FunctionCall`.

Expression	Syntax
Argument	Expr

5

Expressions

Defined in

XPath section 3.2, rule 17.

Used in

`FunctionCall`

Usage

Any expression can be used as an argument to a function. The only reason for defining a separate production rule for `Argument` is to make the rules easier to read.

Note that some expressions when used as arguments might look rather strange if you are thinking in terms of conventional languages. For example «`string-length(..)`» returns the length of the string-value of the parent of the context node, and «`document(@*,/)`» returns a node-set containing the root nodes of the documents whose relative URIs are contained in attributes of the context node, using the system identifier of the root of the source document as the base URI for resolving these relative URIs.

The XPath specification uses the term `Arguments` for the input to an XPath `FunctionCall`. The term **parameters** has a different meaning – it is used in XSLT for the values supplied to a template.

Examples in Context

Any expression can be used as an argument to a function call. Here are some examples of function calls that exploit this flexibility:

Expression	Description
`count(@*)`	Returns the number of attributes on the context node.
`id(string(@idref))`	Returns a node-set containing the element (if there is one) whose ID is equal to the value of the `idref` attribute of the context node.
`not(isbn)`	Returns true if the context node has no child element node named `<isbn>`. The argument here is a `RelativeLocationPath` and is equivalent to «`./child::isbn`».
`generate-id(/)`	Returns a string that uniquely identifies the root node of the document containing the context node.

AxisName

An `AxisName` is used within a `Step` to identify a path to be followed from a given node to other related nodes.

Expression	Syntax
AxisName	«ancestor» | «ancestor-or-self» | «attribute» | «child» | «descendant» | «descendant-or-self» | «following» | «following-sibling» | «namespace» | «parent» | «preceding» | «preceding-sibling» | «self»

Defined in

XPath section 2.2, rule 6.

Used in

AxisSpecifier

Usage

An **axis** is a path through the document tree, starting at a particular node (which I'll call the origin) and following a particular relationship between nodes.

The various axis names have the following meaning:

Axis	Description
ancestor	Selects all the nodes that are ancestors of the starting node, in reverse document order. The first node on the axis is the parent of the origin node, the second is its grandparent, and so on; the last node on the axis is the document root.
ancestor-or-self	Selects the same nodes as the ancestor axis, but starting with the origin node rather than with its parent.
attribute	If the origin node is an element, this axis selects all its attribute nodes, in some arbitrary order. Otherwise, it selects nothing.
child	Selects all the children of the origin node, in document order. For any node except a root node or element node, this selects nothing. Note that the children of an element node do not include its attributes or namespace nodes, only the text nodes, element nodes, processing instructions and comments that make up its content.

Axis	Description
descendant	Selects all the children of the origin node, and their children, and so on recursively. The resulting nodes are in document order. If the origin is an element, this effectively means that the descendant axis contains all the text nodes, element nodes, comments and processing instructions that appear in the original source document between that element's start and end tags, in their original sequence.
descendant-or-self	This is the same as the descendant axis, except that the first node selected is the origin node itself.
following	This selects all the nodes that appear after the origin node in document order, excluding the descendants of the origin node. If the origin is an element node, for example, this effectively means that it contains all the text nodes, element nodes, comments and processing instructions in the document that start after the end tag of the origin element. The following axis will never contain attribute or namespace nodes.
following-sibling	This selects all the nodes that follow the origin node in document order, and that are children of the same parent node. If the origin is a root node, an attribute node, or a namespace node, then the following-sibling axis will always be empty.
namespace	If the origin node is an element, this axis selects all the namespace nodes that are in scope for that element; otherwise it is empty. The order of the namespace nodes is undefined. The namespace nodes correspond to namespace declarations (xmlns="x" or xmlns:y="z") on the element itself or on one of its ancestor elements, but excluding any namespace declaration that cannot be used on this element because it is masked by another declaration of the same namespace prefix.
parent	This axis selects a single node, the parent of the origin node. If the origin node is a root node, the parent axis is empty.
preceding	This selects all the nodes that appear before the origin node, excluding the ancestors of the origin node, in reverse document order. If the origin is an element node, this effectively means that it contains all the text nodes, element nodes, comments and processing instructions in the document that finish before the start tag of the origin element. The preceding axis will never contain attribute or namespace nodes.
preceding-sibling	This selects all the nodes that precede the origin node, and that are children of the same parent node, in reverse document order. If the origin is a root node, an attribute node, or a namespace node, then the preceding-sibling axis will always be empty.

Axis	Description
self	This selects a single node, the origin node itself. This axis will never be empty.

The various axes can also be shown diagrammatically. In each case in the table below the diagram shows the origin node in dark shading, while the nodes on the axis are numbered in the sequence they appear on the axis. The diagram does not show attribute and namespace nodes, and the attribute and namespace axes are therefore excluded from the table.

Axis	Diagram

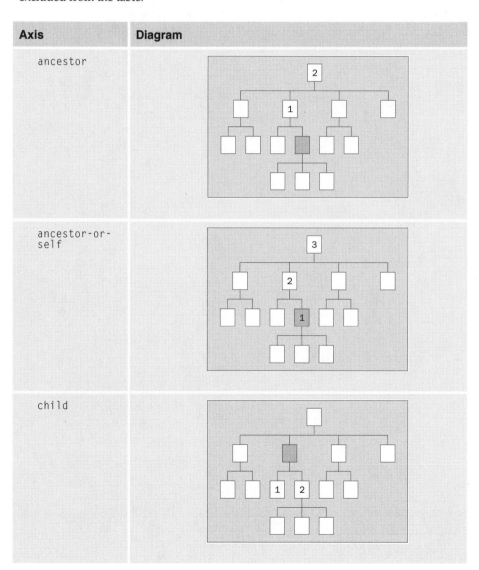

Axis	Diagram
descendant	
descendant-or-self	
following	
following-sibling	

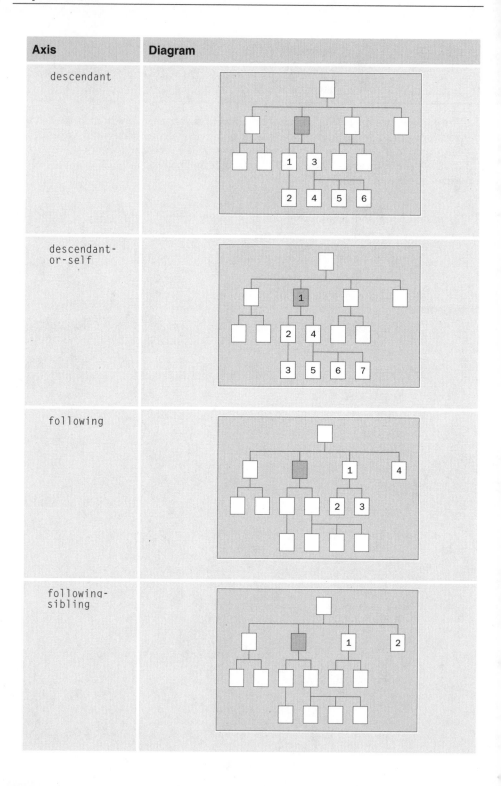

Axis	Diagram
parent	
preceding	
preceding-sibling	
self	

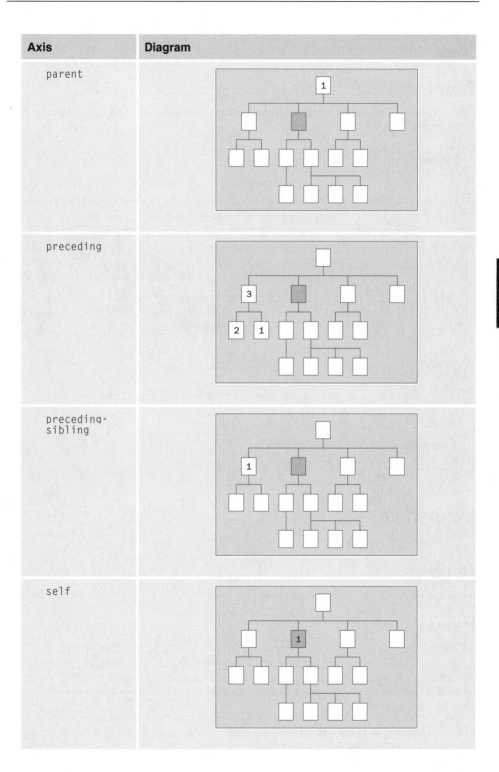

For details of how axes are used in a location path, and examples, see `Step` on page 394.

Examples in Context

An `Axis` is always used as part of a `Step` within a location path. Here are some examples.

Expression	Description
`ancestor::*`	Selects the ancestor elements of the context node.
`child::node()`	Selects the children of the context node. This is usually written in its abbreviated form, «node()».
`attribute::color`	Selects the color attribute of the context node. This is usually written in its abbreviated form, «@color». If the context node is not an element, the result will be empty.
`namespace::*`	Selects all the namespace nodes that are in scope for the context node. If the context node is not an element, the result will be empty.

AxisSpecifier

An `AxisSpecifier` is either an axis name, or a shorthand abbreviation for an axis name.

Expression	Syntax
`AxisSpecifier`	AxisName «::» | AbbreviatedAxisSpecifier

Defined in

XPath section 2.1, rule 5.

Used in

`Step`

Usage

An `AxisSpecifier` is either an axis name followed by a double colon, or an `AbbreviatedAxisSpecifier`. Since an `AbbreviatedAxisSpecifier` is either «@» or nothing, this means that an `AxisSpecifier` can itself be empty, reflecting the fact that in this context «X» is an abbreviation for «child::X».

An `AxisSpecifier` defines a direction of navigation through the document. Given a start node in the document, an `AxisSpecifier` defines an ordered list of nodes that can be visited in turn. Details of each axis are given in the section `AxisName` on page 336.

Examples

Expression	Description
ancestor::	Specifies the ancestor axis.
preceding-sibling::	Specifies the preceding-sibling axis.
@	Specifies the attribute axis.
	Specifies the child axis. (Yes, the entry on the left is blank!).

Digits

Digits is a sequence of decimal digits in the range 0 through 9. The sequence is used as part of a number: either the whole number, or the part before the decimal point, or the part after the decimal point.

Expression	Syntax
Digits	[0-9]+

This production rule is written as a **regular expression** and means that Digits is a sequence of one or more characters, each in the range zero to nine. The square brackets do not mean that the construct is optional, as in some other syntax notations: rather they indicate a range of characters.

Defined in

XPath section 3.7(Lexical Structure), rule 31

Used in

Number

Usage

An instance of Digits is simply a sequence of one or more of the decimal digits zero through nine.

As Number is a lexical token, it cannot contain embedded whitespace; therefore Digits cannot contain whitespace either.

Examples in Context

Expression	Description
89	This Number consists of a single sequence of digits, that is, one instance of Digits.
3.14159	This Number contains two sequences of digits, that is two instances of Digits. The first instance of Digits is «3», the second instance of Digits is «14159».

5

Expressions

EqualityExpr

A non-trivial `EqualityExpr` is used to determine whether two values are equal, or not equal.

Note: for the other comparison operators «<», «<=», «>», and «>=», see `RelationalExpr` on page 389.

Expression	Syntax
EqualityExpr	RelationalExpr | EqualityExpr «=» RelationalExpr | EqualityExpr «!=» RelationalExpr

Defined in

XPath section 3.4, rule 23.

Used in

AndExpr

Usage

A non-trivial `EqualityExpr` consists of one or more `RelationalExpr` operands separated by «=» (equals) or «!=» (not equals) operators. A trivial `EqualityExpr` consists of a single `RelationalExpr` without any «=» or «!=» operator.

The result of an equals (or not-equals) test is always a Boolean value true or false. However, there are many situations where the result of the expression is not obvious, so I'll explain the different cases in some detail.

The harmless looking «=» operator holds many surprises in XPath, so it is well worth studying the rules carefully, even if they seem complicated. Just to warn you of the dangers that lie in wait for the unwary, here are some particular elephant traps:

❑ You can't assume that «$X=$X» is true. It usually will be, but if «$X» is an empty node-set, it will be false.

❑ You can't assume that «$X!=3» means the same as «not($X=3)». When «$X» is a node-set, the first expression is true if any node in the node-set is not equal to 3, while the second is true if no node in the node-set is equal to 3.

❑ You can't assume that if «$X=$Y and $Y=$Z», then «$X=$Z». Again, node-sets are the culprit. Two node-sets are considered equal if there is a value that both have in common, so {2, 3} = {3, 4} is true, and {3, 4} = {4, 5} is true, but {2, 3} = {4, 5} is false.

In this strange Orwellian world where some values seem to be more equal than others, the one consolation is that you can assume that «$X=$Y» always means the same as «$Y=$X».

The left-hand operand of an `EqualityExpr` may be another `EqualityExpr`. This means that the expression «$A = $B = $C» is legal. However, it isn't particularly useful, and probably doesn't have the expected effect. It means the same as «($A=$B)=$C», and tests whether the value of $C, when converted to a Boolean, is the same as the result of comparing $A and $B. This means, for example, that «2=1=0» is true, because «2=1» is false, and 0 when converted to a Boolean is false, and «2=1» therefore equals «boolean(0)».

Comparing Simple Values

First, consider the case where both operands are simple values: Booleans, numbers, or strings. If the two values are of different type, then:

❑   if one is a Boolean, the other is converted to a Boolean, and they are compared as Booleans

❑   otherwise, if one is a number, the other is converted to a number, and they are compared as numbers

❑   otherwise, they are compared as strings.

The effect of these rules is summarized in the following table:

«=»	Boolean	Number	String
Boolean	True if both operands are true or if both are false. False if one operand is true and the other is false.	True if the Boolean is true and the number is not zero and not NaN; or if the Boolean is false and the number is zero or NaN	True if the Boolean is true and the string is not empty, or if the Boolean is false and the string is empty.
Number	True if the Boolean is true and the number is not zero and not NaN; or if the Boolean is false and the number is zero or NaN.	True only if the two operands are numerically equal as defined in IEEE 754.	True only if the string, when converted to a number using the rules for the `number()` function, is numerically equal to the number as defined in IEEE 754.

5

Expressions

«=»	Boolean	Number	String
String	True if the Boolean is true and the string is not empty, or if the Boolean is false and the string is empty.	True only if the string, when converted to a number using the rules for the number() function, is numerically equal to the number as defined in IEEE 754.	True only if the two operands contain the same sequence of Unicode characters.

See Chapter 2, page 81 for details of how IEEE 754 defines numerical equality. For example, positive zero and negative zero are considered equal, but NaN and NaN are considered unequal.

For simple values (including special numeric values such as NaN), the result of applying the «!=» (not equals) operator is always the opposite of applying the «=» operator: if the result of an «=» test is true, the result of «!=» will be false, and vice versa.

Comparisons Involving Node-sets

Now consider the case where at least one operand is a node-set. (And remember that an expression as innocent as «TITLE» or «@HREF» is actually a node-set, even if it only contains a single node.) The result of an «=» or «!=» test is now as shown in the table below. Given that one operand is a node-set (it doesn't matter which), choose the row according to the data type of the other operand.

Data Type of Other Operand	= (equals)	!= (not equals)
Boolean	True if the Boolean is true and the node-set contains at least one node; or if the Boolean is false and the node-set is empty.	True if the Boolean is true and the node-set is empty; or if the Boolean is false and the node-set contains at least one node.
Number	True if the node-set contains a node whose string-value, after converting to a number using the number() function, is numerically equal to the number operand as defined in IEEE 754.	True if the node-set contains a node whose string-value, after converting to a number using the number() function, is numerically not equal to the number operand as defined in IEEE 754.

Data Type of Other Operand	= (equals)	!= (not equals)
string	True if the node-set contains a node whose string-value is equal to the string operand.	True if the node-set contains a node whose string-value is not equal to the string operand.
Node-set	True if there is a pair of nodes, one from each node-set, that have the same string-value. Note that this means that if either or both node-sets are empty, the result is always false. If there is a node that is present in both node-sets, the result will always be true.	True if there is a pair of nodes, one from each node-set, that have different string-values. Note that this means that if either or both node-sets are empty, the result is always false. It also means that if either node-set contains more than one node, then unless the nodes all have the same string-value the result will always be true.

So where a node-set «$N» is compared with a string «'mary'», the test «$N='mary'» is effectively a shorthand for "if there is a node n in $N such that string-value(n) = 'mary'". Similarly, the test «$N!='mary'» is effectively a shorthand for "if there is a node n in $N such that string-value(n) != 'mary'". If $N contains two nodes, whose string-values are "mary" and "john", then «$N='mary'» and «$N!='mary'» will both be true, because there is a node that is equal to 'mary' and another that is not. If $N is an empty node-set, then «$N='mary'» and «$N!='mary'» will both be false, because there is no node that is equal to 'mary', but there is also no node that is not equal to 'mary'.

Note that when we talk about the nodes in a node-set, we are only concerned with the nodes that are members of the node-set in their own right. The children of these nodes are not members of the node-set.

Example: Node-set Comparisons

For example, consider the following piece of XML:

```
<booklist>
  <book><author>Adam</author><title>Penguins</title></book>
  <book><author>Betty</author><title>Giraffes</title></book>
</booklist>
```

Suppose we create a variable whose value is the node-set containing all <book> elements, as follows:

```
<xsl:variable name="all-books" select="//book"/>
```

And now suppose we do the following test:

```
<xsl:if test="$all-books = 'Adam'"/>
```

The result is false, because the node-set $all-books contains two <book> nodes, and neither has a string-value of "Adam". The first <book> element has the string-value "AdamPenguins", and the second has the string-value "BettyGiraffes". The fact that one of them has a child whose string-value is "Adam" is of no consequence: the child is not a member of the node-set.

The string-value of a node depends on the type of node. For a text node, it is the actual characters in the value. For an element node, it is the concatenation of the text in all text nodes that are descendants of the element. For an attribute node, it is the value of the attribute. See Chapter 2 for the detailed rules.

An interesting consequence of the rules for comparing node-sets is that if $N is an empty node-set, the result of the test «$N=$N» is false, because there is no node in the first node-set whose string-value is equal to that of a node in the second node-set.

It is very easy to trip up on these rules, by assuming for example that <xsl:if test="@name != 'James'"> means the same as <xsl:if test="not(@name = 'James')">. It doesn't: if there is no name attribute, the first test is false, while the second is true.

Generally speaking, it is best to steer clear of the «!=» operator unless you know exactly what you are doing. Use «not(x=y)» instead: it is more likely to match the intuitive meaning.

One situation where «!=» can be useful with node-sets, however, is to test whether all values in a node-set have the same value. For example, writing <xsl:if test="not($documents//version!=1.0)"> tests whether there is any node in the node-set «$documents//version» whose numeric value is not 1.0.

It is important to remember that an equality test compares the string values of the nodes, not their identity. For example, «.=/» might seem to be a natural way of testing whether the parent of the context node is the root. In fact this test will also return true if the parent node is the document element, because in a well-formed tree the string-value of the document element is the same as the string-value of the root. So, not only is the test wrong, it could also be very expensive: the string-value of the root contains all the text in the document, so you might be constructing two strings each a million characters long and then comparing them.

A better way to test if the parent node is the root is to write «..[not(..)]»: this is true only for a node that has a parent and no grandparent. Another possibility, which can be used to compare any single-member node-sets, is «generate-id(..)=generate-id(/)». This relies on the generate-id() function, described in Chapter 7, page 463, which returns a string that uniquely identifies a node.

Comparisons Involving Result Tree Fragments

Result tree fragments are not technically part of the XPath specification; rather, they are an extension to XPath defined in XSLT itself. However, it is convenient to treat them here as an intrinsic part of the language.

A result tree fragment is a tree, just like the source document tree: it always has a root, and may have any of the other kinds of nodes that are found on the source document tree. The structure follows the XPath tree model described in Chapter 2. A result tree fragment always arises as a result of an <xsl:variable> or <xsl:param> element with no select attribute. One difference from the source document tree is that the source tree usually represents a well-formed XML document, whose root node has a single element child and no text node children, whereas a result tree fragment only has to be well-balanced: the root may have any number of element nodes and text nodes as its children.

Example: A Result Tree Fragment

The <xsl:variable> element below creates a result tree fragment:

```
<xsl:variable name="rtf">A <emph>very</emph> important person</xsl:variable>
```

A result tree fragment has an equivalent node-set, which always consists of a single root node. The node-set in this example is a root node with three child nodes: a text node for "A♦" (where ♦ represents a space character), an <emph> element node, and a text node for "♦important♦person". These three child nodes are children of the root node, but they are not themselves members of the equivalent node-set: the equivalent node-set contains only one node, namely the root. The equivalent node-set will always contain a single node. It can never be empty, because the value of an <xsl:variable> element that is empty is not a result tree fragment; it is a zero-length string. It can, however, consist of a root node with no children; and as we can see in this example, it does not have to be a well-formed XML document.

The string value of the root node is the concatenation of all the text nodes in the result tree fragment; and the string-value of the tree is the same as the string-value of its root node. So the string-value of this example result tree fragment is "A♦very♦important♦person".

Where one of the operands of the «=» or «!=» comparison is a result tree fragment, it is treated as if the comparison was done with the equivalent node-set. So the result of the comparison will be as follows:

	= (equals)	!= (not equals)
Boolean	True if the Boolean is true, false if it is false; the value of the result tree fragment is immaterial, because it always contains a node.	True if the Boolean is false, false if it is true; the value of the result tree fragment is immaterial, because it always contains a node.
Number	True if the string-value of the result tree fragment, after converting to a number using the number() function, is numerically equal to the number operand as defined in IEEE 754.	True if the string-value of the result tree fragment, after converting to a number using the number() function, is numerically not equal to the number operand as defined in IEEE 754.
String	True if the string-value of the result tree fragment is equal to the string operand.	True if the string-value of the result tree fragment is not equal to the string operand.
Node-set	True if the node-set contains a node whose string-value is equal to the string-value of the result tree fragment.	True if the node-set contains a node whose string-value is not equal to the string-value of the result tree fragment.

These rules actually mean that for all practical purposes, a result tree fragment variable defined as:

```
<xsl:variable name="city">Johannesburg</xsl:variable>
```

behaves in exactly the same way as the string variable:

```
<xsl:variable name="city" select="'Johannesburg'"/>
```

Examples

Expression	Description
@width = 3	Tests whether the width attribute of the context node, after converting to a number, has the numeric value 3. The result will be true if the width attribute is say «3» or «3.00». It will be false if there is no width attribute.

Expression	Description
@width = @height	Tests whether the width attribute and the height attribute of the context node have the same string value. If width is «3» and height is «3.00», the result will be false. It will also be false if either or both attributes are absent. If you want a numeric comparison, use the number() function (described in Chapter 7, page 498) to force a conversion.
@width != $x	If the variable $x holds a numeric value, a numeric comparison is performed; if it holds a string value or a result tree fragment, a string comparison is performed. The result will be true if the values are different. It will be false if there is no width attribute. If $x holds a node-set, the result will be true if there is any node in the node-set whose string-value is equal to the width attribute, using string comparison; it will be false if the node-set is empty or of there is no width attribute.

Expr

Expr is the top-level production rule, representing an XPath expression.

Expression	Syntax
Expr	OrExpr

Defined in

XPath section 3.1, rule 14.

Used in

Expr is the top-level rule for the syntax of an XPath expression.

A nested Expr is also used in the production rules for Argument, PrimaryExpr, and PredicateExpr.

Within an XSLT stylesheet, XPath expressions are used in the following contexts:

Context	Result data type
Attribute value templates. The expression is written between curly braces «{» and «}» in any attribute where attribute value templates are permitted. A list of these attributes is included in Chapter 3, page 119.	string

5

Expressions

Context	Result data type
`<xsl:apply-templates select="">`	node-set
`<xsl:copy-of select="">`	node-set
`<xsl:for-each select="">`	node-set
`<xsl:if test="">`	Boolean
`<xsl:key use="">`	node-set or string
`<xsl:number value="">`	number
`<xsl:param select="">`	Any
`<xsl:sort select="">`	string
`<xsl:value-of select="">`	string
`<xsl:variable select="">`	Any
`<xsl:when test="">`	Boolean
`<xsl:with-param select="">`	Any

Usage

`Expr` (short for *Expression*) is the top-level construct in the production rules defined in this chapter. What the syntax rule says is that every `Expr` is an `OrExpr` (and vice versa, every `OrExpr` is an `Expr`). So it merely delegates the rules to `OrExpr`. The construct `OrExpr` is described on page 378.

The designers of XPath chose to specify the syntax of the language in such a way that the precedence of the various operators is inherent in the production rules. So this rule also tells us that «or» is the lowest-precedence operator. The production rule for `OrExpr` defines it in terms of `AndExpr`, which tells us that «and» is a higher precedence operator than «or», and so on: A consequence of this style of definition is that an `OrExpr` does not necessarily contain an «or» operator; it is merely an expression that occurs in a context where an «or» operator would be recognized.

In XSLT, expressions (that is, sentences conforming to the production rule for `Expr`) occur within stylesheets, and the stylesheet context imposes rules on the `Expr` that are not inherent in the XPath syntax. These include data type rules (for example, certain stylesheet contexts require a node-set, as described in the table above), and also rules about the scope of variables and the assignment of namespace prefixes. For example, «2+2» is a perfectly valid XPath expression, but if you try to write `<xsl:for-each select="2+2"/>` the XSLT processor will report an error, telling you that a node-set is required in this context.

The stylesheet context imposes constraints on the syntactic validity of the expression, and also provides a run-time context when the time comes to evaluate the expression. So we can consider the context of the expression in two parts, a static part and a dynamic part.

The static context of the expression, which can be determined merely by examining the stylesheet, includes:

❑ The list of variable names that are in scope at the point where the expression appears.

❑ The list of namespace prefixes that are in scope at the point where the expression appears, and the corresponding namespace URI for each one. This affects the validity of any QName (loosely, a namespace-qualified name) occurring in the expression, as described in the section QName on page 388.

❑ The required data type (for example <xsl:if> requires a Boolean, <xsl:for-each> requires a node-set, and an expression contained within an attribute value template evaluates to a string).

❑ The set of extension functions (user- or vendor-defined external functions) that is available in the current stylesheet context.

❑ The URI of the stylesheet containing the expression: or more specifically, the URI of the actual XML entity containing the element in which the expression appears (the stylesheet may consist of several separate entities, linked either using <xsl:include> and <xsl:import>, or using XML external general entity references). This URI is in fact needed for one purpose only, to provide a base URI for resolving a relative URI used in the document() function, which is described in Chapter 7.

The dynamic context of the expression, which can only be established while the stylesheet is being used to process a specific source document, includes:

❑ The current values of all variables that are referenced in the expression.

❑ The context node, context position, and context size, which together identify the set of nodes in the source document that the stylesheet is currently processing. These important concepts were explained in Chapter 2.

The XSLT processor may also need information about the static context at run-time. For example, certain functions (such as system-property() and key()) can generate a QName (a name potentially in the form «prefix:localname») as a result of an expression, and just like a QName written directly in the expression, any namespace prefixes this uses must be in scope.

As explained in Chapter 1, page 34, it's a general principle of XPath that expression evaluation is free of side effects: evaluating an expression isn't going to change the values of any variables, write information to log files, or prompt the user for their credit card number. Therefore evaluating the same expression more than once, in the same context, shouldn't make any difference to the answer or to the final output, and equally it shouldn't make any difference in which order expressions are evaluated. As a result, the XSLT and XPath specifications generally say nothing about order of evaluation. The only exceptions are OrExpr and AndExpr, where left-to-right evaluation is explicitly mandated.

The only way side-effects can occur from evaluating an expression is if the expression calls user-written (or vendor-written) extension functions, because the XPath specification doesn't constrain what an extension function can do.

Examples

Examples of expressions occur throughout this chapter. Here is a selection, brought together to indicate the variety of constructs that fall under this heading:

Expression	Description
`$x + ($y * 2)`	Returns the result of multiplying `$y` by two and adding the value of `$x`.
`//book	//magazine`	Returns a node-set containing all the `<book>` and `<magazine>` elements in the same document as the context node.
`substring-before(author, ' ')`	Finds the string-value of the first `<author>` child of the context node, and returns that part of the string-value that precedes the first space character.
`chapter and verse`	Returns the Boolean value true if the context node has a child `<chapter>` element and also a child `<verse>` element.
`93.7`	Returns the numeric value `93.7`.

ExprToken

An `ExprToken` is a lexical unit of the XPath expression language. `ExprToken` defines the lexical rules for separating tokens using whitespace; it is not itself a syntactic unit used in any other production rule.

Expression	Syntax
`ExprToken`	«(» | «)»	«[»	«]»	 «.»	«..»	«@»	 «,»	«::»	 `NameTest`	 `NodeType`	 `Operator`	 `FunctionName`	 `AxisName`	 `Literal`	 `Number`	 `VariableReference`

Defined in

XPath section 3.7 (Lexical Structure), rule 28.

Used in

The production rule is the top-level lexical rule, it is not referenced from anywhere else.

Usage

The production rule defines those constructs in the language that are regarded as lexical tokens. If a construct is a lexical token, it is indivisible: its components must be contiguous and cannot be separated by whitespace. Higher-level constructs consist of a sequence of lexical tokens and are allowed to contain whitespace to separate the tokens. So for example, the expression «child::xsl:*» contains three tokens, «child», «::», and «xsl:*». Spaces and newlines can be used between these tokens, but not within them. This means the expression can contain optional whitespace at all the points marked here with a diamond: «♦child♦::♦xsl:*♦».

> *The spec doesn't explicitly say so, but by implication, whitespace cannot be freely used in the middle of an ExprToken: except, of course, within a Literal. This means, for example, that there can be no space between the two colons in «child::node()», because «::» is a single token.*

Whitespace itself is defined by the ExprWhitespace rule.

Examples

Here are some examples of ExprTokens. No whitespace is permitted within the token, except in the case of a Literal.

Token	Description
[	A punctuation symbol used as part of a Predicate.
item	An NCName.
my-namespace:*	A NameTest. No spaces are permitted before or after the colon.
$weekly-sales-total	A VariableReference. No spaces are permitted after the «$» sign.
93.7	A Number.
"a pinch of salt"	A Literal. Any whitespace occurring within the Literal is significant, it is part of the string value.

ExprWhitespace

The ExprWhitespace rule defines precisely what constitutes whitespace within an XPath expression.

Expression	Syntax
ExprWhitespace	S
S	(#x20 | #x9 | #xD | #xA)+

Defined in

XPath section 3.7, rule 39.
The rule for S is from the XML Recommendation.

Used in

This production rule is not actually referenced from any other. It is used only in the narrative text of the XPath specification.

Usage

The definition of whitespace is taken directly from the XML standard: whitespace is any sequence of space, tab, carriage return, and linefeed characters.

XPath allows whitespace to be used before or after any ExprToken: see the section ExprToken above for a list of constructs that are considered to be lexical tokens and that may therefore not contain any embedded whitespace. It is not intuitively obvious which composite symbols in XPath are tokens and which are not; for example «self::x» consists of three tokens (so spaces can appear before or after the double colon, but not between the two colons), while «xsl:*» is a single token, with no embedded whitespace allowed anywhere. This is because «xsl:*» is a NameTest, and NameTest is one of the constructs listed in the production rule for ExprToken.

The lexical rules for XPath say that any token swallows as many characters as it can: if a character can be treated as part of the previous token, then it is treated as such, even if this causes a syntax error later on. This means it is necessary in some circumstances to insert whitespace to separate tokens; the most common example being the need to use a space before a minus sign to distinguish an arithmetic expression such as «price - discount» from the hyphenated name «price-discount». Whitespace is also required, of course, to separate names from the operators «or», «and», «div», and «mod».

Although it is common practice to write XPath expressions on a single line, because this is how XML attributes are normally written, there is nothing to stop whitespace characters such as tab and newline being used as an alternative to spaces.

Examples

Expression	Description
	The box on the left shows what whitespace usually looks like.
&#xA;	If you really want to see your whitespace characters, you can write them like this.

FilterExpr

A FilterExpr is used to apply one or more Predicates to a node-set, selecting a subset of those nodes that satisfy some condition.

Expression	Syntax
FilterExpr	PrimaryExpr | FilterExpr Predicate

Defined in

XPath section 3.3, rule 20.

Used in

PathExpr

Usage

A non-trivial FilterExpr consists of a PrimaryExpr whose value is a node-set, followed by one or more Predicates that select a subset of the nodes in the node-set. Each predicate consists of an expression enclosed in square brackets, for example «[@name='London']» or «[position()=1]».

The way the syntax is defined, every PrimaryExpr is also a trivial FilterExpr, including simple expressions such as «23», «'Washington'», and «true()».

If there are any Predicates, the value of the PrimaryExpr must be a node-set. Each of the predicates is applied to the node-set in turn; only those nodes in the node-set for which the predicate is true pass through to the next stage. The final result consists of those nodes in the original node-set that satisfy each of the predicates.

A predicate may be either a numeric predicate (for example «[1]» or «[last()-1]»), or a Boolean predicate (for example «[count(*) > 5]» or «[@name and @address]»). If the value of the expression is a number, it is treated as a numeric predicate; otherwise it is converted if necessary to a Boolean (using the boolean() function), and is treated as a Boolean predicate. A numeric predicate whose value is N is equivalent to the Boolean predicate «[position()=N]». So, for example, the numeric predicate «[1]» means «[position()=1]», and the numeric predicate «[last()]» means «[position()=last()]».

It's important to remember that this implicit testing of position() happens only when the predicate expression actually evaluates to a number. For example, «$paras[1 or last()]» does not mean «$paras[position()=1 or position()=last()]», because the result of evaluating «1 or last()» is a Boolean, not a number (and as it happens, it will always be true). Similarly, «book[../@book-nr]» does not mean «book[position()=../@book-nr]», because the result of «../@book-nr» is a node-set, not a number.

As discussed in Chapter 2, every XPath expression is evaluated in some context. For an expression used as a predicate, the context is different from the context of the containing expression. While evaluating each predicate, the context is established as follows:

❑ The **context node** (the node referenced as «.») is the node being tested.

- ❑ The **context position** (the value of the position() function) is the position of that node within the set of nodes surviving from the previous stage, taken in document order.

- ❑ The **context size** is the number of nodes surviving from the previous stage.

To see how this works, consider the FilterExpr «$headings [self::h1] [last()] ». This starts with the node-set that is the value of the variable «$headings» (it is an error if this value is not a node-set). The first predicate is «[self::h1]». This is applied to each node in «$headings» in turn. While it is being applied, the context node is that particular node. The expression «self::h1» is a RelativeLocationPath consisting of a single Step: it selects a node-set. If the context node is an <h1> element this node-set will contain a single node – the context node. Otherwise, the node-set will be empty. When this node-set is converted to a Boolean, it will be true if it contains a node, and false if it is empty. So the first predicate is actually filtering through those nodes in «$headings» that are <h1> elements.

The second predicate is now applied to each node in this set of <h1> elements. In each case the predicate «[last()]» returns the same value: a number indicating how many <h1> elements there are in the set. As this is a numeric predicate, a node passes the test when «[position()=last()]», that is, when the position of the node in the set (taken in document order) is equal to the number of nodes in the set. So the meaning of «$headings [self::h1] [last()] » is "the last <h1> element in the node-set $headings, taking the nodes in document order".

Note that this isn't the same as «$headings [last()] [self::h1] », which means "the node-set containing the last node in $headings, provided it is an <h1> element".

The operation of a Predicate in a FilterExpr is very similar to the application of a Predicate to a Step in a LocationPath, and although they are not directly related in the XPath grammar rules, you can often use Predicates without being fully aware that you are using a FilterExpr or a LocationPath. For example, «$para[1]» is a FilterExpr, while «para[1]» is a RelativeLocationPath consisting of a single Step. The main differences to watch out for are firstly, that in a LocationPath the predicates apply only to the most recent Step (for example in «book/author[1]» the «[1]» means the first author within each book) and secondly, that in a FilterExpr the nodes are always considered in document order (whereas in a Step they can be in forwards or reverse document order depending on the direction of the axis).

Examples

Expression	Description
$paragraphs	This FilterExpr comprises a single VariableReference. It is not necessarily a node-set.
$paragraphs[23]	This FilterExpr consists of a VariableReference filtered by a Predicate. It selects the 23rd node in the node-set that is the value of variable $paragraphs, taking them in document order.

Expression	Description
`document('lookup.xml')`	This `FilterExpr` comprises a single `FunctionCall`. It selects the root node of the document identified by the URI `lookup.xml`.
`key('empname', 'John Smith')[@loc='Sydney']`	This `FilterExpr` comprises a `FunctionCall` filtered by a `Predicate`. Assuming that the key «empname» has been defined in the obvious way, it selects all employees named `John Smith` who are located in `Sydney`.
`(//section|//subsection) [title='Introduction']`	This `FilterExpr` consists of a parenthesized `UnionExpr` filtered by a `Predicate`. It selects all `<section>` and `<subsection>` elements that have a child `<title>` element with the content «Introduction».
`document(//@href) [pricelist][1]`	This `FilterExpr` first selects all documents referenced by URLs contained in `href` attributes anywhere in the source document; from this set of documents it selects those whose outermost element is named `<pricelist>`, and from these it selects the first. The order of nodes that are in different documents is not defined, so if there are several price lists referenced, it is unpredictable which will be selected.

FunctionCall

A `FunctionCall` invokes either a system-defined function or a vendor- or user-supplied extension function.

Expression	Syntax
`FunctionCall`	FunctionName «(» (Argument («,» Argument)*)? «)»

Defined in

XPath section 3.2, rule 16.

Used in

`PrimaryExpr`

Usage

There are two kinds of function call: calls on the standard functions listed in Chapter 7, which will be present in every conforming XSLT product, and calls on extension functions which may be supplied either by the product vendor or by the user. The two kinds can be readily distinguished, because in a call on a standard function, the function name will always be a simple name with no colon, while the name of an extension function will always be in some non-default namespace and will therefore be recognizable by having a name of the form «prefix:localname». The prefix must refer to a namespace declaration that is in scope for the expression containing this function call.

Technically there are two kinds of standard function, core functions which are defined in the XPath specification itself, and additional functions which are defined in the XSLT specification. If you are only using XPath in the context of XSLT stylesheets, however, the difference is of no importance.

A FunctionCall with no arguments takes the form FunctionName «(» «)», while in a call with arguments, the arguments are separated by commas in the usual way. The arguments themselves can be any XPath expression, subject to any type-checking rules or other constraints defined for the particular function in question. This includes expressions such as «/», «.» or «@*», which are not found in conventional programming languages.

A FunctionCall has very similar syntax to a NodeTest such as «node()» or «comment()», but is distinguished simply by use of a set of reserved names for the different node types.

The XSLT standard does not define how extension functions are implemented, and in general this will be different for each vendor's product. If you write an extension function that works with xt, for example, the chances are it will not work with Saxon, and vice-versa. The way that extension functions are written for some popular XSLT implementations is described in Chapter 10.

A FunctionCall always returns a result. This may be a value of any of the five data types: Boolean, number, string, node-set, or result tree fragment (though none of the system-defined functions actually does return a result tree fragment).

There is nothing to say that the same function will always return the same type of result: for example the system-property() function sometimes returns a string and sometimes a number. The specification also states that vendors may allow extension functions to return values of additional data types beyond the standard five, though in this case the only thing the stylesheet can do with the result is to assign the result to a variable or pass it as an argument to another extension function. Several vendors allow extension functions to return an arbitrary Java object, which is a useful way of allowing one extension function to pass data to another.

Many of the standard functions take a fixed number of arguments. In some, an argument is optional (usually defaulting to a node-set containing the context node). The concat() function, which concatenates strings, is exceptional in that the number of arguments is open-ended.

In the case of standard functions, the supplied values will always be converted to the required types if conversion is necessary. The XPath standard also implies that such conversion will happen for extension functions, but it would be unwise to rely on this, particularly if extension functions are defined in a typeless language such as JavaScript.

None of the standard functions have side-effects: they don't change the values of variables, they don't produce any output, and they don't change any settings in the browser or the operating system. There is nothing to stop an extension function from having side-effects; for example, an extension function could print a message or increment a counter, or even do something more radical such as modify the source document or the stylesheet itself. However, extension functions with side-effects are likely to be rather unpredictable, since there is nothing to say in which order things happen. For example, you can't assume that global variables are evaluated in any particular order or that they are evaluated only once; and a global variable that is never accessed might never be evaluated at all.

Calling a function that is not available is an error. However, it is not necessarily an error for a stylesheet to contain an expression that references a function that is not available. You can test whether a particular function is available using the system function `function-available()`, and use the result to avoid calling functions that are not provided. The `function-available()` mechanism works both for extension functions and for system functions: this will be useful as the standard matures, because if new functions are added in version 1.1 of XSLT, you may want to write stylesheets that still work with products that only implement version 1.0.

Examples

Expression	Description
`true()`	A call on a standard function that always returns the Boolean value true.
`string-length($x)`	A call on a standard function that converts the argument to a string, and returns the number of characters it contains.
`count(*)`	A call on a standard function that evaluates the node-set «*» (the set of all element children of the context node) and returns a number indicating how many nodes there are in this node-set.
`xt:intersection($x, $y)`	A call on an extension function. It is identified as an extension function by the presence of a prefix «xt:» which must correspond to a namespace declaration that is in scope. The rules for locating an implementation of this extension function are implementer-defined.
`function-available 'xt:intersection')`	A call on the standard function named `function-available`, which tests whether the extension function named «xt:intersection» is available for use. Note that a positive response doesn't mean that a call on this function will necessarily succeed: for example there is no way of asking how many arguments are expected.

FunctionName

A FunctionName can be any valid name other than a name reserved for a node type.

Expression	Syntax
FunctionName	QName ⌐ NodeType

The "-" sign in this production rule means "but not a": in other words, a FunctionName may be any name other than one used for a NodeType. In practice the choice is a lot more limited than this, since names in the default namespace (names with no colon) can be used only for standard functions, of which there is a fixed list defined in the XPath and XSLT specifications.

Defined in

XPath section 3.7 (Lexical Structure), rule 35.

Used in

PrimaryExpr

Usage

Syntactically, a function name can be any name other than one of the four NodeType names «comment», «text», «processing-instruction», or «node». A function name is recognised in the syntax as a name that is followed by a left parenthesis.

The only function names with no namespace prefix are the system-defined functions listed in Chapter 7. User-defined (or vendor-defined) extension functions will always include a namespace prefix. The prefix is interpreted using the namespace definitions in scope for the stylesheet element containing the expression in which the function name appears.

Examples

Expression	Definition
concat string-length namespace-uri	These are system function names.
sxf:intersection xt:node-set irs:get-tax-rate	These are extension function names.

Literal

A Literal represents a constant string.

Defined in

XPath section 3.7 (Lexical Structure), rule 29.

Syntax

Expression	Syntax
Literal	«"» [^"]* «"» | «'» [^']* «'»

Unless you are familiar with regular expressions you may find this production rule difficult to read, but what it is saying is actually quite simple: a Literal is either a sequence of any characters other than double-quotes, enclosed between double-quotes, or a sequence of any characters other than single-quotes, enclosed between single-quotes.

A Literal is a lexical token. Whitespace within a Literal is allowed, and is significant (whitespace characters are part of the value). Some care is needed when using tab, carriage-return, and newline characters within a literal, because the XML parser is required to replace these by space characters before the XPath expression parser ever gets to see them. Use character references such as «	», «
», and «» to prevent this.

Used in

PrimaryExpr
NodeTest

The appearance of Literal within the syntax rules for NodeTest is for testing the name of a processing instruction: for details of this anomaly, see NodeTest.

Usage

A literal represents a constant string value (note that unlike some other languages, numeric constants are not regarded as literals). It is written enclosed in either single quotes or double quotes; if single quotes are used, there must be no single-quote within the string, while if double-quotes are used, there must be no double-quotes within the string.

It is not possible for a literal to contain both single quotes and double quotes; if such a string is required, use the system function concat(), described in Chapter 7, page 430. Using character entities or entity references doesn't solve the problem, because these are expanded by the XML parser before the XPath parser gets to see them.

In practice the ability to use single and double quotes is further constrained by the fact that in an XSLT context, XPath expressions are always written within XML attributes in the stylesheet. If the XML attribute is written with single quotes, the XPath literal must be in double quotes, and it cannot contain a single quote because that would terminate the attribute value; equally, if the XML attribute is in double quotes, the XPath literal must be in single quotes, and it cannot contain a double quote for the same reasons.

The best way round this problem is to avoid it by using variables defined as result tree fragments in place of the literal. For example, rather than trying to write the expression «message[text="I won't"]», declare a variable as follows:

```
<xsl:variable name="msg-text">I won't</xsl:variable>
```

and write the expression as «message[text=$msg-text]»

Where a literal is used as the entire value of an XPath expression, two pairs of quotes are needed, for example:

```
<xsl:variable name="html-dialect" select="'netscape'"/>
```

If the extra quotes are omitted, «netscape» is assumed to be a node-set expression that finds all <netscape> element children of the context node. This means you won't get a sensible error message when you make this mistake, instead it will probably just lead to your stylesheet producing incorrect results. It's probably clearer to write:

```
<xsl:variable name="html-dialect">netscape</xsl:variable>
```

Although technically this isn't quite the same thing (because the value is now a result tree fragment rather than a string), in practice the result tree fragment can be used anywhere the string could be used, with the same meaning. (The only possible exception is user-defined extension functions, which are free to treat them differently if they choose).

Examples

The following are examples of literals allowed in XPath:

```
'London'
"Los Angeles"
"O'Reilly"
'Never say "never"'
```

Note that the last two examples are fine as far as XPath is concerned, but to write them in an XSLT stylesheet it will be necessary to use XML character or entity references for either the single quotes or the double quotes: whichever kind is used for delimiting the surrounding XML attribute. For example:

```
<xsl:value-of select='"O&apos;Reilly"'/>
<xsl:value-of select="'Never say &quot;never&quot;'"/>
```

You cannot use character or entity references to represent the quotation mark that delimits the literal itself, for example:

```
<xsl:value-of select='"Never say &quot;never&quot;"'/> <!--WRONG -->
```

because once the XML parser has expanded the entity references, the XPath expression seen by the XSLT processor will look like this:

```
"Never say "never""
```

which is clearly wrong. Using variables and the concat() function, as suggested above, is usually simpler.

LocationPath

A LocationPath is a PathExpr that selects nodes by following a path starting either at the root node (an AbsoluteLocationPath) or at the context node (a RelativeLocationPath).

Defined in

XPath section 2, rule 1.

Syntax

Expression	Syntax
LocationPath	RelativeLocationPath | AbsoluteLocationPath

Used in

PathExpr

Usage

A RelativeLocationPath, when used as a LocationPath, is used to select a set of nodes based on their position relative to the context node.

An AbsoluteLocationPath is used to select a set of nodes based on their position in the source document relative to the root node. (If there are several source documents, this will always be the root node of the document that contains the context node, so "absolute" is rather a misnomer).

Examples

Expression	Description
/contract/ clause[3]/ subclause[2]	This AbsoluteLocationPath selects the second <subclause> of the third <clause> of the <contract> that is the document element. If the document element is not a <contract>, or if any of the other components are missing, it produces an empty node-set.

Expression	Description
//figure	The AbsoluteLocationPath selects all the <figure> elements in the document. (See the section AbsoluteLocationPath for advice about the possible poor performance of this construct).
@title	This RelativeLocationPath selects all the title attributes of the context node. The result will either be empty or contain a single attribute node.
book/author/ first-name	This RelativeLocationPath selects the <first-name> elements that are children of the <author> elements that are children of the <book> elements that are children of the context node.
city[not(@name= preceding-sibling ::city/@name)]	This RelativeLocationPath selects all the child <city> elements of the context node that do not have a name attribute that is the same as the name attribute of a preceding <city> element with the same parent. It thus selects a set of child <city> elements with unique names. This is the nearest equivalent in XPath to the SELECT DISTINCT clause in SQL.

MultiplicativeExpr

A non-trivial MultiplicativeExpr performs a multiplication, division, or remainder operation on two numeric operands.

Defined in

XPath section 3.5, rule 26.

Syntax

Expression	Syntax
MultiplicativeExpr	UnaryExpr | MultiplicativeExpr MultiplyOperator UnaryExpr | MultiplicativeExpr «div» UnaryExpr | MultiplicativeExpr «mod» UnaryExpr

Used in

AdditiveExpr

Usage

A non-trivial MultiplicativeExpr consists of two or more UnaryExpr operands separated by the multiply «*» , divide «div», or modulo «mod» operators, whose detailed effect is explained below. A trivial MultiplicativeExpr consists of a single UnaryExpr with no operators.

The reason the `MultiplyOperator`, alone among all the XPath operators, is singled out to have a syntax rule in its own right, is because the meaning of the asterisk character in XPath is very context-dependant: as well as being used as a multiplication operator, it is also used as a wild-card in a NameTest.

The «/» character is not used for division because it is already used for the path operator and as an expression representing the root node.

Although XPath is not intended primarily for doing computations, simple arithmetic functions can be very useful, for example to enable positioning of objects on the output medium.

If either operand of the `MultiplicativeExpr` is not numeric, it is converted to a number as if the `number()` function was used. If the value cannot be converted to an ordinary number, it is converted to the special value NaN (not a number), and in this case the result of the calculation will also be NaN.

Numbers in XSLT are always double-length floating point, so the calculation is carried out using floating point arithmetic. The multiplication and division operations are defined to follow the rules of IEEE 754, which are summarized in Chapter 2. The modulo operation returns the remainder from a division. More technically, it is defined to return "the remainder from a truncating division", which is a division that doesn't use decimals: since this is difficult to understand exactly what this means in all cases, it helpfully explains it by example as follows:

Expression	Result
5 mod 2	1
5 mod –2	1
–5 mod 2	–1
–5 mod –2	–1

To perform an integer division, use «`floor($X div $Y)`»

Arithmetic in XPath never produces an error condition. For example division by zero is not an error, it produces the special number infinity (or minus infinity) as a result.

Examples

Expression	Description
`ceil(count(item) div 3)`	One-third of the number of child `<item>` elements of the context node, rounded upwards. (Useful if you are arranging the items in three columns).
`@margin*2`	Twice the value of the `margin` attribute of the context node.
`item[position() mod 2 = 0]`	Selects the even-numbered child `<item>` elements of the context node.

367

MultiplyOperator

A MultiplyOperator is the symbol used to represent a multiplication sign: an asterisk.

Defined in

XPath section 3.7 (Lexical Structure), rule 34.

Syntax

Expression	Syntax
MultiplyOperator	«*»

The reason the MultiplyOperator, alone among all the XPath operators, is singled out to have a production rule in its own right, is because the meaning of the asterisk character in XPath is context-dependant: as well as being used as a multiplication operator, it is also used as a wild-card in a NameTest.

Used in

MultiplicativeExpr

Usage

See MultiplicativeExpr.

The lexical rules for XPath state that «*» is recognized as a MultiplyOperator if there is a preceding token and the preceding token is not one of «@», «::», «(», «««[», or an Operator. Otherwise, it is assumed to be part of a NameTest.

Examples

Expression	Description
item[$x * 2]	Selects the <item> element whose position is $x multiplied by 2.
***	Converts the string-value of the current node to a number, and multiplies it by itself. (Only the second of the three asterisks is recognized as a multiplication operator, by virtue of the rules above. The other two are examples of a NameTest).

NameTest

A NameTest is either a name, or a generic name specified using wildcards.

Defined in

XPath section 3.7 (Lexical Rules), rule 37.

Syntax

Expression	Syntax
NameTest	«*» | NCName «:» «*» | QName

Note that a NameTest is a token, which means it cannot contain embedded whitespace. This means the second option in the production rule might have been more naturally written as NCName «:*».

Used in

NodeTest

A NameTest, as well as being used in XPath Expressions, is also used in some other XSLT contexts: for example the <xsl:preserve-space> and <xsl:strip-space> elements have an attribute whose value is a whitespace-separated list of NameTests.

Usage

In general a NameTest will match some names and will not match others.

The NameTest «*» matches any name. (But when used as an expression on its own, «*» is short for «child::*», which selects all child elements of the context node. The fact that the result is restricted to element nodes only is because «*», when used in a Step, selects only nodes of the principal node type for the axis: and for all axes except the attribute and namespace axes, the principal node type is element nodes.)

The NameTest «xyz:*» matches any name whose namespace is the one currently bound to the namespace prefix «xyz». It is not necessary that the name being tested should use the same prefix, only that the prefix should refer to the same namespace URI.

The NameTest «xyz:item» matches any name whose namespace is the one currently bound to the namespace prefix «xyz», and whose local part is «item». It is not necessary that the name being tested should use the same prefix, only that the prefix should refer to the same namespace URI.

The NameTest «item» (with no namespace prefix) matches any name whose local part is «item» and whose namespace URI is null. The default namespace is not used.

Examples

Expression	Description
*	Matches any name. If «*» is used on its own, it represents the RelativeLocationPath «child::*», which selects all child elements of the context node, regardless of their name.

Expression	Description
xt:*	Matches any name in the namespace bound to the prefix «xt». If «xt:*» is used on its own, it represents the RelativeLocationPath «child::xt:*», which selects all child elements of the context node that are in the namespace bound to the prefix «xt».
title	Matches a node whose local name is name «title» and whose namespace URI is null.
wrox:title	Matches the name that has local part «title» and whose namespace is the namespace currently bound to the prefix «wrox».

NCName and NCNameChar

An NCName is a name, or part of a name, that contains no colon. XPath adopts the definition from the XML Namespaces Recommendation.

There is no official explanation of the abbreviation NCName but "no-colon-name" is a plausible expansion.

An NCNameChar is a character that may appear in an NCName.

Defined in

XML Namespaces Recommendation.

Syntax

Expression	Syntax
NCName	(Letter | «_») (NCNameChar)*
NCNameChar	Letter | Digit | «.» | «-» | «_» | CombiningChar | Extender

The rules for Letter, Digit, CombiningChar, and Extender are given in the XML specification. The definitions are in the form of long lists of Unicode characters, and little would be gained by repeating them here. The basic principle is that if a name is valid in XML, then it is also valid in XPath.

Informally, an NCName starts with a letter or underscore, and continues with zero or more NCNameChars, which may be letters, digits, or the three punctuation characters dot, hyphen, and underscore. The «Letter» and «Digit» categories include a wide variety of characters and ideographs in non-Latin scripts as well as accented Latin letters, while the «CombiningChar» and «Extender» categories cover accents and diacritics in many different languages.

Used in

QName
NameTest

Usage

An NCName is used in two places in the XPath syntax: as part of a QName, discussed in detail on page 388, and as part of a NameTest, described on page 368.

In both contexts the name is used to match names that appear in the source XML document, which is why the syntax has to match the XML syntax for names.

As well as the XML-defined rules for names, XPath incorporates the additional rules defined in XML Namespaces. The designers of the XPath language made the decision that it would not be possible to use XPath to manipulate an XML document unless the XML document also conformed to the rules defined in XML Namespaces, for example the fact that a name may contain only a single colon.

As in XML, names are case-sensitive, and names are only considered to match when they consist of exactly the same sequence of characters. This is true even when the Unicode standards describe characters as equivalent, for example different ways of writing accented letters.

Examples

The following are examples of valid NCNames:

```
A
a
π
א
system-id
iso-8859-1
billing.address
Straßenüberführung
ΕΛΛΑΣ
... --- ...
```

NodeTest

A NodeTest tests whether a node satisfies specified constraints on the type of node or the name of the node.

Defined in

XPath section 2.3, rule 7.

Syntax

Expression	Syntax
NodeTest	NameTest | NodeType «(» «)» | «processing-instruction» «(» Literal «)»

Note that the second option permits «processing-instruction( )»; the third option is needed only when it is necessary to give the name of the processing instruction.

The third form is unusual in that it is the only place in XPath where the name of a node in the source document is written in quotes. It is hard to see a reason for this: an NCName would have been more natural, since the XML Namespaces specification requires the name of a processing instruction to be an NCName.

Used in

Step

Usage

A NodeTest is used in a Step to specify the type and/or the name of the nodes to be selected by the Step.

In general you specify either the name of the nodes, or their type. If you specify a NameTest, this implicitly selects nodes of the principal node type for the axis used in the Step. For the attribute axis, this selects attribute nodes; for the namespace axis, it selects namespace nodes, and for all other axes, it selects element nodes.

Specifying «node( )» as the NodeType selects all nodes on the axis. You must specify «node( )» if you want the Step to select nodes of more than one type.

Specifying «processing-instruction( )» or «comment( )» or «text( )» as the NodeType selects nodes of the specified type. It doesn't make sense to specify any of these on the attribute or namespace axes, because they can't occur there. These nodes are unnamed, except for processing instructions, which is why there is an option in this single case to specify both the node type and the node name required.

There is no node test for the root node. If an axis (for example the ancestor or parent axis) includes the root node, it will be selected if and only if the NodeTest is «node( )». If you're looking specifically for the root node, you don't need an axis to find it, because the special LocationPath «/» is available.

Examples

Expression	Description
TITLE	This NameTest selects all <TITLE> elements, unless it is used with the attribute axis (in the form «attribute::TITLE» or «@TITLE», when it selects the TITLE attribute, or with the namespace axis (as «namespace::TITLE»), when it selects the namespace node whose prefix is TITLE.
news:article	This NameTest selects all nodes with local name «article» within the «news» namespace. These may be attribute nodes or element nodes, depending on the axis. There must be an enclosing element in the stylesheet that declares the «news» prefix, by having an attribute of the form «xmlns:news="uri"». The node in the source document must have a name that uses this namespace URI, but it does not need to use the same prefix.
MathML:*	This NameTest selects all nodes whose names are in the MathML namespace. These may be attribute nodes or element nodes, depending on the axis. There must be an enclosing element in the stylesheet that declares this prefix, by having an attribute of the form «xmlns:MathML="uri"».
*	This NameTest selects all elements, unless it is used with the attribute axis (in the form «attribute::*» or «@*», when it selects all attributes, or with the namespace axis (as «namespace::*»), when it selects all namespaces.
text()	This NodeTest selects all text nodes on the relevant axis.
processing-instruction()	This NodeTest selects all processing instructions on the relevant axis. Note that the XML declaration at the start of the document is not a processing instruction, even though it looks like one.
processing-instruction('ckpt')	This NodeTest selects all processing instructions that have the name (or PITarget as the XML specification calls it) «ckpt»: for example the processing instruction <?ckpt frequency=daily?>.
node()	This NodeTest selects all nodes on the relevant axis.

NodeType

A NodeType represents a constraint on the type of a node.

Defined in

XPath section 3.7 (Lexical Rules), rule 38.

Syntax

Expression	Syntax
NodeType	«comment» | «text» | «processing-instruction» | «node»

A NodeType is a token, so it can contain whitespace before and after the name, but not within it.

Note that the four NodeType names cannot be used as function names, but apart from this, they are not reserved words. It is quite possible to have elements or attributes called «text» or «node» in your source XML document, and therefore you can use «text» or «node» as ordinary names in XPath. This is why the names are flagged in a NodeTest by the following parentheses, for example «text()».

Used in

NodeTest

Usage

A NodeType can be used within a NodeTest (which in turn is used within a Step) to restrict a Step to return nodes of a particular type. The keywords «comment», «text», and «processing-instruction» are self-explanatory: they restrict the selection to nodes of that particular type. The keyword «node» selects nodes of any type, and is useful because a Step has to include some kind of NodeTest, so if you want all the nodes on the axis, you can specify «node()». For example, if you want all child nodes, specify «child::node()».

Note that there is no way of referring to the other four node types, namely root, element, attribute, and namespace. In the case of the root node, this is because if you only want the root node, you don't need to find it using an axis: just use the special expression «/». In the case of the attribute and namespace nodes, it is because these types of node are exclusive to the attribute and namespace axes: you can only find these nodes by using the axis of the same name, and all the nodes on that axis will be nodes of the appropriate type. In the case of element nodes, all the axes that can contain elements have element as their principal node type, and you can select the nodes of the principal node type using the special NameTest «*».

Examples in Context

Expression	Description
`parent::node()`	Selects the parent of the context node, whether this is an element node or the root node. This differs from «`parent::*`», which selects the parent node only if it is an element. The expression «`parent::node()`» is usually abbreviated to «`..`».
`//comment()`	Selects all comment nodes in the document.
`child::text()`	Selects all text node children of the context node. This is usually abbreviated to «`text()`».
`@comment()`	A strange but legal way of getting an empty node-set: it looks for all comment nodes on the attribute axis, and of course finds none.

Number

A `Number` represents a constant numeric (floating-point) value.

Defined in

XPath section 3.7 (Lexical Rules), rule 30.

Syntax

Expression	Syntax
Number	Digits («.» Digits?)? | «.» Digits

Used in

`PrimaryExpr`

Usage and Examples

A `Number` is a constant numeric value, and is expressed in decimal notation. The production rule is a rather complicated way of saying that there are four ways of writing a number:

Format	Example
Digits	839
Digits «.»	10.
Digits «.» Digits	3.14159
«.» Digits	.001

Note that all numeric values in XPath are treated as double-length floating point values. A more precise definition of the range of possible values is given in Chapter 2, page 81. Functions such as round(), ceiling(), and floor() are available to convert these to integers when required: these are described in Chapter 7.

A Number as such may not have a leading minus sign. However, in any context where a number may sensibly be used, it is also possible to use a UnaryExpr, which can consist of a minus sign followed by a number.

Unlike many programming languages, XPath does **not** allow a number to be expressed in scientific notation: you must write one million as «1000000», not as «1.0e6».

Operator

An Operator is a symbol or name used to denote a processing operation.

Defined in

XPath section 3.7 (Lexical Rules), rule 32.

Syntax

Expression	Syntax
Operator	OperatorName | MultiplyOperator | «/» | «//» | «|» | «+» | «-» | «=» | «!=» | «<» | «<=» | «>» | «>=»

Used in

Each of the operators appears in a different production rule, for example «=» appears in EqualityExpr.

Usage

The production rule for Operator is part of the lexical rules for XPath; an operator is one example of an ExprToken, that is, a lexical token. As operators are tokens, they may always be preceded and followed by whitespace, and must not include any embedded whitespace.

In some cases it is necessary to precede an operator by whitespace to ensure it is recognised. This applies not only to the named operators (such as «and» and «or»), but also to the minus sign «-» which could be mistaken for a hyphen if written with no preceding space.

The numeric comparison operators are written here as XPath sees them; when they appear in an XSLT stylesheet the special characters «<» and «>» can be written «<» and «>» respectively.

The «/» and «//» symbols are regarded as operators, though they have an unusual feature: the right-hand operand is not an expression, but a Step.

Examples

```
and  or  div
*  /  =  !=  <
```

OperatorName

An Operator that is written as a name.

Defined in

XPath section 3.7 (Lexical Rules), rule 33.

Syntax

Expression	Syntax
OperatorName	«and» | «or» | «mod» | «div»

Used in

ExprToken

Usage

The production rule for OperatorName is part of the lexical rules for XPath; an OperatorName is one example of an ExprToken, that is, a lexical token. As operator names are tokens, they may always be preceded and followed by whitespace. In practice the whitespace may be necessary to separate the OperatorName from the adjacent token if that is also made up of letters and digits.

The four operator names are not reserved words. It is perfectly legitimate to have an element in the source XML document named <div> (indeed XHTML defines such an element), and it is possible to refer to that element in the normal way using a path expression such as «ancestor::div» or simply «div». The decision as to whether «div» (or indeed «and», «or», or «mod») is an NCName or an OperatorName is therefore based on context: the rule is that it is recognized as an NCName if it is the first token in the expression, or if the preceding token is «@», «::», «(», «[», or an Operator.

Examples in Context

Expression	Description
$x = 5 or $x = 10	True if the variable $x, after converting to a number, has the value 5 or 10.

Expression	Description
position() mod 2	Zero if the context position is an even number, one if it is odd.
floor(string-length(@name) div 2)	Half the length of the value of the name attribute, rounded down.
@name and @id	True if the context node has both a name attribute and an id attribute.

OrExpr

A non-trivial OrExpr represents a Boolean expression, which is true if either of its operands is true.

Defined in

XPath section 3.4, rule 21.

Syntax

Expression	Syntax
OrExpr	AndExpr | OrExpr «or» AndExpr

Used in

Expr

Usage

A non-trivial OrExpr consists of two or more AndExpr operands separated by the operator «or». A trivial OrExpr consists of a single AndExpr without any «or» operator.

The «or» operator has its usual meaning in Boolean logic: if either or both of the operands are true, the result is true. The operands are first converted to Booleans if necessary by an implicit call of the boolean() function.

The language specification explicitly states that the right-hand operand of an «or» operator is not evaluated if the left-hand operand evaluates to true. (This is one of very few places where the order of evaluation is specified).

Note that there are no null values in XPath, as there are for example in SQL, and there is therefore no need for three-valued logic to handle unknown or absent data. Instead, you may need to test explicitly for absent values, as shown in some of the examples below.

Examples

Expression	Description
`$x = 5 or $x = 10`	True if the variable `$x`, after converting to a number, has the value 5 or 10.
`@name or @id`	True if the context node has a `name` attribute, an `id` attribute, or both.
`not(@id) or @id=""`	True if the context node has no `id` attribute or if it has an `id` attribute and the value is an empty string.
`//para[position()=1 or position()=last()]`	Selects the `<para>` elements that are either the first or the last (or the only) `<para>` children of their parent node.

PathExpr

A `PathExpr` is an expression for selecting a set of nodes by following a path (a sequence of one or more steps) from a given starting point. The starting point may be the context node, the root node, or an arbitrary node-set given, say, by the value of a variable or the result of a function-call.

5

Expressions

Defined in

XPath section 3.3, rule 19.

Syntax

Expression	Syntax
`PathExpr`	`LocationPath` | `FilterExpr` | `FilterExpr «/» RelativeLocationPath` | `FilterExpr «//» RelativeLocationPath`

Used in

`UnionExpr`

Usage

A non-trivial `PathExpr` identifies a node-set. However, because a trivial `FilterExpr` may consist simply of a `Number` or `Literal`, a trivial `PathExpr` may identify a value of any type.

In a non-trivial `PathExpr`, there are several different ways the node-set can be identified:

❑ By a `LocationPath`, representing a set of nodes selected by following a sequence of steps starting either at the document root or at the context node.

❑ By a `FilterExpr`, which might be a variable reference that identifies a node-set, a function call that evaluates to a node-set, a bracketed expression such as «($a | $b)», or any of these followed by one or more predicates.

❑ By a `FilterExpr` followed by the path operator «/» followed by a `RelativeLocationPath`; the `RelativeLocationPath` identifies a sequence of steps in the same way as the `LocationPath`, but starts with the set of nodes identified by the `FilterExpr`, instead of starting at the document root or at the context node.

❑ By a `FilterExpr` followed by the shorthand path operator «//» followed by a `RelativeLocationPath`: as in other contexts, «//» is an abbreviation for «/descendant-or-self::node()/».

Examples

Expression	Description
`para`	This `PathExpr` is a `LocationPath`, and selects all the `<para>` element children of the context node.
`para[@id]`	This `PathExpr` is a `LocationPath`, and selects all the `<para>` element children of the context node that have an `id` attribute.
`para/@id`	This `PathExpr` is a `LocationPath`, and selects the `id` attributes of all the `<para>` element children of the context node. This differs from the previous example in that the result is a set of attribute nodes rather than a set of element nodes.
`/*/para`	This `PathExpr` is a `LocationPath`, and selects all the `<para>` element children of the document element (the outermost element of the document).
`$paragraphs`	This `PathExpr` consists of a `FilterExpr` comprising a single `VariableReference`. It is not necessarily a node-set.
`$paragraphs[23]`	This `PathExpr` consists of a `FilterExpr` comprising a `VariableReference` filtered by a `Predicate`. It selects the 23rd node in the node-set that is the value of variable $paragraphs.
`document('lookup.xml')`	This `PathExpr` consists of a `FilterExpr` comprising a single `FunctionCall`. It selects the root node of the XML document identified by the URI `lookup.xml`.

Expression	Description

`key('empname',`
`  'John Smith')`
`[@location='Sydney']`
	This `PathExpr` consists of a `FilterExpr` comprising a `FunctionCall` filtered by a `Predicate`. Assuming that the key empname has been defined in the obvious way, it selects all employees named John Smith who are located in Sydney.

`(//section | //subsection)` `[title='Introduction']`	This `PathExpr` consists of a `FilterExpr` comprising a parenthesized `UnionExpr` filtered by a `Predicate`. It selects all `<section>` and `<subsection>` elements that have a child `<title>` element with the content «Introduction».
`$sections/body`	This `PathExpr` selects all `<body>` element children of nodes in the node-set identified by the variable `$sections`.
`$sections[3]/body`	This `PathExpr` selects all `<body>` element children of the third node in the node-set identified by the variable `$sections`.
`(//section|//subsection)` `//para`	This `PathExpr` selects all `<para>` descendants of `<section>` and `<subsection>` elements.
`((//section|//subsection)//p` `ara)[last()]`	This `PathExpr` selects the last `<para>` element (in document order) that is a descendant of a `<section>` or `<subsection>` element.

As is evident from the chart at the beginning of this chapter, it's the `PathExpr` construct that accounts for most of the syntactic complexity in the XPath language. The actual production rules are quite complicated and hard to follow, but they are there to make path expressions easy to write, especially if you are familiar with UNIX-style path names for directories and files.

If we forget for a moment the «//» abbreviation, and if we imagine a function call `root()` that finds the root node, then it would become possible to write every path expression in the form `FilterExpr ( «/» Step )*` , which would greatly simplify the production rules. The other options are there to allow the root node to be written as «/», to allow absolute path expressions to be written starting with a «/», and to allow relative path expressions to omit the initial «./».

Predicate

A predicate is a qualifying expression used to select a subset of the nodes in a node-set or a `Step`.

Defined in

XPath section 2.4, rule 8.

5

Expressions

Syntax

Expression	Syntax
Predicate	«[» PredicateExpr «]»

Used in

Step
FilterExpr

Usage

There are two places in the syntax where a predicate can appear: as part of a Step in a PathExpr, or as part of a FilterExpr. The meaning of the two cases is very similar, and it's easy to use them without always being aware of the difference.

For example:

Expression	Description
para[3]	Here the predicate «[3]» is being applied to the Step «para», which is short for «./child::para». It selects the third child <para> element of the context node.
$para[3]	Here the predicate «[3]» is being applied to the variable-reference «$para». Assuming this variable refers to a node-set, the expression selects the third node in the node-set, in document order.

In both cases the effect of a predicate is to select a subset of the nodes in a node-set. The difference comes when a predicate is used with a path expression of more than one step. For example:

Expression	Description
chapter/para[1]	Here the predicate «[1]» is being applied to the Step «para», which is short for «./child::para». It selects the first child <para> element of each child <chapter> element of the context node.
(chapter/para)[1]	This is a FilterExpr where the predicate «[1]» is being applied to the node-set selected by the path expression «chapter/para» The expression selects a single <para> element, the first child <para> of a <chapter> that is a child of the context node.

In effect, the predicate operator «[ ]» has higher precedence (it binds more tightly) than the path operator «/».

Another distinction between the two cases is that in the case of a `FilterExpr`, the nodes are always considered in document order when evaluating the predicate. In the case of a `Step`, the nodes are considered in the order of the relevant axis. This is explained in more detail below.

A predicate may be either a Boolean expression or a numeric expression. These are not distinguishable syntactically, because XPath is not a strongly typed language; for example the predicate «[$p]» could be either. The distinction is only made at run-time. If the value of the predicate is a number, it is treated as a numeric predicate; if it is of any other type, it is converted to a Boolean using the `boolean()` function and is treated as a Boolean predicate. So for example the predicate «[@sequence-number]» is true if the context node has a sequence number attribute, and is false otherwise. The actual numeric value of the attribute `sequence-number` is immaterial: the value of «@sequence-number» is a node-set, so it is treated as «[boolean(@sequence-number)]». If you want to use the sequence number attribute as a numeric predicate, write «[number(@sequence-number)]».

A numeric predicate «[P]» is simply a shorthand for the Boolean predicate «[position()=P]», so you could also achieve the required effect by writing «[position()=@sequence-number]».

As explained in Chapter 2, every expression is evaluated in a particular context. The context in which the predicate is evaluated is not the same as the context for the expression that it forms part of.

The predicate is applied to each node within a node-set separately. Each time it is evaluated:

❑ The context node (the node selected by «.») is the node to which the predicate is being applied.

❑ The context position (the result of the `position()` function) is the position of that node within the node-set, *relative to some axis.*

❑ The context size (the result of the `last()` function) is the number of nodes in the node-set.

The significance of the phrase *relative to some axis* is that the position of a node in a `Step` depends on the direction of the axis used in that step. Some axes (child, descendant, descendant-or-self, following, following-sibling) are forwards axes, so the `position()` function numbers the nodes in document order. Other axes (ancestor, ancestor-or-self, preceding, preceding-sibling) are reverse axes, so `position()` numbers them in reverse document order. The self and parent axes return a single node, so the order is irrelevant. The order of the attribute and namespace axes is undefined.

Where a predicate is used as part of a `FilterExpr` (as distinct from a `Step`), the specification states that the context position is the position relative to the child axis. This is a rather obscure way of saying that for the purpose of evaluating the `position()` function within the predicate, the nodes are considered in document order, regardless of the order in which they were retrieved. It doesn't mean that the nodes have to be children of some common parent, or indeed children of anything at all. It's quite legitimate to write:

```
(document('a.xml') | document('b.xml'))[1]
```

Here we are forming a node-set consisting of two root nodes in different documents, and we are then filtering this node-set to take the one that comes first "in document order". Where nodes in a node-set come from different documents, document order is undefined, so you can't predict which of the two root nodes will be chosen.

In both contexts where predicates can be used, there can be a sequence of zero or more predicates. Curiously, the syntax is defined in different ways in the two cases: in the production rule for Step it is defined by iteration (Step ⇒ AxisSpecifier NodeTest Predicate*), while in the rule for FilterExpr it is defined by recursion (FilterExpr ⇒ FilterExpr Predicate). However, the effect is identical: there can be a sequence of zero or more predicates.

Specifying two separate predicates is not the same thing as combining the two predicates into one with an «and» operator. The reason is that the context for the second predicate is different from the context for the first. Specifically, in the second predicate, the context position (the value of the position() function) and the context size (the value of the last() function) consider only those nodes that successfully passed through the previous predicate. What this means in practice is shown in the examples below:

Expression	Description
book[author="P. D. James"][1]	The first book that was written by P. D. James.
book[1][author="P. D. James"]	The first book, provided it was written by P. D. James.
book[position()=1 and author="P. D. James"]	The first book, provided that it was written by P. D. James. This is the same as the previous example, because in that example the second predicate is not dependant on the context position.

Examples in Context

Expression	Description
para[1]	The first <para> child element of the context node.
para[last()]	The last <para> child element of the context node.
para[position()!=1]	All <para> child elements of the context node, other than the first.
para[@title]	All <para> child elements of the context node that have a title attribute.

Expression	Description
para[string(@title}]	All <para> child elements of the context node that have a title attribute whose value is not the empty string.
para[* or text()]	All <para> child elements of the context node that have a child element or text node.

PredicateExpr

A PredicateExpr is an expression used within a Predicate.

Defined in

XPath section 2.4, rule 9.

Syntax

Expression	Syntax
PredicateExpr	Expr

Used in

Predicate

Usage

A PredicateExpr is syntactically just an Expr: in other words, any XPath expression can be used in a Predicate.

If the result of evaluating the PredicateExpr is a number, it is treated as a numeric predicate, which is true if the value is the same as the context position, and false otherwise.

In all other cases the PredicateExpr is treated as a Boolean value, converting it to a Boolean if necessary using the boolean() function.

Note that the rules for recognising a predicate as a number are very strict. For example, the XSLT variable declared in the examples below is not a number, it is a result tree fragment (see the <xsl:variable> topic in Chapter 4, page 308, for further explanation):

```
<xsl:variable name="index">3</xsl:variable>
```

If you want to use this value as a predicate, either write it so the value of the variable is a number:

```
<xsl:variable name="index" select="3"/>
```

or force it to a number in the predicate:

```
<xsl:value-of select="item[number($index)]"/>
```

or write the Boolean predicate in full:

```
<xsl:value-of select="item[position()=$index]"/>
```

Examples in Context

Any expression can be used as a predicate. Here are some examples: the PredicateExpr is the section between the square brackets.

Expression	Description
section[title]	«title» is a PathExpr; the PredicateExpr is true if the relevant section has at least one child <title> element.
section[@title='Introduction']	Here the predicate is a more conventional Boolean expression.
title[substring-before(.,':')]	The PredicateExpr evaluates to true if the string-value of the title has one or more characters before its first colon: that is, if the substring-before() function returns a non-empty string.
book[not(author=preceding-sibling::author)]	The PredicateExpr here is true if the author of the book is not the same as the author of some preceding book within the same parent element. The effect of this expression is to select the first book by each author.

PrimaryExpr

A PrimaryExpr is essentially an expression that contains no operators. It may also be a parenthesized sub-expression.

Defined in

XPath section 3.1, rule 15.

Syntax

Expression	Syntax
PrimaryExpr	VariableReference | «(» Expr «)» | Literal | Number | FunctionCall

Used in

FilterExpr

Usage

The production rule for PrimaryExpr covers an assortment of different kinds of expressions, which can be used as the basic building blocks of a more complex expression.

The only real thing that these different kinds of PrimaryExpr have in common is the context in which they can be used.

According to the syntax rules, any PrimaryExpr can be followed by a Predicate to form a FilterExpr, so for example «17[1]» and «'Berlin'[3]» are both syntactically legal. The semantic rules, however, say that a predicate can only be applied to a value that is a node-set, so the only primaries that can sensibly be used with a predicate in a FilterExpr are a variable reference, a parenthesised expression, or a function call.

The notable omission from this production rule is PathExpr: a PathExpr is not a PrimaryExpr. This ensures that an expression such as «para[1]» is unambiguously a PathExpr, with the Predicate «[1]» taken as part of the Step, rather than being a FilterExpr consisting of a PrimaryExpr «para» followed by a Predicate «[1]». It is possible to turn a PathExpr into a PrimaryExpr by putting it in parentheses, so «(para)[1]» is a FilterExpr. In this case the meaning is the same, but this will not always be the case.

For example:

Expression	Description
ancestor::*[1]	returns the first ancestor of the context node relative to the ancestor axis, in other words the parent of the context node.
(ancestor::*)[1]	returns the first node in the node-set formed by «ancestor::*», taking the nodes in document order: that is, it returns the document element.
//section/para[1]	returns all <para> elements that are the first <para> child of a <section> parent.
(//section/para)[1]	returns the first element in the document that is a <para> child of a <section> parent.

Examples

Expression	Description
23.5	A Number is a PrimaryExpr
'Columbus'	A Literal is a PrimaryExpr

Expression	Description
`$var`	A `VariableReference` is a `PrimaryExpr`
`contains(@name, '#')`	A `FunctionCall` is a `PrimaryExpr`
`(position() + 1)`	A parenthesized expression is a `PrimaryExpr`

QName

A `QName` (qualified name) is a name optionally qualified by a namespace prefix.

Defined in

XML Namespaces Recommendation

Syntax

Expression	Syntax
`QName`	(`Prefix` «:»)? `LocalPart`
`Prefix`	NCName
`LocalPart`	NCName

Used in

`NameTest`

`QNames` are also used in XSLT stylesheets in a number of other contexts, outside the scope of XPath expressions. They are used both to refer to elements in the source document (for example in `<xsl:preserve-space>` and `<xsl:strip-space>`, and to name and refer to objects within the stylesheet itself, including variables, templates, modes, and attribute sets.

There are also some situations where `QNames` can be constructed dynamically as a result of evaluating an expression. They are used, for example, in `<xsl:element>` and `<xsl:attribute>` to generate names in the result document, and in the `key()` and `format-number()` functions to refer to objects (keys and decimal-formats respectively) defined in the stylesheet. `QNames` constructed at run-time are never used to match names in the source document, and they are never used to match template names, variable names, mode names, or attribute set names in the stylesheet: these references must all be fixed names.

Usage

A `QName` is used in XPath for matching the names of nodes in the source document.

If the name has a prefix, the prefix must be declared by a namespace declaration on some surrounding element in the stylesheet.

For example:

```
<xsl:apply-templates select="math:formula" xmlns:math="http://math.org/"/>
```

Here the namespace is declared on the actual element that uses the prefix, but it could equally be any ancestor element.

The actual element in the source document does not need to have the tag «math:formula», it can use any prefix it likes (or even the default namespace) provided that in the source document the element name is in the namespace URI «http://math.org/».

If the QName does not have a prefix, then the name it matches must use the null URI. This necessarily means the element in the source document will not have a prefix, since the XML Namespaces specification doesn't allow a non-null prefix to be paired with a null URI. However, the converse is not true: a name in the source document with no prefix may be in the default namespace, with a non-null URI, and in this case it will be necessary to use a prefix in the stylesheet to match this element.

A QName with no prefix appearing in an XPath expression uses the null URI, not the default URI.

Examples

Expression	Description
TABLE	Matches a node in the source document whose local name is TABLE and which is in the default namespace, provided the default namespace uses a null URI.
HTML:TABLE	Matches a node in the source document whose local name is TABLE and which is in a namespace whose URI matches the URI currently assigned to the prefix HTML in the stylesheet.

RelationalExpr

A non-trivial RelationalExpr compares the magnitude of two numbers. It provides the usual four operators: less-than, greater-than, less-than-or-equal to, and greater-than-or-equal to. When an operand is a node-set, the comparison applies to the numeric value of the individual nodes in the node-set.

Defined in

XPath section 3.4, rule 24.

5

Expressions

Syntax

Expression	Syntax
RelationalExpr	AdditiveExpr | RelationalExpr «<» AdditiveExpr | RelationalExpr «>» AdditiveExpr | RelationalExpr «<=» AdditiveExpr | RelationalExpr «<=» AdditiveExpr

Used in

EqualityExpr

Usage

A non-trivial RelationalExpr in XPath consists of two or more AdditiveExpr operands separated by one of the operators «<» (less than), «>» (greater than), «<=» (less-than-or-equal to), or «>=» (greater-than-or-equal to).

A trivial RelationalExpr is one that consists of a single AdditiveExpr with no operator.

XPath defines an expression language that can be used in a number of environments. The only environment we are interested in is XSLT stylesheets, where the expression will always appear within an attribute of an XML element. An attribute value can't contain a «<» character, so it must be written either as a numeric character reference or as the entity reference «<». In practice most people choose to represent «>» as «>» as well, though it isn't strictly necessary.

These operators always perform a numeric comparison. There is no mechanism in XPath to compare string values according to their alphabetic sequence.

An expression such as «10 < $x < 30» is a syntactically valid RelationalExpr, but it probably does not have the expected meaning. The actual meaning is to evaluate «(10 < $x)», convert the Boolean result to a number, and then test whether this number is less than 30.

If neither of the operands is a node-set, both operands are converted to numbers by applying the number() function, and they are then compared numerically using the rules given in IEEE 754. For ordinary numbers, this gives the answer you would naturally expect, for example «1.0 < 3.5» is true, and «1.0 > 3.5» is false. If either of the numbers is plus or minus infinity, or negative zero, the result is still what you would expect intuitively, for example «1.0 < 2.0 div 0.0» is true, because the result of «2.0 div 0.0» is positive infinity. If either or both of the numbers is NaN (not a number), however, the result is always false. For example «'zero' <= 'one'» is false, because both operands when converted to numbers give NaN, and NaN <= NaN is false.

If one of the operands is a node-set, the result depends on the type of the other operand, as shown in the following table. In the text, I'll use the word "compares-correctly-with" to mean either "is less than", "is less than or equal to", "is greater than", or "is greater than or equal to", depending on which of the four operators $<$, $<=$, $>$, or $>=$ was actually used. We'll assume first that the node-set is the first operand.

Data type of second operand	Result
Boolean	Testing whether a node-set is less than a Boolean is a singularly odd thing to do, but if you really want to know, the rules are as follows. Let P be the result of converting the node-set to a Boolean, and then to a number: the result is 0 if the node-set is empty, or 1 if it contains one or more nodes. Let Q be the result of converting the Boolean operand to a number: 0 if the Boolean is false, or 1 if it is true. The final result is true if P compares-correctly-with Q.
number	The result is true if there is a node in the node-set whose string-value, when converted to a number, compares-correctly-with the number operand. For example, «//price < 5.00» is true if there is a <price> element in the document whose string-value, when converted to a number, is less than 5.
string	The result is true if there is a node in the node-set whose string-value, when converted to a number, compares-correctly-with the result of comparing the string operand to a number. For example, «//price < '5.00'» is true if there is a <price> element in the document whose string-value, when converted to a number, is less than 5. If the string cannot be converted to a number, the result will always be false.
Result tree fragment	The result tree fragment is converted to a string, and the comparison then proceeds as if it were a string, using the rules above.

If the node-set is the second operand, apply the rules in the table after inverting the expression, so for example «$p < $q» is rewritten as «$q > $p».

Finally, consider the situation if both operands are node-sets. In this case the result is true only if there is a node P in the first node-set and a node Q in the second node-set such that «number(P) compares-correctly-with number(Q)». Another way of defining this is according to the following table, where max() and min() represent the minimum and maximum numeric values of nodes in the node-set.

Expression	Result
M < N	True when min(M) < max(N).
M <= N	True when min(M) <= max(N).

Expression	Result
M > N	True when max(M) > min(N).
M >= N	True when max(M) >= min(N).

In practice these comparisons defined on node-sets are most commonly used when the node-set consists of a single node. For example, the expression «@price > 5.00» is true if there is a price attribute, and its value is numeric, and its numeric value is greater than 5.00; it is false if there is no price attribute, or if the value of the attribute is not numeric, or if its value is 5.00 or less.

Examples

Expression	Description
count(*) > 10	True if the context node has more than ten element children.
sum(SALES) < 10000	True if the sum of the numeric values of the <SALES> children of the context node is less than ten thousand.
position() < last() div 2	True if the context position is less than half the context size, that is, if the position of this node is less than half way down the list of nodes being processed.
not(//@temp <= 0.0)	True if all values of the temp attribute in the document are numeric, and greater than zero.

RelativeLocationPath

When used on its own as an expression, a RelativeLocationPath is a LocationPath that selects nodes by taking one or more steps starting at the context node.

A RelativeLocationPath can also be used within other constructs to represent a sequence of steps starting from some other baseline.

Defined in

XPath section 2, rule 3.

Syntax

Expression	Syntax
RelativeLocationPath	Step | RelativeLocationPath «/» Step | AbbreviatedRelativeLocationPath

Used in

```
LocationPath
AbsoluteLocationPath
AbbreviatedAbsoluteLocationPath
PathExpr
AbbreviatedRelativeLocationPath
```

Usage

A RelativeLocationPath, when used as an expression in its own right, represents a sequence of steps starting from the context node. When used as part of a PathExpr it represents a sequence of steps starting from the nodes in a given node-set, and when used as part of an AbsoluteLocationPath it represents a sequence of steps starting at the root node.

A RelativeLocationPath consists of one or more steps separated by the path operator «/» or the shorthand path operator «//». The production rule uses recursion to specify this: it could equally well have been written as:

RelativeLocationPath $\Rightarrow$ Step ((«/» | «//») Step)*

The «//» can be thought of informally as selecting the descendants of a node. It is handled in a separate syntax rule, AbbreviatedRelativeLocationPath, because it is actually just shorthand. Specifically, if in a RelativeLocationPath one of the steps other than the first or last is «descendant-or-self::node()», then it may be omitted, so that «A/descendant-or-self::node()/B» may be replaced by «A//B». See AbbreviatedRelativeLocationPath on page 328 for more details and examples.

For a description of how the path operator «/» works, see Step on page 394.

Examples

Expression	Description
ancestor::CHAPTER	This is a RelativeLocationPath consisting of a single Step. It selects the ancestors of the context node that are elements with the name <CHAPTER>.
TITLE	This is a RelativeLocationPath consisting of a single Step: this time the Step is an AbbreviatedStep. It selects the children of the context node that are elements with the name <TITLE>.
descendant::PARA/@style	This is a RelativeLocationPath consisting of two Steps. The first Step selects the descendants of the context node that are <PARA> elements; the second Step is an AbbreviatedStep that selects the style attributes of these elements.

5

Expressions

Expression	Description
`section[1]/clause[3]`	This is a `RelativeLocationPath` consisting of two `Steps`, each of which includes a positional predicate. The first `Step` selects the first `<section>` element that is a child of the context node, the second `Step` selects the third `<clause>` element that is a child of the selected `<section>`.
`chapter/section/para/sentence`	This `RelativeLocationPath` selects every `<sentence>` element that is a child of a `<para>` element that is a child of a `<section>` element that is a child of a `<chapter>` element that is a child of the context node.
`.//sentence`	This `AbbreviatedRelativeLocationPath` selects every `<sentence>` element that is a descendant of the context node.

Step

A `Step` selects the set of nodes in the document which are related in a particular way to a supplied baseline; for example given a node-set A, a `Step` can find the nodes that are the children of the nodes in A, or the ancestors of the nodes in A, and so on.

Defined in

XPath section 2.1, rule 4.

Syntax

Expression	Syntax
Step	`AxisSpecifier NodeTest Predicate*` | `AbbreviatedStep`

Used in

```
RelativeLocationPath
LocationPath
```

Usage

There are two ways of defining a step: a long form and a short form. The short form, an `AbbreviatedStep`, can be used only to find the child elements or attributes of the current node. The full form can be used to follow any axis and to find any kind of node.

A step is logically always the right-hand side of the «/» path operator. The left hand side of the path operator evaluates to a node-set; the step defines for each of these nodes a set of related nodes found by navigating from that node in a given direction, and the result of the final expression is the result of applying the step to each node in the left-hand node-set. The left-hand side of the path operator is not always explicit; for example the step «TITLE» is a shorthand for the path «self::node()/child::TITLE», and the path expression «/descendant::FIGURE» can be regarded as shorthand for an imaginary expression «root()/descendant::FIGURE» where «root()» denotes the root node.

Although XPath defines the step operation in rather informal English, some readers may find a more mathematical definition helpful. A step S can be defined as a function $S(X) \Rightarrow N$ that given a node X returns a set of nodes N in the same document. The path operator «/» can be defined as a function $map(A, F) \Rightarrow U$ that takes a node-set A and a step function F as its inputs, and returns the node-set U that is the union of the result of applying the step function F to each of the nodes in its input node-set N.

For example, the step «ancestor::node()», given any node, finds all the ancestors of that node. When the step is used in a path expression such as «$n/ancestor::node()», it returns a node-set containing all the ancestors of all the nodes in $n.

The step itself is defined in terms of a simpler concept, the axis. Each axis returns a set of nodes relative to a specific origin node: for example, its previous siblings or its ancestors. The step returns a subset of the nodes on this axis, selected by node type, node name, and by the predicate expressions. The NodeTest supplies any restrictions on the node type and name of the selected nodes, and the predicate expressions provide arbitrary Boolean conditions that the nodes must satisfy, or positional filters that constrain their relative position.

Note that the step function is defined in terms of sets (which are unordered) and there is no concept of the result being ordered. To understand the meaning of positional predicates in the step it is often useful to think of the step as retrieving nodes in a particular order, but the formal definition doesn't require this. Instead these predicates are defined in terms of the proximity of the node to the origin of the axis. An axis does have direction: every axis that can be used in a step is either a forwards axis or a reverse axis, and the effect of positional predicates (such as «booklist/book[3]») is defined by considering the nodes in the node-set in either document order or reverse document order. If the axis is a forwards axis, the positional predicate «[3]» will return the third node in document order; if it is a reverse axis, the same predicate will return the third node in reverse document order.

So the evaluation of the step function, for a given context node, proceeds as follows:

1. All the nodes on the selected axis are found, starting at the context node.

2. Those that satisfy the node test (that is, those of the required node type and name) are selected.

3. The remaining nodes are numbered from 1 to n in document order if the axis is a forward axis, or in reverse document order if it is a reverse axis.

5

Expressions

4. The first (leftmost) predicate is applied to each node in turn: when evaluating the predicate, the context node (that is, the result of the «.» expression) is that node, the context position (the result of the position() function) is the number assigned to the node in stage 3, and the context size (the result of the last() function) is the largest number allocated in stage 3. A numeric predicate such as «[2]» or «[last()-1]» is interpreted as a shorthand for «[position()=2]» or «[position()=last()-1]» respectively.

5. Stages 3 and 4 are repeated for any further predicates.

Examples

Expression	Description
child::title	Selects child elements of the context node named <title>.
title	Short form of «child::title».
attribute::title	Selects attributes of the context node named title.
@title	Short form of «attribute::title».
ancestor::xyz:*	Selects ancestor elements of the context node whose names are in the namespace with prefix «xyz».
*[@width]	Selects all child elements of the context node that have a width attribute.
text() [starts-with(.,'The')]	Selects all text nodes that are children of the context node and whose text content starts with the characters «The».
*[@code][position() < 10]	Selects the first nine child elements of the context node that have a code attribute.
*[position() < 10][@code]	Selects from the first nine child elements of the context node those that have a code attribute.
self::*[not(@code = preceding-sibling::*/@code)]	Selects the current element node provided that it does not have a code attribute with the same value as the code attribute of any preceding sibling element.
comment()	Selects all comment nodes that are children of the context node.
@comment()	Short for «attribute::comment()», this selects all comment nodes on the attribute axis. The attribute axis can only contain attribute nodes, so this will always return an empty node-set; nevertheless it is a legal *Step*.

UnaryExpr

A non-trivial UnaryExpr is used to change the sign of a number.

Defined in

XPath section 3.5, rule 27.

Syntax

Expression	Syntax
UnaryExpr	UnionExpr | «-» UnaryExpr

Used in

MultiplicativeExpr

Usage

A UnaryExpr consists of a UnionExpr preceded by an optional minus sign. In fact, for generality, the UnionExpr may be preceded by any number (zero or more) minus signs; each one changes the sign of the number.

> *Actually, the XPath specification isn't precise about what a unary minus sign does, so there has been some debate about whether «-0» is negative zero (as in Java and JavaScript) or positive zero (as in most other languages). Since the difference is hardly noticeable the point is a little academic: but the word from the Editor, James Clark, is that negative zero is the intended meaning.*

Intrinsically it may seem strange to be applying a numeric operator (unary minus) to a union, which is a node-set. However, this is simply an accident of the way operator priorities are defined. A UnionExpr does not actually need to contain a union operator, it merely has the potential to do so, and equally a UnaryExpr is not required to contain a minus sign.

In fact it is legal, if not very useful, to write an expression such as «-$a | $b». This forms the node-set that is the union of $a and $b, converts the result to a number, and then negates this number. A node-set is converted to a number by taking the string value of the first node in the node-set (in document order), and parsing that as a number.

Examples

Expression	Description
-2	The numeric value minus two. The minus sign is not part of the number, it is a separate token (and may therefore be separated from the number by whitespace).
- @credit	The negated numeric value of the credit attribute of the context element node. If the context node has no credit attribute, or if its value is not numeric, the result of the expression is NaN (not-a-number).

Expression	Description
1 - - - 1	A not very useful but perfectly legal way of writing the value zero. The first minus sign is a binary subtraction operator; the next two are unary minus signs.

UnionExpr

A non-trivial `UnionExpr` forms the union between two node-sets: that is, the result includes every node that is in either of the input node-sets.

Defined in

XPath section 3.3, rule 18.

Syntax

Expression	Syntax
UnionExpr	PathExpr | UnionExpr «|» PathExpr

Used in

UnaryExpr

Usage

A non-trivial `UnionExpr` consists of two or more `PathExpr` expressions separated by the union operator, «\|».This operator forms the union of two or more node-sets: the resulting node-set contains all the nodes that are in any one of the node-sets, eliminating any duplicates.

A trivial `UnionExpr` consists of a single `PathExpr`, in which case its value is the value of the `PathExpr`.

Both operands to the union operator must be node-sets. The syntax doesn't enforce this: it not only allows expressions such as «$a | $b » where the variables might turn out at run-time to have the wrong type, but it also allows clearly nonsensical expressions such as « 2.0 | "London" ». This is considered to be a semantic rather than a syntactic error.

Examples

Expression	Description
*/figure | */table	Returns a node-set containing all the grandchildren of the context node that are <figure> or <table> elements.

Expression	Description
`book[not(@publisher)]` | `book[@publisher='Wrox']`	Returns all the `<book>` children of the context node that either have no `publisher` attribute, or that have a `publisher` attribute equal to "Wrox". Note that the same result could be achieved, perhaps more efficiently, by using the «or» operator in the predicate.
`(.|..)/title`	Returns all the `<title>` elements that are immediate children of either the context node or the parent of the context node.
`sum(` `(book|magazine)/@sales)`	Returns the total of the `sales` attribute values for all the `<book>` and `<magazine>` children of the context node.
`(//* | //@*)` `[.='nimbus2000']`	Returns a node-set containing all the element and attribute nodes in the document whose string value is "nimbus2000".

There are no equivalent operators in XPath to do other set operations such as intersection and difference, in fact there is no way at all of constructing the intersection or difference of two arbitrary node-sets, other than by using extension functions. Some products supply extension functions to fill the gap: see Chapter 10 for details.

VariableReference

A `VariableReference` is a reference to an XSLT variable or parameter.

Defined in

XPath section 3.7 (Lexical Rules), rule 36.

Syntax

Expression	Syntax
VariableReference	«$» QName

Used in

PrimaryExpr

Usage

The `QName` must match the name of a variable or parameter that is in scope at the point in the stylesheet where the expression containing the variable name appears. Normally this means the name will be exactly the same as the name attribute of the relevant `<xsl:variable>` or `<xsl:param>` element; however, if the name contains a namespace prefix, it is the namespace URI that must match, not necessarily the prefix.

Expressions

5

A `VariableReference` is a lexical token, which means it may not contain whitespace between the $ sign and the `QName`.

The value of the variable reference is whatever value has been assigned to it by the matching `<xsl:variable>` or `<xsl:param>` declaration (in the case of `<xsl:param>`, this value may actually be derived from an `<xsl:with-param>` element in the calling template). The value may be of any type: a Boolean, a number, a string, a node-set, or a result tree fragment. If necessary, the value is converted to the data type required by the context: for example, if a variable holding a node-set is used in a context where a Boolean is required (such as the `test` attribute of `<xsl:if>`), it is converted to a Boolean – which means that it is treated as true if the node-set has one or more nodes in it, false if it is empty. In some cases, however, conversion is not possible, and in this case a run-time error will be reported. For example, it is not possible to use a Boolean value where a node-set is required, such as in the `select` attribute of `<xsl:apply-templates>` or `<xsl:for-each>`.

A variable reference can be used virtually anywhere in an XPath expression where a value is required: that is, an instance of one of the five data types Boolean, number, string, node-set, or result tree fragment. It cannot be used to represent concepts of the language other than values, for example a name, a node type, or an axis.

Examples

```
$x
$lowest-common-denominator
$ALPHA
$my-ns-prefix:param1
$π
```

Summary

XPath expressions used in XSLT to select data from the source document and to manipulate it to generate data to place in the result document. Expressions are the SELECT statement for structured documents – they allow us to select specific parts of the document for transformation, so that we can achieve the required output. However, their use is not restricted to XSLT stylesheets – they can also be used with XPointers to define hyperlinks betweeen documents.

This chapter serves as a comprehensive reference guide for writing these expressions.

The expression language is a superset of the pattern matching syntax used to match specific nodes. Understanding patterns is the next step in understanding how XSLT works and Chapter 6 will examine them in detail.

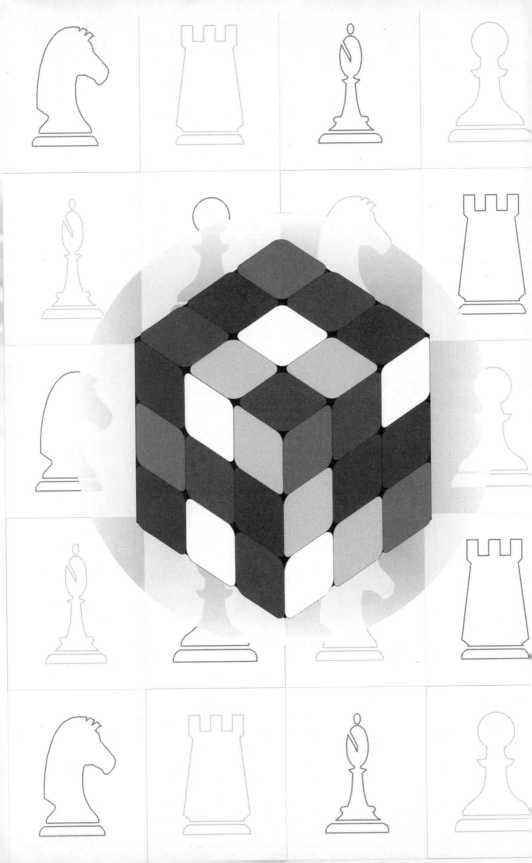

Patterns

This chapter defines the syntax and meaning of XSLT patterns.

Patterns are used in just four places in an XSLT stylesheet:

- ❏ In the match attribute of <xsl:template>, to define to which nodes in the source document a template applies.

- ❏ In the match attribute of <xsl:key>, to define to which nodes in the source document a key definition applies.

- ❏ In the count and from attributes of <xsl:number>, to define which nodes are counted when generating numbers.

In each case the purpose of a pattern is to define a condition that a node must satisfy in order to be selected. The most common use of patterns is in the match attribute of <xsl:template>, where the pattern says which nodes the template rule applies to: so, for example, <xsl:template match="abstract"> introduces a template rule that matches every element.

Most of the patterns found in stylesheets are simple and intuitive, for example:

Pattern	Meaning
title	Matches any <title> element
chapter/title	Matches any <title> element whose parent is a <chapter> element
speech[speaker="Hamlet"]	Matches any <speech> element that has a child <speaker> element whose string-value is «Hamlet».
section/para[1]	Matches any <para> element that is the first <para> child of a <section> element.

The precise rules for the more complex patterns, however, are quite technical, so I'm afraid some of the explanations in this chapter are not going to be easy reading.

Patterns are defined in terms of the name, type, and string-value of a node, and its position relative to other nodes in the tree. To understand how patterns work you therefore need to understand the tree model, which I described in Chapter 2, and the different kinds of node.

Patterns look very similar to XPath expressions, which were described in the previous chapter, and it turns out that they are closely related; however, patterns and expressions are not quite the same thing. In terms of its syntax, every pattern is a valid XPath expression, but not every XPath expression is a valid pattern. It wouldn't make any sense to use the expression «2+2» as a pattern, for example – which nodes would it match?

I described the rules for expressions in the previous chapter. Expressions are defined in the XPath 1.0 Recommendation, which allows them to be used in contexts other than XSLT stylesheets. For example, XPath expressions are used in the XPointer specification to defined hyperlinks between documents, and they are used in some DOM implementations as a way for applications to navigate around the DOM data structure. Patterns, however, are local to the XSLT 1.0 Recommendation (the rules are defined in section 5.2 of the specification), and they are found only in stylesheets.

It would have been quite possible for XSLT to define both the syntax and the meaning of patterns quite independently of the XPath rules for expressions, but this would have created a risk of unnecessary inconsistency. What the XSLT language designers chose to do instead is to define the syntax of patterns in such a way that every pattern was sure to be a valid expression, and then to define the formal meaning of the pattern in terms of the meaning of the expression.

Look at the simplest pattern in the examples above, «title». If «title» is used as an expression, we saw in the previous chapter that it's an abbreviation for «./child::title», and it means "select all the <title> children of the current node". How do we get from that to a definition of the pattern «title» as something that matches all <title> elements?

In the next section, I'll explain how the formal definition of patterns in terms of expressions works. However, in practice it's easier to think of most patterns as following their own rules, rather like the intuitive examples listed above, and referring only to the formal definition in terms of expressions to resolve difficult cases. So I'll follow the formal explanation with an informal one.

The Formal Definition

The formal definition of how patterns are evaluated is expressed in terms of the XPath expression that is equivalent to the pattern. We've already seen that every pattern is a valid XPath expression. In fact, the rules are written so that the only XPath expressions that can be used as patterns are those that return a node-set, and the idea is that you should be able to decide whether a node matches a pattern by seeing whether the node is in the node-set returned by the corresponding expression.

This then raises the question of context. The result of the XPath expression «title» is all the <title> children of the context node. Does that include the particular <title> element we are trying to match, or not? It obviously depends on the context. Since we want the pattern «title» to match every <title> element, we could express the rule by saying that the node we are testing (let's call it N) matches the pattern «title» if we can find a node (A, say) anywhere in the document, which has the property that when we take A as the context node and evaluate the node-set expression «title», the node N will be selected as part of the result. In this example we don't have to look very far to find node A: in fact only as far as the parent node of N.

So the reason that a <title> element matches the pattern «title» is that it has a parent node, which when used as the context node for the expression «./child::title», returns a node-set that includes that <title> element. The pattern might be intuitive, but as you can see, the formal explanation is starting to get quite complex.

In an early draft of the XSLT specification, the rules allowed almost any node-set expression to be used as a pattern. For example, you could define a pattern «ancestor::*[3]», which would match any node that was the great-grand-parent of some other node in the document. It turned out that this level of generality was neither needed nor possible to implement efficiently, and so a further restriction was imposed, that the only axes you could use in a pattern were the child and attribute axes (the various axes are explained on page 337 in Chapter 5). A consequence of this is that the only place where the XSLT processor has to look for node A, (the one to use as a context node for evaluating the expression) is among the ancestors of the node being matched (N), including N itself.

This brings us to the formal definition of the meaning of a pattern (read this slowly):

> **The node N matches a pattern P if and only if
> there is a node A that is an ancestor-or-self of N,
> such that evaluating P as an expression
> with A as the context node
> returns a node-set that contains N.**

In this rule, by saying that A must be an ancestor-or-self of N, I mean that A must either be N itself, or an ancestor of N.

The rule says that the expression is evaluated with A as the context node. It doesn't say what the context size and context position should be, because it makes no difference. Patterns cannot use the position() and last() function except within a predicate, so the question doesn't arise.

This means there is a theoretical algorithm for testing whether a given node N matches a pattern P as follows: for each node starting from N and working through its ancestors up to the root node, evaluate P as an XPath expression with that node as the context node. If the result is a node-set containing N, the pattern matches; otherwise keep trying until you get to the root.

For example:

❑ A <title> element matches the pattern «title» because when the context node is the parent of the <title> element, the expression «title» (which is short for «./child::title») returns a node-set that includes that <title> element.

❑ The node with ID value 'n123' matches the pattern «id('n123')» because the expression «id('n123')» includes that node, regardless of what the context node is at the time.

❑ The pattern «chapter//figure» matches every <figure> element that is a descendant of a <chapter> element because, when the expression «chapter//figure» is evaluated with the parent node of a <chapter> element as the context node, every descendant <figure> of the <chapter> will be returned.

❑ The root node matches the pattern «/» because when the expression «/» is evaluated with the root node as context node, the root is included in the resulting node-set.

❑ An attribute width with value 100 matches the pattern «@width[.=100]» because when its parent element is taken as the context node, the expression «@width[.=100]» includes that attribute.

In practice XSLT processors won't usually use this algorithm: it's only there as a way of stating the formal rules. The processor will usually be able to find a faster way of doing the test – which is just as well, since pattern matching would otherwise be prohibitively expensive.

Although the formal rules usually give the answer you would expect intuitively, there can be surprises. For example, you might expect the pattern «node()» to match any node; but it doesn't. As an expression, «node()» is short for «./child::node()», and the only nodes that this can select are nodes that are children of something. Since root nodes, attribute nodes, and namespace nodes are never children of another node (see the description of the tree model on page 46, in Chapter 2), they will never be matched by the pattern «node()».

Patterns Containing Predicates

The formal equivalence of patterns and expressions becomes especially important when considering the meaning of predicates (conditions in square brackets), especially predicates that explicitly or implicitly use the position() and last() functions.

For example, the pattern «para[1]» corresponds to the expression «./para[position()=1]». This expression takes all the <para> children of the context node, and then filters this set to remove all but the first (in document order). So the pattern «para[1]» matches any <para> element that is the first <para> child of its parent. Similarly the pattern «*[1][self::para]» matches any element that is the first child of its parent and that is also a <para> element, while «para[last()!=1]» matches any <para> element that is a child of an element with two or more <para> children.

An Informal Definition

The formal rules for a pattern such as «book//para», because they are written in terms of expressions, encourage you to think of the pattern as being evaluated from left to right, which means finding a <book> element and searching for all its <para> descendants to see if one of them is the one you are looking for.

An alternative way of looking at the meaning of this expression, and the way in which most XSLT processors are likely to implement the pattern matching algorithm, is to start from the right. The actual logic for testing a node against the pattern «book//para» is likely to be along the lines:

❑   Test whether this is a <para> element. If not, then it doesn't match.

❑   Test whether there is a <book> ancestor. If not, then it doesn't match.

❑   Otherwise, it matches.

If there are predicates, these can be tested *en-route*, for example to evaluate the pattern «speech[speaker='Hamlet']», the logic is likely to be:

❑   Test whether this is a <speech> element. If not, then it doesn't match.

❑   Test whether this element has a <speaker> child whose string-value is «Hamlet». If not, then it doesn't match.

❑   Otherwise, it matches.

Most patterns can thus be tested by looking only at the node itself and possibly its ancestors, its attributes, and its children. The patterns that are likely to be the most expensive to test are those that involve looking further afield.

For example, consider the pattern «para[last() - 1]», which matches any <para> element that is the last but one <para> child of its parent. Most XSLT processors, unless they have an exceptionally good optimizer, are going to test whether a particular <para> element matches this pattern by counting how many children the parent element has, counting how many preceding <para> siblings the test <para> has, and comparing the two numbers. Doing this for every <para> element that is processed could get a little expensive, especially if there are hundreds of them with the same parent. With the pattern «para[1]» or «para[last()]» you've a slightly better chance that the processor will figure out a quicker way of doing the test, but I wouldn't rely on it.

If you write a stylesheet with a lot of template rules, then the time taken to find the particular rule to apply to a given node can make a significant difference. The exact way in which different XSLT processors do the matching may vary, but one thing you can be sure of is that patterns containing complex predicates will add to the cost.

Conflict Resolution

When a pattern is used in the definition a template rule, it is possible that several patterns may match the same node. When this happens, there are rules for resolving this conflict. One of the factors these rules take into account is the default priority of the pattern, which is determined from the way it is written.

The conflict resolution rules, and the way in which the default priority of a pattern is determined, are described under `<xsl:template>` on page 288 in Chapter 4.

How to Read this Chapter

The overall structure of the rules is shown by the hierarchy below. Constructs marked with an asterisk are defined in Chapter 5, *Expressions*.

```
Pattern
    LocationPathPattern
        RelativePathPattern
            StepPattern
                ChildOrAttributeAxisSpecifier
                    AbbreviatedAxisSpecifier *
                NodeTest *
                Predicate *
        IdKeyPattern
            Literal *
```

As this structure is relatively simple and regular, I decided that, unlike Chapter 5, I would present the rules in top-down order, starting with the Pattern construct itself. So you can find the rules on the following pages:

Construct	Page number
Pattern	7
LocationPathPattern	7
RelativePathPattern	10
StepPattern	11
ChildOrAttributeAxisSpecifier	16
IdKeyPattern	17

The production rules use the same syntax notation as in Chapter 5.

Pattern

This is the top-level construct for the XSLT Pattern syntax. A pattern defines a condition that is either true or false for any given node in the source document. The syntax for a `Pattern` is a subset of the syntax for a `UnionExpr` (and therefore for an `Expr`) in the Expression syntax.

Syntax

Expression	Syntax
Pattern	LocationPathPattern | Pattern «|» LocationPathPattern

A `Pattern` is either a `LocationPathPattern` or a sequence of `LocationPathPatterns` separated by the «\|» (union) operator

The syntax of a `LocationPathPattern` is given below.

Used in

match attribute of `<xsl:template>` (page 288)
match attribute of `<xsl:key>` (page 222)
from and count attributes of `<xsl:number>` (page 237)

Usage

Although «\|» is technically a union operator, it is simpler to read it as "or": a node matches the pattern «A | B» if it matches either A or B or both.

Examples

TITLE	«TITLE» is a `LocationPathPattern`, so it is also a `Pattern`
preface | chapter | appendix	A node matches this pattern if it is a `<preface>` element, a `<chapter>` element, or an `<appendix>` element
/ | *	A node matches this pattern if it is either the root node or an element node

LocationPathPattern

A `LocationPathPattern` states conditions that a node must satisfy based on its name, its node type, its position relative to other nodes, and/or its ID and key values.

This construct is a subset of the `PathExpr` construct in the Expression language (and not, as you might expect, of `LocationPath`).

Syntax

Expression	Syntax
LocationPathPattern	«/» *RelativePathPattern ?* | *IdKeyPattern* ((«/»|«//») *RelativePathPattern*) *?* | «//» *? RelativePathPattern*

The above production rule is the way the syntax is defined in the XSLT specification. However, the equivalent production rule below may be easier to understand, and corresponds with the description in the *Usage* section below.

Expression	Syntax
LocationPathPattern	«/» | *RelativePathPattern* | «/» *RelativePathPattern* | «//» *RelativePathPattern* | *IdKeyPattern* | *IdKeyPattern* «/» *RelativePathPattern* | *IdKeyPattern* «//» *RelativePathPattern*

The syntax of a RelativePathPattern is described on page 412, and the syntax of an IdKeyPattern on page 419.

Used in

Pattern (see page 409).

Usage

The syntax rule reproduced above from the XSLT specification can be better understood by listing the seven different kinds of LocationPathPattern, as follows:

«/»	Matches the root node.
RelativePathPattern	Matches a pattern that can appear anywhere in the document.
«/» RelativePathPattern	Matches a pattern defined relative to the immediate children of the root node.
«//» RelativePathPattern	Matches a pattern that can appear anywhere in the document. The inclusion of the leading «//» has no effect on the meaning of the pattern, though it does affect its default priority. The default priority of a pattern comes into play when two template rules match the same node: for details, see the description of <xsl:template> in Chapter 4, page 288.

IdKeyPattern	Matches a node with a given ID attribute or key value.
IdKeyPattern «/» RelativePathPattern	Matches a pattern defined relative to the children of a node with a given ID attribute or key value.
IdKeyPattern «//» RelativePathPattern	Matches a pattern defined relative to the descendants of a node with a given ID attribute or key value.

The pattern «/» matches the root node of any tree. In fact, it is the only pattern that will match a root node. This means that if you have several trees (which will be the case in a stylesheet that uses the document() function described on page 440, in Chapter 7), the pattern «/» will match the root nodes of each one. This means that you can't write different template rules to match the root nodes of different trees. The usual way around this is either to use different modes to process each tree (see the description of <xsl:apply-templates> on page 145 in Chapter 4), or to start processing of secondary documents at the nodes immediately below the root.

A pattern such as «/item» will match an item element that is an immediate child of the root node. This kind of pattern is often useful when your stylesheet is dealing with multiple source documents, because it allows you to distinguish them by the name of the document element.

The pattern «/@width» is legal but meaningless: it would match a width attribute of the root node, but as the root node cannot have attributes, there is no such node.

For the other kinds of LocationPathPattern, see RelativePathPattern on page 412, and IdKeyPattern on page 419.

Examples

/	Matches the root node.
/*	Matches the outermost element node (the document element). In the case of a tree that is not well-formed (see page 51 Chapter 2), it matches any element whose parent is the root node.
/booklist	Matches a <booklist> element whose parent is the root node.
//book	Matches a <book> element that has the root node as an ancestor: in other words, any <book> element.
book	Matches any <book> element.
id('figure-1')	Matches an element with an ID attribute having the value 'figure-1'.

6

Patterns

411

`id('figure-1')//*`	Matches any descendant element of an element with an ID attribute having the value `'figure-1'`.
`key('empnr', '624381')/@dob`	Matches the dob attribute of an element having a value `'624381'` for the key named `empnr`.

RelativePathPattern

A `RelativePathPattern` consists of a `StepPattern` defining conditions a node must satisfy, optionally preceded by a `RelativePathPattern` that a parent or ancestor node must satisfy. The syntax for a `RelativePathPattern` is a subset of the syntax for a `RelativeLocationPath` in the XPath Expression language.

Syntax

Expression	Syntax
`RelativePathPattern`	`StepPattern` | `RelativePathPattern` «/» `StepPattern` | `RelativePathPattern` «//» `StepPattern`

A `RelativePathPattern` is thus a sequence of one or more `StepPatterns` separated by either of the operators «/» (is-parent-of) or «//» (is-ancestor-of).

The syntax of a `StepPattern` is described on page 413.

Used in

`LocationPathPattern`

Usage

With the first form, `StepPattern`, a node matches the pattern if it satisfies the conditions (node name, node type, and predicates) defined in the `StepPattern`. The simplest and most common form of `StepPattern` is simply an element name, for example «title».

With the second form, `RelativePathPattern` «/» `StepPattern`, a node matches the pattern if it satisfies the conditions (node name, node type, and predicates) defined in the `StepPattern`, and if its **parent node** matches the `RelativePathPattern`. This `RelativePathPattern` may in turn include conditions that the parent node's parent or ancestor nodes must satisfy.

With the third form, `RelativePathPattern` «//» `StepPattern`, a node matches the pattern if it satisfies the conditions (node name, node type, and predicates) defined in the `StepPattern`, and if it has an **ancestor** that matches the `RelativePathPattern`. This `RelativePathPattern` may in turn include conditions that the ancestor node's parent or ancestor nodes must satisfy.

Notice that although there is an equivalence between RelativePathPattern in the pattern language and RelativeLocationPath in the expression language, the meaning of a RelativePathPattern is most easily explained by examining the StepPatterns from right to left, starting at the node being tested and working up through its ancestors, if necessary; this is despite the fact that the meaning of a RelativeLocationPath is explained by considering the Steps from left to right, starting at the context node. It's likely that most implementations will adopt a strategy similar to the algorithm as I've explained it here.

In theory everything you can do in a RelativePathPattern could be done in a single StepPattern, since the pattern «A/B» means exactly the same as «B[parent::A]», and the pattern «A//B» means exactly the same as «B[ancestor::A]». However, where several steps are present, the form using «/» and «//» operators is a lot easier to read.

Examples

`title`	This is a StepPattern, and therefore the simplest form of RelativePathPattern. It selects any <title> element.
`section/title`	This is a RelativePathPattern consisting of two StepPatterns joined by the «/» (is-parent-of) operator. It matches a <title> element whose parent is a <section> element.
`chapter//footnote`	This is a RelativePathPattern consisting of two StepPatterns joined by the «//» (is-ancestor-of) operator. It matches a <footnote> element that is a descendant of a <chapter> element.
`chapter/section//footnote`	A more complex RelativePathPattern that matches any <footnote> element that is a descendant of a <section> element that is a child of a <chapter> element.

StepPattern

A StepPattern defines conditions that an individual node must satisfy: typically the node name, node type, and optionally a set of Boolean predicates. The syntax for a StepPattern is a subset of the syntax for a Step in the XPath expression language.

Syntax

Expression	Syntax
StepPattern	*ChildOrAttributeAxisSpecifier NodeTest Predicate *

6

Patterns

The syntax of `ChildOrAttributeAxisSpecifier` *is given on page 418. The constructs* `NodeTest` *(page 371) and* `Predicate` *(page 381) are constructs described in the XPath expression language in Chapter 5.*

The `ChildOrAttributeAxisSpecifier` is mandatory, but if you look at its syntax on page 418 you will see that it may be empty – and in practice it usually is. So unless you choose the long form of the syntax for an axis specifier, a `StepPattern` consists of an optional «@» sign to indicate the attribute axis, then a `NodeTest` which is generally either a node name or a node type such as «text()» or «comment()», followed by zero or more `Predicates`: Boolean expressions enclosed in square brackets.

Used in

`RelativePathPattern`

Usage

We'll look at the usage of each part of the `StepPattern` in turn.

The AxisSpecifier

The `ChildOrAttributeAxisSpecifier` may take the form «attribute::» (abbreviated «@») or «child::» (abbreviated to nothing: «»).

In the formal rules for evaluating a pattern, the steps in a `RelativePathPattern` are evaluated from left to right, and the choice of axis determines whether this step looks at the children or the attributes of the nodes found in the previous step.

Looking at it informally, it simplest to think of the axis specifier as simply a way of saying what node type is required:

❑ If the child axis is used and the `NodeTest` is a `NameTest` (for example «title», «*», or «svg:*»), or the `NodeType` «node()», then we are looking for an element node.

❑ If the attribute axis is used and the `NodeTest` is a `NameTest` (for example «@title», «@*», or «@svg:*»), or the `NodeType` «@node()», and the child axis is used we are looking for an attribute node.

❑ If the NodeTest is anything else (for example «comment()» or «text()»), then it only makes sense to use the child axis, because these nodes will never be found on the attribute axis. Writing «@comment()» or «@text()» is not illegal, just pointless: they are valid patterns that will never match anything.

The Node Test

The form of a `NodeTest` is defined in the XPath expression language; specifically it may be:

❑ a `NameTest` such as «title», «*», or «prefix:*». (The last form matches any element or attribute whose name is in a particular namespace).

❑ a NodeType, one of «comment()», «text()», «processing-instruction()», or «node()».

❑ a named processing instruction, for example «processing-instruction('pi-target')».

The Predicates

The form of a Predicate is defined in the XPath expression language (see Chapter 5, page 381): it is any expression enclosed in square brackets. For example «[speaker='Hamlet']», or «[@width > 100]», or «[*]», or «[1]».

If the predicate is numeric, it is interpreted as a test on the position of the node relative to its siblings. In all other cases, the expression is converted to a Boolean, and if the value is false then the pattern doesn't match.

There are two restrictions on predicates used in patterns:

❑ When a pattern is used in the match attribute of <xsl:template> or <xsl:key>, the predicate must not contain any references to variables. This is to prevent circular definitions: global variables can invoke keys and templates, so if keys and templates were allowed to be defined in terms of global variables, infinite recursion could happen. This restriction doesn't apply to patterns used in <xsl:number>.

❑ Patterns must not use the current() function (described on page 437, in Chapter 7) within a predicate. This is to ensure that the decision as to whether a particular node matches a pattern is predictable and does not depend on the current state of processing. For example, considering the match attribute of the <xsl:key> element, this means that a node is either included in a key or excluded, it can't be included at some times and excluded at other times.

Predicates can be classified into two groups: those that depend on the node's position relative to its siblings, and those that don't. A positional predicate is one whose value is a number, or one that uses the functions position() or last(); all others are non-positional. For example the predicates «[1]», «[position()!=1]», and «[last()-1]» are all positional predicates, whereas «[@name='Tokyo']» and «[*]» are non-positional.

For a non-positional predicate, its meaning is that the StepPattern fails to match a node if the predicate fails to match the node. For example, the predicate «[@security='secret']» is true when the node has a security attribute whose value is 'secret', so any StepPattern that uses this predicate will fail if the node has no security attribute or if the security attribute has any value other than 'secret'.

For a positional predicate, the meaning of the predicate can be deduced from the formal rules given at the start of this chapter. However, it is easier to understand their meaning by using informal rules. A numeric predicate such as «[1]» or «[last()-1]» is equivalent to the Boolean predicate «[position()=1]» or «[position()=last()-1]». So to evaluate a positional predicate, we need to know what position() and last() are.

6

Patterns

The use of positional predicates with the attribute axis doesn't make much sense, because the order of attributes is undefined. So in the following description, I'll assume that you're using the child axis.

If there is only one predicate in the StepPattern, or if this predicate is the first, then:

❑ last() is the number of siblings of the node being tested that satisfy the NodeTest (including the node itself). For example, if we are testing a <para> element against the pattern «para[last()=1]», then last() is the number of <para> elements that are children of the parent of the <para> element being tested. This pattern will match any <para> element that is the only <para> child of its parent.

❑ position() is the position of the node being tested among these siblings, taking them in document order and counting from one. So «para[1]», which means «para[position()=1]», will match any <para> element that is the first <para> child of its parent element, in document order.

Note that it is the position of the node relative to its siblings that counts, not the position in the sequence you are processing the nodes. For example suppose you want to process all the <glossary-entry> elements in a document, in alphabetical order. You can write:

```
<xsl:apply-templates select="//glossary-entry">
    <xsl:sort/>
<xsl:apply-templates>
```

Then suppose you have the following two template rules:

```
<xsl:template match="glossary-entry[1]">
. . .
</xsl:template>

<xsl:template match="glossary-entry">
. . .
</xsl:template>
```

The first template rule will be used for any <glossary-entry> that is the first <glossary-entry> child of its parent. Not, as you might expect, the first <glossary-entry> in alphabetical order, nor even the first <glossary-entry> element in the document. If you want to apply different processing to the <glossary-entry> that is first in alphabetical order, the way to do it is:

```
<xsl:template match="glossary-entry">
<xsl:choose>
<xsl:when test="position()=1">
    . . .
```

```
    </xsl:when>
    <xsl:otherwise>
       . . .
    </xsl:otherwise>
  </xsl:template>
```

This is because the context position within the body of the template rule is the position of the node in the list of nodes being processed, whereas the result for deciding whether a node matches a pattern is the same regardless of the processing context.

If there are several predicates in the StepPattern, then position() and last() in predicates after the first apply to the nodes that survived the previous predicates. So «speech[speaker='Hamlet'][1]» matches a <speech> element that is the first <speech> element among its siblings in which one of the <speaker>s is Hamlet.

The position() and last() functions relate to children of the same parent even when the «//» operator is used. For example, «chapter//footnote[1]» matches any <footnote> element that is a descendant of a <chapter> element and that is the first <footnote> child of its parent. There is no simple way to write a pattern that matches the first <footnote> element in a <chapter>, because the relevant expression «(chapter//footnote)[1]» is not a valid pattern. (Why not? No good reason, it's just that the spec doesn't allow it.)

Positional predicates in patterns need to be used with some attention to performance. Writing a template with the match pattern «para[last()-1]», for example, seems a sensible way to define the processing for the penultimate paragraph of a section. However, a simplistic XSLT processor will expand this predicate to «para[position()=last()-1]», and evaluate it by first determining the position of the current paragraph in its section, then finding the total number of paragraphs in the section, and comparing the two. If the number of paragraphs in a section is large, this could be a very expensive operation. An optimized XSLT processor will find a better strategy, but if performance is critical it would be worth doing some measurements.

Examples

child::title	Matches elements named <title>
title	Short form of «child::title»
attribute::title	Matches attributes named <title>
@title	Short form of «attribute::title»
*[@width]	Matches an element node that has an attribute named width
text()[starts-with(.,'The')]	Matches a text node whose text content starts with the characters «The»
p[@code][position() < 10]	Matches a <p> element that is among the first nine <p> elements of its parent that have a code attribute.

6

Patterns

`p[position() &lt; 10][@code]`	Matches a `<p>` element that is among the first nine `<p>` elements of its parent and that has a code attribute.
`*[not(@code = preceding-sibling::*/@code)]`	Matches an element node provided that it does not have a code attribute with the same value as the code attribute of any preceding sibling element
`comment()`	Matches any comment node
`@comment()`	This matches comment nodes that are found on the attribute axis of their parent node. Since the attribute axis can only contain attribute nodes, this condition can never be satisfied; nevertheless, it is a legal `StepPattern`.

ChildOrAttributeAxisSpecifier

This construct is a subset of `AxisSpecifier` in the Expression syntax. The only two axes used directly in a pattern are the child axis and the attribute axis. Either can be written in its expanded form or its abbreviated form.

Syntax

Expression	Syntax
`ChildOrAttributeAxisSpecifier`	`AbbreviatedAxisSpecifier |` `( «child» | «attribute» ) «::»`

The construct `AbbreviatedAxisSpecifier` is part of the Expression syntax defined on page 327 in Chapter 5, and is either «@», denoting the attribute axis, or nothing, denoting the child axis.

As an `AbbreviatedAxisSpecifier` can be empty, so can a `ChildOrAttributeAxisSpecifier`. What this means in practice is that a `NodeTest` with no explicit axis specifier (for example an element name or a node type such as «text()») implicitly uses the child axis.

A surprising consequence of this is that the pattern «node()» will only match a node that is the child of something, thus it will never match a root node, an attribute node, or a namespace node.

Used in

`StepPattern`

Usage

See StepPattern on page 413.

Unlike expressions, the only two axes that are available directly in a pattern are the child and attribute axes. However, testing for the presence of related nodes on a different axis can be done in the predicate of the StepPattern. Any expression can be used in the predicate, so all axes are available. For example:

```
caption[preceding-sibling::*[1][self::figure]]
```

matches a `<caption>` element whose immediately preceding sibling element is a `<figure>` element.

Examples

child::	Denotes the child axis
	(The box on the left is blank) Denotes the child axis: «child::» is the default axis specifier
attribute::	Denotes the attribute axis
@	Equivalent to «attribute::»

For examples showing a ChildOrAttributeSpecifier in context, see StepPattern on page 413.

IdKeyPattern

This construct allows a pattern to be matched only if the node being tested (or one of its ancestors) has a specified ID attribute or key value.

This construct is a subset of the FunctionCall construct in an Expression, described in Chapter 5, page 359. The only function calls that can be used in a pattern (except within predicates) are the id() and key() functions, and these can only be used with arguments that are literals.

The id() (page 466) and key() (page 469) functions are described in Chapter 7.

Syntax

Expression	Syntax
IdKeyPattern	«id» «(» Literal «)» | «key» «(» Literal «,» Literal «)»

Used in

LocationPathPattern

Usage

This facility provides an equivalent to the ability in CSS to define a style for a specific node in the source document.

There are a number of ways the facility can be used:

❑ If for a particular source document you want to use a general-purpose stylesheet, but want to override its behavior for certain selected nodes, you can write a stylesheet that imports the general-purpose one, and then write the overriding rules in the form of templates that match specific identified elements in the source document.

❑ Sometimes the source document is generated dynamically from a database. Perhaps there is something in the source document you want to highlight, say the search term that was used to locate this record. You could flag this item while generating the source document by giving it a special ID attribute value known to the stylesheet.

In all cases the id() and key() function could be spelled out in terms of a predicate on the ID attributes or the key value expression, so the facility can be seen simply as a shorthand. For example, if <book> elements are keyed on their ISBN property, and implemented as a child element, then the following declarations are equivalent:

(1) using a direct pattern match

```
<xsl:template match="book[isbn='1-861002-68-8']">
```

(2) using a key definition

```
<xsl:key name="isbn-key" match="book" use="isbn"/>
<xsl:template match="key('isbn-key', '1-861002-68-8')>
```

Of course there may be a performance difference between the two, but this depends on how the XSLT processor is implemented.

Examples

| id('figure1') | Matches a node with an ID attribute equal to the string 'figure1'. An attribute is an ID attribute if it is defined in the DTD as having type ID (the name of the attribute is irrelevant). |
| key('empnr', '517541') | Matches a node having a value of '517541' for the key named «empnr» |

The following example shows how this feature can be used in a stylesheet:

Example: Using the key() Pattern to Format a Specific Node

In this example I will show how to use the key() pattern to format one selected node differently from the others.

Source

The source document, itinerary.xml, is a tour itinerary:

```
<itinerary>
<day number="1">Arrive in Cairo</day>
<day number="2">Visit the Pyramids at Gaza</day>
<day number="3">Archaelogical Museum at Cairo</day>
<day number="4">Flight to Luxor; coach to Aswan</day>
<day number="5">Visit Temple at Philae and Aswan High Dam</day>
<day number="6">Cruise to Edfu</day>
<day number="7">Cruise to Luxor; visit Temple at Karnak</day>
<day number="8">Valley of the Kings</day>
<day number="9">Return flight from Luxor</day>
</itinerary>
```

Stylesheet

We'll start with a straightforward stylesheet, itinerary.xsl, to display this itinerary:

```
<?xml version="1.0" encoding="iso-8859-1"?>
<xsl:stylesheet version="1.0"
        xmlns:xsl="http://www.w3.org/1999/XSL/Transform">

<xsl:template match="/">
        <html><head>
                <title>Itinerary</title>
        </head>
        <body><center>
                <xsl:apply-templates select="//day"/>
        </center></body></html>
</xsl:template>

<xsl:template match="day">
    <h3>Day <xsl:value-of select="@number"/></h3>
    <p><xsl:apply-templates/></p>
```

6

Patterns

```
   </xsl:template>
</xsl:stylesheet>
```

Now we'll specialize this by importing it into another stylesheet, `today.xsl`, which displays the activities for day 5 in red:

```
<?xml version="1.0" encoding="iso-8859-1"?>
<xsl:stylesheet
        version="1.0"
        xmlns:xsl="http://www.w3.org/1999/XSL/Transform">

<xsl:import href="itinerary.xsl"/>
<xsl:key name="day-number" match="day" use="@number"/>

<xsl:template match="key('day-number','5')//text()">
    <font color="red"><xsl:value-of select="."/></font>
</xsl:template>

</xsl:stylesheet>
```

Output

The resulting output is as follows:

```
<html>
   <head>
      <META http-equiv="Content-Type" content="text/html; charset=utf-8">
      <title>Itinerary</title>
   </head>
   <body>
      <center>
          <h3>Day 1</h3>
          <p>Arrive in Cairo</p>
          <h3>Day 2</h3>
          <p>Visit the Pyramids at Gaza</p>
          <h3>Day 3</h3>
          <p>Archaelogical Museum at Cairo</p>
          <h3>Day 4</h3>
          <p>Flight to Luxor; coach to Aswan</p>
          <h3>Day 5</h3>
          <p><font
        color="red">Visit Temple at Philae and Aswan High Dam</font></p>
```

```
<h3>Day 6</h3>
        <p>Cruise to Edfu</p>
        <h3>Day 7</h3>
        <p>Cruise to Luxor; visit Temple at Karnak</p>
        <h3>Day 8</h3>
        <p>Valley of the Kings</p>
        <h3>Day 9</h3>
        <p>Return flight from Luxor</p>
    </center>
  </body>
</html>
```

While this example shows one way of using this feature, I have to admit that it's not very convincing. You could achieve the same effect by writing the relevant pattern as «day[@number=5]», without the need to introduce a key at all. And in any practical situation I would want to decide which day's activities to display in red by means of a parameter to the stylesheet: unfortunately there is no way of writing a pattern whose result depends on the value of a parameter, so the logic would have to be coded using <xsl:choose> instead.

Summary

In this chapter I described the syntax and meanings of patterns, whose main use in an XSLT stylesheet is to define which template rules apply to which nodes in the source document, but which are also used in the <xsl:key> and <xsl:number> elements.

Patterns, although their syntax is a subset of that for XPath expressions which we saw described in Chapter 5, are evaluated in a different way to expressions, though we saw that the formal rules express the meaning of a pattern in terms of the corresponding expression.

The next chapter describes the library of standard functions which can be used within XPath expressions in a stylesheet.

6

Patterns

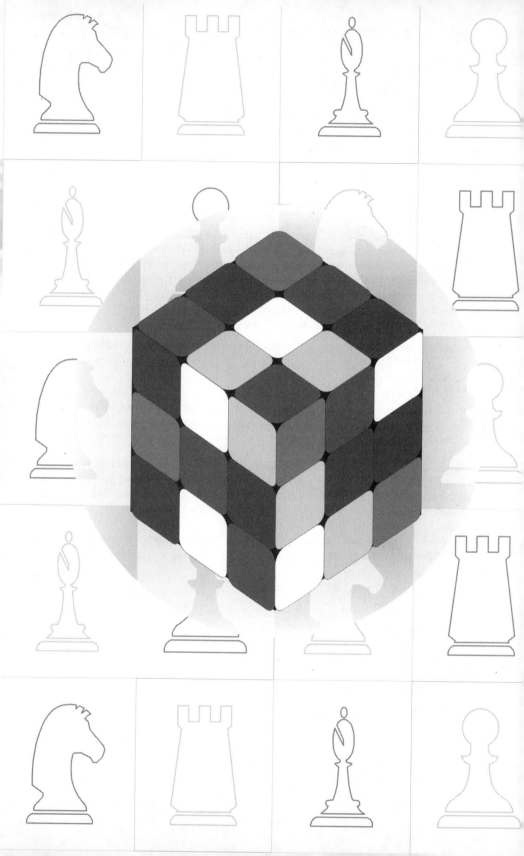

Functions

This chapter describes all the standard functions included in the XPath and XSLT specifications for use in expressions.

For each function, I give: its name, a brief description of its purpose, a reference to where in the XSLT or XPath specifications it is defined, a list of the arguments it expects and the value it returns, the formal rules defining what the function does, and finally usage advice and examples.

Some of these functions are defined in the XPath recommendation, some in XSLT. If you are using them in an XSLT stylesheet, it doesn't matter where they were defined; but if you are using XPath in a context other than XSLT, you should be aware that only the XPath-defined functions (known as *core functions*) are guaranteed to be available. These are shown by a $\rfloor$ in the table below.

The syntax of a function call is described as part of the XPath expression syntax in Chapter 5. This describes where a function call can be used in an expression, and where it can't: the only significant restriction is that you can't use a function call on the right hand side of the path operator «/». Within a function call, the values supplied as arguments can be any XPath expression, subject only to the rules on data types (for example, some functions require an argument that is a node-set). So a function call such as «count(..)», though it looks strange, is perfectly legal: «..» is a valid XPath expression that returns the parent of the context node.

I've arranged the functions in alphabetical order so you can find them quickly if you know what you're looking for. However, in case you only know the general area you are interested in, you may find the following classification useful. In the table the core XPath functions are marked $\rfloor$, while the additional functions defined in XSLT are marked $\rbrace$. The difference is only important when you use XPath expressions in a context other than XSLT stylesheets.

Category	Function
Functions that convert values from one data type to another	﹜ `boolean()` ﹜ `format-number()` ﹜ `number()` ﹜ `string()`
Arithmetic functions	﹜ `ceiling()` ﹜ `floor()` ﹜ `round()`
String manipulation	﹜ `concat()` ﹜ `contains()` ﹜ `normalize-space()` ﹜ `starts-with()` ﹜ `string-length()` ﹜ `substring()` ﹜ `substring-before()` ﹜ `substring-after()` ﹜ `translate()`
Aggregation	﹜ `count()` ﹜ `sum()`
Getting node names and identifiers	﹜ `generate-id()` ﹜ `lang()` ﹜ `local-name()` ﹜ `name()` ﹜ `namespace-uri()` ﹜ `unparsed-entity-uri()`
Boolean functions	﹜ `false()` ﹜ `true()` ﹜ `not()`
Functions that return information about the context	﹜ `current()` ﹜ `last()` ﹜ `position()`
Functions that find nodes	﹜ `document()` ﹜ `key()` ﹜ `id()`
Functions that provide information about the processor	﹜ `element-available()` ﹜ `function-available()` ﹜ `system-property()`

All these functions are in the default namespace: their names do not need to be prefixed. In fact, they are the only functions in the default namespace – extension functions provided by vendors, users, or third parties should always be in a different namespace and will need to have a namespace prefix when called.

boolean

The `boolean()` function converts its argument to a Boolean value.

For example, the expression «`boolean(1)`» returns `true`.

Defined in

XPath section 4.3

Format

```
boolean(value) ⇒ boolean
```

Arguments

Argument	Data type	Meaning
value	any	The value that is to be converted to a Boolean.

Result

A Boolean value: the result of converting the first argument

Rules

Any value may be converted to a Boolean. The rules for conversion are as follows:

Supplied data type	Conversion rules
Number	The number zero converts to false; anything else converts to true
String	A zero-length string converts to false; anything else converts to true
Boolean	The value is unchanged
Node-set	An empty node-set converts to false; anything else converts to true
Result Tree Fragment	The result tree fragment is first converted to a string, and the string is then converted to a Boolean. The resulting Boolean is true if the result tree fragment contains any non-empty text nodes, and is false otherwise.

Usage

In most cases conversion to a Boolean occurs automatically when the context requires it; it is only necessary to call the boolean() function explicitly in order to force a conversion.

7

Functions

Examples

The following example prints a message if the source document contains a `<header>` element and no `<footer>`, or if if contains a `<footer>` and no `<header>`.

```
<xsl:if test="boolean(//header) != boolean(//footer)">
   <xsl:message>Document must contain headers and footers,
                            or neither</xsl:message>
</xsl:if>
```

The conversion of the two node-sets «`//header`» (true if there are any `<header>` elements in the document) and «`//footer`» (true if there are any `<footer>` elements) needs to be explicit here, because we want to do a Boolean comparison, not a node-set comparison.

The following example sets a variable to the Boolean value true or false depending on whether the document contains footnotes. In this case the explicit conversion is probably not necessary, since it could be done later when the variable is used, but it is probably more efficient to retain only a Boolean value in the variable rather than retaining the full set of footnote nodes. Some products may even recognize that the expression «`//footnote`» occurs in a context where a Boolean is required, and scan the document only until the first footnote is found, rather than retrieving all of them.

```
<xsl:variable name="uses-footnotes" select="boolean(//footnote)"/>
```

See also

true() on page 528
false() on page 453

ceiling

The `ceiling()` function returns the smallest integer that is greater than or equal to the numeric value of the argument.

For example, the expression «`ceiling(33.9)`» returns 34.

Defined in

XPath section 4.4

Format

```
ceiling(value)  ⇒  number
```

Arguments

Argument	Data type	Meaning
value	number	The input value. If it is not of type number, it is first converted to a number using the rules for the number() function.

Result

An integer value: the result of converting the first argument to a number and then rounding up, if necessary, to the next highest integer.

Rules

If the value is not numeric, if is first converted to a number. For the detailed rules, see the description of the number() function on page 498. If the value is a node-set, these rules mean that the function applies to the value of the first node in the node-set, in document order.

If the number is an integer, it is returned unchanged. Otherwise, it is rounded up to the next highest integer.

The number data type in XPath supports special values such as infinity, negative zero and NaN (not a number), which are described on page 81 in Chapter 2.

If the argument is NaN (not a number), which will happen if a string is supplied that cannot be converted to a number, the result is not defined in the XPath specification, but most implementations are likely to return NaN. Similarly the effect when the argument is positive or negative infinity is not explicit in the standard, but the most likely result is that the argument is unchanged.

It is undefined whether an argument value that is greater than −1.0 but less than zero will be rounded up to negative zero or to positive zero.

Usage and Examples

The result of this function is illustrated by the following examples:

```
ceiling(1.0) = 1.0
ceiling(1.6) = 2.0
ceiling(17 div 3) = 6.0
ceiling(-3.0) = -3.0
ceiling(-8.2) = -8.0
```

One situation where this function is useful is when calculating the size of a table. If you have a node-set $ns and you want to arrange the values in three columns, then the number of rows needed is: ceiling(count($ns) div 3).

7

Functions

See also

floor() on page 454
round() on page 504

concat

The concat() function takes two or more arguments. Each of the arguments is converted to a string, and the resulting strings are joined together end-to-end.

For example, the expression «concat('Jane', ' ', 'Brown')» returns the string «Jane Brown».

Defined in

XPath section 4.2

Format

concat(value1, value2, value3, …) ⇒ string

Arguments

This function is unique in that it can take any number of arguments (two or more).

Argument	Data type	Meaning
value 1 … value n	string	An input value. If it is not of type string, it is first converted to a string using the rules for the string() function.

Result

A string value: the result of converting each of the arguments in turn to a string and concatenating the results.

Rules

Each of the arguments is converted to a string using the rules of the string() function, and each of the resulting strings is appended to the result string, in the order they appear.

Usage and Examples

The concat() function is often a convenient alternative to using multiple <xsl:value-of> elements to construct an output string. For example:

```
<xsl:value-of select="concat(first-name, ' ', last-name)"/>
```

is equivalent to

```
<xsl:value-of select="first-name"/>
<xsl:text> </xsl:text>
<xsl:value-of select="last-name"/>
```

Another situation where concat() is useful is in defining a key (see <xsl:key> on page 222 in Chapter 4, and the description of the key() function on page 469). XSLT keys cannot be multi-part values, but you can get round this restriction by concatenating the parts of the key with an appropriate separator. For example:

```
<xsl:key name="full-name" match="person"
                    use="concat(first-name, ' ', last-name)"/>
```

This key can then be used to retrieve the person (or persons) with a given name using an expression such as:

```
<xsl:for-each select="key('full-name', 'Peter Jones')"/>
```

A more advanced usage of concat() is to build up a whitespace-separated list of names. As XSLT provides no complex data types for temporary results, a whitespace-separated list is often the best option available for maintaining what in other languages would be an array. You can use other separators, of course, but whitespace is generally the most convenient because it's then easy to separate the components using the functions normalize-space(), substring-before(), and substring-after().

Example: Creating a Comma-separated List

The following example shows a template, which, when supplied with a node-set containing <city> elements with a country attribute, builds a list of cities in the form *city, country*.

Source

The source file is cities.xml:

```
<cities>
    <city name="Paris" country="France"/>
    <city name="Roma" country="Italia"/>
    <city name="Nice" country="France"/>
    <city name="Madrid" country="Espana"/>
    <city name="Milano" country="Italia"/>
    <city name="Firenze" country="Italia"/>
    <city name="Napoli" country="Italia"/>
    <city name="Lyon" country="France"/>
    <city name="Barcelona" country="Espana"/>
</cities>
```

Stylesheet

The stylesheet list-cities.xsl iterates over all the <city> elements using the concat() function to output each one in the format *city, country*.

7

Functions

```
<xsl:transform
 xmlns:xsl="http://www.w3.org/1999/XSL/Transform"
 version="1.0"
>
<xsl:output indent="yes"/>
<xsl:template match="/">
  <out>
    <xsl:for-each select="//city">
      <city><xsl:value-of select="concat(@name, ', ', @country)"/></city>
    </xsl:for-each>
  </out>
</xsl:template>
</xsl:transform>
```

Output

```
<?xml version="1.0" encoding="utf-8" ?>
<out>
   <city>Paris, France</city>
   <city>Roma, Italia</city>
   <city>Nice, France</city>
   <city>Madrid, Espana</city>
   <city>Milano, Italia</city>
   <city>Firenze, Italia</city>
   <city>Napoli, Italia</city>
   <city>Lyon, France</city>
   <city>Barcelona, Espana</city>
</out>
```

See also

```
contains()
substring()  on page 512
```

contains

The contains() function tests whether one string value contains another as a substring.

For example, the expression «contains('Santorini', 'ant')» returns true.

Defined in

XPath section 4.2

Format

```
contains(value, substring)  ⇒  boolean
```

Arguments

Argument	Data type	Meaning
value	string	The containing string. If it is not of type string, it is first converted to a string using the rules for the string() function.
substring	string	The test string. If it is not of type string, it is first converted to a string using the rules for the string() function.

Result

A Boolean value: true if the containing string has a substring that is equal to the test string, false otherwise.

Rules

The result is true if the first string contains a consecutive sequence of characters where each character has the same Unicode value as the corresponding character of the second string.

If the second string is empty, the result is always true.

If the first string is empty, the result is false except when the second string is also empty.

> *The XPath specification does not define the handling of empty strings very precisely, but it is reasonable to assume that implementations will interpret the specification in this way.*

Usage and Examples

The contains() function is often useful where a string has some internal syntax. For example the test:

```
<xsl:if test="contains($name, 'Michael') and contains($name, 'Kay')"/>
```

will succeed if the variable «$name» is the string value «Michael Kay» or «Kay, Michael» or «Michael H. Kay» or «Michaelmas Kayaks Inc.»

Take care if you are using accented or other composite letter forms, as there may be more than one way of representing these in Unicode, and if the representations in the two strings are different, you may not get a match.

7

Functions

See also

`substring()` on page 512
`substring-after()` on page 515
`substring-before()` on page 516

count

The `count()` function takes a node-set as its parameter, and returns the number of nodes present in the node-set.

For example, the expression «`count( . )`» always returns 1.

Defined in

XPath section 4.1

Format

`count(nodes)` ⇒ number

Arguments

Argument	Data type	Meaning
nodes	node-set	The input node-set. An error is reported if the argument is not a node-set.

Result

A number giving the number of distinct nodes in the input node-set.

Rules

The `count()` function takes a node-set as its parameter, and returns the number of nodes present in the node-set.

• Only the nodes that are members of the node-set in their own right are counted. Nodes that are children or descendants of these nodes are not included in the count.

Usage

A node-set is a mathematical set, so all the nodes it contains are distinct (which means they are different nodes – it doesn't mean, of course, that they must have different string-values). If you form a node-set using the union operator «|», any nodes that are in both operands will only be included in the result once. This means, for example, that the result of «`count( . | / )`» will be 1 if and only if the context node is the root.

Since XPath provides no other way of comparing whether two node-sets contain the same node, this can be a useful programming trick. For example, to test whether the context node is one of the nodes in the node-set in variable «$special», write:

```
<xsl:if test="count($special | .) = count($special)"> . . . </xsl:if>
```

Avoid using count() to test whether a node-set is empty, for example by writing:

```
<xsl:if test="count(book[author='Hemingway'])!=0"> . . . </xsl:if>
```

This can be better expressed as:

```
<xsl:if test="book[author='Hemingway']"> . . . </xsl:if>
```

Both examples test whether the current node has any child <book> elements that have a child <author> element whose value is «Hemingway». However, the second example, as well as being more concise, is easier for the XSLT processor to optimize. Many implementations will be able to stop the scan of books as soon as a matching one is found.

Avoid using count() where last() would do the job just as well. This situation arises when you are processing a set of nodes using <xsl:apply-templates> or <xsl:for-each>: the number of nodes in that set is then available from the last() function. For example, it is probably inefficient to write:

```
<xsl:for-each select="book[author='Hemingway']">
   <h2>Book <xsl:value-of select="position()"/> of
           <xsl:value-of select="count(../book[author='Hemingway'])">
   </h2>
   . . .
</xsl:for-each>
```

because – unless the XSLT processor is rather clever – it will have to re-evaluate the expression «../book[author='Hemingway']» each time round the loop.

Instead, write:

```
<xsl:for-each select="book[author='Hemingway']">
   <h2>Book <xsl:value-of select="position()"/> of
           <xsl:value-of select="last()"/>
   </h2>
   . . .
</xsl:for-each>
```

An alternative is to assign the node-set to a variable, so it is only evaluated once.

7

Functions

Examples

The following example outputs the number of `<footnote>` elements in the source document:

```
<xsl:value-of select="count(//footnote)"/>
```

The following example assigns to a variable the number of attributes of the current node:

```
<xsl:variable name="num-atts" select="count(@*)"/>
```

Example: Counting Distinct Values

This example counts how many distinct values of the `country` attribute there are in a list of `<city>` elements.

Source

The source document is `cities.xml`:

```
<cities>
    <city name="Paris" country="France"/>
    <city name="Roma" country="Italia"/>
    <city name="Nice" country="France"/>
    <city name="Madrid" country="Espana"/>
    <city name="Milano" country="Italia"/>
    <city name="Firenze" country="Italia"/>
    <city name="Napoli" country="Italia"/>
    <city name="Lyon" country="France"/>
    <city name="Barcelona" country="Espana"/>
</cities>
```

Stylesheet

The stylesheet is `count-countries.xsl`. It is a complete stylesheet, written using the *Simplified Stylesheet* syntax described on page 104, in Chapter 3. It builds a node-set containing those `<city>` elements that have a different `country` attribute from any preceding `<city>`, and then counts the nodes in this node-set.

```
<count xsl:version="1.0"
       xmlns:xsl="http://www.w3.org/1999/XSL/Transform">
  <xsl:value-of
       select="count(//city[not(@country=preceding::city/@country)])"/>
</count>
```

Output

```
<count>3</count>
```

current

The current() function returns a node-set containing a single node, the current node.

Defined in

XSLT section 12.4

Format

```
current()  ⇒  node-set
```

Arguments

None

Result

A node-set containing a single node, the current node

Rules

It is important to understand the difference between the current node and the context node.

The current node is established as follows:

- ❏ When evaluating a global variable, the current node is the root node of the source document
- ❏ When <xsl:apply-templates> is used to process a selected set of nodes, each selected node in turn becomes the current node. So when a template is invoked, the current node is always the node that caused that template to be selected. On return from <xsl:apply-templates>, the current node reverts to its previous value.
- ❏ Similarly, when the system implicitly invokes a template to process the root node of the source document, the current node is the root node.
- ❏ When <xsl:for-each> is used to process a selected set of nodes, each selected node in turn becomes the current node. When the <xsl:for-each> loop completes, the current node reverts to its previous value.
- ❏ <xsl:call-template> and <xsl:apply-imports> leave the current node unchanged.
- ❏ The current node (unlike the context node) does not change when evaluating a predicate within a path expression.

The context node is the node returned by the XPath expression «.». When used as a freestanding XPath expression, «current()» and «.» return the same result. When used in a predicate, however, the values will generally be different.

7

Functions

The current() function cannot be used in a pattern. This is to ensure that the decision as to whether a node matches a pattern is context-free: it doesn't depend on the circumstances in which the pattern is evaluated.

Usage and Examples

The reason the current() function is provided is to allow you to determine the current node when it is different from the context node – specifically, inside a predicate. The context node can always be determined using the path expression «.» (or its longer form, «self::node()»).

The most common situation where current() is useful is when you want to follow a cross-reference from the current node to some other node. For example, suppose in a book catalogue the <book> elements have an attribute category, whose value is a code such as "CL" or "SF", and that elsewhere there is a lookup table that gives the expansion of these codes, for example CL might be classical literature and SF might be science fiction.

Example: current()

This example lists the books in a catalog; in the description of each book, it also lists other books in the same category.

Source

The source document is booklist.xml:

```
<booklist>
<book category="S">
    <title>Number, the Language of Science</title>
    <author>Danzig</author>
</book>
<book category="FC">
    <title>The Young Visiters</title>
    <author>Daisy Ashford</author>
</book>
<book category="FC">
    <title>When We Were Very Young</title>
    <author>A. A. Milne</author>
</book>
<book category="CS">
    <title>Design Patterns</title>
    <author>Erich Gamma</author>
    <author>Richard Helm</author>
    <author>Ralph Johnson</author>
    <author>John Vlissides</author>
</book>
</booklist>
```

Stylesheet

The stylesheet is list-books.xsl. It processes all the books in an
<xsl:for-each> loop, and for each one it displays the title and the first author.
Then it looks for other books in the same category. Here it uses the predicate
«[./@category = current()/@category]» which is true if the category
attribute of the context element is the same as the category attribute of the
current element. The context element is the one being tested, the current element
is the one whose entry is being displayed. It also tests that these two elements
have different identifiers produced by generate-id(), which is one way of
testing that they are not the same element. Another way of doing this test would
be to write «count(.|current())=2», since the union of the context node and
the current node will contain one element if they are the same, and two if they are
different. In this case you could also get away with writing «.!=current()»,
which tests whether the two nodes have a different string-value, but it can be a
more expensive test, and it doesn't mean quite the same thing.

```
<xsl:transform
 xmlns:xsl="http://www.w3.org/1999/XSL/Transform"
 version="1.0"
>
<xsl:template match="/">
  <html><body>
    <xsl:variable name="all-books" select="//book"/>
    <xsl:for-each select="$all-books">
      <h1><xsl:value-of select="title"/></h1>
      <p><i>by </i><xsl:value-of select="author"/>
        <xsl:if test="count(author)!=1"> and others</xsl:if>
      </p>
      <xsl:variable name="others"
        select="$all-books[./@category=current()/@category and
                           generate-id(.)!=generate-id(current())]"/>
        <xsl:if test="$others">
          <p>Other books in this category:</p><ul>
          <xsl:for-each select="$others">
              <li><xsl:value-of select="title"/></li>
          </xsl:for-each>
          </ul>
        </xsl:if>
    </xsl:for-each>
  </body></html>
</xsl:template>

</xsl:transform>
```

Output

```
<html>
  <body>
    <h1>Number, the Language of Science</h1>
    <p><i>by </i>Danzig
    </p>
    <h1>The Young Visiters</h1>
```

```
            <p><i>by </i>Daisy Ashford
            </p>
            <p>Other books in this category:</p>
            <ul>
                <li>When We Were Very Young</li>
            </ul>
            <h1>When We Were Very Young</h1>
            <p><i>by </i>A. A. Milne
            </p>
            <p>Other books in this category:</p>
            <ul>
                <li>The Young Visiters</li>
            </ul>
            <h1>Design Patterns</h1>
            <p><i>by </i>Erich Gamma and others
            </p>
        </body>
    </html>
```

See also

AbbreviatedStep on page 330, in Chapter 5.

document

The document() function finds an external XML document by resolving a URI reference, parses the XML into a tree structure, and returns its root node. It may also be used to find a set of external documents, and it may be used to find a node other than the root by using a fragment identifier in the URI.

For example, the expression «document('data.xml')» looks for the file data.xml in the same directory as the stylesheet, parses it, and returns the root node of the resulting tree.

Defined in

XSLT section 12.1

Format

```
document(uri)  ⇒  number
document(uri, base-uri)  ⇒  number
```

Arguments

Argument	Data type	Meaning
uri	any	Either: (a) a node-set identifying a set of nodes in the source document whose string-values are URI references, or (b) a value, which, when converted to a string, can be treated as a URI reference
base-uri (optional)	node-set	If the argument is present, it must be a node-set. The base URI of the first node in this node-set is used for resolving any relative URI found in the first argument

Result

The result is always a node-set.

Effect

I'll describe the rules, usage advice, and examples separately for each combination of supplied arguments.

However, first a word about URIs and URLs, which are terms I use rather freely throughout this section.

The XSLT specification always uses the term URI: Uniform Resource Identifier. The concept of a URI is a generalisation of the URLs (Uniform Resource Locators) that are widely used on the web today, and which are nowadays displayed on every cornflakes packet. The idea of a URI is to extend the URL mechanism, which is based on the established Domain Name System (with its hierarchic names such as www.ibm.com and www.cam.ac.uk), to allow other global naming and numbering schemes, including established ones such as ISBN book numbers and international telephone numbers. However, although URIs are a nice idea, the only ones that really work today are the familiar URLs. This is why the terms URI and URL seem to be used rather interchangeably in this section and indeed throughout the book. If you read carefully though, you'll see that I've tried to use both terms correctly.

The XSLT specification leaves it up to the implementation to decide which URI schemes it will support. In the short term, it is likely that most implementations will support conventional URLs only.

A URI used as input to the document() function must identify an XML document. If the URI is invalid, or if it doesn't identify any resource, or if that resource is not an XML document, the specification leaves it up to the implementation what to do: it can either report the error, or return an empty node-set.

7

Functions

The specification doesn't say whether the XML document must be valid: most implementations will provide some way for the user to control whether a validating parser is used.

A URI can be relative rather than absolute. A typical example of a relative URI is `data.xml`. Such a URI is resolved (that is, converted to an absolute, globally unique URI) by interpreting it as relative to some base URI. By default, a relative URI that appears in the text of an XML document is interpreted relative to the URI of the document (or the external XML entity) that contains it, which in the case of the `document()` function is usually either the source document or the stylesheet. So if the relative URI `data.xml` appears in the source document, the system will try to find the file in the same directory as the source document, while if it appears in the stylesheet, the system will look in the directory containing the stylesheet. However, the `document()` function provides a second argument so that the base URI can be specified explicitly if required.

The expansion of relative URIs exploits the fact that in the XSLT tree model, which I described on page 46 in Chapter 2, every node has a Base URI. (Don't confuse this with the namespace URI, which is quite unrelated.) The Base URI of a node will normally be the URI of the XML document or entity from which the node was constructed. In some cases, for example when the input comes from a DOM document, it may be difficult for the processor to determine the Base URI (the concept does not exist in the DOM standard). What happens in this situation is implementer-defined.

The resulting XML document is parsed and a tree is constructed. Whitespace-only nodes are stripped following the same rules as for the source document, based on the `<xsl:strip-space>` and `<xsl:preserve-space>` declarations in force. This is true even if the document happens to be a stylesheet.

If the same URI is used twice (after expansion of a relative URI into an absolute URI), then the same root node is returned each time. You can tell that it's the same root node because the `generate-id()` function will return the same result, and because the `count()` function will treat the two nodes as duplicates. For example, «count(document("a.xml") | document("a.xml"))» should be 1.

A fragment identifier identifies a part of a resource: for example in the URL http://www.wrox.com/booklist#april2000, the fragment identifier is «april2000». In principle, a fragment identifier allows the URI to reference a node or set of nodes other than the root node of the target document.The interpretation of a fragment identifier depends on the media-type (often called MIME type) of the returned document. Implementations are not required to support any particular media types (which means they are not required to support fragment identifiers): and until the standards are better defined, it is likely that few will do so.

The following section describe the behavior of the `document()` function for each possible combination of arguments.

document(node-set)

Note that this includes the common case where the argument is an attribute reference, for example «document(@href)».

Rules

For a simple case such as «document(@href)» the result is a node-set containing one node, namely the root node of the document referenced by the href attribute.

More formally, the result is defined to be the union, for each node N in the supplied node-set, of the result of calling the document() function with two arguments: the first argument being the string-value of node N, and the second argument being a node-set with N as its only member. This is a recursive definition: to see what it means precisely, you'll have to read the section *document (string, node-set-2)* page 449.

What it actually means, however, is that each of the nodes in the supplied node-set should contain a URI as its string-value. If this is a relative URI, it will be resolved relative to the base URI of that node. The base URI of a node (as described on page 56 in Chapter 2) is in layman's language the name of the XML file where the node came from. Normally this will be the URI of the source document itself, but where the node was found in an external entity, or in a document that was itself loaded using the document() function, the base URI may be different. In fact, each node in the supplied node-set could potentially have a different base URI.

This all sounds terribly complicated, but all it really means is that if the source document contains the link «data.xml», then the system will look for the file data.xml in the same directory as the source document.

In the most common case, with a call such as «document(@href)», the supplied node-set contains only a single node, so the result is a node-set containing a single node, namely the root node of the document whose URI is contained in the href attribute of the context node, resolved if this is a relative URI by using the URI of the current node.

Usage

The most common usage of the document() function is to access a document referenced from the source document, typically in an attribute such as href. For example, a book catalogue might include links to reviews of each book, in a format such as:

```
<book>
    <review date="1999-12-28"  publication="New York Times"
                        text="reviews/NYT/19991228/rev3.xml"/>
    <review date="2000-01-06"  publication="Washington Post"
                        text="reviews/WPost/20000106/rev12.xml"/>
</book>
```

If we want to incorporate the text of these reviews in your output document, you can achieve this using the document() function. For example:

7

Functions

```
<xsl:template match="book">
   <xsl:for-each select="review">
      <h2>Review in <xsl:value-of select="@publication"/></h2>
      <xsl:apply-templates select="document(@text)"/>
   </xsl:for-each>
</xsl:template>
```

As the argument @text is a node-set, the result will be the root node of the document whose URI is the value of the text attribute, interpreted relative to the base URI of the <review> element, which (unless it comes from an external XML entity) will be the same as the URI of the source document itself.

Note that in processing the review document, exactly the same template rules are used as we used for the source document itself. There is no concept of particular template rules being tied to particular document types. If the review document uses the same element tags as the book catalogue, but with different meanings, this can potentially create problems. There are two possible ways round this:

❑ Namespaces: use a different namespace for the book catalogue and for the review documents.

❑ Modes: use a different mode to process nodes in the review document: so the <xsl:apply-templates> instruction above would become:

```
<xsl:apply-templates select="document(@text)" mode="review"/>
```

You might find that even if the element names are distinct, the use of modes is a good discipline for maintaining readability of your stylesheet. For more detail on modes, see <xsl:apply-templates> (on page 145) and <xsl:template> (on page 288) in Chapter 4.

Another useful approach, which helps to keep your stylesheet modular, is to include the templates for processing the review document in a separate stylesheet incorporated using <xsl:include>.

Example: Using the document() Function to Analyze a Stylesheet

A stylesheet is an XML document, so it can be used as the input to another stylesheet. This makes it very easy to write little tools that manipulate stylesheets. This example shows such a tool, designed to report on the hierarchic structure of the modules that make up a stylesheet.

This example uses the document() function to examine a stylesheet and see which stylesheet modules it incorporates using <xsl:include> or <xsl:import>. The modules referenced by <xsl:include> or <xsl:import> are fetched and processed recursively.

Source

Any stylesheet, preferably one that uses <xsl:include> or <xsl:import>. A file dummy.xsl is provided for you to use as a sample.

Stylesheet

The stylesheet `list-includes.xsl` uses the `document()` function to access the document referenced in the `href` attribute of `<xsl:include>` or `<xsl:import>`. It then applies the same template rules to this document, recursively. Note that the root template is applied only to the initial source document, to create the HTML skeleton page.

```
<xsl:transform
  xmlns:xsl="http://www.w3.org/1999/XSL/Transform"
  version="1.0"
>

<xsl:template match="/">
  <html><body>
    <h1>Stylesheet Module Structure</h1>
    <ul>
    <xsl:apply-templates select="*/xsl:include | */xsl:import"/>
    </ul>
  </body></html>
</xsl:template>

<xsl:template match="xsl:include | xsl:import">
    <li><xsl:value-of select="concat(local-name(),'s ',@href)"/>
    <xsl:variable name="module" select="document(@href)"/>
    <ul>
    <xsl:apply-templates
        select="$module/*/xsl:include | $module/*/xsl:import"/>
    </ul>
    </li>
</xsl:template>

</xsl:transform>
```

Output

The output for the `dummy.xsl` stylesheet is as shown below:

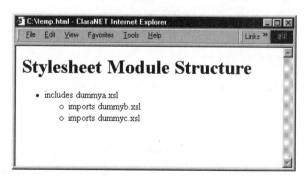

document(node-set-1, node-set-2)

This is the same as the previous case, except that instead of using the node itself as the base for resolving a relative URI, the base URI of the first node in node-set-2 is used. In other words, if a node in node-set-1 contains a relative URL such as «data.xml», the system will look for the file data.xml in the directory containing the XML document from which node-set-2 was derived.

Rules

Most commonly, node-set-2 will contain a single node. For example, the call «document(@href, /)» will use the root node of the source document as the base URI, even if the element containing the href attribute was found in an external entity with a different URI.

More formally, the result is defined to be the union, for each node N in the supplied node-set-1, of the result of calling the document() function with two arguments: the first argument being the string-value of node N, and the second argument being node-set-2. This of course is a recursive definition – to find out what it means, you have to read the section *document (string, node-set-2)* on page 449.

It is not defined what happens if node-set-2 is empty.

Usage

This option is not one you will need to use very often, but it is there for completeness.

If you want to interpret a URI relative to the stylesheet, you can write, for example:

```
document(@href, document(''))
```

This works because the second argument returns the root node of the stylesheet, which is then used as the base URI for the relative URI contained in the href attribute.

document(string)

This format is used when there is a single argument and it is not a node-set. The most common case is a URL hard-coded in the stylesheet, for example «document('tax-rates.xml')».

A common special case is «document('')», which refers to the stylesheet itself. Or to be pedantic, it refers to the stylesheet module, or the XML external entity, containing the element that is the parent of the attribute containing the XPath expression in which «document('')» is used.

Rules

If the argument is not a string, it is converted to a string using the rules of the string() function – but the only data type this really applies to is a result tree fragment, since converting a Boolean or number is unlikely to yield a useful URL, and if it's a node-set, the rules are covered in the previous section.

The string is treated as a URI reference. If it is a relative URI, it is treated as being relative to the base URI of the stylesheet element that contains the expression in which the function call was encountered. This will normally be the URI of the principal stylesheet document , but it may be different if <xsl:include> or <xsl:import> was used, or if pieces of the stylesheet are contained in external XML entities.

Again, all this really means is that relative URLs are handled just like relative URL's in HTML: if you write «document('tax-rates.xml')» in a particular stylesheet module, then the system looks for the file tax-rates.xml in the same directory as that stylesheet module.

If the string is an empty string, then the document referenced by the base URI is used. The XSLT specification states that «document('')» will return the root node of the stylesheet. If the call is contained in a stylesheet brought in using <xsl:include> or <xsl:import>, it returns the root node of the included or imported stylesheet, not that of the principal stylesheet document.

Usage

This form of the document() function is very useful for handling data used by the stylesheet for reference information: for example, lookup tables to expand abbreviations, message files in different languages, or the text of the message of the day, to be displayed on users on the login screen. Such data can either be in the stylesheeet itself (referenced as «document('')»), or in a separate file held in the same directory as the stylesheet (referenced as «document('messages.xml')») or a related directory (for example «document('../data/messages.xml')».

A very convenient use of the document() function is to access the stylesheet itself. XSLT allows data such as look-up tables to appear within any top-level stylesheet element, provided it belongs to a non-default namespace.

Example: a Lookup Table in the Stylesheet

Source

This is the booklist.xml file we saw earlier.

```
<booklist>
<book category="S">
    <title>Number, the Language of Science</title>
    <author>Danzig</author>
</book>
<book category="FC">
    <title>The Young Visiters</title>
    <author>Daisy Ashford</author>
</book>
<book category="FC">
    <title>When We Were Very Young</title>
    <author>A. A. Milne</author>
</book>
<book category="CS">
    <title>Design Patterns</title>
```

7

Functions

```
            <author>Erich Gamma</author>
            <author>Richard Helm</author>
            <author>Ralph Johnson</author>
            <author>John Vlissides</author>
    </book>
    </booklist>
```

Stylesheet

The stylesheet is list-categories.xsl. It processes each of the <book> elements
in the source file, and for each one, finds the <book:category> element in the
stylesheet whose code attribute matches the category attribute of the <book>.
Note the use of current() to refer to the current book: it would be wrong to use
«.» here, because «.» refers to the context node, which is the <book:category>
element being tested.

```
<xsl:transform
  xmlns:xsl="http://www.w3.org/1999/XSL/Transform"
  version="1.0"
  xmlns:book="books.uri"
  exclude-result-prefixes="book"
>

<xsl:template match="/">
  <html><body>
    <xsl:for-each select="//book">
       <h1><xsl:value-of select="title"/></h1>
       <p>Category: <xsl:value-of
                      select="document('')/*/book:category
                                [@code=current()/@category]/@desc"/>
       </p>
    </xsl:for-each>
  </body></html>
</xsl:template>

<book:category code="S" desc="Science"/>
<book:category code="CS" desc="Computing"/>
<book:category code="FC" desc="Children's Fiction"/>

</xsl:transform>
```

Output

```
<html>
    <body>
        <h1>Number, the Language of Science</h1>
        <p>Category: Science</p>
        <h1>The Young Visiters</h1>
        <p>Category: Children's Fiction</p>
        <h1>When We Were Very Young</h1>
        <p>Category: Children's Fiction</p>
        <h1>Design Patterns</h1>
        <p>Category: Computing</p>
    </body>
</html>
```

document(string, node-set-2)

This format is used when there are two arguments and the first argument is **not** a node-set.

Rules

If the first argument is not a string (the only plausible alternative is a result tree fragment), it is converted to a string using the rules of the string() function.

The second argument will normally be a node-set containing a single node: if it contains more than one node, only the first node (in document order) is taken into account. It is not defined what happens if the node-set is empty.

The string is treated as a URI. If it is a relative URI, it is treated as being relative to the base URI of the first node in node-set-2.

Usage

You won't need to use this format very often, but it is there for completeness.

Note: Using keys and ids in Another Document

The functions key() and id() always return nodes in the same document as the context node. It is not possible to retrieve nodes in another document by using an expression such as

```
<!-WRONG-->
<xsl:value-of select="document('a.xml')/key('k1', 'val1')"/>
<!-WRONG-->
```

Instead, the most convenient way to achieve the required effect is to change the context node using <xsl:for-each>, like this:

```
<xsl:for-each select="document('a.xml')">
   <xsl:value-of select="key('k1', 'val1')"/>
</xsl:for-each>
```

See also

id() on page 466
key() on page 469

element-available

This function is used to test whether a particular XSLT instruction or extension element is available for use.

For example, the expression «element-available('xsl:text')» returns true.

Defined in

XSLT section 15

Format

```
element-available(name)  ⇒  boolean
```

Arguments

Argument	Data type	Meaning
name	string	The name of the element being tested. If the value is not a string, it will be converted to a string using the rules for the string() function. The resulting string must take the form of a QName

Result

A Boolean value: true if the named element is available for use as an instruction in a template, false otherwise.

Rules

The first argument must take the form of a QName: that is, an XML name with an optional namespace prefix that corresponds to a namespace declaration that is in scope at the point in the stylesheet where the element-available() function is called.

If this namespace declaration identifies the XSLT namespace http://www.w3.org/1999/XSL/Transform, then the function returns true if the name is the name of an XSLT-defined *instruction*, and false otherwise. The instructions defined in XSLT version 1.0 are as follows:

```
<xsl:apply-imports>          <xsl:fallback>
<xsl:apply-templates>        <xsl:for-each>
<xsl:attribute>              <xsl:if>
<xsl:call-template>          <xsl:message>
<xsl:choose>                 <xsl:number>
<xsl:comment>                <xsl:processing-instruction>
<xsl:copy>                   <xsl:text>
<xsl:copy-of>                <xsl:value-of>
<xsl:element>                <xsl:variable>
```

Instructions are XSLT elements that can appear directly within a template body. Top-level XSLT elements such as `<xsl:template>` and `<xsl:key>` are not instructions, so they should return false. The same applies to elements such as `<xsl:param>`, `<xsl:with-param>`, `<xsl:sort>`, `<xsl:when>`, and `<xsl:otherwise>`, that can only appear in specific contexts and not anywhere in a template body.

If the prefix of the QName identifies any other namespace, then the function returns true if and only if the XSLT processor has an implementation available for the named instruction: that is, if this element can be used as an instruction in a template, rather than being treated simply as a literal result element.

Note that the result of the element-available() function does not depend on whether the namespace has been designated an extension namespace by using the [xsl:]extension-element-prefixes attribute. If the XSLT processor has an implementation of the instruction available, the function should return true whether or not it is currently in a designated extension namespace.

If the QName has no prefix, it's undefined whether the default namespace is used. Generally, for QNames identifying elements, the default namespace is used, but in this case the specification makes no explicit statement either way.

What the spec does say clearly is that if the QName expands to a name with a null namespace URI, the result of the function will always be false. This is because both XSLT instructions and extension elements will always have a non-null namespace URI.

Usage

There are two ways of using this function: it can be used to test for XSLT elements introduced in a later version of XSLT, and it can be used to test for the presence of vendor or third party extensions.

Testing for Features Available in Later XSLT Versions

The ability to test whether a particular XSLT instruction is available is not especially useful with version 1.0 of the specification. It is intended to come into its own when later versions of the specification appear. If you want to use an instruction that only became available in version 1.1 of XSLT, then you can test to see whether it is available with a particular XSLT processor before using it. If it is not available, you can either use <xsl:if> to avoid executing it, or use the <xsl:fallback> mechanism to cope with its absence.

So why specify it as part of version 1.0? The answer is obvious when you think about it: you want to write a stylesheet that uses version 1.1 features, so you call element-available() in order to fail gracefully if you're running with an XSLT processor that only supports version 1.0 features. However, this will only work if the version 1.0 XSLT processor supports the element-available() function, which is why it has been specified now. This is an unusually thoughtful piece of forward planning: the XSLT designers didn't want to get into the same kind of forwards-compatibility problems that have bedeviled HTML. Of course it still means that if you want your stylesheet to run with XSLT processors that support different levels of the language you will have to write and test conditional code in your stylesheet: but at least the capability is there.

In principle you can test whether a version 1.0 instruction is available, on the basis that there may be subset implementations around: unfortunately this will only work if the subset implementation includes the element-available() function, which is not guaranteed.

Note that if you write a stylesheet that uses features in XSLT version 1.1, say, then you must specify «version="1.1"» on the <xsl:stylesheet> element, or «xsl:version="1.1"» on some literal result element, even if you write an <xsl:if> test using element-available() to avoid executing the relevant code. If you specify «version="1.0"», then any use of extension elements is considered an error even if the code is never executed.

Testing for Vendor Extensions

The second way of using the function is to test for vendor or third-party extensions. If you know that a particular extension element is present in some implementations and not others, you can use the element-available() test to see whether it is present at run-time, and again use either <xsl:if> or <xsl:fallback> to handle the situation when it isn't.

For example, the Saxon product provides an extension element to output an entity reference. If you're not using Saxon, you can achieve the same effect by using disable-output-escaping. So to output «$nbsp;» you could write:

```
<xsl:choose xmlns:saxon="http://icl.com/saxon">
<xsl:when test="element-available('saxon:entity-ref')">
    <saxon:entity-ref name="nbsp"
                        xsl:extension-element-prefixes="saxon"/>
</xsl:when>
<xsl:otherwise>
    <xsl:text disable-output-escaping="yes"> </xsl:text>
</xsl:otherwise>
</xsl:choose>
```

An alternative to using the element-available() function is to use the <xsl:fallback> mechanism described in Chapter 4, page 197: an <xsl:fallback> element allows you to define what processing should occur if its containing instruction isn't available. The two mechanisms are essentially equivalent, though a possible limitation of <xsl:fallback> is that it can only be used within an element that permits element children: it could not be used, for example, within <xsl:apply-imports> as currently defined.

Examples

The following code defines a template that can be called to set a debugging breakpoint. It relies on a hypothetical <xsl:breakpoint> instruction introduced in XSLT version 37.1. If the stylesheet is executed with an XSLT processor that does not support this feature, it will ignore the request and continue.

```
<xsl:stylesheet
        xmlns="http://www.w3.org/1999/XSL/Transform"
        version="38.0">
<xsl:template name="set-breakpoint">
    <xsl:if test="element-available('xsl:breakpoint')">
        <xsl:breakpoint/>
    </xsl:if>
```

```
    </xsl:template>
  </xsl:stylesheet>
```

Note that if the version attribute on the <xsl:stylesheet> element were set to "1.0", this stylesheet would be rejected. With version set to any value other than "1.0", *forwards-compatible-mode* is enabled, and the implementation is not allowed to signal <xsl:breakpoint> as an error unless the instruction is actually instantiated. Forwards compatible mode is described in Chapter 3, on page 127.

See also

function-available() on page 459
<xsl:fallback> in Chapter 4, page 197

false

This function returns the Boolean value false.

Defined in

XPath section 4.3

Format

```
false()  ⇒  boolean
```

Arguments

None

Result

The Boolean boolean value false

Usage

There are no Boolean constants available in XPath expressions, so the functions true() and false() can be used where a constant Boolean value is required.

In practice, constant Boolean values are not often required: perhaps the most common usage is when passing a parameter to a template.

Writing «<xsl:if test="false()">» can be useful as a temporary expedient to comment out a section of code in a stylesheet. XML comments are not ideal for this purpose because they cannot be nested.

453

Example

The following code calls a named template, setting the parameter «verbose» to false:

```
<xsl:call-template name="do-the-work">
  <xsl:with-param name="verbose" select="false()"/>
</xsl:call-template>
```

See also

true() on page 528

floor

The floor() function returns the largest integer that is less than or equal to the numeric value of the argument.

For example, the expression «floor(11.3)» returns 11.

Defined in

XPath section 4.4

Format

floor(value) ⇒ number

Arguments

Argument	Data type	Meaning
value	number	The input value. If it is not of type number, it is first converted to a number using the rules for the number() function.

Result

An integer value: the result of converting the first argument to a number and then rounding down, if necessary, to the integer below.

Rules

If the value is not numeric, if is first converted to a number. For the detailed rules, see the description of the number() function on page 498. If the value is a node-set, these rules mean that the function applies to the value of the first node in the node-set, in document order.

If the number is an integer, it is returned unchanged. Otherwise, it is rounded down to the integer below.

If the argument is NaN (not a number), which will happen if a string is supplied that cannot be converted to a number, the result is not defined in the XPath specification; however, most implementations are likely to return NaN. Similarly the effect when the argument is positive or negative infinity is not explicit in the standard, but the most likely result is that the value of the argument is returned unchanged. Details of these special numeric values are given on page 80, in Chapter 2.

Usage and Examples

The result of this function is illustrated by the following examples:

```
floor(1.0) = 1.0
floor(1.6) = 1.0
floor(17 div 3) = 5.0
floor(-3.0) = -3.0
floor(-8.2) = -9.0
```

See also

ceiling() on page 428
round() on page 504

format-number

The format-number() function is used to convert numbers into strings for display to a human user. The format of the result is controlled using the <xsl:decimal-format> element.

For example, the expression «format-number(12.5, '$#.00')» returns the string «$12.50».

Defined in

XSLT section 12.3.

The effect of the function is defined by reference to the Java JDK 1.1 specifications; we have extracted the relevant information for ease of reference.

Format

```
format-number(value, format)  ⇒  string
format-number(value, format, name)  ⇒  number
```

Arguments

Argument	Data type	Meaning
value	number	The input value. If it is not of type number, it is first converted to a number using the rules for the number() function.

7

Functions

455

Argument	Data type	Meaning
format	string	A format pattern. If it is not of type string, it is first converted to a string using the rules for the string() function.
name (optional)	string	The name (a QName) of a decimal format, established using the <xsl:decimal-format> element. If the argument is omitted, the default decimal format is used.

Result

A string value: the result of formatting the first argument using the format pattern supplied in the second argument, applying the rules defined in the decimal format named in the third argument if there is one, or the default decimal format otherwise.

Rules

The decimal-format Name

The third argument, if it is present, must take the form of a QName: that is, an XML name optionally prefixed with a namespace prefix that corresponds to a namespace declaration that is in scope at the point in the stylesheet where the format-number() function is called. There must be an <xsl:decimal-format> element in the stylesheet with the same expanded name, using the namespace URIs rather than prefixes in the comparison.

If the third argument is omitted, the default decimal format is used. A default decimal format can be established for a stylesheet by including an <xsl:decimal-format> element with no name. It is probably intended, though the XSLT specification doesn't say so explicitly, that an implementation should provide a default decimal format if there is none in the stylesheet, and that this should be the same as specifying an <xsl:decimal-format> with no attributes.

The Format Pattern

The rules for the format pattern string are defined in XSLT by reference to the Java JDK 1.1 specification.

The structure of the format pattern is as follows, using the same syntax conventions as in Chapter 5, *Expressions*:

pattern	subpattern (pattern-separator subpattern)?
subpattern	prefix? integer (decimal-point fraction)? suffix?

prefix	`[#x0 - #xFFFD]` - `specialCharacters`
suffix	`[#x0 - #xFFFD]` - `specialCharacters`
integer	`digit* zero-digit* zero-digit` (but also allowing a `grouping-separator` to appear)
fraction	`zero-digit* digit*`
pattern-separator	«;» (by default)
decimal-point	«.» (by default)
grouping-separator	«,» (by default)
digit	«#» (by default)
zero-digit	«0» (by default)
specialCharacters	see table below

In these syntax rules, the characters shown as «;», «.», «,», «#», and «0» are the default representations of `pattern-separator`, `decimal-point`, `grouping-separator`, `digit`, and `zero-digit`. If the relevant `<xsl:decimal-format>` element nominates different characters in these roles, the nominated character is used in its place in the format pattern.

The first `subpattern` is for positive numbers. The second (optional) `subpattern` is for negative numbers.

The special characters used are as follows:

Special character	Meaning
`zero-digit` (default «0»)	A digit will always appear at this point in the result string
`digit` (default «#»)	A digit will appear at this point in the result string unless it is a redundant leading or trailing zero
`decimal-point` (default «.»)	Separates the integer and the fraction part of the number
`grouping-separator` (default «,»)	Separates groups of digits
«E»	Separates mantissa and exponent for exponential formats
`pattern-separator` (default «;»)	Separates the positive and negative format sub-patterns
`minus-sign` (default «-»)	Minus sign
`percent-sign` (default «%»)	Multiply the number by 100 and show it as a percentage
`per-mille` (default «‰»)	Multiply by 1000 and show as per-mille

7

Functions

Special character	Meaning
apostrophe («'»)	Quotes any special characters used in the pattern to give them their ordinary meaning. For example, if you want to output «9» as «#9», set the format pattern to «'#'0».
«¤»	Currency sign (#xA4): this character may not appear in a pattern, except within single quotes. (This is because different versions of Java handle this character differently).

If there is no explicit negative subpattern, «-» is prefixed to the positive form. That is, «0.00» alone is equivalent to «0.00;-0.00». If there is an explicit negative subpattern, it serves only to specify the negative prefix and suffix; the number of digits, minimal digits, and other characteristics are all the same as the positive pattern. That means that «#,##0.0#;(#)» has precisely the same result as «#,##0.0#;(#,##0.0#)».

The exponent character must be immediately followed by one or more digit characters. Example: «0.###E0». The number of digit characters after the exponent character gives the minimum exponent digit count; there is no maximum. Negative exponents are denoted using the same prefix and/or suffix specified for the number itself. The minimum number of integer digits is achieved by adjusting the exponent. The maximum number of integer digits, if any, specifies the exponent grouping. For example, 12345 is formatted using «##0.###E0» as «12.345E3».

The grouping separator is commonly used for thousands, but in some countries for ten-thousands. The number of digits per group in the output string will be equal to the number of digits in the pattern between the last grouping separator and the end of the integer: any other grouping separators in the format pattern are ignored. For example, if you write «#,##,###,####» there will be a grouping separator every four digits.

It is not defined what happens if the format pattern is invalid. This means the implementation is free either to report an error or to display the number in some fallback representation.

Usage

Note that this facility for formatting numbers is completely separate from the facilities available through the <xsl:number> element. There is some overlapping functionality, but the syntax of the format patterns is quite unrelated. The format-number() function formats a single number, which need not be an integer. <xsl:number> is primarily designed to format a list of positive integers. For formatting a single positive integer, either facility can be used.

Examples

The following example shows the result of format-number() using the default decimal-format. Examples with non-default decimal formats are shown under the <xsl:decimal-format> element in Chapter 4, page 187.

number	format pattern	result
1234.5	#,##0.00	1,234.50
123.456	#,##0.00	123.46
100000	#,##0.00	1,000,000.00
-59	#,##0.00	-59.00
1 div 0	#,##0.00	Infinity
1234	###0.0###	1234.0
1234.5	###0.0###	1234.5
.00035	###0.0###	0.0004
0.25	#00%	25%
0.736	#00%	74%
1	#00%	100%
-42	#00%	-4200%
-3.12	#.00;(#.00)	(3.12)
-3.12	#.00;#.00CR	3.12CR

See also

<xsl:decimal-format> on page 187 in Chapter 4

function-available

This function is used to test whether a particular function is available for use. It can be used to test the availability both of standard system functions and of extension functions.

For example, the expression «function-available('concat')» returns true.

Defined in

XSLT section 15.

Format

```
function-available(name)  ⇒  boolean
```

Arguments

Argument	Data type	Meaning
name	string	The name of the function being tested. If the value is not a string, it will be converted to a string using the rules for the string() function. The resulting string must take the form of a QName

7

Functions

Result

A Boolean value: `true` if the named function is available to be called, `false` otherwise.

Rules

The argument must take the form of a `QName`: that is, an XML name, with an optional namespace prefix that corresponds to a namespace declaration that is in scope at the point in the stylesheet where the `element-available()` function is called.

If there is no prefix, or if the namespace URI is null, the call tests whether there is a system function with the specified name. The system functions are those defined in the XPath and XSLT recommendations (and thus in this chapter); vendors are not allowed to supply additional functions in this default namespace, nor are they allowed to omit any. So an XSLT processor that conforms to XSLT version 1.0 will return `true` if the name is one of the following, and `false` otherwise.

boolean	generate-id	round
ceiling	id	starts-with
concat	key	string
contains	lang	string-length
count	last	substring
current	local-name	substring-after
document	name	substring-before
element-available	namespace-uri	sum
false	normalize-space	system-property
floor	not	translate
format-number	number	true
function-available	position	unparsed-entity-uri

If the `QName` includes a non-null namespace, the XSLT processor returns `true` if there is an extension function available with the given name. Since the way that XSLT processors use the extension function namespace to locate an extension function is implementation-defined, the exact way in which this works is likely to vary from one implementation to another. In general, if `function-available()` returns `false` then you are safe in assuming that a call on the function would fail, and if it returns `true`, then there will be some way of calling the function successfully. There is, however, no way of finding out at run-time how many arguments the function expects, or what their data types should be: it still relies on you calling the function with the right arguments.

Usage

There are two ways of using `function-available()`: it can be used to achieve backwards compatibility when using standard functions defined after version 1.0 of the specification, and it can be used to test for the presence of vendor or third-party extensions.

Testing for the Existence of System-defined Functions

The ability to test whether a particular system-defined function is available is not especially useful with version 1.0 of the specification. It is intended to come into its own when later versions of the specification appear. If you want to use a function that was newly defined in version 1.1 of XSLT, then you can test to see whether it is available with a particular XSLT processor before using it. If it is not available, you can use <xsl:if> to avoid executing it. Provided that you enable *forwards-compatible-mode* by setting the version attribute on the <xsl:stylesheet> element to a value other than "1.0", the XSLT processor will not object to the presence of an expression in your stylesheet that calls an unknown function, unless the expression is actually executed.

For example, suppose (as we might hope) that a function node-set() becomes available at version 2.0 of the XSLT specification, with the same functionality as the node-set() extension function currently abailable in Saxon and xt. Then you could test for its existence by writing:

```
<xsl:if test="function-available('node-set')>
```

For a fuller example, see the end of this section.

> *You can't always tell when an expression is going to be executed, for example if it is used as a predicate in a pattern or as the use expression in a key definition. You can, however, make sure that it* won't *be executed, by enclosing it inside an* <xsl:if> *statement that calls* function-available().

Note that it is the XSLT version that is relevant, not the XPath version. It is safe to assume that when a new version of XPath is published, the XSLT specification will be updated to reference it, though this does not necessarily mean that the version numbers will always be synchronized.

In principle you can use function-available() to test whether a version 1.0 instruction is available, on the basis that there may be subset implementations around: unfortunately this only works if the vendor has chosen to implement the function-available() function.

Testing for Vendor or Third-party Extensions

The second way of using function-available() is to test for vendor or third-party extensions. If you know that a particular extension function is present in some implementations and not others, you can use the function-available() test to see whether it is present, and use <xsl:if> to handle the situation when it isn't.

7

Functions

Examples

At least two XSLT implementations, Saxon and xt, provide a `node-set()` function that converts a result tree fragment to a node-set. The following example shows a named template that invokes this function if the stylesheet is run with one of these implementations, and that fails with an error message otherwise. It is also written in the optimistic hope that XSLT 2.0 will provide this function as standard, so the stylesheet will use the function if it's there. (The use of the keyword `<xsl:when>` seems particularly appropriate here!)

The template is written in such a way that it calls `<xsl:apply-templates>` in a specified mode to process the node-set derived from the result tree fragment. (It would be nice to supply the mode as a parameter, unfortunately XSLT doesn't allow this.)

```
<xsl:stylesheet
        xmlns:xsl="http://www.w3.org/1999/XSL/Transform"
        version="2.0">
<xsl:template name="process-tree-fragment"
        xmlns:xt="http://www.jclark.com/xt"
        xmlns:sx=" http://icl.com/saxon">
  <xsl:param name="fragment"/>
  <xsl:choose>
  <xsl:when test="function-available('node-set')">
    <xsl:apply-templates mode="process-fragment"
                         select="node-set($fragment)"/>
  </xsl:when>
  <xsl:when test="function-available('xt:node-set')">
    <xsl:apply-templates mode="process-fragment"
                         select="xt:node-set($fragment)"/>
  </xsl:when>
  <xsl:when test="function-available('sx:node-set')">
    <xsl:apply-templates mode="process-fragment"
                         select="sx:node-set($fragment)"/>
  </xsl:when>
  <xsl:otherwise>
  <xsl:message terminate="yes">
    Cannot convert result tree fragment to node-set
  </xsl:message>
  </xsl:otherwise>
  </xsl:choose>
</xsl:template>
</xsl:stylesheet>
```

This named template can be called as follows, to process all the nodes in the result tree fragment:

```
<xsl:variable name="the-node-set">
  <xsl:call-template name="process-tree-fragment">
    <xsl:with-param name="fragment" select="$supplied-fragment"/>
  </xsl:call-template>
</xsl:variable>
```

See also

element-available() on page 449

generate-id

The generate-id() function generates a string, in the form of an XML Name, that uniquely identifies a node. The only guarantee about the result is that it is different for every node.

For example, the expression «generate-id(..)» might return the string «N015732» when using one XSLT processor, and «b23a1c79» when using another.

Defined in

XSLT section 12.4

Format

```
generate-id()      ⇒  string
generate-id(node)  ⇒  string
```

Arguments

Argument	Data type	Meaning
node (optional)	node-set	The input node-set (only the first node is considered). If the argument is omitted, a node-set containing only the context node is used.

Result

A string value that uniquely identifies the node. This will consist only of ASCII alphanumeric characters, and the first character will be alphabetic. This makes the identifier suitable for use in many contexts, for example as an XML Name.

Rules

If the argument is an empty node-set, the function returns an empty string.

If the input node-set contains more than one node, the target node is the one that is first in document order.

If the argument is omitted, the target node is the context node.

The function returns an arbitrary string: the only constraints are that it will always return the same string for the same node, and that it will always return different strings for different nodes. This includes the case where the nodes are in different documents.

The generated identifiers are unique within a single execution of the stylesheet. If the same stylesheet is used several times, with the same or different source documents, it may generate the same identifiers in each run but is under no obligation to do so.

Usage and Examples

The main intended purpose of the generate-id() function is to create links in the output document. For example, it can be used to generate ID and IDREF attributes in an output XML document, or <a name="X"> and <a href="#X"> pairs in an output HTML document.

Example: Using generate-id() to Create Links

This example takes as input a file resorts.xml containing details of a collection of holiday resorts, each of which includes a list of hotels.

Source

```
<resorts>
    <resort>
        <name>Amsterdam</name>
        <details>A wordy description of Amsterdam</details>
        <hotel>
            <name>Grand Hotel</name>
            <stars>5</stars>
            <address> . . . </address>
        </hotel>
        <hotel>
            <name>Less Grand Hotel</name>
            <stars>2</stars>
            <address> . . . </address>
        </hotel>
    </resort>
    <resort>
        <name>Bruges</name>
        <details>An eloquent description of Bruges</details>
        <hotel>
            <name>Central Hotel</name>
            <stars>5</stars>
            <address> . . . </address>
        </hotel>
        <hotel>
            <name>Peripheral Hotel</name>
            <stars>2</stars>
            <address> . . . </address>
        </hotel>
    </resort>
</resorts>
```

Stylesheet

The stylesheet resorts.xsl constructs an output HTML page in which the hotels are listed first, followed by information about the resorts. Each hotel entry contains a hyperlink to the relevant resort details. The links for the resorts are generated using generate-id() applied to the <resort> element.

This is a complete stylesheet that uses the *Simplified Stylesheet* syntax introduced on page 104, in Chapter 3.

```
<html
  xmlns:xsl="http://www.w3.org/1999/XSL/Transform"
  xsl:version="1.0"
>

<body>
    <h1>Hotels</h1>
    <xsl:for-each select="//hotel">
    <xsl:sort select="stars" order="descending" data-type="number"/>
       <h2><xsl:value-of select="name"/></h2>
       <p>Address: <xsl:value-of select="address"/></p>
       <p>Stars: <xsl:value-of select="stars"/></p>
       <p>Resort: <a href="#{generate-id(parent::resort)}">
              <xsl:value-of select="parent::resort/name"/></a></p>
    </xsl:for-each>

    <h1>Resorts</h1>
    <xsl:for-each select="//resort">
       <h2><a name="{generate-id()}">
          <xsl:value-of select="name"/>
       </a></h2>
       <p><xsl:value-of select="details"/></p>
    </xsl:for-each>
</body>
</html>
```

Notice how generate-id() is used twice, once to generate the identifier of the resort, the other to generate a link from the hotel.

Output

The output below was obtained using Saxon. I have added some extra indentation to show the structure. A different product will generate different identifiers in the <a> elements, but the links will work just as well.

```
<html>
    <body>
        <h1>Hotels</h1>
          <h2>Grand Hotel</h2>
             <p>Address:  . . . </p>
             <p>Stars: 5</p>
             <p>Resort: <a href="#b2ab1">Amsterdam</a></p>
```

```
        <h2>Central Hotel</h2>
          <p>Address:  . . . </p>
          <p>Stars: 5</p>
          <p>Resort: <a href="#b2ab3">Bruges</a></p>
        <h2>Less Grand Hotel</h2>
         <p>Address:  . . . </p>
          <p>Stars: 2</p>
          <p>Resort: <a href="#b2ab1">Amsterdam</a></p>
        <h2>Peripheral Hotel</h2>
          <p>Address:  . . . </p>
          <p>Stars: 2</p>
          <p>Resort: <a href="#b2ab3">Bruges</a></p>
    <h1>Resorts</h1>
        <h2><a name="b2ab1">Amsterdam</a></h2>
          <p>A wordy description of Amsterdam</p>
        <h2><a name="b2ab3">Bruges</a></h2>
          <p>An eloquent description of Bruges</p>
    </body>
  </html>
```

There is no inverse function to generate-id(): specifically, there is no way to find a
node if its generated id is known, other than the very inefficient

```
//node()[generate-id()=$X]
```

It is important to appreciate that the generated ids bear no resemblance to any ID
attribute values in the source document, so the nodes cannot be found using the id()
function.

See also

id() on page 466
key() on page 469

id

The id() function returns a node-set containing the node or nodes with a given ID
attribute.

For example, if the code attribute is defined as an ID attribute, then the expression
«id('A321-780')» might return a node-set containing the single element <product
code="A321-780">.

Defined in

XPath section 4.1

Format

```
id(value)  ⇒  node-set
```

Arguments

Argument	Data type	Meaning
value	any	Specifies the required ID values, in a way that depends on the data type: see below for details

Result

A node-set containing the nodes with the required ID values.

Rules

If the argument is not a node-set, the argument is converted, if necessary, to a string using the rules for the `string()` function, and the resulting string is treated as a whitespace-separated list of tokens. Each token is used as a candidate ID value: if there is a node in the same document as the context node that has an ID attribute equal to this candidate ID value, this node is included in the result node-set.

If the argument is a node-set, this process is applied to each node in the node-set in turn: the node is converted to a string by taking its string-value, this string is treated as a whitespace-separated list of tokens, and each of these tokens is used as a candidate ID value. Note that this is different from simply converting the node-set to a string using the `string()` function, because it uses all the nodes in the node-set, not only the first.

An ID attribute in this context is any attribute declared in the DTD as having type ID.

It is not necessary for the nodes in the argument node-set to be attributes declared as type IDREF or IDREFS, though the function is designed to produce the expected result when they are: that is, it finds the nodes referenced by the IDREF or IDREFS values in the argument node-set.

It is not an error if there is no node with an ID equal to one of the candidate ID values. In this situation, there will simply be no node in the resulting node-set corresponding to this value. In the simplest case, where there is only one candidate ID value supplied, the resulting node-set will be empty if the ID is not present.

7

Functions

Notes

ID values only really work properly if the source document is valid (in the XML sense: meaning, loosely, that it obeys the rules in its own DTD). However, XSLT and XPath are designed to allow invalid documents as well as valid ones to be processed. One possible kind of validity error is that ID values are not unique within the document. This is explicitly covered in the specification – the first node with that ID value is located. Other validity errors are not discussed in the specification, for example what happens if an ID attribute contains embedded spaces. It is best to regard the behavior in such cases as undefined.

A non-validating XML parser isn't required to read attribute definitions from an external DTD. In this situation the XSLT processor will assume there are no ID attributes present, and the id() function will always return an empty result. If this appears to be happening, try a different XML parser. Most good parsers will report the attribute type, even though it isn't absolutely required by the standard.

Usage and Examples

The id() function provides an efficient means of locating nodes given the value of an ID attribute.

In a sense it is a convenience function, because if the attribute named id is always an ID attribute, then the expression

```
id('B1234')
```

is equivalent to the path expression

```
//*[@id='B1234']
```

However, the chances are that in most implementations, the id() function will be much more efficient than the straightforward path expression with a predicate, because the processor is likely to build an index rather than doing a sequential search.

It is also possible to use key() in place of id(). The main advantage of the id() function over using key() is that it handles a whitespace-separated list of IDs in one go. The key() function cannot do this, because there is nothing to stop a key value containing a space.

Note that the id() function always locates elements in the same document as the context node. To locate elements in a different document, use <xsl:for-each> to change the context node, for example:

```
<xsl:for-each select="document('a.xml')">
    <xsl:copy-of select="id('B1234')"/>
</xsl:for-each>
```

Where the source document includes an IDREFS attribute, it is possible to locate all the referenced elements at once. For example, if the <book> element has an attribute authors which is an IDREFS attribute containing a whitespace-separated list of author ids, the relevant <author> elements can be retrieved and processed using a construct such as:

```
<xsl:template match="book">
    . . .
by <xsl:for-each select="id(@authors)">
    <xsl:value-of select="surname"/>
    <xsl:if test="position()!=last()">, </xsl:if>
    <xsl:if test="position()=last()-1">and </xsl:if>
</xsl:for-each>
</xsl:template>
```

See also

key() on page 469

key

The key() function is used to find the nodes with a given value for a named key. It is used in conjunction with the <xsl:key> element described in Chapter 4, on page 222.

For example, if there is a key definition

```
<xsl:key name="vreg" match="vehicle" use="@reg"/>
```

then the expression «key('vreg', 'N498PAA')» might return a node-set containing the single element <vehicle reg="N498PAA">.

Defined in

XSLT section 12.2

Format

```
key(name, value)  ⇒  node-set
```

Arguments

Argument	Data type	Meaning
name	string	Specifies the name of the key. If the argument is not a string, it is converted to a string using the rules of the string() function. The value of the string must be a QName that identifies a key declared using <xsl:key>

7

Functions

Argument	Data type	Meaning
value	any	Specifies the required value of the key, in a way that depends on the data type: see below.

Result

A node-set containing the nodes with the required key values.

Rules

The first argument must take the form of a QName: that is, an XML name optionally prefixed with a namespace prefix that corresponds to a namespace declaration that is in scope at the point in the stylesheet where the key() function is called. If there is no namespace prefix, the relevant namespace URI is null: the default namespace is not used. There must be an <xsl:key> element in the stylesheet with the same expanded name, using the namespace URIs rather than prefixes in the comparison. If there is more than one <xsl:key> element with this name, they are all used: a node is considered to match the key if it matches any of the key definitions with this name.

If the second argument is not a node-set, its value is converted if necessary to a string, using the rules of the string() function. All the nodes in the same document as the context node that have a value for the named key equal to this string are included in the result node-set. Note that one node may have several values for the same key, and there may also be many nodes with the same value for the key.

If the second argument is a node-set, this same process is applied to each node in the node-set. For each node N in this node-set, all the nodes in the same document as the context node that have a value for the named key equal to the string-value of N are added to the result node-set. This isn't the same as simply converting the node-set argument to a string using the string() function, because that would only use the string-value of the first node in the node-set.

Note that with multiple source documents, the resulting nodes will all be in the same document as the context node: but they will not necessarily be in the same document as the nodes from which the key values were obtained.

Usage and Examples

The key() function is provided to make associative access to nodes (finding the nodes given their content) more convenient and more efficient. Efficiency of course depends entirely on the implementation, but it is likely that most implementations will use some kind of index data structure to make the key() function faster than the equivalent location path expression.

For example, to locate the <book> elements having J. B. Priestley as the content of one of their <author> child elements, you could write:

```
<xsl:for-each select="//book[author='J. B. Priestley']">
```

However, it is probably more efficient, if this is done frequently in the stylesheet, to define the author name as a key:

```
<xsl:key name="book-author" match="book" use="author"/>
. . .
<xsl:for-each select="key('book-author', 'J. B. Priestley')"/>
```

The key() function always locates elements in the same document as the context node. To locate elements in a different document, use <xsl:for-each> to change the context node, for example:

```
<xsl:for-each select="document('a.xml')">
    <xsl:copy-of select="key('book-author', 'J. B. Priestley')"/>
</xsl:for-each>
```

The key value supplied can be either a string, or a node-set. In the former case, the key value can be calculated before use: for example it might be the concatenation of several values obtained from different places. In the second case, the key value must always be held as-is within the source document; but the advantage of this usage is that several key values can be supplied in the same call of the key function.

Example: Using keys

This example uses two source files: the principal source document is a file containing a list of books, and the secondary one (accessed using the document() function) contains biographies of authors. The author name held in the first file is used to retrieve the author's biography from the second file, rather like a join in SQL.

Source

The principal source document is an abbreviated version of the booklist.xml file:

```
<booklist>
<book category="FC">
    <title>The Young Visiters</title>
    <author>Daisy Ashford</author>
</book>
<book category="FC">
    <title>When We Were Very Young</title>
    <author>A. A. Milne</author>
</book>
</booklist>
```

The secondary source document, `authors.xml`, reads like this. I've only included two authors to keep it short, but the `key()` function would really come into its own if there were hundreds of entries.

```
<authors>

<author name="A. A. Milne">
<born>1852</born>
<died>1956</died>
<biog>Alan Alexander Milne, educated at Westminster School and Trinity
College Cambridge, became a prolific author of plays, novels, poetry, short
stories, and essays, all of which have been overshadowed by his children's
books. </biog>
</author>

<author name="Daisy Ashford">
<born>1881</born>
<died>1972</died>
<biog>Daisy Ashford (Mrs George Norman) wrote <i>The Young Visiters</i>, a
small comic masterpiece, while still a young child in Lewes. It was found in a
drawer in 1919 and sent to Chatto and Windus, who published it in the same
year with an introduction by J. M. Barrie, who had first insisted on meeting
the author in order to check that she was genuine.</biog>
</author>

</authors>
```

Stylesheet

The stylesheet is in the file `author-biogs.xsl`. It declares a key to match `<author>` elements by their name attribute. This is intended for use with the `authors.xml` file, though there is nothing in the key definition to say so.

Note the use of a global variable to reference the secondary source file. It would be possible to use the `document()` function each time the file is accessed, and any XSLT processor worthy of the name would only actually read and parse the file once, but using a variable in my view makes it easier to see what is going on.

The innermost `<xsl:for-each>` doesn't do any iteration, it is there merely to switch the context to the second document, because the `key()` function only looks in the document containing the context node. Switching the context means it is no longer possible to refer directly to nodes in the principal document, which is why the author's name is first extracted into a variable.

```
<xsl:transform
 xmlns:xsl="http://www.w3.org/1999/XSL/Transform"
 version="1.0"
>
<xsl:key name="biog" match="author" use="@name"/>
<xsl:variable name="biogs" select="document('authors.xml')"/>

<xsl:template match="/">
  <html><body>
```

```
      <xsl:variable name="all-books" select="//book"/>
      <xsl:for-each select="$all-books">
              <!-- for each book in the booklist file -->
        <h1><xsl:value-of select="title"/></h1>
        <h2>Author<xsl:if test="count(author)!=1">s</xsl:if></h2>
        <xsl:for-each select="author">
                <!-- for each author of this book -->
          <xsl:variable name="name" select="."/>
          <h3><xsl:value-of select="$name"/></h3>
          <xsl:for-each select="$biogs">
                  <!-- change the current node to be the authors file -->
                  <!-- then retrieve the entry for this author -->
            <xsl:variable name="auth" select="key('biog', $name)"/>
            <p><xsl:value-of
                    select="concat($auth/born, ' - ', $auth/died)"/></p>
            <p><xsl:value-of select="$auth/biog"/></p>
          </xsl:for-each>
        </xsl:for-each>
      </xsl:for-each>
    </body></html>
  </xsl:template>

</xsl:transform>
```

Output

The output obtained if you run this stylesheet with the subset of the `booklist.xml` file shown above is as follows:

```
<html>
  <body>
    <h1>The Young Visiters</h1>
    <h2>Author</h2>
    <h3>Daisy Ashford</h3>
    <p>1881 - 1972</p>
    <p>Daisy Ashford (Mrs George Norman) wrote The Young Visiters, a
small comic masterpiece, while still a young child in Lewes. It was found in a
drawer in 1919 and sent to Chatto and Windus, who published it in the same
year with an introduction by J. M. Barrie, who had first insisted on meeting
the author in order to check that she was genuine.</p>
    <h1>When We Were Very Young</h1>
    <h2>Author</h2>
    <h3>A. A. Milne</h3>
    <p>1852 - 1956</p>
    <p>Alan Alexander Milne, educated at Westminster School and Trinity
College Cambridge, became a prolific author of plays, novels, poetry, short
stories, and essays, all of which have been overshadowed by his children's
books.</p>
  </body>
  </html>
```

7

Functions

See also

<xsl:key> on page 222 in Chapter 4
id() on page 466

lang

The lang() function tests whether the language of the context node, as defined by the xml:lang attribute, corresponds to the language supplied as an argument.

For example, if the context node is the element <para lang="fr-CA"> (indicating Canadian French), then the expression «lang('fr')» would return true.

Defined in

XPath section 4.3

Format

```
lang(language)  ⇒  boolean
```

Arguments

Argument	Data type	Meaning
language	string	The language being tested. If the argument is not a string, it is converted to a string using the rules of the string() function.

Result

A Boolean: true if the language of the context node is the same as, or a sublanguage of, the language being tested.

Rules

The language of the context node is determined by the value of its xml:lang attribute, or if it has no such attribute, by the value of the xml:lang attribute on its nearest ancestor node that does have such an attribute. If there is no xml:lang attribute on any of these nodes, the lang() function returns false.

The xml:lang attribute is one of the small number of attributes that are given a predefined meaning in the XML specification (in fact, you could argue that it the only thing in the XML specification that has anything to say about what the contents of the document might mean to its readers). The value of the attribute can take one of the following four forms:

- A two-letter language code defined in the international standard ISO 639. For example English is "en" and French is "fr". This can be given in either upper-case or lower-case, though lower-case is usual.

- A two letter language code as above, followed by one or more subcodes: each subcode is preceded by a hyphen «-». For example, US English is "en-US", Canadian French is "fr-CA". The first subcode, if present, must be either a two-letter country code from the international standard ISO 3166, or a subcode for the language registered with IANA. The ISO 3166 country codes are generally the same as Internet top-level domains, for example "DE" for Germany, "CZ" for the Czech Republic, but with the notable exception of the United Kingdom, whose ISO 3166 code (for some reason) is "GB" rather than "UK". These codes are generally written in upper case. The meaning of any subcodes after the first is not defined, but they must contain ASCII letters (a-z, A-Z) only.

- A language code registered with the Internet Assigned Numbers Authority (see www.iana.org), prefixed "i-", for example "i-Navajo".

- A user-defined language code, prefixed "x-", for example "x-Java" if the element contains a Java program.

The xml:lang attribute defines the language of all text contained within the element it appears on, unless it is overridden by another xml:lang attribute in an inner element. So if a document is written in English but contains quotations in German, the xml:lang language code on the document element might say «xml:lang="en"», while an element containing a quotation specifies «xml:lang="de"».

The lang() function in XSLT allows you to test whether the language for the context node is the one you are expecting. For example «lang('en')» returns true if the language is English, while «lang('jp')» returns true if it is Japanese.

Specifically, the rules are as follows:

- If the value of xml:lang for the context node is equal to the string supplied in the argument, ignoring differences of case, the function returns true.

- If the value of xml:lang for the context node, ignoring any suffix starting with a hyphen «-», is equal to the string supplied in the argument, again ignoring differences of case, the function returns true.

- Otherwise, the function returns false.

Usage and Examples

This function provides a convenient way of testing the language used in the source document. Assuming that the source document has been properly marked up using the xml:lang attribute as defined in the XML specification, the lang() function allows you to do language-dependent processing of the data.

The example below shows another way of using lang(): to select language-dependent data from a lookup table held in the stylesheet.

Example: Using lang() for Localizing Dates
Source

The source file issue-dates.xml contains dates in ISO format (yyyymmdd). The dates below happen to be the dates of the various working drafts of the XSLT specification.

```
<issues>
<iso-date>19991116</iso-date>
<iso-date>19991008</iso-date>
<iso-date>19990813</iso-date>
<iso-date>19990709</iso-date>
<iso-date>19990421</iso-date>
<iso-date>19981216</iso-date>
<iso-date>19980818</iso-date>
</issues>
```

Stylesheet

The stylesheet format-dates.xsl contains data and logic to output these dates using English, French, or German month names.

The stylesheet takes a global parameter which is the name of the required language for the output. The way you supply the parameter varies according to which product you are using. For Saxon, use the command line:

```
saxon issue-dates.xml format-dates.xsl language=fr
```

For xt, use:

```
xt issue-dates.xml format-dates.xsl language=fr
```

The language code should be «en», «de», or «fr».

```
<?xml version="1.0" encoding="iso-8859-1"?>
<xsl:transform
 xmlns:xsl="http://www.w3.org/1999/XSL/Transform"
 version="1.0"
>

<xsl:output encoding="iso-8859-1"/>

<data xmlns="data.uri">
<months xml:lang="en">
   <m>January</m><m>February</m><m>March</m><m>April</m>
```

```
        <m>May</m><m>June</m><m>July</m><m>August</m>
        <m>September</m><m>October</m><m>November</m><m>December</m>
    </months>
    <months xml:lang="fr">
        <m>Janvier</m><m>Février</m><m>Mars</m><m>Avril</m>
        <m>Mai</m><m>Juin</m><m>Juillet</m><m>Août</m>
        <m>Septembre</m><m>Octobre</m><m>Novembre</m><m>Décembre</m>
    </months>
    <months xml:lang="de">
        <m>Januar</m><m>Februar</m><m>März</m><m>April</m>
        <m>Mai</m><m>Juni</m><m>Juli</m><m>August</m>
        <m>September</m><m>Oktober</m><m>November</m><m>Dezember</m>
    </months>
    </data>

    <xsl:param name="language" select="'en'"/>

    <xsl:template match="iso-date">
    <date xmlns:data="data.uri" xsl:exclude-result-prefixes="data">
        <xsl:value-of select="substring(., 7, 2)"/>
        <xsl:text> </xsl:text>
        <xsl:variable name="month" select="number(substring(.,5,2))"/>
        <xsl:value-of select="document('')/*/
                    data:data/data:months[lang($language)]/data:m[$month]"/>
        <xsl:text> </xsl:text>
        <xsl:value-of select="substring(., 1, 4)"/>
    </date>
    </xsl:template>
    </xsl:transform>
```

The crux of this is the lengthy path expression (starting with «document('')») that obtains the month name. This expression first locates the stylesheet document («document('')»), then its document element («*», giving the <xsl:stylesheet> or <xsl:transform> element), then the top-level <data> element (the actual element uses «data.uri» as a default namespace, but in the XPath expression it needs to be given an explicit namespace prefix), then the <months> element that matches the required language, and finally the <m> element for the required month. The «[lang($language)]» predicate will be true only for a <months> element whose language code matches the required language.

See the description of the document() function on page 440 for more details on how to use this function to get access to data held in the stylesheet.

I used iso-8859-1 encoding (the character set that Microsoft call Windows ANSI) for this example because that's what my text editor uses. If I had used the default encoding, UTF-8, my text editor wouldn't be able to cope with the accented letters, so it would be harder to see what's going on, though it would still work correctly.

Output

If you selected English, the output is:

```
<?xml version="1.0" encoding="iso-8859-1" ?>
<date>16 November 1999</date>
<date>08 October 1999</date>
<date>13 August 1999</date>
<date>09 July 1999</date>
<date>21 April 1999</date>
<date>16 December 1998</date>
<date>18 August 1998</date>
```

If you selected French, the output is:

```
<?xml version="1.0" encoding="iso-8859-1" ?>
<date>16 Novembre 1999</date>
<date>08 Octobre 1999</date>
<date>13 Août 1999</date>
<date>09 Juillet 1999</date>
<date>21 Avril 1999</date>
<date>16 Décembre 1998</date>
<date>18 Août 1998</date>
```

If you selected German, the output is:

```
<?xml version="1.0" encoding="iso-8859-1" ?>
<date>16 November 1999</date>
<date>08 Oktober 1999</date>
<date>13 August 1999</date>
<date>09 Juli 1999</date>
<date>21 April 1999</date>
<date>16 Dezember 1998</date>
<date>18 August 1998</date>
```

The lang() function only allows you to test whether the language is one of the languages you are expecting; if you want to find out the actual language, you will need to read the xml:lang attribute directly. You can find the relevant attribute using the expression «ancestor-or-self::*[@xml:lang][1]/@xml:lang»

last

The last() function returns the value of the context size. When processing a list of nodes, if the nodes are numbered from one, last() gives the number assigned to the last node in the list.

For example, if you are processing a set of nodes using <xsl:for-each>, then you can output a comma before each node other than the last one by writing:

```
<xsl:if test="position()!=last()">, </xsl:if>
```

Defined in

XPath section 4.1

Format

```
last() ⇒ number
```

Arguments

None

Result

A number, the value of the *context size*. As the name implies, this is context dependant.

Rules

The XPath specification defines the value of the `last()` function in terms of the *context size*. The XSLT specification uses different terminology: it talks about the size of the *current node list*.

When a top-level expression is evaluated (that is, an XPath expression that is not part of another expression), the context size is set to the number of nodes in the current node list. This has three possible settings:

❏ When a global variable is being evaluated, or in certain other contexts such as evaluating the `use` expression in `<xsl:key>`, or evaluating the initial template that matches the root node, it is set to 1 (one).

❏ When `<xsl:apply-templates>` is called to process a set of nodes, the current node list is the list of nodes being processed, and the context size is therefore the number of nodes selected in the call of `<xsl:apply-templates>`.

❏ When `<xsl:for-each>` is called to process a set of nodes, the current node list is the list of nodes being processed, and the context size is therefore the number of nodes selected in the call of `<xsl:for-each>`.

When a predicate is evaluated, either in an expression or in a pattern, the context size is the number of nodes being tested in that step of the expression or pattern evaluation. For more details, see Chapter 5 *Expressions*, and Chapter 6 *Patterns*.

Usage and Examples

To understand the effect of calling `last()`, you need to know what the current node list is.

When `last()` is used as a top-level expression within an `<xsl:template>` (and not within `<xsl:for-each>`), it returns the number of nodes selected by the relevant `<xsl:apply-templates>` select expression. This is because `<xsl:apply-templates>` sets the current node list to be the set of nodes selected by the select expression, after sorting them into the order in which they are processed.

For example, the following code can be used to number all the figures in a document. The `last()` function prints the number of figure elements in the document.

```
<xsl:apply-templates select="//figure"/>
. . .
<xsl:template match="figure">
   <div align="center"/>
   <img src="{@href}"/>
   <p>Figure <xsl:value-of select="position()"/>
      <xsl:text/> of <xsl:value-of select="last()"/></p>
   </div>
</xsl:template>
```

Similarly, when `last()` is used as a top-level expression within `<xsl:for-each>`, it returns the number of nodes selected by the relevant `<xsl:for-each>` select expression. Again, this is because `<xsl:for-each>` sets the current node list to be the set of nodes selected by the select expression, after sorting into the correct order.

The last() function is often used to test whether the current node being processed is the last one in the list. This is illustrated in the following example.

Example: Formatting a List Using position() and last()

This example formats a list of names in the style «Adam, Betsie, Charlie and Diana»

Source

The source file is `booklist.xml`. A relevant subset is shown below:

```
<booklist>
<book category="CS">
     <title>Design Patterns</title>
     <author>Erich Gamma</author>
     <author>Richard Helm</author>
     <author>Ralph Johnson</author>
     <author>John Vlissides</author>
</book>
</booklist>
```

Stylesheet

The stylesheet `format-names.xsl` processes a book by formatting the list of authors into a single element:

```
<xsl:transform
    xmlns:xsl="http://www.w3.org/1999/XSL/Transform"
    version="1.0"
>

<xsl:template match="book">
<auth>
     <xsl:for-each select="author">
```

```
                <xsl:value-of select="."/>
                <xsl:choose>
                    <xsl:when test="position() = last()"/> <!-- do nothing -->
                    <xsl:when test="position() = last()-1"> and </xsl:when>
                    <xsl:otherwise>, </xsl:otherwise>
                </xsl:choose>
            </xsl:for-each>
    </auth>
    </xsl:template>

    </xsl:transform>
```

Output

For the `booklist.xml` file, the output is:

```
<auth>Danzig</auth>
<auth>Daisy Ashford</auth>
<auth>A. A. Milne</auth>
<auth>Erich Gamma, Richard Helm, Ralph Johnson and John Vlissides</auth>
```

`<xsl:call-template>` does not change the context node list, so `last()` will return the same value in the called template as in the calling template.

If the `last()` function is used within the select expression of an `<xsl:sort>` element, then it refers to the number of nodes being sorted. For example, specifying the following sort key:

```
<xsl:sort select="position() mod (ceiling(last() div 3))"/>
```

will sort the nodes A, B, C, D, E, F, G, H into the sequence A, D, G, B, E, H, C, F, which might be useful if you want to arrange them in a table with three columns.

When `last()` is used within an expression used as a predicate applied to a node-set expression, the context size is the number of nodes selected by the current step of the expression, after applying any previous filters. For example, suppose the source document is as follows:

```
<countries>
<country name="France" capital="Paris" continent="Europe"/>
<country name="Germany" capital="Berlin" continent="Europe"/>
<country name="Spain" capital="Madrid" continent="Europe"/>
<country name="Italy" capital="Rome" continent="Europe"/>
<country name="Poland" capital="Warsaw" continent="Europe"/>
<country name="Egypt" capital="Cairo" continent="Africa"/>
<country name="Libya" capital="Tripoli" continent="Africa"/>
<country name="Nigeria" capital="Lagos" continent="Africa"/>
</countries>
```

7

Functions

Then:

- ❏ The expression «countries/country[last()]» returns the country element for Nigeria.

- ❏ The expression «countries/country[@continent='Europe'][last()]» returns the country element for Poland.

- ❏ The expression «countries/country[@continent='Europe'][last()-1]» returns the country element for Italy.

- ❏ The expression «countries/country[@continent='Africa'] [position() != last()]» returns the country elements for Egypt and Libya.

The last() function can be used as a qualifier in a pattern when the last child of a given element is to be treated differently from the others. For example

```
<xsl:template name="normal-p" match="p">
   <xsl:copy>
      <xsl:apply-templates/>
   </xsl:copy>
</xsl:template>

<xsl:template match="p[last()]">
   <xsl:call-template name="normal-p"/>
   <hr/>
</xsl:template>
```

However, this may not perform well, because each <p> element needs to be tested to see if it is the last one, which will probably involve looking at all the children of the parent of the <p> element. Using <xsl:if> will often achieve the same effect more economically:

```
<xsl:template match="p">
   <xsl:copy>
      <xsl:apply-templates/>
   </xsl:copy>
   <xsl:if test="position()=last()">
      <hr/>
   </xsl:if>
</xsl:template>
```

However, note that these two examples are not strictly equivalent. If the <p> elements are processed by a call on <xsl:apply-templates> with no <xsl:sort> specification, they will have the same effect; but if a sort key is specified, then the second template will output an <hr/> element after the last <p> element in the order of the output, whereas the first will output the <hr/> after the last <p> element in document order.

> An easy mistake is to think that last() returns a Boolean value. You can use last() in a predicate to match the last node, for example:
>
> ```
> <xsl:value-of select="para[last()]"/>
> ```
>
> This is a shorthand for the predicate «[position()=last()]», because in a predicate, a numeric value X is equivalent to a test for the condition «position()=X». However, this doesn't extend to other contexts, for example if you write:
>
> ```
> <xsl:if test="last()"/>
> ```
>
> then the numeric value of the last() function is simply converted to a Boolean as if the boolean() function were used. The result will always be true, because last() can never be zero.

See also

position() on page 500
<xsl:number> in Chapter 4, on page 237

local-name

The local-name() function returns the local part of the name of a node, that is, the part of the name after the colon if there is one, or the full name otherwise.

For example, if the context node is an element named <title> the expression «local-name()» returns «title»; for an element named <ms:schema> it returns «schema».

Defined in

XPath section 4.1

Format

```
local-name()     ⇒  string
local-name(node) ⇒  string
```

Arguments

Argument	Data type	Meaning
node (optional)	node-set	Identifies the node whose local name is required. If the node-set contains more than one node, the target node is the one that comes first in document order. If the node-set is empty, the function returns an empty string. If the argument is omitted, the target node is the context node. It is an error if the argument supplied is not a node-set.

7

Functions

483

Result

A string value: the local part of the name of the target node.

Rules

The local name of a node depends on the node type, as follows:

Node type	Local name
root	None, an empty string is returned
element	The element name, after any colon
attribute	The attribute name, after any colon
text	None, an empty string is returned
processing instruction	The *target* used in the processing instruction to identify the application for which it is intended
comment	None, an empty string is returned
namespace	The namespace prefix; or the empty string if this is the default namespace

Usage

This function can be useful if you need to test the local name without also testing the namespace URI. For example if you want to select both <title> and <html:title> elements, you could do this by writing:

```
<xsl:apply-templates select="*[local-name()='title']"/>
```

Or you could define a template rule that matches both:

```
<xsl:template match="*[local-name()='title']">
```

In some ways this can be seen as a misuse of the XML Namespaces facility. The names in one namespace are supposed to bear no relation to the names in another, so any similarity between the names <title> and <html:title> is a pure coincidence.

In practice, this isn't always true. What often happens is that one namespace is adapted from another. For example the US Post Office might devise a schema (and associated namespace) for representing US names and addresses, and the Canadian Post Office might then create a variant of this, with a different namespace URI, for Canadian names and addresses. The two schemas will have many elements in common, and it's quite reasonable to try to write a stylesheet that can handle either. If you want to write template rules that match on both a <us:address> and a <canada:address>, there are two ways of doing it:

Either list both possibilities:

```
<xsl:template match="us:address | canada:address">
```

or match on the local name only:

```
<xsl:template match="*[local-name()='address']">
```

Examples

The following stylesheet fragment outputs an HTML table listing the attributes of the current element, sorted first by namespace and then by local name:

```
<xsl:template match="*" mode="tabulate">
   <table>
      <xsl:for-each select="attribute::node()">
      <xsl:sort select="namespace-uri()"/>
      <xsl:sort select="local-name()"/>
         <tr>
         <td><xsl:value-of select="namespace-uri()"/></td>
         <td><xsl:value-of select="local-name()"/></td>
         <td><xsl:value-of select="."/></td>
         </tr>
      </xsl:for-each>
   </table>
</xsl:template>
```

See also

```
name()
namespace-uri()  on page 490
```

name

The name() function returns a QName that represents the name of a node. Typically this will be the name of the node as written in the original XML source document.

For example, if the context node is an element named <ms:schema>, then the expression «name()» will normally return the string «ms:schema».

Defined in

XPath section 4.1

Format

```
name()  ⇒  string
name(node)  ⇒  string
```

Arguments

Argument	Data type	Meaning
node (optional)	node-set	Identifies the node whose name is required. If the node-set contains more than one node, the target node is the one that comes first in document order. If the node-set is empty, the function returns an empty string. If the argument is omitted, the target node is the context node. It is an error if the argument supplied is not a node-set.

Result

A string value: a `QName` representing the name of the target node.

Rules

The `QName` returned will normally use the same prefix as that which appeared in the original XML source. However, this is not guaranteed: the only guarantee is that it will use a prefix that maps to the same namespace URI. If the source document contains multiple prefixes that map to the same namespace URI the implementation can choose to normalize them, and in theory it is even free to discard the user-selected prefixes entirely and replace them with prefixes of its own choosing.

The name of a node depends on the node type, as follows:

Node type	Name
root	None, an empty string is returned
element	The element name (a `QName`), normally as it appears in the source XML, though a different prefix that maps to the same namespace URI may be substituted.
attribute	The attribute name (a `QName`), normally as it appears in the source XML, though a different prefix that maps to the same namespace URI may be substituted.
text	None, an empty string is returned
processing instruction	The *target* used in the processing instruction to identify the application for which it is intended
comment	None, an empty string is returned
namespace	The namespace prefix; or the empty string if this is the default namespace. (This is **not** prefixed with «xmlns:»)

Except for element and attribute nodes, name() returns the same value as local-name().

Usage

The name() function is useful when you want to display the element name, perhaps in an error message, because the form it takes is the same as the way in which users will generally write the element name.

So, for example, if your stylesheet requires every <book> to have an ISBN attribute, you might write:

```
<xsl:if test="not(@ISBN)">
<xsl:message>The <xsl:value-of select="name()"/> element
             has no ISBN attribute</xsl:message>
</xsl:if>
```

You can also use the name() function to test the name of a node against a string, for example «doc:title[name(..)='doc:section']». However, it's best to avoid this if you can:

❑ Firstly, this fails if the document uses a different prefix to refer to the namespace. There's nothing here to tell the system to treat «doc:section» as a QName, so if the writer of a particular document chose to use the prefix «DOC» instead of «doc» for this namespace, the test would fail, even though the names are equivalent.

❑ Secondly, there is usually a better way of doing it: this particular example can be written as «doc:title[parent::doc:section]». In fact, in most cases where you want to test whether a node has a particular name, you can do it using a predicate of this form. The «self» axis is particularly useful: for example, to test whether the current node is a <figure> element, write <xsl:if test="self::figure">.

There are some occasions when this won't work. For example, suppose your names are structured and you want to do a more complex test on the name; for example «*[starts-with(name(),'private.')]» to select elements whose name starts with the string «private.». This is poor document design: XML names are not intended to carry hidden meaning by means of an internal syntax; if some elements have access restrictions, then rather than giving them names beginning with «private.», it would be better to indicate the restrictions using an attribute such as «private="yes"». However, you may sometimes have to deal with badly-designed documents, so the name() function provides a suitable mechanism. Take care, however, over the handling of namespace prefixes: unless you are certain that prefixes will be used consistently, it is better to test the local-name and the namespace URI rather than the value returned by name(). So the above example would be better written:

```
*[namespace-uri()='' and starts-with(local-name(),'private.')]
```

Another case where you need to use name() to test the name of a node is when you're comparing it against a variable or a parameter to the stylesheet. A common example is if you want to write a stylesheet to produce a sorted list of records, and you want the user to supply the sort key as a parameter. One user might want to sort books by author, another by publisher, and another by price. As the select expression in the <xsl:sort> element must be hard-coded in the stylesheet, the only way to achieve this is by writing:

7

Functions

```
<xsl:sort select="*[name()=$sort-key]"/>
```

where «$sort-key» is the stylesheet parameter containing the name of the field that the user wants to sort by.

Avoid using name() to generate a name in the result document, for example by writing «<xsl:element name="{name()}">». The problem is that any prefix in name() is interpreted in the light of namespace declarations appearing in the stylesheet, not namespace declarations in the original source document. The correct tool for this job is <xsl:copy>. There are cases where <xsl:copy> won't do the job: for example you may want to use the name of an attribute in the input document to generate the name of an element in the output document. In this case use local-name() and namespace-uri() separately, for example:

```
<xsl:element name="{local-name()}" namespace="{namespace-uri()}">
```

Examples

The following stylesheet outputs an HTML table listing the elements that appear in the source document.

Example: Listing the Element Names that Appear in a Document

Source

This stylesheet can be applied to any source document. The output is more interesting if the source document uses namespaces. For example, try applying the stylesheet to itself as its own source document.

Stylesheet

The stylesheet list-elements.xsl is shown below. It processes all the element nodes in the document, sorted by namespace URI and then local name, and for each one it outputs the name, the prefix, the local name, and the namespace URI. There is no attempt to remove duplicate entries.

The only way to determine the namespace prefix is to call name() and extract the part of the string before the colon, if any.

```
<?xml version="1.0" encoding="iso-8859-1"?>
<xsl:transform
 xmlns:xsl="http://www.w3.org/1999/XSL/Transform"
 version="1.0"
>

<xsl:template match="/">
<html><body>
<h1>Table of elements</h1>
<table border="1" cellpadding="5">
<tr><td>Element</td><td>Prefix</td>
```

```
<td>Local name</td><td>Namespace URI</td></tr>
    <xsl:apply-templates select="//*">
        <xsl:sort select="namespace-uri()"/>
        <xsl:sort select="local-name()"/>
    </xsl:apply-templates>
</table></body></html>
</xsl:template>

<xsl:template match="*">
    <xsl:variable name="prefix">
        <xsl:choose>
        <xsl:when test="contains(name(), ':')">
           <xsl:value-of select="substring-before(name(),':')"/>
        </xsl:when>
        <xsl:otherwise/>
        </xsl:choose>
    </xsl:variable>
    <tr>
    <td><xsl:value-of select="name()"/></td>
    <td><xsl:value-of select="$prefix"/></td>
    <td><xsl:value-of select="local-name()"/></td>
    <td><xsl:value-of select="namespace-uri()"/></td>
    </tr>
</xsl:template>

</xsl:transform>
```

Output

The illustration below shows the output when the stylesheet list-cities.xsl is used as the source document:

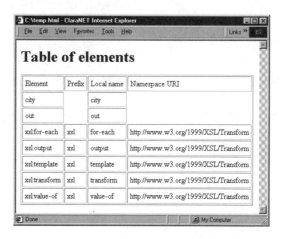

See also

local-name() on page 483
namespace-uri()

namespace-uri

The namespace-uri() function returns a string that represents the URI of the namespace in the expanded name of a node. Typically this will be a URI used in a namespace declaration, that is, the value of an xmlns or xmlns:* attribute.

For example, if you apply this function to the root node of the stylesheet by writing the expression «namespace-uri(document(''))», the result will be the string «http://www.w3.org/1999/XSL/Transform».

Defined in

XPath section 4.1

Format

```
namespace-uri()      ⇒  string
namespace-uri(node)  ⇒  string
```

Arguments

Argument	Data type	Meaning
node (optional)	node-set	Identifies the node whose namespace URI is required. If the node-set contains more than one node, the target node is the one that comes first in document order. If the node-set is empty, the function returns an empty string. If the argument is omitted, the target node is the context node. It is an error if the argument supplied is not a node-set.

Result

A string value: the namespace URI of the expanded name of the target node.

Rules

The namespace URI of a node depends on the node type, as follows:

Node type	Namespace URI
root	None, an empty string is returned.
element	If the element name as given in the source XML contained a colon, the value will be the URI from the namespace declaration corresponding to the element's prefix. Otherwise, the value will be the URI of the default namespace. If this is null, the result will be an empty string.
attribute	If the attribute name as given in the source XML contained a colon, the value will be the URI from the namespace declaration corresponding to the attribute's prefix. Otherwise, the namespace URI will be an empty string.
text	None, an empty string is returned.
processing instruction	None, an empty string is returned.
comment	None, an empty string is returned.
namespace	None, an empty string is returned.

Except for element and attribute nodes, namespace-uri() returns an empty string.

Usage

Let's start with some situations where you **don't** need this function.

If you want to test whether the current node belongs to a particular namespace, the best way to achieve this is using a NameTest of the form «prefix:*». For example, to test whether the current element belongs to the «http://ibm.com/ebiz» namespace, write:

```
<xsl:if test="self::ebiz:*" xmlns:ebiz="http://ibm.com/ebiz">
```

If you want to find the namespace URI corresponding to a given prefix the best solution is to use namespace nodes. You might need to do this if namespace prefixes are used in attribute values: the XSLT standard itself uses this technique in attributes such as extension-element-prefixes, and there is no reason why other XML document types should not do the same. If you have an attribute «@value» which you know takes the form of a namespace-qualified name, you can get the associated namespace URI by writing:

```
<xsl:variable name="prefix" select="substring-before(@value, ':')"/>
<xsl:variable name="ns-uri" select="string(namespace::*[name()=$prefix])"/>
```

7

Functions

The `namespace-uri()` function, by contrast, is useful in display contexts, where you just want to display the namespace URI of the current node, and also if you want to do more elaborate tests. For example you may know that there is a whole family of namespaces whose URIs all begin with `urn:schemas.biztalk`, and you may want to test whether the current node is in any one of these. You can achieve this by writing:

```
<xsl:if test="starts-with(namespace-uri(), 'urn:schemas.biztalk')>
```

Examples

The following stylesheet fragment determines the namespace URI of the current element, and then establishes the outermost ancestor on which that namespace is declared.

```
<xsl:template match="*">
    <xsl:variable name="uri" select="namespace-uri()"/>
    Namespace URI is <xsl:value-of select="$uri"/>
    Declared on element <xsl:value-of
        select="name(ancestor-or-self::*[namespace::*=$uri][last()])"/>
</xsl:template>
```

See also

local-name() on page 483
name() on page 485

normalize-space

The `normalize-space()` function removes leading and trailing whitespace from a string, and replaces internal sequences of whitespace with a single space character.

For example, the expression «`normalize-space(' x&#x9; y ')`» returns the string «x y»

Defined in

XPath section 4.2

Format

```
normalize-space()       ⇒ string
normalize-space(value)  ⇒ string
```

Arguments

Argument	Data type	Meaning
value (optional)	string	The input string. If the argument is not a string, it is converted to a string using the rules of the string() function. If the argument is omitted, it defaults to the string-value of the context node.

Result

A string obtained by removing leading and trailing whitespace from the input string, and replacing internal sequences of whitespace by a single space character.

Rules

Whitespace is defined as in the XML specification, as a sequence of space, tab, newline, and carriage return characters ($\#x9$, $\#xA$, $\#xD$, and $\#x20$).

Usage

It is often a good idea to apply the normalize-space function to any string read from the source document before testing its contents, as many users will assume that leading and trailing whitespace has no significance and that within the string, multiple spaces or tabs are equivalent to a single space.

Don't imagine that <xsl:strip-space> does this for you. The only thing it does is to remove text nodes that contain whitespace only.

One situation where it isn't safe to use normalize-space() is where you are processing mixed element content containing character-level formatting attributes. For example, if you process the nodes that result from the element:

```
<p>Some <i>very</i> traditional HTML</p>
```

then the spaces after «Some» and before «traditional» are significant, even though they appear respectively at the end and the beginning of a text node.

Examples

The following key declaration indexes the titles of books with whitespace normalized:

```
<xsl:key name="book-title" match="book" use="normalize-space(title)"/>
```

This may then be used to locate books by title as follows:

```
<xsl:for-each select="key('book-title', normalize-space($title))">
```

7

Functions

The effect is that it will be possible, without knowing how many spaces and newlines there are, to retrieve a book appearing in the source document as:

```
<book>
    <title>Object Oriented Languages -
                Basic Principles and Programming Techniques</title>
</book>
```

The normalize-space function can be particularly useful when processing a whitespace separated list of values. Such lists are used in some document designs, and they may also be constructed at run-time because there is no other way in XSLT of representing an array of computed values in a variable. Once the string has whitespace normalized, it is possible to use substring-before() to get the next token. To make this easier still, I usually add a space at the end of the string after normalization, so that every token is followed by a single space.

The following example shows how to use normalize-space to obtain a count of the number of words in a string.

Example: Using normalize-space() to get a Word Count

This stylesheet contains a general-purpose template for counting the words in a string. It demonstrates this template by counting the words in the string-value of each element in the document in turn.

Source

This stylesheet can be used with any XML source document. For example, try it with the file authors.xml listed in the example on page 472.

Stylesheet

The stylesheet, called word-count.xsl, contains a named template «word-count» which counts the number of words in the parameter named «text». It does this by using normalize-space() to replace all whitespace sequences with a single space. If the string is now empty, it returns zero, otherwise it calls itself to process the string after the first space character and adds one to the result.

The template rule for the root node is simply a demonstration script that shows how to use the «word-count» template to count the words in every element in the document.

```
<xsl:transform
 xmlns:xsl="http://www.w3.org/1999/XSL/Transform"
 version="1.0"
>

<xsl:template name="word-count">
    <xsl:param name="text"/>
    <xsl:variable name="ntext" select="normalize-space($text)"/>
    <xsl:choose>
```

```
        <xsl:when test="$ntext">
            <xsl:variable name="remainder">
                <xsl:call-template name="word-count">
                    <xsl:with-param name="text"
                            select="substring-after($ntext, ' ')"/>
                </xsl:call-template>
            </xsl:variable>
            <xsl:value-of select="$remainder + 1"/>
        </xsl:when>
        <xsl:otherwise>0</xsl:otherwise>
        </xsl:choose>
    </xsl:template>

    <xsl:template match="/">
        <xsl:for-each select="//*">
            <xsl:variable name="length">
                <xsl:call-template name="word-count">
                    <xsl:with-param name="text" select="."/>
                </xsl:call-template>
            </xsl:variable>
            <element name="{name()}" words="{$length}"/>;
        </xsl:for-each>
    </xsl:template>

</xsl:transform>
```

Output

If you apply this stylesheet to the file authors.xml as suggested, the output is:

```
<element name="authors" words="101"/>;
<element name="author" words="35"/>;
<element name="born" words="1"/>;
<element name="died" words="1"/>;
<element name="biog" words="33"/>;
<element name="author" words="66"/>;
<element name="born" words="1"/>;
<element name="died" words="1"/>;
<element name="biog" words="64"/>;
<element name="i" words="3"/>;
```

See also

concat() on page 430
substring-after() on page 515
substring-before() on page 516

7

Functions

not

The not() function returns the Boolean negation of its argument: if the argument is true, it returns false, and vice versa.

For example, the expression «not(true())» returns false.

Defined in

XPath section 4.3

Format

```
not(condition)  ⇒  boolean
```

Arguments

Argument	Data type	Meaning
condition	Boolean	The input condition. If the argument is not a Boolean, it is converted to a Boolean using the rules of the boolean() function.

Result

The Boolean negation of the argument value: true if the argument is false, false if the argument is true.

Rules

If the argument is not a Boolean, it is converted to a Boolean using the rules of the boolean() function.

If the value (after any conversion) is true, not() returns false; if it is false, not() returns true.

Usage

Note that writing «not($A=2)» is not the same thing as writing «$A!=2». The difference arises when $A is a node-set: «not($A=2)» will be true if $A does not contain a node that is equal to 2, while «$A!=2» is true if A does contain a node that is not equal to 2. For example. if $A is an empty node-set, «not($A=2)» will be true, while «$A!=2» will be false.

It is easy to forget this when testing attribute values: for example the following two examples behave the same way if the attribute go is present (they output «go» if the value is anything other than «no»), but they behave differently if the attribute is absent: the second one outputs «go», but the first one outputs nothing.

```
1: <xsl:if test="@go!='no'">go</xsl:if>
2: <xsl:if test="not(@go='no')">go</xsl:if>
```

When used with node-sets, the relational operators such as «=» and «!=» are subject to an implicit "if there exists" qualifier: «$X=$Y» means "if there exists a node x in $X and a node y in $Y such that x and y have the same string-value". If you want to achieve an "if all" qualifier, for example "if all nodes in the node-set have a size attribute equal to 0", then you can achieve this by negating both the condition and the expression as a whole: «not(@size!=0)».

Examples

The following test succeeds if the current node has no children:

```
<xsl:if test="not(node())">
```

The following test succeeds if the current node has no parent (that is, if it is a root node):

```
<xsl:if test="not(parent::*)">
```

The following <xsl:for-each> statement processes all the child elements of the current node except the <notes> elements:

```
<xsl:for-each select="*[not(self::notes)]">
```

The following test succeeds if the string-value of the current node is zero-length:

```
<xsl:if test="not(.)">
```

The following test succeeds if the name attribute of the current node is absent or is a zero-length string:

```
<xsl:if test="not(string(@name))">
```

The following test succeeds if the name attribute of the first node in node-set $ns is different from the name attribute of each subsequent node in the node-set (we assume that this attribute is present on all nodes in the node-set):

```
<xsl:if test="not($ns[1]/@name = $ns[position()!=1]/@name)">
```

See also

boolean() on page 426
false() on page 453
true() on page 528

number

The number() function converts its argument to a number.

For example, the expression «number('   -17.3')» returns the number –17.3

Defined in

XPath section 4.4

Format

```
number()  ⇒  number
number(value)  ⇒  number
```

Arguments

Argument	Data type	Meaning
value (optional)	any	The value to be converted. If the argument is omitted, the string-value of the context node is used.

Result

A number: the value of the argument after conversion to a number

Rules

The conversion rules depend on the data type of the value supplied, as defined in the following table.

Supplied data type	Conversion rules
Boolean	false becomes zero; true becomes one
number	the value is unchanged
string	leading and trailing whitespace is removed; if the resulting string comprises an optional minus sign followed by an XPath Number it is evaluated as if it were an XPath expression; otherwise the result value is NaN (not a number)
node-set	the node-set is converted to a string using the rules for the string() function, and the resulting string is then converted to a number in the same way as a string argument is converted

Supplied data type	Conversion rules
result tree fragment	the result tree fragment is converted to a string using the rules for the string() function, and the resulting string is then converted to a number in the same way as a string argument is converted

Usage

In most circumstances, conversion to a number is implicit so it is not necessary to use the number() function explicitly.

There is one important situation where conversion needs to be explicit: this is in a Predicate. The meaning of a predicate depends on the data type of the value, in particular, a numeric predicate is interpreted as a comparison with the context position. If the value is not numeric, it is converted to a Boolean.

So for example if a value is held in an attribute or in a result tree fragment is to be used as a numeric predicate, you should convert it explicitly to a number, thus:

```
<xsl:apply-templates select="$sales-figures[number(@month)]"/>
```

To test whether a value (for example, in an attribute) is numeric, use number() to convert it to a number and test the result against NaN (Not a Number). The most direct way to do this is:

```
<xsl:if test="string(number(@value))='NaN'"/>
```

Examples

Expression	Result
number(12.3)	12.3
number("12.3")	12.3
number(true())	1.0
number("xyz")	NaN
number("")	NaN

See also

boolean() on page 426
format-number() on page 455
string() on page 508
<xsl:number> on page 237, in Chapter 4

499

position

The position() function returns the value of the context position. When processing a list of nodes, position() gives the number assigned to the current node in the list, with the first node being numbered as 1.

Defined in

XPath section 4.1

Format

```
position()  ⇒  number
```

Arguments

None

Result

A number, the value of the *context position*. As the name implies, this is context dependant.

Rules

XPath specification defines the value of the position() function in terms of the *context position*. The XSLT specification uses different terminology: it talks about the *current node* and the *current node list*.

When a top-level expression is evaluated (that is, an expression that is not part of another expression), the context position is set to the position of the current node in the current node list. The nodes are numbered starting at 1. There are several possible settings:

❑   When a global variable is being evaluated, or in certain other contexts such as evaluating the use expression in <xsl:key>, the current node list contains a single node (the root), so the context position is always 1. This is also the case when the first template rule is invoked to process the root node.

❑   When <xsl:apply-templates> is called to process a set of nodes, the current node list is the list of nodes being processed, in the order in which they are processed, and the context position is therefore set successively to 1, 2, ... *n* as the nodes are processed. The position reflects the output order of the nodes, in other words the order after sorting, not necessarily the order in the source document.

❑   When <xsl:for-each> is called to process a set of nodes, the current node list is the list of nodes being processed, in the order in which they are processed, and the context position is therefore set successively to 1, 2, ... *n* as the nodes are processed. The position reflects the output order of the nodes, in other words the order after sorting, not necessarily the order in the source document.

❏   If the position() function is used within the select expression of an
    <xsl:sort> key, it refers to the position of the node before sorting. So, for
    example, if you want to sort nodes into reverse document order, you can do
    this by writing:

```
<xsl:sort select="position()" data-type="number" order="descending">
```

A more complex example, where the nodes are sorted into columns for display
in a table, is given in the entry for the last() function on page 478.

When a predicate is evaluated, either in an expression or in a pattern, the context
position is the relative position of the node currently being tested in that step of the
expression or pattern evaluation, counting the nodes in document order if it is a
forwards axis or in reverse document order if it is a reverse axis. For more details, see
Chapter 5 *Expressions*, and Chapter 6 *Patterns*.

Usage and Examples

The two main uses of the position() function are to *display* the current position, and
to *test* the current position.

Displaying the Current Position

In this role the position() function is an alternative to the <xsl:number> instruction,
and can be used for simple numbering of paragraphs, sections, or figures.

There is much less flexibility to control how the numbering is done than when using
<xsl:number>, but the position() function has two important advantages:

❏   It is generally faster

❏   It numbers items in the order they are output, whereas <xsl:number> can only
    allocate a number based on the position of a node in the source document. This
    means <xsl:number> is of little use when a list has been sorted using
    <xsl:sort>.

If you use position(), you can still exploit the formatting capabilities of
<xsl:number> by writing for example:

```
<xsl:number value="position()" format="(a)"/>
```

This determines the position of the node and formats the result according to the given
format pattern: the resulting sequence will be «(a)», «(b)», «(c)», and so on.

Testing the Current Position

It is possible to test the position of the current item either in a Boolean expression in an
<xsl:if> or <xsl:when> element, or in a predicate within a node-set expression or
pattern.

A common requirement is to treat the first or last item in a list differently from the rest. For example, to insert a horizontal rule after every item except the last, the following logic might be used:

```
<xsl:for-each select="item">
<xsl:sort select="@name"/>
   <p><xsl:value-of select="@name"/>:
      <xsl:value-of select="description"/></p>
   <xsl:if test="position() != last()">
      <hr/>
   </xsl:if>
</xsl:for-each>
```

Within a predicate in an expression or pattern, a numeric value represents an implicit test against the result of position(), for example «item[1]» is equivalent to «item[position()=1]», and «item[last()]» is equivalent to «item[position()=last()]».

> You can only use this shorthand in a predicate, that is within square brackets. If you use a numeric value in other contexts where a Boolean is expected, the number is converted to a Boolean on the basis that 0 is false, everything else is true. So <xsl:if test="1"> does *not* mean <xsl:if test="position()=1">; it means the same as <xsl:if test="true()">.

A common requirement when doing more complex processing is to separate the first node in a node-set from the set of nodes after the first.

Example: Using position() to Process a Node-set Recursively

Source

The source file shapes.xml represents a collection of shapes:

```
<shapes>
<rectangle width="10" height="30"/>
<square side="15"/>
<rectangle width="3" height="80"/>
<circle radius="10"/>
</shapes>
```

Stylesheet

The stylesheet area.xsl calculates the total area of these shapes. There is a separate rule for calculating the area of each kind of shape. The recursive template named «total-area» gets the area of the first shape by calling <xsl:apply-templates>, and adds the total area of the remaining shapes by calling itself with a list of shapes containing all the shapes except the first. When the set of shapes is empty, it returns zero.

```
<xsl:transform
 xmlns:xsl="http://www.w3.org/1999/XSL/Transform"
 version="1.0"
>

<xsl:template match="rectangle" mode="area">
    <xsl:value-of select="@width * @height"/>
</xsl:template>

<xsl:template match="square" mode="area">
    <xsl:value-of select="@side * @side"/>
</xsl:template>

<xsl:template match="circle" mode="area">
    <xsl:value-of select="3.14159 * @radius * @radius"/>
</xsl:template>

<xsl:template name="total-area">
    <xsl:param name="set-of-shapes"/>
    <xsl:choose>
    <xsl:when test="$set-of-shapes">
        <xsl:variable name="first">
            <xsl:apply-templates select="$set-of-shapes[1]" mode="area"/>
        </xsl:variable>
        <xsl:variable name="rest">
            <xsl:call-template name="total-area">
                <xsl:with-param name="set-of-shapes"
                    select="$set-of-shapes[position()!=1]"/>
            </xsl:call-template>
        </xsl:variable>
        <xsl:value-of select="$first + $rest"/>
    </xsl:when>
    <xsl:otherwise>0</xsl:otherwise>
    </xsl:choose>
</xsl:template>

<xsl:template match="shapes">
    <xsl:call-template name="total-area">
        <xsl:with-param name="set-of-shapes" select="*"/>
    </xsl:call-template>
</xsl:template>

</xsl:transform>
```

Output

Using Saxon, the output is:

```
1079.1590000000010550138540565967559814453125
```

If you wanted to display this rounded to five places after the decimal point, you could use format-number() with a format pattern of «0.0####».

See also

last() on page 478
<xsl:number> in Chapter 4, on page 237.

round

The round() function returns the closest integer to the numeric value of the argument.

For example, the expression «round(4.6)» returns 5.

Defined in

XPath section 4.4

Format

```
round(value)  ⇒  number
```

Arguments

Argument	Data type	Meaning
value	number	The input value. If it is not of type number, it is first converted to a number using the rules for the number() function.

Result

An integer value: the result of rounding the first argument to the nearest integer

Rules

If the value is not numeric, if is first converted to a number. For the detailed rules, see the description of the number() function on page 498. If the value is a node-set, these rules mean that the function applies to the value of the first node in the node-set, in document order.

Unlike some of the other numeric functions, the XPath specification is very precise about the results of round(). The rules are given in the table below. The concepts of positive and negative zero, and positive and negative infinity, are explained in Chapter 2, starting on page 81.

If the argument is...	Then the result is...
An integer N	N
Between N and N + 0.5	N

If the argument is...	Then the result is...
Exactly N + 0.5	N + 1
Between N + 0.5 and N + 1	N + 1
Between –0.5 and zero	Negative zero
Positive zero	Positive zero
Negative zero	Negative zero
Positive infinity	Positive infinity
Negative infinity	Negative infinity
NaN (not a number)	NaN

Usage

The round() function is useful when you want the nearest integer, for example when calculating an average, or when deciding the geometric coordinates for an object to be displayed.

Examples

Example: Using round() to Arrange Data in a Table

The following example constructs an HTML table in which the number of columns is supplied as a parameter, with the first column taking half the available width, and the remaining columns being of equal width to each other.

Source

The source file is sales.xml:

```
<sales>
   <product>Windows 98
      <period name="Q1">82</period>
      <period name="Q2">64</period>
      <period name="Q3">58</period>
   </product>
   <product>Windows NT
      <period name="Q1">17</period>
      <period name="Q2">44</period>
      <period name="Q3">82</period>
   </product>
</sales>
```

Stylesheet

The stylesheet sales-table.xsl is shown below. It calculates the width of the rows in the table based on the number of columns needed:

7

Functions

505

```
<xsl:transform
 xmlns:xsl="http://www.w3.org/1999/XSL/Transform"
 version="1.0"
>

<xsl:template match="sales">
<html><body>
    <h1>Product sales by period</h1>
    <xsl:variable name="cols" select="count(product[1]/period)"/>
    <table border="1" cellpadding="5" width="100%">
        <tr>
        <th width="50%">Product</th>
        <xsl:for-each select="product[1]/period">
            <th width="{round(50 div $cols)}%">
                <xsl:value-of select="@name"/>
            </th>
        </xsl:for-each>
    </tr>
    <xsl:for-each select="product">
    <tr>
        <td><xsl:value-of select="text()"/></td>
        <xsl:for-each select="period">
            <td>
                <xsl:value-of select="."/>
            </td>
        </xsl:for-each>
    </tr>
    </xsl:for-each>
    </table>
</body></html>
</xsl:template>

</xsl:transform>
```

Output

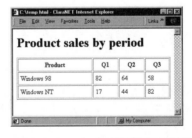

See also

ceiling() on page 428
floor() on page 454

starts-with

The starts-with() function tests whether one string starts with another string.

For example, the expression «starts-with('$17.30', '$')» returns true.

Defined in

XPath section 4.2

Format

```
starts-with(value, substring)  ⇒  boolean
```

Arguments

Argument	Data type	Meaning
value	string	The containing string. If the value is not a string, it is converted to a string using the rules of the string() function.
substring	string	The contained string. If the value is not a string, it is converted to a string using the rules of the string() function.

Result

A Boolean value: true if the first string starts with the second string, otherwise false.

Rules

The strings are compared, character by character, from the beginning. If the second string is exhausted before a pair of non-matching characters is found, the result is true; otherwise it is false. Characters match if they have the same Unicode value.

If the second string is empty, the result is always true. If the first string is empty, the result is true only if the second string is also empty. If the second string is longer than the first, the result is always false.

Usage and Examples

The starts-with() function is useful when the content of text values, or attributes, has some internal structure. For example, the following template rule matches all <link> elements that have an href attribute whose value starts with the character «#»:

```
<xsl:template match="link[starts-with(@href, '#')]">
. . .
</xsl:template>
```

Note

There is no ends-with() function. To test whether a string $A ends with a string $B, the simplest test is:

```
substring($A, string-length($A) - string-length($B) + 1) = $B
```

See also

contains() on page 432
string-length() on page 510

string

The string() function converts its argument to a string value.

For example, the expression «string(4.00)» returns the string «4».

Defined in

XPath section 4.2

Format

```
string()      ⇒  string
string(value) ⇒  string
```

Arguments

Argument	Data type	Meaning
value (optional)	any	The value to be converted. If the argument is omitted, it defaults to a node-set containing only the context node.

Result

A string value: the result of converting the argument to a string.

Rules

Values of any data type can be converted to a string. The rules are as follows.

Data type	Conversion rules
Boolean	The Boolean value false is converted to the string «false». The value true is converted to the string «true».

Data type	Conversion rules
number	NaN is represented as «NaN» Positive and negative zero are both represented as «0» Positive infinity is represented as «Infinity» Negative infinity is represented as «-Infinity» An integer is represented in decimal form with no decimal point and no leading zeros, preceded by a minus sign if it is negative. The result will be a valid XPath Number. Any other number is represented in decimal form with at least one digit before the decimal point and at least one digit after the decimal point, preceded by a minus sign if it is negative; there must be no leading zeros except immediately before the decimal point; after the decimal point there should be as many digits as are necessary to distinguish the number from other IEEE 754 numeric values. The result will be a valid XPath Number.
string	The value is unchanged.
node-set	If the node-set is empty, it is represented as the empty string. Otherwise, it is represented by the string-value of the node that is first in document order. The string value of a text node is the text content. The string value of a comment is the comment. The string value of a processing instruction is the data part The string value of a namespace node is the namespace URI. The string value of an attribute node is the attribute value. The string value of a root node or element node is the concatenation of the values of all its descendant text nodes, taken in document order.
result tree fragment	The string value of a result tree fragment is the concatenation of the values of all its descendant text nodes, in document order. The most common case is the trivial one: `<xsl:variable name="v">New York</xsl:variable>` Here, although the variable is technically a result tree fragment, it can be used to all intents and purposes as if it were a string with the value «New York».

7

Functions

Usage and Examples

It is not usually necessary to call the string() function explicitly, since it will normally be invoked automatically when a string is required and the supplied value is a different type.

An example of a situation where an explicit conversion is appropriate is when you want to force a string comparison of two values rather than a node-set comparison. For example, the following test succeeds if any <author> child of the current node has the value «J. B. Priestley».

```
<xsl:if test="author='J. B. Priestley'">
```

while the following succeeds only if the first <author> child, in document order, has this value:

```
<xsl:if test="string(author)='J. B. Priestley'">
```

However, it would be clearer in this case to write:

```
<xsl:if test="author[1]='J. B. Priestley'">
```

See also

boolean() on page 426
number() on page 498

string-length

The string-length() function returns the number of characters in a string value.

For example, the expression «string-length('Beethoven')» returns 9.

Defined in

XPath section 4.2

Format

```
string-length()        ⇒   number
string-length(value)   ⇒   number
```

Arguments

Argument	Data type	Meaning
value (optional)	string	The string whose length is required. If the value is not a string, it is converted to a string using the rules of the string() function. If the argument is omitted, the string-value of the context node is used.

Result

A number: the number of characters in the value of the argument.

Rules

Characters are counted as instances of the XML Char production. This means that a Unicode surrogate pair (a pair of 16-bit values used to represent a Unicode character in the range #x10000 to #x10FFFF) is treated as a single character.

It is the number of characters in the string that matters, not the way they are written in the source document. A character written using a character reference such as «ÿ» or an entity reference such as «&» is still one character.

Unicode combining and non-spacing characters are counted individually, unless the implementation has normalized them. The implementation is allowed to turn strings into canonical form, but is not required to do so. In canonical form accents and diacriticals will typically be merged with the letter that they modify into a single character. This means that in such cases, the result of the string-length() function is not precisely defined.

Usage

The string-length() function can be useful when deciding how to allocate space on the output medium. For example, if a list is displayed in multiple columns then the number of columns may be determined by some algorithm based on the maximum length of the strings to be displayed.

It is **not** necessary to call string-length() to determine whether a string is empty (null), because converting the string to a Boolean, either explicitly using the boolean() function, or implicitly by using it in a Boolean context, returns true only if the string has a length of one or more. For the same reason, it is not usually necessary to call string-length() when processing the characters in a string using a recursive iteration, since the terminating condition when the string is empty can be tested by converting it to a Boolean.

7

Functions

Examples

The following table shows the result of the `string-length()` function for some example inputs:

Expression	Result
string-length('abc')	3
string-length('')	0
string-length('<>')	2
string-length('&#xFFFD;')	1
string-length('𠀀')	1

See also

substring()

substring

The `substring()` function returns part of a string value, determined by character positions within the string. Character positions are counted from one.

For example, the expression «`substring('Goldfarb', 5, 3)`» returns the string «far».

Defined in

XPath section 4.2

Format

```
substring(value, start)  ⇒  string
substring(value, start, length)  ⇒  string
```

Arguments

Argument	Data type	Meaning
value	string	The containing string. If the value is not a string, it is converted to a string using the rules of the `string()` function.
start	number	The position in the containing string of the first character to be included in the result string. If the value is not a number, it is converted to a number using the rules of the `number()` function.

Argument	Data type	Meaning
length (optional)	number	The number of characters to be included in the result string. If the value is not a number, it is converted to a number using the rules of the number() function. If the argument is omitted, characters are taken from the start position up to the end of the containing string.

Result

A string: the required substring of the containing string.

Rules

Informally, the function returns a string consisting of the characters in the *value* string starting at position *start*; if a *length* is given, the returned string contains this many characters, otherwise it contains all characters up to the end of the *value*.

Characters within a string are numbered 1, 2, 3 ... *n*. This will be familiar to Visual Basic programmers but not to those accustomed to C or Java, where numbering starts at zero.

Characters are counted as instances of the XML Char production. This means that a Unicode surrogate pair (a pair of 16-bit values used to represent a Unicode character in the range #x10000 to #x10FFFF) is treated as a single character.

Combining and non-spacing characters are counted individually, unless the implementation has normalized them. The implementation is allowed to turn strings into canonical form, but is not required to do so. In canonical form accents and diacritics will typically be merged with the letter that they modify into a single character.

The formal rules are surprisingly complex, because they need to take into account conditions such as the start or length being negative, NaN, fractional, or infinite (for a description of the number data type, see Chapter 2, page 81). The rules are as follows:

> **Let start be the numeric value of the second argument.**
> **Let length be the numeric value of the third argument, if specified.**
>
> **If length was specified, the returned string contains those characters for which the position p of the character in the containing string satisfies: p >= round(start) and p < round(start) + round(length)**
>
> **If length was omitted, the returned string contains those characters for which the position p of the character in the containing string satisfies: p >= round(start)**

Rounding is done using the round() function. The comparisons and arithmetic are done using IEEE 754 arithmetic, which has some interesting (but not particularly useful) consequences if values such as infinity and NaN, or indeed any non-integer values are used: the rules for IEEE 754 arithmetic are summarized in Chapter 2.

More usefully, the formal rule tells us that if the *start* argument is less than one, the result always starts at the first character of the supplied string, while if it is greater than the length of the string, the result will always be an empty string. If the *length* argument is less than zero, it is treated as zero, and again an empty string is returned. If the *length* argument is greater than the number of available characters, then characters will be returned up to the end of the containing string.

Usage and Examples

The substring() function is useful when processing a string character-by-character. One common usage is to determine the first character of a string:

```
<xsl:variable name="drive-letter">
    <xsl:if test="substring($filename,2,1)=':')">
        <xsl:value-of select="substring($filename,1,1)"/>
    </xsl:if>
</xsl:variable>
```

Or when manipulating personal names in the conventional American format of first name, middle initial, last name:

```
<xsl:variable name="display-name">
    <xsl:value-of select="first-name"/>
    <xsl:text> </xsl:text>
    <xsl:value-of select="substring(middle-name, 1, 1)"/>
    <xsl:text> </xsl:text>
    <xsl:value-of select="last-name"/>
</xsl:variable>
```

You can use the substring() function in conjunction with string-length() to test whether a string ends with a particular suffix. Remember that character positions are numbered from one:

```
<xsl:variable name="linked-document">
    <xsl:if test="substring(@href, string-length(@href)-3) = '.xml'">
        <xsl:value-of select="document(@href)"/>
    </xsl:if>
</xsl:variable>
```

The following example tests whether a supplied string contains the sequence «#x#» where «x» is any single character:

```
<xsl:if test="contains($s, '#') and
                substring(substring-after($s, '#'), 2, 1)='#'">
```

See also

substring-after()
substring-before() on page 516
string-length() on page 510
contains() on page 432

substring-after

The substring-after() function returns that part of a string value that occurs after the first occurrence of some specified substring.

For example, the expression «substring-after('print=yes', '=')» returns «yes».

Defined in

XPath section 4.2

Format

substring-after(value, substring) ⇒ string

Arguments

Argument	Data type	Meaning
value	string	The containing string. If the argument is not a string, it is converted to a string using the rules of the string() function.
substring	string	The test string. If the argument is not a string, it is converted to a string using the rules of the string() function.

Result

A string containing those characters that follow the first occurrence of the test substring within the containing string.

Rules

If the containing string does not contain the test substring, the function returns an empty string. Note that this could also mean that the containing string ends with the test substring; the two cases can be distinguished by calling the contains() function.

If the containing string does contain the test substring, the function returns a string made up of all the characters that appear in the containing string after the first occurrence of the test substring.

7

Functions

If the test substring is empty, the function returns the containing string.

If the containing string is empty, the function returns an empty string.

Usage and Examples

The `substring-after()` function is useful when splitting a string that contains delimiter characters. For example, when the string is a whitespace-separated list of tokens, the first token can be obtained using

```
substring-before($s, ' ')
```

and the rest of the string using

```
substring-after($s, ' ')
```

It is a good idea to use `normalize-space()` to make sure that each separator is a single space character, and it is also useful to use `concat()` to add an extra space character at the end so that these functions work properly when the list contains a single token.

The following example takes a whitespace-separated list and outputs each token separated by an empty `<br/>` element.

```
<xsl:template name="output-tokens">
  <xsl:param name="list"/>
  <xsl:variable name="nlist"
    select="concat(normalize-space($list),' ')"/>
  <xsl:variable name="first" select="substring-before($nlist, ' ')"/>
  <xsl:variable name="rest" select="substring-after($nlist, ' ')"/>
  <xsl:value-of select="$first"/>
  <xsl:if select="$rest">
    <br/>
    <xsl:call-template name="output-tokens">
      <xsl:with-param name="list" select="$rest"/>
    </xsl:call-template>
  </xsl:if>
</xsl:template>
```

See also

contains() on page 432
substring() on page 512
substring-before()

substring-before

The `substring-before()` function returns that part of a string value that occurs before the first occurrence of some specified substring.

For example, the value of «`substring-before('print=yes', '=')`» is the string «print».

Defined in

XPath section 4.2

Format

```
substring-before(value, substring)  ⇒  string
```

Arguments

Argument	Data type	Meaning
value	string	The containing string. If the argument is not a string, it is converted to a string using the rules of the `string()` function.
substring	string	The test substring. If the argument is not a string, it is converted to a string using the rules of the `string()` function.

Result

A string containing those characters that precede the first occurrence of the test substring within the containing string

Rules

If the containing string does not contain the test substring, the function returns an empty string. Note that this could also mean that the containing string starts with the test string; the two cases can be distinguished by calling the `starts-with()` function.

If the containing string does contain the test substring, the function returns a string made up of all the characters that appear in the containing string before the first occurrence of the test substring.

If either the test substring or the containing string is empty, the function returns an empty string.

Usage and Examples

An example of the use of `substring-after()` and `substring-before()` to process a whitespace-separated list of tokens is given under `substring-after()` on page 515.

If the only reason for using `substring-before()` is to test whether the string has a given prefix, use `starts-with()` instead. You could write:

```
<xsl:if test="substring-before($url, ':')='https'">
```

7

Functions

but the following is simpler:

```
<xsl:if test="starts-with($url, 'https:')">
```

The substring-before() and substring-after() functions can be useful to replace a portion of a string. The translate() function cannot be used to substitute one word for another. For such processing, it is necessary to use a combination of contains(), substring-before(), substring-after(), and possibly concat(). This is illustrated in the example below.

Example: Replacing All Occurrences of a String

This stylesheet replaces all occurrences of a given string by another string, within any text node of the source document. The replaced string is given by the global parameter «replace», the replacement string by the parameter «by».

Source

The stylesheet works with any source document. For example, try it with the file authors.xml, with parameters replace=author by=writer.

Stylesheet

The stylesheet replace.xsl copies all elements and attributes unchanged, but processes text nodes using the named template «do-replace» which replaces all occurrences of the «replace» string with the «by» string. It does the first replacement directly, then calls itself recursively to do the remainder.

To process this stylesheet you need to supply global parameters. The way you do this depends on the product: for example, with Saxon use the command line:

```
saxon source.xml replace.xsl replace=xxx by=yyy
```

With xt, write:

```
xt source.xml replace.xsl replace=xxx by=yyy
```

```
<xsl:transform
  xmlns:xsl="http://www.w3.org/1999/XSL/Transform"
  version="1.0"
>

<xsl:param name="replace"/>
<xsl:param name="by"/>

<xsl:template name="do-replace">
    <xsl:param name="text"/>
    <xsl:choose>
    <xsl:when test="contains($text, $replace)">
        <xsl:value-of select="substring-before($text, $replace)"/>
        <xsl:value-of select="$by"/>
        <xsl:call-template name="do-replace">
```

```
              <xsl:with-param name="text"
                         select="substring-after($text, $replace)"/>
        </xsl:call-template>
    </xsl:when>
    <xsl:otherwise>
       <xsl:value-of select="$text"/>
    </xsl:otherwise>
    </xsl:choose>

</xsl:template>

<xsl:template match="*">
    <xsl:copy>
    <xsl:copy-of select="@*"/>
    <xsl:apply-templates/>
    </xsl:copy>
</xsl:template>

<xsl:template match="text()">
    <xsl:call-template name="do-replace">
        <xsl:with-param name="text" select="."/>
    </xsl:call-template>
</xsl:template>

</xsl:transform>
```

Output

The result of processing the file authors.xml with «replace=author by=***» is shown below:

```
<authors>

<author name="A. A. Milne">
<born>1852</born>
<died>1956</died>
<biog>Alan Alexander Milne, educated at Westminster School and Trinity
College Cambridge, became a prolific *** of plays, novels, poetry, short
stories, and essays, all of which have been overshadowed by his children's
books.</biog>
    </author>

<author name="Daisy Ashford">
<born>1881</born>
<died>1972</died>
<biog>Daisy Ashford (Mrs George Norman) wrote <i>The Young Visiters</i>, a
small comic masterpiece, while still a young child in Lewes. It was found in a
drawer in 1919 and sent to Chatto and Windus, who published it in the same
year with an introduction by J. M. Barrie, who had first insisted on meeting
the *** in order to check that she was genuine.</biog>
    </author>

</authors>
```

7

Functions

519

See also

contains() on page 432
starts-with() on page 507
substring() on page 512
substring-after() on page 515

sum

The sum() function calculates the total of a set of numeric values contained in a node-set.

For example, if the context node is the element `<rect x="20" y="30"/>`, then the expression «sum(@*)» returns 50. (The expression «@*» is a node-set containing all the attributes of the context node).

Defined in

XPath section 4.4

Format

```
sum(nodes)  ⇒  number
```

Arguments

Argument	Data type	Meaning
nodes	node-set	The set of nodes to be totaled. It is an error if the argument is not a node-set.

Result

A number: the result of taking the string-value of each node in the node-set, converting it to a number, and totaling these numeric values.

Rules

The conversion of the string-value of each node to a number follows the rules of the number() function.

The totaling of the numeric values follows the arithmetic rules defined in IEEE 754.

A consequence of these rules is that if there is any node in the node-set whose string-value cannot be converted to a number, the result of the sum() function will be NaN (not a number).

If the node-set is empty, the result is zero.

Usage

The sum() function can be used to create totals and subtotals in a report. It is also useful for calculating geometric dimensions on the output page.

A problem that sometimes arises is how to get a total over a set of values that aren't present directly in the source file, but are calculated from it. For example, if the source document contains <book> elements with attributes price and sales, how would you calculate the total sales revenue, which is obtained by multiplying price by sales for each book, and totaling the result over all books? Or how would you total a set of numbers if each one has a leading «$» sign which you need to strip off first? The short answer is that you can't use the sum() function to do this.

In fact there are two limitations on the use of sum():

❑   All the values to be totaled must be explicitly present as nodes in the source document, it is not possible to perform any preprocessing of the values, for example customized string-to-number conversion, before the calculation is done.

❑   If any value is non-numeric (this includes an absent value), the result will be NaN.

If the data doesn't satisfy these constraints, it will be necessary to process the node-set explicitly using a recursive template. There is an example that does this, calculating the total area of a set of shapes, on page 502.

Examples

Example: A League Table

This example uses the count() and sum() functions to perform various calculations on the results of a set of soccer matches (the Group A matches from the 1998 World Cup Finals)

Source

The source file is soccer.xml:

```
<results group="A">
<match>
<date>10-Jun-98</date>
    <team score="2">Brazil</team>
    <team score="1">Scotland</team>
</match>
<match>
    <date>10-Jun-98</date>
    <team score="2">Morocco</team>
    <team score="2">Norway</team>
</match>
```

```
<match>
    <date>16-Jun-98</date>
    <team score="1">Scotland</team>
    <team score="1">Norway</team>
</match>
<match>
    <date>16-Jun-98</date>
    <team score="3">Brazil</team>
    <team score="0">Morocco</team>
</match>
<match>
    <date>23-Jun-98</date>
    <team score="1">Brazil</team>
    <team score="2">Norway</team>
</match>
<match>
<date>23-Jun-98</date>
    <team score="0">Scotland</team>
    <team score="3">Morocco</team>
</match>
</results>
```

Stylesheet

The stylesheet is in file league.xsl.

The stylesheet creates two global variables: «teams», which is the set of distinct <team> elements in the document (any <team> element that has the same string-value as a preceding <team> element is not included), and «matches» which is the set of all <match> elements.

For each team, the stylesheet calculates the number of matches played, won, drawn, lost, the total number of goals scored by that team, and the total number of goals scored by opposing teams.

```
<xsl:transform
 xmlns:xsl="http://www.w3.org/1999/XSL/Transform"
 version="1.0"
>

<xsl:variable name="teams" select="//team[not(.=preceding::team)]"/>
<xsl:variable name="matches" select="//match"/>

<xsl:template match="results">
<html><body>
    <h1>Results of Group <xsl:value-of select="@group"/></h1>

    <table cellpadding="5">
       <tr>
         <td>Team</td>
         <td>Played</td>
```

```
                    <td>Won</td>
                    <td>Drawn</td>
                    <td>Lost</td>
                    <td>For</td>
                    <td>Against</td>
            </tr>
        <xsl:for-each select="$teams">
                <xsl:variable name="this" select="."/>
                <xsl:variable name="played" select="count($matches[team=$this])"/>
                <xsl:variable name="won"
                    select="count($matches[team[.=$this]/@score &gt;
                                        team[.!=$this]@score])"/>
                <xsl:variable name="lost"
                    select="count($matches[team[.=$this]/@score &lt;
                                        team[.!=$this]/@score])"/>
                <xsl:variable name="drawn"
                    select="count($matches[team[.=$this]/@score =
                                        team[.!=$this]/@score])"/>
                <xsl:variable name="for"
                    select="sum($matches/team[.=current()]/@score)"/>
                <xsl:variable name="against"
                    select="sum($matches[team=current()]/team/@score) - $for"/>
                <tr>
                <td><xsl:value-of select="."/></td>
                <td><xsl:value-of select="$played"/></td>
                <td><xsl:value-of select="$won"/></td>
                <td><xsl:value-of select="$drawn"/></td>
                <td><xsl:value-of select="$lost"/></td>
                <td><xsl:value-of select="$for"/></td>
                <td><xsl:value-of select="$against"/></td>
                </tr>
        </xsl:for-each>
        </table>
</body></html>
</xsl:template>
</xsl:transform>
```

Output

7

Functions

See also

count( ) on page 434

system-property

The system-property( ) function returns information about the processing environment.

For example, until such time as a new version of XSLT is published, the expression «system-property('xsl:version')» always returns 1.0

Defined in

XSLT section 12.4

Format

```
system-property(name)  ⇒  any
```

Arguments

Argument	Data type	Meaning
name	string	Specifies the name of the system property required. If the argument is not a string, it is converted to a string using the rules of the string( ) function. The value of the string should be a QName that identifies a system property. If there is no system property with this name, the function returns an empty string.

Result

The data type of the result, as well as its value, depends on the system property requested.

Rules

The supplied argument is converted into an expanded name using the namespace declarations in scope for the stylesheet element that contains the call on system-property( ).

There are three system properties that every implementation must support: these are all in the XSLT namespace.

System Property Name	Value
xsl:version	A number giving the version of XSLT implemented by the processor. For the current XSLT specification, this is required to be 1.0. Note that this is a number not a string, so if you display it using <xsl:value-of> it will be shown as «1».
xsl:vendor	A string identifying the vendor of the XSLT processor. In practice it will probably also identify the product name, but the actual value is implementer-defined.
xsl:vendor-url	A string: the URL of the vendor's web site

Any additional system properties returned by this function are implementor-defined. There is no explicit rule against these using the default namespace or even the XSLT namespace, but an implementor sticking to the spirit of the standard would normally provide any additional properties in a vendor-specific namespace.

An earlier draft of the XSLT specification stated that this function should give access to operating system environment variables. It would not be surprising to find implementations that provide this capability, but it is not mandatory.

Usage

The system-property() function can be used to determine details about the processor running the stylesheet, either for display purposes (for example, to produce a comment in the generated output), or to apply conditional logic.

Generally it is best to avoid using this function to test whether particular features are available. The functions function-available() and element-available() and the <xsl:fallback> instruction serve this need better, and the forwards compatibility features described on page 127, in Chapter 3 can be used to ensure that a stylesheet can work with processors that implement an older dialect of XSLT.

Examples

The following code outputs a documentary comment into the generated HTML:

```
<HTML>
    <xsl:comment>Generated using XSLT stylesheet abc.xsl
                using <xsl:value-of select="system-roperty('xsl:vendor')"/>
                at XSLT version
        <xsl:value-of select="system-property('xsl:version')"/>
    </xsl:comment>
    . . .
```

7

Functions

See also

element-available() on page 449
function-available() on page 459
<xsl:fallback> on page 197, in Chapter 4

translate

The translate() function substitutes characters in a supplied string with nominated replacement characters. It can also be used to remove nominated characters from a string.

For example, the result of «translate('ABC-123', '-', '/')» is the string «ABC/123».

Defined in

XPath section 4.2

Format

```
translate(value, from, to)  ⇒  string
```

Arguments

Argument	Data type	Meaning
value	string	The supplied string. If the argument is not a string, it is converted to a string using the rules of the string() function.
from	string	The list of characters to be replaced. If the argument is not a string, it is converted to a string using the rules of the string() function.
to	string	The list of replacement characters. If the argument is not a string, it is converted to a string using the rules of the string() function.

Result

A string derived from the supplied string, but with those characters that appear in the second argument replaced by the corresponding characters from the third argument, or removed if there is no corresponding character.

Rules

For each character in the supplied string, one of three possible actions is taken:

❏ If the character is not present in the list of characters to be replaced, the character is copied to the result string unchanged.

❏ If the character is present at position P in the list of characters to be replaced, and the list of replacement characters is of length P or greater, then the character at position P in the list of replacement characters is copied to the result string

❏ If the character is present at position P in the list of characters to be replaced, and the list of replacement characters is shorter than P, then no character is copied to the result string

Note that the third argument must be present, but it can be an empty string. In this case any character present in the second argument is removed from the supplied string.

If a character appears more than once in the list of characters to be replaced, the second and subsequent occurrences are ignored, as are the characters in the corresponding position in the third argument.

If the third argument is longer than the second, excess characters are ignored.

In these rules a *character* means an XML character, not a 16-bit Unicode code. This means that a Unicode surrogate pair (a pair of 16-bit values used to represent a Unicode character in the range #x10000 to #x10FFFF) is treated as a single character, whichever of the three strings it appears in.

Usage and Examples

The translate() function can be used to perform simple case conversion where the alphabet is known and of modest size. For example, if the data uses only unaccented Latin letters, conversion to uppercase can be achieved by writing:

```
translate($X,
  'abcdefghijklmnopqrstuvwxyz',
  'ABCDEFGHIJKLMNOPQRSTUVWXYZ')
```

The translate() function is useful to remove extraneous punctuation or whitespace: for example to remove all whitespace, hyphens, and parentheses from a telephone number, write:

```
translate($X, '&#x20;&#x9;&#xA;&#xD;()-', '')
```

Another use for translate() is to test for the presence of a particular character or range of characters. For example, to test whether a string contains a sequence of three or more ASCII digits, write:

7

Functions

```
contains(translate($X, '0123456789', '9999999999'), '999')
```

Similarly, translate can be used to normalize delimiters before using substring-after() or substring-before() to extract part of the string. If a filename consists of a sequence of names separated by «/» or «\» characters, then the following expression will extract the part of the filename before the first separator:

```
substring-before(translate($X, '\', '/'), '/')
```

See also

contains() on page 432
substring() on page 512
substring-after() on page 515
substring-before() on page 516

true

This function returns the Boolean value true.

Defined in

XPath section 4.3

Format

```
true()  ⇒  boolean
```

Arguments

None

Result

The Boolean value true

Rules

There are no Boolean constants available in XPath expressions, so the functions true() and false() can be used where a constant Boolean value is required.

Usage

There are few occasions where constant boolean values are required; the most common situation is in <xsl:with-param> when supplying a parameter to a template. See the example below.

Writing <xsl:when test="true()"> can be useful as a temporary expedient to force execution down a particular path, perhaps because other paths are still under development.

Example

The following code calls a named template, setting the parameter «verbose» to true:

```
<xsl:call-template name="do-the-work">
  <xsl:with-param name="verbose" select="true()"/>
</xsl:call-template>
```

See also

false() on page 453

unparsed-entity-uri

The unparsed-entity-uri() function gives access to declarations of unparsed entities in the DTD of the source document.

For example, if the DTD contains the declaration:

```
<!ENTITY weather-map SYSTEM "weather.jpeg" NDATA JPEG>
```

then the expression «unparsed-entity-uri('weather-map')» returns either the string «weather.jpeg», or an equivalent absolute URL.

Defined in

XSLT section 12.4

Format

```
unparsed-entity-uri(name)  ⇒  string
```

Arguments

Argument	Data type	Meaning
name	string	Specifies the name of the unparsed entity required. If the argument is not a string, it is converted to a string using the rules of the string() function. The value of the string should be an XML *Name*.

Result

A string containing the URI (the system identifier) of the unparsed entity with the given name, if there is one. Otherwise, an empty string.

Rules

If the document containing the context node includes an unparsed entity whose name is equal to the supplied string, a URI identifying that unparsed entity is returned. If there is no entity with this name, it returns an empty string.

If the system identifier is a relative URI, it is not specified whether the XSLT processor will expand it into an absolute URI before returning it. Generally the XSLT processor will pass on whatever it obtained from the XML parser, and the behavior of different XML parsers varies in this regard. The SAX interface, which many XSLT processors use to receive information from the XML parser, does not say whether the URI should be expanded.

Usage

An unparsed entity is an entity defined in the DTD using a declaration of the form:

```
<!ENTITY weather-map SYSTEM "weather.jpeg" NDATA JPEG>
```

It's the NDATA (meaning "not XML data") that makes it an unparsed entity; and because it is an unparsed entity, it can't be referenced using a normal entity reference of the form «&weather-map;» but must instead be referenced by name in an attribute of type ENTITY or ENTITIES, for example <forecastmap="weather-map">.

As the author of the stylesheet, you are expected to know that the map attribute is of type ENTITY (there's no way within XSLT of finding out), and to pick up the attribute value in a call such as «unparsed-entity-uri(@map)». This call returns the URI of the actual resource, that is the string «weather.jpeg», or, if the parser decides to expand it, something like «file:\c:\documents\forecasts\weather.jpeg». You might use this, for example, to generate an HTML <IMG> element in the output file.

XSLT provides no way of finding out the notation name («JPEG» in our example) or the URI for the notation, nor can you determine the public identifier of the entity if there was one.

> This is not exactly in the spirit of section 4.4.6 of the XML specification, which states: "When the name of an unparsed entity appears as a token in an attribute of declared type ENTITY or ENTITIES, a validating processor must inform the application of the system and public (if any) identifiers for both the entity and its associated notation". However, unparsed entities are hardly XML's most widely used feature, so it is unsurprising that XSLT support for them should be minimal.

The rules in the XSLT specification don't explicitly permit this, but in practice, if you use a non-validating XML parser to process the source document, the parser isn't obliged to pass information about unparsed entities to the XSLT processor, and the unparsed-entity-uri() function is therefore likely to return an empty string. If this happens, try using a validating XML parser – assuming of course that the source document is valid.

Examples

Given the entity definition

```
<!ENTITY weather-map SYSTEM "weather.jpeg" NDATA JPEG>
```

and the entity reference

```
<FORECAST MAP="weather-map"/>
```

the following code will insert an `<IMG>` element into the HTML output:

```
<xsl:template match="FORECAST">
    <IMG HREF="{unparsed-entity-uri(@MAP)}"/>
</xsl:template>
```

See also

Data Model, in Chapter 2 (starting on page 46).

Summary

The exploration of the function library available to the XLST programmer brings the reference part of this book to a close. You now have what I hope is a lucid and definitive reference guide to the XSLT language. The following chapters are designed to help you put the language to work, developing real-world applications. Chapter 8 investigates several possible design patterns for XSLT stylesheets.

7

Functions

531

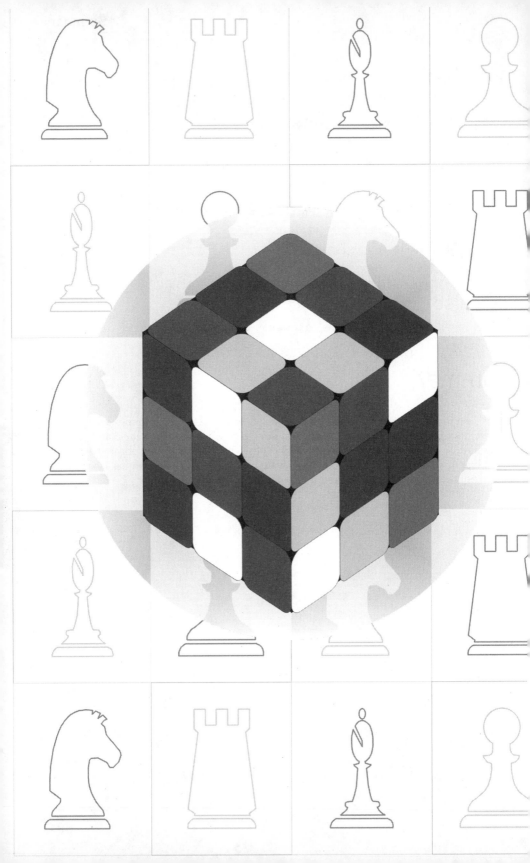

Stylesheet Design Patterns

In this chapter we'll look at four common **design patterns** for XSLT stylesheets.

The concept of design patterns was introduced by Erich Gamma, Richard Helm, Ralph Johnson, and John Vlissides in their classic book *Design Patterns: Elements of Reusable Object-Oriented Software* (Addison-Wesley Professional Computing) ISBN: 0201633612. Their idea was that there was a repertoire of techniques which were useful again and again. They presented 23 different design patterns for object oriented programming, claiming not that this was in some sense a complete list, but that the vast majority of programs written by experienced designers fell into one or more of these patterns.

For XSLT stylesheets, the vast majority of stylesheets I have seen fall into one of four design patterns. These are:

- Fill-in-the-blanks stylesheets
- Navigational stylesheets
- Rule-based stylesheets
- Computational stylesheets

Again, this doesn't mean that these are the only ways you can write stylesheets, nor does it mean that any stylesheet you write must follow one of these four patterns to the exclusion of the other three. It just means that a great many stylesheets actually written by experienced people follow one of these four patterns, and if you become familiar with these patterns, you will have a good repertoire of techniques that you can apply to solving any given problem.

I will describe the first three design patterns rather briefly, because they are not really very difficult. The fourth, the computational design pattern, is explored in much greater depth – not because it is encountered more often, but because it requires a different way of thinking about algorithms than you use with conventional procedural programming languages.

Fill-in-the-Blanks Stylesheets

Many proprietary templating languages have been built up around HTML. The template looks largely like a standard HTML file, but with the addition of extra tags used to retrieve variable data and insert it at a particular point in the HTML data page. The designers of XSLT took care to ensure that in spite of the power of XSLT as a full transformation language, it would still be possible to use it in this simple way, bringing it within the reach of non-programmers with HTML authoring skills.

Here's an example of such a stylesheet. It uses the **simplified stylesheet** syntax (or *literal result element as stylesheet* syntax as it is clumsily-named in the standard), so the `<xsl:stylesheet>` element and the `<xsl:template match="/">` element are implicit.

Example: A "Fill-in-the-Blanks" Stylesheet

Input

This XML document, `orgchart.xml`, represents an organization chart showing the senior management of a certain company at a particular date. It is organized as a recursive structure that directly reflects the management hierarchy:

```
<orgchart date="28 March 2000">
<person>
<name>Keith Todd</name>
<title>Chief Executive Officer</title>
<reports>
   <person>
      <name>Andrew Boswell</name>
      <title>Technical Director</title>
      <reports>
         <person>
            <name>Dave McVitie</name>
            <title>Chief Engineer</title>
         </person>
         <person>
            <name>John Elmore</name>
            <title>Director of Research</title>
         </person>
      </reports>
```

```
    </person>
    <person>
        <name>Alan Gibson</name>
        <title>Operations and Finance</title>
    </person>
    <person>
        <name>Fiona Colquhoun</name>
        <title>Human Resources</title>
    </person>
    <person>
        <name>John Davison</name>
        <title>Marketing</title>
    </person>
    <person>
        <name>Marie-Anne van Ingen</name>
        <title>International</title>
    </person>
    </reports>
    </person>
</orgchart>
```

Stylesheet

There are many creative ways you could display this data: using SVG graphics, explorer-style trees implemented in client-side JavaScript, or just indented lists. I'm not trying to teach you any clever HTML tricks, so in this stylesheet (orgchart.xsl) I'll show the data instead as a rather boring table, with one row per person, and three columns for the person's name, their title, and the name of their boss:

```
<html xmlns:xsl="http://www.w3.org/1999/XSL/Transform"
    xsl:version="1.0">
<head>
    <title>Management Structure</title>
</head>
<body>
    <h1>Management Structure</h1>
    <p>The following responsibilies were announced on
        <xsl:value-of select="/orgchart/@date"/>:</p>
    <table border="2" cellpadding="5">
    <tr>
<th>Name</th><th>Role</th><th>Reporting to</th>
    </tr>
```

```
        <xsl:for-each select="//person">
           <tr>
              <td><xsl:value-of select="name"/></td>
              <td><xsl:value-of select="title"/></td>
              <td><xsl:value-of select="ancestor::person[1]/name"/></td>
           </tr>
        </xsl:for-each>
        </table>
        <hr/>
     </body>
     </html>
```

The key to this design pattern is that the stylesheet has the same structure as the desired output. Fixed content is included directly in the stylesheet as text or as literal result elements, while variable content is included by means of `<xsl:value-of>` instructions that extract the relevant data from the source document. Repeated sections of output, typically rows in a table or items in a list, can be enclosed by `<xsl:for-each>`, and conditional sections by `<xsl:if>` or `<xsl:choose>`.

Output

This kind of stylesheet makes very limited use of XSLT's power, but it is very similar to a wide variety of proprietary templating languages currently in use, and experience has shown that these are easy for experienced HTML authors to learn, even if they have no programming training. This is an important consideration, because on many larger web sites there is a constant need to introduce new page templates at very short notice, and this becomes much easier to achieve if content authors and editors can do the work themselves.

One restriction, of course, is that the input has to come from an XML document. This contrasts with most of the proprietary languages, where the input often comes directly from a relational database. The most elegant way around this restriction is to provide a way of extracting the required data into the tree format used by your chosen XSLT processor, without the need for an actual XML document as an intermediary format. Many XSLT processors accept input in the form of either a DOM tree, or a stream of SAX events, so you could write an interface module that does the database query and delivers the data in this form for use by the stylesheet authors. Another approach is to use the document() function (described in Chapter 7, page 440) with a URI that addresses a servlet with parameters to retrieve the required data. As you might expect, Oracle with their XSQL pages and XSQL servlet technology have probably gone further than most vendors in the direction of XML/XSLT/SQL integration: follow the links given in Chapter 10, page 644.

Navigational Stylesheets

Navigational stylesheets are a natural progression from simple fill-in-the-blanks stylesheets.

Like fill-in-the-blanks stylesheets, a navigational stylesheet is still essentially output-oriented. However, it is now likely to use named templates as subroutines to perform commonly-needed tasks, it is likely to use variables to calculate values needed in more than one place, and it may use constructs such as keys, parameters, and sorting.

Whereas a fill-in-the-blanks stylesheet looks like HTML sprinkled with a few extra control statements, a navigational stylesheet (once you look beyond the angle-bracket syntax) looks very like a conventional procedural program with variables, conditional statements, for loops, and subroutine calls.

Navigational stylesheets are often used to produce reports on data-oriented XML documents, where the structure of the source document is regular and predictable.

8

Design Patterns

Example: A Navigational Stylesheet

Input

Suppose the source document, booklist.xml, looks like this:

```xml
<booklist>
  <book>
    <title>Angela's Ashes</title>
    <author>Frank McCourt</author>
    <publisher>HarperCollins</publisher>
    <isbn>0 00 649840 X</isbn>
    <price>6.99</price>
    <sales>235</sales>
```

```
    </book>
    <book>
        <title>Sword of Honour</title>
        <author>Evelyn Waugh</author><publisher>Penguin Books</publisher>
        <isbn>0 14 018967 X</isbn>
        <price>12.99</price>
        <sales>12</sales>
    </book>
</booklist>
```

Stylesheet

The following navigational stylesheet (booksales.xsl) produces a report on the total number of sales for each publisher.

Note the global variable «$publishers». This is a node-set containing one <publisher> element for each distinct publisher found in the source file. The way it works is that it selects only those publishers that are not the same as any previous publisher, in other words, it filters out the duplicates.

```
<xsl:stylesheet
    xmlns:xsl="http://www.w3.org/1999/XSL/Transform"
    version="1.0">

<xsl:key name="pub" match="book" use="publisher"/>

<xsl:variable name="publishers"
    select="//publisher[not(.=preceding::publisher)]"/>

<xsl:template match="/">
<html>
<head>
    <title>Sales volume by publisher</title>
</head>
<body>
    <h1>Sales volume by publisher</h1>
    <table>
        <tr>
        <th>Publisher</th><th>Total Sales Value</th>
        </tr>
    <xsl:for-each select="$publishers">
        <tr>
        <td><xsl:value-of select="."/></td>
        <td><xsl:call-template name="total-sales"/></td>
```

```
          </tr>
        </xsl:for-each>
      </table>
  </body>
</html>
</xsl:template>

<!-- calculate total book sales for the current publisher -->
<xsl:template name="total-sales">
    <xsl:value-of select="sum(key('pub',string(.))/sales)"/>
</xsl:template>
</xsl:stylesheet>
```

This stylesheet is not very far removed from the fill-in-the-blanks example earlier in the chapter. But because it uses some top-level elements such as `<xsl:key>` and a named template, it now needs to use the full syntax with an `<xsl:stylesheet>` element.

Output

```
<html>
  <head>
      <META http-equiv="Content-Type" content="text/html; charset=utf-8">
      <title>Sales volume by publisher</title>
  </head>
  <body>
      <h1>Sales volume by publisher</h1>
      <table>
        <tr>
            <th>Publisher</th>
            <th>Total Sales Value</th>
        </tr>
        <tr>
            <td>HarperCollins</td>
            <td>235</td>
        </tr>
        <tr>
            <td>Penguin Books</td>
            <td>12</td>
        </tr>
      </table>
  </body>
</html>
```

8

Design Patterns

The obvious difference between a fill-in-the-blanks stylesheet and this navigational stylesheet is that the `<xsl:stylesheet>` and `<xsl:template>` elements are now explicit, which makes it possible to introduce other top-level elements such as `<xsl:key>` and a global `<xsl:variable>`. More subtly, the range of XSLT features used means that this stylesheet has crossed the boundary from being an HTML document with added control instructions, to being a real program. The boundary, though, is a rather fuzzy one, with no visa required to cross it, so many people who have learnt to write simple fill-in-the-blanks stylesheets should be able, as they expand their knowledge, to progress to writing navigational stylesheets of this kind.

Although the use of flow-of-control instructions like `<xsl:if>`, `<xsl:call-template>` and `<xsl:for-each>` gives such a stylesheet a procedural feel, in fact it does not violate the original concept that XSLT should be a declarative language. This is because the instructions do not have to be executed in the order they are written – variables can't be updated, so the result of one instruction can't affect the next one. For example, it's easy to think of the `<xsl:for-each>` instruction in this example processing the selected nodes in document order and adding them one-by-one to the result tree; but it would be equally valid for an XSLT processor to process them in reverse order, or in parallel, so long as the nodes are added to the result tree in the right place. That's why I was careful to call this design pattern *navigational* rather than *procedural*. It's navigational in that you say exactly where to find the nodes in the source tree that you want to visit, but it's not procedural, because you don't define the order in which you will visit them.

Rule-Based Stylesheets

A rule-based stylesheet is one that consists primarily of rules describing how different features of the source document should be processed: rules such as: "if you find a `<species>` element, display it in italics".

Some would say that this rule-based approach is the essence of the XSLT language, the principal way that it is intended to be used. I would say that it's one way of writing stylesheets: often the best way, but not the only way, and not necessarily the best answer in every situation.

Unlike navigational stylesheets, a rule-based stylesheet is not structured according to the desired output layout. In fact, it makes minimal assumptions about the structure of either the source document or the result document. Rather, the structure reads like an inventory of components that might be encountered in the source document, arranged in arbitrary order.

Rule-based stylesheets are therefore at their most useful when processing source documents whose structure is flexible or unpredictable, or which may change a lot in the future. It is very useful when the same repertoire of elements can appear in many different document structures, so a rule like "display dates in the format *23 March 2000*" can be reused in many different contexts.

Rule-based stylesheets are a natural evolution of CSS and CSS2 stylesheets. In CSS, you can define rules of the form "for this set of elements, use this display rendition". In XSLT, the rules become much more flexible, in two directions: the pattern language for defining which elements you are talking about is much richer, and the actions you can define when the rule is fired are vastly more wide-ranging.

A simple rule-based stylesheet will consist of one rule for each element type. The typical rule matches a particular element type, outputs an HTML tag to define the rendition of that element, and calls <xsl:apply-templates> to process the child nodes of the template. This causes text nodes within the element to be copied to the output, and nested child elements to be processed each according to its own template rule.

Example: A Rule-Based Stylesheet

Input

The input scene2.xml is a scene from a play: Act I Scene 2 of Shakespeare's *Othello*. It starts like this:

```
<?xml version="1.0" encoding="iso-8859-1" ?>
<SCENE>
    <TITLE>SCENE II.  Another street.</TITLE>
    <STAGEDIR>Enter OTHELLO, IAGO, and Attendants with
            torches</STAGEDIR>
    <SPEECH>
        <SPEAKER>IAGO</SPEAKER>
        <LINE>Though in the trade of war I have slain men,</LINE>
        <LINE>Yet do I hold it very stuff o' the conscience</LINE>
        <LINE>To do no contrived murder: I lack iniquity</LINE>
        <LINE>Sometimes to do me service: nine or ten times</LINE>
        <LINE>I had thought to have yerk'd him here under the
            ribs.</LINE>
    </SPEECH>
    <SPEECH>
        <SPEAKER>OTHELLO</SPEAKER>
        <LINE>'Tis better as it is.</LINE>
    </SPEECH>
</SCENE>
```

There are some complications that aren't shown in this sample, but which the stylesheet needs to take account of:

❑   The top-level element is not always a <SCENE>; it might also be a <PROLOGUE> or <EPILOGUE>

8

Design Patterns

❑ The <STAGEDIR> element can appear at any level of nesting, for example a stage directive can appear between two speeches, between two lines of a speech, or in the middle of a line.

❑ Several people can speak at the same time. In this case a single <SPEECH> element will have more than one <SPEAKER>. In general a <SPEECH> consists of one or more <SPEAKER> elements followed by any number of <LINE> and <STAGEDIR> elements in any order.

Stylesheet

The stylesheet scene.xsl consists of a number of template rules. It starts by declaring a global variable (used simply as a constant) and a rule for the document element:

```
<xsl:stylesheet
    xmlns:xsl="http://www.w3.org/1999/XSL/Transform"
    version="1.0"
>

<xsl:variable name="backcolor" select="'#FFFFCC'" />

<xsl:template match="SCENE|PROLOGUE|EPILOGUE">
    <HTML>
    <HEAD>
        <TITLE><xsl:value-of select="TITLE"/></TITLE>
    </HEAD>
    <BODY BGCOLOR='{$backcolor}'>
        <xsl:apply-templates/>
    </BODY>
    </HTML>
</xsl:template>
```

The appearance of <xsl:value-of> is a rare departure from the purely rule-based pattern, just to prove that none of the patterns have to be used to the exclusion of the others.

The template rule for the <SPEECH> element outputs a table containing one row and two columns: it puts the names of the speakers in the first column, and the lines of the speech, plus any stage directives, in the second, as follows:

```
<xsl:template match="SPEECH">
    <TABLE><TR>
    <TD WIDTH="160" VALIGN="TOP">
```

```
    <xsl:apply-templates select="SPEAKER"/>
  </TD>
  <TD VALIGN="TOP">
    <xsl:apply-templates select="STAGEDIR|LINE"/>
  </TD>
  </TR></TABLE>
</xsl:template>
```

The remaining template rules are straightforward. Each of them simply outputs the text of the element using an appropriate HTML rendition. The only complication is that for some elements (<STAGEDIR> and <SUBHEAD>, which doesn't actually occur in this particular scene) the HTML rendition is different depending on the element's context, so there is more than one rule defined.

```
<xsl:template match="TITLE">
  <H1><CENTER>
  <xsl:apply-templates/>
  </CENTER></H1><HR/>
</xsl:template>

<xsl:template match="SPEAKER">
  <B>
    <xsl:apply-templates/>
    <xsl:if test="not(position()=last())"><BR/></xsl:if>
  </B>
</xsl:template>

<xsl:template match="SCENE/STAGEDIR">
  <CENTER><H3>
  <xsl:apply-templates/>
  </H3></CENTER>
</xsl:template>

<xsl:template match="SPEECH/STAGEDIR">
  <P><I>
  <xsl:apply-templates/>
  </I></P>
</xsl:template>

<xsl:template match="LINE/STAGEDIR">
  [ <I>
  <xsl:apply-templates/>
  </I> ]
```

```
    </xsl:template>

<xsl:template match="SCENE/SUBHEAD">
   <CENTER><H3>
   <xsl:apply-templates/>
   </H3></CENTER>
</xsl:template>

<xsl:template match="SPEECH/SUBHEAD">
   <P><B>
   <xsl:apply-templates/>
   </B></P>
</xsl:template>

<xsl:template match="LINE">
   <xsl:apply-templates/>
   <BR/>
</xsl:template>

</xsl:stylesheet>
```

Output

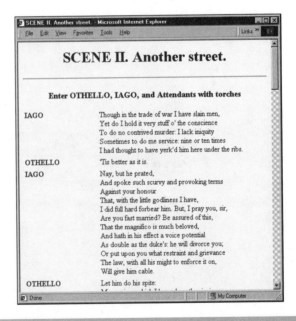

Most of the time a rule-based stylesheet creates a result tree that has quite a similar structure to the source tree, with most of the source text appearing in the same order in the result document, but often with different tags. The closer this describes the transformation you want to do, the closer your stylesheet will be to the example shown above. However, this doesn't mean that the processing has to be purely sequential. You can process chunks of the tree more than once using modes, you can reorder the nodes of the tree, and you can grab data from ancestor nodes, all without deviating from the rule-based design pattern.

The characteristic feature of a rule-based stylesheet is that there is generally one template rule for each type of object found in the source document. Of course it's possible to mix design patterns, particularly if your source document contains a mixture of "data-oriented" and "text-oriented" structures (an example might be a job application form). Then it's quite appropriate to use a navigational pattern for the regular structures and a rule-based pattern for the less regular. The larger and more complex your stylesheet, the more likely it is to contain examples of each of the design patterns.

Computational Stylesheets

Computational stylesheets are the most complex of the four design patterns. They arise when there is a need to generate nodes in the result tree that do not correspond directly to nodes in the source tree. This happens most commonly when there is structure in the source document that is not explicit in its markup. For example:

❏ A text field in the source might consist of a comma-separated list of items that are to be displayed as a bulleted list in the output.

❏ There might be a need to generate `<section>` elements in the output where a section is not explicit in the source, but is defined as comprising an `<h1>` element and all its following sibling elements up to the next `<h1>` element.

Other examples arise where you want to organize data into rows and columns when the input doesn't fall naturally into that structure, or if you need to do complex aggregation of the data, such as constructing a football league table when the source data contains the results of individual matches.

When you write computational stylesheets you will invariably run up against the fact that XSLT does not have an assignment statement, and that it is therefore not possible to write loops in the way you are probably used to in other languages. So you will need to understand some of the concepts of **functional programming**, which the following section tries to explain.

8

Design Patterns

Programming without Assignment Statements

Back in 1968 the renowned computer scientist Edsger Dijkstra published a paper under the title *GoTo Statement Considered Harmful*. His thesis, that programs should be written without `goto` statements, shattered the world as most programmers saw it. Until then they had been familiar with early dialects of Fortran and Cobol in which the vast majority of decisions in a program were implemented by using a construct that mapped directly to the conditional jump instruction in the hardware: «`if condition goto label`». Even the design notation of the day, the ubiquitous flowchart drawn in pencil using a plastic template, represented control flow in this way.

Dijkstra argued that structured programs, written using `if-then-else` and `while-do` constructs instead of `goto` statements, were far less likely to contain bugs and were far more readable and therefore maintainable. The ideas were fiercely controversial at the time, especially among practicing programmers, and for years afterwards the opponents of the idea would challenge the structured programming enthusiasts with arguments of the form, "OK, so how do you do *this* without a `goto` statement?".

Today, however, the battle is won, and the `goto` statement has been consigned to history. Modern languages like Java don't provide a `goto` statement, and we no longer miss it.

But, for just as long there has been another group of enthusiasts telling us that assignment statements are considered harmful. Unlike Dijkstra, these evangelists have yet to convince a skeptical world that they are right, though there has always been a significant band of disciples who have seen the benefits of the approach.

This style of coding, without assignment statements, is called *Functional Programming*. The earliest and most famous functional programming language was Lisp (sometimes ridiculed as *Lots of Irritating Superfluous Parentheses*), while more modern examples include ML and Scheme. (See, for example, *Simply Scheme: Introducing Computer Science* by Brian Harvey and Matthew Wright, MIT Press, 1999)

XSLT is a language without assignment statements, and although its syntax is very different from these languages, its philosophy is based on the concepts of functional programming. It is not in fact a fully-fledged functional programming language, because you cannot manipulate functions in the same way as data; but in most other respects, it fits into this category of language. If you want to do anything at all complicated with it, you'll have to get used to programming without assignment statements. At first it probably won't be easy, because just as those early Fortran and Cobol programmers would instinctively reach for the `goto` statement as the solution to every problem, if your background is in languages like C or Visual Basic or even Java you will just as naturally cherish the assignment statement as your favorite all-purpose tool.

So what's wrong with assignment statements, and why aren't they available in XSLT?

The crux of the argument is that it's the assignment statements that impose a particular order of execution on a program. Without assignment statements, we can do things in any order, because the result of one statement can no longer depend on what state the system was left in by the previous statement. Just as the `goto` statement mirrors the "jump" instruction in the hardware, so the assignment statement mirrors the "store" instruction, and the reason we have assignment statements in our programming languages today is that they were designed to take advantage of sequential von Neumann computers with jump and store instructions. If we want to free ourselves from sequential thinking modeled on sequential hardware architecture, we should find a way of describing what effect we want to achieve, rather than saying what sequence of steps the machine should take in order to achieve it.

The idea of a functional program is to describe the output as a function of the input. XSLT is a transformation language; it is designed to transform an input document into an output document. So, we can regard a stylesheet as a function that defines this transformation: a stylesheet is a function $O=S(I)$ where I is the input document, S is the stylesheet, and O is the output document. Recall the statement made by James Clark at the 1995 Paris workshop, which I quoted in Chapter 1, page 30:

> A DSSSL style sheet very precisely describes a function from SGML to a flow object tree.

This concept clearly remained a key part of the XSLT vision throughout the development of the language.

We're using the word **function** here in something close to its mathematical sense. Languages like Fortran and Visual Basic have borrowed the word to mean a subroutine that returns a result, but the mathematical concept of a function is not that of an algorithm or sequence of steps to be performed, rather it is a statement of a relationship. The square root function defines a relationship between 3 and 9, namely $3=\mathrm{sqrt}(9)$. The essence of a function is that it is a fixed, constant, reliable relationship, and evaluating it doesn't change the world. When you ask me "what's the square root of 9 if you work it out?" I can honestly reply "exactly the same as if I don't". I can say this because square root is a **pure** function: it gives the same answer whoever calls it and however often they call it, and calling it once doesn't change the answer it gives next time; in fact, it doesn't change anything.

The nice property of pure functions is that they can be called any number of times, in any order, and produce the same result every time. If I want to calculate the square root of every integer between zero and a thousand, it doesn't matter whether I start at zero and work up, or start at a thousand and work down, or whether I buy a thousand and one computers and do them all at the same time, I know I will get the same answer. Pure functions have no side-effects.

An assignment statement isn't like that. The effect of an assignment statement "if you work it out" is **not** the same as if you don't. When you write «x = x+1;», the effect depends very much on how often the statement is executed; and when you write several assignment statements, for example

```
temp = x;
x = y;
y = temp;
```

then the effect depends on executing them in the right order.

This means, of course, that a pure function can't update external variables. As soon as we allow assignment, we become dependent on doing things in sequence, one step at a time in the right order.

Don't object-oriented languages achieve the same thing, by preventing one object updating data held in another? No, because although they prevent direct writing to private data, they allow the same effect to be achieved by get() and set() methods. An update to a variable achieved indirectly through a defined interface creates exactly the same dependence on sequence of execution as an update done directly with an assignment statement. A pure function must have no side-effects: its only output is the result it returns.

The main reason that functional languages are considered ideal for a stylesheet language (or a tree transformation language if you prefer) is not so much the ability to do things in parallel or in any order, but rather the ability to do them incrementally. We want to get away from static pages: if you're showing a map of the traffic congestion hotspots in your area, then when the data for a particular road junction changes, you want the map updated in real time, and it should be possible to do this without recalculating and redrawing the whole map. This is only possible if there's a direct relationship – a function – between what's shown at a particular place on the map display and a particular data item in the underlying database. So if we can decompose our top-level stylesheet function, $O=S(I)$, into a set of smaller, independent functions, each relating one piece of the output to one piece of the input, then we have the potential to do this on-the-fly updating.

Another benefit of this incremental approach is that when a large page of XML is downloaded from the network, the browser can start displaying parts of the output as soon as the relevant parts of the input are available. That's the theory, at any rate. There aren't any XSLT processors that can do this yet, because it requires some quite complex analysis of the stylesheet to work out when and to what extent it's possible in any given case – but if the stylesheet were a conventional program with side-effects, it wouldn't ever be possible, because the last bit of input to arrive could change everything.

This is where XSLT template rules come in: they act as the small, independent functions relating one piece of the output to one piece of the input. A template rule has no side-effects, its output is a pure function of its inputs. The inputs are (idealizing slightly) the current position in the input document plus any supplied parameters. It doesn't matter in what order the template rules are executed, so long as we assemble their individual outputs together in the right way to form the result tree. If part of the input changes, then we only need to re-evaluate those template rules that depend on that part of the input, slotting their outputs into the appropriate place in the output tree. In practice, of course, it's not as easy as that, and no-one has yet implemented an incremental stylesheet processor that works like this. However, it will almost certainly come, and the reason assignment statements were left out of the language was to make it possible.

Meanwhile, while the researchers and product developers work out how to implement an incremental stylesheet processor, you as a user are left with a different problem: learning how to program without assignment statements. After this rather lengthy digression into Computer Science theory, in the next section I shall get my feet back on the ground and show you some examples of how to do this.

However, first let's try and separate this from another programming challenge that arises with XSLT, which is the limited number of data types available. In terms of language design principles, the lack of assignment statements and the absence of a rich type system are quite separate matters. In practical terms, however, you often hit the two issues together:

- ❑ The only effect a template can have is via the output it produces (because of the ban on side-effects).

- ❑ And the only output it can produce, if you want to process it further, is a character string (because of the limited range of data types available).

The practical programming challenge is to work round both these restrictions at the same time. If you need convincing that it's possible, take a look at the Knight's Tour example in Chapter 9, page 613

So why are they called Variables?

XSLT, as we have seen, does have variables that can hold values. You can initialize a variable to a value, but what you can't do is change the value of an existing variable once it has been initialized.

So some people have asked, why call it a variable if you can't vary it? The answer lies in the traditional mathematical use of the word variable: a variable is a symbol that can be used to denote different values on different occasions. When I say "area = length × breadth", then **area**, **length**, and **breadth** are names or symbols used to denote values: here they denote properties of a rectangle. They are variables because these values are different every time I apply the formula, not because a given rectangle is changing size as I watch.

Cheating

Just occasionally, you may feel that programming without assignment statements is too mind-boggling, or too slow. In these cases you may be tempted to cheat.

Most XSLT processors actually allow user-written extension functions to have side effects, and some (notably Xalan) go to considerable lengths in their documentation to describe how to exploit this feature to implement a substitute for updateable variables.

The Saxon product goes one step further, and provides an extension element `<saxon:assign>` that allows you to update a variable directly.

8

Design Patterns

Since I've just spent several pages explaining why side-effect-free languages are a "Good Thing", you might find it surprising that I should put a feature in my own product that destroys the principle at a stroke. I have several excuses:

(a) At the time I did it, XSLT was far less advanced as a functional programming language than it finally became.

(b) I thought that although side-effect-free programming is a good thing in theory, many users wouldn't be ready for it.

(c) I wanted to experiment to see whether the costs (in performance and usability) of the pure functional approach exceeded the benefits, and the best way to do this was to launch a genetically modified variant of the language into the wild and see whether the mutation thrived.

These features are a last resort. Most XSLT processors actually do their processing in a predictable way, so you can usually get away with such cheating. If you use a processor that does more optimization, however (as xt does today, and other products may do in the future), then using such extensions might have different side-effects from the ones you wanted: you can find yourself, for example, closing a file before you've written to it, because the order of execution of different instructions is not predictable. These facilities are like the PEEK and POKE of early Basic dialects, a messy escape into a lower level of programming, that you should use only if you are desperate. Having said that, there are situations where they can give a dramatic boost to the speed of a stylesheet with performance problems.

Avoiding Assignment Statements

In the following sections I'll look at some of the common situations where assignment statements appear to be needed, and show how to achieve the required effect without them.

Conditional Initialization

This problem has an easy solution, so I shall get it out of the way quickly.

In conventional languages you might want to initialize a variable to zero in some circumstances and to a value of one in others. You might write:

```
int x;
if (zeroBased) {
    x=0;
} else {
    x=1;
}
```

How can you do the equivalent in XSLT without an assignment statement?

The answer is simple: think of the equivalent:

```
int x = (zeroBased ? 0 : 1 );
```

which has its parallel in XSLT as:

```
<xsl:variable name="x">
   <xsl:choose>
       <xsl:when test="$zeroBased">0</xsl:when>
       <xsl:otherwise>1</xsl:otherwise>
   </xsl:choose>
</xsl:variable>
```

There's only one slight hitch: when you use the content of `<xsl:variable>` to set its value, rather than the `select` attribute, the value of the variable will always be a tree. This doesn't matter if, as here, you want a string or number, because a tree can easily be converted to a string or number, but it's a problem when what you want is a node-set.

Suppose you want the variable `$transactions` to be all the credits or all the debits depending on the value of the Boolean variable `$getCredits`. Here's one way to achieve the desired result:

```
<xsl:variable name="transactions"
          select="//credits[$getCredits] | //debits[not($getCredits)]"/>
```

What this does is to form the union of two node-sets, one of which is always empty. Notice the union operator, «|». If `$getCredits` is true, the first predicate «[`$getCredits`]» is always true and the second predicate «[`not($getCredits)`]» is always false, so the expression is equivalent to «`//credits`»; while if `$getCredits` is false, the situation is reversed, and the expression is equivalent to «`//debits`».

Don't Iterate, Recurse

One of the most common uses of variables in conventional programming is to keep track of where you are in a loop. Whether this is done using an integer counter in a `for` loop, or using an `Iterator` or `Enumerator` object to process a list, the principle is the same: we have a variable that represents how far we have got and that tells us when we are finished.

In a functional program you can't do this, because you can't update variables. So instead of writing a loop, you need to write a recursive function.

In a conventional program a common way to process a list of items is as follows:

```
iterator = list.getIterator();
while (iterator.hasMoreItems()) {
   item = iterator.getNextItem();
   item.doSomething();
}
```

8

Design Patterns

551

The killer assignment statement is «item = iterator.getNextItem()». This assigns a different value to the item each time, and what's more, it relies on the iterator containing some sort of updateable variable that keeps track of how far it's got.

In a functional program we handle this by recursion rather than iteration. The pseudo-code becomes:

```
function process(list) {
    if (!isEmpty(list)) {
        doSomething(getFirst(list));
        process(getRemainder(list));
    }
}
```

This function is called to process a list of objects. It does whatever is necessary with the first object in the list, and then calls itself to handle the rest of the list. (I'm assuming that getFirst() gets the first item in the list and getRemainder() gets a list containing all items except the first.) The list gets smaller each time the function is called, and when it finally becomes empty, the function exits, and unwinds through all the recursive calls.

> It's important to make sure there is a terminating condition such as the list becoming empty. Otherwise the function will keep calling itself forever – the recursive equivalent of an infinite loop.

So the first lesson in programming without variables is to use recursion rather than iteration to process a list. With XSLT this isn't necessary to handle every kind of loop, because XSLT provides built-in facilities such as <xsl:apply-templates> and <xsl:for-each> that process all the members of a node-set without requiring an explicit control variable, as well as functions like sum() and count() to do some common operations on node-sets; but whenever you need to process a set of things that can't be handled with these constructs, you need to use recursion.

Is recursion expensive? The answer is, not necessarily. It's quite possible for a reasonably smart compiler to generate exactly the same code for a recursive procedure as for an iterative one. For example a common compiler technique with functional programming languages is that of *tail recursion*, which recognizes that when a function calls itself as the last thing it does, there's no need to allocate a new stack frame or new variables, you can just loop back to the beginning.

The following example uses a recursive template to process a whitespace-separated list of numbers which, for some reason, have not been marked up as separate elements.

Example: Totaling a List of Numbers

Input

Suppose you have a string that holds a whitespace-separated list of numbers, for example "12 34.5 18.2 −35" and you want to find the total. (Don't ask why: when someone else designs your XML documents for you, these things happen).

For the sake of an example, this is the entire content of the document, `number-list.xml`:

```
<numbers>12  34.5  18.2  -35</numbers>
```

Stylesheet

We need to use some of the string-handling functions provided in the XPath expression language. These are described in Chapter 7; the ones we will use are:

❑ `normalize-space()`, which removes leading and trailing spaces and replaces internal whitespace with a single space character (see page 492).

❑ `concat()`, which concatenates two strings. I shall use this to add a space at the end of the string, so that it works correctly even when there is only one number in the string (see page 430)

❑ `substring-before()`, which I will use to find the part of a string that comes before the first space (see page 516).

❑ `substring-after()`, which I will use to find the part of a string that comes after the first space (see page 515).

❑ `number()`, which converts a string to a number. Actually this would happen automatically, but I will do it explicitly for clarity (see page 498).

Here's the recursive template (in file `number-total.xsl`):

```
<xsl:template name="total-numbers">
   <xsl:param name="list"/>
   <xsl:variable name="wlist"
      select="concat(normalize-space($list), ' ')"/>
   <xsl:choose>
      <xsl:when test="$wlist!=' '">
         <xsl:variable name="first"
            select="substring-before($wlist, ' ')"/>
         <xsl:variable name="rest"
            select="substring-after($wlist, ' ')"/>
```

8

Design Patterns

```
            <xsl:variable name="total">
               <xsl:call-template name="total-numbers">
                  <xsl:with-param name="list" select="$rest"/>
               </xsl:call-template>
            </xsl:variable>
            <xsl:value-of select="number($first) + number($total)"/>
         </xsl:when>
         <xsl:otherwise>0</xsl:otherwise>
      </xsl:choose>
   </xsl:template>
```

Notice how closely this mirrors the pseudo-code structure given earlier.

❑   First, to make tests on the whitespace-separated list easier, it normalizes the supplied list. It uses the `normalize-space()` function to remove leading and trailing spaces and replace all intermediate whitespace with a single space character; then it uses `concat()` to add an extra space at the end, so that the first number in the list will always have a space after it even if it is the only number in the list. (It's actually unnecessary to do this when the template calls itself recursively, because the list will already be in the right format. If you want to write a bit more code to make it go a little faster, there's room for optimization here.)

❑   If the supplied list is empty, the template returns the value zero. The test in the `<xsl:when>` instruction returns false (after normalization, a string containing no numbers will have turned into a single space). So the `<xsl:otherwise>` branch is taken and the template returns, thus terminating the recursion.

❑   Otherwise it extracts the first number from the list into the variable `$first` by calling `substring-before()`, and extracts the remainder of the list into the variable `$rest` by calling `substring-after()`. The template then calls itself recursively to process the remainder of the list, and adds the value of the first number to the total obtained from the other numbers. The `<xsl:with-param>` element sets the parameter for the called template, so that next time around the list it is processing will be the "rest" of the list – the remainder after removing the first element. The `<xsl:value-of>` element writes the result to the current output tree, which may be a variable or a final result tree.

To test this, add the template rule below, and run the stylesheet against the above source document:

```
<xsl:template match="/">
   <xsl:call-template name="total-numbers">
      <xsl:with-param name="list" select="."/>
   </xsl:call-template>
</xsl:template>
```

```
29.7
```

(When I ran this, there were rounding errors, so the result was 29.69999999... If you want to eliminate these, use the `format-number()` function, see page 455) to control the number of decimal places in the output.)

Another example similar to this one was given under `<xsl:call-template>` in Chapter 4, page 167

Here's another example, this time processing a node-set. XPath provides built-in functions for counting nodes and for totaling their values, but they aren't always flexible enough: sometimes you need to walk round the nodes yourself.

Example: Finding the Total Sales Value

The requirement is to find the total sales value of a list of books, using the book list example on page 537. To find the total sales value, you need to multiply the number of sales of each book by its price, which you cannot do using the `sum()` function provided in XSLT.

Input

This example uses the `booklist.xml` file introduced earlier in this chapter. It records sales figures for a number of books, as follows:

```
<booklist>
   <book>
      <title>Angela's Ashes</title>
      <author>Frank McCourt</author>
      <publisher>HarperCollins</publisher>
      <isbn>0 00 649840 X</isbn>
      <price>6.99</price>
      <sales>235</sales>
   </book>
   <book>
      <title>Sword of Honour</title>
      <author>Evelyn Waugh</author>
      <publisher>Penguin Books</publisher>
      <isbn>0 14 018967 X</isbn>
      <price>12.99</price>
      <sales>12</sales>
   </book>
</booklist>
```

8

Design Patterns

Stylesheet

The stylesheet total-sales.xsl is as follows. Once again it defines a recursive template, named «total-sales-value». This is called to process a set of <book> elements passed in the parameter «list». The recursion terminates, returning zero, when the list is empty.

When the list isn't empty, the template multiplies the number of sales times the price for the first book in the list, and adds the total sales value of all the books after the first, which it obtains by calling itself with this shorter list as a parameter. As we're dealing with node-sets this time rather than strings, we use the XPath syntax for manipulating node-sets: in particular, the predicate «[1]» to find the first node in the set, and «[position()!=1]» to find the remainder.

```
<xsl:stylesheet
    xmlns:xsl="http://www.w3.org/1999/XSL/Transform"
    version="1.0">

<xsl:template name="total-sales-value">
    <xsl:param name="list"/>
    <xsl:choose>
        <xsl:when test="$list">
            <xsl:variable name="first" select="$list[1]"/>
            <xsl:variable name="total-of-rest">
                <xsl:call-template name="total-sales-value">
                    <xsl:with-param name="list" select="$list[position()!=1]"/>
                </xsl:call-template>
            </xsl:variable>
            <xsl:value-of select="$first/sales * $first/price + $total-of-rest"/>
        </xsl:when>
        <xsl:otherwise>0</xsl:otherwise>
    </xsl:choose>
</xsl:template>
```

The root template simply calls the recursive template to process the set of all books in the input file, and displays the result in a suitable format by calling the format-number() function, which was described in Chapter 7, page 455.

```
<xsl:template match="/">
   <xsl:variable name="total">
      <xsl:call-template name="total-sales-value">
         <xsl:with-param name="list" select="//book"/>
      </xsl:call-template>
   </xsl:variable>
Total sales value is: <xsl:value-of select="format-number($total,
                        '$#.00')"/>
   </xsl:template>

</xsl:stylesheet>
```

Output

```
Total sales value is: $1798.53
```

Summary

By now the principle should be clear. Whenever you need to find something out by processing a list of items, write a recursive template that is given the entire list as a parameter. If the list isn't empty, deal with the first item, and make a recursive call to deal with the rest of the list after the first item.

As I mentioned, there's another problem that you'll encounter when doing this, which is nothing to do with the lack of an assignment statement, but is to do with the limited range of data types available. The result of a template is always a tree, (or as the standard calls it, a **result tree fragment**) and there are only two things you can do with a tree: you can copy it to the final result tree, or you can convert it to a string. What this means is that if you want to do any more processing on the result of your recursive function, you have to find some way of expressing the result as a string.

This can always be achieved (in one of the worked examples in Chapter 9, on page 613, I show how to encode the state of a chessboard as a string) but it can require a great deal of mental agility. There are several XSLT processors available that get round this by allowing you to convert a tree to a node-set, making it much easier to create complex data structures that can be input to further processing: however, you probably want to avoid using proprietary extensions like this, so I will stick here to the facilities defined in the standard.

Avoid Doing Two Things at Once

Another common requirement for variables arises when you are trying to do two things at once. For example, you are trying to copy text to the output destination, and at the same time to keep a note of how much text you have copied. You might feel that the natural way of doing this is to keep the running total in a variable, and update it as a side-effect of the template that does the copying.

8

Design Patterns

557

Or perhaps you want to scan a set of numbers calculating both the minimum and the maximum value; or while outputting a list of employees, to set a flag for later use if any salary greater than $100,000 was found.

The best answer to this problem is to split the task into two separate templates, and call them separately. Write one function to produce the output, and another to calculate the total. Write one template to find the minimum, and another to find the maximum.

This might mean writing a little more code, and it might take a little longer, because work is being repeated, but it is usually the right approach. The problem of repeated processing can often be solved by using variables for the node-sets used in both calculations: if you need to use a particular node-set as input to more than one process, save that node-set in a variable which can then be supplied as a parameter to the two separate templates.

An alternative is to write a template that returns a composite result; however, as we have seen, XSLT isn't strong on structured data types, so composite values aren't easy to manipulate. If you do need a composite value, the best option is usually a whitespace-separated string.

One situation where it is difficult to save intermediate results and use them as input to more than one process is where the intermediate results are sorted. If you've got a large set of nodes to sort, the last thing you want to do is to sort it more than once. Unfortunately, though, there's no way in standard XSLT of sorting a set of nodes, and then using the sorted result as input to further processing. There are two possible answers, neither of which can be done by pure standard XSLT:

❑ Create a result tree fragment in which the nodes appear in sorted order. Use the proprietary node-set() function (as often as you like) to process the nodes on this tree in their sorted order.

❑ Use a sequence (or **chain**) of stylesheets: the first stylesheet creates a document in which the nodes are sorted in the right order, and subsequent stylesheets take this document as their input.

Note that neither of these techniques violates the XSLT design principle of "no side effects". The node-set() function, which converts a result tree fragment to a node-set, has proved sufficiently popular with both implementers and users that it seems a very strong candidate for inclusion in the next version of the standard.

Grouping

Another common processing task that appears at first sight to need variables is the splitting of data into groups.

Suppose that your souce logged cities and their respective countries in the following format:

```
<cities>
   <city name="CityName" country="CountryName"/>
...etc...
</cities>
```

However, you want to list together all cities found in a particular country:

```
<countries>
   <country name=" CountryName ">
      <city> CityName1</city>
      <city> CityName2</city>
   </country>
...etc...
</countries>
```

In other languages we've probably all written code that achieved similar effects using pseudo-code such as this:

```
sortedCities = cities.sortBy("country");
previousCountry = null;
write("<country>")
for each city in sortedCities {
    thisCountry = city.getAttribute("country");
    if (thisCountry != previousCountry) {
        write("</country>\n<country>");
    }
    write("<city>" + city.getAttribute("city") + "</city>");
    previousCountry = thisCountry;
}
write("</country>")
```

In XSLT, of course, this is a non-starter, for two reasons. Firstly, you need to output a tree, not a text file containing markup tags: this means you can't write the end tag for an element as a separate operation from writing the start tag. Secondly, you can't use assignment statements to spot the change of country as you go through the data.

The best way to tackle this problem in XSLT is to first build a list of unique countries, and then process each one in turn. Let's have a look at an example.

Example: Splitting Data into Groups

Input

This example uses the `cities.xml` file. It logs cities and their respective countries as follows:

```
<cities>
    <city name="Paris" country="France"/>
    <city name="Roma" country="Italia"/>
    <city name="Nice" country="France"/>
    <city name="Madrid" country="Espana"/>
    <city name="Milano" country="Italia"/>
    <city name="Firenze" country="Italia"/>
    <city name="Napoli" country="Italia"/>
    <city name="Lyon" country="France"/>
    <city name="Barcelona" country="Espana"/>
</cities>
```

Stylesheet

You can get a list of unique countries (as a node-set containing the relevant attribute nodes) as follows:

```
<xsl:template match="/">
<xsl:variable name="unique-countries"
    select="/cities
                /city[not(@country=preceding-sibling::city/@country)]
                /@country"
/>
```

The predicate on the `<city>` element rejects any `<city>` whose `country` attribute is the same as the `country` attribute of a preceding sibling, if there is one. In other words, it includes every city that is the first one in its country. Variations on this predicate are possible:

❑   If you know that the cities are sorted by country, you can replace the predicate `preceding-sibling::city` by `preceding-sibling::city[1]`. This means the country would only be compared with that of the immediately preceding city. This might improve performance.

❑   If the `<city>` elements were not all siblings of each other, you could use the `preceding` axis instead of `preceding-sibling`. This, however, would lengthen the search.

Having built a list of unique countries, you can then generate the `<city>` elements for each one. Here goes:

```
<xsl:template match="/">
<xsl:variable name="unique-countries"
    select="/cities
              /city[not(@country=preceding-sibling::city/@country)]
              /@country"
/>
<countries>
    <xsl:for-each select="$unique-countries">
      <country name="{.}">
        <xsl:for-each select="//city[@country=current()]">
          <city><xsl:value-of select="@name"/></city>
        </xsl:for-each>
      </country>
    </xsl:for-each>
</countries>
</xsl:template
```

Output

```
<countries>
    <country name="France">
      <city>Paris</city>
      <city>Nice</city>
      <city>Lyon</city>
    </country>
    <country name="Italia">
      <city>Roma</city>
      <city>Milano</city>
      <city>Firenze</city>
      <city>Napoli</city>
    </country>
    <country name="Espana">
      <city>Madrid</city>
      <city>Barcelona</city>
    </country>
</countries>
```

8

Design Patterns

The main problem with such algorithms is that if there are N nodes to be grouped, then each one may need to be compared with all the previous ones, which gives a total of $N \times (N-1) / 2$ comparisons in total. Double the number of nodes, and it will take about four times as long. The result may be acceptable if there are ten cities, but you will have to be very patient if there are several thousand. Of course a clever XSLT processor might optimize the query and find a more efficient way of doing it, but you can't rely on this. The technology of XSLT processors is still young, and techniques for query optimization have a long way to go.

One answer to this is to sort the nodes first, and then group them; during the grouping stage, each node needs to be compared only to its immediate predecessor, as shown in our example. This requires processing a sorted list, which can only be achieved by using the proprietary node-set() extension function discussed earlier, or by writing one stylesheet to do the sorting and chaining the result into a second stylesheet that does the grouping.

However, comparing each node only with its immediate predecessor may not solve the problem. The crucial expression is:

```
preceding-sibling::city[1]
```

which is shorthand for:

```
preceding-sibling::city[position()=1]
```

This is a lot easier to optimize than the full predicate we had earlier, but it's still likely that some XSLT processors will evaluate it the naïve way, by forming a list of all the preceding siblings, and then looking at the position() of each one to see if it is equal to 1. If the processor works this way, the time taken will still be proportional to the square of the number of cities to be grouped.

Since we're now getting outside the scope of what you can do within standard XSLT, another alternative is to use the <saxon:group> extension element provided by the Saxon product. This is an experimental extension of the XSLT language. The stylesheet to group our list of cities by country would then look like this:

```
<countries>
<saxon:group select="//city" group-by="@country">
   <xsl:sort select="@country"/>
   <country name="{@country}">
      <saxon:item>
         <city><xsl:value-of select="@name"/></city>
      </saxon:item>
   </country>
</saxon:group>
</countries>
```

For more details of this feature, see page of Chapter 10, page 650. A standard way of doing grouping is on the shopping list for the next version of the XSLT standard; but whether it looks anything like the Saxon extension remains to be seen.

Summary

This chapter described four design patterns for writing XSLT stylesheets:

❑   Fill-in-the-blanks

❑   Navigational

❑   Data-driven

❑   Computational

In the last category I described how we need to approach many problems in a way that might seem unfamiliar, because XSLT is a pure functional programming language, with no assignment statements or other side-effects that constrain the order of execution. The result of this is that many of the more complex algorithms need to be written using recursive named templates.

8

Design Patterns

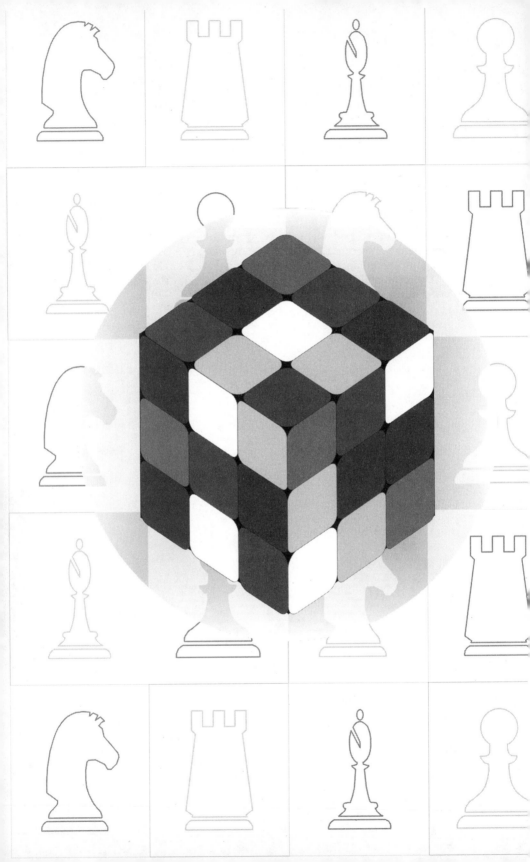

Worked Examples

This chapter aims to show how all the facilities of the XSLT language can work together to solve some real XML processing problems of significant complexity. I have chosen three example applications, and give complete stylesheets for handling them. The code is presented incrementally in this chapter, but the complete stylesheets, and specimen data files, can be downloaded from the Wrox web site at http://www.wrox.com/.

As I described in the previous chapter, XSLT has a broad range of application, and in this chapter I have tried to cover a representative selection of problems. The three examples presented in this chapter are as follows:

❑ The first example is a stylesheet for rendering sequential documents: specifically, the stylesheet used for rendering W3C specifications such as the XML and XSLT Recommendations. This is a classic example of the *rule-based* design pattern described on page 540 in Chapter 8.

❑ The second example is concerned with presenting structured data. I have chosen a complex data structure with many cross-references to illustrate how a navigational stylesheet can find its way around the source tree: the chosen example is a data file containing the family tree of the Kennedys.

❑ The final example stylesheet is quite unrealistic, but fun. It shows how XSLT can be used to calculate a knight's tour of the chessboard, in which the knight visits every square without ever landing on the same square twice. This is not the sort of problem XSLT was designed to solve, but by showing that it can be done I hope it will convince you that XSLT has the computational power and flexibility to deal with the many more modest algorithmic challenges that arise in routine day-to-day formatting applications.

Formatting the XML Specification

In this worked example we'll study the stylesheet used for formatting the XML specifications themselves. You may have noticed that on the W3C web site, you can get the specifications for standards such as XML, XSLT, and XPath either in XML format or in HTML. We'll look at a stylesheet for converting the XML recommendation from its XML form to its HTML form, shown below:

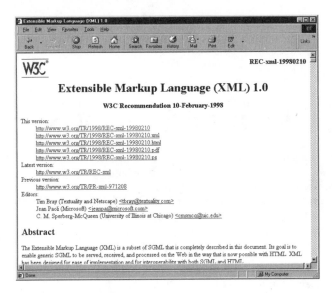

The stylesheets used for the XSLT and XPath specifications are adapted from the version used for the XML specification, and we'll take a quick look at the adaptations too.

This stylesheet was originally written by Eduardo Gutentag and subsequently modified by James Clark. I am grateful to James Clark for placing it in the public domain. I have made changes to the layout and ordering of the rules for the sake of clarity, but I haven't altered the logic. The download file for this chapter on http://www.wrox.com/ contains the original stylesheet from James Clark.

This stylesheet is a classic example of the *rule-based* design pattern, which was introduced on page 540 in Chapter 8. It makes minimal assumptions about where all the different elements in the XML source document appear relative to each other, and it allows new rules to be added freely as the document structure evolves.

You'll probably find it helpful while reading this stylesheet to have the XML source document readily accessible. The official version is on the web at http://www.w3.org/TR/1998/REC-xml-19980210.xml, but you may have problems with that version. You might expect that, since the XML specification was written by XML experts, it would be a perfect example of how to write good XML. Unfortunately this isn't the case, and it uses constructs which some parsers aren't happy with. Specifically:

❑ It contains the entity declaration `<!ENTITY lt "<">` which violates the rule that the replacement text of a parsed entity must be well-formed. This declaration causes IE5 to throw up its hands in horror and refuse to display the document. The declaration is in any case quite unnecessary except for compatibility with SGML.

❑ More subtly, the DTD (called `spec.dtd`) contains references to parameter entities that don't exist, or whose declaration comes after the reference. It happens that these references are all contained within comments in the DTD, but if you read the XML specification very carefully, it says that a parameter entity reference may occur anywhere in the DTD except in an `EntityValue` or `AttValue`. Although this is an acknowledged error in the specification, at least one XML parser (Ælfred) has taken that statement literally, and validates parameter entity references even if they appear within the text of a comment.

So to make your life easier, I've created a modified version of the source document and DTD that avoids these problems, and included them in the download for this book. The source file is called `REC-xml-19980210.xml` and the DTD is called `spec.dtd`. You can view the source either in a text editor, or using the default XML viewer in IE5.

The XML versions of the XSLT and XPath specifications don't suffer from the same problems, and you can view these directly on the W3C web site using the IE5 browser, although copies are included on the Wrox web site for convenience. They don't contain references to a stylesheet, so IE5 will use its default stylesheet, which displays the XML as a collapsible tree. Then you can use View Source to display the source XML, and save it locally on your hard disk if you wish.

Now let's look at the stylesheet, `xmlspec.xsl`.

Preface

Let's start at the beginning:

```
<?xml version="1.0" encoding="ISO-8859-1" ?>

<!-- 1999/01/11 SMI; Style Sheet for the XML and XSL
     Recommendations and Working Drafts;
     written by Eduardo Gutentag -->
<!-- v 1.28 1999/11/15 12:58:16 by James Clark -->

<!DOCTYPE xsl:stylesheet [
<!ENTITY copy    "&#169;">
<!ENTITY nbsp    " ">
]>

<xsl:stylesheet
    version="1.0"
    xmlns:xsl="http://www.w3.org/1999/XSL/Transform">
```

9

Worked Examples

```
<xsl:output method="html"
        doctype-public="-//W3C//DTD HTML 4.0 Transitional//EN"/>

<xsl:param name="w3">http://www.w3.org/</xsl:param>
```

The stylesheet is an XML document, so it starts with an XML declaration; the chosen encoding is ISO-8859-1 because with most editing tools that's easier to edit than UTF–8. Actually, all the characters are ASCII, so specifying UTF-8 would work just as well.

There's then a couple of comments indicating the change history and authorship.

The <!DOCTYPE> declaration doesn't reference an external DTD; this is normal practice for stylesheets because a DTD would restrict your ability to include any element you like in a template and have it treated as a literal result element. What the <!DOCTYPE> does do is to declare a couple of entities for special characters. These allow us to write the copyright symbol as «©» and the non-breaking-space character as « » – if we hadn't declared these entities, we would have to write them each time they appear as «©» and « » respectively.

The fact that we've used entity references rather than numeric character references for these characters in the stylesheet doesn't mean that this is how they will appear in the HTML output. The way the XSLT processor represents these characters in the output is entirely up to the implementer; but whatever representation it chooses, they will display correctly in the browser.

The <xsl:stylesheet> element should be familiar by now. The <xsl:output> element defines the output method as html, and indicates the public identifier of the version of HTML that is being generated, which will be copied into the generated output file. This is good practice. It isn't essential, but of course the W3C want to produce HTML that conforms to their own recommended practice.

The <xsl:param> statement declares a global parameter named w3, and gives it a default value which is the URL for the W3C web site. Making this a global parameter rather than a global variable allows a different value to be supplied during testing, perhaps the URL of a staging server.

Creating the HTML Outline

Now we start with the main template rules for the document. The order is arbitrary, and I've changed the order used by the original authors to present similar rules together.

```
<xsl:template match="spec">
   <html>
      <head>
         <title>
            <xsl:value-of select="header/title"/>
         </title>
```

```
        <link rel="stylesheet" type="text/css"
            href="{$w3}StyleSheets/TR/W3C-{
                substring-before(header/w3c-designation,'-')}"/>

        <!-- This stops Netscape 4.5 from messing up. -->
        <style type="text/css">
            <xsl:apply-templates select="." mode="css"/>
        </style>
    </head>
    <body>
        <xsl:apply-templates/>
    </body>
    </html>
</xsl:template>
```

This is the top-level template rule that generates the HTML outline. There isn't a rule that matches the root node, so the built-in root template kicks in and finds a rule that matches the outermost element, which happens to be <spec>.

Apart from producing the HTML outline, this template does three things: it extracts the document title, it outputs a reference to the CSS stylesheet to be used (in two different formats so it works with different browsers), and within the HTML <body> element it calls <xsl:apply-templates> to process the child elements of the <spec> in the source document.

The call on <xsl:apply-templates mode="css"/> invokes the following little template rule which just outputs some standard content for the <style> element. Note that this could equally well have been done using <xsl:call-template>, or written inline. I don't know why the authors chose to do it this way instead – one possibility is that they wanted to override this rule in another stylesheet module that imports this one. It's also likely that at the time this stylesheet was first written, some XSLT features such as named templates were not yet available in products.

```
<xsl:template match="spec" mode="css">
    <xsl:text>code { font-family: monospace }</xsl:text>
</xsl:template>
```

Formatting the Document Header

We generated the title of the HTML document by accessing the title element within the header element of the source XML file. To understand such queries, you need to take a look at the structure of the <header> element in the source document. In abbreviated form, the structure of the XML specification starts like this:

```
<spec>
    <header>
        <title>Extensible Markup Language (XML) 1.0</title>
        <version></version>
        <w3c-designation>REC-xml-&iso6.doc.date;</w3c-designation>
        <w3c-doctype>W3C Recommendation</w3c-doctype>
        <pubdate>
```

```
            <day>&draft.day;</day>
            <month>&draft.month;</month>
            <year>&draft.year;</year>
        </pubdate>

        <publoc>
            <loc  href="url">url</loc>
            <loc  href="url">url</loc>
        </publoc>
        <latestloc>
            <loc  href="url">url</loc>
        </latestloc>
        <prevlocs>
            <loc  href="url">url</loc>
        </prevlocs>

        <authlist>
            <author>
                <name>Tim Bray</name>
                <affiliation>Textuality and Netscape</affiliation>
                <email href="mailto:tbray@textuality.com">
                            tbray@textuality.com</email>
            </author>
                more authors
        </authlist>

        <abstract>
            <p>The Extensible Markup Language (XML) is a subset of SGML that
                        is completely described in this document... </p>
        </abstract>

        <status>
        <p>This document has been reviewed by W3C Members and
                            other interested parties ...</p>

        <p>This document specifies a syntax… It is a product of the W3C
                    XML Activity, details of which can be found at <loc
                    href='url'>url</loc>.  A list of current W3C
                    Recommendations … can be found at <loc
                    href='url'>url</loc>.</p>

        <p>This specification uses the term URI, which is defined by
                <bibref ref="Berners-Lee"/>, a work in progress expected to update
                <bibref ref="RFC1738"/> and <bibref ref="RFC1808"/>. </p>
        </status>
    </header>
    <body>
        main section of document
    </body>
    <back>
        appendices
    </back>
</spec>
```

Note that some of the tags are structural elements with predictable nesting, while others such as <loc> can appear in all sorts of places, including inline within the text.

The next few template rules are all concerned with processing this header:

```
<xsl:template match="header">
   <div class="head">

      <!-- output clickable W3C logo -->

      <a href="http://www.w3.org/">
         <img src="{$w3}Icons/WWW/w3c_home"
              alt="W3C" height="48" width="72"/>
      </a>

      <!-- output title and version of document -->

      <h1><xsl:value-of select="title"/><br/>
         <xsl:value-of select="version"/>
      </h1>

      <!-- output publication type and date -->

      <h2>
         <xsl:value-of select="w3c-doctype"/>
         <xsl:text> </xsl:text>
         <xsl:value-of select="pubdate/day"/>
         <xsl:text> </xsl:text>
         <xsl:value-of select="pubdate/month"/>
         <xsl:text> </xsl:text>
         <xsl:value-of select="pubdate/year"/>
      </h2>

      <!-- output URLs of successive versions, and authors -->

      <dl>
         <xsl:apply-templates select="publoc"/>
         <xsl:apply-templates select="latestloc"/>
         <xsl:apply-templates select="prevlocs"/>
         <xsl:apply-templates select="authlist"/>
      </dl>

      <!-- output standard copyright statement -->

      <xsl:call-template name="copyright"/>
      <hr title="Separator for header"/>
   </div>

   <!-- output abstract and status sections -->

   <xsl:apply-templates select="abstract"/>
   <xsl:apply-templates select="status"/>
```

```
</xsl:template>

<!-- template rules for document locations -->

<xsl:template match="publoc">
   <dt>This version:</dt>
   <dd><xsl:apply-templates/></dd>
</xsl:template>

<xsl:template match="latestloc">
   <dt>Latest version:</dt>
   <dd><xsl:apply-templates/></dd>
</xsl:template>

<xsl:template match="prevlocs">
   <dt>
      <xsl:text>Previous version</xsl:text>
      <xsl:if test="count(loc)>1">s</xsl:if>
      <xsl:text>:</xsl:text>
   </dt>
   <dd><xsl:apply-templates/></dd>
</xsl:template>

<xsl:template match="publoc/loc | latestloc/loc | prevlocs/loc">
   <a href="{@href}"><xsl:apply-templates/></a>
   <br/>
</xsl:template>

<!-- template rules for authors and affiliations -->

<xsl:template match="authlist">
   <dt>
      <xsl:text>Editor</xsl:text>
      <xsl:if test="count(author)>1">s</xsl:if>
      <xsl:text>:</xsl:text>
   </dt>
   <dd><xsl:apply-templates/></dd>
</xsl:template>

<xsl:template match="author">
   <xsl:apply-templates/><br/>
</xsl:template>

<xsl:template match="author/name">
   <xsl:apply-templates/>
</xsl:template>

<xsl:template match="author/affiliation">
   <xsl:text> (</xsl:text>
      <xsl:apply-templates/>
   <xsl:text>) </xsl:text>
</xsl:template>
```

```
<xsl:template match="author/email">
    <a href="{@href}">
        <xsl:text>&lt;</xsl:text>
        <xsl:apply-templates/>
        <xsl:text>&gt;</xsl:text>
    </a>
</xsl:template>

<!-- templates to display abstract and status paragraphs -->

<xsl:template match="abstract">
    <h2><a name="abstract">Abstract</a></h2>
    <xsl:apply-templates/>
</xsl:template>

<xsl:template match="status">
    <h2><a name="status">Status of this document</a></h2>
    <xsl:apply-templates/>
</xsl:template>
```

So much for the header: nothing very complicated here, though the techniques used to produce a plural label for "previous versions" and "editors" are worth noting, as is the use of `<xsl:text>` to avoid copying white space to the output where it isn't wanted.

The Table of Contents

The next part of the stylesheet deals with the body of the document, and at the same time with the "back" of the document, which has a similar structure. The `<back>` element contains appendices, bibliography, and so on.

```
<xsl:template match="body">
    <h2><a name="contents">Table of contents</a></h2>
    <xsl:call-template name="toc"/>
    <hr/>
    <xsl:apply-templates/>
</xsl:template>

<xsl:template match="back">
    <hr title="Separator from footer"/>
    <xsl:apply-templates/>
</xsl:template>
```

The `<body>` template rule follows a common pattern: it first calls a template to generate the table of contents, then it uses `<xsl:apply-templates>` to process its own children.

9

Worked Examples

Let's see how the table of contents is produced. The structure of the `<body>` element, and also of `<back>`, consists of a sequence of `<div1>` elements representing top-level sections, like this:

```
<div1>
    <head>First-level heading</head>
    <p>Some text</p>
    <div2>
        <head>Second-level heading</head>
        <p>Some more text</p>
        <div3>
            <head>Third-level heading</head>
            <p>Lots more text</p>
        </div3>
    </div2>
</div1>
```

Each `<div1>` element contains a `<head>` element giving its heading, paragraphs of immediate content, and zero or more `<div2>` elements containing level-2 subsections. The `<div2>` elements similarly contain a `<head>` and zero or more `<div3>` elements for level-3 subsections, and so on.

In the `<back>` section, a non-normative appendix is represented by an `<inform-div1>` element instead of the usual `<div1>`, but otherwise the structure is the same.

> *Non-normative is jargon meaning "for information only, not part of the specification".*

So the named template to generate the table of contents looks like this. It first works its way through the nested sections in the `<body>`, and then does the same again for the sections in the `<back>`. The work of actually producing the cross-reference is delegated to another named template, «makeref»:

```
<xsl:template name="toc">
   <xsl:for-each select="/spec/body/div1">
      <xsl:call-template name="makeref"/><br/>
      <xsl:for-each select="div2">
         <xsl:text>    </xsl:text>
         <xsl:call-template name="makeref"/><br/>
         <xsl:for-each select="div3">
            <xsl:text>    </xsl:text>
            <xsl:text>    </xsl:text>
            <xsl:call-template name="makeref"/><br/>
         </xsl:for-each>
      </xsl:for-each>
   </xsl:for-each>

   <h3>Appendices</h3>
```

```
    <xsl:for-each select="/spec/back/div1 | /spec/back/inform-div1">
        <xsl:call-template name="makeref"/><br/>
        <xsl:for-each select="div2">
            <xsl:text>    </xsl:text>
            <xsl:call-template name="makeref"/><br/>
            <xsl:for-each select="div3">
                <xsl:text>    </xsl:text>
                <xsl:text>    </xsl:text>
                <xsl:call-template name="makeref"/><br/>
            </xsl:for-each>
        </xsl:for-each>
    </xsl:for-each>
</xsl:template>

<xsl:template name="makeref">
    <xsl:apply-templates select="." mode="number"/>
    <xsl:choose>
        <xsl:when test="@id">
            <a href="#{@id}">
                <xsl:value-of select="head"/>
            </a>
        </xsl:when>
        <xsl:otherwise>
            <a href="#section-{translate(head,' ','-')}">
                <xsl:value-of select="head"/>
            </a>
        </xsl:otherwise>
    </xsl:choose>
    <xsl:for-each select="head">
        <xsl:call-template name="inform"/>
    </xsl:for-each>
</xsl:template>

<xsl:template name="inform">
    <xsl:if test="parent::inform-div1">
        <xsl:text> (Non-Normative)</xsl:text>
    </xsl:if>
</xsl:template>
```

The «makeref» template first generates a sequence number for the section, then creates a hyperlink to it, using the section's id attribute if it has one, or a name derived from its heading otherwise (spaces are replaced by hyphens). This isn't a particularly brilliant idea, it means that any non-unique headings like "Example" have to be allocated an id manually: presumably the authors would have used the generate-id() function if it had been around at the time. Then if the section is a non-normative one (an <inform-div1> element) it outputs the string "(Non-Normative)".

The way in which this is done is not particularly elegant, though it works. I suspect the template named «inform» was written initially to display the actual section heading in situ, and then reused for the table of contents. A more natural approach would be to include an <xsl:if self::inform-div1> test in the «makeref» template.

9

Worked Examples

The «makeref» template delegates the work of generating a sequence number to a template rule associated with the section being numbered. This uses a special mode, to avoid conflict with the template rule for expanding the content of this section. There are two versions of the rule, one for sections in the body of the document, and one for appendices. There is no need to have different rules for different section levels, because the way the number formatting works is sufficiently flexible to give the right answer at each level.

```
<xsl:template mode="number" match="*">
   <xsl:number   level="multiple"
                 count="inform-div1 | div1 | div2 | div3 | div4"
                 format="1.1 "/>
</xsl:template>

<xsl:template mode="number" match="back//*">
   <xsl:number   level="multiple"
                 count="inform-div1 | div1 | div2 | div3 | div4"
                 format="A.1 "/>
</xsl:template>
```

This use of a list of alternatives in the count attribute is a common way of doing multi-level numbering. It means, in effect, outputting a sequence number for each ancestor element that is either an <inform-div1>, or a <div1>, or a <div2>, etc. Like most template rules in a rule-based stylesheet, it doesn't attempt to do any validation: if the input structure is wrong, it will produce some sort of output regardless, and it's up to the document author to work out what the problem is. This raises an interesting question that you need to consider when designing your own stylesheets: is it the job of the stylesheet to detect and report on errors in the source document?

Creating Section Headers

The next section of the stylesheet is concerned with formatting the section headers. These all have some common logic, concerned with generating the section number and creating a text anchor (<a name="xyz">...</a>) as the target for hyperlinks, so they all call a common named template to do this work. If the section has an id attribute, this is used as the anchor; otherwise an anchor is generated from the section's title. This logic must match the logic used earlier when creating hyperlinks in the table of contents.

Numbers are generated by reusing the template rule we saw while producing the table of contents.

```
<xsl:template match="div1/head | inform-div1/head">
   <h2><xsl:call-template name="head"/></h2>
</xsl:template>

<xsl:template match="div2/head">
   <h3><xsl:call-template name="head"/></h3>
</xsl:template>
```

```
<xsl:template match="div3/head">
   <h4><xsl:call-template name="head"/></h4>
</xsl:template>

<xsl:template match="div4/head">
   <h5><xsl:call-template name="head"/></h5>
</xsl:template>

<xsl:template name="head">
   <xsl:for-each select="..">
      <xsl:call-template name="insertID"/>
      <xsl:apply-templates select="." mode="number"/>
   </xsl:for-each>
   <xsl:apply-templates/>
   <xsl:call-template name="inform"/>
</xsl:template>

<xsl:template name="insertID">
   <xsl:choose>
      <xsl:when test="@id">
         <a name="{@id}"/>
      </xsl:when>
      <xsl:otherwise>
         <a name="section-{translate(head,' ','-')}"/>
      </xsl:otherwise>
   </xsl:choose>
</xsl:template>
```

Note the use of `<xsl:for-each select="..">`. This doesn't do an iteration (a node only has one parent), rather it is there to change the current node from the `<head>` element to its parent `<divX>` element, because that is where the `insertID` template expects to be positioned.

Within the «head» template, the call on the «inform» template simply produces the phrase "(Non-normative)" on appropriate appendices, as before.

Formatting the Text

We now find a number of template rules to process simple textual markup within the body of the document. These are very straightforward, though if you want to understand exactly why they take the form they do, it is worth looking at the source document to understand its structure. In fact, not all the elements mentioned here are used in the XML specification: it's likely that these were present in earlier drafts.

```
<xsl:template match="item/p" priority="1">
   <p><xsl:apply-templates/></p>
</xsl:template>
                  <!-- this template appears to be redundant,
                       it was probably at some time different
                       from the following template -->
```

```
<xsl:template match="p">
   <p><xsl:apply-templates/></p>
</xsl:template>

<xsl:template match="term">
   <b><xsl:apply-templates/></b>
</xsl:template>

<xsl:template match="code">
   <code><xsl:apply-templates/></code>
</xsl:template>

<xsl:template match="emph">
   <i><xsl:apply-templates/></i>
</xsl:template>

<xsl:template match="blist">
   <dl><xsl:apply-templates/></dl>
</xsl:template>

<xsl:template match="slist">
   <ul><xsl:apply-templates/></ul>
</xsl:template>

<xsl:template match="sitem">
   <li><xsl:apply-templates/></li>
</xsl:template>

<xsl:template match="olist">
   <ol><xsl:apply-templates/></ol>
</xsl:template>

<xsl:template match="ulist">
   <ul><xsl:apply-templates/></ul>
</xsl:template>

<xsl:template match="glist">
   <dl><xsl:apply-templates/></dl>
</xsl:template>

<xsl:template match="olist">
   <ol><xsl:apply-templates/></ol>
</xsl:template>

<xsl:template match="item">
   <li><xsl:apply-templates/></li>
</xsl:template>

<xsl:template match="label">
   <dt><b><xsl:apply-templates/></b></dt>
</xsl:template>
```

```
<xsl:template match="def">
   <dd><xsl:apply-templates/></dd>
</xsl:template>

<xsl:template match="quote">
   <xsl:text>"</xsl:text>
   <xsl:apply-templates/>
   <xsl:text>"</xsl:text>
</xsl:template>

<!-- examples -->

<xsl:template match="eg">
   <pre>
      <xsl:if test="@role='error'">
         <xsl:attribute name="style">color: red</xsl:attribute>
      </xsl:if>
      <xsl:apply-templates/>
   </pre>
</xsl:template>

<!-- general-purpose tables -->

<xsl:template match="htable">
   <table border="{@border}"
           cellpadding="{@cellpadding}"
           align="{@align}">
      <xsl:apply-templates/>
   </table>
</xsl:template>
```

An observation here is that «border="{@border}"» will generate the output «border=""» if the element in the source document has no border attribute. It might have been better to write:

```
<table>
   <xsl:copy-of select="@align | @border | @cellpadding"/>
   <xsl:apply-templates/>
</table>
```

The stylesheet continues:

```
<xsl:template match="htbody">
   <tbody><xsl:apply-templates/></tbody>
</xsl:template>

<xsl:template match="tr">
   <tr align="{@align}" valign="{@valign}">
      <xsl:apply-templates/>
   </tr>
</xsl:template>
```

```
<xsl:template match="td">
   <td bgcolor="{@bgcolor}"
       rowspan="{@rowspan}"   colspan="{@colspan}"
       align="{@align}"    valign="{@valign}">
      <xsl:apply-templates/>
   </td>
</xsl:template>

<!-- notes -->

<xsl:template match="ednote">
   <blockquote>
      <p><b>Ed. Note: </b><xsl:apply-templates/></p>
   </blockquote>
</xsl:template>

<xsl:template match="edtext">
   <xsl:apply-templates/>
</xsl:template>

<xsl:template match="issue">
   <xsl:call-template name="insertID"/>
   <blockquote>
      <p><b>Issue (<xsl:text/>
         <xsl:value-of   select="substring-after(@id,'-')"/>
         <xsl:text/>): </b>
         <xsl:apply-templates/>
      </p>
   </blockquote>
</xsl:template>

<xsl:template match="note">
   <blockquote>
      <b>NOTE: </b><xsl:apply-templates/>
   </blockquote>
</xsl:template>

<xsl:template match="issue/p | note/p">
   <xsl:apply-templates/>
</xsl:template>
```

Setting out the Production Rules

Now we get to a more interesting area. The XML recommendation contains syntax production rules, and these are marked up in some detail. A sequence of production rules is contained within a `<scrap>` element, and each rule is a `<prod>` element. Here is an example of a scrap that contains a single production rule:

```
<scrap lang='ebnf' id='document'>
   <head>Document</head>
   <prod id='NT-document'>
      <lhs>document</lhs>
```

```
        <rhs>
            <nt def='NT-prolog'>prolog</nt>
            <nt def='NT-element'>element</nt>
            <nt def='NT-Misc'>Misc</nt>*
        </rhs>
    </prod>
</scrap>
```

This is of course the XML production rule, which appears in the spec as:

Document
[1] document ::= prolog element Misc*

In some cases the production rules within a <scrap> are grouped into <prodgroup> elements, but this grouping is ignored in the output.

Here are the top-level template rules:

```
<xsl:template match="scrap">
    <xsl:if test="string(head)">
        <h5><xsl:value-of select="head"/></h5>
    </xsl:if>
    <table class="scrap">
        <tbody>
            <xsl:apply-templates select="prodgroup | prod"/>
        </tbody>
    </table>
</xsl:template>

<xsl:template match="prodgroup">
    <xsl:apply-templates/>
</xsl:template>

<xsl:template match="prod">
    <!-- select elements that start a row -->
    <xsl:apply-templates
        select="*[self::lhs
                or (self::rhs
                    and not(preceding-sibling::*[1][self::lhs]))
                or ((self::vc or self::wfc or self::com)
                    and not(preceding-sibling::*[1][self::rhs]))]
        "/>
</xsl:template>
```

What is this horrendous select expression doing? A production rule (<prod>) has one left hand side (<lhs>), one or more right-hand-sides (<rhs>), and one or more annotations (<vc>, <wfc>, or <com>). A <vc> element is used to refer to a validation constraint, a <wfc> element to refer to a well-formedness constraint, and a <com> element to refer to a comment. A rule with one <lhs> element, two <rhs> elements, and three <wfc> annotations would be laid out in an HTML table like this:

[17]	lhs1	::=	rhs1	
			rhs2	wfc1
				wfc2
				wfc3

As the comment says, the `select` expression is processing the children of the `<prod>` element that start a new row: here lhs1, rhs2, wfc2, and wfc3. More precisely, the selected elements include any `<lhs>` element, any `<rhs>` element that is not immediately preceded by an `<lhs>` element, and any `<vc>`, `<wfc>` or `<com>` element that is not immediately preceded by an `<rhs>` element. So, this template selects the elements that will start a new row, and calls `<xsl:apply-templates>` to process them.

We'll now look at the template rules that will match these elements. First the `<lhs>`:

```
<xsl:template match="lhs">
  <tr valign="baseline">
  <td><a name="{../@id}"/>
     <xsl:number from="body" level="any"
               format="[1]   "/>
  </td>
  <td><xsl:apply-templates/></td>
  <td>
     <xsl:text>   ::=   </xsl:text>
  </td>
  <xsl:for-each select="following-sibling::*[1]">
     <td><xsl:apply-templates mode="cell" select="."/></td>
     <td><xsl:apply-templates mode="cell"
           select="following-sibling::*[1]
                     [self::vc or self::wfc or self::com]"/>
     </td>
  </xsl:for-each>
  </tr>
</xsl:template>
```

The call on `<xsl:number>` here is a good example of how to generate a sequence of numbers that runs through the document. It creates a sequential number for each `<lhs>` element, that is, for each production rule.

The template then calls `<xsl:apply-templates/>` to process the contents of the `<lhs>` element, which will generally just be the name of the syntactic term being defined, and outputs the « ::= » that separates the term from its definition.

The `<xsl:for-each>` that follows does not do any iteration, it merely moves the current position along to the next sibling. This is because the `select` expression, with its «[1]» predicate, can only ever select a single node.

This node will be the first `<rhs>` element. It calls `<xsl:apply-templates>` to process this first `<rhs>` element with «mode="cell"»; and then, if the element after this is a `<vc>`, `<wfc>` or `<com>` element, it processes that one with «mode="cell"» too. This logic must match the logic used earlier for deciding which elements should start a new row: we must only process those that go on the same row as the `<lhs>` element at this stage.

The next two template rules are used respectively for `<rhs>` elements that start a new row, and for `<vc>`, `<wfc>`, and `<com>` elements that start a new row: that is, rhs2, wfc2, and wfc3 in our example. In each case the template has to generate a number of empty table cells to get the horizontal alignment right.

```
<xsl:template match="rhs">
   <tr valign="baseline">
      <td></td>
      <td></td>
      <td></td>
      <td><xsl:apply-templates mode="cell" select="."/></td>
      <td><xsl:apply-templates mode="cell"
            select="following-sibling::*[1]
                       [self::vc or self::wfc or self::com]"/>
      </td>
   </tr>
</xsl:template>

<xsl:template match="vc | wfc | com">
   <tr valign="baseline">
      <td></td>
      <td></td>
      <td></td>
      <td></td>
      <td><xsl:apply-templates mode="cell" select="."/></td>
   </tr>
</xsl:template>
```

Some people prefer to avoid empty table cells by writing «<td> </td>», but that's only really necessary if the table has borders or a background color.

The `<rhs>` rule uses the same kind of logic as the `<lhs>` rule to process any following `<vc>`, `<wfc>`, and `<com>` elements that belong in the same row.

Now we need to write template rules for elements that go in the same row as a previous element, like rhs1 and wfc1 in the example. These will always be invoked with «mode="cell"». The first two are very simple, because the surrounding `<td>` elements have already been generated.

```
<xsl:template match="rhs" mode="cell">
   <xsl:apply-templates/>
</xsl:template>
```

9

Worked Examples

```
<xsl:template match="com" mode="cell">
    <xsl:text>/*</xsl:text>
    <xsl:apply-templates/>
    <xsl:text>*/</xsl:text>
</xsl:template>
```

For `<vc>` and `<wfc>` elements, we need some logic to generate a hyperlink to the paragraph that describes the validation constraint or well-formedness constraint. The link is represented in the XML by a `def` attribute, and this is used directly to construct the HTML internal hyperlink. The displayed text of the link is formed by retrieving the element whose `ID` is equal to this def attribute, and displaying its text.

For example, if the `<vc>` element has the form `<vc def="vc-roottype"/>`, this points to the following element in the source file:

```
<vcnote id="vc-roottype">
    <head>Root Element Type</head>
    <p>The Name in the document type declaration must match the element type
        of the root element.</p>
</vcnote>
```

so the generated HTML is:

```
<a href="#vc-roottype">Root Element Type</a>
```

Back to the stylesheet:

```
<xsl:template match="vc" mode="cell">
    <xsl:text>[ VC: </xsl:text>
    <a href="#{@def}">
        <xsl:value-of select="id(@def)/head"/>
    </a>
    <xsl:text> ]</xsl:text>
    <xsl:apply-templates/>
</xsl:template>

<xsl:template match="wfc" mode="cell">
    <xsl:text>[ WFC: </xsl:text>
    <a href="#{@def}">
        <xsl:value-of select="id(@def)/head"/>
    </a>
    <xsl:text> ]</xsl:text>
    <xsl:apply-templates/>
</xsl:template>
```

So much for formatting the production rules! This was by far the most complicated part of this stylesheet, the rest should be plain sailing.

Making Cross-references

The next section of the stylesheet is concerned with formatting cross-references. First we'll show the template rules for creating anchors that we can link to – these all generate an element of the form `<a name="xyz">...</a>`. They are used for bibliography items, definitions of terms, and descriptions of validity and well-formedness constraints.

```
<xsl:template match="blist/bibl">
   <dt>
      <a name="{@id}"><xsl:value-of select="@key"/></a>
   </dt>
   <dd>
      <xsl:apply-templates/>
   </dd>
</xsl:template>

<xsl:template match="termdef">
   <a name="{@id}"/><xsl:apply-templates/>
</xsl:template>

<xsl:template match="vcnote">
   <a name="{@id}"/>
   <p><b>Validity Constraint: <xsl:text/>
      <xsl:value-of select="head"/></b></p>
   <xsl:apply-templates/>
</xsl:template>

<xsl:template match="wfcnote">
   <a name="{@id}"></a>
   <p><b>Well Formedness Constraint: <xsl:text/>
      <xsl:value-of    select="head"/></b></p>
   <xsl:apply-templates/>
</xsl:template>
```

And now the template rules that generate the hyperlinks. These all generate an element of the form `<a href="xyz">...</a>` for an external reference or `<a href="#xyz">...</a>` for an internal one.

```
<!-- external references -->

<xsl:template match="p/loc" priority="1">
   <a href="{@href}"><xsl:apply-templates/></a>
</xsl:template>

<xsl:template match="loc">
   <a href="{@href}"><xsl:apply-templates/></a>
</xsl:template>
```

The `priority` attribute on the first template rule is not really necessary; the default priorities would automatically give it higher priority than the rule that follows. In fact it's doubly unnecessary here because the two rules are identical! However, some people prefer to make priorities explicit in such cases, for documentation if nothing else.

```
<xsl:template match="xspecref | xtermref">
    <a href="{@href}"><xsl:apply-templates/></a>
</xsl:template>

<xsl:template match="xnt">
    <a href="{@href}"><xsl:apply-templates/></a>
</xsl:template>

<!-- internal cross-references -->

<xsl:template match="titleref">
    <a href="#{@href}"><xsl:apply-templates/>   </a>
</xsl:template>

<xsl:template match="nt">
    <a href="#{@def}"><xsl:apply-templates/></a>
</xsl:template>

<xsl:template match="termref">
    <a href="#{@def}"><xsl:apply-templates/></a>
</xsl:template>

<xsl:template match="bibref">
    <a href="#{@ref}">
        <xsl:text>[</xsl:text>.
        <xsl:value-of select="id(@ref)/@key"/>
        <xsl:apply-templates/>
        <xsl:text>]</xsl:text>
    </a>
</xsl:template>

<xsl:template match="specref">
    <a href="#{@ref}">
        <xsl:text>[</xsl:text>
        <b>
            <!-- Add the section number and heading of the target -->
            <xsl:for-each select="id(@ref)/head">
            <xsl:apply-templates select=".." mode="number"/>
            <xsl:apply-templates/>
            </xsl:for-each>
        </b>
        <xsl:apply-templates/>
        <xsl:text>]</xsl:text>
    </a>
</xsl:template>
```

Nothing very complicated here. The last template rule is a bit more complicated than the others: it's creating a reference to a section that incorporates its section number, which it obtains by calling `<xsl:apply-templates>` to process the referenced element with «mode="number"».

Filtering Out What We Don't Want

We now have some template rules for elements in the XML source document that we don't want to include in the HTML output at all. An empty `<xsl:template>` element is a "no-op", it says that when this pattern is matched, no output should be produced. If these template rules weren't included, the built-in template rule would kick in for these elements, which would output the text of the element without any markup.

```
<xsl:template match="w3c-designation"/>
<xsl:template match="w3c-doctype"/>
<xsl:template match="header/pubdate"/>
<xsl:template match="spec/header/title"/>
<xsl:template match="revisiondesc"/>
<xsl:template match="pubstmt"/>
<xsl:template match="sourcedesc"/>
<xsl:template match="langusage"/>
<xsl:template match="version"/>
```

These elements are mainly metadata, of interest to the authors but not to the readers. (Actually, the revision history is fascinating if you are interested in that sort of thing. It acts as a reminder that filtering out confidential information in a stylesheet is not the world's most effective security technique).

Boilerplate Text

There is now a template that generates fixed boilerplate text:

```
<xsl:template name="copyright">
  <xsl:variable name="legal"
      select="'http://www.w3.org/Consortium/Legal/'"/>
  <p class="copyright">
    <a href="{$legal}ipr-notice.html#Copyright">Copyright</a>
     &copy;  1999
    <a href="http://www.w3.org">W3C</a>
    (<a href="http://www.lcs.mit.edu">MIT</a>,
    <a href="http://www.inria.fr/">INRIA</a>,
    <a href="http://www.keio.ac.jp/">Keio</a>),
    All Rights Reserved. W3C
    <a href="{$legal}ipr-notice.html#Legal_Disclaimer"
      >liability</a>,
    <a href="{$legal}ipr-notice.html#W3C_Trademarks"
      >trademark</a>,
    <a href="{$legal}copyright-documents.html">document use</a>
    and
    <a href="{$legal}copyright-software.html"
      >software licensing</a> rules apply.
  </p>
</xsl:template>
```

9

Worked Examples

List of Contributors

The last four template rules format the list of contributors at the end of the document. There are two rules that match «orglist/member», the effect is that a semicolon is placed before the name of every member except the first. The priority attribute is necessary this time, because the default priority for both rules would be the same.

```
<xsl:template match="orglist">
   <xsl:apply-templates select="*"/>
</xsl:template>

<xsl:template match="orglist/member[1]" priority="2">
   <xsl:apply-templates select="*"/>
</xsl:template>

<xsl:template match="orglist/member">
   <xsl:text>; </xsl:text>
   <xsl:apply-templates select="*"/>
</xsl:template>

<xsl:template match="orglist/member/affiliation">
   <xsl:text>, </xsl:text>
   <xsl:apply-templates/>
</xsl:template>

<xsl:template match="orglist/member/role">
   <xsl:text> (</xsl:text>
   <xsl:apply-templates/>
   <xsl:text>)</xsl:text>
</xsl:template>
```

And that brings us to the end:

```
</xsl:stylesheet>
```

Variant Stylesheets for the XSLT and XPath Specs

The stylesheet just presented is the one used for the XML specification. The stylesheets used for the XPath and XSLT specifications are slightly different, because these documents use additional element types beyond those used in the XML specification. In each case the XML source document has an internal DTD subset which supplements the base DTD with some additional element types. For example, the XPath document uses special tags to mark up function templates, and the XSLT document has special tags to mark up the proformas used to summarize the syntax of each XSL element.

The stylesheets used for XPath and XSLT therefore consist of a small module that uses <xsl:import> to import the baseline XML stylesheet, and which then defines the extra rules needed for these additional constructs. All three stylesheets are included in the download files for this chapter.

Summary

The example presented here was a real stylesheet, used for a real application, and not just for teaching purposes. It's perhaps slightly atypical in that much of it was written before the XSLT specifications stabilised, so it sometimes does things in a roundabout way. However, it's probably not that dissimilar from many other stylesheets used in document formatting applications.

The phrase "document formatting" is key. The main tasks performed in this stylesheet were applying HTML display styles to different elements, generating hyperlinks, and formatting tables. These are all tasks that lend themselves to using the *rule-based* design pattern.

The next example will be a very different kind of application — one that uses highly-structured data, and displays it in a very different form from the way it arrives in the source document.

A Family Tree

XML is often used for representing information that is a mixture of structured data and text. Rather than taking a simple example of structured data (like the book catalog found in so many XML examples) we will take a look at how to process something rather more complex – a family tree.

I could have used an example with invoices and requisitions and purchase orders. I believe that the techniques used in this worked example are equally applicable to many practical commercial problems, but that you will find a little excursion into the world of genealogy a pleasant relief from the day job.

One caveat, though. Throughout this book I have been talking about tree models of XML, and I have been using words like parent and child, ancestor and descendant, in the context of these data trees. Don't imagine, though, that we can use this tree structure to represent a family tree directly. In fact, a family tree is not really a tree at all, because everyone has two parents: in XML trees, one parent is considered sufficient.

The structure of the family tree is actually quite different from the document tree used to represent it. And in this section, words like parent and child have their everyday meaning!

The Data Model and its XML Representation

The established standard for representing genealogical data is known as GEDCOM, and data in this format is routinely exchanged between software packages and posted on the Internet. The main objects found in a GEDCOM file are records representing individuals (called INDI records), and records representing couples (called FAM records).

An INDI record looks like this:

```
0 @I1@ INDI
1 NAME John Fitzgerald/Kennedy/
1 SEX M
1 BIRT
2 DATE 29 MAY 1917
2 PLAC Brookline, MA, USA
1 DEAT
2 DATE 22 NOV 1963
2 PLAC Dallas, TX, USA
2 NOTE Assassinated by Lee Harvey Oswald.
1 NOTE Educated at Harvard University.
2 CONT Elected Congressman in 1945
2 CONT aged 29; served three terms in the House of Representatives.
2 CONT Elected Senator in 1952. Elected President in 1960, the
2 CONT youngest ever President of the United States.
1 FAMS @F1@
1 FAMC @F2@
```

This is not XML, of course, but we can mechanically convert it to XML, so that it looks like this:

```
<INDI ID="I1">
    <NAME>John Fitzgerald<S>Kennedy</S></NAME>
    <SEX>M</SEX>
    <BIRT>
        <DATE>29 MAY 1917</DATE>
        <PLAC>Brookline, MA, USA</PLAC>
    </BIRT>
    <DEAT>
        <DATE>22 NOV 1963</DATE>
        <PLAC>Dallas, TX, USA</PLAC>
        <NOTE>Assassinated by Lee Harvey Oswald.<BR/></NOTE>
    </DEAT>
    <NOTE>Educated at Harvard University.<BR/>
Elected Congressman in 1945<BR/>
aged 29; served three terms in the House of Representatives.<BR/>
Elected Senator in 1952. Elected President in 1960, the<BR/>
youngest ever President of the United States.<BR/>
    </NOTE>
    <FAMS REF="F1"/>
    <FAMC REF="F2"/>
</INDI>
```

I'll come back later on (page 610) to show how we actually do the conversion into XML.

Each record in a GEDCOM file has a unique identifier (in this case I1 – that's letter I, digit one), which is used to construct cross-references between records. Most of the information in this record is self-explanatory, except the <FAMS> and <FAMC> fields: <FAMS> is a reference to a <FAM> record representing a family in which this person is a parent, and <FAMC> is a reference to a family in which this person is a child.

Note how the fields may be nested to indicate the structure. The GEDCOM specification (which is developed by the Church of Jesus Christ of Latter Day Saints) defines a strict schema saying how the tags can be nested, very much like an XML DTD.

> *An HTML version of the GEDCOM specification can be found at*
> *http://www.tiac.net/users/pmcbride/gedcom/55gctoc.htm.*

However, although the schema is strict, it still allows very varied information to be entered. For example, any number of events or attributes relating to an individual, with full or partial dates, textual notes at any level, and references to sources of information. Examples of events might be birth, death, adoption, or retirement; examples of attributes might be occupation, religion, or health: but the list is open-ended.

9

Worked Examples

The `<INDI>` record contains information about the events and attributes for a person, while the `<FAM>` record defines events for a couple and their family (a "couple" here represents two people who either were married, or had children, or both: either partner may be unknown or unrecorded). A `<FAM>` record, like an `<INDI>` record, has an arbitrary unique identifier. After conversion to XML, it might look like this:

```xml
<FAM ID="F1">
    <HUSB REF="I1"/>
    <WIFE REF="I2"/>
    <CHIL REF="I5"/>
    <CHIL REF="I6"/>
    <CHIL REF="I7"/>
    <MARR>
        <DATE>12 SEP 1953</DATE>
        <PLAC>Newport, RI, USA</PLAC>
    </MARR>
</FAM>
```

The `<FAM>` element contains links to all the individuals making up the family. These are technically redundant in the sense that they could be deduced by finding l links in the opposite direction; but redundancy is not always a bad thing. The element also contains information about events affecting both partners, the most common being their marriage.

To make this clearer, here is a diagram showing how the family relationships are represented.

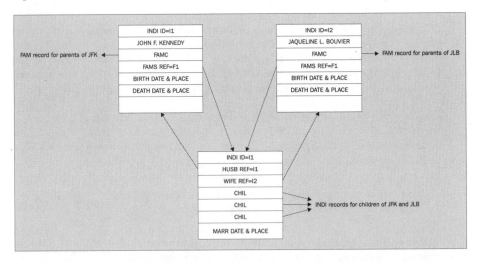

I'm not going to spend time discussing whether this is a good way of representing genealogical information or not. Many people have criticized the data model, either on technical grounds or from the point of view of political correctness, but like the QWERTY keyboard, GEDCOM persists despite its faults simply because so many people are using it.

In GEDCOM, there is no formal way of linking one file to another. XML, of course, creates wonderful opportunities to define how your family tree links to someone else's. But the linking isn't as easy as it sounds (nothing is, in genealogy) because of the problems of maintaining version integrity between two datasets that are changing independently. So I'll avoid getting into that area, and stick to the model that the whole family tree is in one XML document.

Displaying the Family Tree Data

What we want to do is to write a stylesheet that displays the data in a GEDCOM file in HTML format. We'll assume for the moment that the conversion to XML syntax has already been done (I'll discuss how it's done later in the chapter, on page 610). We want the display to look something like the screenshot below:

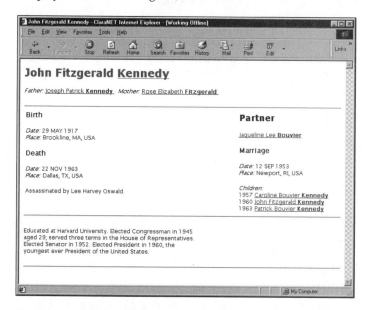

This shows all the details of one individual, with links to related individuals so that you can browse around the family tree. Of course one could attempt many more ambitious ways of displaying this data, and I would encourage you to do so: you can start with the small Kennedy data set included in download for this book, and then continue with any other GEDCOM data set, perhaps one of your own family tree.

Since we will have one HTML page for each individual in the file, we have to think about how to create multiple HTML pages from a single XML input document. There are at least three ways of doing this:

❑   A bulk publishing process, in which you convert the XML input document into a set of HTML pages, and then publish these as static pages on the web server. This has the benefit that you only incur the cost of transformation once. It minimizes your dependence on the facilities available from your Internet Service Provider, and it will work with any browser.

9

Worked Examples

❑   Generating HTML pages on demand in the server, using Java servlets or ASP pages. Again this will work with any browser, but this time you need to find an Internet Service Provider who allows you to run servlets or ASP pages.

❑   Downloading the entire XML file to the client, and generating the display there. This has the advantage that the data is only downloaded once, and the user can then browse it at leisure, with no further interaction with the server. However, this will only work if the user has an XML-capable browser, which today means Internet Explorer 5.

The Netscape 6 / Mozilla browser will support XML and CSS but plans for XSLT support are less clear, though there is a good chance that someone will produce a plug-in. Watch out for news on **http://www.mozilla.org**.

Another disadvantage is security: you have no way of filtering the data, for example to remove details of living persons, and you have no way to stop your entire XML file being copied by the user (for example, the user can do View Source, or can poke around in the browser cache).

The only real difference between the three cases, as far as the stylesheet is concerned, is that the hyperlinks will be generated differently.

There are other differences for the client-side stylesheet, mainly caused by products that don't yet support all features of the standard – but those are hopefully temporary.

We'll handle the differences by writing a generic stylesheet module containing all the common code for the three cases, and then importing this into stylesheets that handle the variations.

The Stylesheet

We're ready to write a stylesheet, `person.xls` that generates an HTML page showing the information relevant to a particular individual. This stylesheet will need to accept the ID of the required individual as a global parameter. If no value is supplied, we'll choose the first `<INDI>` record in the file. Here's the top-level structure:

```
<xsl:transform
    xmlns:xsl="http://www.w3.org/1999/XSL/Transform"
    version="1.0" >

<xsl:param name="id" select="/*/INDI[1]/@ID"/>

<!-- define keys to allow records to be found by their id -->

<xsl:key name="indi" match="INDI" use="@ID"/>
<xsl:key name="fam" match="FAM" use="@ID"/>
```

```
<xsl:template match="/">
   <xsl:variable name="person" select="key('indi', $id)"/>
   <xsl:apply-templates select="$person"/>
</xsl:template>

. . .

</xsl:transform>
```

I've decided to define two keys to give immediate access to <INDI> and <FAM> elements if their ID attributes are known. I could have relied on the id() function, but that would only work if the ID attribute is defined in the DTD as being an attribute of type ID. This makes the stylesheet dependent on having a DTD, so on balance I decided that using the key() function is safer.

The initial template (the one that matches the root node) then calls <xsl:apply-templates> to process the <INDI> element representing the selected person.

The template rule for an <INDI> element creates the shell of the HTML page:

```
<xsl:template match="INDI">
   <html>
      <head>
         <xsl:call-template name="css-style"/>
         <xsl:variable name="name">
            <xsl:apply-templates select="NAME"/>
         </xsl:variable>
         <title><xsl:value-of select="$name"/></title>
      </head>

      <!-- choose background color based on gender -->

      <xsl:variable name="color">
         <xsl:choose>
            <xsl:when test="SEX='M'">cyan</xsl:when>
            <xsl:otherwise>pink</xsl:otherwise>
         </xsl:choose>
      </xsl:variable>

      <body bgcolor="{$color}">

         <!-- Show name and parentage -->

         <h1><xsl:apply-templates select="NAME"/></h1>
         <xsl:call-template name="show-parents"/>
         <hr/>

         <table>
         <tr>
```

9

Worked Examples

```
                <!-- Show events and attributes -->

                <td width="50%" valign="top">
                    <xsl:call-template name="show-events"/>
                </td>
                <td width="20%"/>

                <!-- Show partners, marriages, and children -->

                <td width="30%" valign="top">
                    <xsl:call-template name="show-partners"/>
                </td>
            </tr>
            </table>

            <hr/>

            <!-- Show notes -->

            <xsl:for-each select="NOTE">
                <p class="text"><xsl:apply-templates/></p>
                <xsl:if test="position()=last()"><hr/></xsl:if>
            </xsl:for-each>

        </body>
    </html>
</xsl:template>
```

This template rule works through the process of generating the output page. Some observations:

❑ The title in the HTML header is generated by first creating a variable, and then copying the value of the variable to the <title> element. This is deliberate: it takes advantage of the standard template rules for generating a personal name, but the <xsl:value-of> instruction then removes the tags such as <b> that appear in the generated name, because these clutter the displayed title in some browsers.

❑ The background color of the page depends on the value of the person's SEX attribute. You might consider this to be rather childish, in which case you are welcome to change it, but I left it in because it illustrates another XSLT technique.

❑ The main task of generating the content of the page is split up and delegated to separate named templates, simply for reasons of modularity.

❑ There is no attempt to display all the data that GEDCOM allows to be included in, or referenced from, an <INDI> record, for example citations of sources, multimedia objects such as photographs, etc. Any such data will simply be skipped.

I've chosen to use an internal CSS stylesheet to define font sizes and the like, and the task of generating this is delegated to the template named css-style. This generates fixed output, as follows:

```
<xsl:template name="css-style">
   <style type="text/css">

   H1 {
      font-family: Verdana, Helvetica, sans-serif;
      font-size: 18pt;
      font-weight: bold;
      color: "#FF0080"
   }

   H2 {
      font-family: Verdana, Helvetica, sans-serif;
      font-size: 14pt;
      font-weight: bold;
      color: black;
   }

   H3 {
      font-family: Lucida Sans, Helvetica, sans-serif;
      font-size: 11pt;
      font-weight: bold;
      color: black;
   }

   SPAN.label {
      font-family: Lucida Sans, Helvetica, sans-serif;
      font-size: 10pt;
      font-weight: normal;
      font-style: italic;
      color: black;
   }

   P,LI,TD {
      font-family: Lucida Sans, Helvetica, sans-serif;
      font-size: 10pt;
      font-weight: normal;
      color: black;
   }

   P.text {
      font-family: Comic Sans MS, Helvetica, sans-serif;
      font-size: 10pt;
      font-weight: normal;
      color: black;
   }

   </style>
</xsl:template>
```

It would have been quite possible, of course, to attach these attributes to the various HTML elements individually, or to incorporate them using XSLT attribute sets, but this way seems cleaner, and shows how XSLT and CSS can complement each other. In fact, it might have been even better to use an external CSS stylesheet, since a user displaying many of these HTML pages would then get more benefit from caching.

The next template displays the parents of the current individual, as hyperlinks. Here it is:

```
<xsl:template name="show-parents">

   <xsl:variable name="parents" select="key('fam', FAMC/@REF)"/>
   <xsl:variable name="father" select="key('indi', $parents/HUSB/@REF)"/>
   <xsl:variable name="mother" select="key('indi', $parents/WIFE/@REF)"/>

   <p>
   <xsl:if test="$father">
      <span class="label">Father: </span>
      <xsl:apply-templates select="$father/NAME" mode="link"/> 
   </xsl:if>
   <xsl:if test="$mother">
      <span class="label">Mother: </span>
      <xsl:apply-templates select="$mother/NAME" mode="link"/> 
   </xsl:if>
   </p>
</xsl:template>
```

The template starts by locating the <FAM> record referenced by the <FAMC> field of the current <INDI> record. It does this using the «fam» key defined earlier. Then it selects the <INDI> records for the father and mother, these being the records pointed to by the <HUSB> and <WIFE> fields of the <FAM> record: this time the «indi» key is used.

If the data is not all present, for example if there is no <FAMC> field, or if the <FAM> has no <HUSB> or <WIFE> (no ancestry goes back to infinity), then the «$father» and or «$mother» variables will simply identify an empty node-set. The subsequent <xsl:if> instructions ensure that when this happens, the relevant label is omitted from the output.

The actual hyperlinks are generated by using <xsl:apply-templates> with «mode="link"»: this gets reused for all the other links on the page, and we'll see later how it works. The « » character reference outputs a non-breaking space. It's actually simpler to do this than to output an ordinary space, which would require an <xsl:text> element. If you don't like numeric character references you can define an entity called «nbsp» in the <!DOCTYPE> declaration and then use « » in place of « ».

The next named template is used to display the list of events for an individual, such as birth and death. We will also use it later to display all the events for a couple (such as marriage and divorce).

```
<xsl:template name="show-events">
  <xsl:for-each select="*">
    <xsl:sort select="substring(DATE, string-length(DATE) - 3)"/>

    <xsl:variable name="event-name">
      <xsl:apply-templates select="." mode="expand"/>
    </xsl:variable>

    <xsl:if test="$event-name">
      <h3><xsl:value-of select="$event-name"/></h3>
      <p>
      <xsl:if test="DATE">
        <span class="label">Date: </span>
        <xsl:value-of select="DATE"/><br/>
      </xsl:if>
      <xsl:if test="PLAC">
        <span class="label">Place: </span>
        <xsl:value-of select="PLAC"/><br/>
      </xsl:if>
      </p>
      <xsl:for-each select="NOTE">
        <p class="text"><xsl:apply-templates/></p>
      </xsl:for-each>
    </xsl:if>
  </xsl:for-each>
</xsl:template>
```

The events are presented in an attempt at date order. The logic in <xsl:sort> to extract the last four characters of the <DATE> field is pragmatic, but in the vast majority of cases it gives the year of the event. Simple dates in GEDCOM are in the format «21 APR 1862». The pragmatic approach works even where the date has a form such as «BETWEEN 1865 AND 1868». It fails with a date of «55 BC», but fortunately the Kennedy data doesn't go that far back. A nice enhancement to the stylesheet would be to take the month and day into account when sorting (it is common for two events to occur in the same year, for example death and burial). The best way to achieve this would probably be to use an extension function which converts the GEDCOM date into an ISO date in the form YYYYMMDD.

It's not immediately obvious which elements in the source data relate to events. The GEDCOM standard lists dozens of possible events, and we don't really want to use a union expression of the form select="BIRT | DEAT | BAPM | BURI" that lists them all. Also, we need some kind of translation from the abbreviated tag name (such as BURI) to a more meaningful name or description of the event, such as "Burial". We can kill two birds with one stone by applying another template to the element, in mode «expand»: where the element is recognized as an event, this will return the meaningful name of the event, and where it isn't, it will return an empty string. So we only process those where the returned $event-name is non-empty.

9

Worked Examples

599

So there should now be a long list of templates to expand the tags of individual event types. I won't list them all, just those used most commonly:

```
<xsl:template match="BIRT" mode="expand">Birth</xsl:template>
<xsl:template match="DEAT" mode="expand">Death</xsl:template>
<xsl:template match="BURI" mode="expand">Burial</xsl:template>
<xsl:template match="BAPM" mode="expand">Baptism</xsl:template>
<xsl:template match="MARR" mode="expand">Marriage</xsl:template>
<xsl:template match="EVEN" mode="expand">
   <xsl:value-of select="TYPE"/>
</xsl:template>
<xsl:template match="*" mode="expand"/>
```

The template rule for <EVEN> catches GEDCOM's all-purpose event, which has a <TYPE> child element to give a description of the event. This is used for non-standard events such as "won the jackpot in the National Lottery" that have no explicit tag allocated in the GEDCOM standard. And the final rule ensures that non-event elements return an empty string, and are thus recognized as non-events.

The only part of the HTML display that remains is the right hand panel, where we show information about a person's partner(s) and marriage(s). If multiple partners or marriages are recorded for an individual, there will be multiple <FAMS> fields within the <INDI> element. If there are several, we use headings such as "Partner 1", "Partner 2"; if there is only one, we omit the number.

So the first thing we do is to find all the <FAM> records in which the individual is a spouse: we assign this node-set to the variable $partnerships.

For a woman, to find the name of her partner we need to follow the <HUSB> link, while for a man we need to follow the <WIFE> link. Since the sex may not be recorded, the safest strategy is to look at both partners and list whichever is different from the starting individual. That is also tolerant to situations such as same-sex marriages: when handling genealogical data it's best to be flexible, not only because such things may actually happen whether you approve of it or not, but more importantly, because errors in historical source data are part of life.

The template looks like this:

```
<xsl:template name="show-partners">
   <xsl:variable name="subject" select="."/>
   <xsl:variable name="partnerships"
                 select="key('fam', FAMS/@REF)"/>
   <xsl:for-each select="$partnerships">
      <xsl:sort select="substring(MARR/DATE,
                        string-length(MARR/DATE) - 3)"/>

      <xsl:variable name="partner"
          select="key('indi',
                  (HUSB/@REF | WIFE/@REF)[.!=$subject/@ID])"/>
```

```
            <xsl:variable name="partner-seq">
               <xsl:choose>
                  <xsl:when test="count($subject/FAMS)=1"></xsl:when>
                  <xsl:otherwise>
                     <xsl:value-of select="position()"/>
                  </xsl:otherwise>
               </xsl:choose>
            </xsl:variable>

            <xsl:if test="$partner">
               <h2>Partner <xsl:value-of select="$partner-seq"/></h2>
               <p>
               <xsl:apply-templates select="$partner/NAME" mode="link"/>
               </p>
            </xsl:if>

            <xsl:call-template name="show-events"/>

            <xsl:variable name="children" select="key('indi', CHIL/@REF)"/>
            <xsl:if test="$children">
               <p><span class="label">Children:</span><br/>
               <xsl:for-each select="$children">
                  <xsl:sort select="substring(BIRT/DATE,
                             string-length(BIRT/DATE) - 3)"/>
                  <xsl:value-of select="substring(BIRT/DATE,
                             string-length(BIRT/DATE) - 3)"/>
                  <xsl:text> </xsl:text>
                  <xsl:apply-templates select="NAME" mode="link"/><br/>
               </xsl:for-each>
               </p>
            </xsl:if>
         </xsl:for-each>
      </xsl:template>
```

As before, we try to list the partners in chronological order, based on the year of marriage: if this isn't known, there's not much we can do about it. For each partnership, we list the partner's name, as a hyperlink, then the events associated with the partnership (typically just the marriage), and finally the children's names, again as hyperlinks. The children are found from the <CHIL> fields of the <FAM> record, and are listed in order of year of birth where this is known.

The next group of template rules is used to create the HTML hyperlinks:

```
<xsl:template match="NAME" mode="link">
   <a>
      <xsl:attribute name="href">
         <xsl:call-template name="make-href"/>
      </xsl:attribute>
      <xsl:apply-templates/>
   </a>
</xsl:template>
```

```
<xsl:template match="S">
   <xsl:text> </xsl:text>
   <b><u><xsl:apply-templates/></u></b>
   <xsl:text> </xsl:text>
</xsl:template>

<xsl:template name="make-href">
   <xsl:value-of select="concat(../@ID, '.html')"/>
</xsl:template>
```

The «make-href» template is the only place where the form of a link is defined: in this case it consists of a relative URL reference to another HTML file, with a filename based on the individual's ID attribute, for example I27.html.

The stylesheet ends with a trivial rule for <BR> elements, which are used to separate lines of text:

```
<xsl:template match="BR"><BR/></xsl:template>

</xsl:transform>
```

Putting it Together

We've now got a stylesheet that can generate an HTML page for a single chosen individual. We don't yet have a working web site!

As I suggested earlier, there are three ways you can work. You can do a batch conversion of the entire data file into a collection of linked static HTML pages held on the web server, you can generate each page on demand from the server, or you can generate pages dynamically at the client. I'll show how to do all three: but unfortunately, they all require the use of facilities that go beyond the XSLT standard, and exploit interfaces provided by specific vendor's products.

Publishing Static HTML

To generate HTML files for all the individuals in the data file, we need some kind of script that processes each individual in turn and produces a separate output file for each one. Fortunately many of the XSLT products available include the capability to produce multiple output files from one input file; but unfortunately each product uses different syntax.

In this example I'll use the syntax offered by the Saxon product (Saxon was developed by the author of this book, so it's a natural choice); the equivalent facilities in other products are described in Chapter 10.

We'll need a new template for processing the root element, and because this must override the template defined in person.xsl, we'll need to use <xsl:import> to give the new template higher precedence.

Here is the complete stylesheet, `publish.xsl`, to do the bulk conversion. As well as generating an HTML page for each individual, it also creates an index page listing all the individuals sorted first by surname, then by the rest of the name.

```
<xsl:transform
  xmlns:xsl="http://www.w3.org/1999/XSL/Transform"
  xmlns:saxon="http://icl.com/saxon"
  extension-element-prefixes="saxon"
  version="1.0" >

<xsl:import href="person.xsl"/>

<xsl:param name="dir" select="'.'"/>

<xsl:template match="/">
   <xsl:for-each select="*/INDI">
      <saxon:output file="{$dir}/{@ID}.html">
         <xsl:apply-templates select="."/>
      </saxon:output>
   </xsl:for-each>
   <saxon:output file="{$dir}/index.html">
      <xsl:call-template name="make-index"/>
   </saxon:output>
</xsl:template>

<xsl:template name="make-index">
   <html>
   <head>
      <title>Index of names</title>
   </head>
   <body>
   <h1>Index of names</h1>
   <p>
      <xsl:for-each select="/*/INDI/NAME">
         <xsl:sort select="S"/>
         <xsl:sort select="text()"/>
         <a>
            <xsl:attribute name="href">
               <xsl:call-template name="make-href"/>
            </xsl:attribute>
            <xsl:value-of select="S"/>,
            <xsl:for-each select="text()">
               <xsl:value-of select="concat(' ', ., ' ')"/>
            </xsl:for-each>
         </a>
         <br/>
      </xsl:for-each>
   </p>
   </body>
   </html>
</xsl:template>

</xsl:transform>
```

To run this stylesheet, you will first need to install the Saxon product, which can be found at http://users.iclway.co.uk/mhkay/saxon/. If you are using a Windows platform, it is simplest to install Instant Saxon, which is at :

http://users.iclway.co.uk/mhkay/saxon/instant.html.

You will also need to download the example files from the Wrox website. Create a new directory, copy the stylesheets and the XML data file into it, make this the current directory, and then run the command:

```
saxon kennedy.xml publish.xsl
```

This assumes that you've added saxon.exe to your PATH; if not, change the command to (say) `c:\saxondir\saxon` if you installed the product into `c:\saxondir`

If you want to generate the HTML files in a different directory, you can specify this on the command line, for example:

```
saxon kennedy.xml publish.xsl dir=d:\jfk
```

The new directory should fill with HTML files: double click on the `index.html` file, and you should see an index of names. Click on any of the names to see the screen shown on page 593, in glorious color. Then browse the data by following the relationships.

Generating HTML Pages from a Servlet

An alternative to bulk-converting the XML data into static HTML pages is to generate each HTML page on request. This requires execution of a stylesheet on the server, which in principle can be controlled using ASP pages, Java servlets, or even raw CGI programs. However, as many of the available XSLT processors are written in Java, it turns out to be most convenient to use servlets.

If you aren't familiar with servlet programming, it's probably best to skip this section, because there isn't space here to start from first principles. If you're keen, check out *Professional Java Server Programming* (1-861002-77-7), also published by Wrox Press.

Each XSLT processor currently has a different Java API, so the way you invoke the processor from a servlet will be different in each case. Many of them have some kind of packaged servlet interface, though it's often best to customize it to suit the particular requirements of the application. As there are a lot of variations depending on the environment you are working in, I won't try to give a complete working solution for this situation, but will just sketch out the design.

A particular feature of this application is that there are lots of requests to get data from the same source document, using the same stylesheet, but with different parameters. So ideally we want to hold both the source document and the stylesheet in memory on the server: we don't want to incur the overhead of parsing the full XML document to display each individual.

We would like to accept incoming requests from the browser in the form:

```
http://www.myserver.com/servlets/GedServlet?tree=kennedy&id=I1
```

The parameters included in the URL are firstly, the name of the dataset to use (we'd like the server to be able to handle several concurrently), and secondly, the identifier of the individual to display.

So the first thing that we need to do is to generate hyperlinks in this format. We can do this by writing a new stylesheet module that imports person.xsl and overrides the template that generated the hyperlinks. We'll call this ged-servlet.xsl.

The ged-servlet.xsl stylesheet module looks like this. It has an extra parameter, which is the name of the tree we are interested in, because the same servlet ought to be able to handle requests for data from different family trees. And it overrides the «make-href» template with one that generates hyperlinks in the required format:

```
<xsl:transform
    xmlns:xsl="http://www.w3.org/1999/XSL/Transform"
    version="1.0" >

<xsl:import href="person.xsl"/>
<xsl:param name="tree"/>

<xsl:template name="make-href">
   <xsl:value-of select="concat('/servlet/GedServlet?tree=',
                        $tree, '&amp;id=', ../@ID)"/>
</xsl:template>

</xsl:transform>
```

The stylesheet and the servlet interface could also be extended to generate an index of names, as in the previous example, but as that's a simple task I'll leave you to work that out for yourself.

More tricky is writing the servlet. The details of this will vary according to which product you are using, though the general structure is likely to be similar. For Saxon, the following code (in GedServlet.java) will do the job:

```
import java.io.*;
import javax.servlet.*;
import javax.servlet.http.*;
import java.util.*;

import com.icl.saxon.*;
import com.icl.saxon.output.*;
import com.icl.saxon.expr.*;
import org.xml.sax.*;

public class GedServlet extends HttpServlet {
```

```
/**
* Respond to an HTTP request
*/

public void service(HttpServletRequest req, HttpServletResponse res)
throws ServletException, IOException
{
    ServletOutputStream out = res.getOutputStream();

    try {
        String clear = req.getParameter("clear");
        if (clear!=null && clear.equals("yes")) {
            resetData();
        }

        String tree = req.getParameter("tree");
        String id = req.getParameter("id");

        PreparedStyleSheet style = getStyleSheet();
        DocumentInfo doc = getSourceDocument(tree);

        ParameterSet params = new ParameterSet();
        params.put("id", new StringValue(id));
        params.put("tree", new StringValue(tree));

        StyleSheetInstance transform = style.makeStyleSheetInstance();

        OutputDetails details = new OutputDetails();
        details.setOutputStream (out);
        transform.setOutputDetails(details);
        transform.setParams(params);
        transform.renderDocument(doc, true);

    } catch (SAXException err) {
        out.println("Error applying stylesheet: " + err.getMessage());
    }
    res.setContentType("text/html");
}

/**
* Get the prepared stylesheet from memory; prepare it if necessary
*/

private synchronized PreparedStyleSheet getStyleSheet()
throws SAXException {
    if (stylesheet == null) {
        stylesheet = new PreparedStyleSheet();
        File sheet = new File(
            getServletContext().getRealPath("/ged-servlet.xsl"));
        stylesheet.prepare(new ExtendedInputSource(sheet));
    }
    return stylesheet;
}
```

```
/**
 * Load the source document
 */

private synchronized DocumentInfo getSourceDocument(String tree)
throws SAXException {
    DocumentInfo doc = (DocumentInfo)trees.get(tree);
    if (doc==null) {
        File source = new File(
            getServletContext().getRealPath("/" + tree + ".xml"));
        doc = (new Builder()).build(new ExtendedInputSource(source));
    }
    return doc;
}

/**
 * Reset data held in memory
 */

private synchronized void resetData() {
    trees = new Hashtable();
    stylesheet = null;
}

private Hashtable trees = new Hashtable();
private PreparedStyleSheet stylesheet = null;
}
```

The general logic of this will be similar for other products, although the actual classes and methods will vary.

The XML file holding the family tree data must be in a file tree.xml where tree identifies the specific family tree, in our case kennedy.xml. This must be in the home directory for the web application containing the servlet, as defined by the configuration parameters for your web server. The two stylesheet modules person.xsl and ged-servlet.xsl must also be in this directory.

The servlet keeps in memory a copy of the compiled stylesheet: it makes this copy the first time it is needed. For Saxon this is a PreparedStyleSheet object. It also keeps in memory a data structure representing each XML source document, that is, each family tree. For Saxon this data structure is a DocumentInfo object, for other products it may be a DOM or some other class. The various documents are indexed using a hash table. Note that all accesses to these variables must be in synchronized methods to avoid concurrency conflicts, because in a servlet several threads can be running the same code at once.

The servlet then allocates a new instance or activation of the stylesheet, which is not shared with any other thread, and which is used only once. In Saxon this class is called StyleSheetInstance. The servlet passes this object details of the parameters (extracted from the URL) and the required output destination, before calling on it to process the source document by calling its renderDocument() method.

Generating HTML in the Browser

The third way to display the family tree is to download the whole XML file to the browser as a single chunk, and then use client-side scripts to invoke stylesheet processing whenever the user clicks on a hyperlink. This particular example runs only in Internet Explorer 5, and only with the March 2000 version of Microsoft's XML parser installed (hopefully it will also work with later versions). Information about installing this product is included in Chapter 10, with further details in Appendix A.

I had to make a few changes to the stylesheet to make it run in this environment, partly because of the current restrictions in Microsoft's XSLT implementation, and partly because of the different requirements in this environment.

The application runs within an HTML page `famtree.html` that reads as follows. The `<script>` elements contain client-side Javascript code.

```
<html>
<head>
  <title>Family Tree</title>
  <style type="text/css">
    ... as before ...
  </style>
  <script>
    var source = null;
    var style = null;
    var transformer = null;

    function init() {
      source =
        new ActiveXObject("MSXML2.FreeThreadedDOMDocument");
      source.async = false;
      source.load('kennedy.xml');

      style =
        new ActiveXObject("MSXML2.FreeThreadedDOMDocument");
      style.async = false;
      style.load('ms-person.xsl');

      transformer = new ActiveXObject("MSXML2.XSLTemplate");
      transformer.stylesheet = style.documentElement;
      refresh("I1");
    }

    function refresh(indi) {
      var xslproc = transformer.createProcessor();
      xslproc.input = source;
      xslproc.addParameter("id", indi, "");
      xslproc.transform();
      displayarea.innerHTML = xslproc.output;
    }
  </script>
```

```
        <script for="window" event="onload">
            init();
        </script>
    </head>
    <body>
        <div id="displayarea"></div>
    </body>
</html>
```

The CSS style definitions have moved from the XSLT stylesheet to the HTML page, but they are otherwise unchanged.

The `init()` function on this page is called when the page is loaded. It creates two DOM objects, one for the source XML and one for the stylesheet, and loads these using the relative URLs `kennedy.xml` and `ms-person.xsl`. It then compiles the stylesheet into an object which is rather confusingly called an `XSLTemplate`: this corresponds directly with Saxon's `PreparedStyleSheet` object. Finally it calls the `refresh()` function to display the individual with identifier `I1`.

I've taken a bit of a short cut here. There's no guarantee that a GEDCOM file will contain an individual with this identifier. A more carefully constructed application would display the first individual in the file, or an index of people

The `refresh()` function creates an executable instance of the stylesheet by calling the `createProcessor()` method on the `XSLTemplate` object. It then sets the value of the global `id` parameter in the stylesheet, and applies the stylesheet to the source document by calling the `transform()` method. The HTML constructed by processing the stylesheet is then written to the contents of the `<div id="displayarea">` element in the body of the HTML page.

The stylesheet is written so that a hyperlink to another individual, `I2` say, takes the form:

```
<a href="Javascript:refresh('I2')">Jacqueline Lee Bouvier</a>
```

When the user clicks on this hyperlink, the `refresh()` function is executed, which causes a new execution of the compiled stylesheet, against the same source document, but with a different value for the `id` parameter. The effect is that the contents of the page switches to display a different individual.

The content of the `ms-person.xsl` stylesheet is very similar to the `person.xsl` stylesheet presented earlier, so I will not give it in full here. Again, it is available on the web site. I made the following changes. Some of these were to circumvent restrictions and bugs that will presumably be fixed in later Microsoft releases: this is after all billed as a technology preview.

9

Worked Examples

609

- ❑ The stylesheet no longer generates the `<html>` and `<body>` elements of the HTML page because these are already present.

- ❑ The form of the generated hyperlinks is different.

- ❑ Microsoft's processor does not support `<xsl:import>` so I copied all the relevant template rules into a single stylesheet module.

- ❑ The processor does not support `<xsl:key>` and the `key()` function, so wherever keys were used in the original stylesheet, I substituted a predicate: for example `key('indi', $x)` might be replaced by `../INDI[@id=$x]`

- ❑ I removed the test `<xsl:if test="position()=last()">` because the processor rejected it with a spurious error message. (It says that the `last()` function must have a node-set to operate on).

- ❑ I changed the code `<xsl:if test="$event-name">`, which tests for an empty string, to `<xsl:if test="$event-name!=''">`, because it otherwise gave the wrong answer.

- ❑ I removed the code to set the background color based on the person's sex: partly because I suspect the idea is uncool, and partly because the way of achieving it in this environment would need to be rather different. Similarly with setting the HTML page title.

Converting GEDCOM Files to XML

At the start of this exercise I explained that the GEDCOM format widely used by genealogical software packages is not an XML format, but it can easily be translated into XML. Having got these examples working, you may well want to use them to display your own family tree. There's a wide range of genealogy packages on the market, and any respectable one can do GEDCOM export. For a list of packages, go to http://www.cyndislist.com/software.htm. A good one to start with, which also happens to be free, is Personal Ancestral File or PAF.

The obvious way to translate GEDCOM to XML is to write a program that takes a GEDCOM file as input and produces an XML file as output. However, there's a smarter way: why not write a GEDCOM parser which looks just like a SAX-compliant XML parser, so that any program that can handle SAX input can read GEDCOM directly, just by switching parsers? In particular, many XSLT processors can take input from a SAX-compliant parser, so this enables you to feed GEDCOM straight into a stylesheet.

Equally, many XSLT processors can send the result tree to a user-specified `DocumentHandler` in the form of a stream of SAX events, so if we write a SAX-compatible `DocumentHandler`, our XSLT processor can also output GEDCOM files. This suddenly means we can write stylesheets to transform one GEDCOM file into another, without the hassle of creating an XML file as an intermediate form. As an example, I've included on the web site a stylesheet called `nonliving.xsl` which removes all living individuals from the data set: a sensible courtesy to your relatives if you are publishing your data on the web, quite apart from being a legal requirement in some countries.

A SAX parser for GEDCOM is supplied with the sample files for this chapter on the Wrox web site; it is named `GedcomParser`. GEDCOM uses an archaic character set called ANSEL, so along with `GedcomParser` is another class, `AnselInputStreamReader` to translate the ANSEL characters into Unicode.

Similarly, on the output side, there is a SAX `DocumentHandler` called `GedcomOutputter`, which in turn translates Unicode to ANSEL using an `AnselOutputStreamWriter`.

This structure is shown in the diagram below:

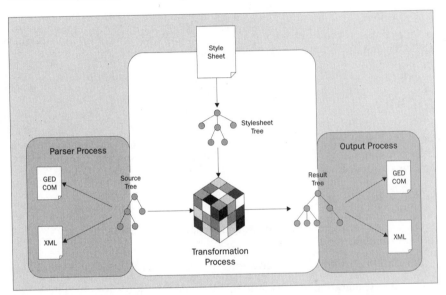

If you do want to see the XML, you can always feed the GEDCOM into a stylesheet that does an identity transformation, the simplest being:

```
<xsl:transform
    xmlns:xsl="http://www.w3.org/1999/XSL/Transform"
    version="1.0" >

<xsl:template match="/">
    <xsl:copy-of select="."/>
</xsl:template>

</xsl:transform>
```

In fact, to create the `kennedy.xml` data file which I used as the input to these example stylesheets, I used a slightly more elaborate stylesheet than this to post-process the output of the GEDCOM parser.

This is called `normalize.xsl`, and it turns various structures found in GEDCOM into a more natural XML representation. Specifically:

❑ A name is represented in GEDCOM in the form «`Michael /Kay/`», but in XML it is easier to handle it if the surname is tagged as «`Michael <S>Kay</S>`».

❑ GEDCOM uses the tags `CONT` and `CONC` to represent continuation lines: with `CONT` the continuation is assumed to represent a new line, with `CONC` it represents a concatenation of the previous line. The `normalize.xsl` stylesheet removes the `CONC` tag, and precedes a `CONT` line with an empty `<BR/>` tag as in HTML.

So, for example, if you want to convert your GEDCOM file `mytree.ged` into XML, you can do it using Saxon by entering the command

```
saxon -x GedcomParser mytree.ged normalize.xsl >mytree.xml
```

Summary

I hope this little excursion into the strange world of genealogical data models has given you some flavor of the power of XSLT as a manipulation and reporting tool for complex structured data.

We've covered a lot of ground:

❑ How to navigate your way around complex linked data within an XML document.

❑ Three different ways of generating an interactive view of a large XML dataset:

❑ Generating lots of static HTML pages in one go at publication time.

❑ Generating HTML pages dynamically using a servlet.

❑ Generating HTML incrementally within the browser.

❑ Using XSLT to transform structured data that wasn't originally in XML format.

The next worked example will venture into even stranger territory, using XSLT to solve a chess problem.

Knight's Tour Stylesheet

This example stylesheet is rather far-fetched, but it does illustrate some advanced use of XSLT features, which you are likely to encounter if you want to do any complex data manipulation.

The purpose of the stylesheet is to produce a knight's tour of the chessboard, in which each square is visited exactly once, as shown in the illustration below. A knight can move to any square that is at the opposite corner of a 3×2 rectangle.

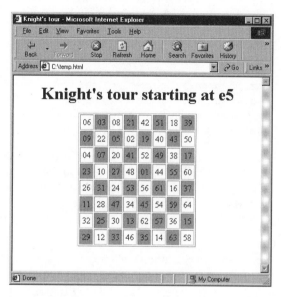

The only input to the stylesheet is an indication of the starting square: in modern chess notation, the columns are denoted by the letters a–h starting from the left, and the rows by the numbers 1–8, starting at the bottom. We'll supply the starting square as a parameter to the stylesheet. The stylesheet doesn't need to get anything from the source document. To meet the requirements of the language, there must be a source document present, but there is nothing that says the stylesheet has to read it.

We'll build up the stylesheet piece-by-piece: you can find the complete stylesheet, tour.xsl, on the Wrox web site.

> *The inspiration for this stylesheet came from Oren Ben-Kiki, who published a stylesheet for solving the eight-queens problem. The concept here is very similar, though the details are quite different.*

The Algorithm

The strategy for getting the knight round the board is based on the observation that if a square hasn't been visited yet, it had better have at least two unvisited squares that are a knight's move away from it, because there needs to be a way of getting in and another way of getting out. That means that if we can get to a square that's only got one exit left, we'd better go there now or we never will.

This suggests an approach where at each move, we look at all the squares we can jump to next, and choose the one that has fewest possible exits. It turns out that this strategy works, and always gets the knight round the board. I don't know a way of proving it, and if any reader does, please let me know: I just know that it seems to work.

The place I usually start design is with the data structures. Here the main data structure we need is the board itself. We need to know which squares the knight has visited, and so that we can print out the board at the end, we need to know the sequence in which they were visited. We don't have a great deal of choice in XSLT about how to represent data structures, so the only practical option is a string. We'll use a string containing 64 values, each representing one square of the board; the value will be an integer between «01» and «64» if the square has been visited (with the number indicating when it was visited), and will be set to the value «- -» if not. It's not essential to the logic, but I actually separate the values with a colon so it's easier to debug. So the string consists of 64 groups of 3 characters.

In a conventional program this data structure would probably be held in a global variable and updated every time the knight moves. We can't do this in XSLT, because variables can't be updated. Instead, every time a template is called, it passes the current state of the board as a parameter, and when the knight moves, a new copy of the board is created, that differs from the previous one only in the details of one square.

It doesn't really matter which way the squares are numbered, but for the sake of convention we'll number them as shown below:

0	1	2	3	4	5	6	7
8	9	10	11	12	13	14	15
16	17	18	19	20	21	22	23
24	25	26	27	28	29	30	31
32	33	34	35	36	37	38	39
40	41	42	43	44	45	46	47
48	49	50	51	52	53	54	55
56	57	58	59	60	61	62	63

So if we number the rows 0 – 7, and the columns 0 – 7, the square number is given as «row * 8 + column».

Having decided on the principal data structure we can decide the broad structure of the program. There are three stages:

❑ Prepare the initial data structures (the empty board with a knight placed on it, somewhere).

❑ Calculate the tour.

❑ Display the final state of the board.

Calculating the tour involves 63 steps, each one taking the form:

❑ Find all the unvisited squares that the knight can move to from the current position.

❑ For each one of these, count the number of exits (that is, the number of unvisited squares that can be reached from there)

❑ Choose the square with the fewest exits, and move the knight there.

We're ready to start coding. The tricky bit, as you've probably already guessed, is that all the loops have to be coded using recursion. That takes a bit of getting used to at first, but it quickly becomes a habit.

The Root Template

Let's start with the framework of top-level elements:

```
<xsl:transform
 xmlns:xsl="http://www.w3.org/1999/XSL/Transform"
 version="1.0"
>

<xsl:param name="start" select="'a1'"/>

<!-- start-column is an integer in the range 0-7 -->

<xsl:variable name="start-column"
   select="number(translate(substring($start, 1, 1),
          'abcdefgh', '01234567'))"/>

<!-- start-row is an integer in the range 0-7, with zero at the top -->

<xsl:variable name="start-row"
   select="8 - number(substring($start, 2, 1))"/>

 . . .

</xsl:transform>
```

All I'm doing here is declaring the global parameter, start, which defines the starting square, and deriving from it two global variables: a row number and column number.

Some observations:

❑ The parameter start has the default value a1. As this is a string value, it needs to be in quotes; these quotes are additional to the quotes that surround the XML attribute. If I had written «select="a1"», the default value would be the string value of the <a1> element child of the document root.

❑ The simplest way of converting the alphabetic column identifier (a-h) into a number (0–7) is to use the translate() function, page 526

❑ The row number is subtracted from 8 so that the lowest-numbered row is at the top, and so that row numbers start from zero. Numbering from zero makes it easier to convert between row and column numbers and a number for each square on the board in the range 0–63.

❑ I haven't yet checked that the supplied start square is valid. I'll do that in the root template.

Now we can move on to the root template. This is invoked when the root node of the source document is matched, but it doesn't actually do anything with the source document.

The root template defines the stages of processing, as follows:

❑ Validate the supplied parameter

❑ Set up the empty board and place the knight on it at the specified starting square

❑ Compute the knight's tour

❑ Print out the tour in HTML format

These tasks are all delegated to other templates, so the root template itself is quite simple:

```
<xsl:template match="/">

    <!-- Validate the input parameter -->

    <xsl:if test="not(string-length($start)=2) or
        not(translate(substring($start,1,1), 'abcdefgh', 'aaaaaaaa')='a') or
        not(translate(substring($start,2,1), '12345678', '11111111')='1')">
        <xsl:message terminate="yes"
            >Invalid start parameter: try (say) 'a1' or 'f6'</xsl:message>
    </xsl:if>

    <!-- Set up the empty board -->
```

```
<xsl:variable name="empty-board">
   <xsl:call-template name="make-board"/>
</xsl:variable>

<!-- Place the knight on the board at the chosen starting position -->

<xsl:variable name="initial-board">
   <xsl:call-template name="place-knight">
      <xsl:with-param name="move" select="1"/>
      <xsl:with-param name="board" select="$empty-board"/>
      <xsl:with-param name="square"
               select="$start-row * 8 + $start-column"/>
   </xsl:call-template>
</xsl:variable>

<!-- Evaluate the knight's tour -->

<xsl:variable name="final-board">
   <xsl:call-template name="make-moves">
      <xsl:with-param name="move" select="2"/>
      <xsl:with-param name="board" select="$initial-board"/>
      <xsl:with-param name="square"
               select="$start-row * 8 + $start-column"/>
   </xsl:call-template>
</xsl:variable>

<!-- produce the HTML output -->

<xsl:call-template name="print-board">
   <xsl:with-param name="board" select="$final-board"/>
</xsl:call-template>

</xsl:template>
```

Notice how most of the calls to <xsl:call-template> are nested within an
<xsl:variable>. This is the only way of returning a result from a called template. The
<xsl:variable> creates a new tree (technically, a result tree fragment), and any
output produced by the called template is directed to that tree. In practice, none of
these trees contain anything but a single text node, so they are treated exactly like
strings.

The code for validating the start parameter is worth examining. It performs three
tests: that the length of the supplied string is two characters, that the first character is
one of the letters a–h, and that the second is one of the digits 1–8. The simplest way to
perform these checks is to use the translate() function in the way shown. If any of
the tests fail, the stylesheet outputs a message using <xsl:message>, and terminates.

Several of the variables (empty-board, initial-board, and final-board) represent a
chessboard containing all or part of a knight's tour. These variables are trees, but we
will treat them as strings. The board is represented by 64 groups of three characters,
each group representing one square.

If the square has been visited, it contains a two-digit sequence number representing the order of visiting (01 for the start square, 02 for the next square visited, and so on), followed by a colon. If the square has not been visited, it contains two hyphens followed by a colon. The colons are not really necessary or relevant, but they are helpful if you need to print out a chessboard for debugging purposes.

Squares on the board are represented by an integer in the range 0–63, which is calculated as $row * 8 + $column.

Setting Up the Board

It's time to look at how the called templates work. I'll start with make-board, whose task is to initialize an empty board. I could have written this out as a string of 192 characters in the stylesheet, but I was too lazy, so I computed it instead:

```
<xsl:template name="make-board">
   <xsl:param name="size" select="64"/>
   <xsl:if test="$size!=0">
      <xsl:text>--:</xsl:text>
      <xsl:call-template name="make-board">
         <xsl:with-param name="size" select="$size - 1"/>
      </xsl:call-template>
   </xsl:if>
</xsl:template>
```

When this template is called from the root template, the parameter $size takes its default value of 64. The template creates one unvisited square (denoted by «--:») and then calls itself to create the other 63. After 64 recursive calls are complete, the $size parameter reaches zero: at this stage 64 unvisited squares will have been written, and the empty board is complete.

The next step is to place the knight in its initial position using the «place-knight» template. Here it is:

```
<xsl:template name="place-knight">
   <xsl:param name="move"/>
   <xsl:param name="board"/>
   <xsl:param name="square"/>

   <xsl:value-of select="substring($board, 1, $square*3)"/>
   <xsl:value-of select="format-number($move, '00:')"/>
   <xsl:value-of select="substring($board, ($square+1)*3 + 1)"/>
</xsl:template>
```

This template takes three parameters: the number of this move, the current state of the chessboard, and the square on which the knight is to be placed. When I call it from the root template, the move number is always one, and the board is always empty, but I will use the same template again later with different parameters.

What the template does is to copy the whole supplied chessboard before and after the square where the knight is to be placed. The number of the required square has to be multiplied by three because my representation of the chessboard uses three characters for each square. This square itself is replaced by three characters representing the move number with a following colon. For example, the fifth move is written as «05:». The move number is converted into this format using the format-number() function (see page 455): the pattern «00:» indicates that the output must be a two-digit number followed by the colon as a punctuation character.

I can't, of course, modify the supplied chessboard in situ. All variables in XSLT are immutable. Instead I create a new board as a modified copy of the original. The result of the template (the value written to its current output destination) is the new state of the chessboard after placing the knight.

Displaying the Final Board

I'll skip the template that computes the knight's tour for the moment, and describe the relatively easy task of outputting the final result as HTML. This actually requires three named templates. The first produces the HTML outline and calls «print-rows» to print the rows:

```
<xsl:template name="print-board">
   <xsl:param name="board"/>
   <html>
      <head>
         <title>Knight's tour</title>
      </head>
      <body>
         <div align="center">
         <h1>Knight's tour starting at <xsl:value-of select="$start"/></h1>
         <table border="1" cellpadding="4">
            <xsl:call-template name="print-rows">
               <xsl:with-param name="board" select="$board"/>
            </xsl:call-template>
         </table>
         </div>
      </body>
   </html>
</xsl:template>
```

The second template prints the rows. Actually it just prints the first row (by calling the «print-columns» template), and then calls itself recursively to print the remaining rows, stopping when it has printed all eight:

```
<xsl:template name="print-rows">
   <xsl:param name="board"/>
   <xsl:param name="row" select="0"/>
   <xsl:if test="$row &lt; 8">
      <tr>
         <xsl:call-template name="print-columns">
            <xsl:with-param name="board" select="$board"/>
            <xsl:with-param name="row" select="$row"/>
```

```
        </xsl:call-template>
    </tr>

    <xsl:call-template name="print-rows">
        <xsl:with-param name="board" select="$board"/>
        <xsl:with-param name="row" select="$row + 1"/>
    </xsl:call-template>
  </xsl:if>
</xsl:template>
```

The «print-columns» template is very similar. It prints the first column, and calls itself to print the remaining columns.

```
<xsl:template name="print-columns">
  <xsl:param name="board"/>
  <xsl:param name="row"/>
  <xsl:param name="column" select="0"/>
  <xsl:if test="$column &lt; 8">
    <xsl:variable name="color">
      <xsl:choose>
        <xsl:when test="($row + $column) mod 2">xffff44</xsl:when>
        <xsl:otherwise>white</xsl:otherwise>
      </xsl:choose>
    </xsl:variable>
    <td align="center" bgcolor="{$color}">
      <xsl:value-of
        select="substring($board, ($row*8 + $column)*3 + 1, 2)"/>
    </td>

    <xsl:call-template name="print-columns">
        <xsl:with-param name="board" select="$board"/>
        <xsl:with-param name="row" select="$row"/>
        <xsl:with-param name="column" select="$column + 1"/>
    </xsl:call-template>
  </xsl:if>
</xsl:template>
```

The template contains a little bit of logic to achieve the traditional checkerboard coloring of the squares, using the «mod» operator to test whether the sum of the row number and the column number is a multiple of 2, and handling the two cases with an <xsl:choose> instruction.

The actual content of each square is the move number, extracted from the relevant place in the data structure representing the board. In the data structure representing the board, there are three characters representing each square, but only the first two are displayed, because the final colon is just a separator.

Finding the Route

So much for the input and output of the stylesheet, now for the substance: the algorithm to calculate the knight's tour.

The basic algorithm we use is that at each move, we consider all the squares we could go to, and choose the one with the fewest exits. For example, if we are on c2 then we could move to a1, e1, a3, e3, b4, or d4, assuming they are all unvisited. Of these, the corner square a1 has only one exit, namely b3, and if we don't visit the corner square now, then we'll never get another chance later. It turns out that this strategy of always visiting the square with least exits always succeeds in generating a complete knight's tour though just in case it doesn't, the algorithm is actually resilient enough to backtrack and try a different route if the first one fails.

The root template makes a call on the template named «make-moves». This template, starting from any given start position, works out all the moves needed to complete the knight's tour. Of course, it does this by recursion: but unlike previous templates which called themselves directly, this one does so indirectly, via another template named «try-possible-moves».

> The first thing the «make-moves» template does is to call the template «list-possible-moves» to construct a list of moves that are legal in the current situation. The result of this template, a list of moves, uses a very similar data structure to that of the chessboard itself. Each move is represented by an integer (the number of the square to which the knight travels), and in the list of moves, a colon follows each integer.

Having established the list of possible moves, the template then calls «try-possible-moves» to select one of these moves and execute it.

Here is the template. Its parameters are the number of this move (starting at move 2, because the knight's initial position is numbered 1), the state of the board before this move, and the number of the square on which the knight is currently sitting.

```
<xsl:template name="make-moves">
    <xsl:param name="move"/>
    <xsl:param name="board"/>
    <xsl:param name="square"/>

    <!-- determine the possible moves that the knight can make -->

    <xsl:variable name="possible-moves">
        <xsl:call-template name="list-possible-moves">
            <xsl:with-param name="board" select="$board"/>
            <xsl:with-param name="square" select="$square"/>
        </xsl:call-template>
    </xsl:variable>
```

```
<!-- try these moves in turn until one is found that works -->

<xsl:call-template name="try-possible-moves">
   <xsl:with-param name="board" select="$board"/>
   <xsl:with-param name="square" select="$square"/>
   <xsl:with-param name="move" select="$move"/>
   <xsl:with-param name="possible-moves" select="$possible-moves"/>
</xsl:call-template>

</xsl:template>
```

The next template to examine is «list-possible-moves». This takes as input the current state of the board and the position of the knight, and it produces a colon-separated list of squares that the knight can move to. For a knight in the center of the board there are eight possible squares it can move to, being those squares that are either two columns and one row, or two rows and one column, removed from the current row. However, we have to consider the case where some of these squares are unavailable because they are off the edge of the board, and we also have to eliminate any squares that have already been visited. The logic I have used is simple, if verbose; it simply examines each of the eight candidate squares in turn:

```
<xsl:template name="list-possible-moves">
  <xsl:param name="board"/>
  <xsl:param name="square"/>
  <xsl:variable name="row" select="$square div 8"/>
  <xsl:variable name="column" select="$square mod 8"/>

  <xsl:if test="$row &gt; 1 and $column &gt; 0
          and substring($board, ($square - 17)*3 + 1, 2)='--'">
     <xsl:value-of select="format-number($square - 17, '00:')"/>
  </xsl:if>
  <xsl:if test="$row &gt; 1 and $column &lt; 7
          and substring($board, ($square - 15)*3 + 1, 2)='--'">
     <xsl:value-of select="format-number($square - 15, '00:')"/>
  </xsl:if>
  <xsl:if test="$row &gt; 0 and $column &gt; 1
          and substring($board, ($square - 10)*3 + 1, 2)='--'">
     <xsl:value-of select="format-number($square - 10, '00:')"/>
  </xsl:if>
  <xsl:if test="$row &gt; 0 and $column &lt; 6
          and substring($board, ($square - 6)*3 + 1, 2)='--'">
     <xsl:value-of select="format-number($square - 6, '00:')"/>
  </xsl:if>
  <xsl:if test="$row &lt; 6 and $column &gt; 0
          and substring($board, ($square + 15)*3 + 1, 2)='--'">
     <xsl:value-of select="format-number($square + 15, '00:')"/>
  </xsl:if>
  <xsl:if test="$row &lt; 6 and $column &lt; 7
          and substring($board, ($square + 17)*3 + 1, 2)='--'">
     <xsl:value-of select="format-number($square + 17, '00:')"/>
  </xsl:if>
```

```
   <xsl:if test="$row &lt; 7 and $column &gt; 1
           and substring($board, ($square + 6)*3 + 1, 2)='--'">
      <xsl:value-of select="format-number($square + 6, '00:')"/>
   </xsl:if>
   <xsl:if test="$row &lt; 7 and $column &lt; 6
           and substring($board, ($square + 10)*3 + 1, 2)='--'">
         <xsl:value-of select="format-number($square + 10, '00:')"/>
   </xsl:if>
</xsl:template>
```

So having found the possible moves we can make, we need to select one of them and make it. This is the job of the try-possible-moves template.

This template is quite complex. It's worth looking at it carefully.

First, it checks whether the list of possible moves is empty. If it is, it takes the <xsl:otherwise> route at the end of the template body, which returns the special value «#/#» indicating that this attempt to find a route through the chessboard failed. As I've mentioned, my "least number of exits" algorithm in fact never does fail, but it's as well to be sure.

In the normal case, there are one or more possible moves, and we call the template find-best-move to find the best one (that is, the one with fewest exits). Just in case we need to backtrack, we also form a list of other possible moves, containing all the moves except the chosen one, so that we can use these later if we need to.

Now we execute the chosen move, which is simply a case of calling the place-knight template, which I described earlier, to place the knight on the chosen square and generate a new board.

And now we can repeat the process: except that as usual in XSLT, when we want to repeat, we recurse. If the board still has unvisited squares (recognized by a value of «--»), we call the «make-moves» template, described above, to calculate the rest of the tour. If not, we output the value of the final board. This output value is passed right down through all 64 levels of recursion to the «$final-board» variable in the root template, which is then passed to the «print-board» template to create the final display.

```
<xsl:template name="try-possible-moves">

   <xsl:param name="move"/>
   <xsl:param name="board"/>
   <xsl:param name="square"/>
   <xsl:param name="possible-moves"/>

   <xsl:choose>
   <xsl:when test="$possible-moves">

       <!-- if at least one move is possible, find the best one -->
```

```
<xsl:variable name="best-move">
   <xsl:call-template name="find-best-move">
      <xsl:with-param name="board" select="$board"/>
      <xsl:with-param name="possible-moves"
                              select="$possible-moves"/>
   </xsl:call-template>
</xsl:variable>

<!-- find the list of possible moves excluding the best one -->

<xsl:variable name="other-possible-moves"
   select="concat(
         substring-before($possible-moves, concat($best-move,':')),
         substring-after($possible-moves, concat($best-move,':')))"/>

<!-- update the board to make the move chosen as the best one -->

<xsl:variable name="next-board">
   <xsl:call-template name="place-knight">
      <xsl:with-param name="move" select="$move"/>
      <xsl:with-param name="board" select="$board"/>
      <xsl:with-param name="square" select="$best-move"/>
   </xsl:call-template>
</xsl:variable>

<!-- now make further moves, until the board is complete -->

<xsl:variable name="final-board">
   <xsl:choose>
   <xsl:when test="contains($next-board, '--:')">
      <xsl:call-template name="make-moves">
         <xsl:with-param name="move" select="$move + 1"/>
         <xsl:with-param name="board" select="$next-board"/>
         <xsl:with-param name="square" select="$best-move"/>
      </xsl:call-template>
   </xsl:when>
   <xsl:otherwise>
      <xsl:value-of select="$next-board"/>
   </xsl:otherwise>
   </xsl:choose>
</xsl:variable>

 <!-- if the final board has the special value '##', we got stuck,
     and have to choose the next best of the possible moves.
     This is done by a recursive call. In practice,
     we never do get stuck, so this path is not taken. -->

<xsl:choose>
<xsl:when test="$final-board='##'">
   <xsl:call-template name="try-possible-moves">
      <xsl:with-param name="board" select="$board"/>
      <xsl:with-param name="square" select="$square"/>
      <xsl:with-param name="move" select="$move"/>
```

```
                    <xsl:with-param name="possible-moves"
                                        select="$other-possible-moves"/>
            </xsl:call-template>
        </xsl:when>
        <xsl:otherwise>
            <xsl:value-of select="$final-board"/>
        </xsl:otherwise>
    </xsl:choose>
    </xsl:when>

    <xsl:otherwise>
        <!-- if there is no possible move, we return the special value '##'
            as the final state of the board, to indicate that we got stuck -->
        <xsl:value-of select="'##'"/>
    </xsl:otherwise>
    </xsl:choose>

</xsl:template>
```

The one thing remaining is to look at the template «find-best-move», which from a set of possible moves chooses the best one, namely the move to the square with fewest exits.

As always, the logic is recursive. We keep track of the best move so far, and the number of exits that the best move so far possesses. If the first move in the list (the *trial move*) is better than the best move so far, it replace the previous best, and we then call the template to process the other moves in the list. The final output is the best move after examining the whole list.

To find the number of exits for a given move, we create a trial board, and make that move by calling the «place-knight» template described earlier. Using this board, we then call the «list-possible-moves» template, also described earlier, to see what moves would be available after the trial move. We aren't interested in the details of these moves, only in how many there are, which we can find out simply by examining the length of the list.

We can now calculate two variables: the best move so far, and the least number of exits, based on whether the trial move is better than the previous best. If the move is the best one so far, it is output. Finally, the «find-best-move» template calls itself recursively to process the remaining moves in the list. On completion, the value returned by the template is the best move, that is, the square to which the knight should move next.

```
<xsl:template name="find-best-move">
    <xsl:param name="board"/>
    <xsl:param name="possible-moves"/>
    <xsl:param name="fewest-exits" select="9"/>
    <xsl:param name="best-so-far" select="'XX'"/>

    <xsl:variable name="trial-move"
                    select="substring-before($possible-moves, ':')"/>
```

```
<xsl:variable name="other-possible-moves"
              select="substring-after($possible-moves, ':')"/>

<!-- try making the first move -->

<xsl:variable name="trial-board">
   <xsl:call-template name="place-knight">
      <xsl:with-param name="board" select="$board"/>
         <xsl:with-param name="move" select="99"/>
         <xsl:with-param name="square" select="$trial-move"/>
      </xsl:call-template>
</xsl:variable>

<!-- see how many moves would be possible the next time -->

<xsl:variable name="trial-move-exits">
   <xsl:call-template name="list-possible-moves">
      <xsl:with-param name="board" select="$trial-board"/>
      <xsl:with-param name="square" select="$trial-move"/>
   </xsl:call-template>
</xsl:variable>

<xsl:variable name="number-of-exits"
              select="string-length($trial-move-exits) div 3"/>

<!-- determine whether this trial move is the best so far -->

<xsl:variable name="minimum-exits">
   <xsl:choose>
   <xsl:when test="$number-of-exits &lt; $fewest-exits">
      <xsl:value-of select="$number-of-exits"/>
   </xsl:when>
   <xsl:otherwise>
      <xsl:value-of select="$fewest-exits"/>
   </xsl:otherwise>
   </xsl:choose>
</xsl:variable>

<!-- determine the best move (the one with fewest exits) so far -->

<xsl:variable name="new-best-so-far">
   <xsl:choose>
   <xsl:when test="$number-of-exits &lt; $fewest-exits">
      <xsl:value-of select="$trial-move"/>
   </xsl:when>
   <xsl:otherwise>
      <xsl:value-of select="$best-so-far"/>
   </xsl:otherwise>
   </xsl:choose>
</xsl:variable>
```

```
<!-- if there are other possible moves, consider them too, using a recursive
       call. Otherwise return the best move found. -->

<xsl:choose>
<xsl:when test="$other-possible-moves">
   <xsl:call-template name="find-best-move">
      <xsl:with-param name="board" select="$board"/>
      <xsl:with-param name="possible-moves"
                            select="$other-possible-moves"/>
      <xsl:with-param name="fewest-exits" select="$minimum-exits"/>
      <xsl:with-param name="best-so-far" select="$new-best-so-far"/>
   </xsl:call-template>
</xsl:when>
<xsl:otherwise>
   <xsl:value-of select="$new-best-so-far"/>
</xsl:otherwise>
</xsl:choose>

</xsl:template>
```

And that's it.

Running the Stylesheet

To run the stylesheet, download it from the Wrox web site, and execute it against an arbitrary source document (for example, against itself). With Saxon, for example, try:

```
saxon tour.xsl tour.xsl start=b6 >tour.html
```

and then display tour.html in your browser. The details of how to supply a global parameter vary for each XSLT implementation: if you don't supply one, the tour will start at the a1 square.

Because of various restrictions in the Microsoft's March 2000 XSLT Technology Preview, this stylesheet does not work within the Internet Explorer 5 browser at the time of writing. Microsoft are committed to implementing the full XSLT standard, however, so it should work eventually.

Observations

The knight's tour not a very typical stylesheet, but it's one that illustrates the computational power of the XSLT language, and in particular the essential part that recursion plays in any stylesheet that needs to do any non-trivial calculation or handle non-trivial data structures. And although you will never need to use XSLT to solve chess problems, you may just find yourself doing complex calculations to work out where best to place a set of images on a page, or how many columns to use to display a list of telephone numbers, or which of today's news stories should be featured most prominently given your knowledge of the user's preferences.

So if you're wondering why I selected this example, there are two answers: firstly, I enjoyed writing it, and secondly, I hope it will have persuaded you that there are no algorithms too complex to be written in XSLT.

9

Worked Examples

627

Summary

In this chapter I've presented three complete stylesheets, all similar in complexity to many of those you will have to write for real applications. I tried to choose three that were very different in character, reflecting three of the design patterns introduced in the previous chapter, namely:

❑   a rule-based stylesheet for converting a document containing semantic markup into HTML. In this stylesheet, most of the logic was concerned with generating the right HTML display style for each XML element, and with establishing tables of contents, section numbering, and internal hyperlinks, with some interesting logic for laying data out in a table.

❑   a navigational stylesheet for presenting selected information from a hierarchical data structure. This stylesheet was primarily concerned with following links with the XML data structure, and it was able to use the full power of XPath expression to achieve this. This stylesheet also gave us the opportunity to explore some of the systems issues surrounding XSLT: when and where to do the XML-to-HTML conversion, and how to handle data in non-XML legacy formats.

❑   a computational stylesheet for calculating the result of a moderately complex algorithm. This stylesheet demonstrated that even quite complex algorithms are quite possible to code in XSLT once you have mastered recursion. The only thing that makes it tricky is the limited range of data types available, but with a little imagination, there is usually a solution available.

To get the second stylesheet to work, I had to use some non-standard interfaces provided by the various XSLT implementations. In the final chapter of the book we'll take a more detailed look at some of the more widely-used XSLT processors available.

9

Worked Examples

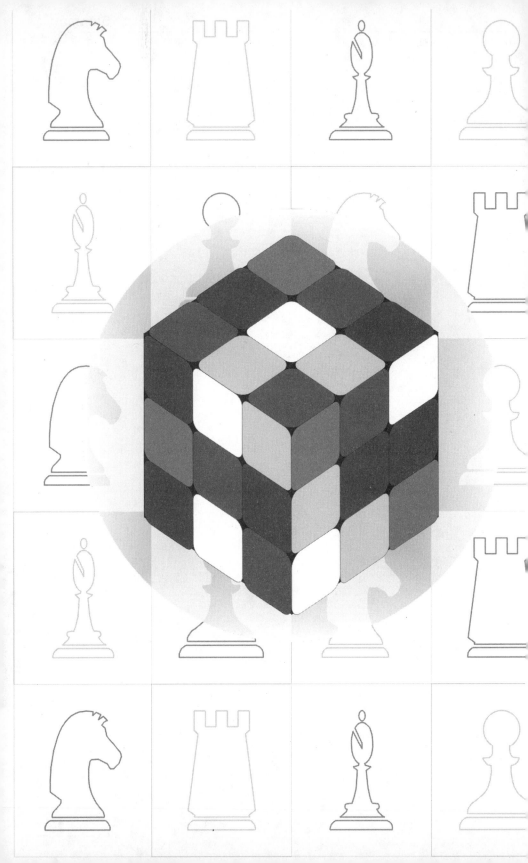

10

XSLT Products

A language is not much use unless you can get hold of software that implements it. Fortunately in the case of XSLT there is a wide range of product implementations available, with a good level of conformance to the standard, and although there are differences in the precise licensing conditions, they are all effectively free, at least for evaluation.

In this section I shall give a quick survey of the most popular XSLT processors. The purpose is not to give you all the information you need to use these products, but to give you an idea of what each one does, and to provide pointers to the vendor's own information.

At the time of writing there are four reasonably complete XSLT processors available which I'll describe in some detail. I shall treat them in alphabetical order: Oracle XSL, Saxon, Xalan, and xt. All four were initially released in Java versions, but Oracle and Xalan now exist also in C++ form.

IBM's LotusXSL product isn't in this list because it is essentially the same thing as Xalan. IBM handed over the LotusXSL code to the Apache Software Foundation, who repackaged it under the Xalan name, and IBM now distribute LotusXSL essentially as a wrapper around Xalan, with some extra APIs and different licensing conditions.

Microsoft's current MSXML3 product isn't yet as complete as these four, but the company is committed to achieving full conformance; and being Microsoft, their product will be of considerable importance anyway. So I'll give them a detailed write-up too. You will find more detailed specifications for this product in Appendix A.

Finally I'll look briefly at some other products which we currently rate only as promising contenders: specifically iXSLT from Infoteria, 4XSLT from FourThought, EZ/X from Activated Intelligence, and Stylus from Excelon. By the time you read this book some of them might have fulfilled their promise and be worthy of a place at the top table, but I had to draw the line somewhere.

Do be aware that everything in this chapter is likely to become out of date quite quickly, certainly far more quickly than the rest of the book. For an update on the current position, there are various useful web sites, for example:

❑ http://www.xmlsoftware.com/xslt/

❑ http://www.xslinfo.com/

❑ http://www.oasis-open.org/cover

If you really want to keep your eye on the ball, subscribe to the XSL mailing list (but be prepared for heavy traffic):

❑ http://www.mulberrytech.com/xsl/xsl-list

In my description of the products, I shall concentrate on describing the extent to which they conform to the XSLT and XPath recommendations, the extensibility mechanisms they offer, and any vendor-supplied extensions. What I won't be doing, in any detail, is to describe the APIs they offer. For that information, you'll have to go to the vendor's own documentation.

There's no independent conformance test for XSLT processors yet, so conformance claims by vendors have to be taken on trust: it all depends on how thoroughly they have read the spec, how thorough their testing has been, and how honest their marketing people are. As an implementer myself, I know how easy it is to miss some of the more subtle requirements in the standard quite unintentionally; and there are a few obscure places where the requirements can be read in different ways, though you have to look hard to find them.

However, before I start with the individual products, I want to describe several features that are similar between several processors, specifically:

❑ the common mechanism that all four Java products have adopted for binding external Java-written functions.

❑ the extension elements available in Saxon, Xalan, and xt to create multiple output files.

❑ the node-set() extension function for converting a result tree fragment to a node-set, which is available in both Saxon and xt, and in modified form in Microsoft MSXML3.

The Common Java Binding Mechanism

All four Java products (Oracle, Saxon, Xalan, and xt) have adopted very similar mechanisms for binding to external functions written in Java, so I will describe this in one place rather than repeat the information for each product. I will call this scheme the Common Java Binding Mechanism. It is not defined in the XSLT or XPath specifications, but is simply a good idea that the vendors have copied from each other in the interests of compatibility.

The XSLT recommendation states that a standard binding to external functions is on the wish list for version 2.0, so it seems quite likely that a similar mechanism to the one described here will be standardized in the future.

Although the vendors have adopted a common approach, there are still differences of detail (for example in the namespaces used) which mean that:

❑ it is difficult to implement an extension function that will work with all four products (in general, you will have to write separate glue to do the interfacing in each case).

❑ it is difficult to write a stylesheet that is portable across products if it uses extension functions, even where the same extension function is available from several vendors.

> **The information here applies to Oracle, Saxon, and xt, and with slight variations also to Xalan.**

A call to an extension function must always use a namespace prefix, for example `ext:function()`. The namespace prefix, `ext`, must be associated with a namespace URI in the normal way, by a declaration such as `xmlns:ext="uri"`.

The Common Java Binding uses this namespace URI to identify the Java class in which the function will be found. The namespace URI must take the form `URI-stem/class-name`, where `URI-stem` is a string defined by the product vendor, and `class-name` is the fully-qualified name of the Java class; for example `java.util.Date` or `com.megacorp.xsllib.WonderClass`. This class must be on the Java class path so that the Java Virtual Machine can find it: for details, see the Java documentation for your particular platform.

The Xalan product differs slightly: here the class name is written as part of the name of the function being called, not as part of the namespace URI.

In the following table, let's assume that you want to invoke methods in the class whose full name is `com.x.Ext`. The table shows how to invoke the static method `m1()` with a single parameter set to 99, how to construct an instance of the class using the default constructor, and how to call an instance-level (i.e., non-static) method `m2()` on that class instance, again with a single parameter set to 99.

Oracle	Namespace declaration:
	`xmlns:j="http://www.oracle.com/XSL/Transform/java/com.x.Ext"`
	
	Static method:
	`<xsl:variable name="result" select="j:m1(99)"/>`
	
	Constructor:
	`<xsl:variable name="instance" select="j:new()"/>`
	
	Instance-level method:
	`<xsl:variable name="result" select="j:m2($instance, 99)"/>`

Saxon	Namespace declaration:
	`xmlns:j="anything/com.x.Ext"`
	
	Static method:
	`<xsl:variable name="result" select="j:m1(99)"/>`
	
	Constructor:
	`<xsl:variable name="instance" select="j:new()"/>`
	
	Instance-level method:
	`<xsl:variable name="result" select="j:m2($instance, 99)"/>`

Xalan	Namespace declaration:
	`xmlns:j="http://xml.apache.org/xslt"`
	
	Static method:
	`<xsl:variable name="result" select="j:com.x.Ext.m1(99)"/>`
	
	Constructor:
	`<xsl:variable name="instance" select="j:com.x.Ext.new()"/>`
	
	Instance-level method:
	`<xsl:variable name="result" select="j:m2($instance, 99)"/>`

xt	Namespace declaration:
	`xmlns:j="http://www.jclark.com/xt/com.x.Ext"`
	
	Static method:
	`<xsl:variable name="result" select="j:m1(99)"/>`
	
	Constructor:
	`<xsl:variable name="instance" select="j:new()"/>`
	
	Instance-level method:
	`<xsl:variable name="result" select="j:m2($instance, 99)"/>`

For this mechanism to work, the XSLT processor has to examine the named class and look for methods that match the function being called (m1() and m2() in our example): Java provides a mechanism called introspection to make this possible (as do other modern object technologies such as COM). Each product applies slightly different rules to this process, particularly if there are several methods in the class with the same name but different numbers or types of arguments, or if the XPath function name uses characters such as hyphens and dots that are not permitted in Java names.

All four products allow a Java method to return an arbitrary object, and allow this object to be held in an XPath variable so it can be passed to other extension functions.

Where the XPath function call has arguments, these will be passed to the Java method. This requires a mapping from XPath data types to Java data types. All the products support the obvious mappings for strings, numbers, and Booleans, but for node-sets and result tree fragments the XPath data types are mapped to Java classes defined by each vendor, as follows:

Product	Java class names

Oracle	node-set:
	`oracle.xml.parser.v2.XMLNodeList`
	
	result tree fragment:
	`oracle.xml.parser.v2.XMLDocumentFragment`

Saxon	node-set:
	`com.icl.saxon.expr.NodeSetValue`
	
	result tree fragment:
	`com.icl.saxon.expr.FragmentValue`

Xalan	node-set:
	`org.w3c.dom.NodeList`
	
	result tree fragment:
	`org.w3c.dom.DocumentFragment`

xt	node-set:
	`com.jclark.xsl.om.NodeIterator`
	
	result tree fragment:
	`com.jclark.xsl.sax.ResultTreeFragment`

Even though the mechanisms used by all four products are very similar, it is therefore not usually possible to write extension functions in a way that is portable. It can be done in a few cases: for example, portability between xt and Saxon is possible for certain methods provided they only take string, double, or Boolean arguments. In general, though, different versions of both the Java method, and the calling code, will be needed for each product.

Example: Using Java Extension Functions

This example shows the use of Java extension functions in Oracle XSL, Saxon, Xalan, and xt.

Rather than write my own extension function, I'll show how to call a method that already exists in the standard Java class library. Specifically, I'll use the class `java.util.Date`, which performs date and time manipulation. The constructor `Date.new()` creates a new `Date` object and initializes it to the current date and time; the method `toString()` creates a printable representation of this date and time.

10

Products

635

Source

Any XML document; there must be a source document, but its contents are not used. You can use `dummy.xml` if you like.

Stylesheet

The stylesheet `xt-date.xsl`, derived from one supplied with the xt product, will work with both xt and Saxon. Its effect is to output the current date. It works with both products because the argument data types are simple, and because Saxon doesn't care what the namespace URI is, so long as it ends with the class name.

Note the use of `xsl:exclude-result-prefixes` to prevent the «date» namespace being included in the result document. This feature isn't implemented in the current version of xt, which ignores this attribute.

```
<xsl:stylesheet
        version="1.0"
        xmlns:xsl="http://www.w3.org/1999/XSL/Transform"
        xmlns:date="http://www.jclark.com/xt/java/java.util.Date">

<xsl:template match="/">
   <html xsl:exclude-result-prefixes="date">
   <body>
      <p><xsl:value-of select="date:toString(date:new())"/></p>
   </body>
   </html>
</xsl:template>

</xsl:stylesheet>
```

The same example will work with Oracle simply by changing the namespace declaration as shown below. The result can be found in `oracle-date.xsl`.

```
xmlns:date="http://www.oracle.com/XSL/Transform/java/java.util.Date"
```

The equivalent for Xalan is `xalan-date.xsl`:

```
<xsl:stylesheet
        version="1.0"
        xmlns:xsl="http://www.w3.org/1999/XSL/Transform"
        xmlns:date="http://xsl.lotus.com/java">

<xsl:template match="/">
   <html xsl:exclude-result-prefixes="date">
   <body>
      <p><xsl:value-of select="date:toString(date:java.util.Date.new())"/></p>
   </body>
   </html>
</xsl:template>

</xsl:stylesheet>
```

Output

The output in each case shows the current date and time, for example:

```
<html>
    <body>
        <p>Tue Apr 04 22:09:39 GMT 2000</p>
    </body>
</html>
```

Writing Multiple Output Files

Another feature which is present in several products (specifically Saxon, Xalan, and xt) is the ability to produce multiple output files. The syntax in each case is slightly different, but the functionality is almost identical.

This feature is something I pioneered in Saxon and which users have adopted with enthusiasm. It's listed in the wish list of enhancements at the back of the XSLT 1.0 Recommendation, so it's very likely to find its way into a future version of the standard. Meanwhile the functionality is there, but not in a portable way.

Generating multiple output files is something I have often found useful when doing transformations. A typical scenario is that a weighty publication, such as a dictionary, is managed as a single XML file, which would be far too big to download to a user who only wants to see a few entries. So the first stage in preparing it for human consumption is to split it up into bite-sized chunks, perhaps one document per letter of the alphabet or even one per dictionary headword. You can make these chunks individual HTML pages, but I usually find it's better to do the transformation in two stages: first split the big XML document into lots of small XML documents, then convert each of these into HTML independently.

The usual model is to generate one principal output file and a whole family of secondary output files. The principal output file can then serve as an index. Often you'll need to keep links between the files so that you can easily assemble them again (using the document() function described on page 440 in Chapter 7), or so that you can generate hyperlinks for the user to follow.

It's best illustrated by an example.

Example: Creating Multiple Output Files

This example takes a poem as input, and outputs each stanza to a separate file. A more realistic example would be to split a book into its chapters, but I wanted to keep the files small.

Source

The source file is `poem.xml`. It starts:

```
<poem>
<author>Rupert Brooke</author>
<date>1912</date>
<title>Song</title>
<stanza>
<line>And suddenly the wind comes soft,</line>
<line>And Spring is here again;</line>
<line>And the hawthorn quickens with buds of green</line>
<line>And my heart with buds of pain.</line>
</stanza>
<stanza>
<line>My heart all Winter lay so numb,</line>
<line>The earth so dead and frore,</line>
. . .
```

Saxon Stylesheet

The stylesheet for use with Saxon is `saxon-split.xsl`.

Note that «saxon» is defined as an extension element prefix, so the
`<saxon:output>` element is recognised as an instruction. Its effect is to switch all
output produced by its template body to a different output file. In fact, it's very
similar to the effect of an `<xsl:variable>` element that creates a tree, except that
the tree, instead of becoming a fragment of the principal result tree, is serialized
directly to an output file of its own.

```
<?xml version="1.0"?>
<xsl:stylesheet xmlns:xsl="http://www.w3.org/1999/XSL/Transform"
                xmlns:saxon="http://icl.com/saxon"
                extension-element-prefixes="saxon"
                version="1.0">

<xsl:template match="poem">
   <poem>
      <xsl:copy-of select="title"/>
      <xsl:copy-of select="author"/>
      <xsl:copy-of select="date"/>
      <xsl:apply-templates select="stanza"/>
   </poem>
</xsl:template>

<xsl:template match="stanza">
   <xsl:variable name="file" select="concat('verse', position(), '.xml')"/>
   <verse number="{position()}" href="{$file}"/>
   <saxon:output file="{$file}">
        <xsl:copy-of select="."/>
   </saxon:output>
</xsl:template>
</xsl:stylesheet>
```

Output

The principal output file contains the skeletal poem below (newlines added for legibility):

```
<?xml version="1.0" encoding="utf-8" ?>
<poem>
<title>Song</title>
<author>Rupert Brooke</author>
<date>1912</date>
<verse number="1" href="verse1.xml"/>
<verse number="2" href="verse2.xml"/>
<verse number="3" href="verse3.xml"/>
</poem>
```

Three further output files verse1.xml, verse2.xml, and verse3.xml are created in the current directory. Here is verse1.xml:

```
<?xml version="1.0" encoding="utf-8" ?>
<stanza>
<line>And suddenly the wind comes soft,</line>
<line>And Spring is here again;</line>
<line>And the hawthorn quickens with buds of green</line>
<line>And my heart with buds of pain.</line>
</stanza>
```

Xalan Stylesheet

The stylesheet for use with Xalan is xalan-split.xsl. It is very similar. In fact the only differences are the namespace declaration:

```
<xsl:stylesheet xmlns:xsl="http://www.w3.org/1999/XSL/Transform"
                xmlns:xalan="org.apache.xalan.xslt.extensions.Redirect"
                extension-element-prefixes="xalan" version="1.0">
```

and the name of the extension element:

```
<xalan:write select="$file">
    <xsl:copy-of select="."/>
</xalan:write>
```

xt Stylesheet

The stylesheet for use with xt is xt-split.xsl.

Again it is very similar; once again the only differences are the namespace declaration:

```
<xsl:stylesheet xmlns:xsl="http://www.w3.org/1999/XSL/Transform"
                xmlns:xt="http://www.jclark.com/xt"
                extension-element-prefixes="xt"
                version="1.0">
```

10

Products

and the name of the extension element:

```
<xt:document href="{$file}">
      <xsl:copy-of select="."/>
</xt:document>
```

The output is the same in all three cases.

It would be nice to write a single stylesheet that works with any of the three processors. Unfortunately, though, xt doesn't yet implement the `element-available()` function or the `<xsl:fallback>` instruction, so this is a bit difficult: the only way to do it would be to test which processor is in use using the `system-property()` function. Another option is to define the common processing in one stylesheet module, and the processor-specific templates in another module which imports this one; there would be one version of this for each processor.

Further details on the exact syntax of the extension elements is provided in the description of each product later in this chapter.

The node-set() extension function

This extension function is provided by two products, Saxon and xt, but I feel it is worth a section of its own because it has a significant effect on the power of the XSLT language. Microsoft's MSXML3 also has a similar capability, though it is provided by an implicit extension to the semantics of the language rather than an explicit extension in its own namespace. Since Microsoft's way of doing it is against the conformance rules of the standard as currently written, they may change it before their final release, unless they can persuade W3C to adopt the way they've done it.

The `node-set()` function (`xt:node-set()` in xt, `saxon:node-set()` in Saxon) allows you to convert a tree to a node-set. The resulting node-set always contains a single node, the root node of the tree, and from this you can navigate to the other nodes using all the XSLT and XPath facilities that you use with the principal source document: for example `<xsl:for-each>`, `<xsl:value-of>`, `<xsl:apply-templates>`, and even the `key()` function (but only for Saxon – xt and MSXML3 don't yet support keys).

What this means is that you can process the data in more than one pass. For example, your first pass can sort the nodes, and the second pass can number them using `<xsl:number>`. Without this capability, `<xsl:number>` is only capable of numbering nodes based on their position in the original source tree. You can sometimes get round this restriction by generating sequence numbers using the `position()` function, but that gives far less flexibility than `<xsl:number>`.

I mentioned right back in Chapter 1 (page 15) that one thing XSLT had in common with SQL was the property of **closure**: the output is the same kind of animal as the input, so you can apply a whole series of transformations in a kind of pipeline.

So complex transformations can be split up into simpler transformations, each of which does just one thing. This is an immensely powerful technique, but it only really becomes possible once the `node-set()` extension is available, because most of XSLT is designed to process node-sets, and there are no other functions in the language that create new node-sets.

Example: Numbering After Sorting, Using node-set()

Source

The source file, `products.xml`, lists sales of various products in each region:

```
<products>
<product name="strawberry jam">
   <region name="south" sales="20.00"/>
   <region name="north" sales="50.00"/>
</product>
<product name="raspberry jam">
   <region name="south" sales="205.16"/>
   <region name="north" sales="10.50"/>
</product>
<product name="plum jam">
   <region name="east" sales="320.20"/>
   <region name="north" sales="39.50"/>
</product>
</products>
```

Stylesheet

The stylesheet, `nodeset.xsl`, first rearranges this into a tree that organizes the data by product within region, then it uses `<xsl:apply-templates>` to process this tree, numbering the nodes as it goes.

As written, it uses Saxon: to run it with xt, simply change the relevant namespace URI.

The variable `$regions` is a set of `<region>` elements with distinct names, formed by filtering out those `<region>` elements that have the same `name` attribute as a preceding `<region>`.

The variable `$tree` is the result tree fragment. The root node of this tree will have several `<region>` elements as its children (trees don't have to be well-formed, only well-balanced), and each `<region>` element will have several `<product>` children.

The template rule for the root element then processes this tree by converting it to a node-set and using `<xsl:apply-templates>` to process the children of the root node. Don't try processing the root node of the tree directly, unless you use a different mode, because then the template rule for «/» will fire again, giving you an infinite recursion.

```xml
<?xml version="1.0"?>
<xsl:stylesheet xmlns:xsl="http://www.w3.org/1999/XSL/Transform"
                xmlns:saxon="http://icl.com/saxon"
                extension-element-prefixes="saxon"
                version="1.0">

<xsl:variable name="regions"
              select="//region[not(@name=preceding::region/@name)]"/>

<xsl:variable name="tree">
    <xsl:for-each select="$regions">
        <xsl:sort select="@name"/>
        <region name="{@name}">
            <xsl:for-each select="//region[@name=current()/@name]">
                <product name="{../@name}" sales="{@sales}"/>
            </xsl:for-each>
        </region>
    </xsl:for-each>
</xsl:variable>

<xsl:template match="/">
<html><body>
    <h1>Sales of Jam by Region</h1>
    <xsl:apply-templates select="saxon:node-set($tree)/region"/>
</body></html>
</xsl:template>

<xsl:template match="region">
    <h1>Region <xsl:number format="A"/>: <xsl:value-of
                                    select="@name"/></h1>
    <xsl:apply-templates/>
</xsl:template>

<xsl:template match="product">
    <h2>Product <xsl:number level="multiple"
                count="product | region" format="A.i"/></h2>
    <p><xsl:value-of select="@name"/></p>
    <p>Total sales: <xsl:value-of
                      select="format-number(@sales, '$###0.00')"/></p>
</xsl:template>

</xsl:stylesheet>
```

Output

I have added extra indentation for readability:

```html
<html>
   <body>
      <h1>Sales of Jam by Region</h1>
      <h1>Region A: east</h1>
      <h2>Product A.i</h2>
```

```
            <p>plum jam</p>
            <p>Total sales: $320.20</p>
        <h1>Region B: north</h1>
        <h2>Product B.i</h2>
            <p>strawberry jam</p>
            <p>Total sales: $50.00</p>
        <h2>Product B.ii</h2>
            <p>raspberry jam</p>
            <p>Total sales: $10.50</p>
        <h2>Product B.iii</h2>
            <p>plum jam</p>
            <p>Total sales: $39.50</p>
        <h1>Region C: south</h1>
        <h2>Product C.i</h2>
            <p>strawberry jam</p>
            <p>Total sales: $20.00</p>
        <h2>Product C.ii</h2>
            <p>raspberry jam</p>
            <p>Total sales: $205.16</p>
    </body>
</html>
```

The Microsoft MSXML3 product appears (though it is not a documented feature) to allow a result tree fragment to be used in exactly the same way as a node-set: this offers the same functionality as the node-set() extension function in the Saxon and xt products, but without the need for an explicit conversion. Although this is a useful feature, it seems unfortunately to have been provided in a way that conflicts with the standard. For example, the following test currently outputs «BUG» with MSXML3 whereas according to the standard it should output nothing, because the string-value of «$tree» is zero-length:

```
<xsl:variable name="tree"><xsl:text/></xsl:variable>
<xsl:if test="$tree">BUG</xsl:if>
```

To circumvent this problem, write:

```
<xsl:if test="string($tree)">
```

Two questions are often asked about the node-set() function:

❏ **Does it violate the "no side-effects" design principle in XSLT?**
The answer to this is no: the node-set() function is a pure function, just like the other conversion functions such as string() and number().

❏ **So why wasn't it included in the standard?**
I simply don't know. There is certainly no good technical objection to it. If there were, you can be sure James Clark wouldn't have implemented it in xt.

That ends our survey of extension features common to several products. It's time now to look at the products individually.

10

Products

Oracle XSL

Oracle's XSLT processor is bundled with their XML parser software. It is available from http://technet.oracle.com/tech/xml/. The Java processor is part of the **XML: Parser for Java v2** product. The software is free, though you have to go through a rather lengthy registration process before you can download it. It is described as an early adopter software. The free license is for internal data processing operations only but permits distribution to third parties under specified conditions. Source code is not provided, and there is no formal support available.

As well as an XSLT processor, Oracle's software includes an XML parser supporting DOM and SAX interfaces, with support for the XML Namespaces recommendation. The parser operates in both validating and non-validating modes.

As one might expect, the Oracle XML development kit includes a number of tools designed to enable XML to be incorporated into a relational database. These tools are designed to work at any of the levels of Oracle's three-tier architecture: client, application server, or database server. The toolkit also includes a Java class generator designed to translate a DTD into a set of Java class definitions reflecting the structure of the DTD. These tools, however, are outside the scope of this book.

Oracle also advertise versions of their parser for C++ and C, these are available for Windows, Linux, Solaris, and HP-UX platforms..

Oracle tell me that the current version of their XSLT implementation (2.0.2.7) is fully conformant with the final (November 1999) XSLT 1.0 and XPath 1.0 recommendations, though their public claims, suprisingly, are more modest: at the time of writing, their web site claims conformance only with the August 1999 draft. They don't say very much about their coverage of features that the standard leaves optional or implementation-defined, so in these areas you may need to do some trial and error. No doubt the documentation will improve as the technology reaches product status.

The Oracle XSLT processor may be invoked either as a Java class, or through a simple command line interface. Once you have installed the Java Virtual Machine and the Oracle software, and set up the PATH and CLASSPATH environment variables, you can run the processor from the command line as follows:

```
java oracle.xml.parser.v2.oraxsl source.xml stylesheet.xsl result.xml
```

The java command invokes Sun's Java Virtual Machine. If you prefer to use Microsoft's Java VM (which will already be installed on your machine if you are running a recent version of Internet Explorer), use the command jview instead.

Stylesheet parameters can be specified using the -p option. I couldn't find any documentation saying how to use this, but discovered by trial and error that the following works (for running the knight's tour stylesheet in Chapter 9, with the knight starting on square d3):

```
java oracle.xml.parser.v2.oraxsl -p start='d3' dummy.xml tour.xsl out.html
```

As with the other products, the command-line interface is really only intended as a development tool. For serious production use, you should write an application that invokes the Java API directly. The detail of the API is well documented, though it could do with a general overview, and there are several sample applications to get you started. The two key classes are XSLStylesheet, which represents a pre-processed (or compiled) stylesheet which you can use as often as you like, and XSLProcessor, which you use to apply a stylesheet to a source document.

Extensions

Oracle XSL supports user-defined extension functions using the Common Java Binding mechanism defined on page 632.

There is no mechanism for creating user-defined extension elements, though they are apparently thinking about this for a future release – so check the latest information.

There are no vendor-supplied extension functions or extension elements. In particular, Oracle does not yet have a facility to produce multiple output files. Again, they have said this is on the agenda for a future release.

Saxon

Saxon is an open source implementation of XSLT produced by the author of this book, Michael Kay. Although the development was sponsored by ICL, the IT services company, it is essentially a one-man effort rather than a corporate product.

Saxon is available at http://users.iclway.co.uk/mhkay/saxon/.

The product is available under the Mozilla Public Licence, which essentially allows you to use it free, for any purpose. The source code is available, and can be modified and enhanced subject to the terms of the license. There is no formal warranty or support. The product is written in Java and runs on any Java 1.1 or Java 2 platform.

The current release, version 5.2, is a complete implementation of the final W3C XSLT 1.0 and XPath 1.0 recommendations, including most of the features that are optional or implementer-defined (the XSLT specification is very open-ended in aspects such as which character encodings and collating sequences should be supported). The documentation available with the product is considerably more detailed than that available for most of the other products described in this chapter.

Invoking the Saxon Processor

Saxon can be invoked as a Java class, or from the command line; there is also a servlet wrapper allowing a stylesheet to be invoked directly from a URL entered at a browser.

If you just want to run the product on a Windows platform, and don't need access to API specifications, source code, or sample applications, it is simplest to download *Instant Saxon*, which is a packaged version designed to run as an executable under Microsoft's Java VM. You can then run a stylesheet using the command:

```
saxon source.xml style.xsl >output.html
```

If the directory containing the `saxon.exe` *file isn't the current directory, and isn't on your PATH, then you'll need to use the full name of the file, for example* `C:\saxon-dir\saxon`.

Other options on the command line allow you to select the stylesheet named in the `<?xml-stylesheet?>` processing instruction, to specify URLs rather than filenames, and to nominate the SAX-compliant XML parser to be used for the source document and for the stylesheet (they can be different; for example one might be a validating parser and one non-validating).

You can specify values for global parameters defined in the stylesheet using a `keyword=value` notation; for example:

```
saxon source.xml style.xsl param1=value1 param2=value2
```

The parameter values are interpreted as strings.

If you download the full Saxon product, you can run it on any platform with a Java VM, and the equivalent command line is then:

```
java com.icl.saxon.StyleSheet source.xml style.xsl param1=value1 param2=value2
```

Saxon can also be invoked from a Java application using a defined API. This allows you to compile a stylesheet into a `PreparedStyleSheet` object, which can then be used repeatedly (in series or in multiple threads) to process different source documents through the same stylesheet. This can greatly improve throughput on a web server. A sample application to achieve this, in the form of a Java servlet, is provided with the product.

Extensibility

Saxon supports a range of extensibility mechanisms, described below.

Writing Extension Functions

Extension functions may be written in Java, using the Common Java Binding described on page 632.

Saxon allows an external Java method to have an extra first argument of class `com.icl.saxon.Context`. This argument, if it is present, is not supplied by the calling XSL code, but by Saxon itself. The `Context` object allows the method to access contextual information such as the current node and current node list; it can also expand namespace prefixes and even read the values of variables. This allows the implementation of powerful functions such as the `evaluate()` function, described on page 649.

Writing Extension Elements

Saxon implements the XSLT element extensibility feature. This feature allows you to define your own instruction types for use in the stylesheet.

If a namespace prefix is to be used to denote extension elements, it must be declared in the `extension-element-prefixes` attribute on the `<xsl:stylesheet>` element, or the `xsl:extension-element-prefixes` attribute on any enclosing literal result element.

Implementing extension elements is rather more complex than implementing simple extension functions. You need to be a fairly dedicated systems programmer to attempt it, especially as the documentation in this area is limited. Saxon supplies a sample set of extension elements that allow the stylesheet to write data to a relational database, and recommends that you use these as an example for writing your own extension elements.

Writing Input Filters

Saxon takes its input as a stream of SAX events. Normally these will come directly from a SAX-compliant XML Parser. Instead, however, you can generate these events from an application.

There are two ways you can exploit this capability (which is also present in several other XSLT processors, though you might have to look carefully to find it):

- ❏ You can write an application that acts as a filter between the XML parser and the stylesheet, performing functions such as normalizing data values and supplying defaulted attributes. It could also split an incoming document into multiple input documents to be processed separately, reducing the size of the tree to be held in memory. For information on writing SAX filters, see the Wrox book *Professional XML*, ISBN 1-861003-11-0.

- ❏ Your application could also supply data from a source that is not originally XML at all: I showed an example of that in Chapter 9, where the Kennedy family tree came from a non-XML data source in GEDCOM format. The application could also be fetching the data from a relational database. In effect, your application is pretending to be an XML parser, so the stylesheet thinks it is getting input from an XML parser when it is actually coming from somewhere else.

Writing Output Filters

The output of a Saxon stylesheet can be directed to a user-defined class, instead of going to an XML or HTML file. This class can be a standard SAX `DocumentHandler`, or an implementation of the Saxon class `com.icl.saxon.output.Emitter`, which is similar to `DocumentHandler` but allows more information to be passed across the interface.

The `DocumentHandler` or `Emitter` to be used is named in the `method` attribute of the `<xsl:output>` or `<saxon:output>` element.

One way of using this is to pass the output of the transformation to the Apache FOP processor, which is a partial implementation of the XSL Formatting Objects specification. This only works if the stylesheet generates XML elements and attributes that conform to this specification.

As an alternative to writing an output filter in Java, Saxon also allows you to process the output through another XSL stylesheet. To do this, simply name the next stylesheet in the next-in-chain attribute of <saxon:output>. This can be useful if you want to do things such as numbering the elements in the result tree: the <xsl:number> instruction always generates numbers that relate to the position of a node in the source tree, which is not very useful if your stylesheet is sorting the data. So you can do sorting with one stylesheet, and then put the data through another stylesheet to add section numbers and a table of contents.

Implementing Collating and Numbering Sequences

Saxon allows you to implement a collating sequence for use by <xsl:sort>. This is controlled through the lang attribute of the <xsl:sort> element. The feature is primarily intended to provide language-dependent collating, but in fact it can be used to provide arbitrary collating sequences: for example, if you want to sort the names of the months January, February, March, etc. in the conventional sequence you could do this by writing and providing a collating sequence for language «x-months».

Similarly, you can define a numbering sequence for use by <xsl:number>. For example, if you have a sequence of items which you want to label as "January", "February", "March" etc. you could implement a special numbering class, and invoke it by specifying <xsl:number format="January" lang="x-months"/>.

Built-in Extensions

As well as supporting user-defined extensions through the above extensibility mechanisms, Saxon also comes with a number of built-in extensions, described in the following sections.

Extension Functions

There are several extension functions (that is, functions not defined in the XSLT standard) supplied with Saxon, listed in the table below. These must be used with a prefix that maps to the namespace URI http://icl.com/saxon.

difference (ns1, ns2)	This returns a node-set that is the difference of the two supplied node-sets; that is, it contains all the nodes that are in ns1 that are not also in ns2.

distinct(ns1)	This returns a node-set containing all the nodes in ns1 that have distinct string-values. Nodes with duplicate string-values are discarded. For example:
	
	 `<xsl:variable name="cities"`
	 `select="distinct(//city)"/>`

`distinct(ns1)` *(cont'd)*	creates a node-set containing one element for each uniquely named `<city>` in the source document. If there were several `<city>` elements with the same name, you can't be sure which of them will be retained, but it generally doesn't matter, because the next step will be to process them all as a group:

```
<xsl:for-each select="$cities">
    <h2>City name is: <xsl:value-of select="."/></h2>
        <xsl:for-each select="//city[.=current()]">
            . . .
```

`evaluate (expression)`	This function allows an XPath expression to be constructed at run-time, as a string, and evaluated. This is useful if a query is not known in advance, but must be constructed based on information supplied by the user in parameters, or read from the source document. For example the following code constructs a node-set consisting of all `<book>` elements that satisfy a predicate passed to the stylesheet as a parameter:

```
<xsl:param name="predicate"/>
<xsl:variable name="selectedBooks" select=
    "saxon:evaluate(concat('//book[', $predicate,
    ']')"/>
```

`has-same-nodes (ns1, ns2)`	This returns a Boolean that is true if and only if `ns1` and `ns2` contain exactly the same set of nodes. Note this is quite different from the «=» operator, which tests whether there is a pair of nodes with the same string-value.
	The equivalent test in standard XSLT is:

```
<xsl:if test="count(ns1)=count(ns2) and count(ns1) =
count(ns1|ns2)">
```

`if(condition. v1, v2)`	The first argument is evaluated as a Boolean; if it is true, the function returns the value `v1`, if it is false, it returns `v2`. The value may be of any type.
`intersection (ns1,ns2)`	This returns a node-set that is the intersection of the two supplied node-sets; that is, it contains all the nodes that are in both `ns1` and `ns2`.
	This function can be useful in conjunction with keys, for example to list all programmers based in Denver, write:

```
<xsl:for-each select="saxon:intersection(
        key('job', 'Programmer'), key('location',
        'Denver'))">
```

line-number( )	This returns the line number of the current node in the source document within the entity that contains it. There are no arguments. This is useful for constructing error messages and for debugging.
node-set (frag)	This takes a single argument that is a result tree fragment. Its function is to convert the result tree fragment to a node-set. The resulting node-set contains a single node, which is a root node; below this are the actual nodes added to the result tree fragment, which may be element nodes, text nodes, or anything else. The node-set returned by this function can be processed in much the same way as a document loaded using the document( ) function.
range(n1, n2)	This constructs a new node-set whose nodes have numeric values in the range n1 to n2. It is designed to provide an equivalent to a conventional for-loop. The following example will create five table cells containing the numbers 1 to 5: ``` <xsl:for-each select="saxon:range(1,5)"> <td><xsl:value-of select="."/></td> </xsl:for-each> ```
system-id( )	This returns the system identifier of the entity containing the current node in the source document (in other words, its Base URI). There are no arguments. This is useful for constructing error messages.
tokenize (string, delimiter?)	This function constructs a new node-set whose nodes result from splitting the supplied string into tokens, separated either the supplied delimiter, or by whitespace. It is designed for operations such as replacing newline characters in the source by elements in the output, or searching for a particular word in the text content of an element.

Extension Elements

Saxon-supplied extension elements are available only if (a) they are used with a namespace prefix that identifies the namespace http://icl.com/saxon, and (b) a prefix for that namespace is listed in the extension-element-prefixes attribute of the enclosing <xsl:stylesheet> element, or in the xsl:extension-element-prefixes attribute of an enclosing literal result element. The prefix saxon is used here as a conventional namespace prefix only: as with the xsl prefix, you can use any prefix you like so long as it maps to the proper namespace URI.

The Saxon extension elements are:

`<saxon:assign>`	This element is used to change the value of a local or global variable that has previously been declared using `<xsl:variable>` (or `<xsl:param>`). For example: `<saxon:assign name="n" select="$n+1"/>` Providing an explicit assignment statement like this blows a gaping hole in the design principle that XSLT is a language where side effects are not allowed. In Chapter 8, I call this "cheating". Use it when only all other options have been exhausted.

`<saxon:entity-ref>`	This element is useful to generate entities such as « » in HTML output. For example:
	
	`<saxon:entity-ref name="nbsp"/>`
	
	You can achieve the same effect within the standard by writing:
	
	`<xsl:text disable-output-escaping="yes"> `
	`</xsl:text>`

`<saxon:group>` and `<saxon:item>`	These elements together provide grouping of items that share a common value. The `<saxon:group>` element operates like `<xsl:for-each>`, but with an additional attribute `group-by` which defines the grouping key. The `<saxon:group>` element must contain somewhere within it an `<saxon:item>` element. The XSL instructions outside the `<saxon:item>` element are executed only once for each group of consecutive elements with the same value for the grouping key; the instructions within the `<saxon:item>` are executed once for each individual item in the `<saxon:group>` selection. For example, to list a collection of books sorted and grouped by author, write:

```
<saxon:group select="book" group-by="author">
  <xsl:sort select="author">
  Books by <xsl:value-of select="author"/>:
  <ul>
  <saxon:item>
    <li><xsl:value-of select="title"/></li>
  </saxon:item>
  </ul>
</saxon:group>
```

10

Products

`<saxon:output>`	The `<saxon:output>` instruction is used to define a new output destination. It takes an attribute `file` which names the output file; all content that results from instantiating the template body of the `<saxon:output>` element is sent to that file instead of the parent file. The effect is that using `<saxon:output>`, a stylesheet can be used to split one large input document into many smaller output documents. All the attributes available on `<xsl:output>` to control the format of the output file are also available on `<saxon:output>`. As an alternative to sending the output to a file, it can also be directed to be processed by another named stylesheet. This allows an XML transformation to be set up as a chain of simpler transformations. An example stylesheet using `<saxon:output>` is shown on page 637.
`<saxon:preview>`	This is an experimental feature for processing very large input documents. Normally XSLT processing requires that the entire source document be constructed as a tree in memory. With very large documents, this may be infeasible. The `<saxon:preview>` extension allows an element to be nominated that acts as a document in its own right; as soon as such an element has been read, it is processed by the stylesheet and is then discarded from the tree, together with all its descendants.

`<saxon: set-attribute>`	This element allows data values to be written to the source tree in the course of processing. The following example sets the `width` attribute of an element to 100 if it has no `width` attribute:
	
	`<xsl:if test="not(@width)">`
	`    <saxon:set-attribute name="width" select="100"/>`
	`</xsl:if>`
	
	Like `<saxon:assign>`, this instruction has side effects, so it is best avoided if you can. Its original purpose was to provide a way of passing data into Java extension functions.

`<saxon:while>`	This element is used to iterate while some condition is true. The condition is given as a Boolean expression in the mandatory `test` attribute. It is generally used with `<saxon:assign>`. For example:

```
<xsl:variable name="n" select="10"/>
<saxon:while test="$n != 0">
   <xsl:value-of select="$n"/>
      <saxon:assign name="n" select="$n - 1"/>
</saxon:while>
```

Xalan

The Xalan product is available from http://xml.apache.org/xalan/overview.html.

Most of the technology in Xalan derived from an earlier product called LotusXSL which was developed by a team under Scott Boag of IBM's Lotus subsidiary before being handed over to the Apache Software Foundation. LotusXSL as currently available from the IBM site (http://www.alphaworks.ibm.com/) is merely a wrapper around the Xalan product.

Xalan is available both in Java and C++ versions. The Java product has received a good level of exposure, enough to justify the developers giving it a version number of 1.0.0. The C++ version, by contrast, is currently at its first release and still has some loose ends to be tidied up, not the least of which is the documentation.

The software is free, and is distributed under the Apache Software License, which essentially allows any kind of use, redistribution, or modification, but disclaims any liability. There is no formal warranty or support. Source code is available.

Xalan uses the Apache XML parser, Xerces. It will also work with any other parser that conforms to the SAX or DOM interfaces, but you have to write the relevant Java glue code (called a *ParserLiaison*) yourself. Xalan will output to a SAX `DocumentHandler` or to a DOM tree as well as supporting the standard output methods of XML, HTML, and text.

Xalan claims complete support for mandatory XSLT 1.0 and XPath 1.0 features. There is no detailed conformance statement, so it is unclear whether all the optional or implementer-defined features of the standard are provided.

The Xalan processor has introduced a novel way of storing the document internally. One of the limitations of XSLT is that the whole source document must be held in memory. The obvious way of implementing a tree structure in Java is to create one object for each node, containing object references to related nodes such as its parent, siblings, and children. This is very hungry in the memory it uses, and it also means that building the tree can account for a significant proportion of the total execution time. Xalan has opted for a different approach, called the Document Table Model, in which the tree is represented internally using arrays. This avoids many of the Java overheads and gives a substantial performance boost, especially for large documents.

10

Products

Invoking the Xalan Processor

The Xalan XSLT processor may be run from the command line, or by calling its Java API. There are also wrappers provided to allow it to be run within an applet or within a servlet.

A typical call from the command line is:

```
java org.apache.xalan.xslt.Process -in a.xml -xsl b.xsl -out c.html
```

The `java` command invokes Sun's Java Virtual Machine. If you prefer to use Microsoft's Java VM (which will already be on your machine if you are running a recent version of Internet Explorer), use the command `jview` instead.

Values of global parameters may be specified on the command line in the form:

```
-PARAM name expression
```

The value can be set to any XPath expression, so if it is a string, it needs to be enclosed in quotes. The expression will be evaluated with the root as the current node.

For example, to run the knight's tour stylesheet described in Chapter 9, the command would be (all on one line):

```
java org.apache.xalan.xslt.Process -PARAM start 'e5' -in dummy.xml
   -xsl tour.xsl -out tour.html
```

This assumes you have changed directory to the directory containing the `tour.xsl` stylesheet. This particular stylesheet works with any source document so the only requirements on `dummy.xml` are that is exists and is XML.

Additional options on the command line are available to provide control over the output format (overriding or supplementing the attributes of any `<xsl:output>` element in the stylesheet), to control tracing and debugging, and to indicate whether warnings are required in the event of conflicts between template rules. Xalan also allows the compiled stylesheet to be saved to disk: but the size is quite large, so by the time you have read it back from filestore it might have been almost as fast to recompile the original.

Xalan also has a Java API, allowing it to be invoked from an application, an applet, or a servlet. The basic classes are:

- ❏ `XSLTProcessor`, which allows you to compile a stylesheet
- ❏ `StyleSheetRoot`, which represents a compiled stylesheet, and which has a `process()` method to run the stylesheet against a particular source document.

Extensibility

Xalan allows you to define both extension functions and extension elements.

In Xalan's extensibility model, a collection of extension elements and functions is bundled together into a **component**, and each component is identified by a namespace URI. The elements and functions available in this component are defined by a `<xalan:component>` element at the top level of the stylesheet.

The Common Java Binding, described earlier in this chapter, is provided as a special variant of this model, in which the `<xalan:component>` element is implicit. Note, however, that if you implement an extension function using this simplified model then testing `function-available()` will always return false.

Extensions may be implemented in Java or JavaScript, or in other languages supported by the Bean Scripting Framework, such as Perl and Python.

JavaScript extensions can be embedded directly within the stylesheet itself, in a `<xalan:script>` element within the `<xalan:component>` element. This is illustrated in the example below.

Example: Using JavaScript Extension Functions with Xalan

Source

This stylesheet can be run with any source document.

Stylesheet

This stylesheet is `xalan-script.xsl`.

The stylesheet creates a Xalan component which is identified by the namespace URI associated with the prefix «user». This component defines an extension element `<user:trace>` and an extension function `user:datePlus()`.

The template rule for the root node shows how this extension element and extension function can be invoked.

```
<xsl:stylesheet xmlns:xsl="http://www.w3.org/1999/XSL/Transform"
                version="1.0"
                xmlns:xalan="http://xml.apache.org/xslt"
                xmlns:user="http://any.user.com/xslt/extension1"
                extension-element-prefixes="user">

<xalan:component prefix="user" elements="trace" functions="datePlus">
    <xalan:script lang="javascript">
        function trace (xslProcessorContext, extensionElement) {
            return "trace called, message=" +
                extensionElement.getAttribute("message");
        }
```

```
        function datePlus (days) {
            var d = new Date();
            d.setDate(d.getDate() + parseInt(days));
            return d.toLocaleString();
        }
    </xalan:script>
</xalan:component>

<xsl:template match="/">
    <html><body>
    <p><user:trace message="starting"/></p>
    <p>In 5 days time it will be <xsl:value-of
      select="user:datePlus(5)"/></p>
    <p><user:trace message="finished"/></p>
    </body></html>
</xsl:template>

</xsl:stylesheet>
```

Output

```
<html>
<body>
<p>trace called, message=starting</p>
<p>In 5 days time it will be 10 April 2000 17:02:26 BST</p>
<p>trace called, message=finished</p>
</body>
</html>
```

Getting scripted extension functions to work properly requires some careful assembly of all the right software. There are five software products that need to be correctly installed and configured to get this example to run:

❑ the Java Virtual Machine

❑ the Xerces XML Parser

❑ the Xalan XSLT Processor

❑ the Bean Scripting Framework

❑ the Rhino JavaScript interpreter

Xerces and Xalan are separate downloads from http://www.apache.org. The Bean Scripting Framework is bundled with Xalan. Rhino Javascript is a separate download from http://www.mozilla.org/rhino/. I found that it had to be version 1.4 release 3, as advised in the Xalan documentation: version 1.5 didn't work. To get all this to run, I used the command:

```
java -cp XXX org.apache.xalan.xslt.Process -in dummy.xml -xsl xalan-script.xsl
```

where XXX is the Java classpath, as follows, all on one line, with no spaces. The actual filenames will depend, of course, on where you installed the software.

```
D:\JavaLib\xerces\xerces-1_0_3\xerces.jar;
D:\JavaLib\xalan\xalan_1_0_0\xalan.jar;
D:\JavaLib\rhino\js.jar;
D:\JavaLib\xalan\xalan_1_0_0\bsf.jar;
D:\JavaLib\xalan\xalan_1_0_0\bsfengines.jar
```

Implementing extension elements more complicated than this trivial example is trickier than implementing extension functions, and the documentation available is rather sparse. The xslProcessorContext argument gives full access to the source document, the stylesheet, the current node and current node list, and other internal information. The extensionElement argument is the node in the stylesheet tree corresponding to the extension element. Xalan uses the DOM to represent its trees internally, so standard DOM interfaces can be used to find related nodes in the tree. The result of the function, if any, is written to the result tree.

Java extensions are defined by reference to the external Java class, which must be present on the classpath. A component written in Java might be represented by a <xalan:script> element as follows:

```
<xalan:script lang="javaclass" src="com.user.class.Extension1"/>
```

The fully-qualified Java class name should be preceded by «class:» if all the methods called are static, that is, if the class does not need to be instantiated. For example:

```
<xalan:script lang="javaclass" src="class:com.user.class.Extension1"/>
```

Multiple Output Files

The only extension currently supplied in Xalan is a facility to produce multiple output files, using an element called <xalan:redirect>. An example of the use of this extension element was given on page 637.

This extension element allows an XSLT transformation to redirect its output to multiple output destinations. You must declare a namespace for the extension prefix (say xmlns:redirect="org.apache.xalan.xslt.extensions.Redirect") and you must declare the extension namespace as an extension (extension-element-prefixes="redirect").

You can either just use <redirect:write>, as in my example, in which case the file will be opened and immediately closed after the write, or you can bracket the write calls by <redirect:open> and <redirect:close>, in which case the file will be kept open for multiple writes until the close call is encountered. Calls can be nested. Calls can take a file attribute and/or a select attribute in order to get the filename. If a select attribute is encountered, it will evaluate that expression for a string that indicates the filename. If the string evaluates to empty, it will attempt to use the file attribute as a default. The element can also have a mkdirs attribute, which, if set to true, will cause any non-existent directories to be created.

10

Products

657

xt

The **xt** product is an open-source implementation of XSLT produced by the editor of the specification, James Clark. It was the first implementation available, and is still the fastest; recently, however, other products have overtaken xt in functionality and have been catching up in performance. Like Saxon, it is a one-man effort rather than a corporate product. It is available under a very flexible license that essentially allows you to do anything you like with the software, but protects the author from any claims. There is no warranty or support. The product is written in Java, and source code is provided.

xt is available at http://www.jclark.com/xml/xt.html.

The current version, referenced as version 19991105, is described as a beta release. It has a few limitations, for example the following features of the XSLT 1.0 and XPath 1.0 Recommendations are not yet implemented:

❑   the element extension mechanism (the `extension-element-prefixes` and `xsl:extension-element-prefixes` attributes, the `<xsl:fallback>` element, and the `element-available()` function)

❑   keys (the `<xsl:key>` element, and the `key()` function)

❑   the `<xsl:decimal-format>` element and the optional third argument on the `format-number()` function, which references an `<xsl:decimal-format>` element

❑   the namespace axis

❑   forwards-compatible processing

❑   the `xsl:exclude-result-prefixes` attribute on literal result elements (however, the `exclude-result-prefixes` attribute on `<xsl:stylesheet>` is implemented)

Another restriction is that errors are not always reported when they should be, which means that an incorrect stylesheet may sometimes appear to work on xt when a strictly conforming XSLT processor would reject it. For example, xt allows a local variable to be declared when another variable of the same name is in scope.

Invoking the xt Processor

The xt processor may be run from the command line, via a Java API, or as a servlet.

With the full product, the typical command line is

```
java com.jclark.xsl.sax.Driver  source.xml  style.xsl  out.html
param1=value1...
```

The product also comes packaged as a Windows executable, in which case you can type:

```
xt  source.xml  style.xsl  out.html  param1=value1...
```

If you are running on Windows, this version is simplicity itself to install and get working.

As the name of the Java class suggests, xt is structured as a SAX filter, taking a stream of SAX events from the XML parser as input, and delivering the result tree to the final formatting process as another stream of SAX events.

xt works with any SAX-compliant XML parser, and the selected parser can be specified by means of a system property. However, the recommended parser is James Clark's xp, which has a specially-extended SAX interface allowing comments to be passed to the application.

The `param1=value1` parameters supply values for any global parameters in the stylesheet; the values must be strings.

The xt product also has a Java API, which can be used to run it in a servlet environment. Unfortunately the speed of James Clark's code is matched only by the brevity of his documentation, so if you want to use this API, be prepared to explore the product structure in some depth. There are, however, some example source files (in `xt.jar`, which you can open using WinZip or any other ZIP file extractor) showing how to use the SAX and DOM interfaces provided by xt, and how to run the processor from a servlet.

Extensibility

The xt product allows user-defined extension functions to be created using the Common Java Binding described on page 632.

xt does not currently support element extensibility, though it implements a subset of the syntax for use with its own extension elements, described below.

Extensions

xt supports several extensions, including multiple output documents, non-XML output, user-defined output handlers, and a number of extension functions. These are described in the following sections.

Multiple Output Documents

XT supports an extension element `<xt:document>` that allows the stylesheet to create multiple output documents. The prefix `xt` (or whatever other prefix you choose to use) must be bound to the namespace URI `http://www.jclark.com/xt`. An example of this feature was given on page 639.

The `<xt:document>` element has a required `href` attribute, which must be a relative URL. The value of the `href` attribute is interpreted as an attribute value template. The content of the `<xt:document>` element is a template body for the result tree to be stored in the location specified by the `href` attribute. The base URL for resolving the `href` relative URL is the URL of the parent output document: either the URL of the main output document or the URL in which the parent `<xt:document>` element was stored. Thus, the same relative URL specified by the `href` attribute can be used in the parent document to reference the document created by the `<xt:document>` element.

The `<xt:document>` element can also have all the same attributes as the `<xsl:output>` element. These attributes are merged with attributes specified on top-level `<xsl:output>` elements to determine the output method for this document. The attributes on the `<xt:document>` element take precedence over the attributes specified on top-level `<xsl:output>` elements.

Non-XML output

It is possible to produce text output using `<xsl:output method="text">`; however this has limitations, for example, it is not possible to output control characters outside the XML character set.

xt therefore provides an alternative method for text output using an output method of «*xt:nxml*» where the prefix xt is bound to the namespace URI `http://www.jclark.com/xt`. This produces an XML tree in which certain elements have special meanings:

❏ The `<char>` element allows the output of a character that is not allowed by XML, for example most of the ASCII control characters below #x20.

❏ The `<data>` element contains data. Within a `<data>` element special characters get escaped.

❏ The `<escape>` element defines a special character and says how it should be escaped.

❏ The `<control>` element contains characters to be output directly without escaping.

Example: Producing Text Output with xt

Source

This stylesheet can be run with any source document.

Stylesheet

This stylesheet is `xt-text.xsl`.

```
<xsl:stylesheet xmlns:xsl="http://www.w3.org/1999/XSL/Transform"
                                        version="1.0">
<xsl:output method="xt:nxml" xmlns:xt="http://www.jclark.com/xt"/>
<xsl:template match="/">
    <nxml>
        <escape char="\">\\</escape>
        <data>&amp;&lt;&gt;\</data>
        <control>&amp;&lt;&gt;\</control>
    </nxml>
</xsl:template>
</xsl:stylesheet>
```

Output

```
&<>\\&<>\
```

User-defined Output Handlers

The method attribute of `<xsl:output>` or `<xt:document>` can take the form «java:package.name.class» where the prefix «java» is bound to the namespace URI `http://www.jclark.com/xt/java` and «package.name.class» is the full name of a Java class that implements the `com.jclark.xsl.sax.OutputDocumentHandler` interface (which extends the SAX interface `org.xml.sax.DocumentHandler`).

This will cause the nodes of the result tree to be streamed to the user-specified document handler.

Extension Functions

xt provides the following extension functions. The namespace URI for these is `http://www.jclark.com/xt`.

`xt:node-set (frag)`	Converts a result tree fragment to the equivalent node-set. The argument must be a node-set or a result tree fragment; the result will be a node-set.
`xt:intersection (ns1, ns2)`	Returns the intersection of two node-sets (the nodes that are present in both the supplied node-sets).
`xt:difference (ns1, ns2)`	Returns the difference of two node-sets (the nodes in the first node-set that are not in the second node-set).

Microsoft Products

Microsoft were one of the earliest vendors to deliver an implementation of XSL, back in 1998 when the first XSL proposals were being made to W3C. Their first implementation was issued as a freestanding component, and this was quickly followed with a second version that was included in Internet Explorer 5.

Unfortunately, the XSLT standard moved on considerably after IE5 was shipped, so in the end Microsoft's early product implemented a language that bore rather little resemblance to the one described in this book. This initial 1998 Microsoft XSL release is described in *XML IE5 Programmer's Reference* by Alex Homer, Wrox Press, ISBN 1-861001-57-6.

However, Microsoft endorsed the W3C Recommendation and made it clear they intended to conform with the final W3C standard when it appeared. And on 26 January 2000, Microsoft shipped a technology preview of version 2 of their XSLT processor, which moved them a long way towards this goal. This was followed quickly by version 3 on 15 March 2000, and Microsoft have warned the world to expect a new version every couple of months until full conformance is achieved. The XSLT processor comes together with a new version of the MSXML parser, and a set of COM interfaces allowing it to be invoked programmatically, including from client-side JScript: the full package is referred to as MSXML3.

The most exciting aspect of Microsoft's technology is that XSLT processing is integrated into the browser. This gives performance benefits (doing XSLT processing on the server can impose a heavy load if site traffic is high) and it also allows the presentation to become much more interactive: for example, it becomes possible to apply XSLT processing in response to user input, without going back to the server, as illustrated in the Kennedy family tree example in Chapter 9.

10

Products

Of course the product can be used on the server as well, always assuming that the server is running under Windows, but in that space there are currently plenty of other products that implement the standard much more fully.

The simplest way to use the Microsoft processor is to put an `<?xml-stylesheet?>` processing instruction in your source XML document. For example:

```
<?xml version="1.0" encoding="utf-8" ?>
<?xml-stylesheet type="text/xsl" href="/styles/doc.xsl"?>
<doc>
. . .
</doc>
```

Note that MSXML3 currently requires the type to be «text/xsl» even though this is not an officially recognized MIME type.

Once you have installed the processor (instructions are given in Appendix A), all you need to do is double-click on the XML document, or type its URL into the browser, and Internet Explorer will display the result of transforming the XML document through its chosen stylesheet.

If life is more complicated, and you want to use different stylesheets to display the same document at different times (depending perhaps on user preferences), then you'll have to do a bit more work and script the stylesheet execution in a web page. Although the technology has moved on a little, the Wrox book *XML IE5 Programmer's Reference* still gives masses of relevant advice on how to do this.

Microsoft's XSLT processor is implemented, as one would expect, in the form of a COM object. This means it can be invoked from any language with COM support, on any Windows platform, client-side or server-side. The product allows XSLT stylesheets to include scripts written in Microsoft scripting languages such as VBScript and JScript, and as usual these can make calls to COM objects in any language.

The March 2000 version of Microsoft's XSLT processor still has some way to go before it implements the full W3C Recommendation. Unlike some vendors, however, they provide fairly detailed information about what's implemented and what isn't (though I've had to supplement this by some trial-and-error investigation of my own). The following table summarizes the situation:

Elements fully implemented	Elements partially implemented	Elements not implemented
`<xsl:apply-templates>`	`<xsl:copy>` omits use-attribute-sets	`<xsl:apply-imports>`
`<xsl:attribute>`		`<xsl:attribute-set>`
`<xsl:call-template>`	`<xsl:element>` omits use-attribute-sets	
`<xsl:choose>`	`<xsl:output>` implements only the method, version, and encoding attributes.	`<xsl:decimal-format>`
`<xsl:comment>`		`<xsl:fallback>`
`<xsl:copy-of>`		`<xsl:import>`
`<xsl:for-each>`		`<xsl:key>`

Elements fully implemented	Elements partially implemented	Elements not implemented
`<xsl:if>`	`<xsl:sort>` omits the `lang` and `case-order` attributes.	`<xsl:namespace-alias>`
`<xsl:include>`		`<xsl:number>`
`<xsl:otherwise>`		`<xsl:preserve-space>`
`<xsl:output>`		`<xsl:strip-space>`
`<xsl:param>`		`<xsl:transform>` (Microsoft say this is not supported, but I tried it and it seems to work)
`<xsl:processing-instruction>`		
`<xsl:stylesheet>`		
`<xsl:template>`		
`<xsl:text>`		
`<xsl:value-of>`		
`<xsl:variable>`		
`<xsl:when>`		
`<xsl:with-param>`		

As far as XPath expressions are concerned, Microsoft claims to implement the full XPath 1.0 specification, with the following exceptions:

❑ Some axes are not implemented: `following`, `preceding`, `following-sibling`, and `preceding-sibling`.

❑ Some functions are not implemented: `document()`, `key()`, and `unparsed-entity-uri()`.

❑ In the format pattern supplied as the second argument of the `format-number()` function, the only characters that may be used are «.», «,», «#», and «0». The third argument, which names a decimal format, cannot be used because the `<xsl:decimal-format>` element is not supported.

Microsoft's parser also allows XPath expressions to be used independently of XSLT stylesheets, as a way of navigating around the DOM.

Extensions

There is no support for extension elements.

Extension functions can be implemented by coding VBScript or JScript modules inside a top-level `<msxsl:script>` element.

10

Products

Here is an example stylesheet that uses such an extension:

Example: Using JScript in an MSXML3 Stylesheet

This example shows a stylesheet that converts dimensions in inches to the equivalent in millimeters.

Source

The source file is `inches.xml`. Enter the full filename into the Address field of IE5 to invoke the stylesheet.

```
<?xml version="1.0" encoding="iso-8859-1"?>
<?xml-stylesheet type="text/xsl" href="to-mm.xsl"?>
<dimensions>
The size of the picture is <inches>5</inches> by
<inches>12</inches>.
</dimensions>
```

Stylesheet

The stylesheet is `to-mm.xsl`

It contains a simple JavaScript function within an `<msxsl:script>` element, and invokes this as an extension function from the template rule for the `<inches>` element.

```
<xsl:stylesheet
        xmlns:xsl="http://www.w3.org/1999/XSL/Transform"
        version="1.0"
        xmlns:ms="urn:anything"
>
<msxsl:script xmlns:msxsl="urn:schemas-microsoft-com:xslt"
              language="VBScript"
              implements-prefix="ms"
>

Function ToMillimetres(inches)
   ToMillimetres = inches * 25.4
End Function

</msxsl:script>

<xsl:output method="html"/>

<xsl:template match="/" >
<html><body><p>
   <xsl:apply-templates/>
</p></body></html>
</xsl:template>
```

```
<xsl:template match="inches">
  .<xsl:text> </xsl:text>
   <xsl:value-of select="ms:ToMillimetres(number(.))"/>
   <xsl:text>mm </xsl:text>
</xsl:template>

</xsl:stylesheet>
```

Output

The following text is displayed in the browser:

```
The size of the picture is 127mm by 304.8mm .
```

These scripts can call COM objects named in the system registry in the usual way. However, if the stylesheet is running in the browser, the user's security settings may prevent your script from instantiating a client-side object.

System Properties

The system-property() function currently returns the following values:

System property name	Value
xsl:version	1
xsl:vendor	Microsoft
xsl:vendor-url	http://www.microsoft.com
msxsl:version	2.6 (but documented as 3.0)

Other Vendors

A number of other vendors have announced XSLT processors, which though I haven't included them in the "big four" earlier in this chapter, are serious contenders if the vendors deliver what they have promised.

Some of the products we include in this category are:

iXSLT from Infoteria

The iXSLT product is available from the Japanese company Infoteria (http://www.infoteria.com).

At the time of writing, this product implemented a rather restricted subset of the XSLT specification. In the press release accompanying the XSLT announcement on 16 November 1999, the company announced they would have a conformant product within 60 days, but as we go to press it has yet to appear.

10

Products

4XSLT from FourThought

This is an open source implementation of XSLT written in the Python language. The vendor is the FourThought company, details on http://opentechnology.org/4Suite/4XSLT/.

Currently, 4XSLT implements an extensive subset of the XSLT recommendation, with a few omissions such as `<xsl:attribute-set>`, `<xsl:decimal-format>`, and `<xsl:fallback>`.

EZ/X From Activated Intelligence

This product is available at http://www.activated.com/products/products.html.

The suppliers made some aggressive performance claims when the product was launched, which were hotly contested by the vendors they made comparisons with, and the claims no longer appear on the product web site.

There is no detailed statement available of which features are implemented, though reports from some users suggest the coverage is rather incomplete.

Stylus from Excelon

For details see http://www.excelon.com/.

The main interest in this product is that it is one of the first products that goes beyond being a simple batch-mode XSLT interpreter to provide something akin to a visual development environment. The tool divides the screen into three panes, containing the input, output, and stylesheet documents respectively; for each of the documents a number of different views are available:

❑ The XML source document can be viewed either as XML or as a tree

❑ HTML output can be viewed either as HTML, or as rendered by Internet Explorer

❑ The stylesheet display allows browsing through the templates according to their match patterns

When a node is selected in the source XML display, the relevant template in the stylesheet is automatically displayed, or it can be created if there is no matching template.

At any stage, pressing Refresh causes the output document to be regenerated, so the effect of any change to the stylesheet can be seen instantly. When a template in the stylesheet is selected, the text in the output document produced by that template is highlighted, making it even easier to see the effects of changes.

Stylus includes an XSLT processor which has recently been re-released at version 2.1.

Early versions caused a certain amount of frustration, because although users liked the visual interface, the supplier failed to provide any information about the restrictions in the XSLT facilities available. The latest version corrects this deficiency, and claims to implement everything except the following:

❑ Namespaces.

❑ `<xsl:apply-imports>`.

❑ `<xsl:decimal-format>`.

❑ `<xsl:namespace-alias>`.

❑ `<xsl:number>` localization features.

❑ `<xsl:output>` attributes except for `method` and `indent`. All other attributes are not supported.

❑ `<xsl:preserve-space>` and `<xsl:strip-space>`. I quote: *Stylus preserves all white space from the source document. All text nodes that contain only white space are stripped.*

❑ Simplified stylesheet syntax.

❑ `<xsl:sort>` attributes lang and case-order.

❑ `unparsed-entity-uri()` function.

❑ Second argument to the `document()` function.

❑ Extension element mechanism.

An evaluation copy of the software can be downloaded for free, but the full product has to be purchased.

Summary

In this chapter I described four products which I consider to be the current leaders in terms of their coverage of the standard, the quality of the implementation, and market share, if that term is meaningful in a world where they are all available for free. These are Oracle's XSL, my own Saxon product, Xalan from Apache, and James Clark's xt. As it happens, they are all written in Java, though Oracle and Xalan now also have C++ versions available.

Then I described the Microsoft technology. Although this is currently behind the others in terms of XSLT support, I expect this situation to change quite rapidly, and Microsoft's unique position in the browser and desktop market means they have the capability to integrate the technology far more effectively into the rest of the client environment, so their processor will undoubtedly become a major player in the market.

10

Products

667

Finally, I described some other contenders to keep an eye on. At the beginning of the chapter I listed some useful web sites where you can track developments.

All these products are very new and there is plenty of time for new players to emerge, for existing leaders to become displaced, and generally for things to change in the way it always does on the Web. So treat anything in this chapter as a snapshot of the state of play in the Spring of 2000: and if you're reading this more than a year after that, it might be wise to treat it as history.

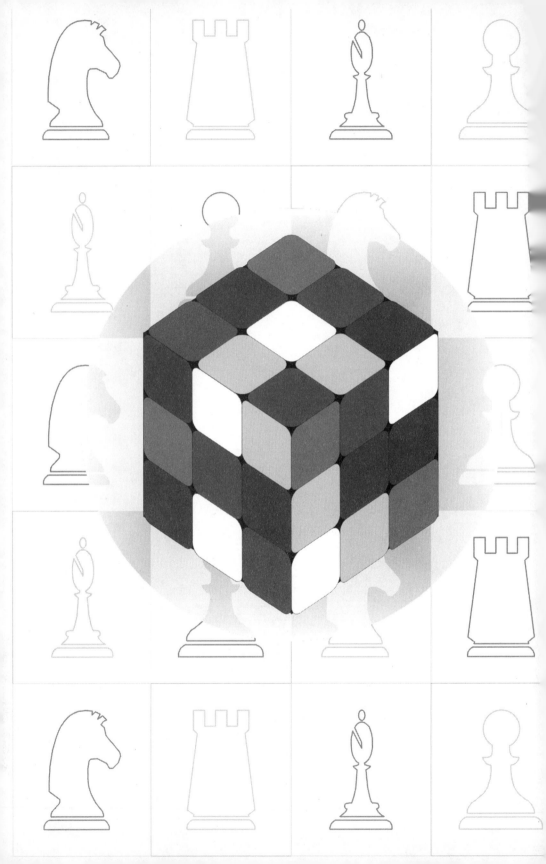

Microsoft MSXML3

This appendix contains information about using Microsoft's MSXML3 technology, which implements a subset of the W3C XSLT recommendation.

MSXML3 is the latest version of Microsoft's XML and XSL technology. It contains an XML parser supporting a DOM interface that is an extended version of the W3C DOM Recommendation, an XSLT processor which currently implements a subset of the W3C XSLT 1.0 Recommendation, an XPath processor which can be used either in conjunction with XSLT stylesheets or directly against the DOM document, and a schema processor which implements Microsoft's own version of XML schemas (which is likely to be significantly different from W3C's definition of an XML schema when that finally appears).

> **Microsoft produced new technology previews of the MSXML product in January 2000 and again in March 2000, and they've promised a steady stream of new releases to follow these, so any information here is a snapshot of the current position: you need to check anything I say here with the latest Microsoft documentation.**

This appendix is **not** designed to cover the original 1998 versions of MSXML, which shipped with IE4 and later with IE5. These implemented a version of XSL based on the draft specifications as they existed at the time, with many Microsoft extensions. This 1998 dialect of XSLT is recognizably similar to XSLT 1.0 as described in this book, but there are so many differences of detail that it is best regarded as a separate language. I shall refer to it as **IE5 1998 XSL**.

A word of warning, though: unless specified otherwise, the documentation on Microsoft's web site refers to their released products, not to the XSLT technology preview. This can be very confusing. For example there are documents on the web site that refer to the "December working draft of the W3C XSL standard" when they mean the December 1998 draft, a very early one. Even some of the documentation included with the technology preview refers to the earlier product rather than the recent ones: you're wandering around a building site here, so wear your hard hat. One useful thing to remember, though, is that when Microsoft refer to "XSL" they usually mean their own 1998 dialect, and when they refer to "XSLT" they mean the W3C XSLT 1.0 Recommendation.

I described the extent to which the latest version of MSXML conforms to XSLT 1.0 and XPath 1.0 in Chapter 10. This Appendix concentrates not on the language level, but on the interfaces for using the MSXML product and integrating it into your applications. With luck, as Microsoft extend the product to give complete coverage of the XSLT language standard, they will not need to make too many changes to the APIs described in this Appendix.

MSXML Versions

At the time of writing, Microsoft has released several versions of the MSXML product. The original beta version 1.0 was quickly superseded by version 2.0, which is supplied with the final release of Internet Explorer 5 and Windows 2000. There is also a full SDK for it, supplied as part of the Internet Explorer and Windows 2000 SDKs. MSXML as a software package includes both an XML parser and an XSLT processor, and although our interest in this book is in the XSLT processor, the product is frequently referred to simply as "the MSXML parser". The version 2.0 product, as we've seen, implemented something close to the December 1998 XSL working draft from the W3C, together with some Microsoft extensions designed to simplify common operations and handle non-W3C-specified activities like loading and saving XML documents.

To confuse the issue, the January 2000 technology preview version of the product – called MSXML2 – is actually version 2.6. The main feature added in version 3, MSXML3, released in March 2000, was support for named templates and the `<xsl:call-template>` instruction. Bear in mind, however, that both the version 2.6 and version 3 products are only technology previews at the time of writing, and Microsoft does not recommend their use in production applications. With good reason: not only are there quite a few bugs around in the code, but the documentation is still very patchy.

MSXML3 continues to support IE5 1998 XSL syntax as well as XSLT syntax. However, you must use one or the other, you can't mix them. They are distinguished by the namespace URI of the `<xsl:stylesheet>` element:

- ❑ IE5 1998 XSL stylesheets use the namespace URI `http://www.w3.org/TR/WD-xsl`
- ❑ XSLT stylesheets use the namespace URI `http://www.w3.org/1999/XSL/Transform`

Installing the MSXML Product

The current release of the MSXML product is available from the XML download page at Microsoft's Web site. To download it, go to :

http://msdn.microsoft.com/downloads/webtechnology/xml/msxml.asp.

After the file `msxmlwr.exe` has been downloaded to your machine, simply double-click on it to install the software.

You will probably want to install the SDK (software development kit) as well, if only to get the documentation: this is available from the same web page. It comes in the form of an executable `msxmlsdk.exe`, which again you can install simply by downloading it to your machine and then double-clicking on it. The documentation is in the form of a compiled Windows Help file `xmlsdk.chm` which the default installation places in `c:\Program Files\msxml` – open it by double-clicking on it in Explorer.

Also on the web site is a page full of useful information about Microsoft's XML initiative and strategy at http://msdn.microsoft.com/xml/default.asp. This includes samples, demos, and articles about XML and related technologies.

The download page also provides links to several tools that you may find useful:

- ❑ Tools for Validating XML and Viewing XSLT Output. These provide a 'shell' where you can view XML files and see the processed XSL output. The shell also validates XML against any embedded schema.

- ❑ Microsoft XSL ISAPI Extension. This Web server-based extension makes it easier to perform server-side XML/XSL transformations. It can automatically execute an XSL style sheet on the server, allowing you to choose alternate style sheets based on browser type. It manages style-sheet caching for improved server performance, has the capability to specify the output encoding, and provides customizable error messages.

- ❑ XSL Stylesheet for XML Schemas. This stylesheet (which uses IE5 1998 XSL) can be used to generate documentation for XML schemas based on the syntax. I haven't discussed XML schemas much in this book. The XSLT specification doesn't use them yet, because the standard isn't finished. But Microsoft implemented their own version of XML schemas, and MSXML takes advantage of these as an alternative to using DTDs.

- ❑ XSL to XSLT Converter. This stylesheet updates IE5 1998 XSL stylesheets to the XSLT-compliant syntax, making them suitable for use with the MSXML2 and MSXML3 products and others. It doesn't do a 100% job of the conversion, but it looks after all of the most common differences.

> **Note that you must install Internet Explorer (version 4.01 with service pack 1, or IE5) in order for MSXML to be fully functional. This is true even if you only want to use MSXML on a server.**

A

MSXML Processor

673

MSXML ProgID and ClassID Information

Rather than use the same file name, ProgID and ClassID for the three versions, Microsoft has given each one different values so that they can be installed and run in parallel:

Parser Version	DLL Name	ProgID and ClassID

MSXML 2.0	`msxml.dll`	`ProgID:`
		`Microsoft.XMLDOM` or
		`MSXML.DOMDocument`
		
		`ClassID:`
		`{2933bf90-7b36-11d2-b20e-`
		`00c04f983e60}`

MSXML 2.6	`msxml2.dll`	`ProgID:`
		`MSXML2.DOMDocument`
		
		`ClassID:`
		`{f6d90f11-9c73-11d3-b32e-`
		`00c04f990bb4}`

MSXML 3.0	`msxml3.dll`	`ProgID:`
		`MSXML2.DOMDocument.3.0`
		
		`ClassID:`
		`{f5078f32-c551-11d3-89b9-`
		`0000f81fe221}`

The terminology here may be confusing. These objects use the name "`DOMDocument`" because when you create an instance, it will hold an in-memory representation of an XML document, conforming to Microsoft's version of the W3C Document Object Model (DOM). The `Document` object has a method `load` which allows this in-memory document to be built from a source XML file. To do this, of course, the XML has to be parsed. There is no separate `Parser` object, rather the XML parser is part of the functionality of the `Document` object. Microsoft has followed the policy of naming objects according to what they are (nouns), not according to what they do (verbs).

The above table shows the `ProgID` and `ClassID` for running the parser in normal apartment-threaded mode. You can also run the parser in free-threaded mode by using an alternative `ProgID` or `ClassID` when you instantiate the component (note that the `ClassID`s vary only on the eighth character):

Parser Version	Free-threaded ProgID and ClassID
MSXML 2.0	ProgID: Microsoft.FreeThreadedXMLDOM or MSXML.FreeThreadedDOMDocument ClassID: {2933bf91-7b36-11d2-b20e-00c04f983e60}
MSXML 2.6	ProgID: MSXML2.FreeThreadedDOMDocument ClassID: {f6d90f12-9c73-11d3-b32e-00c04f990bb4}
MSXML 3.0	ProgID: MSXML2.FreeThreadedDOMDocument.3.0 ClassID: {f5078f33-c551-11d3-89b9-0000f81fe221}

See the topic "*GUID and ProgID Information*" in the MSXML3 SDK help file (you can reach it via *XML Developer's Guide*, then *XML DOM User Guide*) for a full list of the ProgIDs and ClassIDs for the other objects that are implemented by the product – such as the XMLHTTP object, the XSLTemplate object, and the XMLDSO data-binding control.

Running MSXML in Replace Mode

When the version 3 MSXML parser in installed, it also installs a program named xmlinst.exe in your Windows\System or Winnt\System32 folder. This program can be used to change the settings in the system registry to specify how the parser versions are used. Running this program with no parameters (just double-click on it) changes the Registry entries on that machine so that the default ProgID «MSXML.DOMDocument» will actually instantiate the latest version of the parser, rather than the version 2.0 parser. This can be useful if your applications have this original ProgID string hard-coded in. See the topic *Running MSXML3 in Replace Mode* in the help file (you can reach it via *XML Developer's Guide*, then *XML DOM User Guide*) for a list of the command-line arguments that can be used with xmlinst.exe to make other changes to the Registry settings.

A

MSXML Processor

Viewing XML Documents in IE5 with the Default Stylesheet

Internet Explorer 5 can display an XML document directly, as a collapsible tree structure. This makes it easy to examine the document and see the element structure:

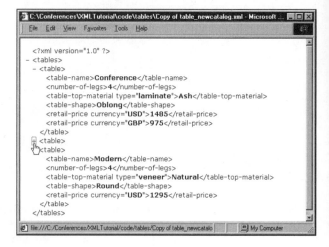

It does this by applying a default stylesheet to the document when it is loaded, and what you see is the result of the transformation specified by this stylesheet. This stylesheet is only used if you don't specify any other. In the next section, I'll show how to specify your own XSLT stylesheet to be used for the transformation.

If you load a document that is not well-formed, or which is invalid against a specified DTD or Schema, an error message is displayed instead:

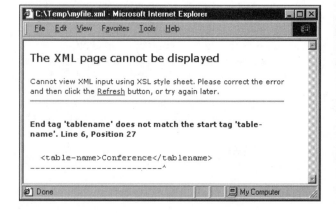

If you want to see the contents of the default stylesheet, type the URL `res://msxml.dll/DEFAULTSS.XSL` into your browser's address bar (the same stylesheet is produced by the URL `res://msxml3.dll/DEFAULTSS.XSL` from the MSXML3 parser).

This default stylesheet is currently written in the IE5 1998 XSL dialect: you can spot this because it uses the old namespace URI «`http://www.w3.org/TR/WD-xsl`», and because it uses obsolete XSL elements such as `<xsl:entity-ref>` and `<xsl:node-name>`.

Viewing XML Documents in IE5 with an XSLT Stylesheet

The easiest way to display the result of an XSL transformation is to attach the specific stylesheet to the XML document using an XML processing instruction. The simplest syntax is:

```
<?xml-stylesheet type="text/xsl" href="url_of_stylesheet"?>
```

For example, if you have a suitable stylesheet named `tablecatalog.xsl` in the same folder as the XML document, you can write:

```
<?xml-stylesheet type="text/xsl" href="tablecatalog.xsl"?>
```

This should be written after the `<?xml version="1.0"?>` XML declaration and any `<!DOCTYPE>` declaration, but before the start tag of the document element. For example:

```
<?xml version="1.0" ?>
<!DOCTYPE tables SYSTEM "tables.dtd">
<?xml-stylesheet type="text/xsl" href="tablecatalog.xsl"?>
<tables>
. . .
</tables>
```

The result could look like this:

MSXML allows only one `<?xml-stylesheet?>` processing instruction in an XML document that specifies an XSL stylesheet (i.e. has «type="text/xsl"»). However, it is possible to display XML documents using Cascading Stylesheets (CSS), and there can be any number of `<?xml-stylesheet?>` processing instructions in an XML document that specify CSS stylesheets (i.e. have «type="text/css"»). Internet Explorer will choose the XSL stylesheet if it is present, otherwise it will will merge the CSS stylesheets together in the same way as it would with multiple HTML `<LINK>` elements that specify CSS stylesheets.

The full list of attributes that can be used in the `<?xml-stylesheet?>` processing instruction is as follows (technically these are *pseudo-attributes* since XML processing instructions contain unstructured text):

Attribute name	Description
alternate	Optional. Values «yes» or «no» (default is «no»). Indicates whether this stylesheet is designed to provide an alternative appearance for the page.
charset	Optional. Specifies the character set or character encoding used in the stylesheet. Examples are «Latin-1» (the same as «ISO-8859-1» and the default if omitted), «ISO-8859-5» (Cyrillic), «EUC-JP» (Japanese) and «UTF-8» (Unicode encoded using a variable number of bytes per character). A full list of the character encodings can be obtained from ftp://ftp.isi.edu/in-notes/iana/assignments/character-sets.
href	Required. The URL or relative path to the stylesheet.
media	Optional. Specifies the intended destination medium for the style information, and may be a single media descriptor or a comma-separated list. The default value is «screen».
title	Optional. Can be used by the application as a name for the stylesheet, or to tell users about the nature of the stylesheet.
type	Required. Specifies the type of the stylesheet, either «text/xsl» (XSL) or «text/css» (CSS). (Technically the value «text/xsl» is not a valid MIME type, but that's what Microsoft decided to use.)

Further information about the `<?xsl-stylesheet?>` processing instruction is in Chapter 3, page 98.

Controlling XSLT Processing with Client-side Script

Using the `<?xml-stylesheet?>` processing instruction is just one of the ways that an XSL stylesheet can be applied to an XML document. An alternative approach is to write script code in an HTML page which explicitly loads the XML document and the stylesheets, and invokes the transformation. This is where the ProgID and ClassID strings for the objects that I showed earlier come into play.

Creating an Instance of an MSXML Document

To create an instance of a DOM Document that will use the version 3.0 MSXML parser, you can use several approaches.

In VBScript:

```
Dim doc
Set doc = CreateObject("MSXML2.DOMDocument.3.0")
```

In JScript:

```
var doc = new ActiveXObject('MSXML2.DOMDocument.3.0');
```

In Visual Basic, you will first need to add a reference to the component DLL using the **Project I References** dialog. You can see the three versions of the parser listed in the screenshot here:

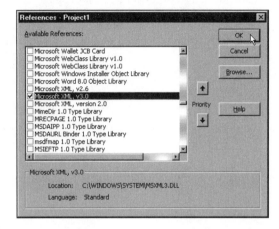

Then you can use the `CreateObject` method:

```
Dim doc
Set doc = CreateObject("MSXML2.DOMDocument.3.0")
```

However, the more usual technique is to use the `New` keyword, which then allows the development environment to display pop-up syntax help and member-lists:

```
Dim doc As New DOMDocument30
```

Loading XML and XSL Documents

Once you've created an instance of a `Document` object, you can use the Microsoft-specific methods to load the content. To load an XML file, use the `load` method:

```
'in VBScript or Visual Basic
doc.Load "c:\temp\myfile.xml"
```

```
//in JScript
doc.load('c:\temp\myfile.xml');
```

If the XML is held in a string rather than in a file (which can arise, for example, because you have read the XML out of a relational database using SQL or ADO) you can use the `loadXML` method:

```
'in VBScript or Visual Basic:
Dim strXML
strXML = "<?xml version='1.0'?><test><testitem/></test>"
doc.LoadXML strXML
```

```
//in JScript
var strXML = '<?xml version="1.0"?><test><testitem/></test>';
doc.loadXML(strXML);
```

You can then set any other properties you need for the MSXML parser. For example, you can set the `async` property to `True` so that parsing of the document is done in the background while processing continues. However, when working with script code that manipulates the documents, it's usually best to leave this at the default value of `False`.

You can also turn on validation in the parser. By default, the parser only checks that the XML is well-formed as it loads and parses documents. By setting the `validateOnParse` property to `True`, you can force the parser to validate the structure of the document against any DTD or Schema that it specifies:

```
'in VBScript or Visual Basic
doc.ValidateOnParse = True
```

```
//in JScript
doc.validateOnParse = true;
```

Checking for Load Errors, Well-Formedness and Validity

After the parser has attempted to load a document, you can check if there was an error by examining the properties of the `parseError` object that the `Document` object exposes. The `parseError` object provides seven properties that reflect the most recent load error:

Property	Description
errorCode	The standard error number of the error that occurred.
filepos	The character position within the entire file where the error was discovered.
line	The number of the line where the error was discovered.
linepos	The character position within this line where the error was discovered.
reason	A text description of the error.
srcText	The source code (text) of the line where the error was discovered.
url	The URL or path of the file that was loaded.

By checking the `errorCode` property, you can tell if an error occurred. The value will be non-zero if the parser has detected an error. The following code samples show how the error details can be retrieved and displayed:

In VBScript or Visual Basic:

```
'check if there was an error while loading
If doc.parseError.errorCode <> 0 Then
  'create the error message
  Dim strError
  strError = "Invalid XML file !" & vbCrlf _
          & "File URL: " & doc.parseError.url & vbCrlf _
          & "Line No.: " & doc.parseError.line & vbCrlf _
          & "Character: " & doc.parseError.linepos & vbCrlf _
          & "File Position: " & doc.parseError.filepos & vbCrlf _
          & "Source Text: " & doc.parseError.srcText & vbCrlf _
          & "Error Code: " & doc.parseError.errorCode & vbCrlf _
          & "Description: " & doc.parseError.reason
  MsgBox strError  'display error message
Else
  'loaded OK so continue processing
  ...
End If
```

In JScript:

```
...
// check if there was an error while loading
if (doc.parseError.errorCode != 0) {
  // create the error message
  var strError = new String;
  strError = 'Invalid XML file !\n'
          + 'File URL: ' + doc.parseError.url + '\n '
          + 'Line No.: ' + doc.parseError.line + '\n '
          + 'Character: ' + doc.parseError.linepos + '\n '
          + 'File Position: ' + doc.parseError.filepos + '\n '
          + 'Source Text: ' + doc.parseError.srcText + '\n '
          + 'Error Code: ' + doc.parseError.errorCode + '\n '
          + 'Description: ' + doc.parseError.reason;
  alert(strError);  // display error message
  }
else {
  // loaded OK so continue processing
  ...
  }
}
```

Both produce a similar result, here showing the effect when a document that is not well-formed is loaded:

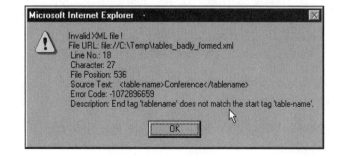

A

MSXML Processor

If you have set the `validateOnParse` property to `True`, and load an XML document that is invalid against its DTD or Schema, the error message shows the details of where the file is invalid. This screenshot shows the VBScript `MsgBox` `dialog` version:

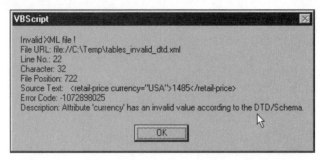

However, not all the properties will always have a value. For example, if you attempt to load an XML document that doesn't exist, you can't expect to get values for the error position or the source text:

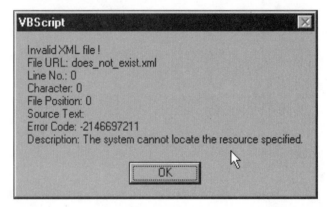

Transforming XML Documents with XSL Using Script

You can load any well-formed XML document using the MSXML parser. This includes XSLT stylesheets and XML schemas, both of which are documents in XML format. If you create two instances of the `Document` object, and load an XML source document into one and an XSL stylesheet into the other, you can then perform a transformation by calling either of the methods `transformNode()` or `transformNodeToObject()`, described below.

This provides an alternative technique to specifying the stylesheet for an XML document by using the `<?xml-stylesheet?>` processing instruction, and has the advantage that different stylesheets can be used to process the same source document at different times.

The transformNode Method

This method is probably the most useful, as it returns a string value containing the result of the transformation.

```
strResult = objXMLNode.transformNode(objStylesheet)
```

The `objXMLNode` parameter will usually be a DOM `Document` object, but it can be a node within a DOM Document, in which case this Node and its descendants are treated as a single standalone XML document.

The `objStylesheet` parameter must also be a DOM object, either a `Document` instance containing a valid XSL stylesheet or a Node within a document that represents an embedded XSL stylesheet (embedded stylesheets were described in Chapter 3, page **99**).

The return value is a string that represents the result of the transformation. Usually it will contain a chunk of HTML which you can then insert into the HTML page to display it. Typically your HTML page will contain a body like this:

```
<body>
<div id="divResults"></div>
</body>
```

and your script will place the transformation results in this place:

```
var objResults = document.all['divResults'];
objResults.innerHTML = objXML.transformNode(objXSL);
```

An example that does this is shown with the Kennedy family tree stylesheet in Chapter 9, page 590; another example can be found on the web site for this book in the file `msxml_transform\default.htm`.

The transformNodeToObject Method

This method is useful when you want to send the result to another object, such as another DOM Document or a `Stream` object:

```
objXMLNode.transformNodeToObject(objStylesheet, objOutput)
```

The `objXMLNode` parameter must be a DOM object, either a `Document` object itself or a Node within an XML document (in which case this node and its descendants are treated as a single standalone XML document).

The `objStylesheet` parameter must also be a DOM object, either a `Document` object containing a valid XSL stylesheet or a Node within a Document representing an embedded XSL stylesheet.

The `objOutput` object will usually be another DOM Document, which will then hold the result of the transformation. For this to work, the transformation must produce a well-formed XML-format document. You can of course use this Document as the input to another transformation.

Example: Using Client-side JScript to Transform a Document

This example demonstrates the way that you can load, parse and transform an XML document using client-side JScript in Internet Explorer 5 or higher. The files are in a folder named `msxml_transform`.

The example shows an HTML page with two buttons on it. The user can click on either of the buttons to select how the data should be displayed. The effect of clicking either button is to apply the corresponding stylesheet to the source XML document.

XML Source

The XML source file for this example is `tables_data.xml`. It defines several tables (real tables, the kind you sit at to eat your dinner), each looking like this:

```
<tables>
<table>
   <table-name>Conference</table-name>
   <number-of-legs>4</number-of-legs>
   <table-top-material type="laminate">Ash</table-top-material>
   <table-shape>Oblong</table-shape>
   <retail-price currency="USD">1485</retail-price>
</table>
...
</tables>
```

Stylesheet

There are two stylesheets, `tables_list.xsl` and `tables_catalog.xsl`. Since this example is designed to show the JScript used to control the transformation rather than the XSLT transformation code itself, I won't list them here.

HTML page

The page `default.htm` contains some simple styling information for the HTML page, then the JScript code that loads the XML and XSL documents, checks for errors, and performs the transformation. Notice that the `transformFiles` function takes the name of a stylesheet as a parameter, which allows you to specify the stylesheet you want to use at runtime:

```
<html>
<head>
<style type="text/css">
       body {font-family:Tahoma,Verdana,Arial,sans-serif; font-size:14px}
       .head {font-family:Tahoma,Verdana,Arial,sans-serif;
                             font-size:18px; font-weight:bold}
</style>

<script language="JScript">
```

```
function transformFiles(strStylesheetName) {

  // get a reference to the results DIV element
  var objResults = document.all['divResults'];

  // create two new document instances
  var objXML = new ActiveXObject('MSXML2.DOMDocument.3.0');
  var objXSL = new ActiveXObject('MSXML2.DOMDocument.3.0');

  // set the parser properties
  objXML.validateOnParse = true;
  objXSL.validateOnParse = true;

  // load the XML document and check for errors
  objXML.load('tables_data.xml');
  if (objXML.parseError.errorCode != 0) {
    // error found so show error message and stop
    objResults.innerHTML = showError(objXML)
    return false;
  }

  // load the XSL stylesheet and check for errors
  objXSL.load(strStylesheetName);
  if (objXSL.parseError.errorCode != 0) {
    // error found so show error message and stop
    objResults.innerHTML = showError(objXSL)
    return false;
  }

  // all must be OK, so perform transformation
  strResult = objXML.transformNode(objXSL);

  // and display the results in the DIV element
  objResults.innerHTML = strResult;
  return true;
}
```

Providing that there are no errors, the function performs the transformation
using the XML file tables_data.xml and the stylesheet whose name is specified
as the strStylesheetName parameter when the function is called. The result of
the transformation is inserted into the <div> element that has the id attribute
value «divResults». You'll see where this is defined in the HTML later on.

If either of the load calls fail, perhaps due to a badly-formed document, a
function named showError is called. This function takes a reference to the
document where the error was found, and returns a string describing the nature
of the error. This error message is then displayed in the page instead of the result
of the transformation:

A

```
function showError(objDocument) {
    // create the error message
    var strError = new String;
    strError = 'Invalid XML file !<BR />'
            + 'File URL: ' + objDocument.parseError.url + '<BR />'
            + 'Line No.: ' + objDocument.parseError.line + '<BR />'
            + 'Character: ' + objDocument.parseError.linepos + '<BR />'
            + 'File Position: ' + objDocument.parseError.filepos + '<BR />'
            + 'Source Text: ' + objDocument.parseError.srcText + '<BR />'
            + 'Error Code: ' + objDocument.parseError.errorCode + '<BR />'
            + 'Description: ' + objDocument.parseError.reason
    return strError;
}


//-->
</script>
```

The remainder of the page is the HTML that creates the visible section. The opening `<body>` element specifies an `onload` attribute that causes the `transformFiles()` function in our script section to run once the page has finished loading:

```
...
</head>
<body onload="transformFiles('tables_list.xsl')">
<p><span class="head">Transforming an XML Document using
        the client-side code</span></p>
...
```

Because it uses the value «tables_list.xsl» for the parameter to the function, this stylesheet is used for the initial display. This shows the data in tabular form.

The next thing in the page is the code that creates the two HTML `<button>` elements, marked **Catalog** and **Simple List**. The `onclick` attributes of each one simply execute the `transformFiles()` function again, each time specifying the appropriate stylesheet name:

```
...
View the tables as a  
<button onclick="transformFiles('tables_catalog.xsl')">Catalog</button>
  or as a  
<button onclick="transformFiles('tables_list.xsl')">Simple List</button>
<hr />
```

Finally, at the end of the code, you can see the definition of the `<div>` element into which the function inserts the results of the transformation.

```
<!-- to insert the results of parsing the object model -->
<div id="divResults"></div>

</body>
</html>
```

Output

When the page is first displayed, it looks like this:

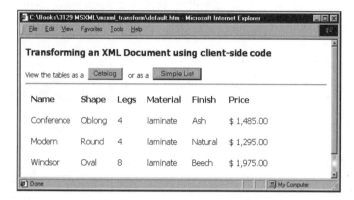

Click on the **Catalog** button, and you will see an alternative graphical presentation of the same data, achieved by applying the other stylesheet.

Using the XSLTemplate Object

In the example above, I created one `Document` object for the source XML file, and another for the stylesheet, and used the `transformNode` method on the source Document to apply the stylesheet and create the resulting HTML.

If you need to use the same stylesheet repeatedly this can be inefficient, because all the work of analysing and validating the stylesheet has to be repeated each time it is used. You can avoid this overhead by compiling the stylesheet into another object, which is rather confusingly called an **XSLTemplate**. The `XSLTemplate` object can then be used repeatedly to do many transformations. I showed an example of this with the Kennedy family tree in Chapter 9, page 590, where each transformation was applied to the same source document, but using different parameter settings to control which part of the XML data would be displayed.

To compile a stylesheet, you create the `XSLTemplate` object and set its `stylesheet` property to the DOM Node (typically the Document itself) containing the `<xsl:stylesheet>` element:

```
objStyle = new ActiveXObject("MSXML2.FreeThreadedDOMDocument");
objStyle.async = false;
objStyle.load('stylesheet.xsl');

objTransformer = new ActiveXObject("MSXML2.XSLTemplate");
objTransformer.stylesheet = objStyle.documentElement;
```

A

The `XSLTemplate` object can be used as often as you like to perform transformations. To perform a transformation, you first need to create an `XSLProcessor` object, which you can regard as holding the information to control one particular transformation. You'll normally create a new one of these each time you want to apply the stylesheet to another source document. You don't need to create the `XSLProcessor` object yourself, the `XSLTemplate` object will do it for you:

```
var objProcessor = objTransformer.createProcessor();
```

You can then perform a transformation by telling the `XSLProcessor` what source document to use, supplying any parameters (these set the values of global `<xsl:param>` elements in the stylesheet), and invoking the `transform()` method. The result of the transformation can then be retrieved from the `XSLProcessor`'s output property:

```
objProcessor.input = source;
objProcessor.addParameter("name1", "value1", "");
objProcessor.addParameter("name2", "value2", "");
objProcessor.transform();
objResults.innerHTML = objProcessor.output;
```

The third argument to `addParameter()` is the namespace URI of the parameter's name, which will usually be an empty string.

Using <object>s and XML Data Islands

Instead of creating an instance of the MSXML `Document` object using script, you can use an `<object>` element in the HTML page. You can also create a data island within an HTML page using the `<xml>` element. Both `<object>` and `<xml>` are HTML elements, not XML.

Creating Document Instances with an <object> Element

You can create instances of the MSXML `Document` object using an HTML `<object>` element, specifying the appropriate `ClassID`, depending on which version of the parser you want to use. In the following code, I'm creating documents that use the version 3.0 MSXML parser, and setting the `async` and `validateOnParse` properties to false:

```
<object id="XMLDocument" width="0" height="0"
  classid="clsid:f5078f32-c551-11d3-89b9-0000f81fe221">
  <param name="async" value="false">
  <param name="validateOnParse" value="false">
</object>

<object id="XSLDocument" width="0" height="0"
  classid="clsid:f5078f32-c551-11d3-89b9-0000f81fe221">
  <param name="async" value="false">
  <param name="validateOnParse" value="false">
</object>
```

The only change required to the code that I used earlier is to get a reference to the two Document objects, rather than creating them directly with script code:

```
// get a reference to the XML document parser
var objXML = document.all['XMLDocument'];

// get a reference to the XSL stylesheet parser
var objXSL = document.all['XSLDocument'];

// load the XML document and check for errors
objXML.load('tables_data.xml');
if (objXML.parseError.errorCode != 0) {
   // error found so show error message and stop
   objResults.innerHTML = showError(objXML)
   return false;
}

// load the XSL stylesheet and check for errors
objXSL.load(strStylesheetName);
if (objXSL.parseError.errorCode != 0) {
   // error found so show error message and stop
   objResults.innerHTML = showError(objXSL)
   return false;
}

// all must be OK, so perform transformation
strResult = objXML.transformNode(objXSL);
```

Using XML Data Islands

Internet Explorer 5 introduces a new HTML element named <xml>, which automatically creates an XML document within an HTML page, as a data island. These documents will use the default version of the MSXML parser. Note that the <xml> element is part of the HTML syntax – it is not an XML element. The following HTML creates two data islands, one containing the source XML document and one containing the XSL stylesheet:

```
<xml id="Source" src="tables_data.xml"></xml>
<xml id="Stylesheet" src="tables_list.xsl"></xml>
```

You can then perform a transformation using similar script code to that shown earlier:

```
function transformFiles() {

   // get a reference to the results DIV element
   var objResults = document.all['divResults'];

   // get a reference to the XML document
   var objXML = document.all['Source'].XMLDocument;

   // get a reference to the XSL stylesheet
   var objXSL = document.all['Stylesheet'].XMLDocument;
```

A

MSXML Processor

689

```
    // perform transformation
    strResult = objXML.transformNode(objXSL);

    // and display the results in the DIV element
    objResults.innerHTML = strResult;
}
```

However, notice that you have to specify that you want the XMLDocument property of the data islands. Unlike the Document objects created directly with script code or an <object> element, the data-island created by the <xml> element is itself just a wrapper for the XML Document. It is an HTML object, and so the XML it contains must be accessed through the XMLDocument property of the <xml> element object.

Using an <xml> data island is simpler than creating Document objects in other ways, but is less flexible as you usually specify the source document in the <xml> element through the src attribute. However, you can set the src attribute value dynamically instead if you wish:

```
    // get a reference to the XSL stylesheet parser
    var objDI = document.all['XSLParser'];
    objDI.src = 'tables_list.xsl';
    var objXSL = objDI.XMLDocument;
```

This gives the same flexibility as using any of the methods described previously.

Finally, as if you weren't spoilt for choice already, you can also create an identical XML data island using the <script> element rather than the <xml> element:

```
    <script language="XML" src="tables_data.xml"></script>
```

Modifying XML Documents Dynamically

As well as providing the ability to transform XML documents using XSLT, the MSXML parser also implements full support for the W3C Document Object Model (DOM), with many Microsoft extensions. This includes a whole range of properties and methods that can be used to access and manipulate an XML document when it is loaded into memory.

For example, you can load an XML document, modify particular values, and then apply a stylesheet to perform a transformation. Or you may wish to use the DOM methods to extract certain sections of an XML document into another document and then apply a transformation to that new document. You might even consider loading an XML document and an XSL stylesheet, then modifying values in both to meet some specific criteria before performing the transformation to obtain the result.

An alternative approach might be to simply create an empty Document instance for either the XML document or the XSL stylesheet, and then populate it directly using the DOM methods. This is obviously more long-winded than just loading a previously created XML file or document string. But it may prove a useful technique in some cases – especially for small documents where the actual transformation operations required vary widely, and are easier built from scratch than as a series of different XSL files on disk.

Modifying an XSLT Stylesheet Dynamically

In many cases you can vary the behavior of an XSLT stylesheet by supplying parameters, in the way I described earlier. There are some things in a stylesheet, however, that have to be hard-coded, and one example is the expression used in the `<xsl:sort>` element to define the sort order. If you're feeling adventurous, however, you can get round this limitation by modifying the stylesheet in memory after it's been loaded.

One way to do this modification, of course, is by applying a stylesheet! But if you just want to make a small change, it's probably more efficient to use the DOM interfaces directly, and make the change *in situ*.

To give you an idea of what's possible, the next example loads an XML document and an XSLT stylesheet and displays the transformation in the HTML page. However, it also provides a set of buttons that can be used to sort the results into different orders.

Example: Varying the Sort Order

The files for this example can be found in the folder `msxml_dynamic`.

XML Source

The XML source file for this example is `tables.data.xml`. It defines several `<table>` elements representing pieces of furniture, each looking like this:

```
<tables>
<table>
  <table-name>Conference</table-name>
  <number-of-legs>4</number-of-legs>
  <table-top-material type="laminate">Ash</table-top-material>
  <table-shape>Oblong</table-shape>
  <retail-price currency="USD">1485</retail-price>
</table>
...
</tables>
```

Stylesheet

The stylesheet is `tables_list.xsl` You can find it in the folder mentioned above; since this example is designed to show the JScript used to control the transformation rather than the XSLT transformation code itself, I won't list it in full here.

The important part of the stylesheet for this example is the `<xsl:apply-templates>` instruction that controls sorting, which looks like this:

A

MSXML Processor

```
<xsl:template match="/">
   <html>
      . . .
      <xsl:apply-templates select="/tables/table">
         <xsl:sort select="table-name" order="ascending"/>
      </xsl:apply-templates>
      . . .
   </html>
</xsl:template>
```

The script in the HTML page will modify the attributes of the <xsl:sort> element to vary the field on which the data is sorted, and the direction of sorting.

HTML page

The HTML code to create the visible part of the page is shown below. It's in file default.htm.

The <body> element's onload attribute has the value «if (preparePage()) sort('table-name', 'ascending')». This executes a function named preparePage() as soon as the HTML page has loaded. If the result of this function is true (that is, the process succeeds), it then calls the sort() function to display the data sorted in ascending order of the «table-name» field.

```
. . .
<body onload="if (preparePage()) sort('table-name', 'ascending')">
<p><span class="head">Modifying an XSLT Stylesheet
                                 using client-side code</span></p>
```

The HTML code then displays a set of buttons allowing the user to change the sort order. Notice that each of the <button> elements executes the sort function when clicked, but with different values for the parameters. These values will be used to modify the select and order attributes of the <xsl:sort> element in the stylesheet.

```
Sort by:  
<button onclick="sort('table-name', 'ascending')">Name</button>
<button onclick="sort('table-shape', 'ascending')">Shape</button>
<button onclick="sort('number-of-legs', 'ascending')">Nr of Legs</button>
<button onclick="sort('table-top-material/@type',
                                  'ascending')">Material</button>
<button onclick="sort('table-top-material', 'ascending')">Finish</button>
<button onclick="sort('retail-price', 'ascending')">Price +</button>
<button onclick="sort('retail-price', 'descending')">Price -</button>
<hr/>
```

The HTML page then defines the objects to hold the source document, stylesheet document, and the output HTML:

```
<object id="XMLDocument" width="0" height="0"
   classid="clsid:f5078f32-c551-11d3-89b9-0000f81fe221">
   <param name="async" value="false">
   <param name="validateOnParse" value="false">
</object>

<object id="XSLDocument" width="0" height="0"
   classid="clsid:f5078f32-c551-11d3-89b9-0000f81fe221">
   <param name="async" value="false">
   <param name="validateOnParse" value="false">
</object>

<!-- to insert the results of parsing the object model -->
<div id="divResults"></div>

</body>
</html>
```

The JScript code that implements the functions is shown next. First the
preparePage() function, which creates some global variables to reference the
output <div> element and the two Document objects, and then loads the XML and
XSL files into these documents:

```
// global variables to hold references to objects
var gobjResults;
var gobjXML;
var gobjXSL;

function preparePage() {

   // get the reference to the results DIV element
   gobjResults = document.all['divResults'];

   // get the reference to the XML document parser
   gobjXML = document.all['XMLDocument'];

   // get the reference to the XSL stylesheet parser
   gobjXSL = document.all['XSLDocument'];

   // load the XML document and check for errors
   gobjXML.load('tables_data.xml');
   if (gobjXML.parseError.errorCode != 0) {
     // error found so show error message and stop
     gobjResults.innerHTML = showError(gobjXML)
     return false;
   }
```

```
    // load the XSL stylesheet and check for errors
    gobjXSL.load('tables_list.xsl');
    if (gobjXSL.parseError.errorCode != 0) {
        // error found so show error message and stop
        gobjResults.innerHTML = showError(gobjXSL)
        return false;
    }

    // all OK, so return true
    return true;
}
```

If either of the `load()` calls should fail, the function `showError()` (the same as the one used in the earlier examples) is used to display the error, and the function returns false. If all is well, it returns true and the `sort()` function can then be executed.

We're now ready to write the `sort()` function which changes the value of the `select` and `order` attributes of the `<xsl:sort>` element. Because the stylesheet is loaded as a DOM Document in memory, we can do this by using the DOM interfaces. It's particularly convenient to use an XPath expression to locate the two attributes directly.

The Microsoft-specific `selectSingleNode()` method takes an XPath expression, and returns the first selected node from the document. Conveniently, our stylesheet contains only one `<xsl:sort>` element.

So we can write the `sort()` function as follows:

```
function sort(strSortBy, strOrder) {

    // get a reference to the 'select' and 'order' attributes from
    // the 'xsl:sort element' in the root template
    var objSelect = gobjXSL.selectSingleNode("//xsl:sort/@select");
    var objOrder = gobjXSL.selectSingleNode("//xsl:sort/@order");

    // change the attribute value to the specified XPath value
    objSelect.nodeValue = strSortBy;
    objOrder.nodeValue = strOrder;

    // perform the transformation
    strResult = gobjXML.transformNode(gobjXSL);

    // and update the contents of the DIV element
    gobjResults.innerHTML = strResult;
}
```

Output

There is a button for each column in the results table. There are two buttons for the Price column, allowing it to be sorted in ascending or descending order.

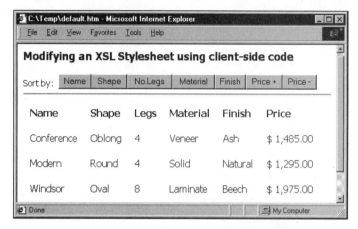

Clicking any of the buttons changes the display without reloading the page, sorting the results into the appropriate order as seen in the next screenshot:

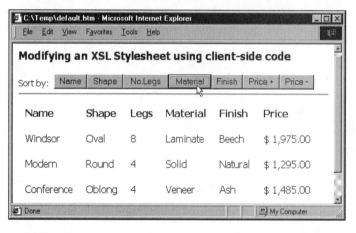

Using XPath Expressions with the DOM

In the previous example I used the method `selectSingleNode()` to select a node from the DOM document by supplying an XPath expression. This works because MSXML allows you to use XPath expressions independently of an XSLT stylesheet.

The following function creates a DOM document and populates it by loading an XML file into it. It then calls the XPath expression «//table/table-name» in the XML DOM's `selectNodes` function, which returns a `NodeList` object containing all the `<table-name>` elements from the document:

A

```
function getTableNames() {

    // get the reference to the results DIV element
    var objResults = document.all['divResults'];

    // create an XML document instance
    var objXML = new ActiveXObject('MSXML2.DOMDocument.3.0');

    // load the XML document and check for errors
    objXML.load('tables_data.xml');
    if (objXML.parseError.errorCode != 0) {
        // error found so show error message and stop
        objResults.innerHTML = showError(objXML)
        return false;
    }

    var strResult = new String;    // to hold the result
    strResult = 'The table names are: ';

    // get a NodeList containing all the <table> elements
    var objTableNodeList = objXML.selectNodes('//table/table-name');
```

Having got a list of the <table-name> elements, it's a simple task to iterate through them extracting the value (from the child text node of each one) and adding it to a string that is then placed into the <div> element elsewhere on the page:

```
    // iterate through all the <table-name> nodes
    for (var i = 0; i < objTableNodeList.length; i++) {

        // get the value of this node from the child text node
        strName = objTableNodeList(i).childNodes(0).nodeValue;
        strResult += '"<b>' + strName + '</b>" ';
    }

    // and update the contents of the DIV element
    objResults.innerHTML = strResult;
}
```

Here's the result using the XML document we've seen earlier:

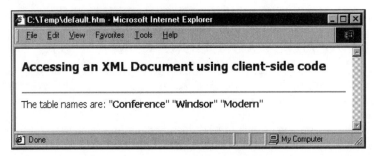

Using the MSXML Parser on the Server

So far in this Appendix we've been using MSXML to perform XSLT transformations on the client. This is great, but it will obviously only work where the client supports the use of the MSXML parser. Even if other browsers offered XSLT support, the scripts we've been writing in our HTML pages will only work with Microsoft's proprietary APIs.

If you have to develop a web site to serve users with a wide variety of browsers installed, then you will need some solution for those who aren't using the latest version of Internet Explorer (not to mention technology previews of XSLT technology that are changing every couple of months). In this situation your only real option is to perform the XML-to-HTML transformation on the server, and then send the resulting HTML to the client. In Chapter 10 I described a number of XSLT processors that can be used on the server, but so long as it's a Windows server, the MSXML3 product can also be used in this role.

The MSXML parser is a standard COM object, so you can instantiate and use it from any COM-enabled language. This includes VBScript and JScript running in an Active Server Pages file on the server, as well as server-based applications built using Visual Basic, C++, Java, Delphi, and so on.

Using MSXML with Active Server Pages

To create an instance of the parser on the server in ASP, we use almost the same techniques as we did on the client. However, to instantiate it in the correct context of the ASP page, we must use the ASP integral `Server` object's `CreateObject` method:

In VBScript:

```
Dim objDocument
Set objDocument = Server.CreateObject("MSXML2.DOMDocument.3.0")
```

In JScript:

```
var objDocument = Server.CreateObject('MSXML2.DOMDocument.3.0');
```

Of course, you can also use the `<object>` element to create the document instance, as we did earlier on the client. This has the advantage that the instance is not actually created until first referenced, whereas the `Server.CreateObject` method will create the instance immediately. Of course, any advantage depends on how you structure your code (that is, on when you execute the `Server.CreateObject` method).

> If you create an instance of the document in ASP within your `global.asa` file, so that it is available for the entire user's session or for the life of the application, be sure to specify the Free-Threaded version of the parser.

Once the document has been created, the techniques for using it are almost identical.

A

MSXML Processor

697

Of course, you can't use message boxes or alert dialogs, and you have to write the output to the client using the `Response.Write` method instead of inserting it onto an element on the page dynamically as we did in our earlier examples.

Example: A Server-Side XSLT Transformation

This ASP page, together with the support files it requires, is provided in a folder named `msxml_asp`. It demonstrates a simple server-side XSLT transformation that sends the result to the client as an HTML page.

Source XML

The source XML file is the same furniture catalog as we used in previous examples in this chapter, which starts:

```
<tables>
<table>
  <table-name>Conference</table-name>
  <number-of-legs>4</number-of-legs>
  <table-top-material type="Veneer">Ash</table-top-material>
  <table-shape>Oblong</table-shape>
  <retail-price currency="USD">1485</retail-price>
</table>
```

Stylesheet

The stylesheet is file `tables_style.xsl` in the same folder. We're not really concerned with the contents of the stylesheet here; it's much the same as in previous examples. The only important thing is that it generates HTML output.

ASP Page

The ASP page reads as follows. It is called `simple_transform.asp`:

```
<%@LANGUAGE="VBScript"%>

<%
' tell client that we're sending an HTML page
Response.ContentType = "text/html"

' error handling subroutine
Sub ShowError(objDoc)
   'create and display error message
   Dim strError
   strError = "Invalid XML file !<BR />" _
          & "File URL: " & objDoc.parseError.url & "<BR />" _
          & "Line No.: " & objDoc.parseError.line & "<BR />" _
          & "Character: " & objDoc.parseError.linepos & "<BR />" _
          & "File Position: " & objDoc.parseError.filepos & "<BR />" _
          & "Source Text: " & objDoc.parseError.srcText & "<BR />" _
          & "Error Code: " & objDoc.parseError.errorCode & "<BR />" _
          & "Description: " & objDoc.parseError.reason
   Response.Write strError
End Sub
```

```
Dim objXML
Dim objXSL

' create two document instances
Set objXML = Server.CreateObject("MSXML2.DOMDocument.3.0")
Set objXSL = Server.CreateObject("MSXML2.DOMDocument.3.0")

' set the parser properties
objXML.ValidateOnParse = True
objXSL.ValidateOnParse = True

' load the source XML document and check for errors
objXML.load Server.MapPath("tables_data.xml")
If objXML.parseError.errorCode <> 0 Then
   'error found so show error message and stop
   ShowError objXML
   Response.End
End If
```

Notice that we have to use the `Server.MapPath` method to convert the XML and XSL document names to a full valid physical path when running under ASP. If not, the `load` method will fail to find the file and report an error.

```
' load the XSL stylesheet and check for errors
objXSL.load Server.MapPath("tables_style.xsl")
If objXSL.parseError.errorCode <> 0 Then
   'error found so show error message and stop
   ShowError objXSL
   Response.End
End If

' all must be OK, so perform transformation
strResult = objXML.transformNode(objXSL)

' and insert the results into the page
Response.Write strResult
%>
```

Output

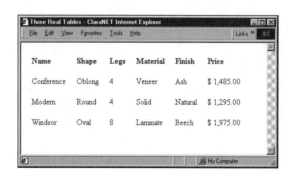

A

MSXML Processor

We could, of course, select the XML document and the XSL stylesheet dynamically when the page is executed, rather than hard-coding the names into the script. For example, a <FORM> section on another page could reference this page and provide a value for the stylesheet name in an HTML control – perhaps named "stylesheet_name". The ASP code then just needs to use this value in the load method:

```
objXSL.load Server.MapPath(Request.Form("stylesheet_name"))
```

Setting the Appropriate Content Type Header

Notice that the previous example uses the ASP statement

```
Response.ContentType = "text/html"
```

to set the HTTP content type header so that the client knows that the data is to be treated as an HTML page. This is because we are creating HTML as the result of our server-side transformation. In this case, if we omitted to include this statement, the page would still work because a Web browser will default to «text/html» if no other content type is specified.

The content type is specified as one of the standard MIME types, and you should always specify this using the Response.ContentType statement. It is particularly important if your are creating something other than an HTML page. For example, if your XSL transformation or other ASP code creates XML-format output, you should use:

```
Response.ContentType = "text/xml"
```

If you are creating an XSL stylesheet to send to the client, use «text/xml». Internet Explorer will also accept «text/xsl», but other browsers might not, because it is not a standard MIME type. For a pure text file, use «text/text». Remember, however, that it is the client itself (or rather the operating system environment in which it is running) that actually decides what to do with the output you send, based on the content type you specify. You can only tell the client what type of output you are creating, and it will decide how to handle it when it arrives.

Conditional XSLT Transformations

Given that some browsers support client-side XSLT transformation and others don't, a natural thing to do is to perform the transformation on the client if it is supported there, or on the server if not. This is easy to do, and simply requires an ASP script that detects the browser version and sends back the appropriate content.

To detect the browser version, you could use a tool like the Microsoft BrowserCapabilities component or CyScape's BrowserHawk component. However, it's easy enough with some simple script code – this example sets a Boolean variable named blnIsIE5 to True if the browser is Internet Explorer 5 or better:

```
blnIsIE5 = False
strUA = Request.ServerVariables("HTTP_USER_AGENT")
If InStr(strUA, "MSIE") Then
  intVersion = CInt(Mid(strUA, InStr(strUA, "MSIE") + 5, 1))
  If intVersion > 4 Then blnIsIE5 = True  'this is IE5 or better
End If
```

Once you know whether you are dealing with a browser that can do the XSL transformation itself, you can send back the correct content. If `blnIsIE5` is `False`, you can use code like that shown earlier to perform the transformation on the server and send back pure HTML.

However, if `blnIsIE5` is `True` you can get the browser to do the transformation. You could create and send back to the client an HTML page that loads the correct source XML file and matching XSL stylesheet, and performs the transformation client-side. This technique has been demonstrated earlier in the example *Using Client-side JScript to Transform a Document* on page 684.

Alternatively, you can send back the pure XML source document. However, to get the client to perform the transformation you need to insert into it a processing instruction that links the correct XSL stylesheet to the XML document. This is easy enough to do by parsing the document on the server before sending it. The following code shows the overall structure of such a page:

```
<%@LANGUAGE="VBScript"%>
<%
'detect browser version and set variable blnIsIE5

If blnIsIE5 Then

    '****************************************
    'tell client that we're sending pure XML
    Response.ContentType = "text/xml"

    'add xsl-stylesheet instruction to XML
    'source document and send it to the client
    '****************************************

Else

    '****************************************
    'tell client that we're sending an HTML page
    Response.ContentType = "text/html"

    'use simple server-based transformation
    'as demonstrated earlier to create the
    'resulting HTML and send it to the client
    '****************************************

End If
%>
```

A

This page, `conditional_transform.asp`, together with the support files it requires, is provided in the folder named `msxml_asp`.

We've already seen how to perform the server-based transformation. What remains is the code (omitted from the above outline) that adds the appropriate `<?xsl-stylesheet?>` processing instruction to the XML document, before sending it to the client. Here is that code in full:

```
If blnIsIE5 Then
    '****************************************
    'tell client that we're sending pure XML
    Response.ContentType = "text/xml"

    'create a parser instance
    Set objXML = Server.CreateObject("MSXML2.DOMDocument.3.0")

    'load the XML document
    objXML.load Server.MapPath("tables_data.xml")

    If objXML.parseError.errorCode = 0 Then

        'get a reference to the outermost <tables> element
        Set objOutermost = objXML.documentElement

        'create the processing instruction attributes
        QUOT = Chr(34)   'double-quote character
        strAttributes = "type=" & QUOT & "text/xsl" & QUOT _
                        & " href=" & QUOT & "tables_style.xsl" & QUOT

        'create the new xsl-stylesheet processing instruction
        Set objNewPI = objXML.createProcessingInstruction( _
                                "xml-stylesheet", strAttributes)

        'insert it into the XML document after the xml version element
        objXML.insertBefore objNewPI, objOutermost

        'and insert the results into the page
        Response.Write objXML.xml

    Else
        Response.Write "Error loading XML document."
    End If
    '****************************************
```

You can see in this code that we're loading the XML source document and getting a reference to the `<tables>` element. We then create a new processing instruction using the `createProcessingInstruction()` method of the XML Document object. Then we can insert our new processing instruction into the XML document before the `<tables>` element (and after the opening xml-declaration) using the `insertBefore()` method of the Document object.

The result is that Internet Explorer 5 and higher will receive the XML source document containing the `<xsl:stylesheet>` instruction, and retrieve this stylesheet for use in a client-side XSL transformation. However, other browsers will receive just the HTML result of performing the transformation on the server:

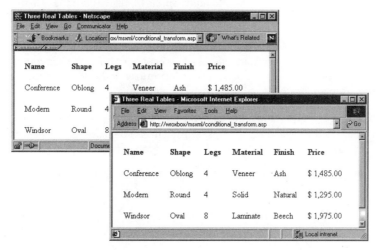

Of course, we could have simplified the operation by just adding the `<?xsl-stylesheet?>` instruction to the XML source document. When loaded into a parser instance with script code, using the load method, any stylesheet instructions are ignored and so the server-side process would still have worked OK. It would also have meant that we didn't need to insert the stylesheet instruction for IE5 browsers using ASP code, which could significantly reduce the processing load on the server. However, the technique we used allows the stylesheet to be chosen dynamically at runtime, perhaps (as shown earlier) in response to a value sent from a `<FORM>` on another page,

Tools for Performing XSL Transformations

While you can easily use and adapt the generic code shown earlier to suit your own applications, it is often useful to take advantage of tools that can make the job easier. One of the tools available from the Microsoft XML download page is an ISAPI extension called `xslisapi.dll`. This can be used to perform the translation on your server with minimal coding required.

You can download the code for this tool from the Microsoft XML Web page at http://msdn.microsoft.com/downloads/webtechnology/xml/xslisapi.asp. The page includes installation and setup instructions, and full documentation.

In its simplest form, the ISAPI extension examines all requests for files with the «.xml» extension, and checks to see if they contain an `<?xml-stylesheet?>` processing instruction. If not, they are passed back to the client with no action taken by the DLL. However, if it finds an `<?xml-stylesheet?>` processing instruction, it checks to see if the browser is IE5 or higher. If it is, it simply passes the XML file on to the client unchanged. But, if the client is not IE5 or higher, the DLL automatically performs the transformation specified by the XSLT stylesheet and sends the client the results.

A

MSXML Processor

You can also specify different stylesheets for the client-side and server-side processing, and even create configuration file entries to provide even more control over the operation. This tool effectively accomplishes what we've been doing in our earlier server-side examples automatically. However, knowing how to perform these tasks yourself is useful and allows you to tailor applications that use them to exactly meet your requirements.

Performing Bulk Transformations

If you use server-based transformations to create output for clients, you do place an extra load on your server. Web servers are optimized to serve pages from disk to the client on demand, rather than carrying out intermediate processing each time. One way to minimize the load is to perform the transformations at specific intervals (based on the frequency with which the source XML or XSLT changes), and write the results to the server's disk as a series of files. The client can then access and download the appropriate file, rather than having the translation performed in real time.

You can easily write the results of a transformation to the server's disk using the `FileSystemObject`:

```
...
'all must be OK, so perform transformation
strResult = objXML.transformNode(objXSL)

'and write the results to the server's disk
Set objFSO = Server.CreateObject("Scripting.FileSystemObject")
Set objFile = objFSO.CreateTextFile("resultpage.htm", True)
                                    'overwrite any existing file
objFile.Write strResult
objFile.Close
```

Alternatively, you might like to look at the `XSLTransform` component that uses a batch file to automatically perform multiple transformations to disk files. See http://www.stonebroom.com for more details.

MSXML3 Quick Reference

The objects, methods, properties and events available with the MSXML3 parser are listed in the Help file that comes with the SDK. Instructions for downloading this appear at the start of this appendix.

The documentation that accompanies the SDK is described by Microsoft as preliminary, and with good reason: in many cases, there are few clues as to how a particular method or property is intended to be used. However, you can get by with quite a small subset of the interface, and I have tried to summarize that subset in this quick reference section.

I have only included here the parts of the interface that are relevant to XSLT and XPath processing. I have covered only the basic interfaces, and have omitted some that look interesting, but which are documented so sketchily (at the time of writing) that a fair bit of trial and error would be needed to get them to work. A full description of the Microsoft DOM interface (the stable parts, not the new additions in the current technology preview) can be found in the Wrox book *Professional XML* - ISBN 1-861003-11-0.

Objects

The objects of particular interest to XSLT and XPath processing are listed below:

Object	Description
IXMLDOMDocument	The root of an XML document
IXMLDOMNode	Any node in the DOM
IXMLDOMNodeList	A collection of Node objects
IXMLDOMParseError	Details of the last parse error that occurred
IXSLProcessor	An execution of an XSL stylesheet
IXSLTemplate	A compiled XSL stylesheet in memory

These objects are described in the sections that follow.

IXMLDOMDocument

The IXMLDOMDocument class inherits all the properties and methods of IXMLDOMNode. This section lists the additional methods and properties of relevance to XSLT and XPath processing, in other words, all the methods and properties that are not also present on IXMLDOMNode, which is described on page 707.

Additional methods

The methods particularly relevent to XPath and XSLT processing are described in detail below.

The validate() method actually belongs to the IXMLDOMDocument2 interface, which is an extension to IXMLDOMDocument introduced with the MSXML2 product.

Name	Returns	Description
abort	(Nothing)	Abort download
load	Boolean	Loads document from the specified XML source
loadXML	Boolean	Loads the document from a string
save	(Nothing)	Saves the document to a specified destination
validate	(Nothing)	Validate the document, using the current DTD or schema

abort() ⇒ Nothing

When a document is being loaded asynchronously, abort() can be called at any time to abandon the process.

load(url) ⇒ Boolean

A

MSXML Processor

The argument is normally a string containing a URL; this URL should identify an XML document. The effect of this method is to clear out any existing content of the `Document` object, and replace it with the result of parsing the XML source from the specified URL. The method returns true if successful, false otherwise.

loadXML(string) ⇒ Boolean

The string contains the text of an XML document. The effect of this method is to clear out any existing content of the `Document` object, and replace it with the result of parsing the XML string. The method returns true if successful, false otherwise.

save(destination) ⇒ Nothing

The destination is usually a filename, given as a string. The effect is to save the Document in XML format as a file. It is also possible to specify various other objects as a destination, for example, it can be another `Document` object, in which case the document is duplicated.

validate() ⇒ Nothing

This method checks that the document is valid, that is, that it conforms to its DTD or schema. If it is valid, the call returns normally, otherwise it raises an error condition.

This is an alternative to validating while the document is being parsed. It can be useful, for example, to ensure that the document created as the output of an XSLT transformation is valid.

A typical call sequence in JScript is:

```
try {
    xmldoc.validate();
} catch(e) {
    alert("Validation error: " + e.description);
}
```

Additional properties

Name	Returns	Description
async	Boolean	True if loaded asynchronously
parseError	IXMLDOMParseError	The last parser error
readyState	Long	Current state of readiness for use
validateOnParse	Boolean	Requests validation

async

If this property is set to true, processing can continue while the document is being parsed and loaded. When using stylesheets, async is normally set to false so that as soon as control returns from the `load()` method, transformation can proceed.

parseError

This property returns an `IXMLDOMParseError` object. To determine if a parsing error occurred, test whether the errorCode of the returned object is non-zero.

readyState

When loading a document asynchronously, this property takes one of the four values:

1	LOADING
2	LOADED
3	INTERACTIVE
4	COMPLETED

You can nominate a function to be called when the state changes, using the `onReadyStateChange` event.

valildateOnParse

If this property is set to true, the document will be validated (against its DTD or schema) as it is loaded.

IXMLDOMNode

This object represents a node in the document tree. Note that the tree conforms to the DOM model, which is not always the same as the XPath model described in Chapter 2: for example, the way namespaces are modeled is different, and text nodes are not necessarily normalized.

There are subclasses of `IXMLDOMNode` for all the different kinds of node found in the tree. I have not included descriptions of all these, since they are not directly relevant to XSLT and XPath processing. The only one I have included is `IXMLDOMDocument`, which can be regarded as representing either the whole document or its root node, depending on your point of view.

Methods

The methods available on `IXMLDOMNode` that are relevant to XSLT and XPath processing are listed below. Most often, these methods will be applied to the root node (the DOM `Document` object) but they can be applied to any node.

Name	Returns	Description
selectNodes	IXMLDOMNodeList	Executes an XPath expression and returns a list of matching nodes
selectSingleNode	IXMLDOMNode	Executes an XPath expression and returns the first matching node

A

Name	Returns	Description
transformNode	String	Applies a stylesheet to the subtree rooted at this node, returning the result as a string
transformNode ToObject	(Nothing)	Applies the stylesheet to the subtree, placing the result into a supplied document or stream

selectNodes(String expression) ⇒ IXMLDOMNodeList

This method takes an XPath expression as its argument, and returns the list of nodes selected by that expression.

Microsoft's documentation on this method is very limited. It seems that the XPath expression must be one that returns a node-set, and that the node to which the expression is applied is used as the context node; also that any namespace prefixes in the expression are interpreted using the namespace declarations in scope for this node.

If no nodes are selected, the method returns an empty list.

The documentation makes no guarantee that the nodes are returned in any particular order.

If the target document supports the IXMLDOMDocument2 interface, which is an extension of the basic IXMLDOMDocument interface, then the IXMLDOMNodeList returned will also implement the IXMLDOMSelection interface.

selectSingleNode(String expression) ⇒ IXMLDOMNode

This method is the same as selectNodes() above, except that it only returns the first selected node in document order.

If no nodes are selected, the method returns null.

transformNode(IXMLDOMNode stylesheet) ⇒ String

This method applies a stylesheet to the document containing this node. The target node is used as the initial context for the stylesheet, but the stylesheet has access to the entire document.

The argument identifies the XSLT stylesheet. This will usually be a Document, but it may be Node representing an embedded stylesheet within a Document.

The result of the transformation is serialized and returned as a string.

transformNodeToObject(IXMLDOMNode stylesheet, Variant result) ⇒ Nothing

This method applies a stylesheet to the document containing this node. The target node is used as the initial context for the stylesheet, but the stylesheet has access to the entire document.

The argument identifies the XSLT stylesheet. This will usually be a Document, but it may be Node representing an embedded stylesheet within a Document.

The result of the transformation is written to the object identified in the second argument. This will usually be a Document. It may also be a Stream.

Properties

The most useful properties are listed below. Properties whose main purpose is to navigate through the document are not listed here, because navigation can be achieved more easily using XPath expressions.

Name	Returns	Description
baseName	String	The local name of the node, excluding any namespace prefix.
namespaceURI	String	The namespace URI.
nodeName	String	The name of the node, including its namespace prefix if any. Note that unlike the XPath model, unnamed nodes are given conventional names such as "#document", "#text", and "#comment".
nodeTypeString	String	Returns the type of node in string form. For example, "element", "attribute", or "comment".
nodeValue	Variant	The value stored in the node. This is not the same as the XPath string-value: for elements, it is always null.
prefix	String	The prefix for the namespace applying to the node.
text	String	Text contained by this node (like the XPath string-value).
xml	String	XML representation of the node and its descendants.

IXMLDOMNodeList

This object represents a list of nodes. For our present purposes, we are interested in this object because it is the result of the selectNodes() method.

An IXMLDOMNodeList is returned as a result of the selectNodes() method: it contains the list of nodes selected by the supplied XPath expression. You can process all the nodes in the list either by using the nextNode() method or by direct indexing using the item property. There is nothing in the documentation that says the nodes will be returned in any particular order.

A

If the document from which the nodes were selected implements the IXMLDOMDocument2 interface introduced in MSXML2, then the node list returned by selectNodes() will also implement the IXMLDOMSelection interface. This offers some additional capabilities, however, the preliminary Microsoft documentation is far from clear as to how these are intended to be used. For details, see the Help file provided with the MSXML3 SDK.

Methods

Name	Returns	Description
nextNode	IXMLDOMNode	Get the next node
reset	(Nothing)	Reset the current position

nextNode() ⇒ IXMLDOMNode

Returns the next node, or null when all the nodes have been processed.

reset() ⇒ Nothing

Resets the node list so that the next node returned by nextNode() will be the first one.

Properties

Name	Returns	Description
item	IXMLDOMNode	The default collection of nodes. A particular node can be referenced as nodeList.item(i).
length	Long	Identifies the number of nodes in the collection.

IXMLDOMParseError

This object is accessible through the parseError property of the IXMLDOMDocument interface. Examples of how to use this object to generate diagnostics are given earlier in this appendix.

Properties

Name	Returns	Description
errorCode	Long	The error code
filepos	Long	The character position of the error within the XML document
line	Long	The line number of the error
linepos	Long	The character position in the line containing the error

reason	String	Explanation of the error
srcText	String	The XML text in error
url	String	The URL of the offending document

IXSLProcessor

An IXSLProcessor object represents a single execution of a stylesheet to transform a source document.

The object is normally created by calling the createProcessor() method of an IXSLTemplate object.

The transformation is achieved by calling the transform() method.

Methods

Name	Returns	Description
addParameter	(Nothing)	Set <xsl:param> value
reset	(Nothing)	Reset state of processor and abort current transform
setStartMode	(Nothing)	Set XSL mode and its namespace
transform	Boolean	Start or resume the XSL transformation process

addParameter(String localName, Variant value, String namespaceURI) ⇒ Nothing

This method supplies a value for a global parameter declared within the stylesheet using a top-level <xsl:param> element. The localName identifies the local name of the parameter, and the namespaceURI its namespace. In the common case that the parameter name has a null namespace URI, the third argument should be an empty string.

The value of the parameter is passed in the second argument. It can be a Boolean, a number, or a string; or a Node or NodeList. The last two cases will both be treated within the stylesheet as a node-set value.

reset() ⇒ Nothing

If a transformation is in progress, this aborts the transformation and resets the processor so it can be used again. It does **not** clear any parameters that have been added, or the startMode.

setStartMode(String mode, String namespaceURI) ⇒ Nothing

A

Normally when a stylesheet is used, processing starts by looking for a template rule that matches the root node and that is defined with no mode attribute. Sometimes it is useful to be able to use the same stylesheet in different ways on different occasions, so MSXML3 allows processing to start in a different mode from the default. Modes are described in Chapter 4, page 296: see the descriptions of the <xsl:apply-templates> and <xsl:template> elements.

Modes are identified by a QName (a namespace-qualified name), so this method allows both the local name and the namespace URI to be specified. Most commonly the second parameter will be an empty string.

transform() ⇒ Boolean

This method applies the stylesheet (from which this XSLProcessor was derived) to the source document identified in the input property. The result of the transformation is accessible through the output property.

If the transformation is completed, the return value is true. If the source document is being loaded asynchronously, it is possible for the transform() method to return false, meaning that it needs to wait until more input is available. In this case, it is possible to resume the transformation by calling transform() again later. The current state of the transformation can be determined from the readyState property.

Properties

Name	Returns	Description
input	Variant	XML source document to transform. This is normally supplied as a DOM Document, but it may also be a Node. The input can also be supplied as an IStream.
output	Variant	Output of the transformation. If you don't supply an output object, the processor will create a String to hold the output, which you can read using this property. If you prefer, you can supply an object such as a DOM Document, a DOM Node, or an IStream to receive the output.
ownerTemplate	IXSLTemplate	The XSLTemplate object used to create this processor object.
readyState	Long	The current state of the transformation. This will be READYSTATE_COMPLETE (3) when the transformation is finished.
startMode	String	Name of starting XSLT mode. See setStartMode() method above.

startModeURI	String	Namespace of starting XSLT mode. See setStartMode() method above.
stylesheet	IXMLDOMNode	The current stylesheet being used.

IXSLTemplate

An IXSLTemplate object represents a compiled stylesheet in memory. If you want to use the same stylesheet more than once, then creating an IXSLTemplate and using it repeatedly is more efficient than using the raw stylesheet repeatedly using transformNode().

Methods

Name	Returns	Description
createProcessor	IXSLProcessor	Create an IXSLProcessor object

createProcessor() ⇒ IXSLProcessor

This method should only be called after the stylesheet property has been set to associate the IXSLTemplate object with a stylesheet.

It creates an IXSLProcessor object which can then be used to initiate a transformation of a given source document.

Properties

Name	Returns	Description
stylesheet	IXMLDOMNode	Identifies the stylesheet from which this IXSLTemplate is derived

Setting this property causes the specified stylesheet to be compiled; this IXSLTemplate object is then reusable representation of the compiled stylesheet.

The DOM Node representing the stylesheet will normally be a DOM Document object, but it may be an Element representing an embedded stylesheet. (Embedded stylesheets are described in Chapter 3, page 99).

The document identified by the stylesheet property must be a free-threaded document object.

Summary

This appendix summarized the techniques and application programming interfaces available for using Microsoft's MSXML3 product, with a particular focus on its XSLT transformation capabilities.

We saw how to view XML directly in the IE5 browser, either with the default stylesheet or with one identified through the <?xml-stylesheet?> processing instruction. Then we saw how to use client-side scripting to control the transformation process, even seeing how it is possible to modify the stylesheet each time it is used.

Finally we looked at the use of MSXML3 as a server-side technology, performing transformations controlled from an ASP page, or doing transformations either on the server or on the client, depending on the capabilities of the user's browser.

Do remember that this is a technology preview. The software is likely to change a lot over the coming months; it is likely to become more reliable, and the documentation will (hopefully) improve a lot. Check Microsoft's web site and news groups to keep up to date with the current position.

B

Glossary

This glossary gathers together some of the more common technical terms used in this book. These terms are not all defined in the XSLT or XPath specifications, some of them are borrowed from XML or other standards in the XML family, and others have been invented for the purposes of this book. So for each definition, I also tell you where the term comes from.

The definitions, however, are my own: in some cases the original specifications have a much more formal definition, but in other cases they are surprisingly vague.

Ancestor Axis

Origin

XPath

Explanation

The ancestor axis selects the parent of the context node, its parent, and so on up to and including the root node. The axis is in reverse document order.

Ancestor-or-Self Axis

Origin

XPath

Explanation

The ancestor-or-self axis selects the context node followed by all the nodes on the ancestor axis. The axis is in reverse document order.

Attribute Axis

Origin

XPath

Explanation

The attribute axis selects all the attributes of the context node. If the context node is not an element, the axis will be empty.

Attribute Node

Origin

XPath

Explanation

A node in a tree that represents an attribute in an XML document. There will be an attribute node attached to an element node for each attribute defined in the start tag of the corresponding element in the original XML document, other than an attribute acting as a namespace declaration. There will also be attribute nodes for attributes given a default value in the Document Type Definition. The string value of the node is the value of the attribute.

Attribute Set

Origin

XSLT

Explanation

A named collection of `<xsl:attribute>` instructions, which when invoked using the `use-attribute-sets` attribute of `<xsl:element>` or `<xsl:copy>`, or the `xsl:use-attribute-sets` attribute of a literal result element, generates a set of attribute nodes to be added to the current output element.

Attribute Value Template

Origin

XSLT

Explanation

An attribute value template is an attribute in the stylesheet that can contain both fixed and variable parts. The fixed parts are written as ordinary characters, while the variable parts are written between curly braces: for example «file="{$dir}/{$fname}.html"» would evaluate to «file="out/page.html"» if the variables $dir and $fname have the values «out» and «page» respectively. Attribute value templates can be used for any attribute of a literal result element, but on XSLT elements they can be used only for those attributes that explicitly allow them.

Attribute

Origin

XML

Explanation

A name=value pair appearing in an element's start tag, for example «category="grocery"».

Axis

Origin

XPath

Explanation

An axis is a direction of travel through the tree. Starting from a particular context node, an axis defines a list of nodes reached from that origin. For example the ancestor axis returns the parent, grandparent, and so on up to the root of the tree, while the following-sibling axis returns all the nodes that appear after the context node and share the same parent.

Base URI

Origin

XSLT

Explanation

Every node has an associated Base URI. For an element, this is the absolute URI of the XML external entity containing the element's start and end tags (most often, of course, this will be the document entity). For other node types, it is defined by reference to an associated element node, typically its parent. The Base URI of a node is used when expanding a relative URI defined in that node, for example a relative URI in an href attribute is considered to be relative to the Base URI of the parent element.

Glossary

Boolean

Origin

XPath

Explanation

One of the allowed data types for the value of an XPath expression. It takes the value true or false.

Built-in Template Rule

Origin

XSLT

Explanation

A template rule that is not explicitly defined in the stylesheet, but which is implicitly available to process a node if there is no explicit template rule that matches it.

CDATA Section

Origin

XML

Explanation

A sequence of characters in an XML document enclosed between the delimiters «<![CDATA[» and «]]>»; within a CDATA section all characters represent text content rather than markup, except for the sequence «]]>».

Character Reference

Origin

XML

Explanation

A representation of a character using its decimal or hexadecimal Unicode value, for example «
» or «↤». Normally used for characters that are difficult or impossible to enter directly at the keyboard.

Child Axis

Origin

XPath

Explanation

The child axis selects all the immediate children of the context node. These can include elements, text nodes, comments, and processing instructions, but not attributes or namespace nodes.

Comment Node

Origin

XPath

Explanation

A node in a tree representing an XML comment. The string-value of the node is the text of the comment.

Comment

Origin

XML

Explanation

An item in an XML document that is conventionally used to carry extraneous information that is not part of the document proper. Written between the delimiters «<!--» and «-->».

Context Node

Origin

XPath

Explanation

For an XPath expression contained directly in the stylesheet (for example, an expression in the `select` attribute of `<xsl:value-of>`, or between curly braces in an attribute value template), the context node is the same as the current node. For an XPath expression used as a predicate within a path expression, the context node is the node for which the predicate is being tested. The context node can be retrieved using the expression «.».

Glossary

B

721

Context Position

Origin

XPath

Explanation

For an XPath expression contained directly in the stylesheet, the context position is the position of the current node in the current node list, all positions being numbered from one. For an XPath expression used as a predicate in a step, the context position is the position of the context node among all the nodes selected by that step of the path expression, in the order of that step's axis. The context position determines the value of the position() function, and is also used in evaluating a numeric predicate such as «[1]».

Context Size

Origin

XPath

Explanation

For an XPath expression contained directly in the stylesheet, the context size is the number of nodes in the current node list. For an XPath expression used as a predicate in a step, the context size is the number of nodes selected by that step of the path expression. The context size determines the value of the last() function.

Current Node List

Origin

XSLT

Explanation

The current node list is a list (an ordered set) of nodes in the source document tree. A new current node list is established by the select expression of <xsl:apply-templates> or <xsl:for-each>. By default the current node list is in document order, but it may be in a different order if an <xsl:sort> element is present. When an XPath expression in the stylesheet is evaluated, the position of the current node in the current node list determines the context position (the value of the position() function), and the size of the current node list determines the context size (the value of the last() function).

Current Node

Origin

XSLT

Explanation

A node in a source tree becomes the current node when it is processed using `<xsl:apply-templates>` or `<xsl:for-each>`. The current node is accessed directly by using the `current()` function. Except within a predicate of a path expression, the current node is the same as the context node, so it can also be accessed using the expression «.».

Current Output Destination

Origin

This book

Explanation

The XSLT specification speaks of instructions such as `<xsl:value-of>` and `<xsl:element>` writing nodes to the result tree. But while an `<xsl:variable>` element is being instantiated, any output is actually redirected to the result tree fragment that will form the value of this variable. In this book we have therefore chosen to refer to whichever tree is currently being written to as the current output destination. Many products also allow multiple output trees.

Current Template Rule

Origin

XSLT

Explanation

When `<xsl:apply-templates>` selects a template rule to process a particular node, that template rule becomes the current template rule. It remains the current template rule through calls of `<xsl:call-template>`, but not though calls of `<xsl:for-each>`. The current template rule is used only in deciding which template to invoke when `<xsl:apply-imports>` is called.

Default Namespace Declaration

Origin

XML Namespaces

Explanation

Takes the form of an XML attribute `xmlns="uri"`. Declares that within its scope, an element name with no explicit prefix will be associated with a particular namespace URI. The default namespace is used only for element names; other objects with no prefix (for example, attributes) have a null namespace URI.

Descendant Axis

Origin

XPath

Explanation

The descendant axis selects all the children of the context node, their children, and so on, in document order.

Descendant-or-Self Axis

Origin

XPath

Explanation

The descendant-or-self axis selects the context node followed by all the nodes on the descendant axis.

Document Element

Origin

XML

Explanation

The outermost element of a document, the one that contains all other elements. The XML standard also refers to this as the root element, but it must not be confused with the root node in the XPath tree model: the root node is the parent of the document element, and represents the document itself.

Document Order

Origin

XPath

Explanation

The nodes in a node-set can always be sorted into document order. For elements from the same document, document order is the same as the order of the start tags in the original source. In terms of the tree structure, a node is ordered after its preceding siblings, and these are ordered after their parent node. The ordering of attribute and namespace nodes, and of nodes from different source documents, is not fully defined.

Document Type Definition (DTD)

Origin

XML

Explanation

The definition of the structure of an XML document, or a collection of XML documents. May be split into an external subset, held in a separate file, and an internal subset, embedded within the document itself.

Document

Origin

XML

Explanation

A parsed entity that conforms to the XML syntax for a Document is said to be a well-formed document; a document that also obeys the rules in its Document Type Definition is said to be valid.

Element Node

Origin

XPath

Glossary

B

Explanation

A node in a tree that represents an element in an XML document. The parent of the element node is either the containing element or the root of the tree; its children are the element nodes, text nodes, comment nodes, and processing instruction nodes derived from the immediate content of the XML element.

Element

Origin

XML

Explanation

A logical unit within an XML document, delimited by start and end tags, for example `<publisher>Wrox Press</publisher>`; an empty element may also be written in abbreviated form, for example `<publisher name="Wrox"/>`.

Embedded Stylesheet

Origin

XSLT

Explanation

A physical stylesheet that does not constitute an entire XML document in its own right, but which is embedded as an `<xsl:stylesheet>` element within some larger XML (or perhaps non-XML) document.

Entity Reference

Origin

XML

Explanation

A reference to an internal or external entity, generally in the form «&name;».

Entity

Origin

XML

Explanation

A physical unit of information that may be referenced within an XML document. Internal entities are embedded within the document in its Document Type Definition; external entities are generally held as a separate file. A parsed entity contains text with XML markup; an unparsed entity contains binary data. A general entity contains material for inclusion in the document; a parameter entity contains material for inclusion in the Document Type Definition.

Expanded Name

Origin

XML Namespaces

Explanation

An identifier obtained from a `QName` by replacing the namespace prefix with the full namespace URI of the namespace to which it refers. An expanded name has two components, the namespace URI and the local name. There is no defined convention for displaying an expanded name, though some products show it as the namespace URI, then a circumflex, then the local name: for example «`http://icl.com/saxon^output`».

Expression

Origin

XPath

Explanation

An XPath construct that can be evaluated to yield a string, a number, a Boolean, a node-set, or a result tree fragment. Used in many contexts such as the `select` attribute of `<xsl:for-each>`, `<xsl:value-of>`, and `<xsl:variable>`, and the `test` attribute of `<xsl:if>` and `<xsl:when>`. Expressions are also used between curly braces in attribute value templates.

Glossary

B

Extension Element

Origin

XSLT

Explanation

An element within a template body that is defined by a product vendor, a user, or a third party, but which otherwise behaves like an XSLT instruction. The XSLT Recommendation defines how extension elements are instantiated but not how they are implemented.

Extension Function

Origin

XSLT

Explanation

A function defined by a product vendor, a user, or a third party, which can be called from within an XPath expression. The XSLT Recommendation defines how extension functions are called but not how they are implemented.

Following Axis

Origin

XPath

Explanation

The following axis selects all the nodes that follow the context node with the exception of attribute and namespace nodes, and the node's own descendants. The axis is in document order.

Following-Sibling Axis

Origin

XPath

Explanation

The following-sibling axis selects all the nodes that follow the context node and that share the same parent node, in document order.

Function

Origin

XPath

Explanation

A procedure that can be called from within an XPath expression; it takes arguments and returns a result. Functions cannot be defined using XPath, only invoked from XPath. A function is either a core function defined in the XPath or XSLT recommendations, or an extension function provided by the vendor or the user.

Global Variable

Origin

XSLT

Explanation

A variable defined in a top-level `<xsl:variable>` element. Global variables are available anywhere in the logical stylesheet, unless masked by a local variable of the same name, or a global variable of the same name and higher import precedence.

ID

Origin

XML

Explanation

An attribute of type ID has a value which is unique within the document (that is, different from any other ID attribute). It is an ID by virtue of being declared as such in the DTD. It is only guaranteed unique if the document is valid (XSLT is not constrained to operate only on valid documents). Elements can be accessed using their ID by means of the `id()` function. Attributes of type IDREF have no special significance in XSLT.

Import Precedence

Origin

XSLT

Glossary

B

729

Explanation

A stylesheet that is loaded using `<xsl:import>` has lower import precedence than the stylesheet doing the importing. The import precedence affects all the top-level elements in that stylesheet, and is used when deciding which top-level elements to use. For example, if two global variables have the same name, the one with higher import precedence is used.

Instantiate

Origin

XSLT

Explanation

Instructions and template bodies in XSLT are not executed, obeyed, or activated: they are said to be instantiated. This term is chosen to avoid any connotation that execution must be sequential.

Instruction

Origin

XSLT

Explanation

One of a number of XSLT elements that is permitted to appear directly within a template body, for example `<xsl:variable>`, `<xsl:choose>`, and `<xsl:message>`. Not all XSLT elements are instructions, for example `<xsl:param>` and `<xsl:when>` are not: this is because these can only appear in a defined context.

Literal Result Element

Origin

XSLT

Explanation

A literal result element is an element appearing within a template body in a stylesheet that is not an XSLT instruction or an extension element. When the template body is instantiated, a literal result element is copied to the current output destination and its content (which is also a template body) is instantiated in turn.

Local Variable

Origin

XSLT

Explanation

A variable defined within a template body. A local variable is accessible only from the following siblings of the `<xsl:variable>` element that defines the variable, and from their descendants. This is analogous to the normal rule in block-structured programming languages.

Mode

Origin

XSLT

Explanation

Modes partition the set of template rules in a stylesheet, so that the same nodes can be processed more than once using different rules each time. The mode named on the call of `<xsl:apply-templates>` must match the mode named on the `<xsl:template>` element that is invoked.

Named Template

Origin

XSLT

Explanation

An `<xsl:template>` element in the stylesheet with a `name` attribute. A named template may be invoked using an `<xsl:call-template>` instruction.

Namespace

Origin

XML Namespaces

Glossary

B

Explanation

A named collection of names. The namespace is named using a URI, which is intended to be formed in such a way as to ensure global uniqueness, but which, in practice, may be any string. Within a particular region of a document, a namespace is also identified by a local name called a prefix; different prefixes can be used to refer to the same namespace in different documents or even within the same document. A name (of an element or attribute in XML, and of a variable, template, mode etc in XSLT) belongs to a specific namespace, and two names can be considered equivalent only if they belong to the same namespace.

Namespace Axis

Origin

XPath

Explanation

The namespace axis selects all the namespace nodes belonging to the context node. If the context node is not an element, the axis will be empty. For elements, there is one namespace node for every namespace that is in scope for the element, whether it relates to a namespace declaration that was defined on this element or on a containing element.

Namespace Declaration

Origin

XML Namespaces

Explanation

A construct in an XML document which declares that within a particular region of the document, a given namespace prefix will be used to refer to the namespace with a particular URI. There are two forms of namespace declaration: `xmlns="uri"` to declare the default namespace (the one with a null prefix), and `xmlns:prefix="uri"` to declare a namespace with a non-null prefix. Both are written in the form of XML attributes and apply to the element they are on and all descendant elements, unless overridden.

Namespace Node

Origin

XPath

Explanation

A node in a tree that represents the binding of a namespace prefix to a namespace URI. A namespace node belongs to an element called its parent: it applies only to that element and not to any descendant elements.

Namespace Prefix

Origin

XML Namespaces

Explanation

A short name used to identify a namespace within a particular region of a stylesheet, so called because it is most often used as the prefix of a QName (the part before the colon). Different prefixes can be used to identify the same namespace, and in different contexts the same prefix can be used to identify different namespaces.

Namespace URI

Origin

XML Namespaces

Explanation

A URI used to identify a namespace. Namespace URIs are unusual in that there is no actual resource that can be obtained using the URI; the URI is simply a unique identifier. In practice, any string can be used as a namespace URI, though «http://» URLs are often used to give some prospect of uniqueness.

NaN

Origin

XPath

Explanation

Not-a-number. This is one of the possible values of a variable whose data type is Number. It results from an operation whose result is not numeric, for example «number('apple')».

Glossary

B

Node

Origin

XPath

Explanation

An object on a tree. There are seven types of node: attribute nodes, comment nodes, element nodes, namespace nodes, processing instruction nodes, root nodes, and text nodes.

Node-set

Origin

XPath

Explanation

A node-set is an unordered collection of distinct nodes from one or more trees. It may be empty, and it may be heterogeneous in the sense that it contains a mixture of nodes of different types.

Number

Origin

XPath

Explanation

One of the allowed data types for the value of an XPath expression. It is a floating point number as defined by IEEE 754.

Output Method

Origin

XSLT

Explanation

XSLT defines three output methods, xml, html, and text. The output method controls the way in which the result tree is output (or serialized) as a stream of characters or bytes.

Parameter

Origin

XSLT

Explanation

A variable whose value is supplied by the caller. A global parameter is a global variable whose value can be set (in a vendor-defined way) when the stylesheet is executed. A local parameter is defined within an `<xsl:template>` element, and its value can be set when the template is invoked using `<xsl:apply-templates>` or `<xsl:call-template>`.

Path Expression

Origin

XPath

Explanation

A path expression is an expression that selects a set of nodes in the source tree. It defines an initial node-set, from which selection starts, and a sequence of steps which define navigation paths from the initial nodes to further nodes. The final result is the set of nodes reached by following each of the steps in turn. For example, the path from the initial nodes to further nodes. The final result is the set of nodes reached by following each of the steps in turn. For example, the path expression «./parent::*» has an initial node-set containing the context node «.», and a single step which navigates to the parent element of that node.

Pattern

Origin

XSLT

Explanation

A construct that defines a condition which every node either satisfies or does not satisfy. The syntax for a Pattern is a subset of the syntax for an XPath expression. Patterns are used in only three XSLT elements: `<xsl:template>`, `<xsl:key>`, and `<xsl:number>`.

Precedence

Origin
XSLT

Explanation
see Import Precedence

Preceding Axis

Origin
XPath

Explanation
The preceding axis selects all the nodes that precede the context node, in reverse document order, with the exception of attribute and namespace nodes, and the node's own ancestors.

Preceding-Sibling Axis

Origin
XPath

Explanation
The preceding-sibling axis selects all the nodes that precede the context node and that share the same parent node, in reverse document order.

Predicate

Origin
XPath

Explanation
An expression used to filter which nodes are selected by a particular step in a path expression, or to select a subset of the nodes in a node-set. A Boolean expression selects the nodes for which the predicate is true; a numeric expression selects the node at the position given by the value of the expression, for example «[1]» selects the first node.

Prefix

Origin

XML Namespaces

Explanation

see Namespace Prefix

Principal Node Type

Origin

XPath

Explanation

Every axis has a principal node type. For most axes, the principal nodes are Elements. For the attribute axis, the principal node type is Attribute, and for the namespace axis, it is Namespace. The principal node type determines the type of nodes selected by the node test «*»: for example, «following-siblings::*» selects elements, while «namespace::*» selects namespace nodes.

Priority

Origin

XSLT

Explanation

Every template rule has a priority. The priority is expressed as a floating-point number. The priority may be specified explicitly, using the priority attribute of the <xsl:template> element; if it is omitted a default priority is allocated based on the pattern. The priority is used to decide which template to instantiate when several template rules match the same node: a rule with numerically higher priority is used in preference to one with lower priority.

Processing Instruction Node

Origin

XPath

Explanation

A node in a tree representing an XML processing instruction.

Glossary

B

737

Processing Instruction

Origin

XML

Explanation

An item in an XML document that is conventionally used to carry instructions to the software that receives the document and processes it. Written between the delimiters «<?» and «?>». Note that the XML declaration at the start of a document, and the text declaration at the start of an external parsed entity, are not processing instructions even though they use the same delimiters.

QName

Origin

XML Namespaces

Explanation

A qualified name. It is either a simple name (an NCName) or a name preceded by a namespace prefix and a colon.

Result Tree

Origin

XSLT

Explanation

The output of a stylesheet. A stylesheet defines a transformation from a source tree to a result tree. Several products have extensions that allow multiple result trees to be created. The final stage of processing is normally to serialize the result tree as a stream of characters or bytes: this is controlled by the selected output method.

Result Tree Fragment

Origin

XSLT

Explanation

This term is misleading: it would be better named a "temporary tree". A result tree fragment is a tree, and it forms the value of a variable. It may be constructed by instantiating an `<xsl:variable>` element with no `select` attribute and non-empty content. It may be used in two ways: by copying it to the result tree or by converting it to a string. Several products also provide an extension function to allow a result tree fragment to be converted to a node-set.

Root Node

Origin

XPath

Explanation

The top-most node in a tree. If the tree represents a well-formed XML document the root node will have exactly one element node as a child, representing the document element, and no text nodes as children. In other cases (for example result tree fragments) it may have zero or more element node children, and zero or more text node children: I refer to such a document as being **well-balanced**. In both cases the root node may also have comment nodes and processing instruction nodes as children.

Simplified Stylesheet

Origin

This book

Explanation

Referred to in XSLT as the *Literal Result Element as Stylesheet Facility*, a simplified stylesheet is a stylesheet consisting solely of a literal result element which is instantiated using the root of the source document as the current node.

Source Document

Origin

XPath

Explanation

The principal source document is the XML document to which the stylesheet is being applied. Secondary source documents can be loaded using the `document()` function.

Glossary

B

739

Step

Origin

XPath

Explanation

A step is used within a path expression to navigate from one node to a particular set of nodes. The step is defined by an axis, giving the direction of navigation, a node test, which defines constraints on the type of and names of the target nodes, and zero or more predicates, which define arbitrary constraints that the target nodes must satisfy.

String

Origin

XPath

Explanation

One of the allowed data types for the value of an XPath expression. It is a sequence of zero or more Unicode characters (the same character set as is used in XML).

String-value

Origin

XPath

Explanation

Every node has a string-value. For a text node the string-value is the textual content; for an element it is the concatenation of the string-values of its descendant text nodes (that is, the textual content of the element after stripping all markup). The string-value of a node is output by the instruction `<xsl:value-of select=".">`.

Stylesheet

Origin

XSLT

Explanation

This term is used to refer either to a single `<xsl:stylesheet>` element and its contents (called in this book a stylesheet module), or to a stylesheet with all the stylesheets that it loads using `<xsl:include>` and `<xsl:import>` elements (called a stylesheet program).

Template Body

Origin

This book

Explanation

A sequence of XSLT instructions, extension elements, literal result elements, and text nodes, forming the content of an `<xsl:template>` element or of various other elements in the stylesheet. When the template body is instantiated, any instructions and extension elements are instantiated according to the rules for each one, while any literal result elements and text nodes are copied to the current output destination. In the XSLT Recommendation the term used is simply *Template*; I have used *Template Body* to avoid confusion with `<xsl:template>` elements.

Template Rule

Origin

XSLT

Explanation

An `<xsl:template>` element in the stylesheet with a `match` attribute. A template rule may be invoked using the `<xsl:apply-templates>` instruction; for each selected node, the appropriate template rule is determined based on a number of criteria including the match pattern and the template rule's import precedence and priority.

Text Node

Origin

XPath

Explanation

A node in a tree representing character data (called PCDATA in XML) within an XML document. Adjacent text nodes will always be merged into a single node. Character references and entity references occurring within the original text will have been replaced by their expansions.

Top-level Element

Origin

XSLT

Explanation

An element in a stylesheet that is an immediate child of the `<xsl:stylesheet>` element.

Tree

Origin

XPath

Explanation

An abstract data structure representing the information content of an XML document. The tree always has a single root node (which contrary to the botanical analogy, is always depicted at the top). The structure of nodes in the tree need not follow the rules for a well-formed document in XML, for example, there may be several element nodes as children of the root.

Unparsed Entity

Origin

XML

Explanation

An unparsed entity is an entity declared in the Document Type Definition with an associated notation. Such entities are unparsed because they generally contain binary data such as images, rather than XML. A function, `unparsed-entity-uri()`, is available in XSLT to access the unparsed entities associated with a source document.

URI

Origin

Internet standards

Explanation

Uniform Resource Identifier: a generalization of the URLs (Uniform Resource Locators) used to uniquely address resources such as web pages on the Internet.

Variable Binding

Origin

XPath

Explanation

The declaration of a variable, in an `<xsl:variable>` or `<xsl:param>` element, in conjunction with the current value of that variable.

Variable Reference

Origin

XPath

Explanation

A reference to a variable within an expression, in the form `$name`.

Well-balanced

Origin

XML Fragment Interchange

Explanation

An XML fragment is well balanced if there is an end tag that matches every start tag. This is a less strict constraint than being well-formed: a well-balanced fragment does not have to have a single element that encloses all the others. XSLT and XPath are defined so they will work on any trees representing a well-balanced XML fragment. The XML and XSLT standards don't use this terminology; instead they refer to the rules for an *external general parsed entity*.

Well-formed

Origin

XML

Explanation

A document is well-formed if it follows the syntax rules in the XML specification. These include the rule that there must be a single outermost element that encloses all others. The XML output of an XSLT stylesheet is not required to be well-formed, only to be well-balanced.

Whitespace

Origin

XML

Explanation

Whitespace is any contiguous sequence of tab, carriage return, newline, and space characters. A whitespace node is a text node whose string-value consists solely of whitespace.

Index A - Elements

A note on the index.

There are three indexes in this book: Index A-Elements, Index B-Functions, and Index C-General. Indexes A and B are flat indexes intended as quick references. The General index has detailed entries arranged hierarchically, covering the entire scope of the book, including elements and functions even though these entries will be listed in their own indexes as well.

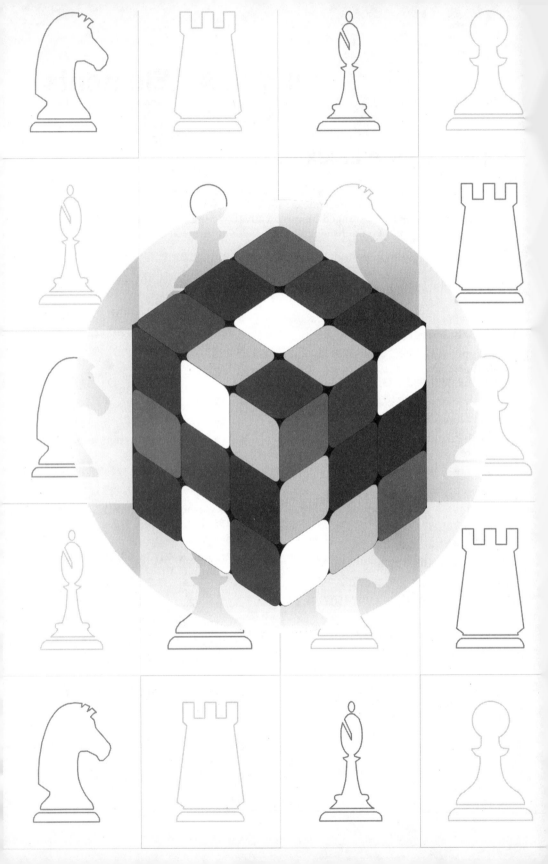

Index B - Functions

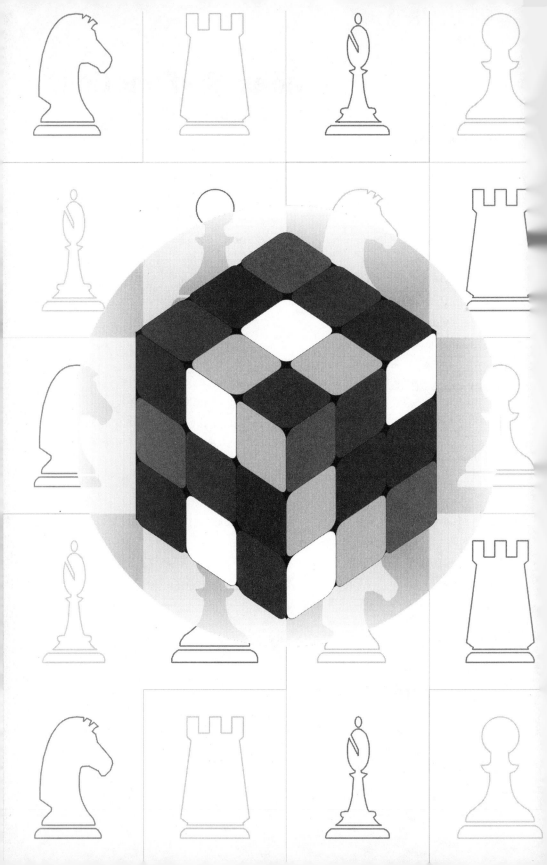

Index C - General

Symbols

S

WROX PRESS INC.

Wrox writes books for you. Any suggestions, or ideas
about how you want information given in your
ideal book will be studied by our team.
Your comments are always valued at Wrox.

Free phone in USA 800-USE-WROX
Fax (312) 893 8001

UK Tel. (0121) 687 4100   Fax (0121) 687 4101

NB. If you post the bounce back card below in the UK, please send it to:
Wrox Press Ltd., Arden House, 1102 Warwick Road, Acocks Green, Birmingham. B27 6BH. UK.

XSLT Programmer's Reference - Registration Card

Name

Address

City _____ State/Region

Country _____ Postcode/Zip

E-mail

Occupation

How did you hear about this book?

☐ Book review (name)

☐ Advertisement (name)

☐ Recommendation

☐ Catalog

☐ Other

Where did you buy this book?

☐ Bookstore (name) _____ City

☐ Computer Store (name)

☐ Mail Order

☐ Other

What influenced you in the
purchase of this book?

☐ Cover Design

☐ Contents

☐ Other (please specify)

How did you rate the overall
contents of this book?

☐ Excellent   ☐ Good

☐ Average   ☐ Poor

What did you find most useful about this book?

What did you find least useful about this book?

Please add any additional comments.

What other subjects will you buy a computer
book on soon?

What is the best computer book you have used this year?

Note: This information will only be used to keep you updated
about new Wrox Press titles and will not be used for any other
purpose or passed to any other third party.

☐ Check here if you DO NOT want to receive further support for this
book.

3129

3129

wrox

PROGRAMMER TO PROGRAMMER™

BUSINESS REPLY MAIL

FIRST CLASS MAIL   PERMIT#64   CHICAGO, IL

POSTAGE WILL BE PAID BY ADDRESSEE

WROX PRESS INC.
29 S.Lasalle Street
Suite 520
CHICAGO IL 60603

NO POSTAGE
NECESSARY
IF MAILED
IN THE
UNITED STATES